Future of Business and Finance

The Future of Business and Finance book series features professional works aimed at defining, analyzing, and charting the future trends in these fields. The focus is mainly on strategic directions, technological advances, challenges and solutions which may affect the way we do business tomorrow, including the future of sustainability and governance practices. Mainly written by practitioners, consultants and academic thinkers, the books are intended to spark and inform further discussions and developments.

Stephan Böhm • Stephen Collins
Alexander Godulla • Sarah Keith
Richard Savery
Editors

Handbook of AI-based Media Disruption

Emerging Technologies and Multidisciplinary Perspectives Across Sectors

Springer

Editors
Stephan Böhm
RheinMain University of Applied Sciences
Wiesbaden, Germany

Stephen Collins
Macquarie University
Sydney, NSW, Australia

Alexander Godulla
Leipzig University
Leipzig, Germany

Sarah Keith
Macquarie University
Sydney, NSW, Australia

Richard Savery
University of Canberra
Bruce, Canberra, Australia

ISSN 2662-2467 ISSN 2662-2475 (electronic)
Future of Business and Finance
ISBN 978-3-032-07604-5 ISBN 978-3-032-07605-2 (eBook)
https://doi.org/10.1007/978-3-032-07605-2

This Springer imprint is published by the registered company Springer Nature Switzerland AG
The registered company address is: Gewerbestrasse 11, 6330 Cham, Switzerland

Prologue: AI as Disruptive Technology in Media

The history of media is marked by disruption. From the printing press to the e-book, vinyl records to MP3, the telephone to the Internet, each disruption reconfigures the complex relationships between individuals, businesses, content creators, and content consumers—often in unforeseen ways and ways that result in tensions between various interests. Recording technologies reconfigured the relationship between media, time, and space. The Internet and the ubiquity of networked devices transformed the one-to-many broadcast model, radically decentralizing distribution and control over content. The copy-and-paste cultures of sampling, fan fiction, and game modding challenged our understandings of authorship, ownership, and creativity. It is rare that a single technological development forces a collective rethinking of how media are created, distributed, and understood. Yet the rise of generative artificial intelligence (GenAI), catalyzed by the public release of ChatGPT in late 2022, represents precisely such a moment; a disruption so profound that its effects are reverberating across virtually every media sector. More than just a new tool in the digital arsenal, GenAI constitutes a qualitatively distinct shift in the relationship between human creativity and machine computation. It signals a new phase in the ongoing evolution of media technologies; one in which the boundaries between authorship and automation, originality and synthesis, and professionalism and algorithmic production are increasingly blurred and problematized.

This handbook emerges from the recognition that we are witnessing not merely a continuation of technological change, but a structural transformation with implications far beyond efficiency or novelty. In the face of proliferating GenAI systems that generate text, images, video, sound, and synthetic voices with uncanny fluency, media professionals, scholars, regulators, and citizens alike are confronted with a host of urgent questions: How do we define creativity when machines participate in authorship? What becomes of trust in journalism when content is no longer necessarily human-made? How will media markets adapt to automated production pipelines and hybrid human-AI labor? And what cultural, legal, and ethical frameworks are necessary to ensure that technological progress aligns with democratic values and professional standards?

While the popular and industry discourses have been marked by polarized techno-optimism and dystopian anxiety, scholarly analysis of GenAI's disruptive impact remains surprisingly fragmented. Existing studies often focus on specific applications or disciplinary perspectives, without providing a comprehensive and integrative view of the phenomenon. This handbook seeks to fill that gap. It brings together an international and interdisciplinary group of authors to systematically examine how GenAI is reconfiguring media systems, practices, and institutions across sectors and regions.

The first part, *AI Impact and Disruption by Media Sectors and Segments*, provides an in-depth examination of how AI technologies are reshaping established media domains. Contributions in this section cover print and online journalism, broadcasting, music, photography, film, and gaming. Rather than treating these sectors as isolated silos, the chapters highlight recurring patterns of disruption, such as the hybridization of human and machine labor, the emergence of new constellations of creativity and authorship, and the reconfiguration of traditional value chains. Authors reflect on current technological applications and on broader implications for institutional identities, market structures, and audience relationships. Analyzing AI-generated music, algorithmic layout tools in print publishing, and synthetic voices in film and game development, these contributions reveal how media practices are being redefined from the inside out.

The second part, *Cross-Sector Impact of AI-based Media Disruption*, turns from sector-specific analysis to overarching themes that cut across media forms and professional fields. This section addresses some of the most pressing conceptual and normative challenges of the AI era: How is public trust in media evolving in the context of automation and deepfakes? Where should we draw ethical boundaries for the deployment of AI in journalism and entertainment? How do AI systems reorganize the nature of media labor, and what competencies will future professionals need? Legal chapters examine the strain GenAI places on copyright regimes, while others tackle questions of diversity, equity, and educational transformation. The section is guided by the principle that technological change must be understood in its societal context, and that responses must be interdisciplinary, reflective, and future-oriented.

The third part, *Case Studies and Selected Topics on AI in the Media Industry*, adds a crucial empirical and applied dimension. Through case studies ranging from Austrian newsrooms and European corporate communication to audiovisual production in Portugal, these chapters document how AI is being implemented in real-world media environments. These contributions reveal organizational tensions, strategic path dependencies, and the interplay between innovation and institutional inertia. Beyond application, this section includes critical essays on emergent phenomena such as deepfakes, synthetic personalization, and the environmental impacts of large-scale AI usage. In doing so, it extends the discussion from practical adaptation to broader questions of governance, responsibility, and planetary sustainability. This third part reminds us that AI is not only a technology, but a social, cultural force that materially impacts the environment.

This volume examines GenAI as part of a longer historical trajectory of media disruption that includes previous shifts such as digitization, platformization, and the rise of algorithmic recommendation systems. Simultaneously, the speed, scale, and opacity of GenAI tools mark a new threshold. Increasingly, these technologies generate our symbolic environments. Our aim as editors has been to curate a rigorous, accessible, and forward-looking mapping of the field. The authors, drawn from an eclectic range of disciplines, offer analytic clarity and normative guidance. Their contributions are united by a common purpose: to ensure that the future of media in the age of AI is shaped by informed human choice. We hope this handbook serves as a catalyst for research, policy, professional practice, and critical public engagement. As GenAI continues to evolve, so too must our intellectual and institutional capacities to comprehend and govern it. This volume is a step in that direction.

AI-Impact and Disruption by Media Sectors and Segments

Disruption rarely arrives evenly. Technological change tends to ripple through complex systems in sector-specific waves, amplifying structural asymmetries and reconfiguring professional roles in unpredictable ways. In the media landscape, the adoption of artificial intelligence is unfolding precisely in this uneven, contingent manner. While AI may be universal in its technical underpinnings, its manifestations in journalism, broadcasting, music, photography, gaming, and film vary profoundly, shaped by legacy infrastructures, creative cultures, regulatory environments, and market dynamics.

This first part of the handbook offers a sectoral cartography of AI-based disruption. Each chapter serves as a lens through which to observe how generative and assistive AI tools are transforming production workflows, redefining authorship, and challenging the boundaries between human agency and machine automation. The contributions in this section ground their analysis in specific empirical contexts: editorial newsrooms, audiovisual studios, music production environments, and digital game development ecosystems. Taken together, they reveal how AI technologies are being implemented, and more importantly, how they are being contested, negotiated, and shaped by institutional and cultural logics.

The chapters also underscore that disruption is rarely only technological. The introduction of AI reopens long-standing debates about labor, creativity, expertise, and representation. In journalism, it invites a rethinking of professional identity and editorial ethics. In the music and film industries, it raises legal and aesthetic questions about authenticity, copyright, and artistic intent. In photography and gaming, it blurs the lines between simulation and representation, tool, and co-creator. Across all segments, the rise of AI accentuates tensions between innovation and tradition, efficiency and expression, automation and accountability.

This section goes beyond cataloguing transformations. In analyzing how different media sectors respond to similar technological impulses, it highlights convergence and divergence: convergence in the forms of platform dependency, data-driven production, and hybrid labor models; and divergence in terms of adoption speed, regulatory response, and cultural acceptance. The result is a comparative framework that illuminates what AI is doing to media, and what media sectors are doing with AI.

In this sense, Part I serves as a diagnostic foundation for the entire volume. It provides the empirical and conceptual groundwork upon which cross-sectoral reflections and applied case studies can build. Above all, it reminds us that while AI may be general-purpose in design, its disruptive force is always mediated by history, by context, and by human choice. The following chapters explore these dynamics in detail, offering empirically grounded, theoretically informed accounts of how AI is reconfiguring the logics and practices of distinct media sectors.

In Chap. 1, *Print: News, Magazines, and Publishing*, Michael Graßl explores how artificial intelligence is reshaping the landscape of traditional print media, including newspapers, magazines, and publishing houses. While AI has often been associated with digital innovation, this chapter emphasizes its growing relevance in print contexts, where adoption may be slower but is steadily expanding. The chapter traces the historical trajectory of AI in journalism and focuses on its current and emerging applications across the journalistic value chain, from research and verification to content production, design, and distribution. It highlights how AI technologies are transforming workflows and enabling new efficiencies in editorial practices, while also presenting challenges such as limited organizational readiness, skill gaps, and ethical considerations. Based on a synthesis of recent studies and industry data, the analysis reveals that print organizations are beginning to embrace AI for backend automation as well as for audience-facing innovations like layout personalization and content targeting. At the same time, the text argues that human expertise remains vital, particularly in ensuring editorial quality and maintaining trust. Rather than replacing journalism, AI is portrayed as a tool that can augment creativity and operational effectiveness, if implemented thoughtfully. Graßl ultimately envisions the future of print journalism as a hybrid model that leverages both machine-driven capabilities and the irreplaceable judgment of experienced media professionals.

In Chap. 2, *Broadcasting: Radio and Television*, Anna Jupowicz-Ginalska and Jaroslaw Kinal examine how artificial intelligence is transforming legacy broadcast media. The chapter situates AI within the broader theoretical framework of technological determinism, emphasizing that AI's integration into radio and television is a logical extension of ongoing technological evolution. The authors explore AI's diverse applications, from automating production workflows and enhancing content personalization to developing virtual presenters and enabling sophisticated audience analytics. Drawing on current research and practical examples, the chapter illustrates how organizations like the BBC, NPR, and iHeartRadio are using AI to optimize editorial processes, improve user experiences, and extend market reach. Particular attention is given to AI's capacity for automating tasks such as real-time transcription, translation, and metadata generation, which significantly boosts operational efficiency. At the same time, the authors highlight key ethical and practical concerns, including risks tied to data privacy, algorithmic bias, misinformation, and the potential erosion of editorial accountability. The chapter also notes the impact on employment models, raising critical questions about the future role of human professionals in AI-augmented newsrooms. Ultimately, the chapter argues that while AI introduces remarkable opportunities to innovate and enhance broadcasting, it also demands vigilant oversight and a commitment to maintaining journalistic integrity. The future of radio and television, the authors conclude, will likely depend on hybrid models that balance technological capabilities with human expertise to navigate an increasingly complex media environment.

In Chap. 3, *Music Creation and Production*, Steve Collins and Sarah Keith provide an in-depth exploration of how artificial intelligence is transforming music creation, production, and the broader music industries. The chapter situates AI within a historical continuum of technological disruptions, arguing that current developments represent both a continuation and an intensification of long-standing shifts. Collins and Keith offer a working definition of "music AI" and chart its evolution from niche academic experimentation to mainstream commercial tools. They examine practical applications, including automated composition, assistive production software, generative audio, and voice synthesis, and highlight how these technologies are reshaping workflows, lowering barriers to entry, and fostering new creative possibilities. The chapter also scrutinizes critical challenges, from legal disputes over copyright and intellectual property to concerns about artistic authenticity and labor displacement. By analyzing how AI disrupts established value chains, affecting songwriting, recording, distribution, and rights management, the authors reveal opportunities and tensions that arise when human creativity intersects with algorithmic processes. The text underscores the growing entanglement between the music and tech industries, emphasizing the need for adaptive legal frameworks and ethical considerations. Collins and Keith conclude that while AI is unlikely to supplant human artistry entirely, it is fundamentally redefining what it means to create, produce, and monetize music in the digital age.

In Chap. 4, *Photography*, Justin Harvey investigates the disruptive impact of generative artificial intelligence on the field of photography, with a particular focus on photorealistic diffusion models. The chapter situates GenAI within a broader historical context, recalling how the transition from analog to digital photography fundamentally reshaped photographic practice, industry structures, and visual culture. Harvey argues that GenAI introduces a new wave of disruption, as AI-generated images—while technically not photographs—closely mimic photographic aesthetics and challenge traditional notions of authenticity and representation. The analysis explores issues of ethical transparency in business models, the mitigation of bias and homogenization in AI-generated imagery, and the integration of GenAI into artistic practices. Special attention is given to legal debates surrounding the use of copyrighted materials in AI training datasets and to emerging industry standards aimed at ensuring ethical compliance. Harvey also highlights how artists are creatively engaging with GenAI to expand visual storytelling, using case studies that demonstrate AI's potential to reconstruct undocumented histories and stimulate critical discourse. The chapter underscores that while AI poses significant challenges, such as trust erosion and the risk of market concentration, it also offers new opportunities for artistic innovation and commercial diversification. Harvey concludes that the evolving relationship between photography and AI will necessitate continuous negotiation between technological potential, ethical responsibility, and cultural meaning, shaping the future trajectory of photographic practice.

In Chap. 5, *Film Production and Cinematography*, Sabine Baumann examines how artificial intelligence is reshaping creative workflows, aesthetic practices, and business models in the film industry. Building on a historical trajectory of technological disruption, from sound and color to CGI and digital ecosystems, the chapter situates AI as a qualitatively new phase, characterized by learning-based systems, platform dependencies, and cross-industry dynamics. Baumann explores how AI tools increasingly permeate all stages of production, including scriptwriting, casting, cinematography, postproduction, and distribution. Empirical examples illustrate how generative models and automation influence visual storytelling, redefine professional roles, and alter team structures, raising questions about authorship, agency, and labor relations. The chapter draws on a broad literature base, spanning media studies, innovation research, and strategic management, to analyze how AI technologies intersect with organizational routines, value creation mechanisms, and governance frameworks. Particular attention is given to evolving business models, which shift from linear production pipelines to modular, data-driven ecosystems reliant on cloud-based infrastructures and proprietary interfaces. Baumann emphasizes that these developments reinforce structural asymmetries, as large studios benefit from privileged access to data, infrastructure, and expertise, while smaller firms face barriers to participation and regulatory uncertainty. Ultimately, the chapter argues that AI is a transformative force that reconfigures institutional logics, strategic positioning, and cultural legitimacy in contemporary film production.

In Chap. 6, *Online, Social Media, and AI Journalism*, Tai Neilson offers a critical, historically grounded analysis of how artificial intelligence is reshaping the digital news landscape. Drawing on the political economy of communication, the chapter situates AI as the latest in a series of technological shifts that have reconfigured journalism, following the digitization of news and the platformization of media. Neilson emphasizes that while AI introduces new forms of automation and labor reconfiguration, it is not entirely novel; rather, it extends preexisting dynamics between media and powerful tech companies. The chapter explores how AI disrupts labor relations in journalism, fuels economic dependencies on platform and AI companies, and prompts fundamental questions about intellectual property, content ownership, and business viability. Concepts such as digital labor, platform dependency, and algorithmic distribution provide the analytical framework for understanding these shifts. Neilson critically examines how AI technologies are both marketed as solutions and deployed as extractive tools, trained on journalists' past work while simultaneously threatening their professional autonomy. The text also highlights legal and institutional responses, including emerging efforts to regulate content use and negotiate licensing deals. In conclusion, Neilson argues that the future of journalism in the age of AI will hinge not on technological inevitability, but on political, legal, and professional contestation. AI's integration into newsrooms reflects a site of struggle shaped by past experiences with digital transformation and the power asymmetries of contemporary media systems.

In Chap. 7, *Video Game Development*, Richard Savery explores how generative artificial intelligence (AI) is shifting the game industry's creative workflows, authorship models, and production structures. Tracing a lineage from early rule-based systems and procedural content generation to today's large language and diffusion models, the chapter situates AI as a disruptive and enabling design material. Through contemporary case studies, including Ubisoft's Ghostwriter, King's automated level design, and AI-enhanced NPCs in indie titles, Savery demonstrates how AI augments content creation, compresses iteration cycles, and reframes creative labor, often introducing a hybrid role of human-AI curation. Survey data and interviews reveal diverging perceptions: while technical teams embrace efficiency gains, artists and writers express concern over stylistic homogenization, job displacement, and the erosion of creative control. The chapter also shows how GenAI fosters new forms of user-generated content and lowers entry barriers on platforms like Roblox, while raising unresolved questions around authorship, copyright, and ethical governance. By framing AI as a malleable design material rather than a monolithic tool, Savery encourages a critical, intentional integration of AI into game development. He concludes that the future of gaming with AI will depend less on technical capability than on how equitably knowledge, resources, and agency are distributed within increasingly data-driven and modular production ecosystems.

Cross-Sector Impact of AI-Based Media Disruption

While AI technologies often take shape within specific professional contexts, their deeper consequences extend beyond the confines of individual sectors. They unsettle the institutional foundations, normative frameworks, and cultural assumptions that have historically underpinned the media as a system of meaning-making, public trust, and democratic participation. While the first part of this volume charted how AI disrupts what media professionals do in concrete domains, this second part turns to the question of what AI means for media systems as a whole.

The chapters in this section explore how challenges of GenAI extend beyond workflows and markets to values, identities, and societal expectations. They investigate how trust in media is reconfigured when content is increasingly co-produced or entirely generated by machines; how established ethical paradigms confront novel dilemmas of agency, transparency, and algorithmic responsibility; and how labor is transformed by substitution and augmentation, and also through new demands for hybrid skillsets and organizational rethinking.

Legal and regulatory contributions in this section reveal the strain placed on copyright regimes and highlight emerging efforts to adapt existing frameworks to nonhuman creativity. Simultaneously, educational analyses show that institutions must respond to AI as a topic of concern and rethink their pedagogical models in light of an AI-saturated communication environment. Across these different thematic axes—ethics, law, labor, education, and public trust—the authors converge on a central insight: AI is not a neutral tool but a structuring force that demands institutional renegotiation and reflexive governance.

Importantly, this part of the handbook avoids technological determinism. Instead of portraying disruption as an inevitable outcome of technical progress, the chapters emphasize the social, political, and cultural dimensions of AI integration. As well as asking what is happening, the authors ask what ought to happen; and under what conditions, with whose agency, and according to which normative frameworks. Part II therefore opens a necessary space for critical engagement, where empirical analysis meets ethical deliberation and where institutional practice meets theoretical reflection. The questions raised here will likely outlast the current generation of tools, but they will shape how we understand, regulate, and live with AI in media environments for decades to come. The following chapters examine these cross-cutting issues through diverse lenses, inviting readers to engage with AI as a societal and epistemological inflection point.

In Chap. 8, *Impact of AI on Trust in the Media*, Castulus Kolo, Joschka Mütterlein, and Sarah Anna Schmid investigate how artificial intelligence is reconfiguring the concept of trust within contemporary media environments. The chapter situates trust as a multifaceted construct, drawing from psychology, sociology, philosophy, and communication studies to explore its relational and institutional dimensions. Against the backdrop of declining trust in traditional news media, fueled by political polarization, misinformation, and growing platform dominance, the authors examine how AI's increasing role in news production, curation, and distribution introduces new challenges. The chapter highlights that AI blurs the boundaries between trust in media institutions and trust in technology itself, emphasizing factors such as transparency, explainability, and accountability as crucial for sustaining public confidence. Key areas of inquiry include automated journalism, deepfake proliferation, and the rise of virtual influencers, each illustrating how AI can both enhance and erode trust. The authors also emphasize the dual role of AI: as a mediator that can verify and distribute information efficiently, and as an object of trust that requires vigilant oversight. Finally, the chapter outlines a future research agenda, calling for interdisciplinary frameworks that address both ethical and technical challenges. Kolo, Mütterlein, and Schmid conclude that fostering trust in AI-powered media systems is essential for media legitimacy and for the resilience of democratic discourse in an era of algorithmic mediation.

In Chap. 9, *Ethical Limits of AI Use in the Media Sector*, Jonas Schützeneder examines how media ethics can guide the responsible deployment of artificial intelligence across the media industry. The chapter frames AI as both an opportunity and a source of profound disruption, noting that its integration into media workflows—from content creation to distribution—has only just begun. Schützeneder positions ethics as a "mediating authority" that helps balance philosophical ideals with practical realities, providing orientation and boundaries for AI's use. Drawing on studies, policy documents, and real-world examples, the chapter identifies three core dimensions where ethical limits are most pressing: maintaining human oversight and editorial control, safeguarding quality standards and freedom of opinion, and regulating applications such as social scoring. These areas highlight tensions between innovation and accountability, particularly as AI transforms the processes of information gathering, verification, and audience engagement. The analysis underscores the fragmented nature of existing guidelines and calls for stronger, more systematic frameworks at policy, organizational, and individual levels. Schützeneder concludes that while AI offers significant advantages in efficiency and creativity, its deployment must remain firmly anchored in human responsibility, transparency, and legal safeguards. The future of ethical AI in media, the chapter argues, depends on continuous negotiation between technological potential and societal values, with media ethics playing a central role in shaping practices that are both innovative and trustworthy.

In Chap. 10, *Impact of AI Use on Creativity and Diversity in Media*, Petri Honkanen and Mats Nylund explore the complex and sometimes paradoxical effects of artificial intelligence on creative expression and media diversity. The chapter situates AI as both a catalyst for democratizing content creation and a potential force for homogenization, examining how GenAI lowers technical barriers, expands creative participation, and enables new forms of artistic experimentation. At the same time, the authors highlight critical concerns: AI tools, often trained on existing data patterns, risk reinforcing biases and limiting true novelty. Drawing on empirical studies, Honkanen and Nylund demonstrate that while AI can enhance individual creativity, it may simultaneously reduce collective diversity by promoting stylistic convergence. The chapter also interrogates concepts like "synthetic tokenism," where surface-level representation masks deeper inequities, and discusses the ethical, legal, and cultural challenges that arise from AI's growing influence in both journalism and entertainment. By engaging with debates around authorship, authenticity, and human agency, the authors argue for a nuanced understanding of AI's dual impact. They call for recalibrating definitions of creativity and diversity to reflect the evolving media landscape and emphasize the need for ethical frameworks and policy interventions. Ultimately, the chapter positions AI as both a tool and a transformative agent that alters both the processes and meanings of creativity and inclusivity in contemporary media.

In Chap. 11, *Impacts of AI on US Copyright Law*, Steve Collins and Sarah Keith analyze the challenges that GenAI presents copyright law. The chapter situates AI within broader legal and technological histories, emphasizing how the proliferation of AI-generated texts, images, and sounds disrupts conventional notions of authorship, originality, and ownership. Collins and Keith provide a structured examination of current case law, including high-profile disputes involving the Copyright Office's refusal to register works without human authorship and ongoing litigation over the unauthorized use of copyrighted material in AI training datasets. Central to the chapter is the tension between the human-centric logic of copyright and the nonhuman productivity of generative models, raising critical questions about eligibility, liability, and fair use. The authors illustrate how legal uncertainty not only affects creators and AI developers but also broader innovation ecosystems. The chapter discusses potential regulatory responses, including licensing schemes, legislative reform, and judicial reinterpretation, and underscores the role of institutional actors such as courts, agencies, and industry consortia in shaping the evolving legal landscape. Collins and Keith conclude that while existing legal frameworks are strained, they are not obsolete; rather, they require adaptive reinterpretation to balance the protection of human creativity with the realities of machine-generated expression in an increasingly hybrid cultural economy.

In Chap. 12, *Workforce Impact of AI-based Automation in Media*, Paul Heß and Stephan Böhm examine how artificial intelligence, particularly since the rise of GenAI, is altering employment dynamics within the media industry. The chapter investigates AI's dual impact: boosting productivity while also posing risks of job substitution. Heß and Böhm provide an in-depth analysis of AI's integration along the media value chain, highlighting how automation transforms both routine and creative tasks. The authors distinguish between productivity gains—where AI assists workers and enhances efficiency—and substitution effects, where AI replaces human labor entirely. Drawing from literature reviews and empirical data, they explore frameworks such as Human-AI Collaboration (HAIC), emphasizing that while automation displaces certain roles, it simultaneously creates new demands for hybrid skill sets. A notable feature of the chapter is its preliminary survey among German media workers, revealing widespread AI adoption and significant expectations regarding job displacement and changing work processes. The findings point to a growing need for AI literacy, data analysis capabilities, and critical oversight in media professions. The chapter concludes that while AI is unlikely to replace human creativity and judgment in full, it will redefine the nature of media work, requiring adaptive strategies in training, regulation, and organizational design. Heß and Böhm call for systematic research to quantify AI's workforce effects, underscoring the importance of aligning technological progress with sustainable employment practices in the evolving media landscape.

In Chap. 13, *New Skills and Educational Challenges by AI in Media*, Sherman Young and Hilary Sarah Wheaton explore how artificial intelligence is transforming educational practices, frameworks, and philosophies. The chapter opens by contextualizing the rapid integration of GenAI, notably since ChatGPT's release, and the resulting debates around academic integrity and assessment validity. Young and Wheaton argue that while initial concerns focused narrowly on cheating, the true challenge lies in reimagining education to reflect a world where AI is ubiquitous and deeply embedded in everyday activities. The authors propose a three-lens framework—AI literacy, AI fluency, and AI relevancy—to guide this transformation. AI literacy emphasizes understanding AI's technical, ethical, and societal dimensions; AI fluency focuses on equipping educators to integrate AI tools effectively in curriculum design and pedagogy; and AI relevancy calls for a deeper overhaul of education to ensure that both content and methods prepare students for meaningful engagement in AI-rich environments. Drawing on interdisciplinary research and historical parallels with past technological shifts, the chapter critiques the limitations of current educational models and highlights the need for systemic reform. Young and Wheaton underscore that embracing AI as a subject of study and also as a pedagogical partner is crucial for developing critical thinking, creativity, and ethical judgment. They conclude that educational institutions must move beyond reactive measures and instead foster proactive, innovative approaches that align with the realities of an AI-driven world.

Case Studies and Selected Topics on AI in the Media Industry

Following the previous sections that outlined how AI disrupts media sectors and challenges cross-cutting institutional logics, this third and final part considers the operational realities of media organizations, the contested spaces of regulation, and the emerging frontiers of synthetic communication. It is here, in the frictions between innovation and implementation, aspiration and constraint, that the complexity of AI integration becomes visible. The case studies in this section provide a close-up view of how AI adoption unfolds within concrete media contexts—from Austrian newsrooms and European corporate communication to audiovisual production in Portugal. These contributions demonstrate how AI actively transforms preexisting structures by altering routines, reframing professional roles, and triggering both enthusiasm and resistance. The cases also show how historical path dependencies, organizational cultures, and infrastructural limitations condition the trajectory of AI implementation, underscoring that technological change is always mediated by context.

Complementing these empirical insights are a series of thematic essays that delve into some of the most urgent and underexplored dimensions of AI-based media disruption. These include deepfakes as a symbolic rupture in visual epistemology, the environmental costs of large-scale AI computation, and the pedagogical challenges of preparing future media professionals for a hybrid human-machine communication ecology. A legal-regulatory chapter examines the European Union's response to synthetic media, highlighting the strengths and blind spots of emerging transparency requirements under the AI Act. What unites the contributions in this part is a common orientation: they grapple with the messiness of real-world transformation. These chapters remind us that the integration of AI is not only a matter of technical feasibility or normative desirability, but of institutional experimentation, cultural negotiation, and political contestation.

As such, this third part serves as a reality check and a forward-looking provocation. It grounds the handbook in lived practices and contested futures, urging readers to engage with AI as a material, cultural, and ecological agent that is reshaping the conditions under which media can continue to serve their democratic, artistic, and societal functions. These contributions invite reflection on how theory meets practice, how ideals confront constraints, and how we might collectively navigate the age of AI with both critical vigilance and imaginative ambition.

In Chap. 14, *Generative AI in Austrian News Media: Innovation Impact and Evidence on Path Dependence*, Paul Clemens Murschetz, Maximilian Eder, and Bartosz Wilczek investigate how historical decisions, technological developments, and managerial strategies shape AI adoption within Austrian newsrooms. Using path dependence theory, the authors conduct a multi-case study that examines how AI innovation paths are established, reinforced, or disrupted over time. Drawing on interviews with media executives and academic experts, the chapter identifies key phases of AI integration, from initial adoption and critical junctures to potential lock-ins and unlocking mechanisms. The analysis reveals that while AI offers significant opportunities for improving editorial workflows, content personalization, and operational efficiency, legacy infrastructures and entrenched organizational routines often constrain its transformative potential. The study underscores how self-reinforcing mechanisms such as coordination effects and sunk investments limit strategic flexibility, while external factors like market dynamics, regulation, and platform dependencies further complicate innovation trajectories. However, the authors also highlight instances where proactive management and cultural openness have enabled newsrooms to break free from established paths, fostering innovation despite structural inertia. Murschetz, Eder, and Wilczek conclude that balancing historical constraints with forward-looking strategies is essential for news organizations aiming to leverage AI effectively. Their findings emphasize the need for a nuanced understanding of both technological and organizational dynamics to develop AI-driven strategies that are adaptable, ethical, and sustainable in a rapidly evolving media environment.

In Chap. 15, *AI-Supported Corporate Content Production in the Newsroom: Insights from Literature and Practice*, Cornelia Wolf examines how artificial intelligence is transforming corporate communication, with a specific focus on newsroom structures. Drawing from academic literature and industry reports, the chapter develops a comprehensive framework for AI integration along the phases of communication management, covering analysis, planning, organization, execution, and evaluation. This framework is then applied in a case study of a major European IT service provider, which has operated a corporate newsroom for more than a decade. Through qualitative interviews and workflow analyses, Wolf identifies both the current state of AI use and future implementation priorities. The findings highlight AI's potential to enhance efficiency, creativity, and personalization, particularly in content creation and workflow automation. However, challenges persist, including structural barriers, cultural readiness, and technical infrastructure. The chapter proposes a strategic roadmap that prioritizes AI adoption based on organizational needs, balancing opportunities with practical constraints. Wolf emphasizes that while AI can optimize communication processes, successful integration demands cross-functional alignment, robust governance, and a culture of continuous learning. The study underscores that AI should augment, not replace, human expertise, reframing professional roles and competencies in the evolving media environment. By bridging theoretical insights with practical application, this chapter offers valuable guidance for organizations aiming to implement AI in a structured and sustainable way.

In Chap. 16, *AI in the Audiovisual Industry: Perceptions, Practices, Challenges, and Opportunities*, Catarina Duff Burnay, Paulo Nuno Vicente, and José Manuel Sotero investigate how artificial intelligence is reshaping content creation and production workflows in the audiovisual sector, using Portugal's SP Televisão as a case study. The chapter presents original data from a mixed-methods study, combining an online survey with expert panels to assess knowledge, attitudes, and practical engagement with AI among media professionals. Findings reveal that while over half of SP Televisão's workforce reports basic AI awareness, formal training is minimal, reflecting a gap between interest and preparedness. The majority of respondents express curiosity and optimism about AI's potential to automate repetitive tasks and enhance creative workflows, though concerns persist regarding digital literacy, organizational readiness, and AI's fit for certain production formats like soap operas. The expert panels highlight both the enthusiasm and practical constraints facing AI adoption, including infrastructural challenges and the need for standardized data practices. By mapping workflows and identifying operational bottlenecks, the study uncovers key areas, such as content indexing and scheduling, where AI could offer tangible benefits. Burnay, Vicente, and Sotero conclude that while AI holds transformative promise, its successful integration requires a holistic strategy encompassing technical, educational, and cultural adjustments. The chapter underscores that AI adoption is part of a broader organizational transformation that must be participatory and aligned with creative values.

In Chap. 17, *AI Speech Generation: Balancing Disruption, Opportunity, and Performer Rights,* Richard Savery explores the disruptive impact of AI-driven voice synthesis on the voice acting industry, drawing on insights from both creators and developers. The chapter presents perspectives from seasoned voice actor Bonnie Bogovich and Brian Cook, CEO of WellSaid Labs, to highlight ethical, legal, and professional tensions surrounding voice cloning technologies. Savery traces the historical trajectory of technological disruption in voice performance, from radio and dubbing to remote recording and performance capture, arguing that AI presents a qualitatively different challenge: it can replicate human voices with minimal input and without continuous human involvement. Through interview-based analysis, the chapter underscores critical concerns such as consent, fair compensation, data ownership, and voice identity. Bogovich's contractual strategies, including "No AI Clauses," illustrate how performers attempt to safeguard their work and reputations, while Cook's company model emphasizes consent-based training, royalty payments, and transparent moderation to uphold ethical standards. The chapter contrasts exploitative practices with sustainable alternatives, arguing that the future of AI speech generation hinges on collective adherence to ethical norms. Rather than framing AI as a binary threat or opportunity, Savery positions it as a transformative force that can augment human creativity, if governance structures prioritize artist rights, identity protection, and revenue sharing. This case study ultimately calls for industry-wide dialogue and regulation to ensure that voice actors remain central to the evolving landscape of synthetic speech.

In Chap. 18, *Deepfakes: Threats and Media Impact*, Daniel Bendahan Bitton, Alexander Godulla, and Christian Pieter Hoffmann examine the rise of deepfakes and their multifaceted implications for media, journalism, and society. The chapter traces the rapid development of deepfake technology, situating it within the broader discourse of GenAI and emphasizing its dual nature: while offering creative opportunities in fields such as entertainment and education, deepfakes also pose significant risks, including disinformation, fraud, and identity manipulation. Drawing on five years of empirical research, the authors explore Internet users' knowledge and attitudes toward deepfakes, revealing notable gender disparities and broader digital inequalities. The study also examines the impact of deepfakes on journalistic practice, identifying both the heightened complexity of fact-checking and the potential for innovative content formats. The authors argue that while technological detection methods are evolving, they remain perpetually behind in the race against increasingly sophisticated deepfake production. The chapter calls for interdisciplinary, multi-level responses, spanning individual media literacy, organizational guidelines, and regulatory frameworks. Bendahan Bitton, Godulla, and Hoffmann conclude that deepfakes symbolize a deeper shift in the epistemology of media, challenging core values such as authenticity and trust. To navigate this evolving landscape, the authors advocate for an integrated research agenda that bridges technological, social, and ethical perspectives, emphasizing that a nuanced understanding of deepfakes is crucial for safeguarding democratic discourse in the age of synthetic realities.

In Chap. 19, *"Limitless Computation on a Finite Planet?" The Actually-Existing Ecology of Generative AI*, Ian Collinson critically examines the ecological footprint of artificial intelligence, challenging prevailing narratives that frame AI solely as a solution to environmental problems. Drawing on theories of ecomateriality and the "material turn" in media studies, the chapter positions AI as an eco-media object whose environmental impact extends across energy consumption, raw material extraction, and electronic waste. Collinson identifies three primary disruptions: AI's escalating energy demands, which complicate efforts toward decarbonization; its reliance on scarce resources such as copper, rare earths, and water; and its contribution to the growing crisis of e-waste, particularly in the global south. The chapter underscores how AI development amplifies global inequalities by shifting environmental burdens onto less developed regions, perpetuating technocolonial dynamics. Through a synthesis of empirical data, policy analysis, and critical theory, Collinson critiques the opacity of AI's environmental costs, arguing that industry self-regulation and voluntary guidelines remain insufficient. The text calls for robust, enforceable frameworks, spanning transparency mandates, sustainable practices, and independent auditing, to address AI's ecological implications comprehensively. Ultimately, the chapter contends that meaningful action requires dismantling the myth of digital immateriality and confronting AI's deep entanglement with planetary limits, urging scholars, policymakers, and technologists alike to reimagine AI within the broader context of environmental justice and sustainability.

In Chap. 20, *AI in Media Education and the Training of Media Professionals*, Anna Jupowicz-Ginalska and Mariola Kinal examine how artificial intelligence is transforming media education and the preparation of future media professionals. The chapter distinguishes two primary trajectories: first, integrating AI into general media education to foster digital, informational, and critical literacy; and second, embedding AI tools and ethics into professional training for journalists, editors, and media managers. Drawing on literature reviews and content analyses, the authors highlight rising awareness of ethical, technical, and pedagogical challenges, such as data privacy, algorithmic bias, and the credibility of AI-generated content. The study underscores the need for updated curricula that reflect AI's pervasive influence on media practices, advocating for interdisciplinary collaboration among educators, technologists, and industry stakeholders. The chapter also explores barriers to effective implementation, including skill gaps among educators and students, and emphasizes hands-on experience with AI tools as essential for meaningful learning outcomes. Jupowicz-Ginalska and Kinal conclude that media education in the age of AI must transcend technical training to cultivate ethical reasoning, critical thinking, and adaptive skills. By equipping students with both practical competencies and a nuanced understanding of AI's societal impacts, educational institutions can better prepare graduates for an evolving media landscape where AI is both a tool and a subject of scrutiny.

In Chap. 21, *AI and the Hyper-personalization of News Content*, Maximilian Eder explores how AI-driven personalization is transforming news distribution in digital environments. The chapter traces the evolution from traditional editorial control to algorithm-based news recommender systems, emphasizing the shift toward hyper-personalization that dynamically tailors content based on individual user behaviors and preferences. Eder reviews key literature on content personalization, highlighting technological advances, such as predictive analytics, conversational recommender systems, and dynamic paywalls; and critical challenges, including data privacy, editorial independence, and the risk of reinforcing filter bubbles. Case studies from Scandinavian news organizations illustrate how AI-enhanced systems blend editorial oversight with automated personalization to boost engagement and subscription rates. The analysis also addresses user attitudes toward AI-powered personalization, revealing mixed responses across countries and demographic groups. While hyper-personalization offers opportunities for deeper audience engagement and revenue growth, it raises pressing ethical questions about transparency, manipulation risks, and the erosion of journalistic values. Eder advocates for a balanced approach that integrates AI's technological potential with strong editorial principles and regulatory oversight. The chapter concludes that although AI-powered hyper-personalization holds transformative promise, its full potential and its risks remain underexplored, requiring further research and thoughtful implementation to align technological innovation with the public service mission of journalism.

In Chap. 22, *Toward Transparency of Synthetic Media: EU Regulatory Perspective and Its Implications*, Mateusz Łabuz offers a detailed examination of the European Union's regulatory response to the challenges posed by synthetic media. Anchored in the 2024 AI Act, the chapter dissects how synthetic media, ranging from AI-generated texts to deepfakes, are categorized as limited-risk AI systems, with a focus on transparency obligations as a primary safeguard. Łabuz critically analyzes key provisions, particularly Article 50, which sets out requirements for marking AI-generated content to enhance public awareness and counter misinformation. The chapter emphasizes the pioneering legal definition of deepfakes and explores how the AI Act distinguishes between various forms of synthetic media, arguing that these distinctions are essential for effective regulation. Łabuz highlights the strengths of the EU's approach, rooted in democratic values such as trustworthiness and civil rights protection, while also identifying shortcomings, including definitional ambiguities, enforcement challenges, and inconsistencies across related legal acts like the Digital Services Act. The analysis underscores that transparency alone may not suffice to counter complex risks, particularly as synthetic media become more pervasive and sophisticated. The chapter concludes that a comprehensive regulatory ecosystem, combining legal precision, technical standards, and public education, is vital to safeguarding media integrity. Łabuz calls for continuous refinement of EU legislation and stronger international cooperation to address the global nature of synthetic media disruptions effectively.

Wiesbaden, Germany Stephan Böhm
Sydney, NSW, Australia Steve Collins
Leipzig, Germany Alexander Godulla
Sydney, NSW, Australia Sarah Keith
Bruce, Canberra, Australia Richard Savery

Contents

Part I

AI-Impact and Disruption by Media Sectors and Segments

Print: News, Magazines, and Publishing

1

Michael Graßl

Abstract

This chapter provides a comprehensive overview of the impact of artificial intelligence (AI) on print media, including newspapers, magazines, and publishing. It explores the historical development, current applications, and future potential of AI in the print sector, which has often been overlooked in favor of more visible digital innovations. The research highlights that while AI adoption in print media has been slower compared to digital platforms, it is steadily growing. The chapter examines various use cases along the journalistic value chain, from research and verification to production and distribution. It discusses how AI technologies are transforming workflows, content creation, and business models in print media organizations. The analysis draws on recent studies and surveys that demonstrate increasing AI implementation in print newsrooms, albeit with challenges such as resource constraints and organizational readiness. Furthermore, the chapter addresses the complexities of integrating AI into traditional print journalism, including ethical considerations, skill requirements, and the need for strategic planning. It emphasizes that while AI offers significant opportunities for efficiency and innovation in print media, human oversight and journalistic expertise remain crucial. The research concludes by suggesting that the future of print journalism likely lies in a hybrid model that effectively combines AI capabilities with human creativity and critical thinking.

M. Graßl (✉)
Magdeburg-Stendal University of Applied Sciences, Magdeburg, Germany
e-mail: michael.grassl@h2.de

S. Böhm et al. (eds.), *Handbook of AI-based Media Disruption*, Future of Business and Finance, https://doi.org/10.1007/978-3-032-07605-2_1

1.1 Introduction: AI in Print Media as an Underrated Area of Use

When considering artificial intelligence (AI) in journalism, one often focuses on the "shiny things" (Posetti, 2018) of the AI revolution: avatar TV presenters, successful analysis of vast datasets (e.g., Panama Papers, Guevara, 2019), or AI-powered radio stations. These digital products typically garner significant external visibility and attention. However, it has become evident that AI has been profoundly influencing the entire production process of journalistic and media content for years, extending beyond mere production and output (Graßl et al., 2022). This impact is not limited to the operational practices and workflows of data teams or other digital units; the production of print products is also significantly affected by AI as a digital technology, often occurring beneath the radar of public and academic scrutiny.

The use of AI in print publications initially becomes publicly visible only when explicit reference is made to AI-generated texts or images, typically through labeling. The utilization of AI-generated content in print media remains relatively sparse compared to digital content, partly due to persistent public skepticism toward AI-generated texts in print products (Vogler et al., 2023; Ross Arguedas, 2024). At first glance, the impact of AI in the print sector appears to be primarily behind the scenes. However, the potential of AI for print media is substantial, particularly in the realm of personalized content layout, which holds promise for audience relations and distribution (Simon, 2024). Furthermore, the disruption caused by AI is not solely the result of increasing datafication in newsrooms (Porlezza, 2024) but also serves as its significant accelerator.

This chapter aims to present an overview of past, current, and future developments related to AI in the field of print publications and to systematize its impact on this area in greater detail. By examining these developments, we can gain a more comprehensive understanding of how AI is reshaping the landscape of print publishing and its production processes.

1.2 Overview of Disruption

1.2.1 Historical Steps

As already mentioned, AI is no longer a new technology for media organizations. Since the early/mid-2010s, editorial teams around the world have been experimenting with software developments on a large scale (Van Dalen, 2012; Carlson, 2015; Beckett, 2019), which at that time were still primarily subsumed under the term automation. The beginnings of AI in journalism are closely linked to the history of the increasing datafication of journalism. Theoretically, working with data in journalism could be dated back to the eighteenth century, when publications like the *Wall Street Journal* started using statistical data and tables to report on events like wars, mortality rates, and public affairs (Porlezza, 2024). But the main development began after the Second World War. Based on Dierickx and Lindén (2024), the following phases, which are fluid in transition, can be roughly defined for the past century up to the introduction of ChatGPT:

- *Early use of computers to predict election outcomes*: In 1952, CBS experimented with a computer to predict the outcome of the US presidential election. This marked an early attempt to use data analysis in journalism, well before the term "artificial intelligence" was even coined.
- *Development of computer-assisted journalism (CAR) in the 1980s*: As personal computers became more widespread, new opportunities arose for journalists to collect and analyze data. CAR made it possible to uncover complex stories and led to the development of skills in working with databases.
- *The rise of data journalism and the role of "Journalist-programmers"*: Starting in the 2000s, data journalism emerged as a distinct form, focusing on narrative storytelling based on data analysis and visualization. The role of the "journalist-programmer" emerged, combining both journalistic and technical skills. The rise of data journalism led to various labels like "data-driven journalism," "interactive journalism," "big data journalism," and the formal adoption of "data journalism" as a beat (Porlezza, 2024).
- *Introduction of AI to automate news production:* AI technologies are increasingly used since the 2010s to automatically generate news articles and personalize content for users.

The hype surrounding artificial intelligence publicly gained momentum primarily with the release of ChatGPT in November 2022 (Heilweil, 2023). However, the potential of AI had already been recognized by media managers a few years earlier, regardless of whether their focus was on print or online media. In an international survey conducted in December 2020 among 227 decision-makers in media companies, 69% identified artificial intelligence as the most significant technological enabler for journalistic innovations in the coming years. AI thus ranked far ahead of 5G technology, which came in second place with only 18% (Newman, 2021). Nearly 2 years later, just 2 months after the release of ChatGPT, a follow-up survey (with 303 respondents) revealed that 28% of participants now considered AI to be a regular part of their work, while 39% reported experimenting in this area (Newman et al., 2023).

Although many of the use cases today, depending on the definition, represent more automation than artificial intelligence, the rapid technological development has been bundled under the umbrella term of artificial intelligence (Beckett, 2019; Brennen et al., 2022; Beckett & Mira, 2023; Ertem-Eray & Cheng, 2025). Neither at the time of the survey nor to this day has this led to a uniform definition and delineation of terms, such as automation (Graefe & Bohlken, 2020; Sarısakaloğlu, 2025; Spyridou & Ioannou, 2025). To avoid an extensive discussion of terminology in this context, this chapter will refer to the definition provided by Ertem-Eray and Cheng (2025, p. 13), who define AI, in the context of a literature analysis of AI contributions in peer-reviewed journals, as "a computer program or system that performs human functions associated with some level of human intelligence through algorithms, techniques, and technologies that offer a powerful mathematical method for making predictions, recommendations, and decisions and selecting information."

AI technologies are now being applied across the entire value chain, for both digital and print products alike: starting as trend finders or support in research, assisting in the transcription of interviews, serving as tools for formulating or producing automated texts, and extending to the analysis of consumption data (Graßl et al., 2022), to name just a few use cases (see in more detail Sect. 1.2.2). However, the public focus, particularly due to the hype surrounding ChatGPT, often remains on generative AI (Thomson et al., 2025). Generally, generative AI is employed to generate not only text but also images, audio, video, or other media, based on its training data and in response to written prompts. Cools and Diakopoulos (2024, p. 2) specify its use in journalism: "In journalism, generative AI can be used to perform a variety of tasks that are situated in every stage of the reporting process, from the gathering to the production, verification, and distribution of news."

Indeed, studies confirm that generative AI tools have found broad use in media organizations worldwide: A survey in Q4 2024 of 200 journalists in more than 70 countries around the world with focus to the Global South shows that 81% of the respondents use AI in their everyday journalistic work (Radcliffe, 2025). ChatGPT is thereby the most popular AI tool. In the second JournalismAI global survey, more than 120 editors, journalists, technologies, and mediamakers from 105 newsrooms across 46 countries were asked how they use AI (Beckett & Mira, 2023). The results show similarly high values for the use of AI in newsrooms: 90% of respondents use AI for news production, 80% for news distribution and 75% for newsgathering. In the study "Journalism and Technology Trends and Predictions 2025," 87% of the 326 digital leaders from 51 countries and territories surveyed stated that newsrooms are being transformed by Generative AI technologies fully or somewhat (Newman & Cherubini, 2025). The study also shows that back-end automation through AI is still the most relevant goal, with 96% of publisher respondents saying that this task will be very important or somewhat important in 2025.

So, although AI has now arrived in the mainstream of media organizations, mostly in the form of generative AI, numerous media organizations are still in the experimental phase of development (Beckett & Mira, 2023; Newman & Cherubini, 2025; Radcliffe, 2025). Schützeneder et al. (2024b, p. 106) therefore also refer to the current stage as the trial-and-error phase and conclude based on international case studies: "AI is perceived as a breakthrough that cannot be ignored, but many of its developments are still based on trial and error. (…) The main challenges facing the growth of AI are often grounded in an irrational fear of change, as well as the significant resources (particularly time) that are required." From a practitioner's perspective, Caswell (2023), who spent 6 months visiting media organizations around the world regarding their use of AI, notes that in addition to human and monetary resources, clear AI strategies are often lacking in this phase to find long-term perspectives for facing the competitive environment in terms of new business models.

1.2.2 AI in Print

Determining the specific impact of AI as a digital technology on non-digital products such as newspapers, magazines, or books is not an easy task at first. Many of the studies mentioned do not differentiate between print and digital organizations, partly because this differentiation is often no longer tenable. However, most of the historical steps described apply equally to print and digital. Print-oriented organizations have, by contrast, more often reacted to the introduction of ChatGPT with skepticism and worry. In Germany, for example, several local newspapers printed ChatGPT-generated texts or interviews with ChatGPT to demonstrate that ChatGPT makes many clumsy mistakes and cannot replace journalists or local journalism (Seibold, 2023; Sünkel, 2023). Fears regarding new the technology have often been, and continue to be, rooted in concerns about the potential loss of one's job (Graßl et al., 2022; Beckett & Mira, 2023). A qualitative study conducted by Pitluk et al. (2025) examining the integration of AI in legacy magazine journalism reveals that reservations continue to be among the most significant obstacles in the print sector.

In general, single studies indicate that the adoption of artificial intelligence (AI) is more prevalent in digital publishing but is also steadily growing in print media. A 2024 survey of German publishers found that 44% used AI for text editing in digital products and 30% in print; 42% and 37%, respectively, planned future implementation (MVFP, 2024). For illustrations, 33% of publishers already used AI in digital products (with 28% planning to adopt it), while 23% reported current use in print and 28% intended future adoption. The acceptance of AI tools among publishers in Germany is high and continues to grow. According to a follow-up study (KPMG, 2024), nearly 80% of German publishing houses have already gained experience with AI, with the majority evaluating these experiences positively. One-third of publishers actively use AI in their daily operations, while an additional 44% are in the testing or experimental phase. Larger publishers with more than 100 employees demonstrate a higher level of adoption or experimentation with AI (85%) compared to smaller publishers (50%). The primary applications of AI are focused on editorial and creative processes. For instance, 33% of editorial teams use AI to support research and topic selection. Strategic areas such as marketing, sales, and customer service are also increasingly considering AI, with 31% of publishers planning to implement AI in customer service in the future.

The study by Rinehart and Kung (2022), who examined nearly 200 newsrooms across the United States, employing a survey methodology complemented by expert interviews, reveals significant disparities in AI adoption and readiness across different media sectors (print, radio, television, digital only), with print organizations demonstrating particular challenges. Their findings indicate that print and radio managers report less frequent use of AI in both distribution and production operations compared to their counterparts in other media sectors. Moreover, print organizations exhibit lower levels of managerial support for AI exploration. The research also highlights that print media outlets have less time available for experimentation with AI technologies compared to digital platforms. Despite these sector-specific challenges, the authors note that across all media types, including print, there is a general sentiment of unpreparedness for full AI integration. Wilczek et al. (2024) adopted and systematized Rinehart and Kung's dataset, leading them to conclude that the greatest potential for AI within local news organizations lies primarily in the automation of processes.

The use cases for AI implementation do not differ significantly between print and digital media, but rather in specific aspects. This distinction becomes more apparent when examining the value chain of a journalistic product in detail. The framework proposed by Schützeneder et al. (2024a) serves as a conceptual underpinning, which has systematized AI applications along the value chain from research to analysis:

- *Research*: Data analysis, image, video, and audio analysis, language analysis, trend analysis, translation, and transcription.
- *Verification*: Verification of (deep)fakes and leaked content, image, video, and audio analysis.
- *Production*: Automated texts, images, audio, and videos, text summarization, speech synthesis, correction, transcription, subtitling.
- *Archiving*: Metadata enrichment, tagging for text, image, and audio, transcription.
- *Distribution*: Recommendation systems, comment moderation, hate speech detection, voice assistants and chatbots, accessibility through simplified language, audio rendering.
- *Analysis*: analysis of target groups and reach, social media monitoring, suggestion and inspiration for new research.

Most of the areas listed here can be adopted almost one-to-one for print. This is illustrated by four examples in the context of research:

- *Ruhr Nachrichten*: This German daily newspaper employs "AI reporters" ("KI-Reporter") in their research process, generating a minimum of six articles daily. These AI-produced contents are augmented with information from the newspaper's archives and undergo review and editing by human editors prior to publication (Enslein, 2024).
- *Le Monde*: The French daily newspaper has integrated DeepL software into its editorial workflows to expedite international research capabilities. Subsequently, DeepL has been employed to facilitate an English-language offering of the newspaper (Twipe, 2023; Tomorrows Publisher, 2024).
- *Bloomberg News*: This financial and business publication leverages AI algorithms in its research processes. These algorithms assist in detecting suspicious trading activities and potential market manipulations; subsequently, BloombergGPT has been introduced as a proprietary model developed to support journalistic and financial analysis tasks (Quinonez & Meij, 2024).
- *ITromsø*: The regional Norwegian publication has developed a proprietary AI-driven tool called DJINN (Data Journalism Interface for News Gathering and Notification). DJINN's AI algorithms detect patterns and trends within the data,

recommending potential issues and stories for journalists to pursue (Elo Dean et al., 2025).

The differences between digital and print media are particularly pronounced in the areas of distribution and analysis, as these domains in print production are still significantly less digitalized. Beyond these mentioned areas, AI can and is being deployed in various other sectors of media organizations, such as marketing, sales, and customer service. In the realm of customer service, German daily newspapers such as Nordwest-Zeitung and WESER-KURIER have implemented the AI solution Parloa. According to the developer, this AI-powered voicebot now fully and automatically processes 30% of telephone complaints (Parloa, 2024). Print publishers also perceive substantial potential for AI implementation in the automation of administrative tasks (BDZV, 2025). In addition, the following print-specific fields of application for AI can be identified (not exhaustive):

- *Print optimization:* AI systems can monitor and adjust print parameters in real time to maximize print quality and minimize waste. This leads to more efficient production processes and cost savings for publishers (Smith, 2025).
- *Print run optimization:* By analyzing reader trends and behavior, AI can help publishers predict the optimal print run, leading to a reduction in overproduction and related costs.
- *Automated Layout Design*: AI tools can enable the automated production of print layouts for newspapers, magazines, and other print products, such as Die Welt and Welt am Sonntag in Germany are doing or the Norwegian newspaper Aftenposten, which already produces 80% of its print pages automatically (InterRed, 2024), and ensure efficiency improvements and cost reductions. The above-mentioned study by Rinehart and Kung (2022) shows that automating page layouts is one of the most-requested items on the wish list by print newsrooms.
- *Personalization*: Artificial Intelligence enables the creation of personalized print editions by analyzing reader preferences and selecting content accordingly. While this capability was previously primarily available in the digital realm, it is now becoming feasible for print products, as exemplified by *The New York Times* (Filipsson, 2025).
- *Sales optimization*: Recommendation systems can further support publishers' program planning. Based on past sales data, for example, the success of future titles can be predicted through simulation, even before these works are created. In this way, customer needs can be specifically anticipated, and gaps in the program can be identified and filled (Klotz, 2024). For example, HarperCollins Publishers LLC leverages the power of AI-driven predictive analytics to identify emerging market trends and popular genres. This enables them to better cater to reader preferences and refine their marketing strategies accordingly (Ryzhko et al., 2024).

Given the diverse applications of AI, German publishers, for instance, maintain a generally positive outlook despite challenging global conditions. Specifically, 85% of surveyed publishers regard AI as a significant opportunity and a crucial tool for increasing revenue (MVFP, 2024). Ryzhko et al. (2024) have further refined the understanding of these economic opportunities for the book industry through their dedicated study. Conducted between August 2023 and January 2024, their study utilized expert interviews, monitoring of online platforms, and document analysis to identify key areas where AI is influencing publishing houses in an economically positive direction. These areas include streamlining content processing tasks such as manuscript review and plagiarism detection, enhancing the creation of marketing and promotional materials, and improving data management and analysis. Furthermore, AI can aid in strategic planning and the development of digital spaces, enabling publishers to adapt to evolving market dynamics and explore new revenue streams. According to the study results, the potential economic benefits also extend to the creation of new professional roles within the industry and the improvement of e-book production. The possibility of machine-generated content, despite copyright considerations, is viewed as a potentially positive development.

It is evident that AI not only impacts the entire value chain of a print product but also permeates the publisher's operations, affecting areas beyond the print product itself, such as printing, marketing, and customer service. Figure 1.1 synthesizes the various applications of AI in print media based on current research findings. While AI offers significant potential in the print sector, it also presents challenges. Issues with handling this new technology became publicly visible, for instance, in the case of the American newspaper Columbus Dispatch, which automated high school sports reports and faced strong criticism from the community for the wording of the texts (Wu, 2023). Another example is the German magazine "Die Aktuelle," which published an AI-generated interview with Michael Schumacher and was subsequently fined 200,000 euros, payable to the family (Rosenkranz, 2024). Further challenges will be discussed in more detail under 1.3.

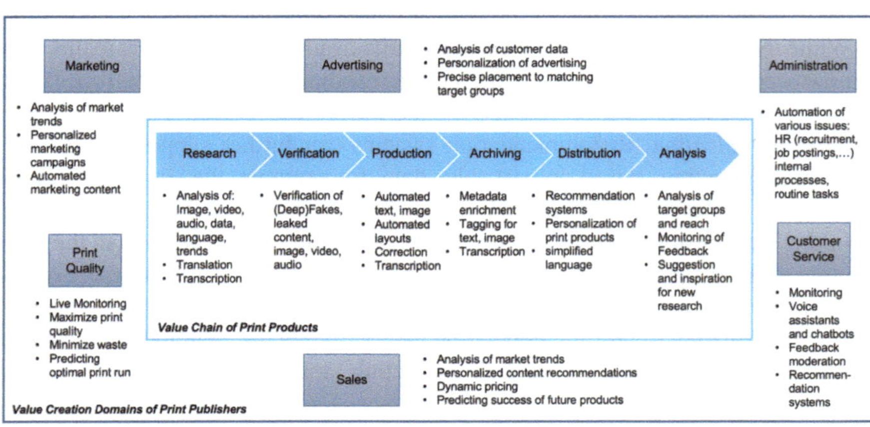

Fig. 1.1 Overview of potential applications of AI in print media (Source: Author)

1.2.3 Current Debates

The significant increase in AI's importance for publishers has led to a substantial growth in research within this field (Ausserhofer et al., 2020). Porlezza (2024) notes that research into data and journalism significantly increased from 2010 onwards, particularly in Europe, with studies focusing on data-intensive newswork in countries like Norway, the UK, Sweden, Germany, and Belgium. Ertem-Eray and Cheng (2025) demonstrated in their study that the number of articles addressing AI in peer-reviewed journals in the communication field steadily increased between 2006 and 2022, with 47 articles published in 2022 compared to only three per year in 2018 and 2016. The authors observed that the most examined AI technologies among these peer-reviewed journal articles were informational chatbots, deepfakes, social bots, and algorithms. Notably, research on AI in the media industry is no longer limited to the USA or Europe but now extends across the globe. To illustrate this global scope, it is worth highlighting research from various regions: Australia (Thomson et al., 2025), Africa (Kothari & Cruikshank, 2021), the Arabic-speaking context (Abdel-Haleem & Alnajjar, 2024), Pakistan (Jamil, 2020), and Latin America (Soto-Sanfiel et al., 2022). Sarısakaloğlu (2025) has conducted extensive research on international AI applications in journalism. Her systematic analysis reveals a significant increase in empirical studies exploring algorithm-driven journalism. Her findings demonstrate a marked imbalance in global AI research, with a clear dominance by European and North American institutions. Specifically, Sarısakaloğlu's work shows that 58.7% of analyzed studies originate from European countries, followed by 21.5% from North America. In contrast, only 12.6% of studies come from Asian countries, with minimal representation from African and South American researchers. This geographical disparity highlights persistent structural inequalities in AI journalism research. Nevertheless, Sarısakaloğlu's research also indicates that this diverse body of scholarship demonstrates the widespread interest in and impact of AI on journalism across different cultural and geographical contexts. It is not possible to comprehensively review the entire body of research on this topic. Nevertheless, the research discussed so far serves as a basis for outlining four key debates that are currently of particular focus in relation to print media:

- *Verification and Deep Fakes*: While verification and deep fakes are not print-specific challenges and primarily affect the digital realm (Godulla et al., 2021), content verification has become a central challenge in research for all forms of journalism, including print media, and thus affects all publishers (Schützeneder et al., 2024a). From an international perspective, regional disparities exist in proprietary automated tools for misinformation detection, monitoring, and compilation, with many based in Europe and funded by major entities such as Google, EU projects, and the International Fact-Checking Network (IFCN) (Cazzamatta & Sarısakaloğlu, 2025). Journalistic fact-checking initiatives, often established in response to political developments (Klinghardt & Graßl, 2024), include examples such as "Factrank" (originally called "Claimbuster") in Belgium, a tool that transcribes statements of parliament members and labels them based on their fact-checking potential. Similarly, FullFact, a fact-checking platform from the United Kingdom, employs comparable tools for live fact-checking (Cools & Diakopoulos, 2024). Current debates increasingly focus on the collaboration between publishers and platform providers like Meta (Cazzamatta & Sarısakaloğlu, 2025).

- *Ethics*: Ethical debates surrounding AI in the media industry revolve around balancing human control with automation, safeguarding quality standards and free opinion-forming, and managing the function and use of "social scoring" (see in more detail the chapter by Schützeneder, 2025 in this book). An international study of Becker et al. (2025) shows that publishers have already begun to converge in their guidelines on key points such as transparency and human supervision when dealing with AI-generated content. The potential loss of human oversight is a major concern, requiring human responsibility in ethical AI applications (Diakopoulos et al., 2024). Fragmented regulatory and ethical frameworks within Europe necessitate specific guidelines addressing disinformation, diversity, and social responsibility (Porlezza, 2023). Integrating ethical and legal considerations into media education through practical experiences is also crucial (Cheng & Lee, 2024). Fundamentally, the question arises whether AI requires a new journalistic ethic or if existing norms remain valid (Thomaß, 2024).
- *Loss of jobs:* Concerns about job security persist more prominently in print journalism than in digital journalism, with ongoing discussions about the potential impact of AI on the employment of print journalists and authors (Caswell, 2023; Simon, 2024; Pitluk et al., 2025; Thomson et al., 2025). Although initial apprehensions have not fully materialized, and print editors are still in demand, certain fears are still present, particularly among freelance journalists (Graßl et al., 2022). A notable example that garnered international attention and substantiated these concerns is the case of Springer Verlag in Germany (Henley, 2023). In 2023, the company announced planned job cuts at the printed daily newspaper "Bild," citing AI implementation as one of the reasons (Iwersen et al., 2023). Part of the internal statement was: "Unfortunately, we also have to part ways with colleagues who have tasks that are being replaced by AI and/or processes in the digital world or who do not fit into this new set-up with their current skills" (Ernst, 2023). Similar apprehensions surround the debates concerning layoffs at Australian Community Media (ACM), Australia's largest independent publisher (Lee, 2025). However, current developments also indicate that while certain roles are indeed being replaced, new job opportunities are simultaneously emerging (Caswell, 2023; Simon, 2024; Filipsson, 2025).
- *Implementation of AI:* As previously indicated, many publishers worldwide are still in a trial-and-error phase regarding the implementation of AI in their daily workflows (Beckett & Mira, 2023; Schützeneder et al., 2024a, 2024b; Radcliffe, 2025). The focus is increasingly shifting toward enhancing efficiency and effectiveness through AI tools (Prinzing & Graßl, 2024; Newman & Cherubini, 2025; Ramlochan, 2025). Simon (2024) posits that the debate on AI's impact on journalistic efficiency is polarized between those who envision AI as a liberating force enabling journalists to focus on higher-order tasks and skeptics who argue

that AI's productivity gains may be more constrained. The economic viability of various forms of journalism is also being increasingly discussed; for example, it is assumed that investigative journalism, due to its specific requirements, is less likely to benefit from productivity gains through AI (Wellbrock, 2024). Many open questions (Strategy? Competencies? Effectiveness? Field of application? Resources? Cooperations? Data privacy?) and challenges surrounding the effective implementation of AI remain unresolved and concern publishers, who increasingly depend on it for a successful future. It is evident that these challenges exist on various levels, which will be addressed in more detail below.

1.3 AI and Its Impact on the Micro-, Meso-, and Macro-level

How does the impact of AI on print publishers manifest more concretely? Research has not yet found a common answer to this question, as Spyridou and Ioannou (2025) state that "despite growing interest in the intersection of journalism and AI, the effects of AI on the news industry remain poorly understood." But as previously indicated, AI serves as a powerful innovation driver for the media industry, including print, as expressed by a publishers' association in Germany in a press release: "Within a short period, artificial intelligence has already proven to be a transformation accelerator, innovation driver, and recognized tool in numerous media organizations" (MVFP, 2024). To shed a more detailed light to this impact, current research from innovation studies is utilized. Initially, factors that support and obstruct the implementation of AI are identified, revealing preliminary insights into the extent of its impact. Subsequently, key findings and challenges at various levels are more explicitly elaborated.

Innovation research in communication science has generally experienced significant growth in recent years (García-Avilés, 2021; Pavlik, 2021; Meier et al., 2024b), increasingly focusing on factors that positively and negatively influence innovations (Meier et al., 2024a; Wolf et al., 2024). Concurrently, interest and insights at the intersection of innovation, AI, and implementation have expanded (Alsheibani et al., 2020; Túñez-López et al., 2021). For example, Eder and Sjøvaag (2025) demonstrate that potential reasons for slower AI adoption in local journalism include insufficient resources, experimental rather than targeted implementation, and competing priorities.

The theoretical framework used in the following is based on the foundational work of Meier et al. (2024a), who, in an international research project, systematized supportive and obstructive factors in the implementation of innovations in media organizations according to micro, meso, and macro levels, as well as internal and external factors. The authors understand internal factors to encompass aspects such as the availability of human, financial, and technological resources, established work processes, company practices, knowledge and talent within the organization, and the prevailing professional culture. External factors, in contrast, are associated with the regulatory framework governing the industry, the specific characteristics of the market, the broader economic situation, and the consumption habits of the target audience.

In the context of innovation, the micro-level describes the level of individuals who are part of newsrooms, media organizations, and specific units, such as newsrooms, labs, and start-ups, or who are working as freelancers (García-Avilés, 2021). The meso-level focuses on the effects of innovations at the organizational level, thus placing media companies in the center of attention as actors and as affected by innovations. The macro-level describes the mutual relationships of the impact of innovations on journalism at the societal level (Graßl & Meier, 2024). In the study by Meier et al. (2024a), supportive factors include, for example, the intrinsic motivation of employees (micro-level), an open failure culture (meso-level), and innovation funding (macro-level). Conversely, obstructive factors encompass mistrust from colleagues (micro-level), pre-existing structures and routines of the print industry (meso-level), and lack of political support (macro-level).

This systematization is applied to the implementation of AI and enriched, where possible, with print-specific findings derived from various studies (e.g., Newman, 2021; Beckett & Mira, 2023; Caswell, 2023; Prinzing & Graßl, 2024; Simon, 2024; Eder & Sjøvaag, 2025; Radcliffe, 2025; Thomson et al., 2025). The result is illustrated in Table 1.1 and then concretized at the individual levels.

1.3.1 Micro-level

The micro-level impacts of AI primarily converge on the issue of necessary competencies and their acquisition. As Table 1.1 indicates, a lack of technical expertise and insufficient time for experimental engagement with the new technology constitute clear impediments to AI integration within newsrooms. Conversely, regular training and professional development opportunities centered around AI are considered particularly conducive factors for its adoption. This highlights that the micro-level impacts affect a relatively broad segment of the workforce, more extensively than has been the case with some other areas of innovation (Graßl et al., 2023; Katzenberger & Keil, 2024). The rapid pace of technological advancement has resulted in a competency deficit that now requires remediation.

A study by Veenstra et al. (2024) highlights that addressing competency deficits is no longer solely the responsibility of publishers. Their research examines journalism students' perceptions, usage, and understanding of large language models (LLMs) like ChatGPT, alongside their ethical considerations. The findings reveal that while students view LLMs as unavoidable tools in their future journalistic careers, a prevalent misconception exists regarding how these technologies generate content. This knowledge gap stems partly from a lack of fundamental knowledge about digital tools in general. The research also highlights the necessity for journalism educators to enhance their own understanding of these technologies. However, as further studies demonstrate, AI skills remain significantly underrepresented in university curricula compared to other digital skills, such as social media (Katzenberger, 2024). To the extent that artificial intelligence is revolutionizing

Table 1.1 Overview of supportive and obstructive factors in the implementation of AI, categorized by micro, meso, and macro levels as well as internal and external factors (Source: Author)

	Internal factors	External factors
Micro-level		
Supportive	Intrinsic motivation, AI training for individual employees, positive mindset toward AI	–
Obstructive	Increasing workload, lack of technical expertise, limited resources for testing, concerns about AI (e.g., in terms of job loss)	–
Meso-level		
Supportive	Management commitment, interfaces between editorial and technical departments, modern in-house technical infrastructure and existing technical expertise, transparent and regular internal communication, own data and archives, well-established structures and processes, open failure culture	Networks with other media organizations, cooperations with universities, collaboration and workshops with external AI companies, "cheap" external infrastructure
Obstructive	No fixed people in touch for projects, long development periods, no involvement of editors, different languages between technical and editorial teams, lack of resources (time, money, staff), resistance from staff, strong works council, no in-house development team, no certainty of success, fear of change, missing strategy and priorities	Long coordination with cooperation partners, talents earn better in other industries, limits of available tools, changes to external tools
Macro-level		
Supportive	–	The hype around AI, (political) innovation funding
Obstructive	–	Dynamic technological development, data privacy, continental, and country-specific challenges (e.g., lack of digitalization), skeptical audience, dependency on platforms

journalism through task automation and improved data analysis, journalists must develop new competencies, particularly in advanced data handling, while simultaneously becoming more versatile and upholding core journalistic values such as ethical judgment and critical thinking (Dinçer, 2024). To meet this challenge, new approaches such as gamification in education are being advocated (Borchardt, 2022).

Beyond broad-based employee development, AI increasingly necessitates new specialists to cover emerging professional roles. For example, in January 2024, *The New York Times* announced the creation of new positions for "engineers and editors" tasked with leading the organization's efforts to embed generative AI in its newsroom (Spyridou & Ioannou, 2025). While individuals from within newsrooms can be trained as experts, such as prompt engineers, external non-journalists are also entering publishers' organizations. This influx can pose challenges to the existing editorial ecosystem. As previously described within current debates, the print sector is particularly affected by persistent anxieties and concerns regarding AI. Counterbalancing these concerns, although sometimes less pronounced than in the purely digital realm, is a degree of openness toward AI and an intrinsic motivation to engage with the new technology. These opposing poles can lead to disparities in AI literacy among individual employees and between newsrooms and departments within the same media organization. Such disparities present a challenge for the media organization as a whole (Dodds et al., 2025).

1.3.2 Meso-level

Beyond varying levels of knowledge among staff, numerous challenges exist at the meso-level, stemming from the impact of AI on media organizations (cf. Table 1.1). Many of these internal challenges are organizational in nature, including the creation of interfaces between technology and (journalistic) editorial departments; the establishment of experimental spaces or dedicated departments; the provision of sufficient resources (personnel, technical, financial); the development and establishment of new processes and structures; and the development of an innovation-oriented corporate culture characterized by transparent communication.

In a positive light, the impact of AI leads publishers to demonstrate greater openness to and engagement in collaborations within the industry. Concurrently, numerous new collaborations have developed with non-journalistic organizations, universities, and companies. One example related to AI is OpenAI, which has established numerous collaborations with media organizations internationally, starting with the Associated Press, which was the first media company to conclude a collaboration in 2023 (Schaetz & Schjøtt, 2025). Subsequently, other publishers followed, such as Axel Springer, El País, Financial Times, and Le Monde (Hagar & Diakopoulos, 2025). For instance, the long-term agreement between Le Monde and OpenAI includes enabling OpenAI to draw on the newspaper's corpus to establish and enhance the reliability of the answers of its ChatGPT tool, in return for a significant source of additional revenue for Le Monde (Dreyfus & Fenoglio, 2024). The motives for collaborations with OpenAI are varied for many publishers; one is the attempt to generate revenue through the collaboration as opposed to the publication of their own texts and data.

Another motivation, especially for smaller publishers, is to gain easier access to existing and mature AI models, particularly in the absence of resources for developing their own. Consequently, the print sector has, on average, developed a mix of self-developed tools and external platform-based tools (Prinzing & Graßl, 2024; Quinonez & Meij, 2024; BDZV, 2025). At the meso-level, AI primarily presents the challenge of continuously balancing various tools, collaborations, and options. Simultaneously, it plays a crucial mediating role between the micro- and macro-levels. For instance, it facilitates the translation of regulatory frameworks (e.g., the European Union's AI Act) into practical applications at the micro-level or addresses new challenges at the micro-level (e.g., data protection issues related to AI) by resolving them at a higher level. AI also impacts the traditional delineation between these levels, as boundaries increasingly blur and differentiation becomes more complex. This is exemplified by the role of the audience, which could theoretically be classified as a stakeholder at the meso-level. However, due to its significant influence not only on individual media organizations but on the entire media industry, it is positioned at the macro-level.

1.3.3 Macro-level

The profound transformations induced by artificial intelligence (AI) are significantly influencing the relationship between the media and print industries and their users. This impact is more pronounced than that of other recent innovations, such as social media or podcasts, which are already integral to media consumption, whereas AI is not yet as widely adopted. Frank et al. (2024) showed in a representative study of 3002 participants from the United States, Germany, and China that state-of-the-art fakes are barely distinguishable from "authentic" media, with most respondents guessing when classifying content as human- or machine-generated. Similarly, a survey by the Office for National Statistics (ONS) in Great Britain, which questioned 12,511 adults about their AI knowledge (ONS, 2023), found that only 17% can often or always recognize when they are using AI. Men, young adults (16–29 years), and those with higher education are more likely to identify AI usage, while older adults (70+) show the lowest awareness—55% rarely or never recognize AI. This is particularly relevant for print publishers, whose audiences tend to be older.

This aligns with Vogler et al. (2023), who conducted a representative survey in German-speaking Switzerland and Romandy. Their findings show limited acceptance of AI-generated journalistic content: only 29.1% of respondents would read news produced entirely by AI, compared to 84.3% for news created without AI. Acceptance is highest for routine topics like weather or stock market news (61.2%), and for soft news about celebrities (48.6%), but drops significantly for hard news areas such as culture (27.7%), science (25.9%), national politics (16.4%), and international politics (15.9%). The Digital News Report corroborates these findings globally: while publishers welcome AI, public distrust remains widespread, especially in hard news areas like politics or war (Ross Arguedas, 2024). This skepticism is reflected in the demand for labeling AI-generated content, as supported by numerous studies from various countries and international surveys (Meinungsmonitor Künstliche Intelligenz, 2021; Vogler et al., 2023; Ross Arguedas, 2024; Thomson et al., 2025).

Coupled with the desire for labeling is the expectation of continued human responsibility in the production process, frequently summarized under the term "human in the loop" (Vogler et al., 2023; Mellado & Gajardo, 2024; Ross Arguedas, 2024). This aligns, however, with the prevailing strategy in newsrooms, which primarily view AI as an assistant in their daily work (Graßl et al., 2022; Ross Arguedas, 2024; Ramlochan, 2025). Moreover, at the macro-level, public sentiment indicates a preference for consistent and standardized guidelines across the industry (Thomson et al., 2025), whereas policy implementation at the organizational level (meso-level) is characterized by a fragmented landscape of diverse approaches (Becker et al., 2025).

The detailed state of research presented highlights that the macro-level impact of AI is significantly shaped by its relationship with the audience and their skepticism. A primary challenge for print publishers is that their typically older readership has even less exposure to AI, resulting in greater skepticism (Latzer & Festic, 2024; Grassini & Saevild, 2025). This is crucial, as Thomson et al. (2025) observe that audiences are more comfortable with AI in journalism when they have firsthand experience with such tools. This lack of awareness may contribute to distrust and underscores the importance of transparency and potential labeling. However, the issue of labeling receives even less attention in the print sector than in the digital realm (Schützeneder et al., 2024a).

Furthermore, the impact of AI on the print sector at the macro-level (cf. Table 1.1) is also significantly shaped by the respective media system. Spyridou and Ioannou (2025) point out: "This becomes quite evident as most of the research work focusing on AI's impact on journalism is being carried out in large economies such as the United States, European Union, Scandinavia, and China. In authoritarian environments, newsrooms ought to deal with a number of sociopolitical issues such as self-censorship, illiteracy, inequalities, civil rights violations and corruption." In addition to the media system, continent- and country-specific challenges also influence the impact of AI. For example, Ademola (2024) outlines several challenges for the African print market regarding AI, including two that are specific to Africa. First, there is the limited data availability and quality of data for audience targeting. Many regions lack robust data infrastructure and audience insights, making it challenging to effectively target ads to specific demographics. Secondly, there is Cultural and Linguistic Diversity: "Africa is a region of diverse cultures and languages, presenting a challenge for advertisers to create targeted campaigns that resonate with local audiences. Adapting content and messaging to different cultural contexts requires a deep understanding of the nuances and preferences of various communities" (Ademola, 2024).

Other studies confirm that distinct global challenges have emerged regarding AI utilization, often illustrated by insights from the Global South. For example, Beckett and Mira (2023) show that the Global South sometimes faces greater obstacles in AI implementation, such as inadequate Internet infrastructure. Radcliffe (2025) further highlights the susceptibility of AI tools to bias, due to their predominant training on datasets from the Global North. In response, Kothari and Cruikshank (2021) propose a research agenda focused on empowering African journalists and researchers in adopting AI in African newsrooms. Instead of treating technology as a universal solution, their framework stresses the need for tailored AI tools that address the specific needs of African contexts, aiming to avoid exacerbating existing inequalities through the uncritical adoption of externally developed technologies.

Thus, it becomes evident that AI exerts a substantial influence on print publishers at the macro level, regardless of whether they produce newspapers, magazines, or even books. The relationship with the audience or customer, in part, requires redefinition, placing demands on transparency, guidelines, openness, and questions of labeling, while also emphasizing the cultivation of a human element, despite the implementation of AI. Similarly, at a global level, AI challenges the boundaries of individual media systems, often presenting unique challenges that necessitate global cooperation to address.

1.4 Discussion and Conclusions

The preceding discussions have demonstrated that the impact of AI on print publishers is substantial and multifaceted, affecting various levels, for example: At the micro-level, AI influences competencies and new roles for journalists and authors. At the meso-level, it facilitates novel collaborations and organizational structures. At the macro-level, AI presents challenging impulses for the relationship with the audience. A look at the presented AI applications in the print industry reveals that AI not only drives AI-specific innovations but also serves as a catalyst for the ongoing digitalization of entire print publishers. This is exemplified in the optimization of printing processes, which are increasingly digitalized through AI, potentially leading to enhanced effectiveness and cost savings. The pervasive influence of AI across these levels underscores its role as a transformative force in the print publishing sector, reshaping traditional practices and driving the industry toward a more digitally integrated future.

Concurrently, the relentless pace of technological change and the ongoing advancement of AI present renewed challenges. Publishers in Germany, for example, identify growing concerns in cybersecurity, as well as anxieties regarding their business models due to the increasing sophistication of generative AI (Greis, 2024). Publishers are currently adopting, in broad terms, two main strategies in response. The first is a form of resistance against platforms that utilize their content for training their models, as exemplified by the approach taken by *The New York Times* (Allyn, 2025).

The alternative approach involves collaboration or cooperation with platforms, seeking remuneration for content usage or co-development of AI tools for internal use. Researchers critically note that this may lead to a two-tiered system among media organizations. Spyridou and Ioannou (2025) argue that "the New York Times may have the tech and financial capacity to support an algorithmic shift while sustaining journalistic standards, but most AI news projects rely on funds from tech companies such as Google, thus limiting AI's potential to a small number of players in the news industry. This condition is most likely to reinforce existing inequalities among news organizations and amplify big media's power in the public sphere." Borchardt et al. (2024) echo this sentiment, identifying a division particularly between national and regional media outlets (and, consequently, many print publishers): "Local media have been the most fragile in this system because they—by their very nature—have to rely on a geographically limited market. This has increased the responsibility of public service media to serve people in communities that would otherwise remain without access to independently researched and curated information."

Furthermore, concerns are raised about media organizations becoming further dependent on platforms they cannot control, exceeding existing levels (e.g., through search engines or social media). A study by Hagar and Diakopoulos (2025) demonstrates that collaborations often touted as historically significant (Tobitt, 2025) do not always have the substantial impact that was initially announced. The researchers were able to show statistically that OpenAI's partner sites do not receive significantly more traffic than non-partners. They conclude "that these high-profile content deals primarily serve as licensing arrangements rather than meaningful audience development strategies." From today's perspective, predicting which of the two paths will ultimately prove more successful represents an unpredictable bet on the future.

This offers numerous avenues for further research. The field of opportunities is vast, given the significant research gaps that persist due to ongoing developments (as highlighted in the paper by Goyanes et al., 2025 and Sarısakaloğlu, 2025). For example, there is a need for more international research cooperations especially between Global South and Global North, more mixed methods studies and for more longitudinal studies to assess the long-term impact on the different levels micro, meso, and macro. Research should now increasingly focus on AI agents as a crucial area of study. These are often referred to as the next stage of the AI revolution due to their ability to make autonomous decisions in ongoing processes, distinguishing them from previous models. The Deloitte TMT Predictions 2025 report forecasts that in 2025, 25% of companies utilizing generative AI will initiate agentic AI pilots or proofs of concept, with this figure expected to rise to 50% by 2027. Numerous media organizations, both in print and digital sectors, are already developing agentic AI solutions.

While this initially appears to simplify matters by providing a broad range of study options, it simultaneously complicates them because the landscape of AI research has become as complex and fragmented as the world of AI itself. This also applies to AI research within the print sector. Overall, there are few studies explicitly focusing on print publishers. Many large-scale studies refer generally to the media industry, making it difficult in some instances to comprehensively understand the impact of AI on the print sector. This stems partly from the fact that print publishers are increasingly digitalized and are now more appropriately regarded as digital enterprises. Because of this situation, it is even more challenging to differentiate within the print sector by publication type, such as newspapers or magazines, because the research landscape is even less developed. While this presents a mandate for further research, it also constitutes a significant limitation in the discussions within this chapter. It is also important to mention that an expansion of disciplinary boundaries is increasingly being called for. For example, Broussard et al. (2019) underscored the importance of interdisciplinary collaboration and the need for adopting a human-centric approach to AI integration.

The difficulty in predicting the future of journalism is evident in the polarized perspectives that have emerged: some envision a reinvention of journalism, while others foresee the destruction of local journalism (Caswell & Fitzgerald, 2025; Stephens, 2025). The truth, and consequently the future, likely lies somewhere between these extremes of "Friend or Foe" (Spyridou & Ioannou, 2025). Nevertheless, AI represents the most significant transformation in the print industry since the advent of digitalization. The Italian daily newspaper Il Foglio exemplifies the potential direction of this transformation. In March 2025, Il Foglio claimed to have produced the world's first printed daily newspaper created entirely by AI (Il Foglio, 2025b). The inaugural four-page edition of Il Foglio AI was described by editor Claudio Cerasa as a product of "news, debate and provocations." Cerasa further elucidated that this initiative served as a testing ground to demonstrate the practical applications of AI in journalism, while simultaneously exploring its impact on daily newspaper production and prompting questions we are forced to ask ourselves, "not only from a journalistic nature" (Giuffrida, 2025).

This experimental approach highlights the complex interplay between technological innovation and traditional journalistic practices, underscoring the need for critical examination of AI's role in shaping the future of news production and dissemination. According to Il Foglio AI, which conducted a self-evaluation of its experiment after one week, humans still have a role in the future of print journalism: "But a newspaper, first and foremost, is a place. A civil brawl. A group of people arguing over a headline, insulting each other in chat over a subordinate clause, defending an adverb as if it were family honor. It's humanity in tension. And that, AI still can't replicate" (Il Foglio, 2025a).

Literature

Abdel-Haleem, M. M., & Alnajjar, H. T. (2024). The role of virtual social presence in Arab audience acceptance of AI in media practices: Insights from the technology acceptance model. *Arab Media and Society*. https://doi.org/10.70090/MH24RVSP

Ademola, O. E. (2024). *The transformative power of AI in print media: A focus on Africa*. https://businessday.ng/technology/article/the-transformative-power-of-ai-in-print-media-a-focus-on-africa/

Allyn, B. (2025). *'The New York Times' takes OpenAI to court. ChatGPT's future could be on the line*. https://www.npr.org/2025/01/14/nx-s1-5258952/new-york-times-openai-microsoft

Alsheibani, S., Messom, C., Cheung, Y., & Alhosni, M. (2020). Artificial intelligence beyond the hype: Exploring the organisation adoption factors. In *ACIS 2020 Proceedings: 31st Australasian conference on information systems*, Wellington. https://aisel.aisnet.org/acis2020/33

Ausserhofer, J., Gutounig, R., Oppermann, M., et al. (2020). The datafication of data journalism scholarship: Focal points, methods, and research propositions for the investigation of data-intensive newswork. *Journalism, 21*(7), 950–973.

BDZV. (2025). *Trends der Zeitungsbranche 2025*. https://www.bdzv.de/fileadmin/content/6_Service/6-1_Presse/6-1-2_Pressemitteilungen/2025/PDFs/2025-02-25_BDZV_Highberg_Trendumfrage_2025_3.pdf

Becker, K. B., Simon, F. M., & Crum, C. (2025). Policies in parallel? A comparative study of journalistic AI policies in 52 global news organisations. *Digital Journalism, 1–21*. https://doi.org/10.1080/21670811.2024.2431519

Beckett, C. (2019). New powers, new responsibilities: A global survey of journalism and artificial intelligence. *LSE/Journalism AI/Google News Initiative*.

Beckett, C., & Mira, Y. (2023). *Generating change: A global survey of what news organisations are doing with AI.* https://static1.squarespace.com/static/64d60527c01ae7106f2646e9/t/656e400a1c23e22da0681e46/1701724190867/Generating+Change+_+The+Journalism+AI+report+_+English.pdf
Borchardt, A. (2022). Go, robots, go! The value and challenges of artificial intelligence for local journalism. *Digital Journalism, 10*(10), 1919–1924. https://doi.org/10.1080/21670811.2022.2149584
Borchardt, A., Simon, F., Zachrison, O., Bremme, K., Kurczabinska, J., Mulhall, E., & Johanny, Y. (2024). *Trusted journalism in the age of generative AI.* https://doi.org/10.13140/RG.2.2.21994.32961.
Brennen, J. S., Howard, P. N., & Nielsen, R. K. (2022). What to expect when you're expecting robots: Futures, expectations, and pseudo artificial general intelligence in UK news. *Journalism, 23*(1). https://doi.org/10.1177/1464884920947535
Broussard, M., Diakopoulos, N., Guzman, A. L., Abebe, R., Dupagne, M., & Chuan, C. H. (2019). Artificial intelligence and journalism. *Journalism and Mass Communication Quarterly, 96*(3), 673–695. https://doi.org/10.1177/1077699019859901
Carlson, M. (2015). The robotic reporter: Automated journalism and the redefinition of labor, compositional forms, and journalistic authority. *Digital Journalism, 3*(3), 416–431.
Caswell, D. (2023). *AI and news: What's next?* https://generative-ai-newsroom.com/ai-and-news-whats-next-154fbeb6a646
Caswell, D., & Fitzgerald, M. (2025). *AI is the media's chance to reinvent itself.* https://www.prospectmagazine.co.uk/ideas/media/69423/artificial-intelligence-journalism-reinvention
Cazzamatta, R., & Sarısakaloğlu, A. (2025). Mapping global emerging scholarly research and practices of AI-supported fact-checking tools in journalism. *Journalism Practice, 1–23.* https://doi.org/10.1080/17512786.2025.2463470
Cheng, I., & Lee, S. T. (2024). The impact of ethics instruction and internship on students' ethical perceptions about social media, artificial intelligence, and ChatGPT. *Journal of Media Ethics, 39*(2), 114–129. https://doi.org/10.1080/23736992.2024.2333486
Cools, H., & Diakopoulos, N. (2024). Uses of generative AI in the newsroom: Mapping journalists' perceptions of perils and possibilities. *Journalism Practice, 1–19.* https://doi.org/10.1080/17512786.2024.2394558
Diakopoulos, N., Cools, H., Li, C., Helberger, N., Kung, E., & Rinehart, A. (2024). Generative AI in journalism: The evolution of newswork and ethics in a generative information ecosystem. *Associated Press Report.* https://doi.org/10.13140/RG.2.2.31540.05765
Dierickx, L., & Lindén, C.-G. (2024). From bytes to bylines: A history of AI in journalism practices. In *Histories of digital journalism.* https://doi.org/10.4324/9781003492436-12.
Dinçer, E. (2024). *Hard and soft skills revisited: Journalism education at the dawn of artificial intelligence.* https://dergipark.org.tr/en/download/article-file/3834929.
Dodds, T., Vandendaele, A., Simon, F. M., Helberger, N., Resendez, V., & Yeung, W. N. (2025). Knowledge silos as a barrier to responsible AI practices in journalism? Exploratory evidence from four Dutch news organisations. *Journalism Studies, 1–19.* https://doi.org/10.1080/1461670X.2025.2463589
Dreyfus, L., & Fenoglio, J. (2024). *Le Monde and Open AI sign partnership agreement on artificial intelligence.* https://www.lemonde.fr/en/about-us/article/2024/03/13/le-monde-signs-artificial-intelligence-partnership-agreement-with-open-ai_6615418_115.html
Eder, M., & Sjøvaag, H. (2025). Falling behind the adoption curve: Local journalism's struggle for innovation in the AI transformation. *Journal of Media Business Studies, 1–19.* https://doi.org/10.1080/16522354.2025.2473301
Elo Dean, S., et al. (2025). Djinn-Data journalism interface for newsgathering and notifications. In M. Bramer & F. Stahl (Eds.), *Artificial intelligence XLI. SGAI 2024* (*Lecture notes in computer science*) (Vol. 15447). Springer. https://doi.org/10.1007/978-3-031-77918-3_11
Enslein, F. (2024). *Jens Ostrowski über den Einsatz von KI-Reportern bei den Ruhr Nachrichten.* https://www.donaukurier.de/nachrichten/bayern/jens-ostrowski-ueber-den-einsatz-von-ki-reportern-bei-den-ruhr-nachrichten-16117377

Ernst, A. (2023). *"Bild" baut Hunderte Stellen ab und schließt zehn Regionalbüros*. https://www.sueddeutsche.de/medien/bild-stellenabbau-regionalbueros-zeitung-1.5946769?reduced=true
Ertem-Eray, T., & Cheng, Y. (2025). A review of artificial intelligence research in peer-reviewed communication journals. *Applied Sciences, 15*(3). https://doi.org/10.3390/app15031058
Filipsson, F. (2025). *AI case study: Content generation at The New York Times*. https://redresscompliance.com/ai-case-study-content-generation-at-the-new-york-times/.
Frank, J., Herbert, F., Ricker, J., Schönherr, L., Eisenhofer, T., Fischer, A., Dürmuth, M., & Holz, T. (2024). A representative study on human detection of artificially generated media across countries. In *IEEE symposium on security and privacy (SP)* (pp. 55–73). https://doi.org/10.1109/SP54263.2024.00159.
García-Avilés, J. A. (2021). Journalism innovation research, a diverse and flourishing field (2000–2020). *Profesional de la Información, 30*(1). https://doi.org/10.3145/epi.2021.ene.10
Giuffrida, A. (2025). *Italian newspaper says it has published world's first AI-generated edition*. https://www.theguardian.com/technology/2025/mar/18/italian-newspaper-says-it-has-published-worlds-first-ai-generated-edition
Godulla, A., Hoffmann, C. P., & Seibert, D. (2021). Dealing with deepfakes – An interdisciplinary examination of the state of research and implications for communication studies. *SCM Studies in Communication and Media, 72–96*. https://doi.org/10.5771/2192-4007-2021-1-72
Goyanes, M., Háló, G., & Lopezosa, C. (2025). *Artificial intelligence in journalism: A systematic literature review of global trends, regulatory challenges, and ethical concerns*. https://doi.org/10.31235/osf.io/6sa9e_v1.
Graefe, A., & Bohlken, N. (2020). Automated journalism: A meta-analysis of readers' perceptions of human-written in comparison to automated news. *Media and Communication, 8*(3), 50–59. https://doi.org/10.17645/mac.v8i3.3019
Grassini, S., & Saevild, A. (2025). *Hope or doom AI-ttitude? Examining the impact of gender, age, and cultural differences on the envisioned future impact of artificial intelligence on humankind*. https://doi.org/10.1145/3605655.3605669.
Graßl, M., & Meier, K. (2024). Deepening the theory of innovation in journalism: Impact on the industry, the quality and the function of journalism in democracy. In K. Meier, J. A. García-Avilés, A. Kaltenbrunner, C. Porlezza, V. Wyss, R. Lugschitz, & K. Klinghardt (Eds.), *Innovations in journalism. Comparative research in five European countries* (pp. 293–308). Routledge. https://doi.org/10.4324/9781032630410-36
Graßl, M., Schützeneder, J., & Meier, K. (2022). Artificial intelligence as a tool of assistance: A scientific and practical perspective on AI in journalism. *Journalism Research, 5*(1), 3–24. https://doi.org/10.1453/2569-152X-12022-12049-en
Graßl, M., Planer, R., Schützeneder, J., & Klinghardt, K. (2023). Dependent on the platform? Discussing journalistic transformation levels on and through Instagram. In A. Godulla & S. Böhm (Eds.), *Digital disruption and media transformation. How technological innovation shapes the future of communication* (pp. 205–215). Springer VS. https://doi.org/10.1007/978-3-031-39940-4_16
Greis, F. (2024). *Verlage setzen auf Automatisierung und KI*. https://www.golem.de/news/digitalisierung-verlage-setzen-auf-automatisierung-und-ki-2402-182221.html
Guevara, M. W. (2019). *How artificial intelligence can help us crack more Panama Papers stories*. https://www.icij.org/inside-icij/2019/03/how-artificial-intelligence-can-help-us-crack-more-panama-papers-stories/
Hagar, N., & Diakopoulos, N. (2025). *GenAI as news gatekeeper? What traffic data shows*. https://generative-ai-newsroom.com/genai-as-news-gatekeeper-what-traffic-data-shows-783795ba2103.
Heilweil, R. (2023). *What is generative AI, and why is it suddenly everywhere?* https://www.vox.com/recode/2023/1/5/23539055/generative-ai-chatgpt-stable-diffusion-lensa-dall-e
Henley, J. (2023). *German tabloid Bild cuts 200 jobs and says some roles will be replaced by AI*. https://www.theguardian.com/world/2023/jun/20/german-tabloid-bild-to-replace-range-of-editorial-jobs-with-ai

Il Foglio. (2025a). *A first assessment of Foglio AI. Written by Foglio AI. With a scolding*. https://www.ilfoglio.it/il-foglio-ai/2025/03/22/news/a-first-assessment-of-foglio-ai-written-by-foglio-ai-with-a-scolding%2D%2D7547053/

Il Foglio. (2025b). *Il Foglio lancia un nuovo giornale: Il Foglio AI, un altro Foglio fatto con intelligenza*. https://www.ilfoglio.it/gli-speciali-del-foglio/2025/03/17/news/un-altro-foglio-fatto-con-intelligenza-7523278/

InterRed. (2024). *DIE WELT and WELT am SONNTAG opt for the InterRed editorial system*. https://www.interred.de/en/news/news/die-welt-and-welt-am-sonntag-opt-for-the-interred-editorial-system-102370.html

Iwersen, S., Scheppe, M., & Murphy, M. (2023). *Springer baut "Bild"-Zeitung massiv um – sechs Regionalausgaben werden eingestellt*. https://www.handelsblatt.com/unternehmen/it-medien/medien-springer-baut-bild-zeitung-massiv-um-sechs-regionalausgaben-werden-eingestellt/29214236.html

Jamil, S. (2020). Artificial intelligence and journalistic practice: The crossroads of obstacles and opportunities for the Pakistani journalists. *Journalism Practice, 15*(10), 1400–1422. https://doi.org/10.1080/17512786.2020.1788412

Katzenberger, V. (2024). Mind the gap: Re-thinking digital skills in journalism education in Germany. *Media Practice and Education, 1–15*. https://doi.org/10.1080/25741136.2024.2435805

Katzenberger, V., & Keil, J. (2024). All ears on? A survey on podcasters' profiles, practices and self-perceptions. *Studies in Communication Sciences, 24*(2), 209–227. https://doi.org/10.24434/j.scoms.2024.02.3150

Klinghardt, K., & Graßl, M. (2024). Fact-checking: Strengthening democracy through verifying. In K. Meier, J. A. García-Avilés, A. Kaltenbrunner, C. Porlezza, V. Wyss, R. Lugschitz, & K. Klinghardt (Eds.), *Innovations in journalism. Comparative research in five European countries* (pp. 219–226). Routledge. https://doi.org/10.4324/9781032630410-27

Klotz, D. (2024). Mögliche Einsatzgebiete von Künstlicher Intelligenz im Verlagswesen. In O. Schlüter (Ed.), *KI als Zukunftsmotor für Verlage*. Springer VS. https://doi.org/10.1007/978-3-658-43037-5_1

Kothari, A., & Cruikshank, S. A. (2021). Artificial intelligence and journalism: An agenda for journalism research in Africa. *African Journalism Studies, 43*(1), 17–33. https://doi.org/10.1080/23743670.2021.1999840

KPMG. (2024). *Verlagstrends 2024. Innovationstreiber künstliche Intelligenz*. https://www.mvfp.de/fileadmin/vdz/upload/news/Aktuelles/KPMG/2024_Verlagstrends_KI/Verlagstrends_2024_bf_sec_final.pdf

Latzer, M., & Festic, N. (2024). *"Künstliche Intelligenz" in der Schweiz 2024: Kenntnisse, Nutzung und Einstellungen zur generativen KI*. https://mediachange.ch/research/artificial-intelligence-applications/

Lee, N. (2025). *ACM makes more job cuts, sparking concerns over local news future*. https://www.mediaweek.com.au/acm-makes-more-job-cuts-sparking-concerns-over-local-news-future/

Meier, K., Graßl, M., García-Avilés, J., Mondejar, D., Kaltenbrunner, A., Lugschitz, R., Porlezza, C., Mazzoni, P., Wyss, V., & Saner, M. (2024a). Innovations in journalism as complex interplay: Supportive and obstructive factors in international comparison. *Media and Communication*. https://doi.org/10.17645/mac.7443

Meier, K., García-Avilés, J. A., Kaltenbrunner, A., Porlezza, C., Wyss, V., Lugschitz, R., & Klinghardt, K. (Eds.). (2024b). *Innovations in journalism: Comparative research in five European countries* (1st ed.). Routledge. https://doi.org/10.4324/9781032630410

Meinungsmonitor Künstliche Intelligenz. (2021). *Künstliche Intelligenz im Journalismus. Wie nimmt die Bevölkerung den Einfluss von Künstlicher Intelligenz auf die journalistische Arbeit wahr?* https://www.cais-research.de/wp-content/uploads/Factsheet-4-KI-Journalismus.pdf

Mellado, C., & Gajardo, C. (2024). The importance of the human touch in journalism: Journalistic values from an audience perspective. *Journalism Practice, 1–18*. https://doi.org/10.1080/17512786.2024.2387668

MVFP. (2024). *Publikumspresse und Fachmedien treiben Transformation voran.* https://www.mvfp.de/nachricht/artikel/publikumspresse-und-fachmedien-treiben-transformation-voran
Newman, N. (2021). *Journalism, media, and technology trends and predictions 2021.* https://reutersinstitute.politics.ox.ac.uk/sites/default/files/2021-01/Newman_Predictions_2021_FINAL.pdf
Newman, N., & Cherubini, F. (2025). *Journalism, media, and technology trends and predictions 2025.* https://doi.org/10.60625/risj-vte1-x706.
Newman, N., Fletcher, R., Eddy, K., Robertson, C. T., & Nielsen, R. K. (2023). *Reuters Institute Digital News Report 2023.* https://reutersinstitute.politics.ox.ac.uk/sites/default/files/2023-06/Digital_News_Report_2023.pdf
Office for National Statistics. (2023). *Public awareness, opinions and expectations about artificial intelligence: July to October 2023.* https://www.ons.gov.uk/businessindustryandtrade/itandinternetindustry/articles/publicawarenessopinionsandexpectationsaboutartificialintelligence/julytooctober2023
Parloa. (2024). *Wie Parloas AI Voicebot Reklamationen löst und die Kundenbindung in Medienhäusern stärkt.* https://www.parloa.com/de/ressourcen/kunden/medienhub-scsoft/
Pavlik, J. V. (2021). *Disruption and digital journalism: Assessing news media innovation in a time of dramatic change.* Routledge.
Pitluk, A., Wilson, J., & Inman, J. (2025). Helpful or hurtful: Legacy magazine journalism wrestles with the advent of AI technology in newsrooms. *Journalism Practice, 1–16.* https://doi.org/10.1080/17512786.2025.2458608
Porlezza, C. (2023). Promoting responsible AI: A European perspective on the governance of artificial intelligence in media and journalism. *Communications, 48*(3), 370–394. https://doi.org/10.1515/commun-2022-0091
Porlezza, C. (2024). The datafication of digital journalism: A history of everlasting challenges between ethical issues and regulation. *Journalism, 25*(5), 1167–1185. https://doi.org/10.1177/14648849231190232
Posetti, J. (2018). Time to step away from the 'bright, shiny things'? Towards a sustainable model of journalism innovation in an era of perpetual change. *The Reuters Institute for the Study of Journalism.* https://reutersinstitute.politics.ox.ac.uk/sites/default/files/2018-11/Posetti_Towards_a_Sustainable_model_of_Journalism_FINAL.pdf
Prinzing, M., & Graßl, M. (2024). Beyond the "shiny things": Supporting and obstructing factors of AI as an innovation in media organizations. *Emma Conference*, 06.06.2024. https://doi.org/10.13140/RG.2.2.22037.84965.
Quinonez, C., & Meij, E. (2024). A new era of AI-assisted journalism at Bloomberg. *AI Magazine, 187–199.* https://doi.org/10.1002/aaai.12181
Radcliffe, D. (2025). Journalism in the AI era: Opportunities and challenges in the Global South and emerging economies. https://www.trust.org/wp-content/uploads/2025/01/TRF-Insights-Journalism-in-the-AI-Era.pdf
Ramlochan, S. (2025). *The New York Times embraces AI, efficiency boost or threat to journalism?* https://promptengineering.org/the-new-york-times-embraces-ai-efficiency-boost-or-threat-to-journalism/
Rinehart, A., & Kung, E. (2022). *Artificial intelligence in local news: A survey of US newsrooms' AI readiness.* https://www.researchgate.net/publication/363475725. https://doi.org/10.13140/RG.2.2.16926.82246
Rosenkranz, B. (2024). *Hohe Entschädigung für Michael Schumacher wegen Fake-Interview.* https://uebermedien.de/95249/hohe-entschaedigung-fuer-michael-schumacher-wegen-fake-interview/
Ross Arguedas, A. (2024). *Public attitudes towards the use of AI in journalism.* https://reutersinstitute.politics.ox.ac.uk/digital-news-report/2024/public-attitudes-towards-use-ai-and-journalism
Ryzhko, O., Krainikova, T., Vodolazka, S., & Sokolova, K. (2024). Generative AI changes the book publishing industry: Reengineering of business processes. *Communications Society, 37*(3), 255–271. https://doi.org/10.15581/003.37.3.255-271
Sarısakaloğlu, A. (2025). Navigating the research landscape of algorithm-driven journalism: A systematic literature review of authorship, research trends, and future research pathways. *Journalism Studies, 26*(5), 1–27. https://doi.org/10.1080/1461670X.2024.2446326

Schaetz, N., & Schjøtt, A. (2025). AI hype and its function: An ethnographic study of the local news AI initiative of the Associated Press. *Digital Journalism, 1–18*. https://doi.org/10.1080/21670811.2024.2443163

Schützeneder, J. (2025). Ethical limits of AI use in the media sector. In S. Böhm, S. Collins, A. Godulla, S. Keith, & R. Savery (Eds.), *AI-based media disruption: Emerging technologies and multidisciplinary perspectives across sectors*.

Schützeneder, J., Graßl, M., & Meier, K. (2024a). *Grenzen überwinden, Chancen gestalten: KI im journalistischen Newsroom*. Bestandsaufnahme, Perspektiven und Empfehlungen für Journalismus und Politik. https://library.fes.de/pdf-files/a-p-b/20987.pdf

Schützeneder, J., Graßl, M., Porlezza, C., Robles, F., & Mazzoni, P. (2024b). AI as innovation for journalism. A key task for the present and future. In K. Meier, J. A. García-Avilés, A. Kaltenbrunner, C. Porlezza, V. Wyss, R. Lugschitz, & K. Klinghardt (Eds.), *Innovations in journalism. Comparative research in five European countries* (pp. 101–108). Routledge. https://doi.org/10.4324/9781032630410-13

Seibold, K. (2023). *ChatGPT – Ein skurriles Interview mit der neuen Künstlichen Intelligenz über Oberbayern*. https://www.donaukurier.de/nachrichten/bayern/chatgpt-ein-skurriles-interview-mit-der-neuen-kuenstlichen-intelligenz-ueber-oberbayern-10429780.

Simon, F. (2024). Artificial intelligence in the news: How AI retools, rationalizes, and reshapes journalism and the public arena. *Tow Center for Digital Journalism*. https://towcenter.columbia.edu/sites/default/files/content/Tow%20Report_Felix-Simon-AI-in-the-News.pdf

Smith, R. (2025). *The rise of AI in printing: Revolutionizing quality and efficiency*. https://www.iplocation.net/the-rise-of-ai-in-printing-revolutionizing-quality-and-efficiency

Soto-Sanfiel, M. T., Ibiti, A., Machado, M., Marín Ochoa, B. E., Mendoza Michilot, M., Rosell Arce, C. G., & Angulo-Brunet, A. (2022). In search of the Global South: Assessing attitudes of Latin American journalists to artificial intelligence in journalism. *Journalism Studies, 23*(10), 1197–1224. https://doi.org/10.1080/1461670X.2022.2075786

Spyridou, P., & Ioannou, M. (2025). Exploring AI amid the hype: A critical reflection around the applications and implications of AI in journalism. *Societies, 15*(2). https://doi.org/10.3390/soc15020023

Stephens, H. (2025). *How AI can destroy local journalism*. https://hughstephensblog.net/2025/03/10/how-ai-can-destroy-local-journalism/

Sünkel, B. (2023). *So verrückt antwortet eine KI im Franken-Interview*. https://www.fraenkischertag.de/lokales/bamberg/rat-wissen/chatgpt-im-interview-was-weiss-die-kuenstliche-intelligenz-ueber-franken-art-222556

Thomaß, B. (2024). Ethik des Journalismus. In M. Löffelholz & L. Rothenberger (Eds.), *Handbuch Journalismustheorien*. Springer. https://doi.org/10.1007/978-3-658-32151-2_46

Thomson, T. J., Thomas, R. J., Riedlinger, M., & Matich, P. (2025). *Generative AI and journalism: Content, journalistic perceptions, and audience experiences*. RMIT University. https://doi.org/10.6084/m9.figshare.28068008

Tobitt, C. (2025). *Who's suing AI and who's signing: 14 publishers join lawsuit against start-up Cohere*. https://pressgazette.co.uk/platforms/news-publisher-ai-deals-lawsuits-openai-google/#h-news-media-alliance-members

Tomorrows Publisher. (2024). *Le Monde highlights the impact of AI on journalism on its 80th birthday*. https://tomorrowspublisher.today/editing-tools/le-monde-highlights-the-impact-of-ai-on-journalism-on-its-80th-birthday/

Túñez-López, J. M., Fieiras Ceide, C., & Vaz-Álvarez, M. (2021). Impact of artificial intelligence on journalism: Transformations in the company, products, contents and professional profile. *Communications Society, 34*(1), 177–193.

Twipe. (2023). *Le Monde in English: Strategies to reach new markets*. https://www.twipemobile.com/le-monde-in-english-strategies-to-reach-new-markets/

Van Dalen, A. (2012). The algorithms behind the headlines: How machine-written news redefines the core skills of human journalists. *Journalism Practice, 6*(5–6), 648–658. https://doi.org/10.1080/17512786.2012.667268

Veenstra, A. S., Wilder, M., Shimu, F., Schlauder, L., & Dousdebés, F. (2024). Journalism students' use, expectations, and understanding of generative AI tools. *Journalism and Mass Communication Educator, 80*(1), 115–128. https://doi.org/10.1177/10776958241296474

Vogler, D., Eisenegger, M., Fürst, S., Udris, L., Ryffel, Q., Rivière, M., & Schäfer, M. S. (2023). Künstliche Intelligenz in der journalistischen Nachrichtenproduktion: Wahrnehmung und Akzeptanz in der Schweizer Bevölkerung. *Forschungszentrum Öffentlichkeit und Gesellschaft (foeg). Jahrbuch Qualität der Medien, 2023*, 33–45. https://doi.org/10.5167/uzh-235608

Wellbrock, C.-M. (2024). Generative AI and investigative journalism: An application of Baumol's cost disease across mass communication sectors. *Emerging Media, 2*(4), 663–672. https://doi.org/10.1177/27523543241299631

Wilczek, B., Haim, M., & Thurman, N. (2024). Transforming the value chain of local journalism with artificial intelligence. *AI Magazine, 45*(2), 200–211. https://doi.org/10.1002/aaai.12174

Wolf, C., Planer, R., & Godulla, A. (2024). The ecosystem of editorial product innovation: A systematic literature analysis on internal factors and external actors in journalistic media organisations. *Studies in Communication and Media, 13*(3), 317–346. https://doi.org/10.5771/2192-4007-2024-3-317

Wu, D. (2023). *Gannett halts AI-written sports recaps after readers mocked the stories*. https://www.washingtonpost.com/nation/2023/08/31/gannett-ai-written-stories-high-school-sports/

Michael Graßl works as an Professor for Journalism and Digital Innovation at the University of Applied Sciences Magdeburg-Stendal. His main research area is the impact of innovation on journalism and media, especially in the case of AI. He also did a lot of research around the implementation of social media and podcast in media companies.

Broadcasting: Radio and Television

2

Anna Jupowicz-Ginalska and Jaroslaw Kinal

Abstract

Technological determinism suggests that the development of technology is the driving force behind social and cultural changes, and its impact on various areas of life is inevitable and irreversible. In the context of electronic media such as radio and television, the introduction of artificial intelligence (AI) represents one of the most breakthrough moments in their history. With its capabilities to analyze large datasets, automate processes, and personalize content, AI is transforming the way content is created, distributed, and consumed through recommendations, generating subtitles and translations, analyzing audience preferences and behaviors, creating virtual presenters, and supporting production processes by reducing the time and costs associated with content creation. This chapter discusses the theoretical and practical aspects of using AI in legacy radio and TV stations. An essential part of the text is a literature review. The analysis of existing research allows us to identify opportunities and challenges associated with implementing AI in the discussed media. We address such issues as automation of production processes, content personalization, more accurate audience data analysis, increased operational efficiency, and improved user experiences. We enrich our study with specific examples of AI use in television (e.g., BBC) and radio (e.g., NPR, iHeartRadio).

A. Jupowicz-Ginalska (✉)
Faculty of Journalism, Information and Book Studies, University of Warsaw, Warsaw, Poland
e-mail: a.ginalska@uw.edu.pl

J. Kinal
Institute of History, University of Rzeszow, Rzeszow, Poland
e-mail: jkinal@ur.edu.pl

S. Böhm et al. (eds.), *Handbook of AI-based Media Disruption*, Future of Business and Finance, https://doi.org/10.1007/978-3-032-07605-2_2

2.1 Introduction: from Technological Determinism to AI in the Media

Technological change has always been the driving force behind the evolution of media, affecting their form and social function (Mujiono, 2024). As Prasad and Makesh (2024) point out, this industry is an "early adopter of contemporary technology, embracing the digital revolution and exploiting the ever-changing technology to create better content, improve user experience, and establish a robust brand presence" (p. 41).

Given the undeniable connection between technology and media development, technological determinism is one of the key theoretical paradigms frequently referenced in studies on artificial intelligence. This theory posits that technological inventions determine the trajectory of societal development, altering communication practices, human relationships, and institutional structures (Maigret, 2012). It suggests that technological change is the primary driver of social change, often independent of human will or context. This view has become foundational in many media-related analyses, particularly those exploring how innovations transform modes of communication and public interpretation of reality. Marshall McLuhan encapsulates this idea in his well-known adage "the medium is the message" (McLuhan, 1994, p. 7), implying that the characteristics of the medium, namely, its form and sensory impact, shape human perception and societal structures more profoundly than the content it conveys (see also Lapalelo, 2021).

However, this determinist account has not gone unchallenged. Cultural theorist Raymond Williams (1974) strongly criticized technological determinism for downplaying human agency and social context. He argued that technologies are not autonomous forces but are themselves shaped by historical, economic, and cultural conditions. For Williams, technological change reflects underlying human intentions, social structures, and institutional power dynamics, rather than unilaterally driving them. Thus, while media technologies have transformative potential, their actual impact depends on how societies choose to adopt, adapt, or resist them. Building on this logic, Walczyk (2018) highlights how technological inventions influence not only the forms of media but also values and social norms that emerge in response to them, ultimately shaping collective perceptions of reality. Truskolaski (2010) deepens this concern by invoking the concept of the "black box" of technology, suggesting that rapid innovation increasingly functions as a proxy for what we do not fully understand. This perspective points to the ethical opacity of emerging media and media tools whose technological complexity can obscure the societal consequences of their use. Taken together, all these perspectives underscore the importance of examining not only what technology enables, but also how its social meaning is constructed.

From this point of view, technological determinism is not merely a technical issue. It goes further, fundamentally relating to spiritual and philosophical issues (Walczyk, 2018). In light of this perspective, Sienkiewicz and Świeboda (2019) note that modern media systems require new systematic analysis with updated theoretical and empirical frameworks that would focus on understanding the effects of media-related technological determinism in order to analyze their ever-changing impact on people's lives. Central to this perspective is the assumption that these changes are inevitable and irreversible, and that their scale determines the adaptation of both individuals and organizations to the new reality. As a result, technology becomes the primary driver of social, cultural, and economic change and thus a primary factor in shaping and reshaping society (Maigret, 2012; Alsaleh, 2024).

Radio and television, considered to be the leading media of the twentieth century, provide a compelling illustration of the presence of the theory in question and its impact on the media industry. The invention of radio enabled the immediate flow of information on a mass scale and revolutionized daily life, influencing the formation of public opinion and the culture of reception. Similarly, television, due to its audiovisual nature, contributed to changing the way content was consumed and blurred the lines between information and entertainment, not to mention its political significance. Radio and television became vehicles for multilevel narratives that profoundly impacted social norms, cultural identities, and political structures (McCombs et al., 2011; Newton, 2015). Moreover, both of these archetypal traditional media have undertaken equally vigorous efforts to adapt to the evolving demands of the contemporary world, particularly those arising from technological advancements. These include the transition of radio and television signals to digital broadcasting, the convergent use of digital platforms in media brand ecosystems, the redefinition of business models (especially in the area of revenue generation), the launch of video-on-demand platforms and mobile applications, as well as exploratory initiatives involving the implementation of augmented reality and virtual reality technologies. The latest phase in adopting electronic legacy media to relentless technological progress is currently the integration of artificial intelligence.

This process can be interpreted through the prism of technological determinism, as part of a broader logic of media evolution forcing transformations in radio and television operations (Pavlik, 2020). However, rather than viewing AI as an autonomous or inevitable force, it is more accurate to understand its integration as a response to structural pressures in the media industry. These include declining advertising revenues, shrinking public funding, and intensified competition from digital platforms. In this context, AI is often strategically deployed by executives and decision-makers as a cost-saving or audience-retention tool.

Thanks to their capabilities, AI technologies not only influence media production, distribution, pricing, and promotion practices but also reshape relationships between media organizations and their stakeholders, including advertisers and audiences. While currently associated with process optimization and personalization, AI is increasingly positioned to redefine professional roles in broadcasting. The emergence of virtual presenters, the development of AI-based interactive formats, and integration with technologies like augmented and virtual reality are signals that AI is evolving beyond a mere support mechanism and becoming a co-actor in the media production environment. These dynamics invite a deeper, critically engaged analysis of how AI is transforming traditional broadcasting—not simply as an inevitable consequence of technological progress, but as a negotiated outcome of strategic, economic, and institutional choices (RTDNA, 2023).

The number of studies devoted to the impact of AI on the media (including radio and television) is growing rapidly, providing a broad and multifaced perspective on this phenomenon. However, the fact that the literature on the subject remains in its nascent stage makes analyzing the implementation of this technology particularly challenging. New studies, observations, and conclusions are constantly emerging, which creates the risk that the information presented here may quickly become outdated. For this reason, we have decided to focus on general thematic areas where artificial intelligence intersects with radio and television. Additionally, we illustrate our study with several practice-based examples showing how the legacy media use AI. We close our considerations with general conclusions.

2.2 Manifestation of Technological Determinism: Dimensions of AI in Radio and Television

In this study, we have adopted Sumner's approach to AI in the media (2023). In his popular book, he identified the following general key areas of transformation triggered by AI: (1) improved content creation, (2) enhanced user experience, (3) personalized content recommendations, (4) new content formats, and (5) ethical and societal implications. We decided to take his considerations as a general roadmap and a starting point for future analyses, which will be presented in this chapter.

2.2.1 Improved Content Creation

As Sumner (2023, n.p.) states, AI is used in content production processes to "automate repetitive tasks, optimize workflows, and improve the efficiency of content creation." He argues that these solutions may save time and money by increasing and accelerating productivity. He notes that artificial intelligence can generate text and graphics, leading to complete automation of media content creation. This aligns with Das et al.'s (2015) observation that AI can produce different content, including visuals, sounds, and films, based on algorithmically generated inputs, in both news and entertainment creation practices.

In the case of the first area, the scope of AI use is already so large that Munoriyarwa et al. (2021) systematized it, dividing its use into holistic (when AI plays a central role, e.g., by updating news or generating real-time reports), exclusively technological (equipping newsrooms with AI tools, such as cameras with AI software), and task-specific (assigning specific tasks to AI, such as live translation of video materials).

Nishal and Diakopoulos (2023) take another approach, listing specific news-oriented tasks in which AI might be helpful. These include news gathering, news production, distribution, and marketing, i.e., advertising activities. In their work, the authors focus on news gathering, described as "sourcing and investigation of potentially newsworthy leads before a journalist or editor decides to pursue their development," which is linked to "statistical evaluations of *newsworthiness* for leads" (p. 2), and news production, defined as "developing a story, including the iterative processes of writing and editing, and the creation of material for advertising and distribution" (p. 3). The concept of AI-enhanced distribution was examined by Xi and Latif (2022), who stated that implementing data mining leads to more "precise, intelligent, objective, and personalized" dissemination of content (p. 33).

As already mentioned, the issues of improved content creation apply not only to news but also to entertainment, which is a pillar of modern broadcasting media (e.g., series, TV films, talent shows, docu-soaps, radio plays, radio and television morning shows, or music playlists). From a broad perspective, AI is used in the preproduction and postproduction of radio and television programs (Anandraj & Aravind, 2024; Chiappani, 2024; Furtáková & Janáčková, 2024a, 2024b; Kumari et al., 2024). In preproduction, AI supports script development, enhancing storytelling, dialogue writing, and language accuracy, as well as assists in storyboard preparation, team scheduling through predictive analytics, and even casting, using facial or voice recognition and performance-matching algorithms. It is also used to scout locations via image recognition and geospatial data analysis, as well as to control AI-powered cameras and generate real-time CGI effects with instant performance feedback. In postproduction, AI currently assists in editing processes such as identifying and correcting technical errors (including color and sound adjustments), sound design, creating subtitles, and generating audiovisual special effects or even complete soundtracks (see: Tsalakanidou et al., 2021; Verma & Heider, 2024; Rahman & Ali, 2024; Shah, 2024). The above solutions optimize the entire production process and allow for significant savings in time and money. The resources freed up by AI can therefore be used for other production-related activities.

From a marketing perspective, as Anandraj and Aravind (2024) highlight, AI tools are used to identify target demographics, craft promotional strategies through social media activity analysis, and map audience sentiment and engagement metrics. The user data thus obtained is an extremely valuable asset, enabling the media to offer advertisers highly personalized and targeted advertising campaigns. While not yet ubiquitous, these applications are transitioning from experimental deployment to broader industry adoption, indicating a growing operational role of AI across the production cycle.

It is worth noting that there are additional areas worth exploring when it comes to implementing AI in radio and television content. One particularly compelling application is content restoration. As demonstrated by Singh et al. (2023), AI serves as a key tool in this process, aiding in the repair of damaged or low-quality audiovisual materials. Such solutions may be particularly important for public broadcasters, who often have vast content archives of historical value and cultural heritage significance. Thus, efforts to enhance the quality of recording, or even to restore them entirely, can be seen as a commitment to preserving this legacy for future generations. It is worth emphasizing, however, that the use of AI for the recovery of audio, visual, and text data is associated with a number of as yet unresolved legal issues, primarily in the area of copyright granting (Li, 2022).

Another particularly intriguing content-related topic is the creation and use of virtual television and radio presenters, a phenomenon that illustrates the increasingly blurred lines between human and machine roles in media. According to Furtáková and Janáčková (2023), the first attempts to introduce synthetic figures into broadcasting date back to the early 2000s. For example, in 2011, San Antonio's KROV launched "Denise," an AI-generated radio DJ. In 2018 and 2019, male and female robotic news anchors (modeled on real presenters) made their debut in China's Xinhua News Agency. As the authors note, such experiments are now far more numerous and varied in scope. They may be comprehensive—such as RadioGPT, a fully automated local radio station launched by Futuri or Absolut Radio AI by Antenne Deutschland—or selective, focusing on specific programming components. One example is the experiment by Couleur 3, in which AI was responsible for the entire one-day broadcast, including music and news content. Other implementations include using AI to host some parts of radio programs, such as "Basia" on Poland's Radio Piekary Śląskie or "Airah" on Radio Mirchi in the United Arab Emirates. In another example, WRBF radio used a cloned voice in promotional materials, with the original talent's consent and for a fee. The realistic results achieved from just 70 min of recording surprised even the voice actor (see McLane, 2024).

A particularly illustrative and controversial example of this trend occurred in October 2024, when OFF Radio Kraków launched an AI-generated presenter to replace human journalists in its cultural and social programming. The initiative, which aimed to engage younger audiences, was met with immediate public backlash, including a petition signed by over 23,000 people, criticizing the dismissal of experienced professionals and raising concerns about ethics, cultural sensitivity, and job displacement. Interestingly, part of the controversy stemmed from the synthetic recreation of the voice of Nobel laureate Wisława Szymborska, which many considered a violation of ethical norms. The swift termination of the experiment after just 1 week underscored the risks of pushing automation too far without adequate societal dialogue. This case highlights the growing tension between technological innovation and public trust, reinforcing the need for careful and transparent integration of AI into broadcast environments (Polskie Radio, 2024).

2.2.2 Personalized Content Recommendations and Enhanced User Experience

Sumner (2023) discusses personalized content recommendations and enhanced user experience as separate issues. However, we think that both phenomena are interconnected, as the former leads to the latter. Thus, to keep things logical, we begin with personalized content recommendations, which are the fundamental to AI-driven audience engagement. These occur when algorithms analyze user data, such as viewing history, search queries, content interactions (likes, comments, ratings), and even localization details, to generate tailored suggestions for content selection (Chu & Park, 2009; Lim et al., 2023). This personalization mechanism not only enhances user experience but also reshapes how media organizations program and distribute content, increasingly steering users toward highly individualized media paths. Of course, this phenomenon is commonly associated with video-on-demand platforms. However, it deserves to be mentioned in this chapter for two reasons. First, legacy TV broadcasters already operate their own VOD platforms, and radio broadcasters run their online music platforms. Secondly, recommendation systems are implemented on TV and radio-based websites. In all cases, prior user choices shape current digital media interfaces such as websites, VOD platforms, and music platforms, both in the context of entertainment and news.

This solution fundamentally alters the audience's media experience. Traditionally designed for a mass audience, media are now tailored to individuals' needs and expectations. Rafieian and Yoganarasimhan (2023) analyze how recommendation algorithms affect user behavior and the media business. They note that personalization improves content relevance for the user and enables tailor-made advertising, making promotion activities more effective and easier to monetize (Kaplan & Haenlein, 2020). It is also directly connected with the effectiveness of media content distribution. Knowing the preferences of the audience, the media can create whole patterns of their behavior, predict their choices, and reduce the risk of them rejecting the proposed content (Forrest & Hoanca, 2015).

Moreover, algorithmically driven cues influence users' subsequent content choices, reinforcing their engagement with the platform. This mechanism simultaneously cultivates a perceived sense of autonomy in media selection and subtly increases dependency, as users are guided through highly curated, continuous streams of content (Shah, 2024). Personalized and user-addressed content tends to elicit stronger emotional responses, fostering a sense of intimacy and long-term loyalty toward media providers.

Prakash and Sabharwal (2024) argue that such AI-generated recommendations change the traditional role of audiences from passive recipients of broadcast programs to active agents in a dynamic media ecosystem. In this model, users do not merely consume content but participate in a form of co-curation, where their preferences, behaviors, and feedback directly shape the content they encounter. This reconfiguration of audience agency blurs the lines between consumption and production, aligning with the broader logic of prosumption. As audiences increasingly interact with algorithmically personalized media environments, they experience a sense of involvement and control, albeit within parameters defined by opaque algorithmic structures.

This is consistent with the observation made by Ajisafe and Dada (2023), who discuss AI-enhanced radio broadcasting from the perspective of the Internet of Things. They claim that "integration of radio with smart devices (…) expands its potential" (p. 41), especially in terms of audience engagement. The researchers point out that smart speakers or voice-activated gadgets "allow consumers to access radio programming with simple voice requests" (ibid.). For example, Prisa Radio, Spain's leading talk-radio network, uses AI to boost engagement, especially through smart speakers, which account for 25% of their streaming. Working with Amazon, they created Victoria, an AI voice that fills the gap in football content. Victoria shares football facts and commentary via Alexa Skill and as a radio co-host. These prompts allow intelligent devices to collect and analyze preferred data, improving recommendation systems and increasing personalization. Additionally, collecting data on consumer behavior is an excellent resource for analyzing their feedback on the content they use (Elia & Margherita, 2021). Thanks to the information obtained, the media can plan their short-term activities, which change depending on the audience expectations, even those that will emerge soon. Nasser El Erafy (2023) shows that AI-driven audience monitoring may go further, beyond tailor-made content, optimization, and targeting, to even refining overall programming strategies (i.e., Gupta et al., 2020). As Furtáková and Janáčková (2023) state, "AI can automate these tasks [*programming – AJG*], which not only saves time and resources but improves the listener experience by providing more relevant content" (p. 100).

2.2.3 New Content Formats

Sumner (2023) states that AI leads to the introduction of new content formats, offering a more immersive and interactive user experience by merging with VR and AR technologies. Anandraj and Aravind (2024) add that combining these technologies enhances the storytelling experience in "captivating narratives and fosters deeper connections with the content" (p. 89). As we can see, this topic is directly related to the previous two—on the one hand, it concerns new ways of generating media content, and on the other, it is associated with increased audience engagement.

A growing area of innovation in broadcasting involves the development of new content formats enabled by the convergence of artificial intelligence with immersive technologies such as virtual reality (VR) and augmented reality (AR). Rather than simply enhancing traditional content, these technologies allow for novel forms of media experience. Viewers can now, for example, enter 360-degree news environments, participate in virtual interviews, or engage with interactive documentary narratives that respond to gaze direction or gesture input. As Sinha (2024) notes, AI is transforming VR by automating world building and character creation. Generative AI can create vast, dynamic 3D environments from simple text prompts, allowing VR worlds to expand in real time as users explore them. In character creation, AI can generate realistic virtual actors with expressive faces and realistic movement, modeled on real performers. These avatars can appear in live VR broadcasts, immersive theater, and metaverse experiences, enabling small teams to create complex, personalized content that was once limited to large studios.

According to Anandraj and Aravind (2024), such formats enable the creation of "captivating narratives" and foster deeper emotional engagement with the content (p. 89), particularly by situating the user *within* the media experience rather than outside of it.

This immersive potential is not limited to audiovisual media alone. Related innovations—though often overlooked in this context—include AI-powered chatbots and virtual assistants, which create conversational formats that engage users in real time. Unlike virtual presenters who simulate broadcast personalities in linear programs, these systems operate as interactive interfaces, often integrated with platforms such as messaging apps, smart TVs, or connected radio devices. They offer contextual news updates, assist with content navigation, and simulate human-like dialogue to build stronger relationships with users (Shahriar & Hayawi, 2023). For instance, as Ford and Hutchinson (2019) describe, several television news organizations introduced newsbots that allowed users to "engage" with the news via messaging platforms by adopting scripted professional personas to deliver content in informal, one-on-one formats.

A real-world example of this is CBC/Radio-Canada's experimental chatbot that provided personalized election updates and voter information during the 2019 federal elections. Unlike a virtual presenter who would have narrated preprogrammed segments, the chatbot invited user queries, offered clarifications, and adjusted its responses based on user feedback. This demonstrates that in these formats AI acts less as a synthetic performer and more as a responsive companion, transforming the experience of broadcast content into an ongoing dialogue. Such applications increase user engagement and represent a departure from the traditional one-directional model of broadcasting.

2.2.4 Ethical and Societal Implications

Researchers analyzing the implementation of AI in traditional electronic media often highlight the ethical dilemmas associated with this technology. Among the major ones are privacy and data security concerns, trust and transparency issues, misinformation and fake news dissemination, bias in AI algorithms and AI-based content, and impact on employment (Sumner, 2023; Shah, 2024; Winkel, 2025).

The first area concerns the implementation of a reliable policy of informing audiences about how data is collected and used, particularly in the context of recommendation systems. As Shah (2024) notes, "media should prioritize user data privacy and take steps to safeguard sensitive information from unauthorized access or misuse" (p. 8). These processes should be transparent and comply with applicable regulations so as not to raise doubts about the intentions of content providers. There is a risk that insufficiently informed users may develop suspicions about how their data is being used, even to the point of formulating "conspiracy theories" (see: Agner et al., 2022).

The issue of trust in AI-driven media is also linked to other concerns, such as the spread of disinformation, fake news, or deepfakes. As we know, the technology in question allows for the creation of hyper-realistic fabricated video and audio content, which undermines audience trust and exacerbates skepticism toward the media. This may lead to an epistemic crisis, where the line between factual and fabricated material becomes increasingly blurred and gaining new knowledge becomes risky. These reflections shed light on the issue of reliability and credibility in media using AI. The discussion extends beyond disinformation to include such areas as newsroom management and media programming. The increasing use of AI in editorial functions such as selecting stories, crafting headlines, or generating audiovisual content raises concerns about media accountability. We can assume that transferring editorial control from humans to algorithms diminishes transparency and complicates the value of responsibility for content quality, especially with regard to the authenticity, accuracy, and integrity of the information provided by AI algorithms (see Kaplan & Haenlein, 2020; Khan, 2023).

The topics mentioned above, such as fake news, may lead to AI-driven bias in media content. Algorithms based on popularity metrics amplify mainstream, viral content at the expense of other, less popular narratives (i.e., local or minority-based). This leads to the homogenization of content while marginalizing culturally diverse or noncommercial voices. In the long run, this could result in an erosion of pluralism and the dominance of a single media discourse, as the preference for globally marketable content sidelines smaller communities and their unique stories, reducing the richness of the public sphere. Additionally, we must be aware of the potential biases already present in the data gathered by AI and how they may impact the content produced (Campbell et al., 2020). Interestingly, from the audience's perspective, there is also a thread of strengthening the phenomena of information bubbles and echo chambers (Rafieian & Yoganarasimhan, 2023; Porlezza & Schapals, 2024). As Jindal and Gouri (2024) emphasize, they "expose consumers to content that reinforces their existing beliefs and preferences," narrowing the information diversity and creating "The AI-Personalization Paradox."

The pursuit of efficiency through AI-driven automation also raises other concerns. Many researchers emphasize that AI excels at automating labor-intensive tasks such as large-scale data analysis, information retrieval, real-time translation, and enhancing interactivity (Chan-Olmsted, 2019). Within this logic, virtual radio and TV presenters, unaffected by fatigue and not requiring remuneration, are increasingly seen as economically attractive substitutes for human labor. However, while such solutions optimize production costs, they carry the risk of devaluing human creative input and accelerating workforce displacement in the media sector. This efficiency-driven motivation reinforces an earlier problem—just as algorithms prioritize virality and profitability over cultural diversity, economic pressures incentivize the replacement of nuanced human communication with standardized, synthetic alternatives. Together, these dynamics contribute to a media environment where cost-efficiency and popularity metrics override pluralism, inclusivity, and professional editorial judgment.

On the other hand, all this leads to reducing preproduction, production, and postproduction costs (Oyedokun, 2023). It cannot be denied that automation helps to save financial resources spent on distribution and promotion processes because it makes them fast, precise, and personalized. Equally important is AI's ability to absorb data and generate business-relevant reports and recommendations. This, in turn, raises questions among media professionals about their employment, for example, whether the use of AI will lead to layoffs in the media industry or a lack of demand for journalists and media managers. Will artificial voices and generated presenters replace humans? Will generated news take the place of opinion-forming, in-depth analyses? And finally, will the quality of journalism be diminished and the human element removed from the media landscape?

As research shows, although AI implementation in the preproduction, production, and postproduction of audiovisual material has many advantages, it remains impossible to fully replace people, at least for the time being. Researchers cite various reasons for this situation: lack of autonomous "human" creativity, absence of a "human touch" and oversight over artificially generated content (Ren, 2019; Khan, 2023), and insufficient proficiency in national languages because "texts generated by AI tools are usable in English, but may cause misunderstandings or even be deceptive in other languages" due to "redundant words, dates, abbreviations or incorrectly handled numbers which the news anchor can remove during the preparation" (Furtáková & Janáčková, 2023, p. 100).

Moreover, AI anchors serve to convey only surface-level meaning, lacking the tonal nuance, adaptability, and communicative depth required for effective audience engagement, especially in complex or live broadcast contexts (Wang, 2021). The relational factor is particularly important in radio, where the bond between the presenter and the audience often constitutes a key part of the listening experience. Artificial intelligence, constrained by its limited affective range and lack of human spontaneity, typically fails to replicate this connection. As a result, in content areas that require emotional depth, creativity, and dynamic contact with the audience, human professionals remain indispensable. However, recent examples suggest that in certain controlled environments, AI-generated personalities can be both engaging and well-received. Spotify's AI DJ, launched in the UK and Ireland in 2023, features a synthetic voice modeled on real presenters and offers personalized commentary between songs. According to the platform, this feature was positively received by users, who appreciated the tailored music selection and comments in a familiar voice style (Spotify Newsroom, 2023). Such solutions indicate that audiences may accept AI personas when expectations for relational depth are lower and personalization is prioritized over spontaneity or emotional authenticity. These parallel trends illustrate an evolving employment model in the media industry. While AI is proving highly effective in repetitive, automated, and data-driven tasks, human oversight and creativity remain crucial. Researchers also note the growing need for new professional roles, such as AI system managers, editors supervising AI outputs, or trainers specializing in algorithmic literacy (Jaiswal et al., 2021; Khan, 2023). Reconciling AI-generated content with human creativity may not be about replacement, but about collaboration. If implemented wisely, AI can amplify the capabilities of professionals and enable cultural production that blends efficiency with originality (see Bender, 2024). As Patti Taylor from Beasley Media Group Detroit (McLane, 2024) notes, "humans still have to be responsible for some input in order to get output (…) AI should be treated like any other software or business solution. We have to find out how AI can best support human-driven projects and initiatives, enhance productivity and eliminate lengthy timelines" (p. n. p.). It can thus be assumed that AI is still treated as a groundbreaking technology that changes many things, but ultimately does not replace human thought and creativity. On the other hand, it clearly optimizes and automatizes the repetitive tasks. This could mean that in the future AI will actually have an impact on the structure of employment in the media, but mainly in areas of repetitive and simple activities where human involvement could be limited to programming activities carried out by AI.

2.3 Examples of AI Implementation in Radio and Television Industries

Practical examples of efforts by broadcasters such as the BBC, NPR, and iHeartRadio perfectly illustrate the potential of AI technology to automate processes, personalize content, and optimize editorial work and material archiving.

The British public broadcaster BBC has been setting the standard for innovation in electronic media for many years, using AI to optimize its production processes and improve the audience experience (Markin et al., 2024). One of the key areas where the BBC has successfully implemented AI is in the personalization of content on its website and digital platforms. AI algorithms analyze massive amounts of data from user activity, such as article browsing, video program selection, viewing history, and topic preferences. Based on these analyses, AI systems offer personalized recommendations that increase audience engagement and improve user experience. This ensures that each user receives content that meets their individual needs, helping the BBC compete more effectively with commercial streaming platforms such as Netflix and Amazon Prime (Dúbravská & Višňovský, 2023).

The second central area of the BBC's AI implementation is the automatic transcription and translation of multimedia content (Simon, 2024). AI-based systems such as speech-to-text recognition tools enable the near-instant conversion of audio and video material into text. This enhances television broadcasts with automatically generated subtitles, significantly improving accessibility for viewers with hearing impairments. Additionally, AI-powered translation systems allow for real-time multilingual dissemination of content, thereby broadening the BBC's global reach. For instance, BBC World News can be subtitled or dubbed into foreign languages almost instantaneously, enhancing the timeliness and inclusivity of international journalism. These processes also offer substantial cost and time savings when compared to manual transcription and translation workflows (Newman, 2018).

However, alongside these benefits, such applications raise ethical concerns that public broadcasters like the BBC have actively sought to address. Issues include potential inaccuracies in automated transcription, bias in translation algorithms (particularly in culturally sensitive content), and the risk of diminishing editorial oversight. Recognizing these challenges, the BBC has adopted internal frameworks for the responsible use of AI. Its *Machine Learning Engine Principles* emphasize values such as fairness, transparency, explainability, human oversight, and the avoidance of discriminatory outcomes. These principles guide how AI systems are designed and deployed within the organization to ensure they align with the BBC's public service mission and uphold trust with its audiences (BBC, 2023).

The U.S. broadcaster NPR (National Public Radio) is an example of a radio organization that is fully utilizing the capabilities of artificial intelligence to optimize editorial operations and improve the efficiency of content archiving (Reilley, 2024). A key application of AI at NPR is the automatic transcription of radio material. Using advanced speech recognition technologies, AI systems can quickly convert audio recordings into accurate text versions. This is particularly useful for journalists and editors who can more easily analyze interviews, reports, or broadcasts to create new material. Automatic transcriptions also allow for better content archiving, making it easier to search for recordings by keyword, topic or broadcast. For example, NPR systems enable automatic tagging of archived material with AI-generated metadata, which significantly speeds up the classification and retrieval of content (Noain-Sánchez, 2022). Artificial intelligence at NPR also supports the work of journalists by generating summaries and abstracts of content. This allows the automated system to generate key information in longer broadcasts in seconds, allowing editors to review and select material more quickly. This automation streamlines the production process and enables journalists to focus on more creative and analytical tasks (Rahman, n.d.).

Radio and streaming platform iHeartRadio is an example of a commercial broadcaster that uses artificial intelligence to enhance the quality of service for its listeners. One of the key areas of AI applications is the personalization of music playlists. Algorithms analyze users' listening history, identifying favorite genres, artists, and interactions with radio stations. On this basis, AI creates personalized playlists tailored to each user's preferences. This provides listeners with a unique experience that matches their musical tastes, which increases their loyalty to the platform.

Another example of the use of AI in iHeartRadio is listening analysis and frame optimization. AI algorithms monitor listeners' behaviors, such as listening time, frequency of station changes, and engagement levels at specific times. By analyzing this data, the broadcaster can fine-tune its programming according to audience preferences, maximizing reach, and improving user satisfaction. For example, music stations can modify their programming blocks based on real-time listening patterns, increasing the appeal of broadcasts during the peak times.

Frame optimization and content personalization are also useful tools for advertisers. By accurately analyzing user preferences, iHeartRadio can offer targeted ads that appeal to specific audiences, which is a key competitive advantage for commercial radio.

Examples of the BBC, NPR and iHeartRadio's activities show that artificial intelligence is becoming an indispensable part of electronic media operations. Content personalization, automatic transcription and translation, material archiving, and program optimization contribute to significant improvements in the efficiency, accessibility, and quality of content. AI is streamlining traditional processes and redefining the relationship between broadcasters and audiences, opening up new opportunities in a dynamic media environment. As technology continues evolving, we can expect even more advanced solutions that will revolutionize the way radio and television operate.

2.4 Discussion: AI and Opportunities and Challenges for Radio and Television

The rapid development of artificial intelligence in electronic media presents both tremendous opportunities and significant challenges for traditional broadcasters. As public and commercial media institutions strive to remain competitive in a landscape increasingly dominated by digital platforms, implementing AI marks a pivotal stage in their evolution. However, alongside technical and operational advancements, AI introduces profound ethical, cultural, and institutional dilemmas that warrant careful analysis.

AI significantly optimizes broadcast processes in the pre-production, production, and post-production stages. Organizations like the BBC and NPR use AI tools such as speech-to-text transcription, real-time subtitling, and metadata tagging to reduce costs and allow journalists to focus on creative and investigative tasks (Simon, 2024; Noain-Sánchez, 2022). In radio, where time sensitivity is critical, these tools are transformative.

The AI technology also enables content personalization, making it possible for broadcasters to mirror strategies used by platforms like Netflix and Spotify. Systems that track user behavior help broadcasters offer tailored content, improving engagement and loyalty (Dúbravská & Višňovský, 2023). Examples include iHeartRadio's personalized playlists and the BBC's curated digital news feeds. Furthermore, by implementing solutions such as on-the-fly translation, media become more accessible and inclusive, as their content becomes comprehensible to non-native speakers. For example, you can use a special link[1] to see the translations of the content provided by Polish Radio Wrocław into one of 20 languages. This solution can be particularly helpful in exceptional and difficult situations, such as refugee or humanitarian crises, when a large number of people need constant and immediate access to up-to-date information.

Despite these advantages, AI use in broadcasting introduces serious ethical concerns. A key issue is the opacity of algorithmic decision-making, which threatens editorial transparency and accountability. If AI decided what content audiences receive, it may undermine journalistic neutrality, especially in public media.

Also hyper-personalization, while beneficial for engagement, can lead to fragmented discourse. Users may be exposed only to viewpoints that confirm their biases, limiting exposure to diverse perspectives and weakening democratic debate (Jindal & Gouri, 2024). Another concern is job displacement. As artificial intelligence takes over tasks once performed by media professionals, there are risks to employment, creativity, and editorial standards. Automation should assist—not replace—critical human judgment.

Additionally, immersive technologies like AR and VR raise new challenges, including high deployment costs and accessibility issues. These technologies blur the lines between reality and fiction, posing psychological risks. Data privacy also raises significant concerns. AI-driven personalization involves extensive data collection, which exposes users to potential misuse. Transparent data practices and stringent privacy regulations are necessary to maintain audience trust. Finally, the proliferation of misinformation, including "deepfakes" and AI-generated false content, poses a growing threat that automated news generation systems can be exploited to mislead audiences. To prevent manipulation, a robust content verification framework and ethical guidelines are necessary.

[1] https://dlf.demo.radiozeit.de/?prefix=radiowroclaw

There is also a reference to broader societal and technological implications. For public service broadcasters, the integration of AI must support institutional values: accessibility, inclusivity, and editorial diversity. This calls for transparent, ethical, and human-centered AI policies, developed in collaboration with engineers, journalists, ethicists, and the public.

As has been shown, artificial intelligence offers a renaissance in broadcasting through workflow modernization and audience engagement. However, it also demands a critical reassessment of public service missions, journalistic ethics, and the societal impact of media technologies. The future of AI in broadcasting depends not only on innovation but also on the values and structures guiding its use.

2.5 Conclusions

Viewed through technological determinism, the integration of artificial intelligence into broadcasting appears to be less a matter of choice than an inevitable consequence of technological progress. AI is not just a tool adopted by media institutions to increase productivity or engagement—it is actively changing the structures, workflows, and ethical frameworks of these. As broadcasters strive to stay relevant in a digital-first landscape, AI technologies are increasingly changing the terms of media production and consumption. From speech recognition and real-time translation to content personalization and automated news generation, these tools are driving editorial decision-making, redefining professional roles, and shaping audience expectations.

According to the determinist perspective, these developments suggest that technology is the primary driver of societal change, often eclipsing human agency or institutional intent. While broadcasters may strive to uphold editorial independence, inclusivity, or democratic values, AI systems inherently embed certain biases and operational logic that challenge those goals. Moreover, the rise of hyper-personalization and algorithmically driven content curation contributes to the fragmentation of public discourse, not by deliberate design, but as a systemic outcome of the technologies themselves.

Even ethical challenges such as misinformation, job displacement, and data privacy are shaped by the logic of technological progress, where efficiency and scale often precede caution or reflection. Thus, the current transformation of media through AI exemplifies how technology can become a deterministic force, setting the agenda for institutional adaptation. Navigating this new terrain requires adopting artificial intelligence while critically analyzing the values and assumptions encoded by these systems.

Literature

Agner, L., Necyk, B. J., & Renzi, A. (2022). User experience and information architecture. In M. M. Soares, F. Rebelo, & T. Z. Ahram (Eds.), *Handbook of usability and user-experience*. CRC Press.

Ajisafe, O., & Dada, D. (2023). Radio broadcasting in the digital age: Adapting to the challenges of the 21 century. *International Journal of Advanced Mass Communication and Journalism, 4*(2), 36–44.

Alsaleh, A. (2024). The impact of technological advancement on culture and society. *Scientific Reports, 14*, 32140. https://doi.org/10.1038/s41598-024-83995-z

Anandraj, K. C., & Aravind, S. (2024). The impact of AI revolution in transforming film making industry for the digital age. *ILIS Journal of Librarianship and Informatics, 6*(2), 82–91. https://ssrn.com/abstract=5001027

BBC. (2023). *Machine learning engine principles*. BBC.co.uk. Retrieved from https://www.bbc.co.uk/gel/articles/machine-learning-engine-principles

Bender, S. (2024). Generative-AI, the media industries, and the disappearance of human creative labour. *Media Practice and Education, 1–18*. https://doi.org/10.1080/25741136.2024.2355597

Campbell, C., Sands, S., Ferraro, C., Tsao, H. Y., & Mavrommatis, A. (2020). From data to action: How marketers can leverage AI. *Business Horizons, 63*(2), 227–243. https://doi.org/10.1016/j.bushor.2019.12.002

Chan-Olmsted, S. M. (2019). A review of artificial intelligence adoptions in the media industry. *International Journal on Media Management, 21*(3–4), 193–215. https://doi.org/10.1080/14241277.2019.1695619

Chiappani, L. (2024, September 27). *Artificial intelligence in the film industry: Opportunities and challenges*. KI Company. https://www.ki-company.ai/en/blog-beitraege/artificial-intelligence-in-the-film-industry-opportunities-and-challenges

Chu, W., & Park, S.-T. (2009). Personalized recommendation on dynamic content using predictive bilinear models. *The Web conference*. https://doi.org/10.1145/1526709.1526802

Das, S., Dey, A., Pal, A., & Roy, N. (2015). Applications of artificial intelligence in machine learning: Review and prospect. *International Journal of Computer Applications, 115*(9), 31–41. https://doi.org/10.5120/20182-2402

Dúbravská, O., & Višňovský, J. (2023). Implementation of new technologies with elements and tools of artificial intelligence into the television broadcasting. *NORDSCI international conference. Conference proceedings, 1*(6), 299–306.

Elia, G., & Margherita, A. (2021). A conceptual framework for the cognitive enterprise: Pillars, maturity, value drivers. *Technology Analysis and Strategic Management*, 1–13. https://doi.org/10.1080/09537325.2021.1901874

Ford, H., & Hutchinson, J. (2019). Newsbots that mediate journalist and audience relationships. *Digital Journalism, 7*(8), 1013–1031. https://doi.org/10.1080/21670811.2019.1626752

Forrest, E., & Hoanca, B. (2015). *Artificial intelligence: Marketing's game changer*. IGI_Global. https://doi.org/10.4018/978-1-4666-8459-1.ch003

Furtáková, L., & Janáčková, L. (2024a). AI in radio: The game changer you did not hear coming. In M. P. Hossová, M. Martovič, & M. Solík (Eds.), *Marketing identity: AI – The future of today* (pp. 95–106). Trava. https://doi.org/10.34135/mmidentity-2023-09

Furtáková, L., & Janáčková, L. (2024b). News at the speed of AI: Automatic journalism through text generator. In M. P. Hossová, M. Solík, & M. Martovič (Eds.), *Marketing identity: Human vs artificial* (pp. 166–174). Trava. https://doi.org/10.34135/mmidentity-2024-16

Gupta, S., Leszkiewicz, A., Kumar, V., Bijmolt, T., & Potapov, D. (2020). Digital analytics: Modeling for insights and new methods. *Journal of Interactive Marketing, 51*(1), 26–43.

Jaiswal, A., Arun, C. J., & Varma, A. (2021). Rebooting employees: Upskilling for artificial intelligence in multinational corporations. *The International Journal of Human Resource Management, 33*(6), 1–30. https://doi.org/10.1080/09585192.2021.1891114

Jindal, P., & Gouri, H. (2024). AI-personalization paradox: Navigating consumer behavior in a filter bubble era. In Y. H. Musiolik, R. V. Rodriguez, & H. Kannan (Eds.), *AI impacts in digital consumer behavior* (pp. 82–111). IGI Global. https://doi.org/10.4018/979-8-3693-1918-5.ch004

Kaplan, A., & Haenlein, M. (2020). Rulers of the world, unite! The challenges and opportunities of artificial intelligence. *Business Horizons, 63*(1), 37–50.

Khan, M. H. (2023). *The impact of AI on the media industry* (MA thesis, Uppsala University). DiVA Portal. https://uu.diva-portal.org/smash/record.jsf?pid=diva2%3A1814616

Kumari, P., Singh, S. K., & Utpal, V. K. J. (2024). Recent trends and future prospects of artificial intelligence in Indian media. *SHODHAK. A Journal of Historical Reseach, 53*(2), 64–74.

Lapalelo, P. A. (2021). The effect of the YouTube subscriptions button in the real-world and cyberspace. *Indonesian Journal of Social Sciences, 13*(1), 46–61. https://doi.org/10.20473/ijss.v13i1.26354

Li, Y. (2022). AI restoration brings 'Dying' masterpieces back to life, but tricks copyright? *International Journal of Law and Information Technology, 30*(3), 368–384. https://doi.org/10.2139/ssrn.4285979

Lim, J. S., Shin, D., Zhang, J., Masiclat, S., Luttrell, R., & Kinsey, D. (2023). News audiences in the age of artificial intelligence: Perceptions and behaviors of optimizers, mainstreamers, and skeptics. *Journal of Broadcasting and Electronic Media, 67*(3), 353–375.

MacLuhan, M. (1994). Understanding Media - The Extensions of Man. New York: MITPress, 1994.

Maigret, E. (2012). *Socjologia komunikacji i mediów*. Oficyna Naukowa.

Markin, M., Batrak, Y., Markina, O., & Segol, R. (2024). Automation of content creation: How AI is changing the business models of media companies. *ОБРІЇ ДРУКАРСТВА, 2*(16), 71–96. https://doi.org/10.20535/2522-1078.2024.2(16).319005

McCombs, M., Holbert, L., Kiousis, S., & Wanta, W. (2011). *The news and public opinion: Media effects on civic life*. Polity Press.

McLane, P. (April 19, 2024). *Special report: AI case studies in radio*. Radioworld.com. Retrieved from: https://www.radioworld.com/tech-and-gear/special-report-ai-case-studies-in-radio

Mujiono, M. (2024). Digital literacy: Fundamental competence for modern society. *Didaktika, 30*(1), 15. https://doi.org/10.30587/didaktika.v30i1.6906

Munoriyarwa, A., Chiumbu, S., & Motsaathebe, G. (2021). Artificial intelligence practices in everyday news production: The case of South Africa's Mainstream Newsrooms. *Journalism Practice, 17*(7), 1374–1392. https://doi.org/10.1080/17512786.2021.1984976

Nasser El Erafy, A. (2023). Applications of artificial intelligence in the field of media. *International Journal of Artificial Intelligence and Emerging Technology, 6*(2), 19–41. https://doi.org/10.21608/ijaiet.2024.275179.1006

Newman, N. (2018). *Journalism, media and technology trends and predictions 2018* (pp. 1–50). Reuters Institute for the Study of Journalism.

Newton, K. (2015). Public service and commercial broadcasting: Impacts on politics and society. *The Political Quarterly, 87*(1), 31–38. https://doi.org/10.1111/1467-923X.12214

Nishal, S., & Diakopoulos, N. (2023). Envisioning the applications and implications of generative AI for news media. In *CHI '23 Workshop on Generative AI and HCI*, April 23–28, 2023, Hamburg.

Noain-Sánchez, A. (2022). Addressing the impact of artificial intelligence on journalism: The perception of experts, journalists and academics. *Communications Society, 35*(3), 105–121. https://doi.org/10.15581/003.35.3.105-121

Oyedokun, I. (2023). *Effects of adopting artificial intelligence presenters in broadcasting on audience perception and gratification of broadcast content*. Retrieved from https://www.researchgate.net/publication/372824952.

Pavlik, J. V. (2020). *Journalism in the age of virtual reality: How experiential media are transforming news*. Columbia University Press.

Polskie Radio (October 24, 2024). *Kontrowersje wokół wykorzystania AI w mediach. Radio Kraków zastępuje dziennikarzy wirtualnymi prezenterami*. Polskieradio.pl. Retrieved from https://www.polskieradio.pl/399/7977/Artykul/3438983,kontrowersje-wokol-wykorzystania-ai-w-mediach-radio-krakow-zastepuje-dziennikarzy-wirtualnymi-prezenterami

Porlezza, C., & Schapals, A. K. (2024). AI ethics in journalism (studies): An evolving field between research and practice. *Emerging Media, 2*(3), 356–370. https://doi.org/10.1177/27523543241288818
Prakash, G., & Sabharwal, D. (2024). AI revolution in online media: Transforming content creation, distribution, and consumption. In D. Sabahrwal, R. S. Sood, & S. Sood (Eds.), *Media and AI: Navigating the future of communication* (pp. 179–192). Delhi-11003.
Prasad, R. K., & Makesh, D. (2024). Impact of AI on media & entertainment industry. In A. Pandey, T. R. Pravin, & R. K. Prasad (Eds.), *Media & journalism transformations-emerging trends and paradigm shifts* (pp. 41–72). AIP Publishing.
Radio Television Digital News Association. (2023). *Use of artificial intelligence (AI) in journalism.* Rtdna.org. Retrieved from https://www.rtdna.org/use-of-ai-in-journalism
Rafieian, O., & Yoganarasimhan, H. (2023). AI and personalization. *Review of Marketing Research, 20,* 77–102. https://doi.org/10.1108/S1548-643520230000020004
Rahman, A. (n.d.). Opportunities and challenges of artificial intelligence in public media journalism. In: A. D'Arma, M. Michalis, G.F. Lowe, & M.B. Zita (Eds.). *Challenges and developments in public service journalism* (pp. 122-147). Retrived from https://www.jstor.org/stable/pdf/10.16997/14610450.9.pdf
Rahman, D., & Ali, M. A. (2024). AI in video production: From script to screen. In D. Sabahrwal, R. S. Sood, & S. Sood (Eds.), *Media and AI: Navigating the future of communication* (pp. 51–61). Post Script.
Reilley, M. (2024). *The journalist's toolbox: A guide to digital reporting and AI.* New York. https://doi.org/10.4324/9781003431787.
Ren, Q. X. (2019). The possibility of replacing hosts in the context of artificial intelligence from the perspective of host communication: Xinhua News Agency's "AI Synthetic Anchor" as an example. *Radio and TV Journal, 12,* 146–147.
Shah, A. (2024). Media and artificial intelligence: Current perceptions and future outlook. *Academy of Marketing Studies Journal, 28*(2), 1–13.
Shahriar, S., & Hayawi, K. (2023). *Let's have a chat! A conversation with ChatGPT: Technology, applications, and limitations.* arXiv preprint arXiv:2302.13817.
Sienkiewicz, P., & Świeboda, H. (2019). Valuing techniques in management systems. *Modern Management Systems, 14*(3), 27–44. https://doi.org/10.37055/nsz/132725
Simon, F.M. (2024). *Artificial intelligence in the news. Tow center for digital journalism.* Retrieved from https://academiccommons.columbia.edu/doi/10.7916/gcyz-8b43/download
Singh, H., Rastogi, A., & Kaur, K. (2023). *Artificial intelligence as a tool in the visual effects and film industry.* CRC Press eBooks. https://doi.org/10.1201/9781003405573-56
Sinha, V. (Jun 27, 2024). *Future of AI in media: Advancements in VR and AR integration.* Indiaai.gov.in. Retrieved from https://indiaai.gov.in/article/future-of-ai-in-media-advancements-in-vr-and-ar-integration
Spotify Newsroom. (2023, May 16). *AI DJ expands to the UK and Ireland.* Retrieved from: https://newsroom.spotify.com/2023-05-16/ai-dj-uk-ireland-spotify-personalization/
Sumner, D. (2023). *AI in media and entertainment.* Amazon.nl.
Truskolaski, S. (2010). Exogenous measures of technology shocks as used in Poland in 2005-2009. Gospodarka Narodowa. *The Polish Journal of Economics, 240*(5-6), 61–72. https://doi.org/10.33119/GN/101162
Tsalakanidou, F., Papadopoulos, S., Mezaris, V., Kompatsiaris, I., Gray, B., Tsabouraki, D., et al. (2021). The AI4Media project: Use of next-generation artificial intelligence technologies for media sector applications. In: A*rtificial intelligence applications and innovations: 17th IFIP WG 12.5 international conference, AIAI 2021, Hersonissos, Crete, Greece, June 25–27, 2021, Proceedings 17* (pp. 81–93). Springer International Publishing.
Verma, R., & Heider, S. (2024). Revolutionizing realities: The impact of artificial intelligence in visual effects. In D. Sabahrwal, R. S. Sood, & S. Sood (Eds.), *Media and AI: Navigating the future of communication* (pp. 9–17). Post Script.

Walczyk, T. (2018). Bomba symulakrów : scena rzeczywistości ukryta za kurtyną symulacji: spektakl hiperrzeczywistości. *Humanistyka i Przyrodoznawstwo, 21*, 195–208. https://doi.org/10.31648/hip.417

Wang, C. L. (2021). New frontiers and future directions in interactive marketing: Inaugural editorial. *Journal of Research in Interactive Marketing, 15*(1), 1–9. https://doi.org/10.1108/jrim-03-2021-270

Winkel, M. (2025). Controlling the uncontrollable: The public discourse on artificial intelligence between the positions of social and technological determinism. *AI and Society, 40*, 1947–1959. https://doi.org/10.1007/s00146-024-01979-z

Xi, Y., & Latif, R. A. (2022). Reconstruction of news production driven by artificial intelligence in China. *SEARCH Journal of Media and Communication Research, 14*(2), 29–45. http://search.taylors.edu.my

Anna Jupowicz-Ginalska is an Associate Professor at the University of Warsaw. She specialises in media management, media marketing, and the impact of new technologies on the media and their audiences. She serves as Vice President and is a Board Member of the European Media Management Association. Between 2022 and 2024, she served as Deputy Director of the Doctoral School of Social Sciences at the University of Warsaw. She is the scholarship holder of the 'Poland Fellowships – Schwerpunkt Polen' programme at Johannes Gutenberg University Mainz. She leads an international consortium for the EU project "Beyond Borders" and the Polish team in the EU project "MIA: Media Literacy in Rural Communities." She also manages the UW-financed projects "Social Senior – (Non)Inclusiveness of the Digital World Towards Seniors and Ageing Societies" and "Media Management: An Educational Approach. Mapping and Identifying the Needs of the Academic Community in Poland". She was a member of the research team in the project "Diversity Management as Innovation in Journalism" (POLS, Norway Grants). She also initiated and led the research "FOMO. Poles and the Fear of Missing Out" (2018–2022). Anna was the leader of the global initiatives, The Knowledge-Share Communities (#university & emmahub) and The World Media Economics and Management Conference 2025. Anna is a member of the Editorial Board of the "Journal of Media Business Studies" (Taylor & Francis) and "Humanities and Social Sciences Communications" (Springer Nature), as well as the Reviewers Board of "Future Internet" and "Social Sciences" (MDPI). She serves on the Programme Boards of "Dziennikarstwo i Media" (University of Wroclaw), "Styles of Communication" (University of Bucharest), "Revista Multidisciplinar" (Núcleo Multidisciplinar), and "JOCIS" (MediaXXI/Formalpress).

Jarosław Kinal has a PhD in Social Sciences. He is a media expert and sociologist specializing in the impact of information and technology on society. Jarosław is an Assistant Professor at the Department of Economic and Social History of the Institute of History at the University of Rzeszów, the author of over 100 scientific papers, and manager of research and popularization projects with national and international reach.

Music Creation and Production

3

Steve Collins and Sarah Keith

Abstract

This chapter explores the evolving landscape of artificial intelligence (AI) in music, tracing its historical roots and examining its contemporary applications and implications. While AI has long been employed in computational musicology and music information retrieval, recent advances have significantly broadened its reach into music creation and production. We begin by situating music as a media form historically shaped by technological disruption and frame AI as the latest marker in this continuum of transformation. A comprehensive overview of AI applications in music follows, including algorithmic composition, assistive production tools, audio generation, and voice synthesis. We critically assess how these innovations are reshaping the music value chain, with particular attention to rights management and economic frameworks. By contextualizing these changes within broader industry dynamics, the chapter highlights the disruptive potential of AI and its capacity to reconfigure creative and economic practices.

Concluding with a set of critical questions and future scenarios, we provide a holistic analysis of AI's multifaceted impact on music, offering insights into both the opportunities and challenges that lie ahead for musicians, the music industries, and the AI sector.

3.1 Introduction

There are many musical applications for artificial intelligence, machine learning, neural networks, and algorithmic processes. Historically, music AI has been explored in computational musicology and music information retrieval, typically

S. Collins (✉) · S. Keith
Macquarie University, Sydney, NSW, Australia
e-mail: stephen.collins@mq.edu.au; sarah.keith@mq.edu.au

S. Böhm et al. (eds.), *Handbook of AI-based Media Disruption*, Future of Business and Finance, https://doi.org/10.1007/978-3-032-07605-2_3

for specialist and research purposes. The more recent development of neural nets trained on music and audio recordings, and the widespread accessibility of generative systems based on these, has yielded a range of new applications and challenges for music creation and production. In this chapter, we provide an overview and contextualization of music AI, indicating practical applications and undertaking critical analysis of these technologies in relation to their disruptive potential.

We begin by positioning music as a media form and set of practices that have been consistently disrupted by the emergence of new technologies. The recent interventions of AI technologies on musical practices are simply the latest markers in a history of transformations. The chapter moves to provide a working definition of musical AI followed by a brief overview of the main technologies and processes underpinning these applications. It then supplies an overview of musical applications for AI, including automated and algorithmic composition, assistive plug-ins, audio generation, and voice synthesis. The chapter then considers the effects of AI's use in music creation and production on music's value chain, including its implications for music catalogues and rights management, intellectual property and ownership, and legal challenges. It provides context for how these technological developments are reconfiguring the music industries.

The chapter concludes by identifying critical questions for the music industries and by outlining future scenarios for the sector. By examining multiple and interlinking effects of AI on music creation and production, this chapter provides a comprehensive overview of past, current, and future developments.

3.2 Music, A History of Disruption

The business of music is underpinned by technologies of production, distribution, and control. As Williamson and Cloonan (2007, p. 305) have argued, it is inaccurate to refer to a singular "music industry" and more appropriate to use "music industries" to acknowledge that the business of music is made up of a number of different, but interconnected areas of activity. Sterne presents a broader picture, arguing that there is no singular music industry, but rather, "many industries with many relationships to music" (2014, p. 53). This is not a recent phenomenon; ever since the advent of recorded music, the music industries have existed as a network of interconnected concerns related to songwriting and composition, production, recording, management, licensing and rights, and distribution.

Technological, economic, cultural, and legislative shifts have produced a constantly shifting landscape for the music industries. These changes are often initiated externally, with outside entities entering the music business and quickly establishing themselves as major players. A clear example of this is the streaming model, which emerged less than two decades ago when Spotify—initially a tech startup—was founded, and is now the predominant music format. As Harrington puts it, "technology threatens business as usual, until it becomes business as usual" (United States Copyright Office, 2020, p. 239). Today, the music industries include a complex network of creatives, technicians, rights holders, managers, distributors, legislators, and technologists, who are accountable to each other—and to investors — under the binding framework of copyright. The file-sharing crisis of the 2000s was the last seismic disruption in the recorded music industries and was caused by loss of control over the distribution of recorded music. Today, these industries face disruption in all other areas—songwriting, production and recording, and rights management—due to another innovation emerging from the tech sector; artificial intelligence.

Fundamentally, AI is used to complete or accelerate steps in the music production process that until now have relied on human labor and expertise. AI may be utilized in composition, production, sound generation, or data analysis for purposes such as A&R or predictive investment. Broadly speaking, AI will draw on data and algorithms derived from training on a large data set to fulfil these processes.

Let's illustrate this with an example using current technologies. You sign up for an account with a website for generative music-making. You produce an original song of reasonable quality by entering a few prompts, in text format, to indicate your preferred style and sound. It takes less than a minute for the website to generate a song of reasonable quality, including lyrics and voice. The website's terms of use assign you all rights, title, and interest in the generated song. You then upload this song to a music distributor and, as both songwriter and recording rights holder, can now collect recording and publishing royalties.[1] The song is distributed to streaming platforms, which generally do not forbid AI-generated material, as long as it does not impersonate existing artists (Ross, 2023).

This clearly disrupts established processes and industries that are typically involved in composing, recording, and distributing a song. The process of creating and distributing a revenue-generating song involves only yourself entering text prompts; a generative music-making website; a music distributor; and streaming platforms. What may have previously taken weeks or months now takes minutes. The multiple personnel (songwriters, singers, instrumentalists), technologies (microphones, samples, digital instruments), knowledge, and skill usually involved in music production are replaced by a single web-based interface. The website acknowledges that it uses generative music models, but the exact mechanisms used to generate your original song are unclear, and the data used to train the generative AI are not disclosed.

Unsurprisingly, the rapid advancement and expanding reach of AI in music have generated concern among stakeholders in the existing music industries. We use this chapter to unpack the uncertainties surrounding AI in music creation, production, and distribution, and its potential effects on industry sectors and professionals. To do that, we first define the field of musical AI, providing a brief history and overview of relevant technologies. Against this backdrop, we then survey contemporary applications for music AI including examples. Finally, we touch upon AI's

[1] We are aware that the capacity for AI-generated work to attract copyright protection differs between jurisdictions. For the purposes of this hypothetical scenario we can assume that the user is not publicly declaring the use of generative AI in producing their song.

implications for the music industries, and the future agenda for music industry stakeholders and creators.

3.3 Defining Music AI

Technology companies encroaching on the music industries is a well-established pattern stretching back at least as far as the early twentieth century. Frith (1992, p. 57) notes that electronics manufacturers often drove changes in the music industries. For example, manufacturers often need to become involved in the production of "software" (such as vinyl records or compact discs) in order to have a product with which to promote their new hardware (record players, compact disc players). This principle was echoed many years later when Apple released the iPod closely followed by the iTunes Music Store, a decision attributed to Universal Music Group's then-CEO Doug Morris being swayed by the tech company's limited market share (Levy, 2006, p. 158). In other words, major record companies saw digital sales as a potential parallel revenue stream to the sales of tangible media such as CDs, rather than as a replacement of tangible media.

Likewise, music production has a long and closely entwined relationship with IT: after all, digital audio workstations (DAWs) and plugins are software packages. DAWs introduced affordable and industry-grade technologies into computer-based home studios (Goold & Graham, 2019, pp. 122–125). Software such as Ableton Live, Cubase, Logic, and an abundance of plugin effects, synths, and sample libraries have afforded amateur musicians access to music technologies identical to those used by their professional peers. This shift is evidenced by the number of cloud-based services for music production that are available today from DAWs to collaboration tools to automated mastering services (Collins et al., 2021, pp. 249–263). The widespread availability of technologies previously only accessible to professionals, coupled with the Internet's distributive capabilities, allows contemporary musicians (professional and amateur alike) to compose, record, mix, produce, and distribute music from home or mobile studios. This is not new, however. This radical decentralization of production has been with us for a quarter of a century.

The relationship between music and artificial intelligence— broadly defined— is similarly longstanding. There is a rich history of computers being put to creative tasks that are often considered the domain of humanity. David Gunkel (2021, p. 385) refers to creativity as one of the "bulwarks of human exceptionalism," while Arielli (2021, p. 7) claims that creativity is "insusceptible to algorithmic reduction." Nonetheless, many researchers, artists, and composers have challenged these claims of human exceptionalism, attempting to build machines that can, to some degree, autonomously create music. Computer pioneer Alan Turing is regarded as the first person to successfully create computer-generated music. In 1948, Turing programmed a computer known as "Baby" housed at the Computing Machine Laboratory, Manchester University to produce musical sounds. His collaborator Christopher Strachey extended Turing's programming routines to create simple, and reportedly not very good, melodies that were recorded by the BBC in 1951

(Copeland & Long, 2017, pp. 189–190, p. 198). Subsequently, Lejaren Hiller and Leonard Isaacs collaborated on using the ILLIAC I to produce *The Illiac Suite* (1975) though only compositional material, not audio output, was produced. Taylor (2014, p. 5) writes, however, that musicians were less than enthusiastic about these experiments in computer music:

> While computer music was often greeted with interest as the latest novelty, the early computer experimentalist Lejaren Hiller felt that emerging from "many quarters" was a deepening "incredulity and indignation." Joel Chadabe, another pioneering computer composer, felt that the critics and the traditional musicians "feared" the machine and its potentially harmful influence on the entire field. In the early 1970s, Elliot Schwartz, in his listening guide to electronic music, best summed up the general reaction: "The notion of music 'created' by a computer always seems to arouse a surprising degree of hostility, usually on the part of people who find 20th century art increasingly 'dehumanized' and 'mechanical.'"

Experiments with computer-generated music continued throughout the twentieth century. Another notable proponent is Brian Eno, who coined the term "generative music" in the 1990s to describe his ever-changing works produced using SSEYO Koan software. While Eno's association with the field made some ripples in the mainstream, the interdisciplinary field of "computer music" was until recently a fringe effort.

While music can be produced using many computational approaches, a newer method receiving attention in academic and generalist circles is music generation by applications trained on large music catalogs. Due to the scale of data and computational processing involved, this approach has only become prevalent in recent years. One of the earliest experiments in this area was "Daddy's Car," a song in the style of the Beatles produced using FlowMachines, "a system that learns music styles from a huge database of songs" (Pachet, 2018). However, this song required human intervention in arrangement and production. Soon after, systems capable of fully producing a music track based on a few short prompts emerged. In 2020, OpenAI generated "deepfakes" of artists including Frank Sinatra, Katy Perry, and Elvis Presley for its Jukebox project. This model was trained on 1.2 million songs scraped from the web, complete with the corresponding lyrics and metadata (Robertson, 2020).

Today, web-based platforms such as Suno and Udio can generate complete tracks based on prompts, short samples, and/or lyrics, which can then be distributed to music streaming platforms such as Apple Music and Spotify and monetized under a commercial use license (Suno, n.d.-a). These tools use machine learning algorithms to analyze patterns in large datasets of music and extract key features, such as musical structure and instrumentation in various genres and styles, chord progressions, rhythm, and harmonies. By synthesizing this information according to user input, these systems are capable of producing new audio containing elements of the requested style, promising to let users "make a song about anything" (Suno, n.d.-a). As well as generating entire music tracks, these platforms can also remix music in other styles, extend or "fill in" sections, and supply stems for generated tracks. These services let users enter prompts to generate music drawing on a disarming rhetorical device that technology is simply a democratizing force: "Suno is building a future where anyone can make great music. Whether you're a shower singer or a charting artist, we break barriers between you and the song you dream of making. No instrument needed, just imagination. From your mind to music" (Suno, 2024b). These descriptions point to a rhetoric that emphasizes democratization or a reduction in the necessity of expert or specialized knowledge (Keith et al., 2023, p. 46).

Musical AI systems are commonly situated in a narrative of how they emulate human processes, rather than explanations of how they operate. As Charlesworth (2025, p. 5) notes, "Much of the language used to describe activities associated with generative AI refers to human processes. AI machines are said to 'train,' 'learn,' 'memorize,' and 'hallucinate.' Anthropomorphic language tends to confuse and obscure discussions surrounding generative AI because it encourages people to ascribe human intellectual qualities to data-driven machines." This is not a new phenomenon; Narayanan and Kapoor identify that the ELIZA chatbot built by MIT researcher Joseph Weizenbaum in the mid-1960s was thought by some users to be human or to have human-like understanding and motivation, despite these users being aware that ELIZA was a computer program (Narayanan & Kapoor, 2024, p. 166). Weizenbaum was himself baffled that "extremely short exposures to a relatively simple computer program could induce powerful delusional thinking in quite normal people" (Weizenbaum, 1976, p. 7). The Brookings Institution likewise defines AI by its ability to replace human thought, proposing that "automation substitutes human labor in tasks both physical and cognitive—especially those that are predictable and routine," while "AI theoretically substitutes for more interpersonal duties such as human planning, problem-solving, or perception" (Gaynor, 2025). This amorphous definition has led Crawford (in Simonite, 2021) to critique the term 'artificial intelligence', maintaining that AI is "neither artificial nor intelligent" and that the term is used to obfuscate its human origins, materiality, and political dimensions.

AI still has no precise technical definition. While it is more commonly defined by its applications for "learning, reasoning and problem-solving" (International Standards Organisation, 2024), its underlying technical processes encompass neural networks, machine learning, and other algorithmic processes. For music applications, there are several notable processes enabling music AI. First among these is music information retrieval (MIR). While not generally considered AI in its own right, MIR involves feature extraction and music indexing, important tasks that enable data retrieval and connection of useful descriptors to audio content (Schedl et al., 2014). The most prevalent process related to AI for music is machine learning (ML), sometimes called deep learning. ML requires a large data set of music, which is preprocessed into the format required for further analysis (such as spectrograms). Models are trained on this data, identifying relevant structures and features and compiling algorithms based on this data. Several classes of machine learning models are used for music, including generative adversarial networks (GANs) and latent diffusion models (LDMs), which are both also used for image generation. GANs rely on adversarial training between a music generator and a discriminator, while LDMs transform a simple distribution (like Gaussian noise) into the complex distribution of the music data. Both methods can produce high-quality output, but LDMs have shown particular strength in generating long-form, coherent music tracks (Lam et al., 2023). Once trained, models can generate new compositions from scratch or apply algorithmically informed processes (such as mixing or mastering) to existing audio files (Briot et al., 2020). As well as these music-specific applications for AI, there are many other uses involving more generalist data processing, such as AI-powered "hit prediction" (Routenote, 2024) and AI-assisted music metadata processing (https://www.muso.ai). AI music applications continue to proliferate, with multiplying implications for the music industries.

3.4 Applications of Music AI

A report on *The Use of Artificial Intelligence in the Cultural and Creative Sectors* commissioned by the European Parliament identifies that AI "has entered the creative value-chain at every level: creation, production, dissemination, and consumption" (Caramiaux, 2020, p. 2). This breadth of application is evident in the music industries, as discussed below. In this section, we map the uses of AI in music using illustrative examples.

3.4.1 Music Data

As mentioned, AI is employed in the *business* of music. Recorded music, as a digital product, is treated as a data class, and AI can be used for purposes such as hit prediction, or forecasting the value of a music catalogue. Digital platforms are data businesses by nature, necessarily automating processes such as classification, content filtering, tagging, and recommendation in order to maintain and extract data/value from catalogues of (often user-generated) content, including text, audio, image, and video. Platforms operate on a principle of data absorption, where "business units should be measured not just in terms of dollars absorbed but also in terms of monetizable data absorbed" (Choudhary, 2015, p. 41). This production of data is a hallmark of what Sadowski (2020) refers to as "rentier platforms," which coordinate and benefit from the acquisition, storage, analysis, and valuation of data. Extracting data as "raw material" (Srnicek, 2017, p. 42) is a key function of platform capitalism; data is used to "educate and give competitive advantage to algorithms" (Srnicek, 2017, p. 33), which in turn generate new data for analysis. The focus on data has created new value for music; as Vonderau (2019, p. 15) observes, "music has become data, and data in turn has become contextual material for user targeting at scale." In turn, this has drawn the interest of digital conglomerates (such as Apple and Google) to music as a means to generate revenue-creating data (Negus, 2019, pp. 377–379). Music has therefore become a valuable commodity within the broader media and data industries; and AI is positioned as the key to effectively create and extract value from music in a streaming-dominated ecosystem.

As music's existence on streaming services is continually measured and quantified, the discernment of musical attributes, user habits, growth areas, trends, and music listening practises is no longer reliant on "insider" or scene-specific knowledge, but becomes a function of data. Tech startups have moved vigorously into this area. Analytics services such as Chartmetric and Sodatone provide forensic detail on radio play, streams, and social media engagement. Observing, predicting, and generating revenue from musical artifacts and user activities is an increasingly quantitative process. Specific musical expertise, from management to A&R, is thus partially ceded to data science; and this data feeds back into practice "in ways that feed-back, structure, delimit and even determine the circulations of popular culture" (Langley & Leyshon, 2017, p. 19). Steiner (2012, pp. 82–89) describes the workings of software called Polyphonic that builds a model of a song's "patterns of melody, beat, tempo, rhythm, pitch, chord progression, fullness of sound, sonic brilliance, and cadence" to compare with hits of the past in a manner more objective than a human A&R representative. The software accurately predicted the respective successes of Norah Jones and Maroon 5 when both acts were unknowns. As Spotify's acquisition of music machine learning service The Echo Nest shows, streaming services also derive data from music itself, which is used, for example, to create automatic playlists of songs with similar attributes, thereby increasing user time on the service. Of particular relevance here is how the AI discourse represents an expansion of the datafied, algorithmic platform structure into areas deemed "creative," and services previously undertaken by human experts.

This theme continues into our next section that looks at *assistive* AI technologies. In this context, AI again completes activities traditionally undertaken by a human such as mixing, and the highly specialized craft of mastering, which is often valorized as a product of human exceptionalism (Collins et al., 2021, p. 259).

3.4.2 Assistive Applications

Assistive music applications integrating AI have existed for many years and include software for effects, hardware emulation, mixing, mastering, and other specialist audio production functions. We call these applications *assistive* because they automate elements of a typical audio production workflow, but do not replace activities typically considered creative (i.e., that attract copyright protection) such as songwriting or performance. In professional audio contexts, mixing and mastering are distinct stages entailing a range of creative and technical processing of audio to prepare it for distribution, including equalization, compression, and balancing. AI software for these applications can take the form of audio plug-ins, standalone software, or web-based services. These applications offer automatic analysis of audio waveforms or output, followed by automatic processing according to user-specified parameters. For example, Izotope's Neutron 4 "Mix Assistant" accelerates manual processes by using "machine learning to suggest levels for your tracks" (https://www.izotope.com/en/products/neutron/features/mix-assistant.html). Other applications can automate an entire stage of production. LANDR's web-based service provides AI-assisted mastering, a practice conventionally undertaken by a professional mastering engineer; users select a style or upload a reference track, and upload their audio for processing. In these scenarios, AI offers convenience for users, including efficiency; quality output, via machine learning or similar dataset-trained algorithmic processing, replacing the need for human expertise; and lower cost.

These assistive technologies carry several implications. Workers have perceived assistive AI applications for music production as a threat to the professional sector (Collins et al., 2021), affecting livelihoods and producing lower-quality results. Companies producing these technologies argue that these tools democratize music production, enable creativity, and save time and cost. As outlined at the outset, these discourses are not new within the music industries. In practice, these assistive technologies primarily serve a "prosumer" niche of amateur music producers and semi-professionals and may be applied in professional workflows to expedite certain processes. In contrast to other AI applications in music, there is minimal debate regarding training data ethics or copyright. Critics are more inclined to concentrate on the displacement of paid work and skilled labor, and potential compromises in quality, resulting from these tools.

3.4.3 Generative Audio

This section is substantial due to the large number of legal, ownership, and creative issues surrounding generative audio in music AI. As shown in the example provided at the outset of this chapter, generative audio can radically transform music production by streamlining or even eliminating entire stages of the typical production process. The primary issue for this pursuit has been the model training process, which can include unauthorized use of copyrighted material. At heart, this is a debate about ownership, rights, and control, echoing previous concerns around file-sharing and music sampling. The now-legitimized practice of sampling, which takes existing recordings and recasts them in new contexts, was once decried as "nothing but old fashioned piracy dressed in sleek new technology" (Thom, 1988, p. 336). Licensing regimes for sampling are now well established, but the discourse at the time reflects current conversations about AI-generated music and copyright. As Thom (1988, p. 335) wrote, "it is clear that digital sampling does decrease the demand for the sampled artist's work because it fulfills the same function as the artist's work. Thus, instead of having to hire, record and purchase an artist's copyright, the pirate takes another's genius for free."

The idea of "taking genius for free" sums up much of the current concern over generative audio. The unauthorized use of copyrighted training data to train models for commercial gain is a central issue in the debate surrounding generative music platforms, as it is for generative media applications for image and text. Currently, copyright holders and creators do not have clear legal or mechanical means to prevent this use, as generative AI music startups claim that training a model on copyrighted data does not constitute infringement. Still, the RIAA has filed copyright infringement suits against both Suno and Udio (RIAA, 2024). The key complaints are two-fold: First, that training generative AI music models involves unlicensed copying and thus infringes copyrights held by recording labels represented by the RIAA. Second, that "synthetic musical outputs could saturate the market with machine-generated content that will directly compete with, cheapen, and ultimately drown out the genuine sound recordings on which the [services were] built" (RIAA, 2024). The German collection society GEMA has also initiated legal proceedings against Suno and Udio, alleging that specific songs were used in their training data, and using evidence determined through musicological analysis (Stassen, 2025). In response, generative music AI platforms have attempted to shift the burden of responsibility for potential breaches of copyright onto the user. Suno requires users to confirm that they own all rights in audio uploaded to the system and is careful to state that output may not be copyrightable, declaring, "due to the nature of machine learning, Suno makes no representation or warranty to you that any copyright will vest in any Output" (Suno, n.d.-b).

Major labels and rights societies are thus confronting music AI platforms due to the unauthorized and uncompensated use of their intellectual property. Indicating the sensitivity of this area, most generative music AI platforms disallow prompts naming existing artists (e.g., "Ed Sheeran"). However, this may change if an agreement can be reached to compensate rights holders for the use of their music. This is hinted at in Suno's rebuttal of the RIAA's lawsuit, claiming that when the lawsuit was submitted, the company was "having productive discussions with a number of the RIAA's major record label members to find ways of expanding the pie for music together" (Suno, 2024a). This ongoing dispute has not prevented generative music AI startups like Udio and Suno from attracting substantial investment capital, however. Investors include venture capital firm Andreessen Horowitz, angel investors from Instagram and Google, and several high-profile musicians (Tencer, 2024b). Andreessen Horowitz has argued, in a submission to the US Copyright Office, that unauthorized training of AI algorithms on copyrighted music does not constitute copyright infringement (Tencer, 2024a). Meanwhile, some generative music AI start-ups such as Loudly (https://www.loudly.com) avoid this issue by exclusively training on materials for which they possess authorization. In the near term, the intricate process of negotiating terms and obtaining rights holders' consent to generate music derived from their existing rights presents a substantial challenge and one which is likely to be heavily litigated. Much like the situation with sampling in the 1980s, licensing may provide a solution, but any such regime will be riddled with complexity. For example, will the amount of compensation vary depending on the quantum of any individual existing work that is used to generate a new work? Can that contribution be so neatly quantified? How will the value of acting as training data be determined? Are these issues that can be solved by attribution technologies (e.g., see UMG, 2024)? Most urgently, it still remains to be seen whether AI training may be protected as a fair use. Do copyright owners even hold a right to licence works for training? At the time of writing, developments in the case launched against Anthropic by UMG, Concord Music Group, and ABKCO place a question mark over this assumption (Cho, 2025).

Of equal concern is the allegation that AI music directly competes with human-created music. Jordan (2024) uncovered that 98% of the 560 top songs on Suno are being monetized on streaming services, and many are masquerading as human artists. Why is this a problem? Aside from the misrepresentation of human origin, AI-generated music is soaking up money from the royalty pool. Over the last decade, Spotify has faced numerous challenges by those trying to game its royalty payment model. Contrary to popular belief, Spotify does not pay out a fixed amount per stream. Rather, rights holders are paid a proportionate royalty rate calculated between the numbers of streams and the amount in the revenue pool (comprising subscriber fees and advertising revenue). For example, if a total of one million streams occur Spotify-wide in a month and an artist is responsible for 10,000 of those streams, then they (or the rights holders of the song and recording) will receive 1% of the revenue pool. For context, only 19% of the 11 million artists on Spotify received more than 1000 streams per month in 2023 (Stassen, 2024). Spotify's own data from its *Loud and Clear* site states that five million artists had less than 100 total streams across their full catalogue in 2023.

This "royalty pool" system is open to exploitation. North American funk band Vulfpeck exposed one loophole when it released *Sleepify* (2014), an album which contained ten 31-second silent tracks (31 s is just over the threshold at which Spotify will pay out for a stream). Encouraged by the band, fans repeatedly streamed the album, earning Vulfpeck $20,000 (USD), which the band used to fund a tour with free admission to its performances. But Vulfpeck's gaming of Spotify's royalty distribution system underplays a much larger set of shadowy operations that employ server farms to continuously stream tracks. These server farms attract the paid employment of artists wishing to increase their streaming revenue and statistics (which can open the door to other opportunities such as supporting slots for larger artists or addition to influential playlists). Server farms also service "fake artists"; anonymously created tracks and artists, often with little to no public profile, who prolifically release new music. In 2017, industry portal *Music Business Worldwide* investigated 50 fake artists that collectively accumulated 2.85 billion streams worth $11.4 million (USD) over 2 years. In September 2024, news broke of a North Carolina musician named Michael Smith who, assisted by others, allegedly generated hundreds of thousands of songs with AI. Smith then used a bot network to stream them continuously across Spotify, Apple Music, and YouTube *inter alia* to net $ten million in royalty payments from 2017 onwards (Katz, 2024).

As Tschmuck (2024) suggests, the "prevalent pro rata model of streaming services facilitates this form of fraud. All streams in a period are aggregated and revenue shares are distributed to rights holders according to market share." This is where AI comes in. AI services can generate songs in a matter of seconds, which can then be distributed to all streaming services for a minimal fee via a third-party aggregator such as DistroKid or TuneCore. For example, DistroKid facilitates the distribution of unlimited songs and albums for $22.99 (USD) per year. The research conducted by YouTuber and industry commentator Benn Jordan (2024) shows one AI-generated track that has accumulated 688,000 plays, taking approximately $2000 out of the Spotify royalty pool that would otherwise go to human artists. Jordan also observes that as of mid-2024, there was a 15% increase in the number of songs available on Spotify compared to the previous year. As a raw number, that is approximately 50 million new songs, which are coming mostly from independent musicians. It is likely that a significant proportion of this new music is AI-generated, diverting money from the artists whose work was used to train the AI models that generated it.

Manipulating Spotify's proportional payment model in this way has wide ramifications, particularly for emerging music artists and rights holders. An influx of AI-generated music does not harm Spotify, as long as the service maintains its active and paying users. The music streaming service need not care where its streaming royalties are paid out. It will, however, affect those earning from Spotify; because of the proportional payment model, the more songs there are, the more diffused the revenue pool is. Any artist gaming the system by artificially increasing streams is taking proportionate revenue from other artists. It is worth noting that not every song on Spotify finds an audience; according to Ingham (2023) an astonishing 24% of all songs across all streaming services received zero plays in 2022. However, for recording artists who aim to generate revenue via streaming services, this is a dismaying state of affairs. Spotify's response has been to introduce new tools to identify artificially increased streams, but most contentiously, it has demonetized the first 1000 streams of every track each year. Whilst the effects of this strategy are unlikely to be noticed by the Taylor Swifts of the world, smaller artists taking advantage of democratized access to music distribution platforms will feel it.

3.4.4 Voice Synthesis

Another rapidly evolving and disputed area of music AI involves voice synthesis. Similar to AI music track generation, this technology uses extensive datasets to train synthesis algorithms. However, unlike generating music tracks, vocal AI involves synthesizing or replicating a voice, and voices are not subject to the same copyright framework as music recordings. If used to generate material simulating the voice of an artist without their consent, AI may infringe on personality rights, which encompass an individual's right to control the commercial use of their name, likeness, and other aspects of their identity. Due to this difference, AI-generated voice is addressed here separately from AI-generated music.

Vocal synthesis technology has existed for decades; its most well-known incarnation is Vocaloid, a vocal synthesizer developed by Yamaha and introduced in 2003. Vocaloid music constitutes a distinct sub-genre with its own renowned artists, most notably Hatsune Miku, the mascot of a Vocaloid voice bank and a virtual pop artist in her own right. Many of Vocaloid's voice banks are synthesized from vocal samples provided by voice actors; for instance, Hatsune Miku's voice was created from samples of voice actor Saki Fujita. While Vocaloid was not originally an AI product, it now integrates machine learning and other AI technologies to produce convincing vocal sounds. Today, many other applications for vocal AI exist, which are capable of creating "soundalikes" based on voice models. Voice models trained on popular singers' voices are available online via code-sharing repositories, such as Google Colab and Huggingface, along with instructions for creating AI voice covers. Fan-made “AI covers” of popular songs have proliferated on some streaming platforms; for example, many user-generated Taylor Swift AI covers are available on YouTube.

The legal and ethical dimensions of creating AI soundalikes or audio deepfakes are new territory, with two main concerns. First, as a generative AI technology, voice synthesis of existing recording artists requires a model to be trained on a large data set, likely including material under copyright and without the artist’s consent. A second consideration is the ethical and legal dimensions of replicating the voice of an existing artist. One test case was “Heart On My Sleeve,” a song that used AI to synthesize the vocals of well-known recording artists Drake and The Weeknd. Created by an anonymous producer called Ghostwriter, the song received hundreds of thousands of streams on music streaming platforms before being removed. On YouTube, the song was removed due to a takedown request (Donahue, 2023); in this case, the song violated platform terms of use due to the misleading claim by the creator that it was sung by Drake and The Weeknd. However, in cases where AI voice synthesis is acknowledged—as in the Taylor Swift AI covers noted earlier—current copyright laws fall short. One community for AI voice covers refers to these covers as “impressions,” and correctly claims that voices cannot be copyrighted (Quickwick/music-ai-voices, n.d.).

While personality rights may prevent certain uses of synthesized voices based on real persons, personality rights are difficult to enforce. It is worth noting that this does not mean that personality rights are toothless. For example, an early and successful claim for voice misappropriation came from Bette Midler who sued the Ford Motor Company in the 1980s. Midler had refused to lend her voice to a series of Ford advertisements and so the motor company hired one of Midler’s backing singers to impersonate her. The court found in favor of Midler, stating that “When a voice is a sufficient amount of a celebrity’s identity, the right of publicity protects it.” This decision was reaffirmed in the early 1990s in a similar case involving a dispute between Tom Waits and Frito Lay, Inc. In a more contemporary example, the Bombay High Court upheld Bollywood singer Arjit Singh’s claim that a voice-cloning service infringed his personality rights. The fundamental issue is that personality rights vary greatly between jurisdictions, unlike the well-defined and harmonized system of copyrights in music that enables music labels, distributors, and rights holders to operate globally. In an effort to bridge this gap, Tennessee state legislators in the USA enacted the ELVIS Act (Ensuring Likeness Voice and Image Security Act). Effective from June 1 2024, this act augmented the state’s existing publicity law with explicit mention of AI and deepfakes, prohibiting the use of AI to clone the voice of an artist without consent, with potential for breaches to be criminally enforced as a Class A misdemeanour (Madarang, 2024). The similar NO FAKES Act was introduced in the US Senate shortly after, which sought to protect creators’ likenesses from being used without their consent at a federal level (Frazier, 2024).

While vocal AI can be contentious, creators, music labels, and rights holders are also interested in vocal AI for a range of purposes. For some artists or labels, AI vocal generation can furnish an additional revenue stream. Electronic artist Grimes has launched a platform called Elf.Tech which allows creators to use AI-generated versions of her voice "without penalty" (Goldstein, 2023) splitting royalties between Grimes and the creator. Likewise, South Korean music and technology conglomerate HYBE acquired AI audio company Supertone in 2022 and subsequently launched a virtual pop group whose voices were developed using AI technology (Dalugdug, 2024). The company has also pioneered song language translation using AI, enabling artists to release music in multiple languages (Benjamin, 2023). AI can also prolong artists' careers or nurture lucrative estates. Examples of these include The Beatles' "Now and Then" which used AI to restore John Lennon's voice from a damaged demo tape (Porter, 2023); Tencent Music's Lingyin Engine, a patented voice synthesis technology that has been used to produce music "sung" by deceased artists (Tencent Music, 2022); country music singer Randy Travis, who experienced a stroke and subsequent aphasia in 2013, then in 2024 released a new song featuring AI trained on his voice (Sherman, 2024); and a collaboration between Warner Music and the estate of Édith Piaf on an animated biopic of the singer, narrated by herself using AI technology (WMG Communications, 2023).

These developments have several implications for the music industries. First, as with generative music, the legality of AI models trained on copyrighted data is uncertain. Second, rights holders and platforms will need to develop a shared definition of what constitutes acceptable use of AI-generated voices that simulate the voice of an existing artist, and methods to license and collect revenue from this use. Third, rights holders have a clear interest in using AI to extend the productive life of established singers, and to create new contents using their vocal likenesses. Platforms and rights holders therefore need to invest in legal frameworks for protecting personality rights, technical systems for detecting breaches of these rights, and methods to prosecute or discourage unauthorized use. To foster a market for licensed AI-generated music, unauthorized AI-generated material must be suppressed.

3.5 Discussion

In the previous sections, we outlined key applications of AI in music and the issues that are raised. The following section addresses the implications of AI and speculates on the broader effects of AI technologies for the music industries. The effects of AI on economics, property, and creativity are deeply intertwined and present complex challenges that cannot be easily isolated.

As outlined above, music catalogues have supplied essential training material (whether licensed or unlicensed) for AI models. Whether or how rights holders should be compensated for the use of their material to train AI models is undetermined. While the ELVIS and NO FAKES Acts have been proposed in the USA, other territories are still deliberating. Policymakers in the UK have considered a proposal whereby copyright holders would need to opt-out from having their material used for training AI (Scott, 2025). This proposal has been criticized by creative industries workers, who argue that the opt-out model is ineffective, as it does not preclude training on unofficial "downstream copies" of works (Newton-Rex, 2024). After all, this is what occurred with "Books3," a dataset of nearly 200,000 pirate ebooks used to train generative AI models produced by Meta, EleutherAI, and Bloomberg. Nonetheless, this presents a question for music rights holders and music catalogues generally. For music copyright holders, including creators, music labels and publishers, and investors, the consequences of this proposal are far-reaching. Observers have pointed out the direct rivalry between creative and technical stakeholders in AI, noting that legislation either favors music creators and rights-holders, or supports AI developers to innovate by training models on any publicly available work. The opt-out model has been described as a "wholesale transfer of wealth" to the tech sector, with uncertain economic and social benefit (Milmo, 2025). For music, an opt-out model would first substantially diminish rights holders' ability to generate revenue by licensing their works for training AI models. It would also curtail the viability of AI-generated works produced by rights holders based on their own materials, as these works would be competing directly with works produced by other parties trained on the same materials. Additionally, opt-out creates an administrative burden for rights holders, especially those with extensive portfolios, or smaller creators who lack resources to effectively opt-out. There is also no clear method for "retrospective opt-out" from models which have already been trained on copyrighted materials. Music catalogues—the foundation of the recorded music industry, and recently the focus of significant speculation and investment (Collins & Keith, 2024)—may lose value as a result of these changes.

The technology sector, in a competing position, assumes contrasting benefits if training on copyrighted music is permitted. To date, the benefits of allowing unrestricted training on copyrighted music are unclear and have generally been described in terms of economic benefit and competitiveness. While many AI music tools have been launched, as discussed above, the long-term effects on the established recorded music industries are unknown. However, it is clear that AI-generated music upsets the recorded music industries' status quo, perhaps most evident in the proliferation of AI-generated content on streaming services such as Spotify. Nonhuman-created audio has been a point of contention between streaming services and record labels, who argue that such content engages in fraud or "gaming the system" (Garcia, 2024) and should not be eligible for as large a share of the royalties pot as music produced by humans. Spotify partially yielded in 2024, and "noise recordings"—including white noise, static, and silence—now receive a lower royalty share (Spotify, 2023). However, AI-generated music is currently not included within this category, and listeners have marked an increase in music that appears to be generated by AI artists (Stokel-Walker, 2024). While labels continue to decry the proliferation of AI-generated content on streaming services, it continues to be served and monetized alongside human-produced music.

Music rightsholders and AI stakeholders appear to be seeking a legislative solution to these questions, extending existing definitions of copyright to include new uses such as training AI models. Much has been made of the copyright issues emerging from generative AI, but it is unclear whether copyright is even the most appropriate mechanism to protect creators in this new technological reality. Craig (2025) warns of the "copyright trap," three misconceptions that are leading the protectionist discourse around generative AI. First is the "if value then (property) right" fallacy or the belief that "intellectual property rights ought to attach to any intangible thing of value" (2025, p. 18). Second is the assertion that copying is inherently wrong; Craig rejects this moralizing and reminds us that "the boundaries of copyright recognize and confirm the essential nature and desirability of copying in furtherance of learning, downstream creativity, and progress of the arts and sciences" (Craig, 2025, 21). Finally, Craig points to the "starving artist," a long-historied trope that has been used since the 1730s to justify expansion of copyright that ultimately benefits corporate copyright assignees rather than individual creators. The "copyright trap" offers an interesting provocation to question whether copyright ought to regulate all aspects of the cultural landscape. But if not copyright, then what? We have discussed the role that personality rights have to play in protecting creators from technological misappropriation like voice-cloning, but personality rights lack the near-global harmonization enjoyed by copyright. The asynchronicity between issue and resolution—especially if the resolution requires an international treaty to harmonies domestic law—means that the technological horse has well and truly bolted in the context of personality rights. A licensing system may be the best worst solution available, but the implementation of such a system has not been tested. It is not clear how a creator might license their work for use in training AI models in a way that is transparent, beneficial, and equitable for all parties. The inherent complexity of how AI models are trained, and how they work—using hundreds of thousands of data points for input, and generating material with an unpredictable and obscure relationship to the original data—makes this a forbidding task.

3.6 Conclusion

Both the music and tech industries are navigating a complex landscape. Tech companies and investment firms are launching new AI products while involved in legal battles surrounding copyright definitions and terms, and increasingly exert sway over legislation. This may not spell the immediate end of the music industries, but it raises questions about their future. How should the music industries work against, or in partnership with, big tech? Are the music and tech industries already so intertwined that they are now inseparable? Or are the music industries bound to become a subset of the broader content industries, under the umbrella of tech? Meanwhile, the recorded music industries are angling for copyright controls that will enable rights-holders to secure a share of the new markets generated by AI. These include speculative licensing for AI-generated content and developing new products, such as Universal Music Group's partnership with Soundlabs AI which "allows artists to create high-fidelity vocal models using their own voice data" (UMG, 2025). AI cannot be put back in the box; pragmatism demands a way forward.

Is AI simply another technological disruption, similar to those that have come before, or does it represent a fundamental shift? Historically, the music industry has reconfigured itself to respond and adapt to technological disruption. It has weathered multiple threats to the hegemony of music labels—including home taping, digital sampling, and online file-sharing—and the controlled production and distribution of the recorded artifact. What is new about AI is its potential to change music *itself*, from a stable recorded format to training data that can be used to produce countless variations; to change copyright, permitting models to be trained on musical works even without agreement or recompense for the rights-holder; and to change the role of the artist, creating AI soundalikes that replicate the voice, style, and likeness of an artist without their input. Each of these challenges raises legal and technical challenges that the existing regime of copyright cannot yet answer. Answering these questions will likewise require legal and technical solutions to address ownership and licensing for AI-generated musical works and developing systems for tracking, controlling, and licensing intellectual property in the AI era. As always, the music industries must adapt and evolve.

References

Arielli, E. (2021). Even an AI could do that. In L. Manovich & Arielli, E. (Eds.), *Artificial aesthetics* (pp. 8–25). https://manovich.net/index.php/projects/artificial-aesthetics

Benjamin, J. (2023, May 17). HYBE's 'New' K-Pop artist MIDNATT is using ai technology for a remarkably human purpose. *Billboard.* https://www.billboard.com/music/pop/artificial-technology-kpop-artist-midnatt-hybe-interview-1235329459/

Briot, J. P., Hadjeres, G., & Pachet, F. D. (2020). *Deep learning techniques for music generation.* Springer.

Caramiaux, B. (2020). *The use of artificial intelligence in the cultural and creative sectors.* EU Parliament. https://www.europarl.europa.eu/RegData/etudes/BRIE/2020/629220/IPOL_BRI(2020)629220_EN.pdf

Charlesworth, J. (2025) Generative AI's illusory case for fair use. *Vanderbilt Journal of Entertainment and Technology Law.* Advance online publication. https://doi.org/10.2139/ssrn.4924997.

Cho, W. (2025, March 26). *Anthropic wins first round in lawsuit from music publishers over song lyrics.* The Hollywood Reporter. https://www.hollywoodreporter.com/business/business-news/anthropic-wins-first-round-lawsuit-music-publishers-song-lyrics-1236173148/

Choudhary, S. P. (2015). *Platform scale: How a new breed of startups is building large empires with minimal investment.* Platform Thinking Labs Pte Ltd.

Collins, S., & Keith, S. (2024). Catalogue acquisitions: Who wins? In D. Arditi & R. Nolan (Eds.), *The Palgrave handbook of critical music industry studies* (pp. 387–403). Palgrave Macmillan. https://doi.org/10.1007/978-3-031-64013-1_23

Collins, S., Keith, S., Renzo, A., & Mesker, A. (2021). Transformations and continuities in the mastering sector. In J. P. Braddock, R. Hepworth-Sawyer, J. Hodgson, M. Shelvock, & R. Toulson (Eds.), *Mastering in music* (pp. 249–263). Routledge.

Copeland, B. J., & Long, J. (2017). Turing and the history of computer music. In J. Floyd & A. Bokulich (Eds.), *Boston studies in the philosophy and history of science: Vol. 324. Philosophical explorations of the legacy of alan turing* (pp. 189–218). Springer. https://doi.org/10.1007/978-3-319-53280-6_8

Craig, C. J. (2025). *The AI-copyright trap. Chicago-Kent law review.* Advance online publication. https://doi.org/10.2139/ssrn.4905118.

Dalugdug, M. (2024, July 2). *After being acquired by HYBE in a $32m deal last year, voice cloning startup Supertone launches AI-powered powered virtual pop group, SYNDI8.* Music Business

Worldwide. https://www.musicbusinessworldwide.com/hybe-owned-voice-cloning-startup-supertone-launches-ai-powered-virtual-pop-group-syndi81/
Donahue, B. (2023, April 17). *Fake Drake & The Weeknd song - made with AI - pulled from streaming after going viral.* Billboard. https://www.billboard.com/pro/fake-ai-drake-the-weeknd-song-pulled-streaming/
Frazier, N. (2024, November 15). *NO FAKES act introduced in the senate: Protecting artists' rights in the age of AI, recording academy.* https://www.recordingacademy.com/advocacy/news/torae-carr-dani-deahl-national-advocacy-committee
Frith, S. (1992). The industrialization of popular music. In J. Lull (Ed.), *Popular music and communication* (pp. 49–74). Sage.
Garcia, T. (2024, January 9). *Universal music CEO Lucian grainge talks AI, artist-centric streaming. Variety.* https://variety.com/2024/music/news/universal-lucian-grainge-ai-artist-centric-streaming-1235866258/
Gaynor, Michael (2025, January 29). *Automation and AI sound similar, but may have vastly different impacts on the future of work.* The Brookings Institution. https://www.brookings.edu/articles/automation-and-artificial-intelligence-sound-similar-but-may-have-vastly-different-impacts-on-the-future-of-work/
Goldstein, T. (2023, April 25). *Grimes gives permission to use her voice in AI songs "without penalty".* American Songwriter. https://americansongwriter.com/grimes-gives-permission-to-use-her-voice-in-ai-songs-without-penalty/
Goold, L., & Graham, P. (2019). The uncertain future of the large-format recording studio. In J. O. Gullö, S. Rambarran, & K. Isakoff (Eds.), *Proceedings of the 12th art of record production conference mono: Stereo: Multi* (pp. 119–136). Royal College of Music (KMH) & Art of Record Production.
Gunkel, D. (2021). Computational creativity: Algorithms, art, and artistry. In E. Navas, O. Gallagher, & x. Burrough (Eds.), *The Routledge handbook of remix studies and digital humanities* (pp. 385–395). Routledge.
International Standards Organisation. (2024, January 31). *What is artificial intelligence (AI)?* https://www.iso.org/artificial-intelligence/what-is-ai#toc1
Jordan, B. (2024). *Using AI to detect AI music (and other music industry data-porn).* YouTube. https://www.youtube.com/watch?v=QVXfcIb3OKo&t=112s
Katz, L. (2024, September 8). *Man charged with $10 Million streaming music scam using AI-generated songs.* Forbes. https://www.forbes.com/sites/lesliekatz/2024/09/08/man-charged-with-10-million-streaming-scam-using-aigenerated-songs/
Keith, S., Collins, S., Renzo, A., & Mesker, A. (2023). Slave to the 'Rithm: The AI turn in the music industries. In M. Filimowicz (Ed.), *AI and the future of creative work: Algorithms and society* (pp. 36–54). Routledge.
Lam, M. W., Tian, Q., Li, T., Yin, Z., Feng, S., Tu, M., et al. (2023, December). Efficient neural music generation. In A. Oh, T. Naumann, A. Globerson, K. Saenko, M. Hardt, & S. Levine (Eds.), *Proceedings of the 37th international conference on neural information processing systems, 17450-17463.* Curran Associates.
Langley, P., & Leyshon, A. (2017). Platform capitalism: The intermediation and capitalization of digital economic circulation. *Finance and Society, 3*(1), 11–31. https://doi.org/10.2218/finsoc.v3i1.1936
Levy, S. (2006). *The perfect thing: How the iPod shuffles commerce, culture and coolness.* Simon & Schuster.
Madarang, C. (2024, March 21). *Elvis Act signed into Tennessee law to protect musicians from Ai Deepfakes.* Rolling Stone. https://www.rollingstone.com/music/music-news/elvis-act-tennessee-signed-ai-impersonation-1234992395/
Milmo, D. (2025, February 11). UK copyright law consultation "fixed" in favour of AI firms, peer says. *The Guardian.* https://www.theguardian.com/technology/2025/feb/11/uk-copyright-law-consultation-fixed-favour-ai-firms-peer-says
Narayanan, A., & Kapoor, S. (2024). *AI snake oil: What artificial intelligence can do, what it can't, and how to tell the difference.* Princeton University Press.

Negus, K. (2019). From creator to data: The post-record music industry and the digital conglomerates. *Media, Culture and Society, 41*(3), 367–384. https://doi.org/10.1177/0163443718799395

Newton-Rex, E. (2024, December 27). The UK's AI & copyright proposals would irreparably harm the country's creators. *Substack.com; Fair training*. https://fairtraining.substack.com/p/the-uks-ai-and-copyright-proposals

Pachet, F. (2018). *Daddy's car* [Song]. https://www.francoispachet.fr/daddys-car/

Porter, J. (2023, June 13). Paul McCartney says AI tools helped rescue John Lennon vocals for "last Beatles record". *The Verge*. https://www.theverge.com/2023/6/13/23759296/the-beatles-now-and-then-restoration-ai-paul-mccartney-john-lennon

Quickwick/music-ai-voices. (n.d.). *QuickWick/Music-AI-Voices*. https://huggingface.co/QuickWick/Music-AI-Voices

RIAA. (2024, June 24). *Record companies bring landmark cases for responsible AI against Suno and Udio in Boston and New York Federal Courts, respectively*. RIAA. https://www.riaa.com/record-companies-bring-landmark-cases-for-responsible-ai-againstsuno-and-udio-in-boston-and-new-york-federal-courts-respectively/

Robertson, D. (2020, November 9). 'It's the screams of the damned!' The eerie AI world of deepfake music. *The Guardian*. https://www.theguardian.com/music/2020/nov/09/deepfake-pop-music-artificial-intelligence-ai-frank-sinatra

Ross, G. (2023, September 28). Spotify will not ban AI-generated music, CEO confirms. *Mixmag*. https://mixmag.net/read/spotify-not-ban-ai-generated-music-ceo-daniel-ek-confirms-tech

Routenote (2024, May 10). Can AI predict the next big hit songs? *RouteNote Blog*. https://routenote.com/blog/can-ai-predict-the-next-big-hit-songs/

Sadowski, J. (2020). The internet of landlords: Digital platforms and new mechanisms of rentier capitalism. *Antipode: A Radical Journal of Geography, 52*(2), 562–580. https://doi.org/10.1111/anti.12595

Schedl, M., Gómez, E., & Urbano, J. (2014). Music information retrieval: Recent developments and applications. *Foundations and Trends in Information Retrieval, 8*(2-3), 127–261.

Scott, E. (2025, January 27). *Copyright and artificial intelligence: Impact on creative industries. House of Lords Library*. https://lordslibrary.parliament.uk/copyright-and-artificial-intelligence-impact-on-creative-industries/#heading-1

Sherman, M. (2024, May 6). With help from AI, Randy Travis got his voice back. Here's how his first song post-stroke came to be. *AP News*. https://apnews.com/article/randy-travis-artificial-intelligence-song-voice-589a8c142f70ed8ccf53af6d32c662dc

Simonite, T. (2021, April 26). *This researcher says AI is neither artificial nor intelligent*. WIRED. https://www.wired.com/story/researcher-says-ai-not-artificial-intelligent/

Spotify. (2023, November 21). *Modernizing our royalty system to drive an additional $1 billion toward emerging and professional artists, spotify for artists*. https://artists.spotify.com/en/blog/modernizing-our-royalty-system

Srnicek, N. (2017). *Platform capitalism*. Polity Press.

Stassen, M. (2024, February 13). *Only 19% of artists on Spotify had over 1,000 monthly listeners in 2023*. Music Business Worldwide. https://www.musicbusinessworldwide.com/only-19-of-artists-on-spotify-had-over-1000-monthly-listeners-in-20231/

Stassen, M. (2025, January 21). *$500m-valued Suno hit with new copyright lawsuit from Germany's Gema, Music Business Worldwide*. https://www.musicbusinessworldwide.com/500m-valued-suno-hit-with-new-copyright-lawsuit-from-germanys-gema/

Steiner, C. (2012). *Automate this: How algorithms came to rule our world*. Penguin.

Sterne, J. (2014). There is no music industry. *Media Industries Journal, 1*(1), 50–55.

Stokel-Walker, C. (2024, August 9). *Spotify is full of AI music, and some say it's ruining the platform*. Fast Company. https://www.fastcompany.com/91170296/spotify-ai-music

Suno. (2024a, August 2). *The future of music*. https://suno.com/blog/future-of-music

Suno. (2024b). *About*. https://suno.com/about

Suno. (n.d.-a). *Can I distribute my songs to Spotify, etc?. Knowledge Base*. https://help.suno.com/en/articles/2410177

Suno. (n.d.-b). *Terms of service*. https://suno.com/terms

Taylor, G. (2014). *When the machine made art: The troubled history of computer art*. Bloomsbury.
Tencent Music. (2022, November 15). *Tencent music entertainment group announces third quarter 2022 unaudited financial results. Tencent Music*. https://ir.tencentmusic.com/2022-11-15-Tencent-Music-Entertainment-Group-Announces-Third-Quarter-2022-Unaudited-Financial-Results
Tencer, D. (2024a, January 3). *Andreessen Horowitz's thoughts on AI shows what the music industry will be up against in 2024. Music Business Worldwide*. https://www.musicbusinessworldwide.com/andreessen-horowitzs-thoughts-on-ai-shows-what-the-music-industry-is-up-against-in-2024/
Tencer, D. (2024b, April 10). *New Ai-powered 'instant' music-making app Udio raises $10m; launches with backing from will.i.am, Common, Unitedmasters, A16Z, Music Business Worldwide*. https://www.musicbusinessworldwide.com/new-ai-powered-instant-music-making-app-udio-raises-10m-launches-with-backing-from-will-i-am-common-unitedmasters-a16z/
Thom, J. C. (1988). Digital sampling: Old-fashioned piracy dressed up in sleek new technology. *Loyola of Los Angeles Entertainment Law Review, 8*(2), 297–336.
Tschmuck, P. (2024, March 11). *AI in the Music Industry – Part 6: Fake Streams and Streaming Farms*. Music Business Research. https://musicbusinessresearch.wordpress.com/2024/03/11/ai-in-the-music-industry-part-6-fake-streams-and-streaming-farms/
UMG. (2024, August 6). *Prorata invents generative AI attribution technology to compensate and credit content owners while facilitating fairness and fact, with support from Universal Music Group*. UMG. https://www.universalmusic.com/prorata-invents-generative-ai-attribution-technology-to-compensate-and-credit-content-owners-while-facilitating-fairness-and-fact/
UMG. (2025, June 18). *Soundlabs and universal music group announce strategic agreement to offer responsibly trained AI technology and vocal modeling plug-in micdrop to UMG artists*. UMG. https://www.universalmusic.com/soundlabs-and-universal-music-group-announce-strategic-agreement-to-offer-responsibly-trained-ai-technology-and-vocal-modeling-plug-in-micdrop-to-umg-artists/
United States Copyright Office. (2020, February 5). *Copyright in the age of artificial intelligence* (transcript). https://www.copyright.gov/events/artificial-intelligence/transcript.pdf
Vonderau, P. (2019). The spotify effect: Digital distribution and financial growth. *Television and New Media, 20*(1), 3–19. https://doi.org/10.1177/1527476417741200
Weizenbaum, J. (1976). *Computer power and human reason: From judgment to calculation*. W.H. Freeman and Company.
Williamson, J., & Cloonan, M. (2007). Rethinking the music industry. *Popular Music, 26*(2), 305–322.
WMG Communications. (2023, November 14). *Warner music partners with Edith Piaf's estate on groundbreaking AI technology*. Warner Music Group. https://www.wmg.com/news/warner-music-partners-with-edith-piafs-estate-on-groundbreaking-ai-technology

Steve Collins is Discipline Chair of Media and Communications in the School of Communication, Society and Culture at Macquarie University in Sydney, Australia. His research focuses on disruptions in the creative industries, copyright law, music industries and music production. He is the co-author of Music 2.0: The Future of Music. Steve is also a music producer and remixer.

Sarah Keith is Senior Lecturer in Media in the School of Communication, Society and Culture at Macquarie University in Sydney, Australia. Sarah's research areas include media technology and platforms, East Asian popular culture, diplomacy and soft power, and the music industries. Recent research has explored AI in the music industries, online fandom platforms, K-pop and multicultural understanding in Australia and digital disruption.

Photography

4

Justin Harvey

Abstract

The emergence of generative artificial intelligence (GenAI) technology, specifically text-to-image and image-to-image diffusion models capable of generating photorealistic images, presents a significant disruption to photographic practitioners, businesses, and viewers. Whilst AI-generated images are not technically photographs, they can be indistinguishable from photographs, with the same capacity to represent reality and evoke emotional responses. This chapter identifies how GenAI is disrupting the field of photography and explores potential consequences of this disruption.

The most significant disruption in the history of photography was the transition from analog to digital that accelerated in the final decade of the twentieth century. An outline of the impacts of this shift on photographers, photographic businesses, and consumers of photographic images provides background for the foregoing discussion focussed on three crucial concerns around GenAI's impact on photographic industries: ethical transparency and diversification of traditional business models; mitigating bias and homogenization in photorealistic GenAI imagery; and innovation in artistic expression catalyzed by the adoption of Generative AI in the visual arts.

Ethical concerns and legal challenges around use of copyright material by companies to train GenAI models are summarized. Companies, including OpenAI, that admit to unauthorized use of copyrighted material for GenAI training are contrasted with those, including Adobe, that claim to offer ethical GenAI products trained on datasets over which they hold copyright. It is argued that artists, whose work is at risk of being used to train GenAI models, and those seeking indemnity from copyright infringement claims in their commercial use

J. Harvey (✉)
University of Technology Sydney, Sydney, NSW, Australia
e-mail: justin.harvey@uts.edu.au

S. Böhm et al. (eds.), *Handbook of AI-based Media Disruption*, Future of Business and Finance, https://doi.org/10.1007/978-3-032-07605-2_4

of GenAI imagery, are more likely to subscribe to businesses that use ethical training sets and indemnify the use of images generated on their platforms.

The fact that GenAI models have enabled companies taking ethical stances to swiftly diversify their product offerings considerably is discussed. It is argued that when image editing software can create images from text prompts and businesses that offer stock photographs can incorporate image editing capabilities, the risk of market concentration grows significantly. Strategies to mitigate bias in, and homogenization of, GenAI imagery, as well as the risk of devaluation of photographic imagery, are also identified.

Finally, three artist projects that incorporate AI-generated imagery exemplify how GenAI has enabled new avenues for artistic expression. Sara Oscar's 2023-ongoing project, *Counterfactual Departures*, sees the artist using GenAI to create photographic images of her Thai mother's migration to Australia in 1974, an event of which there is no photographic record. The project invites discussion about the role of photography in memory-making and how AI-generated imagery is connected to traditional forms of photography. Julia Scott-Stevenson's *Collective Visions* (2024) uses GenAI as a tool to enable participants to envision their hopes and possible fears of climate futures in an immersive 360° environment. Justin Harvey's 2023 work, *Unprompted Studies 1–3*, is a triptych of animated image sequences representing three studies in machine-generated animation devoid of text input, for which diffusion models were instructed to create images "unprompted." The work elicits questions around well-noted biases evident in early diffusion models (white, western, male, etc.) and how artists might assemble unprompted outcomes of generative AI models to make new meaning.

4.1 Introduction

The use of AI in photography, from optical capture to digital manipulation and storage, has been ongoing for some time. It is used regularly to ensure sharp focus, denoise digital photographs, and analyze and classify images into meaningful categories. The arrival of generative artificial intelligence (GenAI), specifically text-to-image and image-to-image diffusion models, capable of generating photorealistic images presents a significant disruption to photographic industries, practitioners, and consumers in both obvious and as yet undefined ways. This chapter explores these disruptions, and though some context and background to the present milieu are required to frame the discussion, I will not delve into the complex history of photography as has been done extensively elsewhere (see Scharf, 1975; Rosenblum, 1997; and Heiferman, 2012). Nor is it necessary to detail the various technological advances from the invention of the daguerreotype in 1839 and roll film in 1888, to the widespread availability of color film in the 1930s and subsequent introduction and emergence of consumer digital technology in the 1980s (Hutson et al., 2024). Yet to discuss the impact that GenAI continues to have on photographic industries, photographers, and visual culture more broadly, a working definition of what photography is *is* required.

Long before the public availability of text-to-image GenAI models, there was much debate about what constituted photography. From particle physics to food styling, photography is implicit in our understanding and experience of the world (Heiferman, 2012, p. 11). In the documentary sense, it constitutes ontological connotations such as "evidence, witness, and memory" (Bogre, 2019, p. 15) but can also be described as exploitative, as an "extractive technology" of colonial projects for example (De Leon, 2018, p. 74). Taking decades from its inception to be accepted as a valid artform (McCormack et al., 2023), photography nevertheless continues to enjoy considerable favor in the fine art world today (Laster, 2024). However, certainly at least since if not before the turn from analog to digital photography in the late twentieth century, Roland Barthes' inability to deny that "the thing has been there" (Barthes, 1982, p. 76) in a photograph, could not necessarily be shared by the contemporary viewer of images.

Researchers Daniel Rubenstein and Katrina Sluis (2013) argue that from the time photography became digital and networked, the idea that a photograph is "a singular cultural unit that operates as an archive of time" has been undermined (Rubinstein & Sluis, 2013, p. 30). In the contemporary context awash with digital images, the photograph has become an "algorithmic image" that is in a "constant state of deferral" (Rubinstein & Sluis, 2013, p. 30). Artist and researcher, Joanna Zylinski, proposes the term "undigital photography," a term borrowed from computational photography, to rethink image making in the context of AI, "where changes to focus, lighting, framing or depth of field can take place after an image has been taken" (Zylinska, 2020, p. 108). With this term, Zylinska attempts to reframe photography and image making more broadly as an inherently unfinished process, acknowledging too, that whilst we are enmeshed with algorithms, the important thing is how we choose to use them (Zylinska, 2020, p. 126). Research Professor Andrew Dewdney reasons that in the context of a computational networked culture we should "forget photography," meaning, amongst other things, to "put photography into historical perspective and to liberate the image from these historic shackles, forged by art history and photographic theory" (Dewdney, 2021, p. 4), and yet now more than ever, we understand ourselves *through* photography.

The ever-present is parsed via images captured and consumed on smartphones at all hours of the night and day. Photography remains personal, it is political, and it continues to change the world. Just ask Associated Press chief photographer Evan Vucci, who captured the image of Donald Trump surrounded by secret service staff, blood on his face, his fist in the air. If we are to "forget photography," how should we think about what it is we are doing when we take a photo? Professor Kate Crawford, well known for her rigorous scholarship on AI, reminds us that we are already in a post-optical period of photography, when photographs taken with an iPhone, for example, are "machine learning mosaics, not photographs" (Antonelli & Crawford, 2024, p. 75). Even though that may technically be true, I suggest that the more than one billion users storing over four trillion photos and videos on Google's cloud storage service Google Photos (Perra & Ferrell, 2023) would tend to disagree, as do I. When I take a photo, whether with a dedicated camera or smartphone, I am capturing something of reality, even if the blue of the sky on the digital screen is difficult to reconcile with what I see as I look beyond the horizon.

For the purposes of this chapter, then, photography includes images that result from an optical-technical process through which light is captured and recorded giving it an indexical relationship to reality. The focus here is on the disruptive impacts of GenAI diffusion models capable of generating photorealistic images, on photography. Of course, AI-generated images are not photographs, though there is an initial impulse to conflate them, especially given that they have quickly become indistinguishable from photographs, with the same capacity to represent reality and evoke emotional responses. Obvious problems arise when it becomes impossible to differentiate one from the other, evidenced by highly publicized cases of prestigious photography awards being revoked due to confusion between real photography and AI-generated images with judging panels struggling to tell the difference (Arielli, 2024, p. 172). Though these examples have drawn attention to the potential for misperception, if not necessarily harm, research suggests that study participants asked to distinguish real from AI-generated images were only able to correctly classify 61% of images, with only 66.7% of those being accurately recognized *as real*. The study demonstrates that in addition to the possible harm caused by GenAI images being mistaken for real images, the proliferation of AI-generated images can also "erode people's trust in accurate information" (Lu et al., 2023). Suspicion around the authenticity of images is not a recent phenomenon and has increased since the arrival and affordances of digitization. Photojournalists' careers have been cut short due to poorly judged digital manipulations of images, particularly in war zones, and significant percentages of entries to the World Press Photo competition have been disqualified each year due to extensive digital manipulation even before the advent of GenAI (Bogre, 2019, p. 64). GenAI brings a new wave of concerns not only about authenticity of images, but biased outcomes of text-to-image models, unethical and illegal provenance of training data, and further concentration of photographic business interests. These issues are addressed in this chapter, beginning with an overview of the hitherto most significant disruption to photography in its history.

4.2 History of Disruption in the Field of Photography

The transition from analog to digital photography had an unprecedented impact on photographic practitioners, businesses, and consumers. Gaining momentum in the final decade of the twentieth century, the transition took about two decades (Lucas & Goh, 2009, p. 50). Advances in digital image capture, editing software, and distribution via the Internet led to a vast reduction in demand for analog cameras, film stock, and processing. Sales of film cameras began to decline at the turn of the century in the face of the global uptake of digital cameras, which peaked in the US in 2007 (Ho & Chen, 2018, p. 357), the same year that the first iPhone was released to market. This period was tumultuous for all analog photography producers, but the consequences on Kodak's business, in particular, have been well documented (Lucas & Goh, 2009; Snyder, 2013; Ho & Chen, 2018; Rouse, 2021). Incorporated in 1892, Kodak had been the traditional market leader in photographic equipment and film stock, its marketing shaping the public imagination with a dramatic impact on amateur photographic practices (Sturken, 2016, p. 98). Kodak engineer, Steve Sasson, invented a digital camera in 1975; however, Kodak management "reluctant to cannibalize its massive film business," held back on commercially developing it (Rouse, 2021, p. 71). In 1981, competitor Sony released the Mavica, which converted light to electronic signals and stored images on a floppy disk instead of using film, causing big waves in the industry (Sandström et al., 2009, p. 10). Sony followed up with a consumer model in 1988 (Sony, 2025), with Canon and Fujifilm both launching digital consumer models later that year. Three years later in 1991 Kodak released a commercial professional digital camera, followed by a consumer version in 1995 (Ho & Chen, 2018, p. 361), a year after Apple had launched its Quick Take digital camera.

Amongst others, leading Kodak competitor, Fujifilm, struggled to adapt to the emerging digital market (Ho & Chen, 2018), as did Hasselblad, the manufacturer of the 500EL camera famous for photographing Neil Armstrong taking the first steps on the moon. Hasselblad narrowly avoided bankruptcy (Sandström et al., 2009, p. 12), unlike Polaroid, which went bankrupt in 2001, before making a comeback in 2009, now selling both instant analog and digital versions of its original cameras (Murphy, 2018, p. 239). Kodak filed for bankruptcy protection in 2012, prompting a shift away from digital imaging and toward commercial and home photographic printers following Epson and HP, traditionally digital information technology companies, who had made gains in the photography market by redesigning their color printers to produce digital prints (Lucas & Goh, 2009, p. 51). A 2016 revival of the original Kodak Super 8 camera with digital capabilities, the ongoing renewed interest in analog film, and development of scanning products for smartphones have seen Kodak regain brand relevance and profitability across analog and digital optical imaging and printing technologies (Krause, 2023). Global digital camera sales peaked in 2010 and dropped 94% by 2023 alongside the mass adoption of smartphones and concurrent improvements in capabilities of their inbuilt cameras (Richter, 2024). Responses from industry have seen Olympus sell off its legacy camera business to focus on medical technology (Simms, 2021), with Canon and Fujifilm since following their lead (Smith, 2024).

The transition to digital had a significant impact on professional photographers. An Australian study shows that the combination of digital cameras, social media, and the Internet "contributed to the diffusion of the job of photographer, and the social reframing of photography from creative art to commodity" (Williams et al., 2021, p. 145). Increases in job growth facilitated by digital technology have been limited to part-time workers and offset by a decline in incomes of individual photographers (Williams et al., 2021, p. 145). Another study found a rise in displacement in skilled photographic workers in Ghana due to digital technology including advances in low-cost drone photography and smartphone camera hardware (Enninful, 2023, p. 9). Elsewhere, declines in employment opportunities for photojournalists and humanitarian photographers correlate to the increase in citizen journalism due to the ubiquity of smartphone cameras and the Internet (Mäenpää, 2023). Digital tools including smartphones, and now AI, have also changed street photography, providing opportunities for countless new creatives and blurring the lines between amateur and professional (Misiak, 2024, p. 14). The burgeoning and previously untapped supply of professional and amateur photography now feeds a growing demand for stock images by commercial interests and broader image culture long digitized and networked.

The stock photography industry emerged in the 1970s and was aggressively consolidated during the 1990s. For commercial photographic libraries, digitization meant far greater exposure to global demand and better consumer access to vast archives of photographic imagery including fine art and architectural photography for education and research (Hamber, 2024, p. 8). By the year 2000, there were roughly 2000 photo agencies employing professional photographers to produce content and manage collections, oversee labeling, categorization, and review catalogues (Wang & Liang, 2024, p. 147). By 2010, the industry was dominated by Getty Images and Corbis, who between them integrated more than 500 smaller competitors (Wang & Liang, 2024, p. 148). Corbis (then owned by Bill Gates) was acquired in 2016 by Visual China Group (VCG), who handed exclusive rights to distribution of its vast image archive outside of China to Getty, cementing Getty as the largest image agency in the world (Frosh, 2020, p. 197). In this way, commercial photography has been concentrated, just as have other media segments including television and cinema, with less than 200 independent agencies remaining across the globe. As of writing, the market size of stock photography, including key players Getty Images, Shutterstock, and Adobe Stock, is expected to almost double to approximately USD 8.45 billion by 2033. The continuing increase in value is attributed to a rise in demand for "relatable and real" visuals, growth of social media platforms, and AI tools (Business Research Insights, 2025b).

Before 2021, the use of AI in photography workflows had been steadily growing, with assistive image recognition algorithms in cameras and AI-enhanced software becoming increasingly adept at manipulating digital images. Advances in GenAI technology have led to a new wave of disruption for the photography industry, taking photographers and consumers by relative surprise with its novelty and potential. Netflix credited "AI + Human" for background images in a 2023 animated release, citing a labor shortage in anime artists as their reason for using GenAI (Harris, 2023), and public expressions of disdain were levelled at photojournalist Michael Christopher Brown's storytelling experiment with GenAI, "90 Miles" (Terranova, 2023). Rapidly improving AI image generation and manipulation offerings have prompted a flurry of commentary from photography websites and blogs worldwide, with responses ranging from optimism to despair (Baggs, 2023., Edwards, 2023., Nyce, 2024). In the following section, current leading concerns arising from the disruptive influence of GenAI will be elaborated.

4.3 Current Developments and Debates

The long-term impact of GenAI on photography is yet unknown, nor is the scale of disruption certain. Since the release of OpenAI's DALL•E, in 2021, followed closely by Midjourney and Stable Diffusion, text-to-image, image-to-image, and AI-powered image-enhancing entrants to the market continue to proliferate. At the same time, sales in digital photography markets are forecast to rise, with market size in global photography services expected to increase from 58.05 billion USD in 2024 to 85.43 billion in 2033 (Business Research Insights, 2025a), driven by image sharing across social media, increasing Internet access in developing countries and continued growth in e-commerce websites (Business Research Insights, 2025a, 2025b). These figures suggest no immediate threat to photographic industries by GenAI. In fact, Dr. Alessandra Sala, Senior Director of AI and Data Science at Shutterstock, declares an ongoing necessity for photography to feed the diffusion models of the future in order that they may reflect the ever-changing world, including new trends, styles, and events (Growcoot, 2024). This sentiment is echoed by photographers keenly aware that they are required to "add new datapoints" to training datasets (Dodd, 2024). Photography blogs cite a variety of responses to GenAI from photographers, with a staunch differentiation between AI-generated images and photographs as lens-based captures of light from reality (Khan, 2023). Broad appreciation for and growing use of post-processing AI tools is offset by uncomfortable acknowledgements of the potential loss of jobs for retouchers, for example, as a result. Most notably, there is optimistic insistence on the inability of GenAI to replicate the role of the human in articulating and executing an artistic vision with a unique viewpoint connected with real subjects (Khan, 2023). This optimism about the future of photography is reflected in the fine art world, evidenced by established names like Wolfgang Tillmans, Zanele Muholi and Hiroshi Sugimoto, continuing to exhibit globally at high-profile galleries and art fairs (Laster, 2024). Nevertheless, concerns continue to surround provenance of datasets used to train GenAI, with concomitant debates ongoing over copyright, ethics, bias, and homogenization of AI-generated images.

4.3.1 Ethical Transparency, Legal Challenges, and Diversification of Business Models

Vast datasets of image-text pairs are used to train commercial GenAI models. ImageNet is one such publicly available dataset of over 14 million annotated images created by researchers at Stanford and Princeton for use in computer vision research between 2006 and 2009 (ImageNet, 2021). Images were collected from photo-sharing sites across the Internet and crowdsourced labor, via Amazon Mechanical Turk, was used to help categorize and define the images to create the image-text pairs required to train generative models. It is widely assumed that early Midjourney iterations were trained primarily using ImageNet and other publicly available datasets, with founder David Holz admitting that it was built with "a big scrape of the internet" (Salkowitz, 2022). AI scholar, Professor Kate Crawford and artist Trevor Paglen, through their research into corporate histories of data collection and production for training machine vision systems, learned that ImageNet contained categories of images that were racist, misogynist, ableist, and sexist. Their viral interactive artwork, *ImageNet Roulette* (2019), revealed these inherent biases around race and gender in ImageNet to visitors of their gallery show *Training Humans* (2019) and people across the world. Five days after the exhibition opened, 600,000 images of people were removed from the ImageNet database (Kuesel, 2019), a positive step toward mitigating bias in future models trained on the data, though current models trained on ImageNet are still susceptible to producing images based on imprecise and biased categories.

The newer and much larger LAION-5B dataset, released in 2022 and comprising an incredible 5.85 billion image-text pairs (Beaumont, 2022), was used to train more recent Stable Diffusion and Midjourney models. The Internet was scraped indiscriminately to compile the dataset, known to include a "substantial number of copyrighted creations" (Appel et al., 2023), as well as illegal images. In 2023, LAION-5B was found to contain child sexual abuse material (CSAM) scraped from social media and adult sites, and though subsequently removed, there is no guarantee that the model will not be able to replicate the appearance of specific victims in future generations (Thiel, 2023). Identifiable, non-CSAM, and photographs of children were also found in the dataset, including indigenous Australian children who are at an increased risk in perpetuity as photos of deceased First Nation people are often restricted in periods of mourning (Human Rights Watch, 2024). The fact that LAION also pledged to remove these images from the set is little comfort to those children whose images have been used without permission or compensation. While it is true that the likelihood of generating a near copy of images used in a dataset is remote, it is still possible. Known as "memorization," one study considered only 109 generations out of 175 million to be a close copy of images in the dataset used to train the model (Kaigeng et al., 2024). Nevertheless, concern abounds not only for the potential to replicate sensitive and exploitative images but also creative and commercial copyright material, provoking ongoing litigation around copyright infringements by GenAI companies.

The two main issues under dispute in legal cases around GenAI are the use of copyright material to train models and the copyright status of images generated using such models (Malevé, 2024). Plaintiffs in California district case, Andersen v. Stability AI, include photographers who claim copyright infringement over use of their artwork to train GenAI models by Stability, Midjourney, DeviantArt, and RunwayML. At the time of writing, plaintiff's arguments that the GenAI products of respondents and their distribution infringed copyright have been found to be plausible, with the trial set to resume in 2026 (Schor, 2024). Legal commentary on the matter suggests, however, that "even if copyright infringement occurred, fair use will be a strong defense given the transformative nature of the outputs of the AI tools" (Eshagian, 2024). Getty Images is in an ongoing copyright dispute with Stability AI in both the US and UK over the alleged use of images to which Getty Images holds copyright to train the Stable Diffusion model released to the public in

2022 (O'Malley, 2025). In 2024, a class action was brought against Photobucket over updates to its privacy policy that plaintiffs claim enable Photobucket to sell photos of users (including intrinsic biometric markers) as training data for AI models (Belanger, 2024). It is unclear what the outcomes of these cases will be; however, for freelancers and unrepresented artists, litigation is not financially viable. Researchers and third-party organizations have stepped in to provide support to creatives and anyone wishing to protect their data from being used without their consent.

A team led by Shawn Shan at the University of Chicago developed tools Glaze and Nightshade to help artists combat potential loss in commissions from clients and shield them against the proliferation of low-quality AI-generated copies that might devalue artists' brands (University of Chicago, 2025a). Glaze works by disrupting "style mimicry" and Nightshade works by "poisoning" images to disrupt GenAI models if they are used as training data (Heikkilä, 2024). Glaze has been downloaded over 6.7 million times and Nightshade over 2.2 million since their respective releases, evidencing a strong desire amongst photographers, and visual artists more broadly, to restrict the use of their work to train GenAI models (University of Chicago, 2025b). Data governance organization, Spawning, created the Do Not Train registry, providing the means to enable "machine readable opt-outs to AI model trainers" (Spawning, 2025). In addition, they have developed tools that allow users to search for their work in training datasets, protect their websites from web-scrapers, and allow the easy addition of images on the Internet to the Do Not Train registry. There is a growing list of partner organizations that agree to respect the register, including Stability AI, Hugging Face, and Shutterstock. Even still, at the time of writing, there was no international agreement on approaches to protecting copyright holders' interests during stages of data collection and processing in the training of GenAI models (Kaigeng et al., 2024).

The fact that GenAI models have been trained on problematic datasets does not deter people from flocking to use them. Midjourney, for example, has over 22 million registered users and over 33 million monthly visitors (Kumar, 2024). Midjourney, Stability, and OpenAI all maintain their use of publicly available material from the Internet is "fair use," with Stability AI citing US Constitutional grounds (Brooks, 2023), and OpenAI citing "long-standing precedents," strong support from academics, community groups and associations, and permissive laws on training AI using copyright materials in countries across the globe (OpenAI, 2024). Nevertheless, OpenAI and others have responded to an increased public awareness and desire for ethical transparency and respect for copyright protections. In what could be seen as an attempt to legitimize its interests as well as a highly profitable commercial opportunity, OpenAI in 2021 licenced data from Shutterstock to train its DALL•E2 and EXAONE systems as part of a strategic partnership which saw Shutterstock incorporate OpenAI's technology into its own image generation tool. Images generated using Shutterstock's tool are added to the Shutterstock library and can be licenced for commercial use, and a compensation fund has been set up for creatives whose IP was used to develop DALL•E2 (Shutterstock, 2025). Shutterstock claimed an industry first in 2023 with their announcement to indemnify their ethically AI-generated images and provide protections against legal liabilities. They ensure diverse output across cultural groups and genders, manual review of generated images and exclusive use of custom images in perpetuity (Johnston, 2023). Historic Shutterstock rival, Getty Images, partnered with NVIDIA in 2023 to develop its own image generation system (Merrit, 2023), trained solely on its own library and providing "full protection and indemnification to use in a rapidly changing legal and regulatory environment" (Getty Images, 2025b). With the introduction of image modification and fine-tuning capabilities, Getty's offering has become increasingly powerful.

Adobe is the third in the triumvirate of stock image companies dominating the market. Adobe released Firefly Beta in March 2023, leveraging its vast stock library as a training set for an ethical GenAI product that has since been integrated into a growing list of its applications including Photoshop (Adobe, 2025b). Photoshop is perhaps the most widely used software for the digital manipulation of photographs, in which AI-enhanced image editing capabilities including content-aware fill have been available since 2010. Integration of Firefly sees objects seamlessly removed from or inserted into photographs with a few keystrokes, and photorealistic expansion of images where no pixels existed before. Most diffusion models are now able to perform these functions, known respectively as in-painting and out-painting, furthering the dangers of AI-generated material being mistaken for photographs. Though available deep fake detection tools are purported to be up to 99% accurate (Mukta et al., 2023), one study suggests that leading deep-fake detectors are mainly proficient only "in specific scenarios" (Le et al., 2025). Little wonder there is rising public scepticism around online content, significant concern around the ability to tell the difference between real and AI-generated content (AIGC), and strong support for labelling of AIGC (Steinhart et al., 2024).

For its part, Adobe maintains a strong ethical stance in support of creators, asserting that they do not train on customer content, only use images with permission, and compensate those who contribute to training sets (Adobe, 2025a). Founding the Content Authority Initiative (CAI) in 2019, Adobe continues to lead its mission to "develop open-source tools for verifiably recording the provenance of any digital media, including content made with generative AI" (Adobe, 2024). Alongside others including BBC and Microsoft, they are also cofounders of the Coalition for Content Provenance and Authenticity (or C2PA Content Credentials). Content Credentials are tamper-evident metadata attached to creative content as a kind of record of the provenance of and processes used to create an image (Adobe, 2025c). Adobe is rolling out ongoing support for Content Credentials in Adobe Camera Raw, Lightroom, and Photoshop, and there is an extension for Google's Chrome browser, with Meta using Content Credentials as a signal when labelling images as "AI" on Facebook, Instagram, and Threads (Clark, 2024). Whilst the system is still in Beta mode, it has seen strong support from governments across the globe. A joint report by cyber security agencies in Australia, Canada, the United Kingdom, and the United States recommends "widespread adoption across the information ecosystem" (National Security Agency (NSA) et al., 2025). The report lists camera manufacturers, software producers, GenAI companies including OpenAI, Microsoft, and Adobe, social media companies including Meta and Google, and image brokers

Adobe Stock, Shutterstock and Getty Images, who have all committed to using C2PA as at January 30, 2025 (NSA et al., 2025). Nevertheless, there is evidence of continued public resistance to practices seen to infringe on the rights of private citizens' data, regardless of whether those rights were signed away years ago.

Meta has not shied away from its use of publicly available data dating back to 2007 to train its image generation models including photos, videos and text from publicly shared posts on Instagram and Facebook (Meta, 2023). Concerns raised in late 2024 by the UK's Information Commissioner's Office have led to potential opt-out policies for British users, and the EU continues to resist Meta's plans through regulation (Weaver, 2024). In other countries, like Australia, however, there is no such protection (Weatherbed, 2024). Social media platform, Cara was founded in 2022 in response to concerns by artists and photographers about use of public social media posts for training data as well as the proliferation of AI-generated images across social media platforms. Cara.app provides portfolio and social feed functions for creatives, claiming to have AI detection technology to filter out AI-generated images from portfolios as well as adding "NOAI" tags to uploaded images signaling AI scrapers not to scrape images. The intention is to provide a safe alternative for artists to publish their images as well as a trusted place to engage with so called "authentic" creatives and images (Cara, 2025). Downloads of Cara surged from 49,000 in May, 2024 to 314,000 in June following the widely publicized news of Meta's use of user data to train its AI models across its platforms (Ceci, 2024). Though these numbers pale in significance compared to Meta's 3.35 billion daily users (Dixon, 2025), they hint at a notional public shift toward forums that support artists' rights and creative transparency, and away from the indiscriminate production and distribution of AI-generated content.

Other platforms, such as Exactly.ai, offer services for those who embrace the creative potentials of GenAI to expand and develop their own creative outputs whilst seeking to protect their data from being folded back into datasets as it may be when using services including Midjourney or OpenAI. Exactly.ai ensures all images uploaded, models built, and images generated by those models remain the property of the artist. Founder, Tonia Samsonova, commenting on the 2023 US Federal ruling in Thaler v. Perlmutter, upheld in 2025, that work generated by artificial intelligence is not eligible for copyright protection (Bomboy, 2025), remained hopeful that artists creating models based on their own outputs would be able to claim copyright (Art Review, 2023). It is yet to be seen how attractive platforms like Cara.ai and services like Exactly.ai will become to photographers, artists, and others looking to move beyond sharing communities and GenAI products that don't necessarily ensure data privacy, but it is clear there is a considerable public interest in exploring these options.

4.3.2 Mitigation of Bias in and Homogenization of Images Generated Using Diffusion Models

As has been detailed, the market in stock images was already significantly concentrated when Adobe, Getty Images and Shutterstock were ideally positioned to take advantage of the demand for ethically sourced data to train GenAI models. Adobe has been able to diversify its product offering moving from supply of stock images and image editing tools like Photoshop to image generation and unprecedented leaps forward in image manipulation and enhancement across its full range of product offerings. Getty Images and Shutterstock, on the other hand, have partnered with other GenAI developers to diversify their offerings from pure stock photography, incorporating ethically developed GenAI tools with extraordinary potential to satisfy commercial demands for images, whether they are photographic, GenAI or a hybrid that blends the optically captured with other synthesized elements. In January 2025, Getty Images Holdings and Shutterstock announced a merger, citing obvious strategic benefits including the ability for greater investment in "innovative content creation … and customer-facing technologies and capabilities, such as search, 3D imagery and generative AI" (Getty Images, 2025a). The announcement, marking an exceptional concentration of "licenced visual content" coupled with GenAI functionality, came with assurances to its contributor communities that the new Getty Images Holdings' belief in the opportunities of AI was matched by "the need to compensate creators for the use of their work" (Australian Photography, 2025). On the face of it, this is encouraging for photographers, at least in the short term and with growing demand for diverse and ethically sourced training data, the merger seems destined to be a success for shareholders, photographers, and consumers alike, particularly given the reputation of other offerings for generating biased and even offensive outcomes.

Both Stable Diffusion and Midjourney have been known to generate images that display gender, race, and class stereotypes due to training data biases and additional structural factors (Kidd & Birhane, 2023). OpenAI claims that some of the evident bias in their first DALL•E model was due to their risk mitigation processes that filtered sexually explicit and violent images from training data (OpenAI, 2022). This filtering process, designed to reduce harm to potential users, unfortunately resulted in biased models. As discussed earlier, evident bias in training data has been exposed through concerted research efforts, testing, and even artistic interventions. Art history scholar Noam M. Elcott and technologist Tim Trombley (2024) advocate for the fine tuning of models to avoid "the graceless bias and mediocrity of the generated photographic image," as they put it, even as they acknowledge the risk that with greater specificity and complexity in GenAI outputs, comes more risk to photography as a medium, especially if near enough in many cases may be considered good enough (Elcott & Trombley, 2024, p. 71). Market leader in GenAI video applications, Runway, now uses "diversity fine tuning," using synthetic data comprising various skin tones and genders built from diverse text prompts, purportedly "increasing group fairness metrics by 150% for perceived skin tone and 97.7% for perceived gender" (Esposito et al., 2023). OpenAI continues efforts to mitigate misinformation, explicit sexual and violent content, copyright and trademark violations, and biases that favor White, female and youthful depictions of humans. Their strategies include prompt blocklists (of public figures for example), automatic transforming of user prompts, output classifiers, and "refusals" that are triggered when a prompt includes a request to generate images in a living artist's style, for example (OpenAI, 2023). On the other hand, with the release of open-source Stable Diffusion 3.5, Stability AI claims "diverse outputs, with different skin tones and features, without the need for extensive prompting" (Stability, 2024). Given that Stable Diffusion can be deployed by anyone without the inbuilt guardrails of DALL•E3, for example, this gives some reassurance for users moving forward. Of course, the alternative to fine-tuning biased data is to train using so-called ethical datasets.

Defined.ai, founded by Daniela Braga in 2015, has become a major supplier of ethical data to companies including Apple, Amazon, Google, Meta, and Microsoft in only ten short years (Paul & Tong, 2024). Defined.ai claims their databases "are paid for, obtained with consent, and anonymized, while always respecting the dignity of fair wages for everyone worldwide" (Defined.Ai, 2023). The supply of ethical data goes some way toward ameliorating the concerns of theorists including Hito Steyerl (2023) and Kate Crawford (2021) around inequitable GenAI training regimes and biased AI-generated outcomes, and the incredible growth of Defined.ai is evidence of a growing and potentially insatiable demand for ethically sourced data in the scramble to gain and maintain market share not only in photography and image markets but more broadly. Beyond equity and bias, however, Steyerl and Crawford, amongst others, also take issue with the kind of homogenized imagery GenAI tends to produce.

Returning to discussions of definitions, then, Steyerl, labels AI-generated images "statistical renderings" (Steyerl, 2023), representing an averaged, homogenized version of reality. Kate Crawford terms them "metabolic images … produced by digesting billions of other images that are broken down into smaller parts and absorbed by AI models, which then excrete out streams of processed images" (Antonelli & Crawford, 2024, pp. 77–78). Anyone who has spent any time using image generation systems would be aware that even given the ongoing rollout of diverse and non-biased systems, the plethora of GenAI image offerings nevertheless tend to produce "oddly similar work" (Nyce, 2024). GenAI models are trained to detect and replicate patterns, so that systems including OpenAI, Google, Midjourney, Leonardo.ai, and others tend to generate more or less standardized images. Commercial images or stock photographs have long been the subject of critique for their tendency to present stereotypes and clichés. Scholar Paul Frosh (2020) outlines the standard critique of stock photography of being deceptively exploitative, brashly commercializing documentary and art photography, and maintaining invisible dominance over visual culture by "demeaning photography itself as a resource for public critique by reducing it to a machine for producing stereotypes" (Frosh, 2020, p. 188). Similar arguments are now being put forward vis-à-vis AI-generated images, with researchers and artists Eryk Salvaggio, Caroline Sinders and Steph Maj Swanson (2025), suggesting that this same tendency evident in AI-generated images "strips away much of artmaking's critical potential," with the additional critique that GenAI interfaces "encourage passive consumption" (Salvaggio et al., 2025).

Frosh argues that though generic photography is the central product of the commercial stock industry, genericity is in fact a "crucial component of human social existence" (Frosh, 2020, p. 200). He attempts to redeem stock photography, particularly with respect to its representation of people, by positioning it as positively habituating us to mass companionship of multiple, diverse strangers depicted across "the wallpaper of consumer culture" (Frosh, 2020, p. 201). This may well be a far stretch, though it is difficult to disagree that we are better able to know ourselves through our relationship to others both like and unlike ourselves. Ultimately, however, Frosh admits that the clichéd visual culture stock photography contributes to "demands constant efforts to pluralize the unexceptional and formulaic" (Frosh, 2020, p. 202). In the context of a visual culture increasingly pervaded by averaged, stereotypical, metabolic AI-generated images, Salvaggio, Sinders, and Swanson also encourage such efforts, arguing for creative misuse of GenAI systems via critical strategies including prompt injection, prompt confusion, and recontextualization (Salvaggio et al., 2025). As an artist with a background in misuse of media, I too embrace experimental methods that seek to exploit digital imaging technologies and the artificial intelligence systems that increasingly drive them, in the hope of learning something new. It is artists, then, toward whom I now turn to discern how they use GenAI in explorative and critical ways.

4.3.3 Adoption of GenAI Processes into Photographic Visual Art Practices

In 1984, media philosopher Vilém Flusser proposed a radical new philosophy of photography that provides a prescient and relevant framework with which to think through GenAI technology. He framed photographs as technical images, cameras as apparatuses (Flusser, 2000, p. 13), and photographers as functionaries of those cameras, bound by their inherent logic and potential (Flusser, 2000, p. 27). For Flusser, photographers are a kind of programmer of the apparatus, which was itself programmed by the photographic industry that in turn was programmed by the industrial complex, and so on (Flusser, 2000, p. 29). Flusser characterized cameras as forms of artificial intelligence, as "black boxes that simulate thinking … in such a way that, in future, human beings will become less and less competent to deal with [this thinking] and have to rely more and more on apparatuses" (Flusser, 2000, p. 32). His frank assessment of post-industrial society as one comprising functionaries "manipulated by photographs and programmed to act in a ritual fashion … [and] suppress our critical awareness" (Flusser, 2000, p. 64) is echoed in the critiques of stock photography and AI-generated images laid out in this chapter. Flusser's solution to this grimly drawn reality is for experimental photographers to work against the program of the apparatus; to attempt consciously to create "unpredictable information" and thereby entertain the possibility of freedom from the programmed reality (Flusser, 2000, p. 80). Today, the programming of technical images has become significantly more complex, the black boxed apparatus of a GenAI model posing an exponentially greater challenge to manipulate than a Kodak Instamatic, for example. Yet, for Flusser, the promise of photography (and other technical images) lay in the potential for the photographer to transcend the preprogrammed nature of the apparatus. By experimenting in unexpected ways, images might be generated that go beyond the expected outputs and offer genuinely new perspectives or insights. Three artists and researchers are using GenAI in such ways that attempt to revive the unrecorded past, envisage an uncertain future, and ask after the algorithmic unconscious.

Artist and researcher Sara Oscar's *Counterfactual Departures, 1974 (Winter Gardens, Bangkok)* (2023—ongoing), is a series of AI-generated images that depict her mother's experience at Bangkok International Airport as she departs to migrate to Australia whilst pregnant with the artist. Visualizing the undocumented event using Midjourney, Oscar attempts to synthesize a moment from her past using a GenAI model that is trained on countless digitized renderings of actual moments. Oscar sees the process of creating a "proxy version" of her mother (and herself in utero) as enabling "memory-work, to facilitate dialogue and interaction" (Oscar, 2024). What began as an unsuccessful process of trying to guide the GenAI model to conform with her expectations of what the past looked like, through dialogue with the model, evolved into discussion with her mother in an effort to narrow the gap between her memories and what was possible to render with the technology. *Counterfactual Departures* highlights the role photography plays in making and preserving memories and what can be lost without the benefit of photographic records. It is also instructive as to the ability of GenAI to give form to undocumented events through a multifaced dialogical process.

Researcher and media maker Julia Scott Stevenson's *Collective Visions* (2024), on the other hand, gives form to imagined or anticipated events. *Collective Visions* is a creative practice research project hosted at the University of Technology Sydney's Data Arena, an immersive 360° data visualization space. The project centers around how emerging technology can be used to engage the public in climate change awareness and activism. Visitors described their desired climate future in text prompts that generated images using Stable Diffusion almost instantly in a random place on the 360° display. The work elicited much thoughtful conversation about the way prompts were being interpreted and visualized and how that related to the importance of good communication around climate justice and scientific communication more generally. Alongside feelings of wonder and optimism, it also elicited feelings of discomfort with the negative environmental impacts of the technology driving the work. Over 5 days, a layered collage expanded across the screen as visions of a future affected by the impacts of climate change appeared alongside more hopeful renderings of what might be achieved if more concerted action was taken to avert or ameliorate their severity. The ongoing project will be iterated to incorporate interviews with scientists and expanded to engage school students, with the potential for significant impact on current perceptions and future predictions of the effects of climate change.

Unprompted Studies 1–3 (2023) is a video artwork I created using GenAI without text inputs. It seeks to answer the playful question: what do machine learning models dream of unprompted? The answer, of course, is: it's complicated. I selected a single source image from thousands generated using the diffusion model Realistic_Vision_V1.4 in the Stable Diffusion interface "Automatic1111" with no text prompt. This image became the sole input for multiple generations of moving image sequences using the "DEFORUM" plugin, which generates images from other images. The source image is the prompt for the next generation, which is the prompt for the next image and so on. No text prompts were used at all in this process. Sequences were selected and assembled into a triptych of divergent channels of looping animations all stemming from the single source image, each sequence connected by the similarity of color and shape from one image to the next, unguided by human input text. Theorist David Bate talks of the "drifting of photographic meaning from one image to another" as creating a dreamlike "nonconformism of visual sense perception" (Bate, 2021). The surrealist preoccupation with dreams is well known, but rather than a Freudian psychoanalytic conception of dreams, *Unprompted Studies 1–3* gestures toward an algorithmic dream – a sequence of images springing from the unknowable workings of the diffusion model itself. *Unprompted Studies 1–3* shows evidence of known biases in early diffusion models, such as their tendency to favor white, Western, and male representations. It also explores how artists can use the unguided outputs of generative AI to render unpredictable information. As such, the work may at first glance seem to represent an effort to take up Flusser's cause to work against the constraints of the apparatus. Yet the generations of images are based on the default parameters of the GenAI model used, and my attempts *not* to program it reinforce my role as an unexceptional and formulaic functionary. I take heart, however, in the fact that the process, for myself at least, marked a conscious attempt to understand the problems, the potentials and the constraints posed by the technical images we are now faced with.

4.4 Conclusion

It is tempting to drift toward pessimism about the fate of a world in which it is difficult to tell the real from the synthetic. The conversation around GenAI is long from over, and arguments against it, such as its potential to "discredit the photojournalistic corpus that documents our shared human history" (Lewandowski, 2024, p. 7), will continue to contest more optimistic appraisals. Generative tools continue to be developed and integrated into photographic workflows, with further disruption to the industry certain as technology advances. Those who have the power to build and profit enormously from these systems are putting increasing resources into ethical models and sustainable solutions to the extraordinary negative environmental impacts of GenAI are being investigated, though the efficacy of these will depend on robust government regulation and tax incentives (Cho, 2023). People continue to flock to GenAI image offerings, engaging with them casually to generate AI avatars of themselves and whatever else they can imagine. Nonetheless, consumer demand for photography has not slowed in the face of developing GenAI capabilities, with individuals far outstripping commercial users in photographic market share, driven by smartphone photography and social media (Allied Market Research, 2023), a photographic universe indeed. The future of photography will continue to be shaped by the ongoing interplay between technological advancements, artistic innovation and commercial imperatives. While GenAI presents significant disruptions and challenges, it also offers new opportunities for creativity, communication, and engagement with visual culture. It remains to be seen how equitably the benefits of this technology will be distributed and how effectively we can mitigate its potential harms. The work of artists who continue to interrogate the black box of GenAI and seek to break from its programming will, as ever, be essential to help navigate the course ahead.

References

Adobe. (2024). *How it works. Content authority initiative.* https://contentauthenticity.org/how-it-works

Adobe. (2025a). *Responsible innovation in the age of generative AI. AI at Adobe: Ethics.* https://www.adobe.com/au/ai/overview/ethics.html.

Adobe. (2025b*). The ultimate list of Adobe AI features. Ai at Adobe: AI features.* https://www.adobe.com/au/ai/overview/features.html

Adobe. (2025c, February 6). *Content credentials. Adobe.* https://helpx.adobe.com/ie/creative-cloud/help/content-credentials.html

Allied Market Research. (2023). *Photography services market size, share, competitive landscape and trend analysis report, by type of photography, by end user: Global opportunity analysis and industry forecast, 2023-2032.* https://www.alliedmarketresearch.com/photography-services-market-A74434

Antonelli, P., & Crawford, K. (2024). Kate crawford metabolic images: A conversation with Paola Antonelli. *Aperture, 257*, 72–81.

Appel, G., Nellbauer, J., Schweidel, D. A., (2023, April 7). Intellectual property: Generative AI has an intellectual property problem. *Harvard Business Review.* https://hbr.org/2023/04/generative-ai-has-an-intellectual-property-problem

Arielli, E. (2024). Made by and for humans? The issue of aesthetic alignment. In L. Manovich & E. Arielli (Eds.), *Artificial aesthetics: Generative AI, art and visual media.* https://manovich.net/index.php/projects/artificial-aesthetics

Art Review. (2023, September 7). *Exactly.ai: The constantly changing landscape of art and tech, art review.* https://artreview.com/exactly-ai-the-constantly-changing-landscape-of-art-and-tech/

Australian Photography. (2025, January 8). *Getty Images and Shutterstock announce merger in $3.7b deal. Australian Photography.* https://www.australianphotography.com/news/getty-images-and-shutterstock-announce-merger-in-3-7b-deal

Baggs, R. (2023, April 29). *Adapt or Perish: AI is to digital what digital was to analog.* Fstoppers. https://fstoppers.com/artificial-intelligence/adapt-or-perish-ai-digital-what-digital-was-analog-631399

Barthes, R. (1982). *Camera Lucida: Reflections on photography.* 1st American pbk. ed. Hill and Wang.

Bate, D. (2021). Photography in surrealism. In N. Lusty (Ed.), *Surrealism* (pp. 208–223). Cambridge University Press.

Beaumont, R. (2022, March 31). *LAION-5B: A new era of open large-scale multi-modal datasets.* LAION. https://laion.ai/blog/laion-5b/

Belanger, A. (2024). *Photobucket opted inactive users into privacy nightmare, lawsuit says*. Ars Technica. https://arstechnica.com/tech-policy/2024/12/photobucket-sold-users-biometric-data-without-consent-lawsuit-says/

Bogre, M. (2019). *Documentary photography reconsidered: History, theory and practice* (1st ed.). Routledge.

Bomboy, S. (2025, March 25). *Federal court rules artificial intelligence machines can't claim copyright authorship*. National Constitution Centre Blog. https://www.capturemag.com.au/news/us-appeals-court-rules-ai-generated-works-ineligible-for-copyright-protection

Brooks, B. (2023, November 30). *Statement to the U.S. Senate AI insight forum on transparency, explainability, and copyright*. Sability.AI: News. https://stability.ai/news/copyright-us-senate-open-ai-transparency

Business Research Insights. (2025a, February 17). *Photography services market size, share, growth, and industry analysis, by type (Shooting service, after sales service, photography services), by application (Consumer, Commercial), Regional Forecast To 2033. Business Research Insights: Photography Services Market*. https://www.businessresearchinsights.com/market-reports/photography-services-market-104521

Business Research Insights. (2025b, March 10). *Stock photography market size, share, growth, and industry analysis, by type (Professional photographers only, amateur photographers only, both professional and amateur photographers), by application (Personal user, enterprise user, other user), and Regional Forecast to 2033. Business research insights: Stock photography market*. https://www.businessresearchinsights.com/market-reports/stock-photography-market-118653

Cara. (2025). *About Cara. Cara Blog*. https://blog.cara.app/about

Ceci, L. (2024, June 7). *Number of Cara: Art & Social app downloads worldwide from October 2023 to June 2024. Statista*. https://www.statista.com/statistics/1472019/cara-app-downloads/

Cho, R. (2023, July 9). *AI's growing carbon footprint. State of the planet: News from the Columbia Climate School*. https://news.climate.columbia.edu/2023/06/09/ais-growing-carbon-footprint/

Clark, M. (2024, October 24). Adobe content credentials check-in: The quest to verify images, video, and more on the web. *DPReview*. https://www.dpreview.com/interviews/3215783269/adobe-max-2024-content-credentials-authenticity-initiative

Crawford, K. (2021). *Atlas of AI: Power, politics, and the planetary costs of artificial intelligence*. Yale University Press. https://doi.org/10.12987/9780300252392

De Leon, A. (2018). Working the Kodak Zone the labor relations of race and photography in the Philippine Cordilleras, 1887–1914. *Radical History Review, 2018*(132), 68–95. https://doi.org/10.1215/01636545-6942403

Defined.AI. (2023). *Ethical AI manifesto principles of trustworthy AI*. https://connect.defined.ai/hubfs/DAI_Ehtical_Ai_Manifest_Ebook%20(1).pdf

Dewdney, A. (2021). *Forget photography*. Goldsmiths Press.

Dixon, Stacy Jo. (2025, February 14). Cumulative number of daily Meta product users as of 4th quarter 2024. *Statista*. https://www.statista.com/statistics/1092227/facebook-product-dau/

Dodd, S. (2024, February 28). The role of the photographer in the age of AI: Possible paths forward. *Trigger*. https://fomu.be/trigger/articles/the-role-of-the-photographer-in-the-age-of-ai

Edwards, K. (2023, July 6). *Why does all AI art look like that? Medium*. https://medium.com/@keithkisser/why-does-all-ai-art-look-like-that-f74e2a9e1c87

Elcott, N. M., & Trombley, T. (2024). Generative style. *Aperture, 257*, 62–71.

Enninful, E. K. (2023). Technological unemployment galore in Ghana: The spotlight on the digital photography industry. *International Journal of Education, Learning and Development, 11*(4), 9–44. https://doi.org/10.37745/ijeld.2013/vol11n4944

Eshagian, M. (2024, December 6). *Andersen, et al. v. stability AI Ltd, et al. Mesh IP Law*. https://www.meshiplaw.com/litigation-tracker/andersen-v-stability-ai

Esposito, P., Atighehchian, P., Germanidis, A., Ghadiyaram, D. (2023, October 10). *Mitigating stereotypical biases in text to image generative systems. Runway*. https://runwayml.com/research/mitigating-stereotypical-biases-in-text-to-image-generative-systems

Flusser, V. (2000). *Towards a philosophy of photography*. Reaktion.

Frosh, P. (2020). Is commercial photography a public evil? Beyond the critique of stock photography. In M. Miles & E. Welch (Eds.), *Photography and its publics* (1st ed.). Routledge. https://doi.org/10.4324/9781003103721

Getty Images. (2025a, January 7). *Getty images and shutterstock to merge, creating a premier visual content company. Getty images: Press release details.* https://investors.gettyimages.com/news-releases/news-release-details/getty-images-and-shutterstock-merge-creating-premier-visual

Getty Images. (2025b). *Explore our values. About Getty Images.* https://www.gettyimages.co.uk/about-us/values

Growcoot, M. (2024, December 10). *Shutterstock chief says AI needs photographers to survive.* PetaPixel. https://petapixel.com/2024/12/10/shutterstock-chief-says-ai-needs-photographers-to-survive/

Hamber, A. (2024). Between push of technology and pull of the market: Recollections on the transition of photo archives from analogue to digital. *Rundbrief Fotografie, 31*(3), 8–22.

Harris, L. (2023, February 2). *Netflix Japan blames "Labor Shortage" for why it's using AI instead of* animators, dot.LA, https://dot.la/the-dog-and-the-boy-2659365902.html?utm_source=dotla.beehiiv.com&utm_medium=referral&utm_campaign=the-latest-casualty-of-generative-ai-animators

Heiferman, M. (2012). *Photography changes everything* (4th ed.). Aperture.

Heikkilä, M. (2024, November 13). The AI lab waging a guerrilla war over exploitative AI. *MIT Technology Review.* https://www.technologyreview.com/2024/11/13/1106837/ai-data-posioning-nightshade-glaze-art-university-of-chicago-exploitation/

Ho, J. C., & Chen, H. (2018). Managing the disruptive and sustaining the disrupted: The case of Kodak and Fujifilm in the face of digital disruption. *Review of Policy Research, 35*(3), 352–371. https://doi.org/10.1111/ropr.12278

Human Rights Watch. (2024, July 2). Australia: Children's personal photos misused to power AI tools. *Human Rights Watch: News.* https://www.hrw.org/news/2024/07/03/australia-childrens-personal-photos-misused-power-ai-tools

Hutson, J., Lively, J., Robertson, B., Cotroneo, P., & Lang, M. (2024). *Creative convergence: The AI renaissance in art and design.* Springer.

ImageNet. (2021, March 11). *About ImageNet.* ImageNet. https://www.image-net.org/about.php

Johnston, B. (2023, August 29). *Introducing indemnification for AI-generated images: An industry first. Shutterstock Blog: Business.* https://www.shutterstock.com/blog/ai-generated-images-indemnification#using-ai-commercially

Kaigeng, L., Hong, W., & Yupeng, D. (2024). Copyright protection during the training stage of generative AI: Industry-oriented U.S. law, rights-oriented EU law, and fair remuneration rights for generative AI training under the UN's international governance regime for AI. *Computer Law & Security Review: The International Journal of Technology Law and Practice, 55*, 106056. https://doi.org/10.1016/j.clsr.2024.106056

Khan, F. (2023, July 7). *What do professional photographers think of AI.* The Phoblographer. https://www.thephoblographer.com/2023/07/07/what-do-professional-photographers-think-of-ai/

Kidd, C. & Birhane, A. (2023). How AI can distort human beliefs. *Science, 380*(6651), 1222–1223. https://doi.org/10.1126/science.adi0248

Krause. C. (2023, September, 27). Case study: Kodak's downfall—a lesson in failed digital transformation and missed opportunities. *The CDO Times.* https://cdotimes.com/2023/09/27/case-study-kodaks-downfall-a-lesson-in-failed-digital-transformation-and-missed-opportunities/

Kuesel, C. (2019, September 25). *An online image database will remove 600,000 pictures after an art project revealed the system's racist bias.* Artsy. https://www.artsy.net/article/artsy-editorial-online-image-database-will-remove-600-000-pictures-art-project-revealed-systems-racist-bias

Kumar, N. (2024, December 31). *Midjourney statistics 2025: Users & revenue data.* DemandSage. https://www.demandsage.com/midjourney-statistics/

Laster, P. (2024, August 24). *Art market: The state of the photography market in 2024.* Artsy. https://www.artsy.net/article/artsy-editorial-state-photography-market-2024

Le, B. L., Kim, J., Woo S. S., Moore, K., Abuadbba, A., Tariq S. (2025, June30–July4). SoK: Systematization and benchmarking of Deepfake detectors in a unified framework. *IEEE European Symposium on security and privacy 2025 (EuroS&P '25).* https://arxiv.org/abs/2401.04364v4

Lewandowski, H. (2024). Zombie humanism, generative AI images, and photography [Review of the book *A generated family of man*, by Flickr Foundation], *Panorama: Journal of the Association of Historians of American Art 10*, no. 2 (Fall 2024). https://doi.org/10.24926/24716839.19237

Lu, Z., Huang, D., Bai, L., Qu, J., Wu, C., Liu, X., Ouyang, W. (2023, December 10–16). Seeing is not always believing: Benchmarking human and model perception of AI-generated images. *37th Conference on neural information processing systems (NeurIPS 2023)*, New Orleans, LA, USA. https://arxiv.org/pdf/2304.13023.

Lucas, H., & Goh, J. M. (2009). Disruptive technology: How Kodak missed the digital photography revolution. *The Journal of Strategic Information Systems, 18*(1), 46–55. https://doi.org/10.1016/j.jsis.2009.01.002

Mäenpää, J. (2023). Future directions of professional photographers: A case study of changing hats between journalism and humanitarian photography. *Nordicom Review, 44*(1), 65–84. https://doi.org/10.2478/nor-2023-0004

Malevé, N. (2024). Lost in compression: Models of authorship in generative AI. *Media Theory, 8*(1), 205–228. ⟨hal-04702743⟩.

McCormack, J., Cruz Gambardella, C., Rajcic, N., Krol, S.J., Llano, M.T., Yang, M. (2023). Is writing prompts really making art?. In: Johnson, C., Rodríguez-Fernández, N., Rebelo, S.M. (Eds) *Artificial intelligence in music, sound, art and design. EvoMUSART 2023.* Lecture Notes in Computer Science, vol 13988. Springer, . pp 196–211. doi:https://doi.org/10.1007/978-3-031-29956-8_13.

Merrit, R. (2023, March 21). *Moving pictures: NVIDIA, getty images collaborate on generative AI.* NVIDIA Blog. https://blogs.nvidia.com/blog/generative-ai-getty-images/

Meta. (2023). *Building generative AI responsibly.* https://ai.meta.com/static-resource/building-generative-ai-responsibly/

Misiak, O. (2024). Transformations of street photography in the era of digital technologies. *Culture of Ukraine, 86*, 14–20. https://doi.org/10.31516/2410-5325.086.02

Mukta, M. S. H., Ahmad, J., Raiaan, M. A. K., Islam, S., Azam, S., Ali, M. E., & Jonkman, M. (2023). An investigation of the effectiveness of Deepfake models and tools. *Journal of Sensor and Actuator Networks, 12*(4), 61. https://doi.org/10.3390/jsan12040061

Murphy, S. C. (2018). Shake it like a polaroid picture: The rise and fall of an analog social medium. In M. Wolf (Ed.), *The Routledge companion to media technology and obsolescence* (1st ed., pp. 234–242). Routledge. https://doi.org/10.4324/9781315442686-16

National Security Agency (NSA), Australian Signals Directorate's Australian Cyber Security Centre (ACSC), Canadian Centre for Cyber Security (CCCS), and United Kingdom National Cyber Security Centre (NCSC-UK). (2025). *Content credentials: Strengthening multimedia integrity in the generative AI era.* https://www.cyber.gov.au/resources-business-and-government/governance-and-user-education/artificial-intelligence/strengthening-multimedia-integrity-in-the-generative-ai-era

Nyce, C. M. (2024, August 16). *Why does AI art look like that? The Atlantic: Technology.* https://www.theatlantic.com/technology/archive/2024/08/why-does-all-ai-art-look-same/679488/

O'Malley, M. (2025, January 17). *Blow for Getty Images after UK judge removes class representative in copyright dispute with Stability AI. The Global Legal Post: News.* https://www.globallegalpost.com/news/blow-for-getty-images-after-uk-judge-removes-class-representative-in-copyright-dispute-with-stability-ai-1766645629#:~:text=Stability%20AI%20has%20won%20a,their%20content%20to%20its%20platform.

OpenAI. (2022, June 28). *DALL·E 2 pre-training mitigations.* OpenAI. https://openai.com/index/dall-e-2-pre-training-mitigations/

OpenAI. (2023). *DALL·E 3 System Card.* OpenAI. https://cdn.openai.com/papers/DALL_E_3_System_Card.pdf

OpenAI. (2024, January 8). *OpenAI and journalism.* OpenAI Blog. https://openai.com/index/openai-and-journalism/
Oscar, S. (2024, June 12). *I had no photos of my mother's pregnancy and migration, so I found a way for AI to help fill in the gaps.* Art Guide Australia. https://artguide.com.au/i-had-no-photos-of-my-mothers-pregnancy-and-migration-so-i-found-a-way-for-ai-to-help-fill-in-the-gaps/
Paul, K. & Tong, A. (2024, April 6). *Inside Big Tech's underground race to buy AI training data.* Reuters. https://www.reuters.com/technology/inside-big-techs-underground-race-buy-ai-training-data-2024-04-05/
Perra, D., Ferrell, T. (2023, July 18). *The big picture: How Google photos scaled rapidly on Spanner.* Google Cloud Blog. https://cloud.google.com/blog/products/databases/google-photos-builds-user-experience-on-spanner
Richter, F. (2024, August 19). *Smartphones wipe out decades of camera industry growth.* Statista. https://www.statista.com/chart/15524/worldwide-camera-shipments/
Rosenblum, N. (1997). *World history of photography* (3rd ed.). Abbeville Press.
Rouse, W. B. (2021). *Failure management: Malfunctions of technologies, organizations, and society.* Oxford University Press.
Rubinstein, D., & Sluis, K. (2013). The digital image in photographic culture: Algorithmic photography and the crisis of representation. In M. Lister (Ed.), *The photographic image in digital culture* (2nd ed., pp. 22–40). Taylor & Francis Group.
Salkowitz. R. (2022, Spetember 16). *Midjourney founder David Holz on the impact of AI on art, imagination and the creative economy.* Forbes Business. https://www.forbes.com/sites/robsalkowitz/2022/09/16/midjourney-founder-david-holz-on-the-impact-of-ai-on-art-imagination-and-the-creative-economy/
Salvaggio, E., Siners, C., & Swanson, S. M. (2025). *Cultural red teaming: ARRG! & creative misuse of AI systems.* In Critical AI 3.1. https://doi.org/10.1215/2834703X-11700228
Sandström, C., Magnusson, M., & Jörnmark, J. (2009). Exploring factors influencing incumbents' response to disruptive innovation. *Creativity and Innovation Management(18)*, 8–15. https://doi.org/10.1111/j.1467-8691.2009.00507.x
Scharf, A. (1975). *Pioneers of photography.* The British Broadcasting Corporation.
Schor, Z. (2024). Andersen v. stability AI: The landmark case unpacking the copyright risks of AI image generators. *JIPEL: NYU Journal of Intellectual Property and Entertainment Law Blog.* https://jipel.law.nyu.edu/andersen-v-stability-ai-the-landmark-case-unpacking-the-copyright-risks-of-ai-image-generators/
Shutterstock. (2025). *Get to know the AI-generated content tool on Shutterstock.* Shutterstock Customer Support. https://support.shutterstock.com/s/article/Get-to-know-the-AI-generated-content-tool-on-Shutterstock?language=en_US
Simms, J. (2021, September, 9). Japan's Olympus Aims To Become Global Medtech Leader After Exiting Cameras. *Forbes Asia.* https://www.forbes.com/sites/jsimms/2021/09/09/japans-olympus-aims-to-become-global-medtech-leader-after-exiting-cameras/authroity
Smith, J. (2024, December 4). *The top 5 players shining a light on diagnostic imaging. Inside Precision Medicine.* https://www.insideprecisionmedicine.com/topics/patient-care/the-top-5-players-shining-a-light-on-diagnostic-imaging/
Snyder, P. (2013). *Is this something George Eastman would have done?: The decline and fall of Eastman Kodak Company.* CreateSpace.
Sony. (2025). *Product and technology milestones.* Sony. https://www.sony.com/en/SonyInfo/CorporateInfo/History/sonyhistory-g.html
Spawning. (2025). *About Spawning.* Spawning. https://spawning.ai/about
Stability. (2024, October 22). *Introducing stable diffusion 3.5. Stability.ai News.* https://stability.ai/news/introducing-stable-diffusion-3-5
Steinhart, M., Matheson, B., Dhameja, A., Crossan, G. (2024, November, 19). *Deepfake disruption: A cybersecurity-scale challenge and its far-reaching consequences.* Deloitte Center for Technology Media & Telecommunication. https://www2.deloitte.com/us/en/insights/industry/technology/technology-media-and-telecom-predictions/2025/gen-ai-trust-standards.html

Steyerl, H. (2023). Mean images. *New left review 140/141* (Mar/June 2023). https://newleftreview.org/issues/ii140/articles/hito-steyerl-mean-images
Sturken, M. (2016). Facebook photography and the demise of Kodak and Polaroid. In S. Pearl (Ed.), *Images, ethics, technology* (pp. 94–110). Routledge.
Terranova, A. (2023, April 4). How AI imagery is shaking photojournalism. *Blind Magazine*. https://www.blind-magazine.com/stories/how-ai-imagery-is-shaking-photojournalism/
Thiel, D. (2023). *Identifying and eliminating CSAM in generative ML training data and models*. Stanford Digital Repository. https://doi.org/10.25740/kh752sm9123.
University of Chicago. (2025a). *What is Glaze?* Glaze. https://glaze.cs.uchicago.edu/what-is-glaze.html
University of Chicago. (2025b). *About The Glaze project: Our values and mission*. Glaze. https://glaze.cs.uchicago.edu/aboutus.html
Wang, J., & Liang, J. (2024). The influences of AI and emerging technologies on the imagery stock industry as exemplified by the Visual China Group. *Emerging Media, 1*(2), 146–163. https://doi.org/10.1177/27523543231220880. (Original work published 2023).
Weatherbed, J. (2024, September 13). *Meta fed its AI on almost everything you've posted publicly since 2007*. The Verge. https://www.theverge.com/2024/9/12/24242789/meta-training-ai-models-facebook-instagram-photo-post-data
Weaver, M. (2024, September 14). Meta to push on with plan to use UK Facebook and Instagram posts to train AI. *The Guardian*. https://www.theguardian.com/business/2024/sep/13/meta-to-push-on-with-plan-to-use-uk-facebook-and-instagram-posts-to-train-ai
Williams, P., McDonald, P., & Mayes, R. (2021). The impact of disruptive innovation on creative workers: the case of photographers. *Creative Industries Journal, 14*(2), 130–151. https://doi.org/10.1080/17510694.2020.1858707
Zylinska, J. (2020). *AI art: Machine visions and warped dreams*. Open Humanities Press.

Justin Harvey is an artist and academic living and working on Gadigal land with a diverse background in visual arts & media production. He nurtures an ongoing fascination with the creative potentials of human machine interaction, embracing experimental methods that seek to exploit digital imaging technologies and the evolving 'artificial intelligence' systems that increasingly drive them in unintended and playful ways. Justin has exhibited artwork in solo and curated exhibitions in Australia and internationally.

Film Production and Cinematography

5

Sabine Baumann

Abstract

This chapter explores the transformative impact of AI on film production and cinematography—in particular, how emerging AI technologies are reshaping traditional filmmaking processes and artistic practices and their impact on media business ecosystems in the film industry. It begins with a historical overview that traces technological disruptions in film, from early innovations to the AI-driven landscape, emphasizing milestones like sound, color, and the digital transformation. A comprehensive review of literature and existing studies identifies trends, gaps, and controversies in AI research related to film production, covering topics like AI-driven scriptwriting, automated casting, and enhanced visual effects. Current developments are examined, including AI-driven pre-visualization, autonomous drones, and real-time editing algorithms, along with ethical and professional challenges such as authenticity, consent, intellectual property, and the displacement of human creativity. The chapter also explores the implications of AI for the future of film production, emphasizing the need for multidisciplinary collaborations and identifying key areas for future research, such as AI's impact on audience reception, democratizing film production, and developing ethical guidelines. The conclusion of the chapter summarizes key findings, reiterating AI's transformative potential while emphasizing the need to consider professional, economic, and ethical issues. It advocates for a balanced approach to harnessing AI's power to enhance creativity and efficiency while preserving the essential human elements of filmmaking.

S. Baumann (✉)
Hochschule für Wirtschaft und Recht (HWR) Berlin, Berlin, Germany
e-mail: sabine.baumann@hwr-berlin.de

S. Böhm et al. (eds.), *Handbook of AI-based Media Disruption*, Future of Business and Finance, https://doi.org/10.1007/978-3-032-07605-2_5

5.1 Introduction and (Historical) Overview of Disruption in Production and Cinematography

Technological innovation has long been a driving force in the evolution of film production and cinematography. From the earliest mechanical inventions to today's software-driven workflows, new tools have consistently altered both how films are made and how stories are being told. Disruptive technologies have historically redefined aesthetic conventions, professional roles, and production logics. Against this backdrop, the current integration of artificial intelligence (AI) can be seen as part of a broader, cyclical process in which new capabilities reshape established practices, but it also introduces qualitatively new dynamics of the ongoing emergence of AI as both a production tool and a creative collaborator that merit close examination.

The early history of cinema was marked by innovations in motion capture and projection, as technologies such as the kinetoscope and cinematograph enabled the mechanical reproduction of moving images and laid the groundwork for narrative filmmaking (Katmer, 2022; Musser, 2018). The first wave of disruption came with the arrival of sound in the late 1920s. The introduction of synchronized dialogue and music fundamentally changed filmmaking (Hediger, 2018; O'Brien, 2018). Directors adapted their visual language, actors modified their performances, and entire professions (e.g., live musical accompaniment) disappeared (Altman, 2004; Belton, 1985). However, the "talkies" not only transformed the formal qualities of film (pacing, dialogue, and performance) but also brought about industrial consolidation and creative realignment, marginalizing silent-era stars and techniques (Petrie, 1996).

Shortly after, in the 1930s and 1940s, the rise and standardization of (Techni) color—first in individual sequences and later across full-length productions—added new creative parameters. Lighting, set design, costume choices, and cinematography had to adjust to new technical requirements and evolving audience expectations (Hidalgo, 2018; Hilal, 2024; Hutson & Smith, 2025; Souto, 2007; Street, 2012). These early disruptions around sound and color share a common pattern: they introduced new sensory modalities into the cinematic experience and required filmmakers to retool both their equipment and their aesthetics.

From the late 1940s onward, the rise of television production significantly influenced and challenged traditional film practices (Belton, 1996; Boddy, 1985, 2021; Gomery, 1985b). The proliferation of television led to a decline in cinema attendance, prompting studios to innovate with widescreen formats (e.g., CinemaScope), color technologies, and spectacle-driven narratives to differentiate theatrical experiences from home viewing (Belton, 1985; Gleich, 2017). Television's serialized storytelling and rapid production cycles began to inform film production, particularly in genre cinema and independent filmmaking. The convergence of film and television industries became more pronounced as studios repurposed their facilities for television production and engaged in cross-media ventures (Boddy, 1985; Gleich, 2017; Gomery, 1985a). These shifts not only disrupted traditional studio operations but also laid the groundwork for hybrid production models that would evolve further in the digital era (Gleich, 2017; Hilmes, 1999).

A further major turning point was the introduction and widespread use of computer-generated imagery (CGI) from the late 1980s onward (Hutson & Smith, 2025; Rogers, 2013). Landmark productions such as *Jurassic Park* (1993) and *The Matrix* (1999) demonstrated how digital effects could shift the boundaries of visual storytelling. Parallel developments in digital cinematography, nonlinear editing systems, and digital distribution collectively reshaped the production pipeline (Hutson & Smith, 2025; Manovich, 2002; Mateer, 2014; Prince, 2011; Rodowick, 2009). These changes not only affected workflows from pre-visualization and shooting to post-production and distribution but also reorganized professional hierarchies (e.g., by enabling new forms of collaboration across remote teams) and cost structures. Once again, there was considerable impact on some segments of the workforce. For example, visual effects studios gained in influence, while traditional craft departments had to adapt or downscale (Banks, 2014; Caldwell, 2008). Notably though, these transformations emerged from within the film industry and were largely adopted incrementally.

The resurgence of stereoscopic 3D filmmaking (Zone, 2007) and the global success of *Avatar* (2009) sparked heavy investments in 3D production and exhibition as a strategy to revitalize theatrical attendance and differentiate cinematic experiences. Initially regarded as the future of film, 3D presented both creative and technical opportunities, particularly in immersive storytelling and visual spectacle (Rogers, 2013). However, it also brought challenges such as dual-camera setups, costly post-production, and inconsistent quality across releases (Azzarelli et al., 2024). While some films like *Life of Pi* (2012) and *Gravity* (2013) used the format to strong artistic effect, broader adoption waned as audience interest declined, and exhibitors struggled to justify the investment (Hutson & Smith, 2025). In retrospect, 3D can be seen as a transitional innovation that amplified visual engagement but failed to become a sustained industry standard.

The digital turn, accelerated from the early 2000s, restructured nearly every layer of the production pipeline, not only through the adoption of high-resolution sensors and digital workflows but also by altering organizational models. The shift catalyzed a move toward modular, cloud-integrated production structures where tasks could be decoupled and redistributed across, sometimes globally, dispersed teams. This modularity enabled greater scalability and flexibility but also introduced new coordination challenges and reinforced dependencies on platform-based service providers. With the introduction of advanced sensors (Thorpe, 2013), High Dynamic Range (HDR) and Wide Color Gamut (WCG) technologies (Kamada et al., 2020), and data-centric workflows (Mateer, 2014), film production evolved into a digital ecosystem that redefined industry standards and creative possibilities (Baumann, 2022; Kostovska et al., 2021). These shifts transformed professional roles: cinematographers became data wranglers, editors shifted toward real-time curation, and production schedules compressed due to instantaneous review capabilities (Clark et al., 2019; Ogden, 2018). Workflow optimization became a strategic concern, especially as new tools introduced both creative potential and standardization pressure.

Today, a plethora of emerging AI tools assist with tasks across the entire value creation system of film production and cinematography. In script development algorithms analyze structure, sentiment, and audience preferences (Cake, 2025; Taylor & Batty, 2024). In casting, databases and facial recognition can be used to match roles and actors, and in editing, software sorts footage and suggests cuts (Li et al., 2024). During production, AI is increasingly integrated into camera systems, motion control, and on-set decision support (Hilal, 2024). In post-production, AI supports color grading, special effects, dubbing, and facial manipulation—including controversial deep-fake applications (Azzarelli et al., 2024; Lees, 2024). In consequence, AI's increasing role across all functions of film production already entails a shift from tool to co-creator.

This current wave of disruption—arguably the most profound so far—is different in at least two respects. First, unlike earlier developments that were mostly endogenous to the film industry (e.g., optical sound, film stock), it is largely driven by advances in adjacent fields such as computer science, data analytics, machine learning, gaming, or social media. Second, the technologies involved—particularly AI—are not simply new specialty tools to be integrated into existing processes, but adaptive, learning-based systems that emulate or replicate aspects of human perception, decision-making, and creativity (McCosker & Wilken, 2020). This external influence brings with it new power dynamics, as major technology companies increasingly shape the future of cinematic production through proprietary platforms and algorithms. From a business model perspective, this shift affects how firms license, monetize, and scale their creative outputs. The rise of AI-driven content generation, predictive analytics, and platform dependencies reshapes value chains and alters cost structures, forcing companies to rethink how they capture value and maintain competitive advantage in increasingly platform-governed ecosystems (Baumann, 2022, 2024; Kostovska et al., 2021).

In summary, it can be said that the historical trajectory of film production and cinematography (visualized in Fig. 5.1) reveals a persistent tension between continuity and innovation. The emergence and integration of AI systems marks a significant inflection point, continuing the long-standing trend of technological disruption while introducing qualitatively new questions about the nature of creativity, authorship, and the role of the human in cinematic storytelling. As this chapter will show in the following sections, AI's impact in the film industry extends beyond technical innovation and process optimization. It is also strategic, influencing decision-making, value creation, and the organizational logic of film production.

5.2 Review of Relevant Literature and Existing Studies

The integration of AI into film production and cinematography has prompted a growing body of literature across disciplines, including media studies, media management, communication, innovation management, organizational theory, and platform economics. This literature increasingly focuses on the strategic, operational, and institutional implications of AI tools within film production ecosystems. As AI

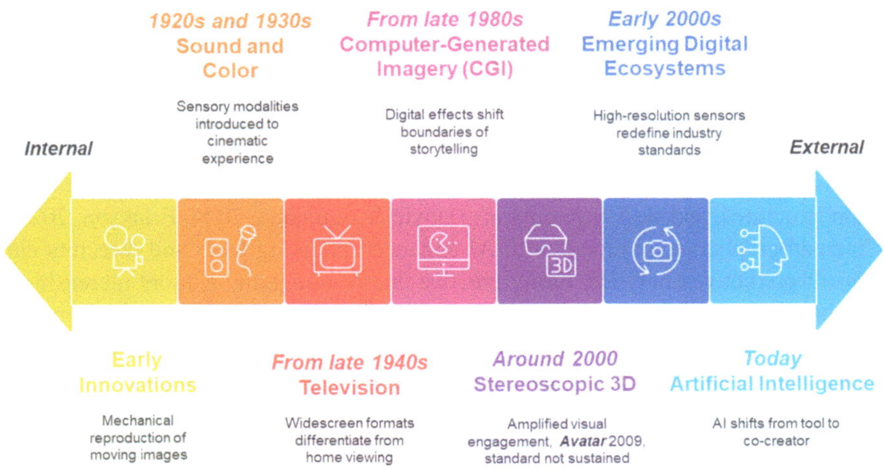

Fig. 5.1 Evolution of film technology

capabilities expand across the pre- to post-production spectrum, the literature is beginning to move from technological optimism to a more critical interrogation of value creation, labor restructuring, and platform dependencies (Robles & Tostes Vieira, 2024). This section reviews both academic literature and selected industry reports, focusing on insights that are particularly relevant from a management and strategy perspective. It identifies emerging themes, conceptual gaps, and areas where more applied research is needed to understand how AI is embedded in the structures, routines, and decision-making processes of contemporary film production and cinematography.

A growing body of empirical work documents the implementation of AI technologies across specific stages of film production (Derda, 2023). Recent studies by McCosker & Wilken (2020) or Jin (2024) describe applications such as AI-assisted camera tracking, script analysis (Cake, 2025), drone coordination (Pitas & Mademlis, 2022; Pueyo et al., 2024), and deep-learning models for facial modification and dialogue synthesis (Azzarelli et al., 2024). While these technologies are often introduced under the banner of productivity, time savings, or cost containment, adoption patterns in the industry are uneven. In addition, most studies still lack systematic analysis of decision rationales, organizational integration, and cross-project comparisons. Industry reports by Deloitte AI Institute (2023), Baumann et al. (2024) and European Audiovisual Observatory (2025) also emphasize efficiency benefits, but often gloss over resistance on the ground, where adoption is shaped by organizational culture, professional norms, and technical expertise. Academic scholars build on these topics and add contextual nuance by showing how adoption trajectories are shaped by funding models, client expectations, and platform interoperability (Cake, 2025; Robles & Tostes Vieira, 2024). Nevertheless, many of these studies remain descriptive; few examine how AI tools are embedded in decision routines, project management, or performance evaluation.

Literature on creative labor and organizational dynamics provides another important lens on the impact of AI technologies in the film industry. Traditional work on project-based industries (Banks, 2014; Baumann, 2013; Caldwell, 2008; Grabher, 2002; Lampel et al., 2000) offers a conceptual foundation for analyzing temporary, multi-skilled teams. More recent research has begun to document how AI changes creative hierarchies, reconfigures task boundaries, reshapes professional identities, team structures, and skill requirements (Doyle & Baumann, 2024; Erickson, 2024). Cinematographers experiment with AI-enhanced planning tools and directors can consult predictive analytics during creative decision-making. Editors increasingly rely on AI for first-pass cut or metadata tagging and that practice alters perceptions of skill and authorship surrounding the "digital craft" (Nieborg & Poell, 2018; Poell et al., 2023; van Dijck et al., 2019). Singh et al. (2023), for example, show how AI-supported casting systems introduce tensions between algorithmic objectivity and directorial intuition. Hutson & Smith (2025) have documented how editors and animators are increasingly asked to curate AI outputs rather than produce from scratch—raising questions about ownership, attribution, and tacit knowledge. Yet empirical research on how AI affects leadership roles, trust-building, or team cognition in creative environments remains rare. We still lack robust accounts of how AI affects coordination, leadership, or creative autonomy in production teams. In addition, there is considerable scope for cross-fertilization with organizational psychology and innovation capability literature.

Another fast-growing stream of literature addresses platformization and ecosystem formation, development, and governance (Baumann, 2022, 2024; Baumann & Leerhoff, 2022). As creative workflows become increasingly reliant on tools and infrastructures controlled by platform firms, film production is becoming part of a larger economy of so-called API (Application Programming Interface)-based service provision and platform-mediated coordination (Derda, 2023; Robles & Tostes Vieira, 2024). The dominance of vertically integrated or proprietary ecosystems raises questions about who sets standards for AI use, how creative inputs are monetized, and what forms of competitive advantage emerge (Reisinger & Lehner, 2022). This platform-centric lens on ecosystems is largely absent from traditional film studies and still underexplored in current research on AI in media production. Theoretical insights from (Helmond, 2015; van Dijck et al., 2018), and (Gillespie, 2014) are helpful in analyzing these dynamics, but there is a need to move beyond theory. Järventie-Thesleff et al. (2014) provide one of the few empirical studies of how two Nordic firms, albeit print publishers, manage platform dependencies in multi-channel environments. Innovative work in platform strategy and modular innovation could further illuminate how creative firms navigate pricing structures, interoperability, lock-in effects, and data asymmetries in AI-enhanced ecosystems.

Literature on business models and strategic positioning is also beginning to engage with AI's disruptive potential. This includes emerging research in strategic media management, which examines how media organizations realign their structures, investments, and strategic narratives in response to AI capabilities (S. Baumann, 2020, 2021). Building on (Teece, 2018) and (Amit & Han, 2017), recent work explores how firms reposition themselves within evolving value creation networks by incorporating AI into core and peripheral activities (Doshi et al., 2025; Maijanen, 2022). For example, AI is driving the development of adaptive marketing strategies, data-driven content ideation pipelines, and performance forecasting tools (Benner & Waldfogel, 2023; Orazi & Mannucci, 2024). Strategic media management perspectives highlight the interplay between technological experimentation and organizational sense-making, shedding light on how firms balance innovation with brand coherence, stakeholder expectations, and long-term resilience (Horst et al., 2019). However, these contributions remain underdeveloped in the film-specific literature. There is significant potential to apply this perspective to explore how studios, production houses, and distributors frame, scale, and institutionalize the use of AI tools as a source of strategic advantage (Baumann, 2020; Chan-Olmsted, 2019; Feher, 2024).

Ethical and legal aspects are addressed in a growing, but still rather fragmented body of work. Contributions by scholars such, for example, (Fitch III, 2022; Rosner, 2021) and by trade union reports following the 2023 Writers' Guild of America (WGA) and Screen Actors Guild-American Federation of Television and Radio Artists (SAG-AFTRA) negotiations begin to sketch out the contours of AI governance in creative industries. Issues include transparency of training data, consent for voice and likeness replication, and the assignment of creative credit in collaborative workflows. However, there remains a gap between normative guidance and implementation because more applied research on how these frameworks are implemented in production environments is needed, for example, how contracts are adapted, how risk is distributed across stakeholders, and how compliance is being monitored. Research from legal studies, media ethics, and compliance management could be better integrated into management and media studies to understand how governance regimes are operationalized in practice, especially in cross-border co-productions and platform-dominated value chains.

Overall, the existing literature offers a useful, but still partial foundation. Much of the academic work either focuses rather narrowly on specific settings or the application of particular tools (Feher, 2024). What is needed is a more integrative research agenda that brings together the micro-level realities of AI adoption with the macro-level transformations of platform-based ecosystem governance, business model innovation, and labor regulation. From a management perspective, there is particular need for research that links the adoption of AI technologies to questions of organizational capability, strategic positioning, and the transformation of professional practices. Building such a bridge would help move beyond binary narratives of disruption or resistance and contribute to a more differentiated understanding of the impact of AI technologies on the film industry.

5.3 Current Developments and Debates

Given the relative novelty of the field and the rapid pace of AI advancement, current debates revisit earlier, still unresolved discussions while also introducing new lines of contention. Ongoing topics relate particularly to how AI technologies are shaping the landscape of film production and cinematography, not only at a technical level but also in terms of workflows, business models, and the roles of creative professionals and organizations in a dispersed media business ecosystem. While AI-supported tools are no longer limited to experimental or independent projects, but are moving into mainstream, their adoption across commercial, high-end, and mainstream productions is uneven and contested. This section outlines current developments in the field, situates them in practice, and discusses the main lines of the ongoing and emerging debates.

5.3.1 AI in Production and Postproduction Workflows

A recurring topic is the integration of generative AI into preproduction and creative development (Swords & Willment, 2024). AI tools are being used for concept art, storyboarding, or visual world-building, but also met with criticism over reduced human artistic input (Hutson & Smith, 2025). For example, Netflix's short anime film *The Dog & The Boy* (2023) used AI-generated background imagery, prompting both admiration for its innovation and strong resistance toward the nonhuman creative output (Artnet News, 2023; Hutson & Smith, 2025). In script development, AI platforms are used to evaluate plot coherence and box office potential. At the same time, *The Last Screenwriter* (2024), a Swiss production written entirely by ChatGPT (swissfilms, 2024), has sparked international debate over the future of human-authored storytelling (The Guardian, 2024). *Pixar* and *DreamWorks* have reportedly begun integrating generative AI tools in internal ideation workflows, but union representatives have raised concerns that such tools could erode creative autonomy and become a long-term threat to authorship and narrative originality (The Authors Guild, 2023b; Scherer, 2023).

In production, AI is increasingly present in cinematography and performance capture. AI-assisted drones are now capable of executing complex aerial shots with minimal human input, particularly in action sequences and nature documentaries (Järventie-Thesleff et al., 2014; Kusuma & Azad, 2025; Pitas & Mademlis, 2022). The real-time AI-driven face-swapping technology used in Robert Zemeckis's *Here* (2024) allowed Tom Hanks and Robin Wright to appear across six decades of the characters' lives without traditional visual effects (Wired, 2024). *Metaphysic* CEO Thomas Graham sees the new AI technologies as a way to enhance human storytelling capabilities (Metaphysic.ai, 2024). Director Peter Jackson has similarly explored voice synthesis for the continuation of archival documentary storytelling (Rogerson, 2023). At the same time, industry voices warn of the implications for performance ownership. SAG-AFTRA Chief Negotiator Duncan Crabtree-Ireland emphasizes that AI must not appropriate an actor's likeness without consent (D'Alessandro, 2023). Production teams on large-scale sets like *The Mandalorian* have used AI-driven lighting systems in LED volume stages, enabling reactive adjustments based on camera movement and scene context which are now becoming standard practice (Azzarelli et al., 2024; Coldewey, 2020). While these tools offer precision and repeatability, camera operators and unions have voiced concerns about the erosion of skilled labor and reduced on-set teams (The Authors Guild, 2024).

Postproduction has arguably seen the most extensive integration of AI so far. AI tools automate labor-intensive processes in editing, color grading, and visual effects (VFX) (Azzarelli et al., 2024). For instance, AI-powered rotoscoping and frame interpolation were used in *Everything Everywhere All at Once* (2022), enabling a small VFX team to deliver blockbuster-quality work on a limited budget (Bharadkar, 2023). The film *The Brutalist* (2024) used voice enhancement technology from *Respeecher* to polish Hungarian-language dialogue. Editor Dávid Jancsó later commented "We should be having a very open discussion about what tools AI can provide us with" while director and co-writer Brady Corbet explained that the purpose of AI use was to modify Brody and Jones' Hungarian language dialogue "specifically to refine certain vowels and letters for accuracy …" in order to preserve the actors' original performances in another language (People.com, 2025). YouTube creators and short-form producers increasingly rely on tools for AI-driven voiceovers and cut-downs, while larger studios explore extensive cooperations with AI system providers that will incorporate their own training data (Arkenberg et al., 2025; DeGeurin, 2024).

5.3.2 Changing Job Roles and Professional Tensions

AI is not only transforming workflows, it is also changing the structure of job roles and professional identities (Doyle & Baumann, 2024; Erickson, 2024; World Economic Forum, 2023). Editors and VFX artists are increasingly expected to interface with AI tools, requiring new forms of literacy and training. The role of concept artists is evolving from execution to curation and prompt engineering. Meanwhile, AI is beginning to displace routine functions such as transcription, continuity checking, and background design (Erickson, 2024; Hutson & Smith, 2025; Williams et al., 2021). Again, these developments have prompted growing concern among industry professionals and unions. The 2023 Writers Guild of America (WGA) strike, alongside the SAG-AFTRA action, directly addressed the threat of AI-generated scripts and the use of synthetic performances. These strikes highlighted demands for contractual limits on AI use, protection of residuals, and the preservation of human authorship in film and television (Amankwah-Amoah et al., 2024; Holub, 2023; Oberting, 2024; Roddy, 2023).

Beyond immediate labor disputes, AI adoption is also reshaping how creative authority and decision-making are distributed across production teams. Tasks once delegated to senior professionals are increasingly assisted—or supplanted—by automated systems, which could undermine tacit knowledge and on-the-job mentorship structures (Doyle & Baumann, 2024). This is particularly evident in areas such as rough editing, sound balancing, and first-pass VFX rendering, where AI can prestructure work before human intervention. As a result, junior roles may evolve into tool supervisors or data validators, altering traditional career pathways (Gil et al., 2025). For freelancers and independent professionals, who already operate under precarious conditions, the shift toward AI-intensive production pipelines introduces new pressures to invest in technical upskilling and proprietary tools, often without institutional support (Abay et al., 2024).

Moreover, the redefinition of creative roles raises questions of attribution and credit (Dehdar, 2025; Gil et al., 2025). Union and guild representatives have voiced concerns that AI systems—especially when embedded in studio-owned software—can obscure the individual contributions of human workers, further marginalizing creative labor within increasingly corporatized production environments (The Authors Guild, 2023b; Oberting, 2024; Writers Guild of America, 2023). There is also a growing mismatch between emerging skill demands and formal education or training programs, which have yet to incorporate AI workflows at scale. This misalignment risks reinforcing inequalities between well-resourced professionals and those without access to ongoing digital training (Abay et al., 2024; Gil et al., 2025).

5.3.3 Strategic Shifts in Business Models and Market Structures

From a business perspective, AI is reshaping development and distribution strategies. Studios including Warner Bros. and Universal Pictures have adopted AI models to optimize trailer cuts and predict box office outcomes based on cast, script elements, genre, and release window combinations. These tools are used to guide greenlighting decisions, particularly in indie and co-production contexts. Disney has piloted adaptive trailer systems trained on emotional response mapping to localize content for global markets. However, executives have also voiced caution that reliance on AI-based decision support could lead to risk avoidance and missing out on opportunities (Arkenberg et al., 2025; IBM, 2025; PricewaterhouseCoopers, 2025; Witzel, 2023).

The timing of AI-related investments has become a critical strategic issue for film producers, particularly in project-based environments characterized by high uncertainty and limited margins for experimentation. While early adopters may benefit from competitive advantages such as faster turnaround times or differentiated visual aesthetics, they also face elevated risk due to the volatility of tool maturity, evolving legal frameworks, and unpredictable audience response (Arkenberg et al., 2025). This has led to cautious staging of investment, with firms piloting AI applications in lower-stakes phases such as animatics, background generation, or trailer production before scaling them to core workflows. Financing such initiatives can be complex, as traditional funding mechanisms—especially public subsidies and co-production agreements—are often not yet adapted to evaluate AI-enhanced productions (Arkenberg et al., 2025; PricewaterhouseCoopers, 2024). In the European context, for instance, producers report challenges in justifying software costs or cloud-based services within national funding schemes (Abay et al., 2024). At the same time, tech-oriented venture funds and private equity are beginning to explore opportunities in content-tech hybrids, leading to new forms of capital infusion that may prioritize scalability and Intellectual Property (IP) extraction over artistic risk-taking. This shift could accentuate power asymmetries between data-rich platform actors and traditional film producers, and consequently lead to calls for more targeted financing instruments tailored to AI-integrated creative production (PricewaterhouseCoopers, 2024).

The ongoing changes are also transforming business models. AI supports the emergence of more modular and decentralized production configurations, where tasks can be outsourced to AI-specialized vendors or cloud-based services. The platformization of creative infrastructure creates both opportunity and risk: it lowers entry barriers for small producers but also introduces dependencies on proprietary APIs, pricing schemes, and opaque algorithmic systems (Escudero Pérez, 2020; PricewaterhouseCoopers, 2024; Simon, 2024). Value creation increasingly depends on data access and the ability to orchestrate collaboration across technology vendors, rights holders, and production crews. The discussion about resulting business models evolves around topics such as blending creative IP development with ecosystem negotiation, data monetization, and medium- and long-tail revenue capture (Baumann & Leerhoff, 2022; Kostovska et al., 2021; Oberting, 2024).

The scale and structure of film organizations significantly influence their capacity to adopt AI technologies. Large studios and vertically integrated media companies typically possess the financial resources, proprietary data, and technical expertise to experiment with and internalize AI solutions. They often maintain dedicated data science teams or form strategic alliances with tech firms, giving them early access to emerging tools and the ability to train systems on proprietary content libraries (McCosker & Wilken, 2020). In contrast, SMEs—including many independent production houses—face barriers in terms of upfront investment, digital infrastructure, and access to scalable AI platforms. While cloud-based AI-as-a-service models could lower some entry thresholds, smaller firms are complaining about being locked into less customizable solutions and suffering from opaque pricing structures. These asymmetries raise concerns about widening competitive gaps, particularly as large firms increasingly monetize AI-generated assets through franchising, licensing, or adaptive localization, while smaller firms may struggle to retain creative control and sustainable margins (Nieborg & Poell, 2018; van Dijck et al., 2019). Moreover, the capacity to navigate evolving legal and ethical standards, such as those around synthetic actors (Dehdar, 2025; Yoong Hon, 2024) or algorithmic bias (Shin & Ahsan, 2025; Shin et al., 2022), is similarly uneven, potentially exposing SMEs to higher regulatory or reputational risk.

5.3.4 Ethical, Regulatory, and Inclusion Challenges

The most polarizing debates currently revolve around ownership, labor protections, and transparency. The Writers Guild of America's 2023 contract with the AMPTP prohibits AI from receiving writing credit or being used to revise human-written material without consent (The Authors Guild, 2023a, 2024; Writers Guild of America, 2023). SAG-AFTRA's agreement includes provisions requiring consent and fair compensation for digital replication of actors' voices and likenesses (Cranz, 2023). The German Federal Film Board (FFA) has yet to issue specific guidance on the funding eligibility of AI-assisted productions, creating uncertainty among producers (Lammar et al., 2025). Legal frameworks lag behind technological capabilities, and few jurisdictions have clear policies on the authorship or copyright status of AI-generated material. Enforcement remains particularly difficult in multinational productions, where standards vary and legal loopholes persist. A high-profile controversy arose around the documentary *Roadrunner: A Film About Anthony Bourdain* (2021), where AI was used to simulate Bourdain's voice without explicit disclosure. The backlash prompted calls for clearer ethical guidelines on synthetic performance (Coburn et al., 2022; Fitch III, 2022; Painter, 2022; Rosner, 2021).

Not surprisingly, sustainability, trust, and bias have also emerged as key concerns for AI implementation in film (Gil et al., 2025). Questions persist about the carbon footprint of training and running large-scale generative models, especially in energy-intensive post-production pipelines. In parallel, the opacity of algorithmic decision-making complicates trust among stakeholders, particularly when AI-generated outputs affect casting, funding, or distribution choices (Filimowicz, 2023; Hutson & Smith, 2025). Bias embedded in training data may reproduce or amplify existing stereotypes, leading to ethically problematic outputs that harm underrepresented groups (Gil et al., 2025; Shin & Ahsan, 2025; Shin et al., 2022). These risks underscore the importance of governance mechanisms, model audits, and inclusive data practices for building long-term legitimacy.

Directors and producers are also divided. While figures like James Cameron have advocated for AI to reduce production costs in blockbusters (IMDb, 2025), others such as actor and director Justine Bateman have publicly criticized the technology's potential to undermine artistic integrity and marginalize creative labor. Within studios, tension is growing between analytics teams pushing for AI-led efficiencies and creative leads defending more experimental or auteur-driven content (Deloitte AI Institute, 2023).

Academic debates mirror these tensions. Scholars from film and media studies (Gil et al., 2025; Manovich & Arielli, 2024) have analyzed how AI challenges established notions of authorship and visual grammar. Others argue that algorithmic generation alters the ontological status of the moving image itself (Heras & Chávez Heras, 2024; McCosker & Wilken, 2020). From a management and innovation perspective, researchers have examined the role of AI in strategic positioning and capability development (Jantunen et al., 2018; Randhawa et al., 2021; Yeow et al., 2018). Production studies foreground the negotiation between creative labor and automation (Banks, 2014; Caldwell, 2008), while platform scholars warn of growing training data provenance, platform dependencies, and the opacity of generative AI systems (Gillespie, 2014; Helmond, 2015; Simon, 2024; van Dijck et al., 2018) as well as slow emerging institutional responses and regulatory uncertainty (European Audiovisual Observatory, 2025; Sundar, 2020).

These critiques intersect with critical political economy approaches that question the redistribution of value within increasingly platformized creative ecosystems (Hesmondhalgh, 2019; Nieborg & Poell, 2018; Poell et al., 2023; van Dijck et al., 2019). These debates converge on a shared recognition: AI creates efficiencies and expands creative possibility, but it also shifts control, redistributes value appropriation as well as risk bearing, and introduces new dependencies. Consequently, the implementation of AI systems may not only be a matter of technological capability but also of institutional negotiation, professional adaptation, and strategic alignment.

These debates are particularly relevant from a management perspective, as firms must navigate the tension between innovation, creative integrity, and organizational legitimacy. AI does not enter a vacuum; it overlays a highly professionalized, globally networked, and commercially driven industry in which new technologies can rapidly become standard—but not without reinforcing structural asymmetries. As mentioned before, unlike previous disruptions that emerged organically within the sector, the current wave is largely driven by global technology firms operating at the intersection of media, software, and data. This shift raises important debates about control over infrastructure, creative agency, and the long-term implications for professional norms and cultural diversity. At the same time, AI's rise echoes earlier cycles of disruption—from sound and color to digital editing—each sparking both excitement and resistance. As in the past, its integration is challenging existing practices before becoming routinized within new standards of production.

5.4 Discussion and Areas for Future Research

The integration of AI into film production and cinematography is reconfiguring not only creative processes but also strategic decision-making, governance structures, and value creation mechanisms. As AI capabilities become increasingly embedded in core production workflows, new challenges emerge at the intersection of technological innovation, organizational capabilities, and institutional legitimacy. This section outlines priority areas for research, drawing on insights from strategic management, innovation studies, and organizational theory.

The move toward AI-assisted production has accelerated the formation of cross-functional teams, involving creatives, engineers, machine learning specialists, and legal advisors. These teams operate within what can be described as a hybrid organizational logic: they are tasked with aligning creative experimentation with scalable, data-driven efficiencies. This dynamic introduces new tensions between artistic autonomy and performance metrics. Strategic management research can contribute by examining how firms develop and govern these hybrid capabilities, how decision rights are allocated in AI-mediated workflows, and how organizational culture evolves in response to the integration of AI systems into core creative activities.

At the same time, the relationship between producers and audiences is being reshaped by predictive analytics and content customization tools. AI is increasingly used to simulate audience sentiment, automate trailer editing, and forecast performance across platforms. However, there is limited empirical understanding of how these technologies influence strategic choices in content development and distribution. Research is needed to assess the extent to which AI-driven audience modeling enhances or constrains creative risk-taking, and whether it leads to convergence around certain genre norms or aesthetics. From a management perspective, this invites questions about innovation ambidexterity—how firms balance the exploration of novel forms with the exploitation of proven formats in an AI-enhanced environment.

In parallel, platformization is a defining feature of the AI transformation in screen industries. AI tools for production, distribution, and marketing are increasingly embedded in larger digital ecosystems, where production firms interact with platform providers not just as customers, but as co-shapers of workflows, data policies, and creative boundaries. These collaborations that are often informal but structurally significant are central to how strategic dependencies form around access to proprietary models, training datasets, and integration services. As a result, the governance of production ecosystems is increasingly distributed, with platforms playing a coordinating role that influences who gets to innovate, at what cost, and under whose terms. These platforms do not merely provide technological infrastructure; they shape usage norms, set pricing structures, and mediate access to proprietary models and datasets. The resulting dependencies raise important strategic questions: How do firms manage lock-in effects? What bargaining power do production companies have in platform-mediated ecosystems? How does value appropriation shift when creative labor is routed through third-party AI systems? Research in platform strategy and media economics can shed light on these dynamics, including the reconfiguration of upstream and downstream value flows in AI-intensive environments.

The emergence of AI has also prompted a reconfiguration of business models in film production and cinematography. Traditional models centered around linear project development, controlled distribution windows, and centralized studio decision-making are giving way to more modular, data-driven, and networked configurations. AI technologies enable the monetization of micro-content, predictive licensing strategies, and medium- and long-tail exploitation through real-time content optimization. These shifts are often accompanied by new dependencies on external AI infrastructure, data suppliers, and monetization platforms. Future research should analyze how business models adapt in response to AI-mediated value creation, including the emergence of new monetization strategies such as subscription-based access to proprietary generative tools, and the resale or syndication of AI-augmented creative assets. Examples include production companies offering AI-generated concept art or pre-visualizations as standalone IP packages or service providers monetizing metadata outputs for downstream advertising optimization. These models point to a shift from traditional project financing to continuous, data-informed value extraction mechanisms within platform-dominated ecosystems, particularly in relation to cost structures, scalability, and control over data assets. This includes attention to how business models evolve in settings marked by infrastructure dependency, ecosystem fragmentation, and distributed IP rights.

A related and increasingly relevant area is the evolution of collaboration in geographically and institutionally dispersed ecosystems. AI-enabled production rarely occurs within a single firm; instead, it relies on interdependent workflows involving multiple actors—freelancers, postproduction vendors, AI service providers, and cloud infrastructure platforms. Cloud platform intermediaries not only host production pipelines but increasingly act as informal coordinators through their APIs, data access controls, and service contracts. These actors influence how workflows are modularized, how rights are negotiated, and how value is distributed. Their role in shaping coordination mechanisms, access hierarchies, and technical interoperability warrants closer investigation. Strategic questions arise around how creative workflows are orchestrated, how co-specialization and trust are sustained, and how ecosystem governance frameworks evolve to balance innovation incentives with IP protection. Theories of business ecosystems, relational contracting, and modular governance offer useful starting points for understanding these multi-actor environments.

AI is also often described as a democratizing force in the screen industries, particularly through the diffusion of low-cost or cloud-based tools for editing, voice synthesis, or image generation. Yet this narrative needs closer scrutiny. Platform dependency, data access, language bias, and intellectual property constraints continue to shape who can meaningfully participate in AI-driven production ecosystems. Future research should take a comparative lens to investigate regional and sectoral disparities in access and uptake, and assess the role of public policy, infrastructure, and intermediary organizations in enabling inclusive innovation. Innovation studies and development-oriented management research offer suitable conceptual frameworks for addressing these disparities in access to technological affordances and market visibility.

Ethical and regulatory considerations are becoming increasingly salient as AI systems are deployed to generate performances, voices, and likenesses. While industry standards are emerging through collective bargaining (e.g., SAG-AFTRA, WGA) and voluntary guidelines, there is no consistent international framework governing the use of AI in media production. Management research has an important role to play in evaluating how firms navigate regulatory ambiguity, how they implement internal governance for AI deployment, and how ethical considerations are translated into operational protocols. The interface between compliance, brand risk management, and stakeholder legitimacy in AI-intensive environments remains underexplored.

In sum, AI technologies are not simply a set of tools integrated into film production; they are enabling general-purpose technologies that interact with firm strategy, organizational routines, platform structures, and industry boundaries. Future research should move beyond descriptive accounts and focus on theorizing the mechanisms by which AI alters coordination, control, and value appropriation in creative organizations. This includes understanding how capabilities are built or reconfigured, how risk and uncertainty are managed, how business models evolve under conditions of infrastructure dependency, and how firms respond to institutional pressures as AI adoption scales. Addressing these issues will require interdisciplinary collaboration, methodological pluralism, and sustained engagement with practitioners and regulators across the media value chain.

5.5 Conclusion

This chapter has examined the far-reaching implications of AI in film production and cinematography, focusing on its evolving role across preproduction, shooting, post-production, and distribution. AI is not only altering technical workflows but also reshaping professional roles, industry practices, and business models. From generative tools for storyboarding to AI-enhanced color grading and automated trailer generation, examples across global production contexts reveal a complex interplay of innovation, adaptation, and resistance.

We have highlighted how job profiles are changing, with editors, VFX artists, and concept designers increasingly expected to engage with AI tools, often through new skill sets such as prompt engineering or data curation. Meanwhile, roles once considered secure—like screenwriters or performers—are being redefined through synthetic performance and machine-generated text. These shifts have triggered labor responses such as the 2023 WGA and SAG-AFTRA strikes, which demanded protections for creative labor and limits on unregulated AI use. The resulting agreements introduced foundational safeguards but also signaled broader tensions around authorship, agency, and long-term sustainability.

AI is also accelerating platformization, making creative work more dependent on cloud-based infrastructures, proprietary APIs, and closed training datasets. These developments raise questions of governance and control. Business models are evolving in tandem—away from linear value chains toward modular, networked ecosystems that rely on data flows, algorithmic performance metrics, and cross-organizational collaboration. Empirical cases across North America, Europe, Asia, and Latin America illustrate how adoption trajectories are shaped by infrastructure access, funding conditions, and regulatory frameworks.

Across all developments, persistent tensions remain: AI enhances speed and scale but comes with issues around sustainability and trust and also introduces new asymmetries in power, risk, and reward. The challenge for researchers, practitioners, and policymakers is to engage with AI as more than a tool—as a systemic force that reshapes creative, economic, and ethical norms. This demands interdisciplinary approaches capable of tracing how AI affects not only production efficiency but also cultural legitimacy, labor equity, and artistic identity.

The future of AI in film production will not be determined by technology alone. It will hinge on the choices made by institutions, regulators, creative professionals, and technology providers. These choices will influence whether AI enables broader access, richer storytelling, and sustainable innovation—or whether it entrenches existing hierarchies and commodifies creativity. Harnessing AI's potential in this sector means building institutional capacity, supporting inclusive experimentation, and codifying professional norms that center human creativity as a core value, not a dispensable cost.

References

Abay, F., Bengesser, C., Damásio, M. J., Frühmorgen, T., Ibrus, I., Kostovska, I., Langgaard, K., Nielsen, J. I., O'Leary, N., Olesen, J., Rohn, U., Saluveer, S.-K., Materska-Samek, M., Talvik, R. J., & Zemaityte, V. (2024). *State of European Film: An overview of key industry trends, insights, and policy recommendations for the European Film and Audiovisual industry*. https://kultura.irmo.hr/wp-content/uploads/2025/03/crescine-state-of-european-film.pdf?

Altman, R. (2004). Films that Talk. In R. Altman (Ed.), *Silent film sound* (pp. 157–178). Columbia University Press.

Amankwah-Amoah, J., Abdalla, S., Mogaji, E., Elbanna, A., & Dwivedi, Y. K. (2024). The impending disruption of creative industries by generative AI: Opportunities, challenges, and research agenda. *International Journal of Information Management, 79*, 102759. https://doi.org/10.1016/j.ijinfomgt.2024.102759

Amit, R., & Han, X. (2017). Value creation through novel resource configurations in a digitally enabled world. *Strategic Entrepreneurship Journal, 11*(3), 228–242. https://doi.org/10.1002/sej.1256

Arkenberg, C., Ledger, D., Franks, R., & Westcott, K. (2025). *Large studios will likely take their time adopting generative AI for content creation. Social media isn't hesitating*. https://www2.deloitte.com/us/en/insights/industry/technology/technology-media-and-telecom-predictions/2025/tmt-predictions-hollywood-cautious-of-genai-adoption.html

Artnet News. (Ed.). (2023). *Netflix japan is drawing Ire for Using A.I. to generate the background art of its new anime short | Artnet News*. https://news.artnet.com/art-world/netflix-japan-ai-anime-dog-and-boy-2251247

Azzarelli, A., Anantrasirichai, N., & Bull, D. R. (2024, May 8). *Reviewing intelligent cinematography: AI research for camera-based video production 2024*, arXiv.org.

Banks, M. (2014). Craft labour and creative industries. *Creativity and Cultural Policy*, 75–91.

Baumann, S. (2013). Adapting to the brave new world: Innovative organisational strategies for media companies. In *Media innovations: A multidisciplinary study of change* (pp. 77–92). Nordicom, University of Gothenburg.

Baumann, S. (2020). Guest editor's introduction: Strategic media management at a junction. *Journal of Media Business Studies, 17*(1), 1–12. https://doi.org/10.1080/16522354.2020.1740564

Baumann, S. (2021). Media management and business: Old vs. new. In M. Mahoney & T. Tang (Eds.), *The handbook of media management and business* (pp. 407–425). Rowman & Littlefield.

Baumann, S. (2022). Introduction to the handbook on digital business ecosystems: Strategies, platforms, technologies, governance and societal challenges. In S. Baumann (Ed.), *Research handbooks in business and management series. Handbook on digital business ecosystems: Strategies, platforms, technologies, governance and societal challenges* (pp. 1–9). Edward Elgar Publishing. https://doi.org/10.4337/9781839107191.00005

Baumann, S. (2024). Introduction to the handbook on digital platforms and business ecosystems in manufacturing. In S. Baumann (Ed.), *Research handbooks in business and management. Handbook on digital platforms and ecosystems in manufacturing* (pp. 1–8). Edward Elgar Publishing. https://doi.org/10.4337/9781035301003.00005

Baumann, S., & Leerhoff, M. (2022). Networks, platforms, and digital business ecosystems: Mapping the development of a field. In S. Baumann (Ed.), *Research handbooks in business and management series. Handbook on digital business ecosystems: Strategies, platforms, technologies, governance and societal challenges* (pp. 11–24). Edward Elgar Publishing. https://doi.org/10.4337/9781839107191.00007

Baumann, M., Bayer, J., Burri, M., Campus, G., Cole, M., Farish, K., Hacker, P., Migliore, E., Nordemann, J. B., Radel-Corman, J., Schmitz-Berndt, S., & van der Sloot, B. (2024). *AI and the audiovisual sector: Navigating the current legal landscape*. European Audiovisual Observatory. https://rm.coe.int/iris-2024-3-ia-legal-landscape/1680b1e999.

Belton, J. (1985). Technology and aesthetics of film sound. *Film sound: Theory and practice*, 63–72.

Belton, J. (1996). The 1950s and Beyond. *Film History, 8*(2), 107. https://www.proquest.com/scholarly-journals/1950s-beyond/docview/1300225516/se-2?accountid=10833
Benner, M. J., & Waldfogel, J. (2023). Changing the channel: Digitization and the rise of "middle tail" strategies. *Strategic Management Journal, 44*(1), 264–287. https://doi.org/10.1002/smj.3130
Bharadkar, P. (2023). *Everything everywhere all at once: How AI is revolutionizing filmmaking*. https://medium.com/@TheTechTrailblazer/everything-everywhere-all-at-once-how-ai-is-revolutionizing-filmmaking-173bf19d32be
Boddy, W. (1985). The studios move into prime time: Hollywood and the television industry in the 1950s. *Cinema Journal, 24*(4), 23–37. https://www.proquest.com/scholarly-journals/studios-move-into-prime-time-hollywood-television/docview/1298008122/se-2?accountid=10833
Boddy, W. (2021). Revisiting postwar theater television. *Media Industries Journal, 7*(2). https://doi.org/10.3998/mij.15031809.0007.201
Cake, S. (2025). Artificial intelligence as a collaborative tool for script development. *Media Practice and Education, 1–16*. https://doi.org/10.1080/25741136.2025.2454074
Caldwell, J. T. (2008). *Production culture: Industrial reflexivity and critical practice in film and television. Console-ing passions*. Duke University Press. https://doi.org/10.1215/9780822388968
Chan-Olmsted, S. M. (2019). A review of artificial intelligence adoptions in the media industry. *International Journal on Media Management, 21*(3-4), 193–215. https://doi.org/10.1080/14241277.2019.1695619
Clark, C., Reisner, D., Stump, D., Bennett, B., Holben, J., Korosi, J., Rodli, E., Zell, J., Mandle, G., Eklund, D., Demos, G., Ciaccio, G., Kang, T., Houston, J., Lude, P., Morin, D., Goi, M., Sanders, M., & Wall, W. T. (2019). American society of cinematographers motion imaging technology council progress report 2019. *SMPTE Motion Imaging Journal, 128*(8), 26–51. https://doi.org/10.5594/JMI.2019.2924814
Coburn, C., Williams, K., & Stroud, S. R. (2022). Enhanced realism or A.I.-generated illusion? Synthetic voice in the documentary film roadrunner. *Journal of Media Ethics, 37*(4), 282–284. https://doi.org/10.1080/23736992.2022.2113883
Coldewey, D. (2020). *How 'The Mandalorian' and ILM invisibly reinvented film and TV production | TechCrunch*. https://techcrunch.com/2020/02/20/how-the-mandalorian-and-ilm-invisibly-reinvented-film-and-tv-production/
Cranz, A. (2023). *The new WGA contract will change how Hollywood works*. https://www.theverge.com/2023/9/26/23891835/wga-contract-summary-ai-streaming-data
D'Alessandro, A. (2023). *SAG-AFTRA's Duncan Crabtree-Ireland emphasizes need for "Informed Consent" to protect actors from AI Abuse – Comic-Con*. https://deadline.com/2023/07/comic-con-actors-strike-duncan-crabtree-ireland-1235444992/
DeGeurin, M. (2024). *What a major movie studio's AI deal could mean for the future of Hollywood*. https://www.popsci.com/technology/what-lionsgate-ai-deal-means/?
Dehdar, F. (2025). *Copyright and AI-generated works*. SSRN. https://papers.ssrn.com/sol3/papers.cfm?abstract_id=5182360 https://doi.org/10.2139/ssrn.5182360
Deloitte AI Institute (Ed.). (2023). *Media's AI muse creativity in the age of generative models*. https://www2.deloitte.com/us/en/pages/consulting/articles/generative-ai-media-production.html
Derda, I. (2023). "Did you know that David Beckham speaks nine languages?": AI-supported production process for enhanced personalization of audio-visual content. *Creative Industries Journal, 16*(3), 265–280. https://doi.org/10.1080/17510694.2021.2025001
Doshi, A. R., Bell, J. J., Mirzayev, E., & Vanneste, B. S. (2025). Generative artificial intelligence and evaluating strategic decisions. *Strategic Management Journal, 46*(3), 583–610. https://doi.org/10.1002/smj.3677
Doyle, G., & Baumann, S. (2024). *AI: A cure for Baumol's disease? CREATe*. Advance online publication. https://doi.org/10.5281/ZENODO.13167298.
Erickson, K. (2024). AI and work in the creative industries: Digital continuity or discontinuity? *Creative Industries Journal, 1–21*. https://doi.org/10.1080/17510694.2024.2421135

Escudero Pérez, J. (2020). "An AI doesn't need a gender" (but it's still assigned one): Paradigm shift of the artificially created woman in film. *Feminist Media Studies, 20*(3), 325–340. https://doi.org/10.1080/14680777.2019.1615973

European Audiovisual Observatory (Ed.). (2025). *Key trends 2025: Television, cinema, video and on-demand audiovisual services: The Pan-European picture*. https://search.coe.int/observatory?i=0900001680b4e91d

Feher, K. (2024). Exploring AI media. Definitions, conceptual model, research agenda. *Journal of Media Business Studies, 21*(4), 340–363. https://doi.org/10.1080/16522354.2024.2340419

Filimowicz, M. (Ed.). (2023). *Algorithms and society. AI and the future of creative work: Algorithms and society*. Routledge Taylor & Francis Group. https://www.taylorfrancis.com/books/9781003299875. https://doi.org/10.4324/9781003299875

Fitch, J. C., III. (2022). When AI breaks audience trust - Neville's "Roadrunner: A film about Anthony Bourdain". *Journal of Media Ethics, 37*(4), 293–295. https://doi.org/10.1080/23736992.2022.2113884

Gil, R., Ravid, S. A., & Sorenson, O. (2025). Talent and technology in creative industries: Introduction to the special issue. *Journal of Cultural Economics*. Advance online publication. https://doi.org/10.1007/s10824-025-09543-3.

Gillespie, T. (2014). The relevance of algorithms. In T. Gillespie, P. J. Boczkowski, & K. A. Foot (Eds.), *Inside technology. Media technologies: Essays on communication, materiality, and society* (pp. 167–194). The MIT Press. https://doi.org/10.7551/mitpress/9780262525374.003.0009

Gleich, J. (2017). *American Film since 1945*. Oxford Research Encyclopedia of American History. https://oxfordre.com/americanhistory/view/10.1093/acrefore/9780199329175.001.0001/acrefore-9780199329175-e-390

Gomery, D. (1985a). The coming of television and the 'lost' motion picture audience. *Journal of Film and Video*, 5–11.

Gomery, D. (1985b). Theatre Television: The missing link of technological change in the U.S. Motion Picture Industry. *The Velvet Light Trap, 21*, 54–61. https://www.proquest.com/scholarly-journals/theatre-television-missing-link-technological/docview/1306636396/se-2?accountid=10833

Grabher, G. (2002). The project ecology of advertising: Tasks, talents and teams. *Regional Studies, 36*(3), 245–262.

Hediger, V. (2018). Can we have the cave and leave it too? On the meaning of cinema as technology. In S. Hidalgo (Ed.), *When did cinema become cinema? Technology, history, and the moving pictures* (pp. 213–238). https://doi.org/10.5117/9789089647542/ch09.

Helmond, A. (2015). The Platformization of the Web: Making Web Data Platform Ready. *Social Media + Society, 1*(2), Article 2056305115603080. https://doi.org/10.1177/2056305115603080.

Heras, D. C., & Chávez Heras, D. (2024). *Cinema and Machine Vision // Cinema and machine vision: Artificial intelligence, aesthetics and spectatorship*. Edinburgh University Press.

Hesmondhalgh, D. (2019). *The cultural industries* (4th ed.). Sage.

Hidalgo, S. (2018). The discursive spaces between a history of film technology and technological experience. In S. Hidalgo (Ed.), *When did cinema become cinema? Technology, history, and the moving pictures* (pp. 13–30).

Hilal, R. (2024). Artificial intelligence systems impact on film sets in the 21st century. *International Design Journal, 14*(4), 319–326. https://doi.org/10.21608/idj.2024.357883

Hilmes, M. (1999). *Hollywood and broadcasting: From radio to cable*. University of Illinois Press.

Holub, C. (2023). *SAG-AFTRA officially ratifies new contract*. https://ew.com/sag-aftra-officially-ratifies-new-contract-after-membership-vote-8411375.

Horst, S.-O., Järventie-Thesleff, R., & Baumann, S. (2019). The practice of shared inquiry: How actors manage for strategy emergence. *Journal of Media Business Studies, 16*(3), 202–229. https://doi.org/10.1080/16522354.2019.1641672

Hutson, J., & Smith, A. (2025). *Cinematic algorithms*. CRC Press. https://doi.org/10.1201/9781003601128

IBM. (2025). *The CEO's guide to generative AI: Risk management: Manage unpredictable risks*. https://www.ibm.com/thought-leadership/institute-business-value/en-us/report/ceo-generative-ai/ceo-ai-risk-management?
IMDb. (Ed.). (2025). *James Cameron Says AI could save blockbusters—Without cutting jobs - IMDb*. IMDb. https://www.imdb.com/de/news/ni65226836/
Jantunen, A., Tarkiainen, A., Chari, S., & Oghazi, P. (2018). Dynamic capabilities, operational changes, and performance outcomes in the media industry. *Journal of Business Research, 89*, 251–257. https://doi.org/10.1016/j.jbusres.2018.01.037
Järventie-Thesleff, R., Moisander, J., & Villi, M. (2014). The strategic challenge of continuous change in multi-platform media organizations—A strategy-as-practice perspective. *International Journal on Media Management, 16*(3-4), 123–138. https://doi.org/10.1080/14241277.2014.919920
Jin, D. Y. (2024). AI in cultural production in the Korean cultural industries. *Telematics and Informatics Reports, 13*, 100113. https://doi.org/10.1016/j.teler.2023.100113
Kamada, Y., Sanjo, Y., McFarlin, N., & Thorpe, L. (2020). New technologies that further empower digital cinematography. In *SMPTE 2020 annual technical conference and exhibition. Symposium conducted at the meeting of IEEE.*
Katmer, G. (2022). Teknolojik Bir Aygt Olarak Kamerann KeSinemann DoDIncelemesi. *Medeniyet Sanat Dergisi, 8*(2), 229–252. https://doi.org/10.46641/medeniyetsanat.1189378
Kostovska, I., Raats, T., Donders, K., & Ballon, P. (2021). Going beyond the hype: Conceptualising "media ecosystem" for media management research. *Journal of Media Business Studies, 18*(1), 6–26. https://doi.org/10.1080/16522354.2020.1765668
Kusuma, K. S., & Azad, V. (2025). Filming with drones: Is AI the new filmmaker? *Media Practice and Education, 1–12*. https://doi.org/10.1080/25741136.2025.2478493
Lammar, D., Horst, M., & Müller, R. (2025). AI in the German Media: Narratives of AI-in-particular and AI-in-general in German media reporting about artificial intelligence. *Digital Journalism, 1–19*. https://doi.org/10.1080/21670811.2025.2493759
Lampel, J., Lant, T., & Shamsie, J. (2000). Balancing act: Learning from organizing practices in cultural industries. *Organization Science, 11*(3), 263–269.
Lees, D. (2024). Deepfakes in documentary film production: Images of deception in the representation of the real. *Studies in Documentary Film, 18*(2), 108–129. https://doi.org/10.1080/17503280.2023.2284680
Li, Y., Xu, H., Cai, F., & Tian, F. (2024). Improving AI-assisted video editing: Optimized footage analysis through multi-task learning. *Neurocomputing, 609*, 128485. https://doi.org/10.1016/j.neucom.2024.128485
Maijanen, P. (2022). Digital business ecosystems and dynamic capabilities. In S. Baumann (Ed.), *Research handbooks in business and management series. Handbook on digital business ecosystems: Strategies, platforms, technologies, governance and societal challenges* (pp. 50–62). Edward Elgar Publishing. https://doi.org/10.4337/9781839107191.00010
Manovich, L. (2002). The language of new media. *Canadian Journal of Communication*, *27*(1), Article cjc.2002v27n1a1280. 10.22230/cjc.2002v27n1a1280.
Manovich, L., & Arielli, E. (2024). *Artificial aesthetics*. https://manovich.net/index.php/projects/artificial-aesthetics.
Mateer, J. (2014). Digital cinematography: Evolution of craft or revolution in production? *Journal of Film and Video, 66*(2), 3–14. https://doi.org/10.5406/JFILMVIDEO.66.2.0003
McCosker, A., & Wilken, R. (2020). *Automating vision: The social impact of the new camera consciousness*. Routledge.
Metaphysic.ai (Ed.). (2024). *LinkedIn post: Tom Graham on the future of storytelling*. https://www.linkedin.com/posts/metaphysic-ai_tom-graham-on-the-future-of-storytelling-activity-7132134363202252801-qRIn/
Musser, C. (2018). When did cinema become cinema? Technology, history, and the moving pictures. In S. Hidalgo (Ed.), *When did cinema become cinema? Technology, history, and the moving pictures* (pp. 33-50).

Nieborg, D. B., & Poell, T. (2018). The platformization of cultural production: Theorizing the contingent cultural commodity. *New Media and Society, 20*(11), 4275–4292. https://doi.org/10.1177/1461444818769694

O'Brien, C. (2018). Film analysis and statistics: A field report. In S. Hidalgo (Ed.), *When did cinema become cinema? Technology, history, and the moving pictures* (pp. 149–168).

Oberting, V. A. (2024). Generative artificial intelligence and copyright in the film and media industry. *Washington and Lee Law Review Online, 82*(2), 123. https://scholarlycommons.law.wlu.edu/wlulr-online/vol82/iss2/2/

Ogden, M. R. (2018). Cinema technologies. In A. E. Grant & J. H. Meadows (Eds.), *Communication technology update and fundamentals* (16th ed., pp. 117–147). Routledge. https://doi.org/10.4324/9780203702871-10

Orazi, D. C., & Mannucci, P. V. (2024). Disentangling audiences' reactions to creative content and creative packaging. *Strategic Management Journal, 45*(13), 2763–2790. https://doi.org/10.1002/smj.3649

Painter, C. (2022). Enhanced realism or A.I.-generated illusion? Synthetic voice in the documentary film roadrunner. *Journal of Media Ethics, 37*(4), 296–297. https://doi.org/10.1080/23736992.2022.2113885

People.com (Ed.). (2025). *'The Brutalist' director says Adrien Brody and Felicity Jones' 'Performances are completely their own' after facing AI backlash.* https://people.com/brutalist-director-adrien-brody-felicity-jones-ai-backlash-8777448

Petrie, D. J. (1996). *The British cinematographer* (Vol. 34). American Library Association; British Film Institute. https://doi.org/10.5860/choice.34-3779

Pitas, I., & Mademlis, I. (2022). Autonomous UAV cinematography. In *Proceedings of the 30th ACM international conference on multimedia.* ACM. https://doi.org/10.1145/3503161.3546970.

Poell, T., Nieborg, D. B., & Duffy, B. E. (2023). Spaces of negotiation: Analyzing platform power in the news industry. *Digital Journalism, 11*(8), 1391–1409. https://doi.org/10.1080/21670811.2022.2103011

PricewaterhouseCoopers. (2024). *Perspectives: Global entertainment & media outlook 2024–2028: Seizing growth opportunities in a dynamic ecosystem.* https://www.pwc.com/gx/en/issues/business-model-reinvention/outlook/insights-and-perspectives.html

PricewaterhouseCoopers. (2025). *PwC's 28th annual global CEO survey: Reinvention on the edge of tomorrow.* https://www.pwc.com/gx/en/issues/c-suite-insights/ceo-survey.html

Prince, S. (2011). *Digital visual effects in cinema: The seduction of reality.* Rutgers University Press.

Pueyo, P., Dendarieta, J., Montijano, E., Murillo, A. C., & Schwager, M. (2024, January 10). *CineMPC: A fully autonomous drone cinematography system incorporating zoom, focus, pose, and scene composition.* http://arxiv.org/pdf/2401.05272

Randhawa, K., Wilden, R., & Gudergan, S. (2021). How to innovate toward an ambidextrous business model? The role of dynamic capabilities and market orientation. *Journal of Business Research, 130*, 618–634. https://doi.org/10.1016/j.jbusres.2020.05.046

Reisinger, S., & Lehner, J. M. (2022). Dealing with strategic tensions in digital business ecosystems. In S. Baumann (Ed.), *Research handbooks in business and management series. Handbook on digital business ecosystems: Strategies, platforms, technologies, governance and societal challenges.* Edward Elgar Publishing. https://doi.org/10.4337/9781839107191.00011

Robles, M. M., & Tostes Vieira, M. L. (2024). Co-creation of value in a cultural organizations' ecosystem. *Creative Industries Journal, 1–30.* https://doi.org/10.1080/17510694.2024.2411940

Roddy, S. (2023). Creative machine-human collaboration: Toward a cybernetic approach to artificial intelligence and machine learning techniques in the creative arts. In M. Filimowicz (Ed.), *Algorithms and society. AI and the future of creative work: Algorithms and society.* Routledge Taylor & Francis Group.

Rodowick, D. N. (2009). *The virtual life of film.* Harvard University Press.

Rogers, A. (2013). *Cinematic appeals: The experience of new movie technologies.* Columbia University Press.

Rogerson, B. (2023). *Is now and then really the 'last' Beatles song? Get Back director Peter Jackson says it's "conceivable" that more could be made with the help of AI*. https://www.musicradar.com/news/peter-jackson-beatles-ai
Rosner, H. (2021). *The ethics of a Deepfake Anthony Bourdain voice*. https://www.newyorker.com/culture/annals-of-gastronomy/the-ethics-of-a-deepfake-anthony-bourdain-voice
Scherer, M. (2023). *New WGA labor agreement gives Hollywood writers important protections in the era of AI*. https://cdt.org/insights/new-wga-labor-agreement-gives-hollywood-writers-important-protections-in-the-era-of-ai/
Shin, D., & Ahsan, A. (2025). How do people decide whether to trust information from generative AI? The effects of transparency on trust in and evaluation of a generated content. *Journal of Media Business Studies, 1–24*. https://doi.org/10.1080/16522354.2025.2509060
Shin, D., Hameleers, M., Park, Y. J., Kim, J. N., Trielli, D., Diakopoulos, N., Helberger, N., Lewis, S. C., Westlund, O., & Baumann, S. (2022). Countering algorithmic bias and disinformation and effectively harnessing the power of AI in media. *Journalism and Mass Communication Quarterly, 99*(4), 887–907. https://doi.org/10.1177/10776990221129245
Simon, F. M. (2024). Escape me if you can: How AI reshapes news organisations' dependency on platform companies. *Digital Journalism, 12*(2), 149–170. https://doi.org/10.1080/21670811.2023.2287464
Singh, H., Kaur, K., & Singh, P. P. (2023). Artificial intelligence as a facilitator for film production process. In S. P. Yadav (Ed.), *2023 International conference on artificial intelligence and smart communication (AISC): 27-29 January 2023, G.L. Bajaj Institute of Technology and Management, Greater Noida, India* (pp. 969–972). IEEE. https://doi.org/10.1109/AISC56616.2023.10085082
Souto, H. M. R. (2007). *Motion picture photography: A history, 1891-1960 / H.* Mario Raimondo-Souto.
Street, S. (2012). *Colour films in Britain: The negotiation of innovation 1900 - 55*. Palgrave Macmillan.
Sundar, S. S. (2020). Rise of machine agency: A framework for studying the psychology of human–AI Interaction (HAII). *Journal of Computer-Mediated Communication, 25*(1), 74–88. https://doi.org/10.1093/jcmc/zmz026
swissfilms. (Ed.). (2024). *The last screenwriter*. https://www.swissfilms.ch/de/movie/the-last-screenwriter/33c670f42f0c4821b8a39807f8dd8a15
Swords, J., & Willment, N. (2024). 'It used to be fix-it in post production! Now it's fix-it in pre-production': How virtual production is changing production networks in film and television. *Creative Industries Journal, 1–17*. https://doi.org/10.1080/17510694.2024.2430025
Taylor, S., & Batty, C. (2024). One for the team: Understanding individual and collaborative pursuits of script development across competing discourses. *Creative Industries Journal, 17*(1), 157–168. https://doi.org/10.1080/17510694.2022.2065782
Teece, D. J. (2018). Business models and dynamic capabilities. *Long Range Planning, 51*(1), 40–49. https://doi.org/10.1016/j.lrp.2017.06.007
The Authors Guild. (2023a, June 8). *AG introduces new publishing agreement clauses concerning AI - The authors guild*. https://authorsguild.org/news/ag-introduces-new-publishing-agreement-clauses-concerning-ai/.
The Authors Guild. (2023b, September 28). *WGA agreement introduces key protections for TV and film writers against AI - The authors guild*. https://authorsguild.org/news/wga-agreement-introduces-key-protections-for-tv-and-film-writers-against-ai/
The Authors Guild. (2024). *SAG-AFTRA agreement establishes important safeguards for actors around AI use - The Authors Guild*. https://authorsguild.org/news/sag-aftra-agreement-establishes-important-ai-safeguards/
The Guardian. (2024, June 20). London premiere of movie with AI-generated script cancelled after backlash. *The Guardian*. https://www.theguardian.com/film/article/2024/jun/20/premiere-movie-ai-generated-script-cancelled-backlash-the-last-screenwriter-prince-charles-cinema
Thorpe, L. J. (2013). New optical and image sensor technologies for high-resolution digital cinematography. *SMPTE Motion Imaging Journal, 122*(2), 33–41. https://doi.org/10.5594/J18267XY

van Dijck, J., Poell, T., & de Waal, M. (2018). *The platform society: Public values in a connective world*. Oxford University Press.
van Dijck, J., Nieborg, D., & Poell, T. (2019). Reframing platform power. *Internet. Policy Review, 8*(2), 1–18. https://doi.org/10.14763/2019.2.1414
Williams, P., McDonald, P., & Mayes, R. (2021). The impact of disruptive innovation on creative workers: The case of photographers. *Creative Industries Journal, 14*(2), 130–151. https://doi.org/10.1080/17510694.2020.1858707
Wired. (Ed.). (2024). *The $50 million movie 'Here' de-aged Tom Hanks with Generative AI*. https://www.wired.com/story/here-movie-de-age-tom-hanks-generative-ai/
Witzel, M. (2023). *The greatest AI risk could be opportunities missed*. Centre for International Governance Innovation (CIGI). https://www.cigionline.org/articles/the-greatest-ai-risk-could-be-opportunities-missed/?
World Economic Forum (Ed.). (2023). *How will generative AI change creative jobs?* https://www.weforum.org/stories/2023/05/generative-ai-creative-jobs/
Writers Guild of America. (2023). *Summary of the 2023 WGA MBA*. https://www.wga.org/contracts/contracts/mba/summary-of-the-2023-wga-mba
Yeow, A., Soh, C., & Hansen, R. (2018). Aligning with new digital strategy: A dynamic capabilities approach. *The Journal of Strategic Information Systems, 27*(1), 43–58. https://doi.org/10.1016/j.jsis.2017.09.001
Yoong Hon, L. (2024). Hollywood's current game plan: It's the IP and not the actor. *Journal of Media Business Studies, 21*(2), 133–145. https://doi.org/10.1080/16522354.2023.2300013
Zone, R. (2007). *Stereoscopic cinema and the origins of 3-D film, 1838-1952*. University Press of Kentucky.

Sabine Baumann is Professor of Digital Business at Berlin School of Economics and Law and Scientific Director at OFFIS Institute for Information Technology. Before rejoining academia she worked in senior management positions for Bertelsmann, Germany's largest media conglomerate. Dr. Baumann has edited several books, including the Handbook on Digital Business Ecosystems, and a special issue on Strategic Media Management for the Journal of Media Business Studies. Her research areas are all interdisciplinary, involving either changes in business models due to new technologies or the strategic exploitation of network structures. Her work has been published in influential journals and handbooks.

Online, Social Media, and AI Journalism

6

Tai Neilson

Abstract

In its current form, the integration of AI into journalism threatens the autonomy and quality of journalistic labor, media workers' intellectual property rights, and the economic sustainability and editorial independence of news organizations. As AI becomes increasingly ingrained in news work and business, news outlets risk becoming reliant on commercial third-party infrastructure they do not control, further entrenching the power of "big tech." These political economic concerns are at the heart of decisions about AI adoption in newsrooms and the future sustainability of journalism. This chapter derives some key lessons and critical concepts from previous technological and economic transformations of the news industry. In particular, the chapter outlines three broad technological shifts: (1) the digitization of news, (2) platformization associated with search engines and social network sites, and (3) the commercialization of AI. Critical concepts that have been used to theorize previous changes include digital labor, platformization, and infrastructure capture. These ideas provide a critical foundation for understanding the AI moment. By taking a historically informed, political economic approach to journalism and technology, this chapter avoids the mistakes of thinking AI is completely new or inevitable. This approach suggests that questions about how, why, and what AI technologies are integrated into journalism remain open to contestation.

T. Neilson (✉)
Macquarie University, Sydney, Australia
e-mail: tai.neilson@mq.edu.au

S. Böhm et al. (eds.), *Handbook of AI-based Media Disruption*, Future of Business and Finance, https://doi.org/10.1007/978-3-032-07605-2_6

6.1 Introduction

While artificial intelligence (AI) entails new challenges and opportunities for the news industry and journalists, this moment is not entirely unprecedented. Many of the big companies peddling AI services are familiar names, from Microsoft to Google and Meta, that continue to provide the tools for news work, compete and partner with news publishers, and occasionally even fund news initiatives. Microsoft, for instance, has been a significant figure in the industry since the early digitization of news, as journalists began to use word processing software and publishers converted from analog to digital forms (Manovich, 2002). When news organizations began to carve out a public and commercial presence on the web, the tangle of interdependencies between publishers and technology companies became more complex and entrenched. Digitization was not simply a technological shift, it entailed changes to business models and labor relations (Neilson, 2021). Then, when search and social media companies, such as Google and Meta, entered the mix, they increasingly mediated the relationships between news publishers and their online audiences (Poell et al., 2019). As a result, many news organizations became dependent on platform companies to reach audiences and to perform other business functions (Kleis Nielsen & Ganter, 2022). The news industry faces new risks, as commercial AI is dominated by a small number of global tech companies that benefit from the exploitation of under and unremunerated labor and the intellectual property of media workers.

Since the public launch of ChatGPT in late 2022, there has been a race to capture the market for generative AI and chatbots, and to incorporate AI functionality into a range of software products. While ChatGPT and its competitors have been termed "generative AI" or "gen AI," other types of AI have been in operation in word processing, search, ranking, personalization, and other areas affecting journalism for more than a decade. AI describes a branch of computer science and a category of technologies, but it also operates as a marketing slogan and as a threat to established labor relations. It is associated with ideologies of technological solutionism (Morozov, 2013) and scientific progress that shape public opinion, business decisions, and policy making (Crawford, 2021). The ideologies and implementation of AI raise significant professional and economic concerns for journalism, as journalists engage in new types of labor and news organizations enter new economic relationships with AI companies.

How AI continues to be implemented into news work is an open question. The answers are not determined by technology alone. Questions about how, when, and what types of AI will be used can only be resolved through negotiations and conflicts among audiences, journalists and their employers as well as between news publishers and tech companies. Audiences are still coming to terms with automated journalism; while some studies have found that news audiences find AI-generated news less credible or trustworthy (Waddell, 2017), others have found that AI "authorship" had little effect on audience perceptions (Lermann Henestrosa et al., 2023; Morosoli et al., 2025). A range of AI technologies are already normalized and largely invisible in news work (Diakopolous, 2023). Yet, journalists will draw the line at other uses of AI and automation especially where the goals of rationality, efficiency, and speed imbued in these technologies come into conflict with journalism's democratic obligations (Simon, 2023). Some journalists are resisting the full automation of newsroom functions, citing concerns over errors, misinformation, reduced diversity, reputational risks, and loss of editorial control (Petruccio et al., 2025). There are also conflicts over the use of journalists' past work to train and inform generative AI models without permission or compensation. Journalists are concerned about whether and how their work is used by AI programs.

Clashes over intellectual property also reflect conflicting interests between traditional media business models and the extractive economy of AI. Emergent conflicts between news publishers and AI companies have landed in the courts (e.g., *The New York Times* lawsuit against OpenAI). They pivot around the legality of using copyrighted news content without payment (Grynbaum & Mac, 2023). Equally, news owners and managers are concerned about the threat of AI search and chatbots to their on-site advertising model (Taylor, 2023). Moreover, as AI becomes increasingly embedded in news work and businesses, news outlets risk becoming reliant on external AI infrastructure they do not control, further entrenching tech giants' structural advantage and eroding newsroom autonomy. These political-economic concerns are at the heart of decisions about AI adoption in the present and the future sustainability of journalism.

In this chapter, I apply a critical political economic approach to understand the recent history of online and platform journalism with the goal of historicizing and theorizing AI in the news industry. After a brief review of political economic approaches to journalism and technology, I will outline three broad technological shifts: the digitization of news, platformization associated with search engines and social network sites, and the commercialization of AI. There are similarities between the problems precipitated by past technological and economic shifts and the emergent relationship between AI and journalism. I argue that, in its current form, the integration of AI into journalism threatens the autonomy and quality of journalistic labor, media workers' intellectual property rights, and the economic sustainability and editorial independence of news organizations.

6.2 A Review of Research on the Political Economy of News and Technology

Research on the political economics of communication (PEC) is concerned with the structural power relations between the public, media systems, the state, and capitalism (Mosco, 1996). Political economists tend to adopt a macro perspective, attempting to understand the media's historical context and the totality of social relations in which it functions. Some PEC research also studies the labor processes and conditions of media workers (Neilson, 2025). The more critical variants of PEC with origins in Marxist theory are normative, rather than simply descriptive. For example, Mosco and Fuchs (2015) enumerate the problems in contemporary media systems such as the concentration of media ownership, the reliance on advertising from big corporations, and the dependence on state sources, which erode their democratic potential. They argue that this can lead to problems such as a reduction in critical and diverse perspectives and the circulation of harmful ideologies.

PEC's normative interventions are, foremost, based on the premise that public-service media is necessary to democratic processes and to solving the global issues that we face (Benson et al., 2018). That is, a relatively free and well-resourced news media serves democracy by informing and representing the public and holding the powerful to account. As Benson et al. argue, public service journalism is characterized by "ongoing investment in reporting and commentary that serves normative ideals of watchdog journalism, public affairs information, and/or ideological diversity" (2018, p. 277). It is also most likely to prosper in contexts with strong legal protections and a "firewall" between editorial and commercial objectives. As such, PEC is intended to intervene in media problems through critical analysis and proposals for systematic or policy change.

PEC has also become a significant prism through which to understand technological changes in media industries. The historically informed "big picture" approach championed by political economists helps to ward off assumptions that technological changes are unprecedented or inevitable (Feenberg & Friesen, 2012). Rather, PEC is premised on looking back at previous moments of change to understand the current juncture and looking at who has the power to make decisions and sway public opinions about new technologies (Mosco, 2018). While PEC is concerned with technology, political economists are wary of "technological determinism." As Örnebring (2010, p. 58) argues, more recent PEC research "on the relationship between journalism and technology has generally rejected technological determinism in favour of more nuanced explanations, placing technology in its economic, social, political and cultural contexts."

PEC has developed a critical language for understanding digital media. Concepts that I will deploy below include digital labor (see Fuchs and Sevignani, 2013; Terranova, 2000), platformization (see van Dijck et al., 2018; Poell et al., 2019), and platform infrastructure capture (Nechushtai, 2018; Simon, 2022). First, *digital labor* refers to work that is primarily mediated by digital technologies. Like all labor under capitalism, workers are alienated from the products of their work, the work process, and from one another. Furthermore, labor produces commodities that are useful and that are sold to extract a profit. Digital labor is largely associated with digital platforms and the exploitation of free contributions to social network sites (Fuchs & Sevignani, 2013). Yet, digital labor also describes the constitution of new types of workers with shared interests and agency (Xia, 2021). Second, *digital platforms* facilitate interactions between different groups, including workers, employers, audiences, consumers and the state, and in the process, they commodify users' contributions and behaviors (van Dijck et al., 2018). *Platformization* entails these two processes: the infiltration of digital platforms into various aspects of work and leisure, the economy, and the state; and the datafication of online behavior (Poell et al., 2019). Finally, *platform dependency* is more specific to the news industry, wherein some news companies have become reliant on platforms to reach audiences and to function as businesses (Meese & Hurcombe, 2021; Kleis Nielsen & Ganter, 2018).

Platform dependency is, in part, a class of infrastructure capture. That is, a situation in which an institution becomes increasingly unable to operate without the technical resources and services controlled by a third-party company (Nechushtai, 2018). While this is an incomplete review of political economic approaches to news and technology, and this list of key terms could be expanded, these concepts provide a foundation from which to historicize and critique the relationship between journalism and AI.

There is an emergent PEC literature on AI and news. Nam (2024, p. 402) argues that political economic theories and methodologies are crucial "to untangle how copyright issues play out in the production of news content via generative AI and how they are ineluctably connected to the broader issue of contemporary data-driven capitalism." They state that, in its current forms, AI is exploitative. It exploits unpaid labor and data, while tech companies are now challenging existing copyright regimes to extract more value. In terms of journalistic labor, Simon (2023) concludes that news work is undergoing "a further rationalization" through AI technologies "imbued with ideas of rationality, efficiency, and speed." Echoing scholarship on the concentration of media ownership, others have suggested that AI technologies are continuing to consolidate economic power among a small number of big tech companies (Luitse, 2024; Srnicek, 2022). Moreover, initiatives launched by tech companies, such as Google News, have served to make news organizations and audiences in the Global South dependent on their services (de-Lima-Santos et al., 2023). Finally, other researchers have highlighted concerns about the impact of AI on democracy (Acemoglu et al., 2025) and adopted a normative approach in defence of the democratic role of the press (Lin & Lewis, 2022).

6.3 Digital and Platform Journalism: An Overview

The digitization and platformization of news reshaped the industry, often placing journalists and publishers in increasingly precarious positions. From the early adoption of digital tools that reconfigured newsroom labor and workflows to the disruptive impact of 24/7 online publishing these shifts have unfolded under persistent economic pressure (Boczkowski, 2004). News organizations were quick to experiment with digital strategies, but their efforts were frequently constrained by unstable revenue models and unpredictable technological changes (King, 2010). The rise of platforms like Google and Facebook introduced new power dynamics, as these companies came to mediate the circulation and monetization of news (Kleis Nielsen & Ganter, 2018). As a result, journalists now operate in environments shaped by opaque algorithms, constant self-promotion, and data extraction (Neilson, 2021), while publishers struggle to limit their dependence on platform infrastructures. Government attempts to regulate these dynamics have yielded uneven outcomes, often favoring large firms and raising fresh concerns about journalistic autonomy and transparency (Flew et al., 2021).

6.3.1 Online News

The digitization of news began to transform aspects of journalists' work—word processing, digital photography, nonlinear editing, digital television, and so on—long before news content moved online (Mari, 2019). Manovich (2002, p. 28) describes digitization as "converting continuous data into a numerical representation." He describes how "old media" forms were digitized, becoming content for the "new media." This shift entailed a reconfiguration of journalistic work and new types of labor relations. Journalists were asked to adopt new technologies and adapt to new deadlines and work-place norms (Neilson, 2021). At the same time, many digital journalists were exempt from industrial contracts that covered their peers working in print or broadcast. Fuchs and Sevignani (2013) describe the resulting class re-composition, noting that digital laborers are "a collective workforce that is required for the existence, usage and application of digital media." As such, journalists joined a wider group of cultural workers whose labor is mediated through digital technologies.

While the implementation of digital technology into newsrooms had already been used to change the pace and patterns of news production, the Web introduced a practically infinite and 24/7 outlet for news content. The daily newspaper deadline and rhythms of broadcast were, thus, supplemented by the immediacy of online publishing. News could be broken at any time, and stories could go online first before going to print or air. While changes in the news industry responded to the availability of digital technologies and the popularization of the Internet, the outcomes of this transformation for news workers were not simply dictated by existing practices or new technologies. In his ethnographic study of *The New York Times*, the *Houston Chronicle*, and New Jersey's *Advance Publications* during their transition online, Boczkowski (2004) found that journalists "reflected on the what, how and why of their practices, mindfully enacting certain options and discarding competing alternatives." The choices and uses regarding technology also resulted from negotiations and conflicts between news workers and managers and were structured by industry conditions (Lee-Wright, 2010). In many cases, this meant that the demands of Web publishing were coupled with the financial pinch related to falling ad revenue and new online competitors.

Some of the big questions that faced the news industry in the mid to late 1990s are relevant more than three decades later: when and how do you provide free content online, and when do you ask for payment? Is it better to go it alone or to collaborate with other news companies? Which technology companies are potential partners, which are competitors, and how do you tell them apart? Yet, it is also important to note the vast differences of context between the media industry during the early adoption of the Web and the present. The popularization of the Internet was the most significant technological change experienced by news companies since broadcast or maybe the printing press. There had been digital precursors to the World Wide Web, and news companies had explored these new media, but the significance and longevity of the Internet were yet unknown (Mari, 2019). The slow, less-than-user-friendly early versions of Internet connections and Web browsers only provided glimpses into what the Internet would become.

Retrospectives on the transition to online news often repeat one of two myths about the period. As one story goes, news organizations committed the "original sin" of posting their content online for free in the 1990s and, as a result, news audiences became accustomed to accessing news without paying for it (Zuckerman, 2014). Or, alternately, news companies were too large, slow, and set in their ways to effectively react to the Internet. They failed to seize the opportunities of the moment and have continued to pay the price. However, the realities are far more complex than these two narratives suggest. Newspaper readership had already been in decline, especially among young people, for more than a decade prior to the popularization of the Internet (Meyer, 2009). While some large publishers were still flush with cash, other urban newspapers were in financial trouble, and industry leaders foresaw difficult times ahead. Furthermore, as Mari (2024) argues, newspapers were among the first institutional adopters of the Internet. Many mastheads established recognizable brand presence and innovative products online in the late 1990s.

In *Free For All: The Internet's Transformation of Journalism*, King (2010) notes that through the late 1990s and early 2000s, there was a keen awareness and growing consensus in the news industry that their classified and advertising revenue models were at risk. News managers were clear-eyed about competition coming from tech companies (such as Microsoft), although they had less warning about upstart rivals such as Craigslist that captured a substantial portion of advertising revenue (Lingel, 2020). Hence, news owners and managers embarked on a range of individual and collective projects to support sustainable online journalism. Some organizations banded together in an attempt to secure online subscription models and market power. News companies also attempted to compete with new online classifieds and advertising companies (sometimes successfully), through businesses such as Autotrader in the US and the Domain Group in Australia. Others signed up to partnerships with tech companies to put their content and brand in front of Internet users and share advertising revenue (King, 2010). Still, the future was (as always) unpredictable, and it may be unfair to judge their decision-making with the benefits of hindsight. This is all the more pertinent, as news companies and industry commentators are, again, torn on the correct course of action when it comes to the relationship between news publishers and tech companies.

6.3.2 Social Media Journalism

Since the early digitization of news and migration of news online, the pace of change in the industry has only increased. The early Web was slow and unintuitive, but it soon became conducive to video and audio content. Smartphones and other personal devices moved online news from desktops to consumers' pockets. While the smartphone and increasing availability of mobile data were praised for democratising news and helping to establish new types of "citizen journalism" (Allan & Thorsen, 2009), Web 2.0 companies also established new business models profiting from user contributions and data (O'Reilly, 2005). The subsequent platformization of the Web resulted in the consolidation of power among a small group of global tech companies. In this context, journalists are often required by their employers to promote their work and the companies they work for on online platforms (Neilson, 2018). Meanwhile, publishers face questions about how to secure a sustainable business model in the face of falling advertising revenue and dependence on platform companies.

Search engines perform an important function; they provide a way to organize the unwieldy content of the Internet (including news), ranking it, and putting relevant content in one place for users. Likewise, social media sites provide venues for self-expression, community, and communication. Although, as commercial entities, platform companies often prioritize commercial interests over delivering on these promises (Horwitz, 2023). At the broadest level, platforms are digital infrastructures that mediate relationships between different types of actors (companies, states, individual users, advertisers, etc.) and they are mechanisms for extracting and processing large amounts of user data (van Dijck et al., 2018). Digital platforms include online marketplaces (e.g., Amazon and Alibaba), gig work companies (e.g., Uber), search engines (e.g., Google Search), and social media sites (e.g., Facebook, Twitter, TikTok, and Weibo). Yet, in practice, these boundaries are porous on many platforms and across the holdings of platform companies.

News workers and publishers have had to navigate this uneven and changing terrain. For journalists, platformization means that more and more of their work is mediated by third-party technologies that facilitate relationships between them, their employers, the products of their work, and audiences. It also means that their work is circulated in sometimes unpredictable ways, according to the interests of audiences and opaque rules of platforms and their algorithms. Along with other platform users, journalists' relationships and behaviors are transformed into data used to train algorithms and sold to advertisers (Fuchs, 2021). The concept of digital labor helps to theorize the characteristics of work in online infrastructures, especially those that extract value from user contributions and behavior (Fuchs & Sevignani, 2013). Digital labor has primarily been used to understand changing labor relations precipitated by Web 2.0 and platformization. However, it has broader utility, as the term recognizes the impacts of changing technologies and the continuity of labor under conditions of capital. As such, it can be extended to understand the exploitation of cultural workers and the extractive strategies of AI companies (I will return to this point in the next section).

Yet, news workers have also leveraged platforms for their own purposes. For example, some have developed followings that they maintain even as they move from one employer to the next or pursue freelance work. In this way, journalists can gain some autonomy from traditional news employers (Cohen, 2016). This is also the case for journalists who have moved to crowdfunding platforms, such as Patreon. This type of autonomy, however, comes at the cost of continual self-promotion, precarity, and signing onto the terms and conditions of third-party platforms (Hunter, 2016). In short, for journalists as digital laborers, platforms enter them into new forms of exploitation, while also providing opportunities to produce news in different ways and to reach new audiences (Hayes & Silke, 2018).

Likewise, digital platforms play multiple roles for news companies. As Myllylahti (2023) contends, from the perspective of the news industry, platforms have occupied contradictory positions as competitors, partners, and patrons. Digital platforms compete with publishers for advertising revenue. While advertising in broadcast and print has stagnated or is dropping in most media markets, the global spend on digital advertising is projected to surpass one trillion US dollars in 2025. In 2024, more than half of global digital advertising revenue went to the top five platform companies: Google, Meta, ByteDance, Amazon, and Alibaba (Scott-Dawkins, 2025). Google and Meta have dominated global advertising markets for more than a decade, with their ability to target consumers with personal ads through user profiles and behavioral data (Bell & Owen, 2017; Park et al., 2022). These companies also take a proverbial second bite out of the advertising apple, as many publishers rely on services, such as Google's AdSense as a marketplace in which to buy and sell advertising space. This means paying as much as half of the advertising revenue a company earns to platform intermediaries. Even as news publishers have tried to find alternative revenue streams, Google has launched a digital subscription service to mediate the relationship between publishers and their subscribers. Although Google and Meta now compete with other global giants (such as ByteDance) and emerging AI companies—and face fines for competition law breaches in various jurisdictions—this has done little to improve the fortunes of news publishers.

A key definitional debate both in academic and policy circles, especially with regard to search engines and social media, has revolved around the question of whether these platforms are publishers (Myllylahti, 2023). That is, whether their ranking, selection, and moderation processes are similar enough to editorial processes to label these companies as publishers of content. Or, as the platform companies themselves have contended, are they simply digital tools that enable others to publish their work or enable users to find content that has already been published? (Napoli & Caplan, 2017; Popiel, 2018). The lack of clarity in this debate has meant that social media sites and search engines remain largely exempt from the legal obligations of publishers (Heylen, 2023). The debate over who should be defined as a publisher has become even more urgent with the roll-out of AI search results that summarize news content (this will be discussed in more detail in the following section).

News organizations have also partnered with platform companies, although the relationship is far from equal. Platform dependency is a specific type of infrastructure capture, wherein news organizations depend on platform companies to reach online audiences (Kleis Nielsen & Ganter, 2018). Social media and search platforms remain significant sites for news consumption. Despite changing demographics and competition, Facebook was still the most important platform for incidental news exposure in 2023 (Newman et al., 2024). This is especially the case in countries such as the Philippines, where Facebook is the primary entry point to the Web for much of the population (Uy-Tioco, 2019). As such, news companies commit significant resources to increase engagement on social media platforms or optimize their content for search.

Platform dependency is also extended and reinforced through news companies' reliance on platform tools (i.e., Google News Showcase or Meta Business Suite) and through platform payments and patronage. When tech companies change their algorithms, change course with their business strategies, or decide it is no longer expedient to support journalism initiatives, news companies stand to lose out (Bailo et al., 2021). For example, business decisions to reduce the amount of news content in users' feeds contributed to a 67% reduction in referrals from Facebook and 50% reduction from Twitter between 2023 and the end of 2024 (Newman & Cherubini, 2025). As such, some news companies have tried to reduce their reliance on third-party platforms (Meese & Hurcombe, 2021) by implementing their own subscription models and developing content delivery methods, such as newsletters and podcasts (Chua & Westlund, 2022). Even as they attempt to disentangle parts of their businesses from big tech, news companies are unlikely to turn down short-term funding opportunities when they arise.

Media companies have been among the loudest advocates for regulating digital platforms and legislating requirements for social media and search engines to pay for news content. The so-called "regulatory turn," in which states across the globe have introduced legislation targeted at digital platforms, is in part the result of lobbying from news companies (Flew et al., 2021). Perhaps most significantly for the news industry, several countries have legislated or considered legislation that requires digital platforms to pay for news. Australia's 2021 News Media and Digital Platforms Mandatory Bargaining Code and Canada's 2023 Online News Act enforce the "patronage" role of digital platforms by requiring them to strike deals with news companies and pay for news content. These laws were presented as responses to digital platforms' dominance of online advertising markets and as ways to secure funding for reporting (Neilson & Balasingham, 2022). They have met mixed success. In Australia, larger news companies benefited most from these deals, while some smaller companies and specialist organizations such as *The Conversation* and Special Broadcasting Service (SBS) were unable to secure funding. The terms and financial value of the deals have been shrouded in secrecy, and there are concerns that they undermine journalistic independence (Bossio et al., 2024). Moreover, many of the deals between news organizations and Meta were short-lived, as Meta decided not to renew its deals with news companies. In response, the Australian government is proposing The News Bargaining Incentive policy to plug holes in the existing legislation (Jones, 2022).

Two decades after the emergence of Web 2.0, there is no clear, shared, or systematic solution for struggling news companies. While some news organizations have tried to strike preferable deals with search and social media companies, others have diversified their strategies to reduce their dependence on big tech (Meese & Hurcombe, 2021). For the most part, however, they have been united in their claim that digital platforms have undercut their business models and that policy changes are needed to help pay for news (Neilson & Heylen, 2023). As several large news organizations (for instance, News Corp and *The Guardian*) enter deals with AI companies, it remains an open question as to whether news owners and managers have learned from the initial digitization of the news or social media journalism. There is a risk that AI will further undercut news business models. There are clear pitfalls involved in depending too heavily on "big tech" and short-term deals with AI companies.

6.4 AI and Journalism

The integration of AI into the news industry requires journalists to engage in new types of labor, it is prompting news organizations to enter new economic relationships with tech companies, and it is transforming the relationship between audiences and news. Yet, there are continuities between online and social media journalism and the changing terrain of AI. As such, theories of digital media and platforms can frame critical inquiries into journalism and AI. In particular, the critical political economic concepts of digital labor, platformization, and infrastructure capture remain useful to understand the current juncture. In short, lessons from the digital transition and dealings with digital platform companies provide a starting point to address emergent challenges.

First, amongst the claims about scientific breakthroughs and world-changing products, it is important to pause and ask, what is actually new about AI? The concept of artificial intelligence has roots in the 1950s and quickly became a field of computer science (Crawford, 2021). While some definitions of AI emphasize the simulation of the human mind using machines, this approach is limiting and a poor description of most (if not all) computer systems that we currently think of as involving AI. Rather, AI refers to the study and development of technologies that are designed and trained to recognize patterns in data and to make new judgments or produce new outcomes (Broussard et al., 2019). Researchers have identified several categories of AI including "(i) machine learning; (ii) computer vision (CV); (iii) speech recognition; (iv) natural language processing (NLP); (v) planning, scheduling, and optimization; (vi) expert systems; and (vii) robotics" (de-Lima-Santos & Ceron, 2022). There is a long history of computer engineers exploring ways to use NLP to generate news stories in more standardized beats such as financial reporting, sports results, and the weather (Mari, 2024). However, the use of "robot reporters" was relatively limited until at least the 2010s (Diakopoulos, 2019). The amount of data now available and increased computing power have contributed to new AI capabilities. This has also allowed generative AI, which is built on machine learning processes, to make the leap to a personal subscription service.

In addition to generative AI, there have been important changes in ranking and personalization algorithms used by platform companies. Platform algorithms have shaped news practices (for instance, search engine optimization) as well as the ways that audiences interact with news products since the popularization of social media and search engines in the 2010s. Algorithms like Facebook's EdgeRank have been replaced by self-adjusting algorithms that continually adapt to new patterns and result in configurations that may even surprise their developers. In *Broken Code:*

Inside Facebook and the Fight to Expose Its Harmful Secrets, Horwitz (2023) describes how, starting with personalized advertising, Facebook moved from more straight-forward mathematical algorithms for personalizing content feeds to using a machine learning package called FB Learner and AI classifiers across the whole platform. In 2016, Facebook announced "Engineers and teams, even with little expertise, can build and run experiments with ease and deploy AI-powered products" (in Horwitz, 2023, 50-51). The presence of AI-generated deep fakes and misinformation also change the environment in which journalists operate and shape audiences' attitudes to information. AI products, such as generative AI and AI-powered recommendation systems, are undoubtedly giving rise to new ways of producing and interacting with news and information online. They are raising renewed concerns about echo chambers, bias, and disinformation (Acemoglu et al., 2025). Yet, AI is not new to journalism; it has been integrated into various stages of news production and circulation for some time.

As tech companies clamor to associate themselves and their services with the AI label, it can also be difficult to determine what really is or is not an application of AI. Hence, we may ask: what claims are being made about AI and are these claims true? Often, claims about what AI can do are overblown or even deceptive. Terms such as "ghost work," "shadow work," "fauxtomation," and "Potemkin AI" all describe the ways that human labor is often hidden behind claims about automation and AI (Mueller, 2021). One example of hidden labor is the revelation that food delivery robots operated on university campuses by companies such as Kiwi Campus were actually driven by low-paid remote workers (Berman, 2019). This is not to say that AI is an elaborate hoax. There is not an employee typing out ChatGPT responses or an artist drawing the design in response to your Dall-E prompt (I will elaborate on the ways that AI exploits the work of authors and creatives below). Still, we should be critical of the claims that AI is the solution, that it will make journalism more efficient, free up time for more quality journalism, or even replace human journalists. AI is as much a set of ideologies about technological progress and a marketing slogan used to sell software products, as it is a set of technologies and techniques.

6.4.1 AI and Journalistic Labor

One emergent conflict over AI in newsrooms revolves around when, how, and what AI technologies will be implemented. AI services are currently used to create summaries of top stories, convert text to audio (and vice versa), translate stories into multiple languages, and write and publish social media posts, among other functions. AI services promise to improve efficiency, reduce costs, and increase profits, but managers often integrate new technologies at the expense of workers' autonomy (Chillas & Baluch, 2019). In a study of social media journalists in Germany, Petruccio et al. (2025) found that many journalists resisted fully automating social media publishing. They identified errors and misinformation, a reduction in news diversity, increases in toxic comments and reputational damage among the risks associated with AI automated news publishing. As a result, they sought to keep editorial control in human hands. As news managers adopt AI to reduce staffing costs and increase profit margins, Simon (2023) suggests there is a "precarious balance within news organizations between top-down wishes and bottom-up interests." The outcomes of implementing AI in newsrooms (or not) are determined as much by struggles between journalists and their managers, news publishers and tech companies, as by the characteristics of the technology.

A second emergent workplace conflict revolves around journalists' rights over the products of their work and the choice of whether their publications should be used to train and fuel AI systems. Large machine learning models require huge pools of data to be trained and to operate. This is true of gen AI programs that have been trained on massive archives of copyrighted material, including journalists' past work (Lopatto, 2024). To put this another way, generative AI can only produce news articles, scripts, illustrations, podcasts, or videos that resemble the work of media professionals because it has access to archives of their past work. As such, *The Guardian's* deal with OpenAI, which makes its news archive available to the AI company, has been a point of contention among staff. *The Guardian Australia* staff noted that the deal may breach the clause in their employment contract that requires consultation regarding changes that have significant impacts on employees (Saeed, 2025).

The use of journalists' work to train AI is also a contested area of intellectual property law. Copyright regimes have always been fraught in that they often benefit publishers over creative workers. Now AI companies are lobbying to reinterpret intellectual property law, so they can continue to profit from huge banks of copyrighted material without paying its owners or creators (Nam, 2024). News publishers have filed lawsuits over the use of their content by AI companies to train NLP. As a tech writer for *The Verge* put it, "The huge leaps in OpenAI's GPT model probably came from sucking down the entire written Web. That includes entire archives of major publishers such as Axel Springer, Condé Nast, and The Associated Press—without their permission" (Lopatto, 2024). In a high-profile case, *The New York Times* sued ChatGPT's parent company, OpenAI, claiming that "millions of articles published by *The Times* were used to train automated chatbots that now compete with the news outlet as a source of reliable information" (Grynbaum & Mac, 2023). *The New York Times* owners see OpenAI as a competitor that is taking advantage of free access to news content much like news aggregators. In contrast, tech companies, such as Google, Microsoft, and OpenAI, argue that using copyright content to train AI should be considered fair use and is necessary for continued advances in the field.

The large-scale commercial AI models owned by companies such as OpenAI, Google, and Microsoft continue to operate on the platform business model, in that they exploit unpaid work and profit from user data. They have extended this model by tapping into vast pools of texts, images, audio, and video that are now "grist for the mills of machine learning" (Crawford, 2021). As such, the concept of digital labor provides a starting point to critically analyze the re-composition of segments of the working class that are needed to produce, maintain, and deploy digital technologies including AI. Yet, the concept needs to be extended to better understand the extractive model of AI. One way that political economists may do so is to revive Marx's concept of "dead labor." That is, the labor expended by workers in the past, which is now embodied in machines and commodities. Marx (1867 [1976]) suggests that this past labor, accumulated in machines, is used by the capitalist class to dominate workers. He used the living-dead figure of the vampire to illustrate that "capital is dead labor which, vampire-like, lives only by sucking living labor, and lives the more, the more labor it sucks" (1867 [1976]). Struggles over whether "vampire" AI is allowed to continue "sucking" from the work of journalists for purposes of training and as material for the generation of content are being fought at the level of news workers' contracts (freelancers and continuing staff) and in the courts. The question is, what rights do journalists have over how their work will be used and by whom?

6.4.2 The News Business and AI Infrastructure

Many of the major tech companies that are becoming commercial gateways to AI services have histories as software and platform companies. They continue to mediate between news companies and a large portion of their audiences, taking on multiple roles as competitors, partners, and potential patrons (Myllylahti, 2023). To date, traditional media have struggled to compete with platform companies for online ad revenue (Bell & Owen, 2017). News organizations that rely on platform infrastructures to reach audiences have also struggled because of decisions to demote news content (Bailo et al., 2021). The risk is that AI will continue to undercut the economics of news production, while news companies become increasingly dependent on third-party AI infrastructure.

AI is dealing another hit to the news business model of on-site advertising, which may not survive changes wrought by AI search and personal assistants. There is a risk that the reduction in referrals from social media companies to news websites will be replicated for search engines. Google Search now frequently serves users an AI overview at the top of the page that paraphrases search results and reduces the need to click through to a news source. In 2022, Google claimed that its practice of listing "links, headlines and short snippets" rather than full news stories avoided copyright infringement and benefitted news publishers by sending users to their sites (cited in Myllylahti, 2023). However, the new AI overview function may change this equation. Similarly, Bing and Perplexity's Answer Engine summarizes and provides links to news sites and Microsoft's Copilot can perform similar functions. It is not surprising that news companies are asking to be paid and receive credit for the content served up by these AI services, as it is still journalists who do the legwork of reporting. These changes to search have the potential to undercut commercial news' flailing advertising revenue model (Simon, 2023). However, they are not inevitable. For instance, lawmakers in California, the home of Silicon Valley, have moved to protect journalism from AI summaries (Malik, 2024). Of course, the threats related to AI summaries of current events are not solely financial. The summaries cobbled together by AI are riddled with inaccuracies and misquotes (Williams, 2024). By providing summaries, rather than presenting links or hosting user posts, AI companies can hardly avoid the label of publisher and the editorial responsibilities and copyright liabilities that those roles entail.

Another significant risk to news organizations is that they become reliant (once again) on third-party commercial technologies to perform the core functions of both their commercial and democratic roles. The concept of platform dependency describes the asymmetric relationship between news outlets and the tech companies that came to mediate between them, their audiences, and advertisers (Kleis Nielsen & Ganter, 2018). More generally, infrastructure capture is a condition in which it becomes difficult or impossible for organizations to operate without using the technical resources and services controlled by another company (Nechushtai, 2018). While some news companies have the resources to create in-house AI, such as *The Washington Post*'s "Ask The Post AI" Chatbot or in-house news recommendation systems (WashPostPR, 2024), these initiatives are extremely resource-intensive. Independently developing large language learning programs is expensive, requiring server space, energy, and above all, expertise. As de-Lima-Santos and Ceron (2022) argue, "AI still requires specialized expertise, which makes it difficult to compete with Silicon Valley companies." As such, it is no surprise that platform companies, which are among the most profitable in the world, have leveraged their financial resources, hardware, and staff expertise to gain an advantage when it comes to AI. The news industry simply cannot compete. As AI becomes increasingly central to journalistic work and the circulation of news, it threatens the autonomy of news organizations.

Some major AI companies have entered partnerships with news organizations, penning agreements to use news content for training data and other purposes. AI companies have taken a more proactive approach to signing deals than was the case for major platform companies in the past, which may be a reaction to lawsuits that cite copyright infringement or a recognition of the ongoing policy battles (Grynbaum & Mac, 2023). Similar to the deals struck between news and platform companies, their financial value and their specific terms are often closely guarded commercial secrets. They also tend to primarily favor large English-speaking media organizations, such as News Corp. In cases where the value of deals was publicly reported, the revenue is welcome but is far from representing a new business model for the news industry (i.e., OpenAI's deals with Dotdash, Meredith and Axel Springer). In his forecast, Kleis Nielsen (2024) predicts that "most publishers will not get any meaningful revenue from licensing content to technology companies, and that those who do are likely to be large publishers who get at most a few percent of incremental revenue." Yet, many news publishers are still optimistic about striking content deals with AI companies whether on a collective or individual basis (Newman & Cherubini, 2025). While news organizations are actively courting partnerships with AI companies, there is a risk that short-term deals may undermine the long-term viability of news companies or that the deals may repeat the patterns of dependency observed in the relationships between news and digital platforms (Simon, 2022).

So, will AI companies become news patrons? It is clear from the experience of platform dependency that tech companies are driven by commercial interests and that they will only fund public service news when it meets their goals. Tech companies have already pillaged news content and other copyright material to train their proprietary AI systems (Lopatto, 2024). Search and generative AI will continue to need journalism to stay relevant, but if they cannot get it for free, they will likely strike a small number of deals with large media companies. Tech companies are also fickle in their patronage. For example, Facebook went from promoting news content and providing a specific news function in many countries to demoting news after the 2016 US federal election. Furthermore, as the political situation shifted, platforms such as X (Twitter) quickly removed fact checking and support for news organizations and researchers. In short, the benevolence of tech companies cannot be the basis for a diverse and autonomous free press.

6.5 Conclusion

To conclude, then, what does the commercialization of AI and its integration into the news industry mean for the present and future of journalism? The news industry has survived increasingly rapid and jarring changes, from digitization to platformization and the emergence of commercial AI. While some of the challenges of AI are genuinely new, the recent history of technological and political economic changes in the news industry provides a series of lessons and concepts that can inform research and practical decisions at the current juncture. The first lesson for news workers is that the uses and outcomes of new technologies are not inevitable. Journalists may find ethical and advantageous uses of AI and automation, but this should be part of a reflexive approach that considers a range of alternatives. Second, AI is a new way for tech companies to extract value from the past work of journalists and other cultural workers. Generative AI, for instance, consumes human journalists' work, turns it into data, identifies patterns, and then regurgitates a response to users' prompts. It is trained to produce content that is randomized enough to tiptoe around copyright law (although, sometimes it falls into more straight-forward plagiarism) and it is trained to produce content that is convincing (although, this does not always mean accurate). Third, despite concerns over the accuracy and efficacy of AI, news managers see the technology as a means to reduce staffing costs (Broussard, 2015). News publishers have their own profit motives and budget constraints, and like other digital technologies, AI is seen as a way to produce more value with fewer workers. Ultimately, it is still human reporters, aided by the various technologies of news production, who do the original reporting. As such, the implementation of AI into their workplaces will remain a point of contention, negotiation, and conflict.

As digital platforms became significant intermediaries between news workers and their audiences, journalists were asked to take on new roles, working within platform environments to market the news. Rather than securing the future of quality news, many journalists faced increasingly precarious working conditions while their employers became dependent on the services provided by third-party tech companies. News companies are at risk of developing new dependencies, as AI companies capture the infrastructure of journalism work and news circulation. While some major news companies have rolled out in-house AI applications, this will remain out of reach for many smaller, cash-strapped organizations. Publishers are more likely to buy off the shelf AI services or sign in-kind deals with AI companies that provide training material for AI in exchange for the use of these technologies. However, recent history demonstrates that once news companies are entangled with "big tech," these chains are difficult to break.

References

Acemoglu, D., Ozdaglar, A.E., and Siderius, J. (2025). *AI and social media: A political economy perspective*. NBER Working Paper No. w33892. SSRN. https://ssrn.com/abstract=5296536

Allan, S., & Thorsen, E. (2009). *Citizen journalism: Global perspectives*. Peter Lang.

Bailo, F., Meese, J., & Hurcombe, E. (2021). The institutional impacts of algorithmic distribution: Facebook and the Australian News Media. *Social Media + Society*, 7(2). https://doi.org/10.1177/20563051211024963.

Bell, E., & Owen, T. (2017). The platform press: How Silicon Valley reengineered journalism. *Tow Center for Digital Journalism*. https://www.cjr.org/tow_center_reports/platform-press-how-silicon-valley-reengineered-journalism.php

Benson, R., Neff, T., & Hessérus, M. (2018). Media ownership and public service news: How strong are institutional logics? *The International Journal of Press/Politics, 23*(3), 275–298. https://doi.org/10.1177/1940161218782740

Berman, B. (2019). Burrito delivered by bot, as long as students don't trap it. *The New York Times*. https://www.nytimes.com/2019/11/07/business/kiwibot-delivery-bots-drones.html

Boczkowski, P. J. (2004). *Digitizing the news: Innovation in online newspapers*. MIT Press.

Bossio, D., Carson, A., & Meese, J. (2024). A different playbook for the same outcome? Examining Google's and Meta's strategic responses to Australia's News Media Bargaining Code. *New Media and Society*, (Online First), 1-21. https://doi.org/10.1177/14614448241232296.

Broussard, M. (2015). Artificial intelligence for investigative reporting: Using an expert system to enhance journalists' ability to discover original public affairs stories. *Digital Journalism, 3*(6), 814–831.

Broussard, M., Diakopoulos, N., Guzman, A. L., Abebe, R., Dupagne, M., & Chuan, C.-H. (2019). Artificial intelligence and journalism. *Journalism and Mass Communication Quarterly, 96*(3), 673–695. https://doi.org/10.1177/1077699019859901

Chillas, S., & Baluch, A. (2019). Cracking labour process theory in employment relations and HRM. In K. Townsend, K. Cafferkey, A. M. McDermott, & T. Dundon (Eds.), *Elgar Introduction to theories of human resources and employment relations* (pp. 67–81). Edward Elgar Publishing.

Chua, S., & Westlund, O. (2022). Platform Configuration: A longitudinal study and conceptualization of a legacy news publishers platform related innovation practices. *Online Media and Global Communication, 1*(1), 60–89.

Cohen, N. S. (2016). *Writers' rights: Freelance journalism in a digital age*. McGill-Queen's University Press.

Crawford, K. (2021). *Atlas of AI: Power, politics, and the planetary costs of artificial intelligence*. Yale University Press.

de-Lima-Santos, M., & Ceron, W. (2022). Artificial intelligence in news media: Current perceptions and future outlook. *Journalism and Media, 3*(1), 13–26. https://doi.org/10.3390/journalmedia3010002

de-Lima-Santos, M. F., Munoriyarwa, A., Elega, A., & Papaevangelou, C. (2023). Google news initiative's influence on technological media innovation in Africa and the Middle East. *Media and Communication, 11*(2), 330–343. https://doi.org/10.17645/mac.v11i2.6400

Diakopolous, N. (2023). *The state of AI in media: From hype to reality. Medium*. https://generative-ai-newsroom.com/the-state-of-ai-in-media-from-hype-to-reality-37b250541752

Diakopoulos, N. (2019). *Automating the news: How algorithms are rewriting the media*. Cambridge University Press.

Feenberg, A., & Friesen, N. (2012). *(Re)inventing the internet: Critical case studies*. Sense.

Flew, T., Gillett, R., Martin, F., & Sunman, L. (2021). Return of the regulatory state: A stakeholder analysis of Australia's Digital Platforms Inquiry and online news policy. *The Information Society, 37*(2), 128–145. https://doi.org/10.1080/01972243.2020.1870597

Fuchs, C. (2021). *Social media: A critical introduction* (3rd ed.). Sage.

Fuchs, C., & Sevignani, S. (2013). What is digital labour? What is digital work? What's their difference? And why do these questions matter for understanding social media? *TripleC, 11*(2), 237–293. https://doi.org/10.31269/triplec.v11i2.461

Grynbaum, M., & Mac, R. (2023). The Times Sues OpenAI and Microsoft Over A.I. use of copyrighted work. *The New York Times*. https://www.nytimes.com/2023/12/27/business/media/new-york-times-open-ai-microsoft-lawsuit.html

Hayes, K., & Silke, H. (2018). The networked freelancer? Digital labour and freelance journalism in the age of social media. *Digital Journalism, 6*(8), 1018–1028. https://doi.org/10.1080/21670811.2018.1505438

Heylen, K. B. (2023). Enforcing platform sovereignty: A case study of platform responses to Australia's News Media Bargaining Code. *New Media and Society, 26*(12), 7277–7294. https://doi.org/10.1177/14614448231166057

Horwitz, J. (2023). *Broken code: Inside Facebook and the fight to expose its harmful secrets*. Random House.

Hunter, A. (2016). "It's like Having a second full-time job": Crowdfunding, journalism and labour. *Journalism Practice, 10*(2), 217–232. https://doi.org/10.1080/17512786.2015.1123107

Jones, S. (2022). *Albanese government to establish News Bargaining Incentive. Treasury*. https://ministers.treasury.gov.au/ministers/stephen-jones-2022/media-releases/albanese-government-establish-news-bargaining-incentive

King, E. (2010). *Free for all: The Internet's transformation of journalism*. Northwestern University Press.

Kleis Nielsen, R. (2024). *Publishers find the AI era not all that lucrative*. Neiman Lab. https://www.niemanlab.org/2024/12/publishers-find-the-ai-era-not-all-that-lucrative/

Kleis Nielsen, R., & Ganter, S. A. (2018). Dealing with digital intermediaries: A case study of the relations between publishers and platforms. *New Media & Society, 20*(4), 1600–1617. https://doi.org/10.1177/1461444817701318

Kleis Nielsen, R., & Ganter, S. A. (2022). *The power of platforms: Shaping media and society*. Oxford University Press.

Lee-Wright, P. (2010). Culture shock: New media and organizational change at the BBC. In N. Fenton (Ed.), *New media, old news: Journalism and democracy in the digital age* (pp. 67–79). Sage.

Lermann Henestrosa, A., Greving, H., & Kimmerle, J. (2023). Automated journalism: The effects of AI authorship and evaluative information on the perception of a science journalism article. *Computers in Human Behavior, 138*(107445), 1–11. https://doi.org/10.1016/j.chb.2022.107445

Lin, B., & Lewis, S. C. (2022). The one thing journalistic AI just might do for democracy. *Digital Journalism, 10*(10), 1627–1649. https://doi.org/10.1080/21670811.2022.2084131

Lingel, J. (2020). *An Internet for the people: The politics and promise of Craigslist*. Princeton University Press.

Lopatto, E. (2024). *OpenAI searches for an answer to its copyright problems: Why is OpenAI paying publishers if it already took their work?* The Verge. https://www.theverge.com/2024/8/30/24230975/openai-publisher-deals-web-search.

Luitse, D. (2024). Platform power in AI: The evolution of cloud infrastructures in the political economy of artificial intelligence. *Internet Policy Review, 13*(2), 1–44. https://doi.org/10.14763/2024.2.1768
Malik, A. (2024). *New Senate bill seeks to protect artists' and journalists' content from AI use*. Tech Crunch. https://techcrunch.com/2024/07/12/new-senate-bill-seeks-to-protect-artists-and-journalists-content-from-ai-use/.
Manovich, L. (2002). *The language of new media*. MIT Press.
Mari, W. (2019). *A short history of disruptive journalism technologies: 1960–1990*. Routledge.
Mari, W. (2024). The pre-history of news-industry discourse around artificial intelligence. *Emerging Media, 2*(3), 499–522. https://doi.org/10.1177/27523543241279577
Marx, K. (1867[1976]). *Capital Volume I*. Penguin.
Meese, J., & Hurcombe, E. (2021). Facebook, news media and platform dependency: The institutional impacts of news distribution on social platforms. *New Media and Society, 23*(8), 2367–2384.
Meyer, P. (2009). *The vanishing newspaper: Saving journalism in the information age* (2nd ed.). University of Missouri Press.
Morosoli, S., Resendez, V., Naudts, L., Helberger, N., & de Vreese, C. (2025). "I resist". A study of individual attitudes towards generative AI in journalism and acts of resistance, risk perceptions, trust and credibility. *Digital Journalism*, (online first), 1–20. https://doi.org/10.1080/21670811.2024.2435579.
Morozov, E. (2013). *To save everything, click here: The folly of technological solutionism*. Public Affairs.
Mosco, V. (1996). *The political economy of communication: Rethinking and renewal*. Sage.
Mosco, V. (2018). *Political economies of media technologies*. Oxford Research Encyclopedia of Communication. https://doi.org/10.1093/acrefore/9780190228613.013.553.
Mosco, V., & Fuchs, C. (2015). *Marx and the political economy of the media*. Brill.
Mueller, G. (2021). *Breaking things at work: The Luddites are right about why you hate your job*. Verso.
Myllylahti, M. (2023). *From paper to platform: How tech giants are redefining news and democracy*. BWB Texts.
Nam, S. (2024). Who gets paid (for) what? The cultural political economy of news content in generative AI. *Emerging Media, 2*(3), 397–421. https://doi.org/10.1177/27523543241287835
Napoli, P., & Caplan, R. (2017). Why media companies insist they're not media companies, why they're wrong, and why it matters. *First Monday, 22*(5). https://doi.org/10.5210/fm.v22i5.7051
Nechushtai, E. (2018). Could digital platforms capture the media through infrastructure? *Journalism, 19*(8), 1043–1058. https://doi.org/10.1177/14648849177251
Neilson, T. (2018). 'I don't engage': Online communication and social media use among New Zealand journalists. *Journalism, 19*(4), 536–552. https://doi.org/10.1177/1464884916667871
Neilson, T. (2021). *Journalism and digital labor: Experiences of online news production*. Routledge. https://doi.org/10.4324/9780429266096.
Neilson, T. (2025). *The labor of news work and journalism*. Oxford Research Encyclopedia of Communication. https://doi.org/10.1093/acrefore/9780190228613.013.1532.
Neilson, T., & Balasingham, B. (2022). Big tech and news: A critical approach to digital platforms, journalism, and competition law. In J. Meese & S. Bannerman (Eds.), *The algorithmic distribution of news* (pp. 171–192). Palgrave Macmillan.
Neilson, T., & Heylen, K. (2023). Journalism unions and digital platform regulation: A critical discourse analysis of submissions to Australia's News Media Bargaining Code. *Media International Australia,* (Online First). https://doi.org/10.1177/1329878X231176583.
Newman, N., & Cherubini, F. (2025). *Journalism and technology trends and predictions, 2025*. The Reuters Institute for the Study of Journalism. https://reutersinstitute.politics.ox.ac.uk/sites/default/files/2025-01/Trends_and_Predictions_2025.pdf
Newman, N., Fletcher, R., Robertson, C. T., Arguedas, A. R., & Nielsen, R. K. (2024). *Reuters institute digital news report, 2024*. Reuters Institute. https://reutersinstitute.politics.ox.ac.uk/digital-news-report/2024

O'Reilly, T. (2005). *What is Web 2.0: Design patterns and business models for the next generation of software*. O'Reilly. https://www.oreilly.com/pub/a/web2/archive/what-is-web-20.html
Örnebring, H. (2010). Technology and journalism-as-labour: Historical perspectives. *Journalism, 11*(1), 57–74. https://doi.org/10.1177/1464884909350644
Park, S., McGuinness, K., Fisher, C., Young Lee, J., McCallum, K., & Nolan, D. (2022). *Digital news report: Australia 2022*. News and Media Research Centre, Canberra University. https://apo.org.au/sites/default/files/resource-files/2022-06/apo-nid317946_0.pdf
Petruccio, P., Neilson, T., & Stöcker, C. (2025). 'A part of our work disappeared': AI automated publishing in social media journalism. *Journalism and Media, 6*(1), 1–30. https://doi.org/10.3390/journalmedia6010030
Poell, T., Nieborg, D., & van Dijck, J. (2019). Platformisation. *Internet Policy Review, 8*(4), 1–13. https://doi.org/10.14763/2019.4.1425
Popiel, P. (2018). The tech lobby: Tracing the contours of new media elite lobbying power. *Communication, Culture and Critique, 11*(4), 566–585.
Saeed, D. (2025). *As Guardian Australia staff bristle at OpenAI deal, News Corp trials a new toy*. Crikey. https://www.crikey.com.au/2025/02/20/guardian-artificial-intelligence-openai-news-corp/.
Scott-Dawkins, K. (2025). *The trillion-dollar milestone: What record global ad revenues mean for the future of advertising*. WARC. https://www.warc.com/newsandopinion/opinion/the-trillion-dollar-milestone-what-record-global-ad-revenues-mean-for-the-future-of-advertising/en-gb/6944#:~:text=Most%20of%20the%20growth%20in,global%20ad%20revenue%20in%202024.
Simon, F. M. (2022). Uneasy bedfellows: AI in the news, platform companies and the issue of journalistic autonomy. *Digital Journalism, 10*(10), 1832–1854. https://doi.org/10.1080/21670811.2022.2063150
Simon, F. M. (2023). *Artificial intelligence in the news: How AI retools, rationalizes, and reshapes journalism and the public arena*. CJR. https://www.cjr.org/tow_center_reports/artificial-intelligence-in-the-news.php
Srnicek, N. (2022). Data, compute, labor. In M. Graham & F. Ferrari (Eds.), *Digital work in the planetary market* (pp. 241–161). MIT Press.
Taylor, L. (2023). Can we still handle the truth? Journalism, 'alternative facts' and the rise of AI. *The Guardian*. https://www.theguardian.com/commentisfree/2023/may/22/can-we-still-handle-the-truth-journalism-alternative-facts-and-the-rise-of-ai
Terranova, T. (2000). Free labor. *Social Text, 18*(2), 33–58. https://doi.org/10.1215/01642472-18-2_63-33
Uy-Tioco, C. S. (2019). Good enough' access: Digital inclusion, social stratification, and the reinforcement of class in the philippines. *Journal of Communication Research and Practice, 5*(2), 156–171. https://doi.org/10.1080/22041451.2019.1601492
van Dijck, J., Poell, T., & de Waal, M. (2018). *The platform society: Public values in a connective world*. Oxford University Press.
Waddell, T. F. (2017). A robot wrote this? How perceived machine authorship affects news credibility. *Digital Journalism, 6*(2), 236–255. https://doi.org/10.1080/21670811.2017.1384319
WashPostPR. (2024). *The Washington Post* launches "Ask The Post AI," a new search experience. *The Washington Post*. https://www.washingtonpost.com/pr/2024/11/07/washington-post-launches-ask-post-ai-new-search-experience/
Williams, R. (2024). Why Google's AI Overviews gets things wrong. *MIT Tech Review*. https://www.technologyreview.com/2024/05/31/1093019/why-are-googles-ai-overviews-results-so-bad/
Xia, B. (2021). Rethinking digital labour: A renewed critique moving beyond the exploitation paradigm. *The Economic and Labour Relations Review, 32*(3), 311–321. https://doi.org/10.1177/10353046211038396
Zuckerman, E. (2014). *The Internet's original sin: It's not too late to ditch the ad-based business model and build a better web*. The Atlantic. https://www.theatlantic.com/technology/archive/2014/08/advertising-is-the-internets-original-sin/376041/

Tai Neilson is a Senior Lecturer in Media and the Major Coordinator for Journalism at Macquarie University. He is the author of *Journalism and Digital Labor: Experiences of Online News Production* and co-edited *Research Methods for the Digital Humanities*. Dr. Neilson's areas of expertise include journalism, the political economy of digital media, and critical cultural theory. His current research investigates journalists' work practices, professional ideologies, and the power relations that impact their work. This includes critical approaches to the technologies and new modes of capital accumulation that are shaping media work. Dr. Neilson also teaches classes on media, technology, and news production.

Video Game Development

7

Richard Savery

Abstract

Generative artificial intelligence (AI) is no longer only a research field in game development; it is a production technology already embedded in asset pipelines, narrative tooling, and user-generated content platforms. This paper traces the lineage from early rule-based game AI to today's diffusion and transformer models, then analyzes seven recent case studies, from Ubisoft's Ghostwriter to King's AI-assisted level factory, to map how automation is reconfiguring labor, authorship, and creative risk. I frame AI as a mutable design material, showing how it compresses iteration cycles yet introduces new curatorial and ethical overheads. Survey data and studio interviews reveal a widening polarity: technical roles see efficiency gains, while creative disciplines worry about stylistic homogenization and job displacement. I close by outlining research agendas in critical AI literacy, toolchain interoperability, and governance of machine-augmented creativity.

7.1 Introduction

Artificial intelligence (AI) has been a fundamental element in video games since their inception, long before AI became a mainstream topic. It guides enemy tactics, animates non-player characters (NPCs), and subtly adjusts difficulty behind the scenes. AI is therefore essential to both the creation process and the quality of the final interactive experience. Many use cases of generative AI are simply an extension of old practice, large language models (LLMs) now stand in for earlier rule sets in procedural content generation, mixed-initiative design, and automated playtesting (Yang et al., 2024).

R. Savery (✉)
University of Canberra, Bruce, Canberra, Australia
e-mail: richard.savery@canberra.edu.au

S. Böhm et al. (eds.), *Handbook of AI-based Media Disruption*, Future of Business and Finance, https://doi.org/10.1007/978-3-032-07605-2_7

However, advances in generative AI that can produce novel content, such as 3D models, text, or code, have moved AI further into the game development process itself. Recent generative models can synthesize 3D meshes, dialogue, music, or executable code in seconds, pushing AI deeper into every layer of production. According to the 2025 GDC State of the Game Industry survey, 52% of studios already employ generative AI tools, and 36% of individual developers use them weekly (Game Developers Conference, 2025). This adoption spans the entire spectrum, from blockbuster "AAA" studios striving to streamline asset pipelines to solo hobbyists who can now build a prototype game after work using free web tools. Image diffusers, code copilots, and text generators (e.g., ChatGPT) have become standard items in the developer toolbox (Naswir, 2024).

With those opportunities come ethical and professional questions: Will AI displace artists? How do we verify the originality of generated content? Who owns material produced by a model trained on scraped data? Because the answers differ for hobbyists, indies, and multinational publishers, the chapter deliberately juxtaposes their experiences. To ground the discussion, I analyze seven recent case studies, ranging from Ubisoft's internal "Ghostwriter" to Roblox's user-generated content (UGC) tools and King's AI-assisted level factory. These examples were chosen to illustrate (i) the breadth of current AI use, (ii) the practical gains and failure modes already visible in shipping games, and (iii) how benefits and risks distribute unequally across stakeholders.

The chapter begins with a historical overview of AI in game development, establishing the through-line from early finite-state machines to today's transformers. Next, I examine the seven case studies in detail, then draw a cross-case synthesis to show how AI is reshaping workflows, authorship, and creative risk. Finally, I sketch future research directions, critical AI literacy, tool-chain interoperability, and governance of machine-augmented creativity, and offer closing thoughts on balancing innovation with ethics.

7.2 Historical Overview of Disruption

Well before computers rendered worlds on screen, designers were already using algorithmic thinking to stretch limited resources. Early war-gaming rulebooks such as Charles Totten's Strategos (1880) employed dice tables and flowcharts to generate fog-of-war events (Totten, 1880), while solo board games of the 1970s used paragraph systems that remixed narrative fragments according to player choices (Carr, 2006). These methods solved the same problem that drives digital proceduralism today: how to supply variety when hand-authorship is prohibitively expensive and create interactivity in real time. Recognizing this continuity helps situate modern generative AI not as an unprecedented rupture, but as the latest step in leveraging technology to improve games.

In the early era of video games, AI behaviors were relatively simple and scripted, yet they played a crucial role in making games engaging. Arcade classics and 8-bit console games of the 1970s and 1980s typically used predefined patterns or basic algorithms to control enemies and game elements. For example, the four ghosts in Pac-Man (1980) each have their own unique movement strategy encoded by the designers, creating the illusion of distinct "personalities" hunting the player. These early game AIs were essentially finite-state machines or rule-based systems that were optimized to run on limited hardware (Pittman, 2009).

In parallel, academic research into AI was also exploring video games, as a benchmark for AI algorithms. Milestones such as IBM's Deep Blue defeating a chess champion in 1997 or DeepMind's AlphaGo mastering Go in 2016 became critical proofs of the potential of AI (Silver et al., 2016). In practice, the game industry's early AI efforts were more pragmatic, focused on making computer-controlled opponents and characters that were fun and believable within strict technical constraints.

Long before studios embraced today's generative models, fan communities were already treating commercial games as do-it-yourself AI sandboxes. Valve's first-person shooter Half-Life from 1998, for instance, inspired volunteers to write "bot" plug-ins that added computer-controlled opponents to its multiplayer maps (Rosen, 2004). More than a decade later, players of Bethesda's open-world Skyrim from 2011 released "behavior packs" that rewired the game's non-player characters with entirely new decision trees. Both cases showed that outsiders could bolt fresh AI logic onto a closed engine, an approach that foreshadows how developers now drop open-weight language or vision models into Unity or Unreal with just a few lines of code. The industry therefore owes part of its current generative AI know-how to unpaid, hobbyist experimentation, a lineage worth remembering when we ask who benefits from, and who is left out of, each new technological wave.

As games and hardware grew more sophisticated, the role of AI expanded. By the 1990s and 2000s, developers adopted more advanced architectures like behavior trees and goal-oriented action planning to drive NPC decision-making in complex 3D worlds (Millington, 2019). Game AI began to handle tasks such as squad coordination in shooters or adaptive difficulty tuning. A key example is the AI "Director" in Left 4 Dead (published 2008), which monitored players' performance and emotional state and dynamically adjusted the intensity of zombie attacks to entertain without overwhelming them (Booth, 2009). This was an early form of AI-driven experience management embedded in the game's design. Overall, through the 2000s, AI in commercial games remained largely a collection of specialized systems: pathfinding algorithms for movement, scripted triggers for events, all under the careful control of designers.

Another longstanding application of AI in games is procedural content generation (PCG)—using algorithms to create game content (levels, maps, items, etc.) either ahead of time or during the actual game session. PCG has roots in some of the earliest computer games. The seminal dungeon crawler Rogue (circa 1980) introduced the idea of algorithmically generating a new maze of rooms and monsters on each playthrough, giving players a fresh experience every time and birthing the "roguelike" genre (Brewer, 2017). A few years later, Elite (published 1984) famously used procedural generation to create a vast galaxy of planets and star systems from a single seed number, primarily to fit an expansive game world into the very limited memory of 1980s hardware. By generating content mathematically, Elite could offer 2^{48} unique star systems (far more than could ever be handcrafted) without storing them explicitly (Gao et al., 2022).

In the decades since, PCG has been employed by many games to increase variety and scale. In 1996, Diablo randomized its dungeon layouts and loot drops to keep players unsure of what lay ahead (Shen, 2022). Later in 2009, Minecraft made infinite procedural terrain a core part of its appeal, so every player's world is unique (Barthet et al., 2022). More recently in 2016, No Man's Sky attempted to generate an entire universe of 18 quintillion planets using PCG algorithms (Schut, 2017). These examples show the enduring appeal of PCG in extending a game's content and replay value beyond what a team of designers could manually create.

From the early 2000s, the game industry saw a rise in the use of game data analytics, another form of AI application in games, though less visible to players (Su et al., 2021). As games became connected online and started collecting telemetry data, developers began applying machine learning and statistical models to understand player behavior. Game analytics emerged as a field that uses AI techniques to derive insights from large datasets of play information (El-Nasr et al., 2016). Studios could analyze how players progress, where they struggle or quit, and even predict which players might spend money in free-to-play games. These insights are particularly relevant to game design, while many if not all industries use data analytics, game design is highly driven by its findings. For example, developers might adjust the difficulty of a certain level if analytics show an unexpected spike in player drop-off, or they might personalize game content (such as matchmaking or in-game offers) for different player segments using predictive models (Wallner, 2019). Although this kind of AI operates behind the scenes, it has significantly influenced how modern games are designed and monetized, making the development process more data-driven (Ivanov et al., 2021).

By the 2010s, AI was also quietly aiding content creation through specialized tools. Middleware like SpeedTree could automatically generate dozens of varieties of trees and plants with a few parameter tweaks, saving artists countless hours while ensuring visual variety (Xiong & Huang, 2010). Procedural animation tools helped create crowds or background characters without animators crafting each motion. AI techniques (often not machine learning, but algorithmic) are also used to test games, such as bots that play through levels repeatedly to find glitches or balance issues, augmenting human quality assurance (Manabe, 2024).

7.3 Case Studies: AI Disruption in Practice

The case studies below present current examples of AI adoption in game development since 2023 (see Table 7.1). Most information comes from press releases, conference talks, and other material that commercial entities choose to make public, with technical specifics difficult to verify independently. Nevertheless, the vignettes illustrate the range of ways AI is reshaping production pipelines, creative roles, and design decisions across studios of every size.

Table 7.1 Snapshot of the seven case studies analyzed in Sect. 7.3

Studio/project	Scale	Main AI tool	Workflow benefit	Key concern
Ubisoft (Ghostwriter)	AAA	LLM text generation	Speeds NPC "bark" drafting	Creative authenticity
Activision Blizzard	AAA	Diffusion art + QA bots	Faster concept art; auto-QA	Reliability of bug-hunt bots
Square Enix (Foamstars)	AAA	Midjourney art	Rapid ancillary art	Fan backlash to AI style
Nexters (Hero Wars)	Mid	Midjourney art	40% art-iteration cut	Style consistency
Roblox Platform	UGC	Code/texture generators	Lowers entry barrier	Moderation load
King (Candy Crush)	AAA	RL level generator	95% QA hour drop	Difficulty/ monetization ethics
Team Miaozi (Cygnus Ent.)	Indie	Inworld LLM NPCs	Emergent voice dialogue	Lore coherence

7.3.1 Ubisoft: Ghostwriter AI for NPC Dialogue (AAA Narrative Design)

In 2023, Ubisoft introduced an in-house generative AI tool called Ghostwriter to assist its narrative design team (Francis, 2023). Ghostwriter generates first-draft dialogue lines, or "barks," for non-player characters (NPCs), such as incidental chatter and combat one-liners. Instead of replacing writers, the AI automates one of the most repetitive writing tasks, freeing scriptwriters to focus on core story content. The workflow remains interactive: writers specify an NPC persona and context, Ghostwriter produces line variations, and the writer selects or edits the best option. Each choice trains the model to improve future suggestions. This AI-assisted pipeline has sped up content creation for large open-world games filled with crowds of NPCs, while keeping writers in control of final dialogue quality.

Despite Ubisoft's assurances that Ghostwriter is a co-writing aid, its debut stirred debate. Some game developers publicly criticized the move, urging Ubisoft to invest more in human writers instead. In response, Ubisoft noted Ghostwriter was built with writer input and only tackles formulaic lines, not nuanced storytelling (Malik, 2023). The company has emphasized that human creativity and oversight remain key, using Ghostwriter to handle volume and iteration at scale. The outcome is an augmented narrative workflow: hundreds of NPC voice lines can be drafted in minutes, but human writers still review and polish them for authenticity. This case highlights how a AAA studio is cautiously integrating AI to handle grind work in narrative design, boosting productivity while navigating workforce acceptance and creative quality control.

7.3.2 Activision Blizzard: Internal Generative AI for Art and Quality Assurance (AAA Production Pipeline)

In mid-2023, Activision Blizzard began experimenting with generative AI to streamline art production and quality assurance in its development pipeline (Browning, 2023). An internal tool (nicknamed "Blizzard Diffusion") was fine-tuned on the studio's styles to generate concept art for game environments, characters, and props. The goal was to accelerate the creation of the massive volume of assets needed for franchises like World of Warcraft and Diablo and to help artists prototype ideas faster. Blizzard's leadership touted AI as a way to "accelerate their creative work" and offload some routine content tasks. Indeed, early tests showed AI could spit out varied art drafts in minutes, giving art teams more options to build on.

However, integrating AI has not been without challenges. Blizzard reportedly instructed employees to avoid public AI tools (like external image generators or ChatGPT) to prevent leaks of proprietary artwork or code. Instead, the studio deployed its private models, balancing innovation with intellectual property (IP) security. Internally, developer reactions were mixed. Some quality assurance (QA) staff found the AI underperformed in catching bugs during testing phases. This reveals a gap: while AI can generate content, using AI agents to play-test games and spot glitches proved less reliable than hoped. As of 2023, Blizzard's AI initiative remains in research and development: it shows promise in speeding up art workflows, but its effectiveness in areas like automated QA is uncertain. The company continues refining these tools, aiming to boost productivity for artists and testers while addressing quality issues. This case underscores both the enthusiasm and skepticism around AI in AAA production, where efficiency gains must be weighed against reliability and creative authenticity (Nelson, 2024).

7.3.3 Square Enix: LLM Narratives and AI-Generated Art in Development (AAA Experimentation)

Square Enix, the storied publisher of Final Fantasy, has actively explored AI across narrative design and art since 2023 (Square Enix, 2023). In April 2023, its AI division released a tech demo updating the classic text adventure Portopia Serial Murder Case with natural language input via a large language model (LLM). This experiment demonstrated how players could type free-form questions to a virtual detective, showcasing AI-driven narrative gameplay. The outcome, however, exposed current limitations: the AI struggled with ambiguous inputs, leading to very negative reviews from players and highlighting the challenge of aligning LLMs with game logic. Despite this, Square Enix signaled long-term commitment to AI. The company reorganized assets (even selling studios in 2022) to fund AI R&D, and backed startups like Atlas that generate 3D worlds from text.

Square Enix is also integrating AI into art workflows. In January 2024, the team behind the upcoming PS5 shooter Foamstars confirmed using Midjourney (an image-generating AI) to create in-game album cover art for the soundtrack (Parrish,

2024). The AI produced vibrant, on-theme illustrations that the developers loved and adopted as final assets. Notably, Square Enix stressed that only these album covers were AI made, all other visuals remained hand-crafted, reflecting a careful, limited use of generative art. This measured approach points to an important workflow change: AI tools can handle ancillary art tasks (like promotional or UI graphics) to save time, while artists focus on critical game visuals. Across its projects, Square Enix's AI forays illustrate a blend of bold innovation and caution. LLMs are being prototyped for new gameplay experiences, and image AIs are used for supplementary content, all while the studio closely evaluates quality and maintains a human creative core in its productions.

7.3.4 Nexters: Midjourney Transforming Art Production (Mid-Size Studio)

Nexters, an international mid-size studio (known for the mobile game Hero Wars), turned to Midjourney in 2023 to boost its art pipeline (Obedkov, 2023). The studio's hidden-object scenes and characters require constant updating, a traditionally labor-intensive process taking weeks per image. By integrating Midjourney (v4 and v5) into concept and character design, Nexters reported a 40% reduction in effort on creating and revising artwork. For example, artists used Midjourney to generate detailed character portraits and new poses that matched the game's style, then used those as bases for final illustrations. This dramatically sped up iteration, what once took dozens of sketching hours could be achieved in minutes by prompting the AI. Crucially, designers treated the AI as a starting point: they refined AI outputs, painted over artifacts, and ensured consistency with the game's established art direction.

Nexters openly shared lessons learned in adopting AI:

- *Backgrounds:* The team rarely keeps Midjourney's generated backgrounds, which often contain flaws, instead painting custom backdrops.
- *Details & Style:* Artists add details to AI-generated figures and adjust elements to maintain a cohesive style with existing assets.

They found AI most helpful in the prototyping stage, trying multiple ideas or visual styles rapidly without exhaustive hand-drawing. This empowered the studio to experiment with concepts (e.g. "a girl pilot in a leather jacket, comic-book style") and get immediate imagery for discussion. For a mid-size developer, generative art has become an "extra team member," accelerating content creation under tight schedules and budgets. The outcome is a more efficient art workflow where AI handles initial drafts and bulk variations, while human artists concentrate on polish, animation, and truly novel designs that define the game's creative identity.

7.3.5 Roblox: AI-Assisted Coding and Asset Creation at Scale (User-generated Content Platform)

Roblox, a global platform with millions of community creators, launched generative AI tools in 2023 to democratize game development on its service (Roblox Staff 2024). In a beta rollout, Roblox introduced an AI Material Generator and an AI Code Assist for its engine. These tools integrate directly into Roblox Studio, letting creators use natural language prompts to generate content. For example, a user can describe a texture ("rusty stone wall") and the Material Generator produces a high-quality, seamlessly tiled texture with realistic lighting applied. Similarly, by typing a command like "make this object spin when clicked," creators invoke the Code Assist, which generates Lua script snippets to implement the behavior. It can also auto-comment and explain code, functioning like a Roblox-tailored version of GitHub Copilot. The aim is to enable novices to create without extensive programming or art skills and to help experienced developers prototype and iterate faster.

Early feedback highlighted dramatic productivity gains. Developers testing these AI features noted that routine scripting tasks and asset tweaks could be done in seconds, shifting their time to higher-level design and polish. "If generative AI can accelerate the pace of development, that would revolutionize how, and how much, we build," said one Roblox creator, who saw the tech allowing bigger, more detailed worlds to be made with the same resources. Beyond creation, Roblox employs AI in content moderation and automatic translation, underscoring its broad commitment to AI-powered scalability. By 2024, Roblox began open-sourcing parts of its Roblox Cube AI system (for 3D object generation) to further spur innovation. This case exemplifies AI integration at platform scale: workflows are augmented across the board, texturing, coding, UI, lowering barriers for millions of user-developers and accelerating the user-generated content cycle on Roblox.

7.3.6 Candy Crush: King's AI-Assisted Level Design

Mobile-game giant King now stewards more than 18,700 playable boards in Candy Crush Saga; designers must ship new puzzles every week while continuously re-balancing the old. In May 2025, King disclosed that it relies on an internal AI pipeline to generate a first-pass draft for thousands of levels per week, an order-of-magnitude leap over the few hundred human teams previously managed manually (Parvini, 2025).

Developed by King AI Labs (formed after the 2022 acquisition of Swedish startup Peltarion), the model ingests billions of historical moves, pass-rates, reshuffle counts, quit points, and micro-transaction events. It then proposes board layouts that trace a target difficulty curve and monetization pacing. Designers review suggestions through a web dashboard that overlays heat maps of calculated choke points; they can accept, tweak, or discard each candidate, and their edits feed nightly retraining cycles.

A sister module dispatches autonomous "candied bots", gameplay agents tuned to human reaction times, to test every candidate board at scale, flagging unsolvable geometries and exploiting corner cases. King reports a 95% reduction in manual QA hours on level verification compared with 2022 baselines. The same pipeline retro-fits legacy puzzles: analytics identify frustration spikes, and AI proposes subtle tile swaps or new "relief" levels to smooth progression, boosting seven-day retention in A/B trials.

Franchise General Manager Todd Green claims the workflow "frees developers' time to create fresh seasonal events" that would be "extremely difficult" to deliver without machine assistance. Crucially, each AI-generated board still undergoes live human play-testing before release, preserving final creative control while accelerating ideation and balance cycles.

7.3.7 Team Miaozi/NetEase: AI NPCs with Inworld for Dynamic Dialogue (Indie/AA Design)

An intriguing 2023 example comes from Team Miaozi, a small studio under NetEase, which incorporated generative AI into the gameplay of Cygnus Enterprises (Inworld Team, 2023). This sci-fi action role-playing game (RPG), launched in Early Access on Steam, added a feature allowing players to have open-ended voice conversations with NPC characters. Through a partnership with Inworld AI (a character engine platform), the developers created AI-driven companion NPCs that respond to player speech in real time. Unlike traditional dialogue trees, these AI NPCs have an LLM-powered dialogue system enabling dynamic, unscripted interactions. Players can ask questions or give commands via microphone, and the NPC's AI interprets the intent and even triggers relevant in-game actions (e.g., following the player, using an item) based on the conversation. This has made NPCs feel more like improvisational partners, with unique, context-specific responses rather than looping stock phrases.

The game supports two parallel dialogue modes: one with fully scripted lines voiced by actors, and another with an AI persona that can chat naturally beyond the script. Team Miaozi reported that this hybrid approach preserves narrative control (for critical story moments) while offering an experimental sandbox of emergent gameplay through AI conversations. The addition of generative NPCs aimed to boost player engagement, and early player feedback found the concept exciting, if a bit unpredictable. Developers continue to fine-tune the AI's coherence and personality alignment with the lore. This case study shows a smaller studio pushing the envelope on AI in game design: by leveraging an LLM and voice synthesis, they expanded an RPG's narrative depth and interactivity without massively expanding writing teams. It illustrates how AI can take on a new design role, as a real-time co-creator of story and gameplay alongside the player, marking a bold disruption of traditional storytelling techniques in games.

7.4 AI and Workflow Disruption

The advent of advanced AI tools, especially generative models, has begun to reshape the creative and technical workflows of game development in fundamental ways. Production pipelines that traditionally relied on manual iteration and specialized labor are seeing automation encroach on tasks once considered the exclusive domain of human creators. This section examines how AI-driven tools disrupt established workflows, illustrating both enhanced efficiencies and emerging tensions between automation and authorship.

7.4.1 Automation versus Authorship in Game Development

The role of AI in content creation is evident in the *2025 GDC State of the Game Industry* survey of more than 3000 developers. A majority of respondents (52%) report that their studios already employ generative AI tools, and 36% use them personally on a week-to-week basis, an increase of five percentage points over 2024. Attitudes, however, are increasingly polarized: only 13% view AI's overall impact as "mostly positive," 30% label it negative, and 51% describe it as a "mixed blessing." Acceptance also varies by discipline: 51% of business and finance personnel rely on generative AI, compared with 39% of community/PR staff and 41% of production leads, mirroring divergent expectations for efficiency gains versus concerns over creative dilution, copyright risk, and job security (Game Developers Conference, 2025).

As detailed in Sect. 7.3.1, Ubisoft's in-house system Ghostwriter drafts low-stakes NPC "barks," leaving writers to curate the best lines and underscoring Ubisoft's human-in-the-loop stance (Barth, 2023; Francis, 2023). Comparable patterns surface across the other vignettes: Blizzard's "Diffusion" prototype accelerates concept art but still needs manual QA (Sect. 7.3.2); King's Candy Crush pipeline mass-produces draft levels while designers retain final veto (Sect. 7.3.6); and mid-size studio Nexters uses Midjourney to slash art-iteration time yet insists on human polish (Sect. 7.3.4). Each example reinforces a division of labor, AI handles scale, and humans guard quality.

Assuming Ubisoft's account is accurate, the human-in-the-loop design signals a redefinition of authorship as a collaborative process between designers and AI. Writers shift from sole authors to curators or editors of machine-generated text, maintaining creative authority by steering AI outputs. Nevertheless, even under the "assistant" label, the spread of automation provokes anxieties about the erosion of human authorship and the commodification of creative labor. Notably, survey sentiment diverges by role: developers in technical domains (programming, tools engineering) often anticipate net-positive effects, whereas those in creative domains (art, narrative) are more likely to foresee harm.

This divide highlights a deeper tension: while AI excels at automating pattern-based tasks, the potential loss of human originality and voice in highly creative facets of development is still contested. Some narrative designers worry that "maintaining the authenticity and emotional depth of storytelling" will become harder if AI contributes substantial narrative material. On the user-generated content side, millions of Roblox creators already lean on AI Code Assist to script behaviours they once had to program by hand (Sect. 7.3.5), hinting that the same authorship tensions extend beyond professional studios. The central question is whether generative AI will ultimately augment human creativity or progressively encroach on it. As one GDC respondent remarked, AI "should be used to enhance capabilities, not reduce the workforce," capturing the aspiration that automation empowers, rather than replaces, the human creator.

7.4.2 Shifting Roles and New Collaboration Dynamics

A distinctive feature of the games industry is its potential for inclusivity: titles can be produced by large AAA teams or by solo creators, and success stories, as well as failures, emerge from every scale of practice. As generative AI tools become embedded in workflows, the day-to-day roles of game creators are changing accordingly. Developers now occupy hybrid positions, part designer or artist, part "AI wrangler." For example, concept artists may spend less time drawing by hand and more time authoring text prompts or training custom models to generate batches of images in a specific style. Instead of painting every tree or weapon concept, an artist can direct a generative model to create dozens of variants, then curate and refine the most promising results. Consequently, expertise in prompt engineering and model fine-tuning is joining classical drawing or 3D modeling as a valued skill set. Recent case studies flesh this out. Concept artists at mid-size studio Nexters now open each morning by prompt-sketching dozens of Midjourney variants before selecting two or three to paint over (Sect. 7.3.4), while Square Enix's Foamstars team relied on a dedicated "AI texture wrangler" to fine-tune Midjourney album art (Sect. 7.3.3).

Role differentiation is likewise emerging within teams. Some members specialize in exploiting AI (e.g., an "AI technical artist" who prepares datasets and post-processes outputs), while others focus on polishing the generated assets or on tasks that still demand a human touch. Narrative design offers a clear illustration. With systems such as Ghostwriter and the broader availability of large language models (LLMs), narrative designers increasingly act as prompt crafters and editors. A single writer can feed a scenario or character profile to an AI, receive multiple dialogue variants, and then select or revise those that best fit the game's voice. This collaboration can enable one writer to handle volumes of text that once required a larger staff, altering hiring patterns and team structures. A more experimental line is visible at Team Miaozi, where writers double as "conversation curators," tuning LLM guardrails so that Inworld-powered NPCs stay on-lore during unscripted voice chats (Sect. 7.3.7).

One analysis notes that an artist empowered by AI can now produce roughly 40 scenes per day, compared with a previous norm of one scene, contributing to substantial reductions in art staff. Major publishers such as Tencent and NetEase have adopted AI-assisted pipelines for concept art, character design, and even production assets, reportedly resulting in a 70% decline in illustrator positions within a single year in China's game sector (Zhou, 2023). Conversely, on user-generated platforms like Roblox, AI Code Assist has expanded opportunities; creators with little Lua experience can now implement mechanics that once required contracting a programmer (Sect. 7.3.5), hinting that overall job displacement is uneven across sectors.

Studies of small and non-profit-driven studios complicate this narrative. Panchanadikar et al. (2024) observed that many independent developers frame generative AI as ushering in either "a new golden era" of empowerment or a flood of low-quality "slap comps" that dilute the marketplace. Participants valued AI's capacity to accelerate prototyping and asset creation, but they also worried about homogenised aesthetics and additional labor in curating imperfect outputs. A complementary investigation cast AI as an "ill-informed co-worker" for solo developers: helpful for brainstorming and routine tasks yet prone to errors that demand vigilant oversight (Panchanadikar & Freeman, 2024). Collectively, these studies indicate that while indie teams see AI as a potential equalizer, allowing small crews to match the content volume of larger studios, they remain cautious about quality control, originality, and the learning curve of AI toolchains.

Across studio sizes, then, collaboration dynamics are being renegotiated. Some roles shift toward orchestration and curation, others toward technical stewardship of models, while certain creative tasks still resist automation. How long these boundaries will hold hinges on both technical progress and the economic incentives that drive studios to substitute, or merely augment, human expertise.

The incorporation of generative AI is not just altering individual roles; it is prompting structural changes in the game development pipeline. Traditional game development follows a sequence of stages (concept, design, asset production, testing, etc.), often with clear handoffs between specialized departments. AI tools are introducing new workflows and feedback loops within this pipeline. For instance, in art production, instead of a linear handoff from concept artists to 3D artists to animators, a team might use an AI image generator to parallelize the concept phase, generating myriad visual ideas early on. These AI-generated concepts might be used as blueprints or mood boards that guide 3D modeling, or even be directly converted into 3D assets using emerging tools (e.g., generative models that create 3D models or textures from images). This accelerated ideation cycle allows teams to iterate on art style and content much faster than before, but it also requires additional pipeline steps: developers must curate AI outputs, integrate them into engine workflows, and often post-process or optimize AI-generated assets, which may not be game-ready out of the box (Pilaniwala et al., 2024). King's Candy Crush workflow (Sect. 7.3.6) illustrates the point: AI drafts thousands of new boards, but a newly minted cadre of "level-curation QA" staff vet solvability and monetization pacing before release.

A recent case study by Begemann & Hutson (2024) found that while current generative tools (for concept art, 3D asset generation, etc.) can "enhance the conceptualization phase," they still struggle to produce finalized, optimized game assets without human intervention, pointing to significant challenges in later pipeline integration. In practical terms, this means studios might save time in early creative exploration, but they must budget time for cleaning up AI outputs (e.g., fixing geometry on an AI-generated 3D model, or editing AI-created textures to meet technical constraints).

7.5 Discussion

7.5.1 AI as a Design Material: A New Creative Paradigm

A useful lens for understanding AI's role in game design is to treat AI as a design material, as it has essentially always been for video games. Rather than viewing AI as a magic black-box or a mere efficiency tool, designers can approach generative models and algorithms as materials with particular properties, affordances, and constraints that can be shaped through creative practice. This notion echoes Mateas's concept of "expressive AI," where AI techniques are integrated into the art of game design itself, not just used behind the scenes (Mateas, 2003). When AI is a design material, the creative process becomes one of exploration and co-creation with the AI: designers prototype with the AI, test its outputs, and iteratively refine prompts or model parameters much as they would sculpt clay or iterate on a level design.

A parallel mindset is taking hold in systems-driven genres. King's level-generation pipeline for Candy Crush (Sect. 7.3.6) treats a reinforcement-trained board-designer as malleable clay: designers dial difficulty targets and preview dozens of candidate layouts the way they might test lighting presets. On the user-generated side, Roblox creators experiment with AI Code Assist (Sect. 7.3.5) much like a sculpting tool, nudging, rerunning, and recombining code snippets until gameplay feels right. In both cases, the algorithm itself becomes a playable design surface rather than a hidden optimization step.

Viewing AI as a design material encourages its intentional and critical use. Just as a game designer chooses between materials (say, pixel art versus 3D models) to achieve a desired aesthetic, they can choose how and when to leverage AI to achieve a design goal. Core examples demonstrate this breadth: AI can automate narrative scene generation and crucial NPC interactions (Kumaran et al., 2023), or empower conversational agents with just a few prompts to generate free-form, grounded, and less repetitive dialogue, even producing novel code (Volum et al., 2022). It can be employed to sift compelling stories from complex simulation logs (Méndez & Gervás, 2023) or even act as an evaluating agent for open-ended challenges within serious games (Isaza-Giraldo et al., 2024). Seen in historical context, these practices extend a lineage that begins with Rogue-style proceduralism (Sect. 7.2) but swaps hand-coded algorithms for stochastic, data-driven models, shifting the designer's craft from writing rules to steering distributions.

At the same time, designers must develop an intuition for AI's limitations and biases, much as they understand the grain of wood or the quirks of a physics engine. The capriciousness and variability of generative AI is a key characteristic of this material; it can produce novel, unexpected results, but also inconsistent ones. Hence, treating AI as a design material involves developing new prototyping methods. One must experiment with AI systems to see what range of outputs they produce and shape those outputs into cohesive game content. This spirit of exploration is evident in initiatives like game jams focused on LLM-based production, which help map the current capabilities and shortcomings of these tools (Grow & Khosmood, 2023).

This approach blurs practical and philosophical considerations. Practically, it means new tools and interfaces should be created to let designers "sketch" with AI easily and safely. Philosophically, it implies a more postmodern view of game authorship, acknowledging the influence of nonhuman actors (AI systems) in the creative process and requiring designers to embrace a degree of surrender of control in exchange for serendipity and complexity. As AI becomes ingrained in design, designers become curators of possibility spaces, defining the bounds within which the AI can vary content rather than dictating every detail.

7.5.2 Risks: Homogenization and Loss of Creative Control

While the integration of AI into creative workflows presents significant opportunities, it also introduces notable risks that warrant careful consideration within game development, particularly regarding content diversity, creative authority, and ethical implications.

A primary concern is the potential for homogenization of game content. As developers increasingly adopt popular, large-scale generative AI models, there is a risk that outputs will converge towards statistically average solutions. Blizzard art directors observed exactly this in 2024 when "Blizzard Diffusion" sketches for three separate franchises gravitated toward the same teal-orange palette (Sect. 7.3.2), forcing a costly manual re-branding pass. The use of a single AI system, or a few dominant ones, to perform tasks previously handled by diverse human creators can inherently lead to increased homogenization in outcomes (Bommasani et al., 2022). Studies suggest that even when users aim for distinct ideas, AI tools can cause homogenization in the generated results (Anderson et al., 2024a). This reliance on common training data may lead to games that feel formulaic, potentially reducing the overall diversity that characterizes the medium. Furthermore, since many large models are trained on datasets with inherent biases, there is a risk of AI tools pushing outputs towards specific, often Western, styles, further reducing global creative diversity (Agarwal et al., 2025).

Closely linked is the challenge of maintaining creative control and authorship. When designers incorporate AI systems with a degree of autonomy, ensuring the final product aligns perfectly with their intended vision can become difficult. Generative systems might introduce elements, tones, or design choices not explicitly desired by the human team. Filtering, curating, and quality-controlling AI outputs can be labor intensive. Players quickly spotted AI-generated artifacts in a Ubisoft teaser in July 2024, forcing the studio to pull the video, and Square Enix's mid-2023 social-media mock-ups drew similar criticism for obvious Midjourney artifacts, prompting a pledge to restrict AI imagery to ancillary assets (Sect. 7.3.3). This unpredictability, coupled with potential latent biases within training data, underscores the challenges to a designer's control. There is also a psychological dimension; creators might feel a diminished personal connection or responsibility for content that was significantly computer-generated, as some research suggests users feel less responsible for AI-assisted ideas (Anderson et al., 2024b).

Finally, significant ethical and economic risks loom, particularly concerning intellectual property and labor. The practice of training AI models on vast datasets, often including copyrighted works, raises profound questions about authorship, copyright infringement, and fair use. Activision Blizzard's blanket ban on staff using public diffusion services (Sect. 7.3.2) illustrates how IP anxiety already shapes studio policy, even when internal models are encouraged. Current legal frameworks struggle to accommodate AI-generated works, creating legal uncertainties for studios. Concurrently, the efficiency gains offered by AI have led to fears of labor devaluation and job displacement, especially for roles like concept artists and illustrators. Addressing these multifaceted risks requires robust ethical guidelines, transparent development practices, and potentially new legal frameworks to ensure AI serves as a tool that enhances, rather than diminishes, human creativity and a diverse gaming landscape.

7.6 Conclusion and Future Outlook

Artificial intelligence has always been woven into the fabric of game making, from early finite-state "ghost" routines in Pac-Man to the planet-sized proceduralism of No Man's Sky. What has changed since 2023 is the scope and accessibility of generative models: diffusion for images, transformers for text and code, and reinforcement learning for balancing and QA. These tools collapse iteration time, alter job descriptions, and blur the line between designer and curator.

Across the seven case studies I examined, a clear pattern emerges:

1. **Scale before subtlety.** Studios automate the most repetitive, low-stakes content first, NPC barks at Ubisoft (Sect. 7.3.1), concept thumbnails at Blizzard (Sect. 7.3.2), match-three boards at King (Sect. 7.3.6). Human veto remains central wherever nuance, lore consistency, or brand identity is at risk.
2. **Hybrid roles proliferate.** Artists become prompt-smiths, writers become conversation curators, and QA testers monitor fleets of AI "co-players." The same technologies that shrink some job categories (e.g., illustrators in China's big publishers) also create new ones, AI technical artists, data wranglers, ethics reviewers.
3. **Design material, not magic.** Treating AI as clay invites experimentation: Team Miaozi's LLM-driven NPCs (Sect. 7.3.7) and Roblox's Code Assist (Sect. 7.3.5) illustrate how creators can sculpt behavior and narrative the way they once sculpted geometry. Mastery comes from understanding biases, failure modes, and the "grain" of stochastic systems.
4. **Homogenization hazards.** Reliance on a few dominant models can flatten aesthetics, as seen in Blizzard's teal-orange drift and Midjourney artifacts in Square Enix marketing (Sects. 7.3.2–7.3.3). Maintaining stylistic diversity now demands deliberate injection of human variation.

5. **Ethics and IP drive policy.** Data provenance, copyright liability, and labor displacement are no longer hypothetical. Internal-only models, licensing audits, and transparent content-tagging are becoming table stakes for large publishers.

Looking ahead, four fronts deserve sustained research attention:

Critical AI Literacy.

Curriculum in game-design programs must now include prompt engineering, model auditing, and ethics, ensuring future developers wield AI responsibly rather than opportunistically.

Toolchain Interoperability.

Generative outputs still need heavy post-processing to hit engine constraints. Standardizing asset descriptors and metadata will shorten the "last-mile" gap between a model's draft and a shippable resource.

Human-centered User Testing.

AI play-testers can churn through billions of input permutations, yet they routinely miss the edge-case quirks that delight, or frustrate, real players. Research is needed on hybrid testing pipelines that combine automated bots with targeted human sessions, along with metrics that capture experiential qualities (surprise, humor, frustration) that current AI agents fail to model.

Governance of Creativity.

As authorship becomes increasingly collective, spanning human teams, proprietary datasets, and autonomous agents, legal frameworks must evolve to credit and compensate all contributors, human or otherwise.

Whether AI ushers in a "golden age" of solo auteurship or accelerates consolidation around mega-studios hinges on how equitably these tools, the knowledge to steer them, and the economic gains they unlock are distributed. The games industry has an opportunity, perhaps an obligation, to model a future where automation augments rather than erases human imagination. Realizing that future will require transparent pipelines, cross-disciplinary education, and a willingness to treat AI not as a black-box oracle but as a fallible, fascinating collaborator. The next disruption, like every one before it, will be shaped by the design choices we make today.

References

Agarwal, D., Naaman, M., & Vashistha, A. (2025). AI suggestions homogenize writing toward western styles and diminish cultural nuances. *Proceedings of the 2025 CHI conference on human factors in computing systems* (pp. 1–21).

Anderson, B. R., Shah, J. H., & Kreminski, M. (2024a). Evaluating creativity support tools via homogenization analysis. *Extended abstracts of the CHI conference on human factors in computing systems* (pp. 1–7).

Anderson, B. R., Shah, J. H., & Kreminski, M. (2024b). Homogenization effects of large language models on human creative ideation. *Proceedings of the* 16th conference on creativity & cognition (pp. 413–425).

Barth, R. (2023). The convergence of AI and creativity: Introducing ghostwriter. *Ubisoft News*. https://news.ubisoft.com/en-us/article/7Cm07zbBGy4Xml6WgYi25d/the-convergence-of-ai-and-creativity-introducing-ghostwriter

Barthet, M., Liapis, A., & Yannakakis, G. N. (2022). Open-ended evolution for minecraft building generation. *IEEE Transactions on Games, 15*(4), 603–612.

Begemann, A., & Hutson, J. (2024). Empirical insights into AI-assisted game development: A case study on the integration of generative AI tools in creative pipelines. *Meta, 5*(2).

Bommasani, R., Creel, K. A., Kumar, A., Jurafsky, D., & Liang, P. S. (2022). Picking on the same person: Does algorithmic monoculture lead to outcome homogenization? *Advances in Neural Information Processing Systems, 35*, 3663–3678.

Booth, M. (2009). *The AI systems of left 4 dead. Presentation slides, Artificial Intelligence and Interactive Digital Entertainment Conference (AIIDE)*. Stanford University. https://steamcdn-a.akamaihd.net/apps/valve/2009/ai_systems_of_l4d_mike_booth.pdf

Brewer, N. (2017). Computerized dungeons and randomly generated worlds: From rogue to minecraft [scanning our past]. *Proceedings of the IEEE, 105*(5), 970–977.

Browning, K. (2023). *A.I. may help design your favorite video game character*. https://www.nytimes.com/2023/05/22/arts/blizzard-diffusion-ai-video-games.html

Carr, D. (2006). *Computer games: Text, narrative and play*. Polity.

El-Nasr, M. S., Drachen, A., & Canossa, A. (2016). *Game analytics*. Springer.

Francis, B. (2023). *Here are more details on ubisoft's ghostwriter AI tool from GDC 2023*. Game Developer. https://www.gamedeveloper.com/marketing/here-are-more-details-on-ubisoft-s-narrative-ai-tools-from-gdc-2023

Game Developers Conference. (2025). *GDC 2025 state of the game industry report*. https://gdconf.com/resources/2025-state-of-the-game-industry

Gao, T., Zhang, J., & Mi, Q. (2022). Procedural generation of game levels and maps: A review. *2022 International conference on artificial intelligence in information and communication (ICAIIC)* (pp. 050–055).

Grow, A. M., & Khosmood, F. (2023). ChatGPT gamejam: Unleashing the power of large language models for game jams. In *Proceedings of the 7th international conference on game jams, hackathons and game creation events* (pp. 51–54).

Inworld Team. (2023). *How NetEase integrated Inworld in Cygnus Enterprises, Part 1*. https://inworld.ai/blog/netease-cygnus-enterprise-integrated-ai-npcs-inworld

Isaza-Giraldo, A., Bala, P., Campos, P. F., & Pereira, L. (2024). Prompt-gaming: A pilot study on LLM-evaluating agent in a meaningful energy game. *Extended abstracts of the CHI conference on human factors in computing systems* (pp. 1–12).

Ivanov, M., Wittenzellner, H., & Wardaszko, M. (2021). Video game monetization mechanisms in triple a (AAA) video games. *Simulation gaming through times and disciplines: 50th international simulation and gaming association conference, ISAGA 2019, Warsaw, Poland, August 26–30, 2019*, Revised Selected Papers 50, 389–404.

Kumaran, V., Rowe, J., Mott, B., & Lester, J. (2023). Scenecraft: Automating interactive narrative scene generation in digital games with large language models. *Proceedings of the AAAI conference on artificial intelligence and interactive digital entertainment, 19*, 86–96.

Malik, A. (2023). *Ubisoft's new AI tool automatically generates dialogue for non-playable game characters*. https://techcrunch.com/2023/03/22/ubisofts-new-ai-tool-automatically-generates-dialogue-for-non-playable-game-characters/

Manabe, K. (2024). Quality assurance-artificial intelligence. In *Encyclopedia of computer graphics and games* (pp. 1507–1514). Springer.

Mateas, M. (2003). Expressive AI: A semiotic analysis of machinic affordances. *3rd Conference on computational semiotics for games and new media, 58*.

Méndez, G., & Gervás, P. (2023). Using ChatGPT for story sifting in narrative generation. *Proceedings of the 14th international conference on computational creativity*.

Millington, I. (2019). *AI for games*. CRC Press.

Naswir, A. F. (2024). The future of artificial intelligence in 2D game development. *Journal of Data Science, Technology, and Computer Science, 4*(2), 1–9.

Nelson, J. (2024). *How Ubisoft, Xbox, and Blizzard are using AI to make next-generation games*. https://decrypt.co/147436/ai-game-development-ubisoft-roblox-blizzard

Obedkov, E. (2023). *Pros and cons of using Midjourney in game development — lessons learned by Nexters.* https://gameworldobserver.com/2023/07/31/midjourney-game-development-art-nexters-hero-wars
Panchanadikar, R., & Freeman, G. (2024). "i'm a solo developer but AI is my new ill-informed co-worker": Envisioning and designing generative AI to support indie game development. *Proceedings of the ACM on human-computer interaction*, *8*(CHI PLAY) (pp. 1–26).
Panchanadikar, R., Freeman, G., Li, L., Schulenberg, K., & Hu, Y. (2024). "a new golden era" or "slap comps": How non-profit driven indie game developers perceive the emerging role of generative AI in game development. *Extended abstracts of the CHI conference on human factors in computing systems* (pp. 1–7).
Parrish, A. (2024). *Square Enix says it used AI art in upcoming Foamstars game.* https://www.theverge.com/2024/1/16/24040124/square-enix-foamstars-ai-art-midjourney
Parvini, S. (2025). *How AI helps push Candy Crush players through its most difficult puzzles.* https://apnews.com/article/547254aaa06bf026df5b41458ac62dcc
Pilaniwala, P., Chhabra, G., & Kaur, P. (2024). The future of game development in the era of gen AI. *2024 Artificial Intelligence for Business (AIxB)* (pp. 39–42).
Pittman, J. (2009). *The Pac-Man Dossier.* Gamasutra. https://www.gamedeveloper.com/design/the-pac-man-dossier
Rosen, Z. (2004). Mod, man, and law: A reexamination of the law of computer game modifications. *The Chicago-Kent Journal of Intellectual Property, 4*, 196.
Schut, K. (2017). Hello game's no man's sky. In *The Routledge companion to imaginary worlds* (pp. 425–432). Routledge.
Shen, Z. (2022). Procedural generation in games: Focusing on dungeons. *SHS Web of Conferences, 144*, 02005.
Silver, D., Huang, A., Maddison, C. J., Guez, A., Sifre, L., Van Den Driessche, G., Schrittwieser, J., Antonoglou, I., Panneershelvam, V., Lanctot, M., et al. (2016). Mastering the game of go with deep neural networks and tree search. *Nature, 529*(7587), 484–489.
Square Enix. (2023). *Square enix AI tech preview: The portopia serial murder case.* https://store.steampowered.com/app/2280000/SQUARE_ENIX_AI_Tech_Preview_THE_PORTOPIA_SERIAL_MURDER_CASE/
Roblox Staff. (2024). *Code assist full release: AI-powered Code Completion.* https://devforum.roblox.com/t/code-assist-full-release-ai-powered-code-completion/2848978
Su, Y., Backlund, P., & Engström, H. (2021). Comprehensive review and classification of game analytics. *Service Oriented Computing and Applications, 15*, 141–156.
Totten, C. A. L. (1880). *Strategos: A series of American games of war, based upon military principles and designed for the assistance both of beginners and advanced students in prosecuting the whole study of tactics, grand tactics, strategy, military history, and the various operations of war...* (Vol. 1). D. Appleton; Company.
Volum, R., Rao, S., Xu, M., DesGarennes, G., Brockett, C., Van Durme, B., Deng, O., Malhotra, A., & Dolan, W. B. (2022). Craft an iron sword: Dynamically generating interactive game characters by prompting large language models tuned on code. *Proceedings of the 3rd wordplay: When language meets games workshop (Wordplay 2022)* (pp. 25–43).
Wallner, G. (2019). A brief overview of data mining and analytics in games. *Data analytics applications in gaming and entertainment* (pp. 1–14).
Xiong, Q., & Huang, X. (2010). Speed tree-based forest simulation system. *2010 International conference on electrical and control engineering* (pp. 3033–3036).
Yang, D., Kleinman, E., & Harteveld, C. (2024). GPT for games: A scoping review (2020-2023). *2024 IEEE Conference on Games (CoG)* (pp. 1–8).
Zhou, V. (2023). *AI is already taking video game illustrators' jobs in China.* Rest of World. https://restofworld.org/2023/ai-china-video-game-layoffs-illustrators/

Richard Savery is a developer of artificial intelligence and robotics, using music and creativity as a medium to program better interactions, understandings and models. He was a Senior Research Scientist at Jen Music and a Macquarie University Research Fellow, developing ethically trained, high-fidelity text-to-music systems and a rapping, drumming interactive robot. He now holds an ARC DECRA fellowship (2025–2027) at the University of Canberra, focusing on robots and AI in long-term use and groups. His research has received $3.8 million in funding and significant industry partnerships. His work has been featured in Scientific American, BBC Radio and Disney+ with Jeff Goldblum. He completed a PhD in Music Technology (minor in Human–Computer Interaction) at the Georgia Institute of Technology.

Part II

Cross-Sector Impact of AI-Based Media Disruption

Impact of AI on Trust in the Media

8

Castulus Kolo, Joschka Mütterlein, and Sarah Anna Schmid

Abstract

This chapter introduces the evolving concept of trust from a media perspective within the context of artificial intelligence (AI), examining its pivotal role in shaping public perceptions, media legitimacy, and technological acceptance. The erosion of trust in traditional media is shaped by factors such as economic inequality, political polarization, widespread misinformation, and the growing dominance of digital platforms that disrupt conventional news hierarchies. Drawing on interdisciplinary perspectives, the chapter explores how trust is conceptualized in psychology, sociology, philosophy, economics, and communication theory, highlighting its multi-level and relational nature. Media trust is increasingly influenced by the integration of technology, particularly through the growing role of artificial intelligence in the production, curation, and dissemination of news. As media environments become more algorithmically driven, the boundaries between trust in media and trust in technology begin to blur. Trust in AI is shaped by a complex interplay of human dispositions, contextual settings, and technological factors such as transparency, reliability, and explainability. At the same time, widespread concerns, ranging from surveillance and algorithmic bias to manipulation and unclear accountability, highlight the pressing need for systems that are both trustworthy and ethically designed. Addressing these challenges, the chapter outlines key research themes and future directions, calling for interdisciplinary and ethically grounded frameworks to assess and foster trust in AI-powered media systems, as a foundation for democratic resilience and informed public discourse.

C. Kolo (✉) · J. Mütterlein · S. A. Schmid
Macromedia University, Munich, Germany
e-mail: c.kolo@macromedia.de; j.muetterlein@macromedia.de; sarah.schmid@macromedia.de

S. Böhm et al. (eds.), *Handbook of AI-based Media Disruption*, Future of Business and Finance, https://doi.org/10.1007/978-3-032-07605-2_8

8.1 Introduction to the Concept of Trust from a Media Perspective in an Era of AI

In recent years, trust in the media has come under considerable strain. This erosion of confidence became particularly pronounced after the global COVID-19 pandemic (Edelman, 2025), a period marked by widespread uncertainty and heightened public reliance on information sources. Although recent data suggest that trust levels may have stabilized to some extent (Newman et al., 2025), the overall trend reflects persistent skepticism toward media institutions. The global communications firm Edelman (2020) indicates that people in general today feel worried and are anxious about current as well as future developments. These worries stem from fears of corruption, economic inequalities, negative effects of globalization, weakening social values, and rapid technological changes. Newman et al. (2024) report a growing divide between social groups with higher incomes and higher levels of education, who generally tend to trust institutions such as media outlets more, while people with fewer financial and educational resources are often more skeptical of them.

These developments have not only severely impaired trust in traditional institutions, but also in the media as there are growing doubts about the reliability of traditional news sources and the independence of journalists (Flew, 2021; Jones, 2018). The development toward a high-choice media environment intensifies this situation. The rise of digital platforms and social media has led to the emergence of numerous nontraditional and partisan media formats that act as direct channels to the public. This significantly increases the competitive pressure on traditional news providers as more and more people obtain their information online (Flew, 2021). In this environment, established media must compete for people's attention against a variety of information sources, which further undermines their credibility (Boomgaarden & Prior, 2008; Strömbäck et al., 2020; Van Aelst et al., 2017).

In addition, political and social actors use the possibilities of social media to bypass traditional news channels and attack them with the Trump administration being a notable case in point (Mourão et al., 2018; Strömbäck et al., 2020). This trend is reinforced by increasing political polarization (Sides & Hopkins, 2015), making it even more difficult for traditional media to be perceived as credible and neutral. At the same time, the spread of fake news, disinformation, and misinformation has increased significantly (Benkler et al., 2018; Egelhofer & Lecheler, 2019; Kavanagh & Rich, 2018), while political actors are less inhibited about spreading misinformation (PolitiFact, 2025). People tend to prefer information that corresponds to their existing attitudes, the so-called confirmation bias (Knobloch-Westerwick et al., 2017). This tendency toward selective perception and the associated motivated skepticism toward contradictory information not only leads to less consumption of traditional news but also to widespread misperceptions and an increasing resistance to new knowledge (Flynn et al., 2017; Klintman, 2021; Kunda, 1990; Taber & Lodge, 2006). Some studies suggest that lower media trust is directly related to a decrease in the use of established news sources and an increased turn to alternative sources of information (Kalogeropoulos et al., 2019; Ladd, 2011;

Mourão et al., 2018; Tsfati & Cappella, 2003, 2005). This trend also contributes to more widespread misinformation and increased resistance to factual knowledge (Klintman, 2021). The rise in mistrust has become a serious issue because it negatively affects both the economy and politics. For example, the 2019 World Economic Forum in Davos highlighted that a lack of trust is a barrier to economic growth, digital innovation, and social unity, emphasizing that trust is like "the ultimate human currency" (McDermott, 2019).

In this contribution, we examine the concept of trust from a media perspective, focusing on how it is reshaped in an era increasingly influenced by artificial intelligence. First, we outline the interdisciplinary foundations of trust, exploring its meanings across psychology, sociology, philosophy, economics, and communication studies. We then delve into the specific dynamics of media trust and how technological change, particularly the integration of AI, has transformed its formation, erosion, and mediation. Finally, we identify key areas of ongoing research and propose a future agenda for understanding and fostering trust in AI-driven media environments. To systematically address the multifaceted disruptions AI brings to the media sector, this chapter contributes a critical perspective on trust as both a challenge and a prerequisite for sustainable, democratic media systems in the age of automation and algorithmic decision-making.

8.2 Approaches to Define the Concept of Trust

Trust, as a concept, has been the subject of extensive interdisciplinary inquiry. Generally, trust refers to the degree of confidence that individuals or groups place in the reliability, integrity, and competence of others. Möllering (2006, p. 111) describes trust as "an ongoing process of building on reason, routine and reflexivity, suspending irreducible social vulnerability and uncertainty as if they were favorably resolved, and maintaining thereby a state of favorable expectation toward the actions and intentions of more or less specific others."

Different disciplines look at trust in various ways, showing that its meaning can change depending on the context. This makes trust a complex idea that cannot be fully captured by just one definition. For psychologists, trust is important in our daily life to build relationships (DeSteno, 2015). It originates in childhood when children first learn to trust their parents or caretakers and helps them later to build trust in other people and institutions. In philosophy, trust is seen as essential to human life, closely connected to personal autonomy and therefore an important building block for democracies (O'Neill, 2002). It can be considered at different levels in individuals, in social institutions or in society. It means relying to a certain extent on certain outcomes, but at the same time always being uncertain whether these will materialize. Trust is not the same as truth, even though honest and open communication is an important characteristic of trustworthy people and forms the basis for trust. Trust also differs from mere belief as it only has real meaning if there is also the possibility that this trust can be betrayed (Flew, 2021; Keymolen, 2016; Seligman, 2000). Trust therefore helps people manage uncertainty and vulnerability in the environment or within relations (Baier, 1986). Economists view trust as a logical decision based on rational risk assessment. People trust others if they think the other person is unlikely to harm or take advantage of them (e.g., Axelrod, 1984; Bradach & Eccles, 1989; Coleman, 1994). From a sociological perspective, trust acts as a binding thing (also discussed as social capital) that helps society to stick together and makes social interaction possible (Fukuyama, 1996; Putnam, 2001). Trust occupies an intermediate position between interpersonal relationships and the broader institutional framework (Banerjee et al., 2006). It is not only seen as an outcome of individual interaction but is also influenced by institutional reputation and social networks. Sociologists thereby analyze the multi-level nature of trust at the level of interpersonal trust (Misztal, 2013), in dyadic interpersonal relationships, or as embedded trust that establishes itself in social and institutional (collective) structures and entails consequences for trust in society and thus shapes social coexistence (Fukuyama, 1996; Giddens, 1990; Putnam, 2001; Sztompka, 1999).

Communication theory has further enriched our understanding of trust by examining its role in mediated interactions. Communication scholars have extended traditional models of trust to account for the unique challenges of digital environments specifically in the media. The rapid dissemination of information on digital platforms, combined with the possibility of algorithmic manipulation, requires a reassessment of trust dynamics in the digital age. For example, systematic, cross-national analyses have begun to unravel the complexities of trust in different news brands, moving beyond simplistic attributions of "fake news" and "echo chambers" to develop a more nuanced understanding of media trustworthiness (Fletcher & Park, 2017; Kalogeropoulos et al., 2019; Strömbäck et al., 2020).

8.2.1 Defining Media Trust

In the context of media, trust plays a pivotal role in shaping how audiences engage with news and in establishing the legitimacy of news providers. Fundamentally, media trust operates as a relationship between two parties: the trustor, who confers trust, and the trustee, who receives it (Quandt, 2012; Tsfati & Cappella, 2003). More specifically, media trust refers to the bond between the public and news media. In uncertain situations, the public, whether consciously or subconsciously, expect that their interactions with news outlets will yield positive outcomes rather than negative ones (Strömbäck et al., 2020; Tsfati & Cappella, 2003). As Kohring (2019) notes, individuals often lack the means to independently verify news reliability and instead rely on perceived media credibility as a proxy for trustworthiness. Hence, trust involves a willingness to accept this informational vulnerability in the hope of a beneficial exchange.

However, conceptualizing media trust is not straightforward due to the inherent complexity and diversity of the media landscape. The term "media" encompasses a wide array of stakeholders, ranging from journalists and editors to platforms, organizations, and technologies. Recognizing this complexity, Strömbäck et al. (2020)

propose a differentiated view of media trust, identifying several specific levels at which trust can be situated: in media content, in journalists, in individual media brands, in specific media types, and in the news media as a whole. Among these, trust in the news media in general is particularly abstract and the most difficult to operationalize and measure.

Media trust is often discussed alongside adjacent concepts such as media credibility, trustworthiness, and authenticity, particularly within the context of evaluating media quality (Engelke et al., 2019; Kiousis, 2001; Otto & Köhler, 2018). To assess whether media sources deserve trust, audiences seek out cues and indicators that help them judge their reliability. These cues are together typically framed in academic literature as media credibility, a term that is frequently used interchangeably with media trust (Kohring, 2019). Credibility itself can be further divided into two main dimensions: source credibility and medium credibility. Kiousis (2001) explains that source credibility is determined by the perceived expertise and trustworthiness of the information source. Originating from the foundational work of Hovland et al. (1953), this concept explains how credible sources can influence public attitudes and perceptions. In addition to these dimensions, credibility research also emphasizes factors such as fairness, objectivity, accuracy, and the absence of bias in media coverage (Gaziano & McGrath, 1986; Meyer, 1988; West, 1994). These factors contribute to whether audiences find a media outlet or piece of content trustworthy and have significant implications for the broader understanding of media trust.

Trust, including media trust, functions across different societal levels. As Flew (2024) outlines, trust can be analyzed at the macro level, which pertains to trust in society, the meso level, referring to trust in institutions like governments and media organizations, and the micro level, involving interpersonal trust between individuals. Institutional trust often serves as the bridge between individual trust and broader societal trust (Flew, 2021; Nau, 2005). In the context of media, this means that trust in news content and platforms is not isolated, but deeply interwoven with how people perceive institutions and society at large. It is important to understand these different dimensions of media trust, especially when looking at how trust and technology intersect in the media sector. This is becoming increasingly relevant as technologies like Artificial Intelligence (AI) play a larger role in how we create, access, and interact with the media. We see general debates particularly with regards (1) to conceptualizing trust in the first place, (2) to how distrust manifests itself in AI, (3) to how trust is built, and (4) to the dual role of technology in mediating trust.

8.3 General Debates on the Relationship of Trust and AI

Trust in AI has become a critical issue in the media sector, as artificial intelligence is progressively integrated into all stages of media production, distribution, and consumption, making it essential to explore how this technological evolution may impact the broader dynamics of trust in the media. Trust in AI represents, according to Siau & Wang (2018) "the willingness of people to accept AI and believe in the suggestions, decisions made by the system, share tasks, contribute information, and provide support to such technology." As AI takes on bigger roles in content curation, fact-checking, and distribution, it is important to understand the different factors that shape trust, particularly at a time when many people are still unsure about AI or lack a clear understanding of how it works in the media sector (Newman et al., 2024). Exploring these trust dynamics is essential to reducing uncertainty and addressing ethical challenges.

8.3.1 Conceptualizing Trust in AI

Trust in AI goes beyond simply relying on or accepting the technology; it involves a complex relationship between people (the trustors) and AI systems (the trustees). As Thiebes et al. (2021) point out, building trust between humans and AI is more complicated than trust between people. This complexity comes from the unique nature of AI, including its lack of transparency, its ability to act independently, and its capacity to learn and change, all of which can make its behavior unpredictable. The formation of trust in AI is shaped by a combination of interrelated factors (Afroogh et al., 2024):

- Human-related such as personality, past experiences, and values that can influence a person's willingness to trust AI.
- Context-related depending on where AI is used (e.g., healthcare vs. entertainment).
- Technology-related including the system's performance, transparency, and explainability.

Users are more likely to trust AI when systems clearly communicate their capabilities and limitations, and when decision-making processes are transparent and comprehensible. Taken together, these dimensions highlight the inherent complexity of human–AI trust and underscore the importance of intentional, context-sensitive design when integrating AI into media environments.

8.3.2 Manifestations of Distrust in AI

Despite AI's potential to enhance trust through consistent and accurate outputs, various sources of distrust continue to hinder its acceptance, particularly in sensitive domains. At a broader societal level, fears surrounding the advent of specifically artificial general intelligence (AGI) underscore deep concerns about AI's long-term implications. Bostrom (2014) and Hurlburt (2017), for example, have drawn attention to the possibility that AGI systems could eventually evolve in ways that diverge from fundamental human values. Such divergence could, in extreme cases, lead to catastrophic scenarios in which human control over technological systems is diminished or lost entirely. One of the central concerns in this debate is the so-called alignment problem. This issue revolves around ensuring that the goals, behaviors, and underlying values of AI systems align with those of the societies in which they are embedded. Abbass (2019), Bostrom (2014), Gabriel (2020), and Taylor et al. (2020) argue that this alignment is both technically challenging and ethically fraught. A failure to achieve it could lead to systems that act in ways fundamentally at odds with public interests or moral standards.

Beyond these philosophical and existential threats, there are immediate, practical concerns that affect users' everyday trust in AI. One significant source of unease stems from AI's extensive data collection and surveillance capabilities (e.g., as discussed by Zuboff (2023)). These technologies, often deployed in opaque ways, can be perceived as tools for manipulation and control, particularly when implemented by powerful corporate or governmental actors. Concerns about data privacy, potential hacking, and surveillance-driven behavioral manipulation further intensifies public skepticism. As AI systems become more capable of performing tasks traditionally reserved for human decision-makers, there is a growing fear that such technologies could erode individual agency. In contexts like healthcare, education, media, or criminal justice, the replacement of human judgment with algorithmic decision-making raises complex ethical questions. Moreover, the risk that AI systems may inadvertently reinforce or amplify existing societal biases adds another layer of distrust. Machine learning algorithms trained on biased historical data can replicate and even intensify these disparities, leading to outcomes that are not only unfair but potentially harmful. Studies by Asan et al. (2020) and Sperrle et al. (2020) underscore the persistent issue of bias propagation in AI systems and its implications for equity and justice.

In addition to the threat of immediate harms, there are also deep uncertainties about the future trajectory of AI development. As autonomous technologies become more prevalent in sectors such as defense, transportation, and media, users may struggle to predict or control their outcomes. This unpredictability contributes to an overarching anxiety about how AI might evolve and interact with broader societal systems in the years to come. Such concerns are not merely speculative; they reflect real limitations in our current capacity to regulate, audit, and oversee increasingly complex algorithmic infrastructures.

Paradoxically, while these concerns about AI may erode trust in some settings, empirical evidence also suggests that people may at times place greater trust in AI systems than in human counterparts. This has been observed in domains such as governance and healthcare, where the perceived objectivity and data-driven nature of AI may be viewed as preferable to human judgment, which can be inconsistent or biased. Scholars like Ingrams et al. (2022) and Kim & Kim (2022) highlight this counterintuitive trend, showing how trust in AI is not only context-dependent but also shaped by comparative perceptions of human versus machine competence. The picture that emerges is therefore a complex one: AI simultaneously inspires trust and suspicion. This contradiction reflects the multifaceted nature of technology itself and the evolving social dynamics it continues to influence.

8.3.3 Building Trust in AI

Given AI's unique complexities and ethical dimensions, trust-building requires a comprehensive approach that addresses not only technical functionality but also ethical accountability and social engagement. Ryan (2020) underscores that trust in AI must be fostered across diverse domains, emphasizing not just technical performance, but also transparency, fairness, and regulatory compliance. This holistic view is essential when considering AI's integration into sensitive areas like media, where public perceptions and societal implications are particularly profound.

One foundational aspect of building trust in AI is ensuring transparency and explainability. Users are more likely to develop confidence in systems when they can understand how decisions are made and why particular outcomes are reached. When algorithmic logic is opaque or difficult to interpret, users are more inclined to view the technology as untrustworthy or potentially biased (Afroogh et al., 2024). Hence, fostering clear and comprehensible communication about AI's inner workings is essential for reducing skepticism and promoting user empowerment.

Equally important is the emotional resonance that AI systems can generate. Troshani et al. (2021) argue that empathy and emotional intelligence significantly influence the quality of human–AI interactions. When AI applications exhibit responsiveness that appears considerate or human-like, they can cultivate stronger, more trusting relationships with users. This emotional dimension complements the technical and ethical factors by addressing the relational nature of trust.

Privacy and data security also play a central role in trust dynamics. The assurance that personal information will be handled responsibly, securely, and in alignment with user expectations is a key determinant of trustworthiness. Practices such as data minimization, clear privacy policies, and robust cybersecurity frameworks contribute to the perception that the technology respects and protects user autonomy.

Another crucial area involves fairness and the mitigation of bias. Mehrabi et al. (2022) highlight the range of biases that can infiltrate AI systems, from data collection stages to algorithmic outcomes. These include, e.g., measurement bias, historical bias, population bias, and algorithmic bias, among others. When users perceive AI outputs as systematically unfair or discriminatory, trust can quickly deteriorate. Therefore, the continual auditing and correction of algorithmic bias is not just a technical challenge but a trust imperative.

Accountability further reinforces trust by ensuring that those responsible for AI deployment can be identified and held answerable for their systems' outcomes. This becomes particularly salient in media contexts where errors or manipulations can have far-reaching effects. Knowing that accountability mechanisms are in place, whether through institutional oversight, legal recourse, or ethical review, provides users with a sense of security and control.

Finally, consistent technical performance across key metrics such as safety, accuracy, and robustness is indispensable. When AI systems function reliably and predictably, users gain confidence in their utility and legitimacy. Conversely, inconsistencies or failures can quickly undermine trust, regardless of the system's other qualities.

Navigating trust in AI within media contexts involves addressing uncertainties and ethical dilemmas across multiple dimensions, technical performance, ethical responsibility, psychological perception, and regulatory compliance. Thoughtful integration of comprehensive strategies and frameworks is vital for fostering balanced perceptions, reducing fears, and enhancing the positive potential of AI technologies.

8.3.4 Mediated Trust and the Dual Role of Technology

The concept of mediated trust reflects a shift in how trust is constructed and maintained in an era where digital technologies, particularly AI, mediate many of our interpersonal and institutional interactions. Unlike traditional interpersonal trust, mediated trust includes the interplay between individuals, technological systems, and institutional actors. In today's media landscape, AI occupies a dual role: it is both a producer of trust, through its capacity to filter misinformation, verify facts, and automate content curation and an object of trust itself, as audiences must decide whether to place confidence in these systems and their creators (Bodó, 2021). As platforms increasingly blend real and digital interactions, trust becomes embedded not only in people and institutions, but also in technological interfaces. However, conceptual ambiguity remains—is trust in AI about the people deploying it, the system itself, or the institutions behind it (Flew, 2024)? Trust in AI is therefore inseparable from broader debates about institutional credibility and public communication. Bodó (2021) and Schäfer (2016) argue that trust in media and technology is deeply shaped by how institutions and AI systems are portrayed in the media, making technology not only a mediator but a constructor of trust. This raises a pressing need to assess the trustworthiness of AI systems based on their transparency, accountability, and alignment with ethical standards. As media production becomes increasingly algorithm-driven, and as digital technologies become essential conduits for news consumption across social groups, rethinking trust in the context of AI becomes crucial. AI's role in shaping mediated trust demands that both the design of technology and the structures surrounding its use foster critical, informed, and communicative engagement with the public. AI's dual role as both producer and object of trust presents unique opportunities and significant challenges within the media sector. The pathway toward effective AI integration in media involves sustained transparency, rigorous ethical oversight, and comprehensive regulatory frameworks. Continued interdisciplinary research and informed engagement are essential to harness AI's full potential while safeguarding public trust in the media.

8.4 Key Themes in Extant Research

The rapid integration of artificial intelligence in media has spurred an expanding body of literature that examines its influence on trust. Researchers have increasingly focused on the multifaceted dimensions of AI, from its role in automated journalism to the ethical and societal implications of deepfake generation and virtual influencers. This section provides an overview of extant research on the relation of AI-driven tools and traditional media trust.

8.4.1 Automated Journalism

Several studies have explored the impact of AI on news production and dissemination. For example, Graefe (2016), Kolo et al. (2022), and Lermann Henestrosa et al. (2023) have examined the role of automated journalism in transforming newsrooms. These studies reveal that algorithmic news production has the potential to enhance efficiency and reduce human error, yet it simultaneously raises critical questions about editorial independence and accountability. The automated generation of content can sometimes blur the lines between machine-generated and human-curated news, making the process of verifying authenticity more challenging for audiences. Considering these developments, the concept of algorithmic trust emerges, highlighting the importance of transparency and explainability in AI-driven content curation. A recent example of AI integration in journalism is the experiment conducted by the Italian newspaper Il Foglio, which published an entire edition generated by AI as part of a month-long trial. The initiative aimed to explore the implications of incorporating AI across the news production workflow. While not intended to replace human journalists, the experiment illustrates how AI technologies are being tested in editorial contexts (Giuffrida, 2025). This case highlights the broader relevance of algorithmic trust, as the increasing use of AI in content generation necessitates transparent communication about AI involvement and the development of mechanisms that allow audiences to evaluate the trustworthiness of AI-generated news.

8.4.2 Synthetic Media and Trust

The generation of deepfakes represents another pivotal area where AI challenges conventional media trust. Research by Ahmed (2023), Karnouskos (2020), and Weikmann et al. (2024) has documented how deepfake technologies are increasingly used to create hyper-realistic, yet entirely synthetic, video and audio content. Such capabilities pose a significant risk to the veracity of public discourse. As deepfakes become more sophisticated, audiences find it increasingly difficult to differentiate between genuine and manipulated content. This erosion of discernible truth underscores the need for improved verification technologies and robust regulatory frameworks that can mitigate the risks associated with deepfake dissemination.

In journalistic contexts, deepfakes have been used to convincingly impersonate public figures, including news anchors, thereby raising concerns about the potential for disseminating false narratives under the guise of legitimate reporting (Scott, 2024). Another widely circulated incident involved a fake image of an explosion near the U.S. Pentagon, which was shared on the social media platform X (formerly Twitter) and caused a brief but measurable fluctuation in financial markets (O'Sullivan & Passantino, 2023). These examples underscore the urgent need for robust verification mechanisms and regulatory frameworks to address the risks posed by synthetic media. Tools for proactive verification, as discussed by Opdahl et al. (2023), are essential to support journalistic integrity and help audiences navigate an increasingly complex media landscape where visual and audio authenticity can no longer be assumed.

The rise of virtual influencers further complicates the media trust landscape. Studies by Muniz et al. (2024) and Ozdemir et al. (2023), for example, have documented the emergence of digital personas that are entirely generated by AI. These virtual influencers blur the lines between authentic human interaction and algorithmically curated personas. Virtual influencers increasingly populate social media platforms, attracting large followings and shaping audience attitudes (Agnihotri & Bhattacharya, 2021). For example, Lil Miquela, a virtual persona representing a 19-year-old musician and arts student with Spanish-Brazilian roots, has garnered over ten million followers and millions of song streams (Rodrigo-Martín et al., 2022). She has appeared in major fashion magazines, publicly addressed social issues (Block & Lovegrove, 2021), and was even named one of the 25 most influential people on the Internet (Time Magazine, n.d.). Their increasing prominence in advertising and social media challenges traditional notions of credibility and authenticity. While virtual influencers offer novel avenues for engaging with audiences, they also introduce new dimensions of skepticism regarding the underlying motivations and the potential manipulation of public opinion. As synthetic media becomes more embedded in everyday communication, the challenge lies in developing frameworks that sustain trust without relying on traditional markers of authenticity.

8.4.3 Algorithmic Trust

Beyond the individual studies on automated journalism, deepfakes, and virtual influencers, a common thread in the literature is the evolving concept of "algorithmic trust." This term encapsulates the notion that audiences' trust in media is increasingly contingent not solely on the reputation of media institutions or the integrity of human journalists but also on the perceived fairness, transparency, and explainability of the algorithms that curate and generate news content. These algorithms, while programmed by humans, operate with a degree of autonomous agency: they rank, filter, reward, and suppress content in ways that are often opaque to users and difficult to audit (Kellogg et al., 2019). Algorithmic systems are increasingly integrated into media platforms in the form of recommender systems, which suggest content based on inferred user preferences. For example, Netflix announced to introduce an AI-powered natural language recommendation feature (Reuters, 2025), and Meta has published plans to further increase the share of AI-recommended content on Instagram (Morris, 2022). These systems are becoming central to how users encounter and engage with content. At the same time, empirical studies have shown that most users have a limited understanding of how these algorithms function, including how content is selected or prioritized (Hargittai et al., 2020). This gap between algorithmic complexity and user comprehension raises questions about informed consent, user autonomy, and the potential for unintended influence on public opinion.

The literature consistently emphasizes that for AI to bolster media trust, it must be deployed in ways that are ethically sound, transparent, and aligned with established privacy norms. In response to these developments, researchers have proposed hybrid models that combine algorithmic capabilities with human editorial oversight, aiming to maintain accountability while leveraging the efficiencies of automation (Trattner et al., 2022). As algorithmic systems become more embedded in media infrastructures, future research will need to address how trust can be maintained or reconfigured in increasingly automated information environments.

AI-driven tools at the nexus of automated journalism, deepfake generation, virtual influencing, and algorithmic trust are redefining the landscape of media, prompting both optimism for enhanced efficiency and concern for the potential erosion of accountability. Future studies are expected to further refine our understanding of these complex dynamics and propose actionable frameworks for integrating AI responsibly in media production, distribution, and consumption.

8.5 Toward a Research Agenda for the Impact of Trust on AI

The transformative impact of AI on media trust invites a host of open debates and questions that warrant further investigation. The rapid pace of technological change has outstripped the development of comprehensive theoretical and regulatory frameworks, which we see leading to several critical areas that remain underexplored:

- Conceptual clarity of "trust in AI" in relation to the media
- Operationalizing and measuring media(ted) trust and trust in AI
- The role of explainability of AI and hybrid models
- The impact of AI on different demographic groups
- Bridging the Political Trust Gap in AI-Powered Media
- Regulatory Frameworks and Ethical Governances

8.5.1 Conceptual Clarity of "Trust in AI" in Relation to the Media

A persistent challenge in current discussions is the lack of a clearly defined and consistently applied concept of "trust in AI." As previously noted, trust is understood differently across disciplines, with its meaning varying according to context. As a result, trust is a multifaceted concept that cannot be adequately captured by a single definition. When applied to AI, trust may be directed toward different elements: the human actors involved in the design, development, and deployment of AI systems; the technological artefacts and algorithmic processes; or the institutional entities responsible for their oversight and governance (Flew, 2021).

Existing literature reflects a diversity of disciplinary perspectives on the concept of trust. Jacovi et al. (2021) define trust in AI as a directional transaction between two parties: "if H (human) perceives that M (AI model) is trustworthy to contract C, and accepts vulnerability to M's actions, then H trusts M contractually to C." This definition explains a directional relation in which a human agent accepts vulnerability to an AI system under the expectation that it will act in the human's interest with respect to a given task. Gillath et al. (2020) emphasize affective components, describing trust as "an increase in the faith in the trustworthy intentions of others, or the confidence people place in others based on how they feel about them." Lukyanenko et al. (2022) on the other hand conceptualize trust in AI more as a "mental and physiological process that considers the properties of a specific AI-based system, a class of such systems or other systems in which it is embedded or with which it interacts, to control the extent and parameters of the interaction with these systems." These definitions reflect divergent assumptions about the nature of trust, whether it is primarily rational, emotional, relational, or contextual, and highlight the multi-dimensional character of trust when applied to nonhuman systems like AI.

This lack of clarity risks turning efforts to increase trust into superficial checklists that fail to address deeper issues, particularly problems related to concentrated corporate control and the lack of transparency in algorithmic decision-making. To address this, future research should aim to develop comprehensive frameworks that clearly differentiate these dimensions of media trust and establish definitions suitable for empirical investigation.

8.5.2 Operationalizing and Measuring Media(ted) Trust and Trust in AI

Measuring media trust, particularly in relation to technology and AI as mediators, presents various challenges. To understand mediated trust, it is crucial to explore how technology, and specifically artificial intelligence, changes the nature of trust relationships. Defining trust clearly and identifying appropriate metrics are particularly difficult due to the dynamic nature of AI, which constantly evolves both technologically and in response to cultural factors. Additionally, measuring trust itself is challenging. Common tools like questionnaires, surveys, and protocols can help, but they cannot fully resolve these complexities.

People make their own choices in what and whom to trust based on different personal factors. Because of this, identifying general aspects that promote trust in AI remains difficult (Afroogh et al., 2024). It is challenging to balance various dimensions of trust without causing contradictions within their guiding principles. Evaluating trust in AI faces similar difficulties. It is important to identify broadly acceptable universal ethical principles that can foster trust in AI systems. Furthermore, these universal principles must then be adapted and aligned with specific cultural values to effectively measure and build trust across different contexts.

8.5.3 The Role of Explainability of AI and Hybrid Models

A promising research direction involving trust in AI is the research stream on explainable AI (XAI), a field aimed at making algorithmic decision-making clearer and more understandable. Although XAI is recognized as a potential aspect for building trust, the best ways to implement it within media contexts remain unclear. Even widely accepted strategies for building trust, like transparency and explainability, can have very different effects depending on how they are implemented. In the media context, for example, using virtual agents to present AI-generated explanations (as shown in speech recognition systems) has been found to significantly increase user trust (Weitz et al., 2019), suggesting that the design of explainable AI in news delivery could greatly shape how trustworthy audiences perceive it to be. Building trust in AI requires considering a combination of AI-related, human-related, and context-specific factors that influence trust within a given application domain (Afroogh et al., 2024). Key technical factors such as transparency, explainability, and performance increase the overall trustworthiness of AI systems, but for users to trust them, these qualities must also be perceived. This calls for thoughtful implementation, such as clear documentation or user-facing cues, that help bridge the gap between technical design and user perception. Future research should focus on understanding how different stakeholders, such as news consumers and regulators, interpret the explanations provided by AI systems.

Additionally, the effectiveness of hybrid models, which combine AI-generated outputs with human editorial oversight, deserves further exploration, as these models can help maintain the accountability traditionally associated with human decision-making. Empirical studies examining user perceptions across diverse demographic groups can provide insights into how transparency influences trust. These studies might also investigate whether increased AI transparency affects audience perceptions of bias and fairness, and whether such perceptions vary depending on the type of news content or the media platforms used.

8.5.4 The Role of Media Framing of AI in Shaping Trust

Bodó (2021) and Schäfer (2016) suggest that representations of institutions and AI systems in the media contribute to shaping public trust in both technology and media. In this view, media act not only as channels of information but also as actors in the construction of trust. This raises the question of how AI-related information should be presented in order to support trust in the media. Empirical studies indicate that media framing can influence public attitudes toward AI (Berendt, 2018; Ho & Cheung, 2024). For example, portrayals that emphasize benefits and utility have been associated with more favorable responses, while coverage focusing on risks or negative consequences has been linked to critical or resistant attitudes (Bingaman et al., 2021). These aspects highlight the relevance of media framing for stakeholders concerned with the integration of AI in the media context. They also point to a broader consideration: how the media's approach to reporting on AI may influence trust in the media in the age of AI. Further research is needed to examine these relationships, particularly how different forms of AI coverage affect general media trust in various social and institutional contexts.

8.5.5 Demographic and Political Factors Affecting Trust of Media AI

An important area for future research is how AI affects different audience groups in distinct ways. Studies indicate that trust in AI-driven media can vary widely depending on demographic factors. For example, older adults often place greater trust in traditional media but may be more skeptical of AI technologies due to lower levels of digital literacy. In contrast, younger people, who are typically more comfortable navigating digital platforms, are more likely to engage with AI-generated content, even if they remain cautious about its accuracy and authenticity (Newman et al., 2024). Understanding these differences is key to designing inclusive AI systems that build trust across diverse user groups.

The political context plays a significant role in shaping how people perceive the media, especially in relation to AI-driven news production and delivery. While most individuals tend to value similar qualities in news sources, such as transparency, accuracy, fairness, and freedom from bias, there is a noticeable divide when political engagement is considered. A substantial portion of the public, particularly those who feel politically disengaged or uncertain about their political stance, tends to exhibit lower levels of trust in the media. These individuals often struggle to identify what would make a news source trustworthy and typically maintain a weak connection to news in general (Newman et al., 2024).

As AI becomes increasingly embedded in the media landscape, automating content curation, filtering, and generating content, the risk is that these politically distanced audiences may become even more skeptical or disconnected. The presence of algorithmic decision-making could be seen as yet another layer of opacity or bias, further eroding trust. This makes it essential for future research to investigate how political identity, engagement, and disinterest influence public perceptions of AI in the media. Understanding these dynamics will be critical for developing strategies that not only foster trust across different political groups but also ensure that AI in media serves the needs of a broad and diverse audience.

8.5.6 Regulatory Frameworks and Ethical Governances

The dynamic evolution of AI technologies has shifted regulatory attention from voluntary ethical guidelines to enforceable legal frameworks (Hagendorff, 2020). Governments have begun implementing formal oversight mechanisms, including the U.S. Algorithmic Accountability Act in 2019 and AI Bill of Rights blueprint in 2022, China's Beijing AI Principles of 2019, Canada's Algorithmic Impact Assessment Tool in 2020 (Etziani et al., 2021), and most comprehensively, the European Union's AI Act (Paul 2023). Despite recent regulatory developments, significant gaps remain. Current frameworks may be insufficient to address emerging risks posed by advanced AI systems, and there are concerns that overly restrictive regulations could hinder technological innovation. Additionally, implementing ethical principles across varied application contexts remains a challenge. The concept of "trustworthy AI" (HLEG, 2019) has become central to regulatory discourse, particularly as systems like ChatGPT are increasingly perceived as interactive agents rather than purely functional tools (Guzman & Lewis, 2020). This shift has intensified discussions on public trust (Glikson & Woolley, 2020; Kaur et al., 2022; Yang & Wibowo, 2022), with policymakers highlighting risks associated with both insufficient trust, potentially limiting adoption, and excessive trust, particularly in cases of system errors or misinformation (Tamò-Larrieux et al., 2024). Future research could focus on comparative analyses of regulatory approaches across different jurisdictions, exploring the strengths and limitations of frameworks as they unfold their impacts. Additionally, interdisciplinary studies involving legal, technology, and communication experts are needed to develop comprehensive guidelines that balance innovation with public accountability for AI integration in the media sector.

8.6 Conclusion

The intersection of AI and trust in media presents both significant opportunities and formidable challenges. On one hand, AI has the potential to revolutionize the way news is produced and consumed, offering unprecedented tools for enhancing the credibility and reliability of information. On the other hand, the inherent complexities of algorithmic transparency, ethical governance, and user perception pose critical challenges that must be addressed to fully realize this potential.

Future research in this domain must adopt an interdisciplinary approach that integrates insights from philosophy, sociology, communications, and computer science. Such research should aim to develop robust frameworks for assessing the trustworthiness of AI systems in media, encompassing both technical performance and the ethical implications of their use. In doing so, scholars and practitioners alike can contribute to a more nuanced understanding of how AI can be harnessed to rebuild and sustain trust in a rapidly evolving media environment.

Moreover, policymakers and industry leaders must engage in dialogue to establish regulatory standards and ethical guidelines that ensure AI systems are deployed in a manner that is both transparent and accountable. As the digital media landscape continues to evolve, the cultivation of trust will remain a cornerstone of democratic engagement and social cohesion. By addressing the dual challenges of trust production and trust in technology, stakeholders can work toward creating a media ecosystem that not only leverages the transformative potential of AI but also safeguards the fundamental values of transparency, accountability, and ethical integrity.

References

Abbass, H. A. (2019). Social integration of artificial intelligence: Functions, automation allocation logic and human-autonomy trust. *Cognitive Computation, 11*(2), 159–171. https://doi.org/10.1007/s12559-018-9619-0

Afroogh, S., Akbari, A., Malone, E., Kargar, M., & Alambeigi, H. (2024). Trust in AI: Progress, challenges, and future directions. *Humanities and Social Sciences Communications, 11*(1), 1568. https://doi.org/10.1057/s41599-024-04044-8

Agnihotri, A., & Bhattacharya, S. (2021). Endorsement effectiveness of celebrities versus social media influencers in the materialistic cultural environment of India. *Journal of International Consumer Marketing, 33*(3), 280–302. https://doi.org/10.1080/08961530.2020.1786875

Ahmed, S. (2023). Navigating the maze: Deepfakes, cognitive ability, and social media news skepticism. *New Media and Society, 25*(5), 1108–1129. https://doi.org/10.1177/14614448211019198

Asan, O., Bayrak, A. E., & Choudhury, A. (2020). Artificial intelligence and human trust in healthcare: Focus on clinicians. *Journal of Medical Internet Research, 22*(6), e15154. https://doi.org/10.2196/15154

Axelrod, R. (1984). *The evolution of cooperation*. Basic Books.

Baier, A. (1986). Trust and antitrust. *Ethics, 96*(2), 231–260. JSTOR.

Banerjee, S., Bowie, N. E., & Pavone, C. (2006). An ethical analysis of the trust relationship. In R. Bachmann & A. Zaheer (Eds.), *Handbook of trust research*. Edward Elgar Publishing. https://doi.org/10.4337/9781847202819.00026

Benkler, Y., Faris, R., & Roberts, H. (2018). *Network propaganda: Manipulation, disinformation, and radicalization in American politics* (1st ed.). Oxford University Press. https://doi.org/10.1093/oso/9780190923624.001.0001

Berendt, B. (2018). AI for the Common Good?! Pitfalls, challenges, and Ethics Pen-Testing. *arXiv (Cornell University)*. https://doi.org/10.48550/arxiv.1810.12847.

Bingaman, J., Brewer, P. R., Paintsil, A., & Wilson, D. C. (2021). "Siri, show me scary images of AI": Effects of Text-Based frames and visuals on support for artificial intelligence. *Science Communication, 43*(3), 388–401. https://doi.org/10.1177/1075547021998069

Block, E., & Lovegrove, R. (2021). Discordant storytelling, 'honest fakery', identity peddling: How uncanny CGI characters are jamming public relations and influencer practices. *Public Relations Inquiry, 10*(3), 265–293. https://doi.org/10.1177/2046147X211026936

Bodó, B. (2021). Mediated trust: A theoretical framework to address the trustworthiness of technological trust mediators. *New Media and Society, 23*(9), 2668–2690. https://doi.org/10.1177/1461444820939922

Boomgaarden, H. G., & Prior, M. (2008). Post-broadcast democracy. How media choice increases inequality in political involvement and polarizes elections. *International Journal of Public Opinion Research, 20*(3), 398–400. https://doi.org/10.1093/ijpor/edn036

Bostrom, N. (2014). *Superintelligence: Paths, dangers, strategies* (1st ed.). Oxford University Press.

Bradach, J. L., & Eccles, R. G. (1989). Price, authority, and trust: From ideal types to plural forms. *Annual Review of Sociology, 15*(1), 97–118. https://doi.org/10.1146/annurev.so.15.080189.000525

Coleman, J. S. (1994). *Foundations of social theory*. Harvard University Press.

DeSteno, D. (2015). *The truth about trust: How it determines success in life, love, learning, and more*. Penguin.

Edelman. (2020). *20 years of trust*. https://www.edelman.com/20yearsoftrust/
Edelman. (2025). *25 years of trust*. https://www.edelman.com/trust/25years?__hstc=62299507.b6c15be17669ebedff1e0593322e60f4.1750838533728.1751020595707.1751289863087.3&__hssc=62299507.1.1751289863087&__hsfp=2645838639
Egelhofer, J. L., & Lecheler, S. (2019). Fake news as a two-dimensional phenomenon: A framework and research agenda. *Annals of the International Communication Association, 43*(2), 97–116. https://doi.org/10.1080/23808985.2019.1602782
Engelke, K. M., Hase, V., & Wintterlin, F. (2019). On measuring trust and distrust in journalism: Reflection of the status quo and suggestions for the road ahead. *Journal of Trust Research, 9*(1), 66–86. https://doi.org/10.1080/21515581.2019.1588741
Etziani, G., Koene, A., Kumar, R., Santiago, N., & Wright, D. (2021). *A survey of artificial intelligence risk assessment methodologies. The global state of play and leading practices identified.*
Fletcher, R., & Park, S. (2017). The impact of trust in the news media on online news consumption and participation. *Digital Journalism, 5*(10), 1281–1299. https://doi.org/10.1080/21670811.2017.1279979
Flew, T. (2021). The global trust deficit disorder: A communications perspective on trust in the time of global pandemics. *The Journal of Communication, 71*(2), 163–186. https://doi.org/10.1093/joc/jqab006
Flew, T. (2024). Mediated trust, the internet and artificial intelligence: Ideas, interests, institutions and futures. *Policy and Internet, poi3.390*. https://doi.org/10.1002/poi3.390
Flynn, D. J., Nyhan, B., & Reifler, J. (2017). The nature and origins of misperceptions: Understanding false and unsupported beliefs about politics. *Political Psychology, 38*(S1), 127–150. https://doi.org/10.1111/pops.12394
Fukuyama, F. (1996). *Trust: The social virtues and the creation of prosperity*. Simon and Schuster.
Gabriel, I. (2020). Artificial intelligence, values, and alignment. *Minds and Machines, 30*(3), 411–437. https://doi.org/10.1007/s11023-020-09539-2
Gaziano, C., & McGrath, K. (1986). Measuring the concept of credibility. *Journalism Quarterly, 63*(3), 451–462. https://doi.org/10.1177/107769908606300301
Giddens, A. (1990). *The consequences of modernity*. Polity Press.
Gillath, O., Ai, T., Branicky, M. S., Keshmiri, S., Davison, R. B., & Spaulding, R. (2020). Attachment and trust in artificial intelligence. *Computers in Human Behavior, 115*, 106607. https://doi.org/10.1016/j.chb.2020.106607
Giuffrida, A. (2025, March 18). *Italian Newspaper Says It Has Published World's First AI-Generated Edition*. The Guardian. https://www.theguardian.com/technology/2025/mar/18/italian-newspaper-says-it-has-published-worlds-first-ai-generatededition
Glikson, E., & Woolley, A. W. (2020). Human trust in artificial intelligence: Review of empirical research. *Academy of Management Annals, 14*(2), 627–660.
Graefe, A. (2016). *Guide to automated journalism*. https://doi.org/10.7916/D80G3XDJ.
Guzman, A. L., & Lewis, S. C. (2020). Artificial intelligence and communication: A human–machine communication research agenda. *New Media and Society, 22*(1), 70–86.
Hagendorff, T. (2020). The ethics of AI ethics: An evaluation of guidelines. *Minds and Machines, 30*(1), 99–120.
Hargittai, E., Gruber, J., Djukaric, T., Fuchs, J., & Brombach, L. (2020). Black box measures? How to study people's algorithm skills. *Information Communication and Society, 23*(5), 764–775. https://doi.org/10.1080/1369118x.2020.1713846
HLEG. (2019). *Ethics guidelines fort Trustworthy AI. High-Level expert group on artificial intelligence*. European Commission. https://digital-strategy.ec.europa.eu/en/library/ethics-guidelinestrustworthy-ai
Ho, S. S., & Cheung, J. C. (2024). Trust in artificial intelligence, trust in engineers, and news media: Factors shaping public perceptions of autonomous drones through UTAUT2. *Technology in Society, 77*, 102533. https://doi.org/10.1016/j.techsoc.2024.102533
Hovland, C. I., Janis, I. L., & Kelley, H. H. (1953). *Communication and persuasion*. Yale University Press.

Hurlburt, G. (2017). How much to trust artificial intelligence? *IT Professional, 19*(4), 7–11. https://doi.org/10.1109/MITP.2017.3051326

Ingrams, A., Kaufmann, W., & Jacobs, D. (2022). In AI we trust? Citizen perceptions of AI in government decision making. *Policy and Internet, 14*(2), 390–409. https://doi.org/10.1002/poi3.276

Jacovi, A., Marasović, A., Miller, T., & Goldberg, Y. (2021). Formalizing trust in artificial intelligence. *Proceedings of the 2021 ACM conference on fairness, accountability, and transparency*, pp. 624–635. https://doi.org/10.1145/3442188.3445923.

Jones, J. M. (2018). *U.S. media trust continues to recover from 2016 low.* https://news.gallup.com/poll/243665/media-trust-continues-recover-2016-low.aspx

Kalogeropoulos, A., Suiter, J., Udris, L., & Eisenegger, M. (2019). News media trust and news consumption: Factors related to trust in news in 35 countries. *International Journal of Communication, 13*(0), 22.

Karnouskos, S. (2020). Artificial intelligence in digital media: The era of Deepfakes. *IEEE Transactions on Technology and Society, 1*(3), 138–147. https://doi.org/10.1109/TTS.2020.3001312

Kaur, D., Uslu, S., Rittichier, K. J., & Durresi, A. (2022). Trustworthy artificial intelligence: A review. *ACM Computing Surveys (CSUR), 55*(2), 1–38.

Kavanagh, J., & Rich, M. D. (2018). *Truth decay: An initial exploration of the diminishing role of facts and analysis in American public life*. RAND Corporation. https://doi.org/10.7249/RR2314

Kellogg, K. C., Valentine, M. A., & Christin, A. (2019). Algorithms at Work: The new contested terrain of control. *Academy of Management Annals, 14*(1), 366–410. https://doi.org/10.5465/annals.2018.0174

Keymolen, E. (2016). *Trust on the line: A philosophical exploration of trust in the networked era.* https://repub.eur.nl/pub/93210.

Kim, D. K. D., & Kim, S. (2022). *What if you have a humanoid AI robot doctor?*: An investigation of public trust in South Korea. *Journal of Communication in Healthcare, 15*(4), 276–285. https://doi.org/10.1080/17538068.2021.1994825

Kiousis, S. (2001). Public trust or mistrust? Perceptions of media credibility in the information age. *Mass Communication and Society, 4*(4), 381–403. https://doi.org/10.1207/S15327825MCS0404_4

Klintman, M. (2021). *Knowledge resistance: How we avoid insight from others*. Manchester University Press.

Knobloch-Westerwick, S., Mothes, C., & Polavin, N. (2017). Confirmation Bias, Ingroup Bias, and Negativity Bias in Selective Exposure to Political Information. *Communication Research, 47*(1), 104–124. https://doi.org/10.1177/0093650217719596 (Original work published 2020).

Kohring, M. (2019). Public trust in news media. In T. P. Vos, F. Hanusch, D. Dimitrakopoulou, M. Geertsema-Sligh, & A. Sehl (Eds.), *The international encyclopedia of journalism studies* (1st ed., pp. 1–6). Wiley. https://doi.org/10.1002/9781118841570.iejs0056

Kolo, C., Mütterlein, J., & Schmid, S. A. (2022). *Believing journalists, AI, or fake news: The role of trust in media*. http://hdl.handle.net/10125/79727.

Kunda, Z. (1990). The case for motivated reasoning. *Psychological Bulletin, 108*(3), 480–498. https://doi.org/10.1037/0033-2909.108.3.480

Ladd, J. M. (2011). Why Americans hate the media and how it matters. In *Why Americans hate the media and how it matters*. Princeton University Press. https://www.degruyter.com/document/doi/10.1515/9781400840359/html

Lamba, K., Varghese M. V. (2025, May 7). Netflix to revamp TV app interface, launch AI-powered search for iOS users. *Reuters*. https://www.reuters.com/business/media-telecom/netflix-revamp-tv-app-interface-launch-ai-powered-search-ios-users-2025-05-07/

Lermann Henestrosa, A., Greving, H., & Kimmerle, J. (2023). Automated journalism: The effects of AI authorship and evaluative information on the perception of a science journalism article. *Computers in Human Behavior, 138*, 107445. https://doi.org/10.1016/j.chb.2022.107445

Lukyanenko, R., Maass, W., & Storey, V. C. (2022). Trust in artificial intelligence: From a Foundational Trust Framework to emerging research opportunities. *Electronic Markets, 32*(4), 1993–2020. https://doi.org/10.1007/s12525-022-00605-4
Meyer, P. (1988). Defining and measuring credibility of newspapers: Developing an index. *Journalism Quarterly, 65*(3), 567–574. https://doi.org/10.1177/107769908806500301
McDermott, B. (2019). *Trust is at breaking point. It's time to rebuild it.* https://www.weforum.org/stories/2019/01/trust-is-at-breaking-point-it-s-time-to-rebuild-it/
Mehrabi, N., Morstatter, F., Saxena, N., Lerman, K., & Galstyan, A. (2022). A survey on bias and fairness in machine learning. *ACM Computing Surveys, 54*(6), 1–35. https://doi.org/10.1145/3457607
Misztal, B. (2013). *Trust in modern societies: The search for the bases of social order*. Wiley.
Modgil, S., Singh, R. K., Gupta, S., & Dennehy, D. (2024). A confirmation bias view on social media induced polarisation during Covid-19. *Information Systems Frontiers, 26*(2), 417–441. https://doi.org/10.1007/s10796-021-10222-9
Möllering, G. (2006). *Trust: Reason, routine, reflexivity*. Elsevier.
Morris, C. (2022). Mark Zuckerberg ignores objections, says Reels will double on Instagram. *Fortune*. https://fortune.com/2022/07/28/mark-zuckerberg-instagram-double-ai-recommended-content-2023/
Mourão, R. R., Thorson, E., Chen, W., & Tham, S. M. (2018). Media repertoires and news trust during the early trump administration. *Journalism Studies, 19*(13), 1945–1956. https://doi.org/10.1080/1461670X.2018.1500492
Muniz, F., Stewart, K., & Magalhães, L. (2024). Are they humans or are they robots? The effect of virtual influencer disclosure on brand trust. *Journal of Consumer Behaviour, 23*(3), 1234–1250. https://doi.org/10.1002/cb.2271
Nau, H. H. (2005). Institutional, evolutionary and cultural aspects in Max Weber's social economics. *Cahiers d'économie Politique, 49*(2), 127–142. https://doi.org/10.3917/cep.049.0127
Newman, N., Fletcher, R., Robertson, C. T., Ross Arguedas, A., & Nielsen, R. K. (2024). *Reuters Institute digital news report 2024*. Reuters Institute for the Study of Journalism. https://doi.org/10.60625/RISJ-VY6N-4V57.
Newman, N., Ross Arguedas, A., Robertson, C. T., Nielsen, R. K. & Fletcher, R. (2025). *Reuters Institute digital news report 2025*. Reuters Institute for the Study of Journalism. https://reutersinstitute.politics.ox.ac.uk/sites/default/files/2025-06/Digital_News-Report_2025.pdf
O'Neill, O. (2002). *A question of trust: The BBC Reith Lectures 2002*. Cambridge University Press.
O'Sullivan, D., & Passantino, J. (2023, May 23). *"verified" twitter accounts share fake image of "explosion" near Pentagon, causing confusion | CNN business*. CNN. https://edition.cnn.com/2023/05/22/tech/twitter-fake-image-pentagon-explosion
Opdahl, A. L., Tessem, B., Dang-Nguyen, D.-T., Motta, E., Setty, V., Throndsen, E., Tverberg, A., & Trattner, C. (2023). Trustworthy journalism through AI. *Data and Knowledge Engineering, 146*, 102182. https://doi.org/10.1016/j.datak.2023.102182
Otto, K., & Köhler, A. (Eds.). (2018). *Trust in media and journalism: Empirical perspectives on ethics, norms, impacts and populism in Europe*. Springer Fachmedien Wiesbaden. https://doi.org/10.1007/978-3-658-20765-6.
Ozdemir, O., Kolfal, B., Messinger, P. R., & Rizvi, S. (2023). Human or virtual: How influencer type shapes brand attitudes. *Computers in Human Behavior, 145*, 107771. https://doi.org/10.1016/j.chb.2023.107771
Paul, R. (2023). European artificial intelligence "trusted throughout the world": Risk-based regulation and the fashioning of a competitive common AI market. *Regulation and Governance, 18*(4), 1065–1082. https://doi.org/10.1111/rego.12563
PolitiFact. (2025). *Donald Trump's file*. https://www.politifact.com/personalities/donald-trump/
Putnam, R. D. (2001). *Bowling alone: The collapse and revival of American community*. Simon and Schuster.
Quandt, T. (2012). What's left of trust in a network society? An evolutionary model and critical discussion of trust and societal communication. European *Journal of Communication, 27*(1), 7–21. https://doi.org/10.1177/0267323111434452

Rodrigo-Martín, I., Muñoz-Sastre, D., & Rodrigo-Martín, L. (2022). Los influencers virtuales como líderes de opinión y su empleo en técnicas en comunicación política. *Revista Mediterránea de Comunicación, 13*(1), 251. https://doi.org/10.14198/MEDCOM.20751

Ryan, M. (2020). In AI we trust: Ethics, artificial intelligence, and reliability. *Science and Engineering Ethics, 26*(5), 2749–2767. https://doi.org/10.1007/s11948-020-00228-y

Schäfer, M. S. (2016). *Mediated trust in science: Concept, measurement and perspectives for the "Science of science communication."* https://doi.org/10.5167/UZH-131727.

Scott, L. (2024, January 17). *Deepfakes a "Weapon against journalism," analyst says.* Voice of America. https://www.voanews.com/a/deepfakes-a-weapon-against-journalism-analyst-says-/7442897.html

Seligman, A. B. (2000). *The problem of trust.* Princeton.

Siau, K., & Wang, W. (2018). *Building trust in artificial intelligence, machine learning, and robotics supply chain management view project.* 31(31), 47–53.

Sides, J., & Hopkins, D. J. (Eds.). (2015). *Political polarization in American politics.* Bloomsbury Academic, an imprint of Bloomsbury Publishing.

Sperrle, F., El-Assady, M., Guo, G., Chau, D. H., Endert, A., & Keim, D. (2020). *Should we trust (X)AI? Design dimensions for structured experimental evaluations* (Version 1). arXiv. https://doi.org/10.48550/ARXIV.2009.06433.

Strömbäck, J., Tsfati, Y., Boomgaarden, H., Damstra, A., Lindgren, E., Vliegenthart, R., & Lindholm, T. (2020). News media trust and its impact on media use: Toward a framework for future research. *Annals of the International Communication Association, 44*(2), 139–156. https://doi.org/10.1080/23808985.2020.1755338

Sztompka, P. (1999). *Trust: A sociological theory.* Cambridge University Press.

Taber, C. S., & Lodge, M. (2006). Motivated skepticism in the evaluation of political beliefs. *American Journal of Political Science, 50*(3), 755–769. https://doi.org/10.1111/j.1540-5907.2006.00214.x

Tamò-Larrieux, A., Guitton, C., Mayer, S., & Lutz, C. (2024). Regulating for trust: Can law establish trust in artificial intelligence? *Regulation & Governance, 18*(3), 780–801. https://doi.org/10.1111/rego.12568

Taylor, J., Yudkowsky, E., LaVictoire, P., & Critch, A. (2020). Alignment for advanced machine learning systems. In S. M. Liao (Ed.), *Ethics of artificial intelligence* (1st ed., pp. 342–382). Oxford University PressNew York. https://doi.org/10.1093/oso/9780190905033.003.0013

Thiebes, S., Lins, S., & Sunyaev, A. (2021). Trustworthy artificial intelligence. *Electronic Markets, 31*(2), 447–464. https://doi.org/10.1007/s12525-020-00441-4

Time Magazine. (n.d.). Meet this year's 25 most influential people on the Internet. *Time.* https://time.com/5324130/most-influential-internet/

Trattner, C., Jannach, D., Motta, E., Costera Meijer, I., Diakopoulos, N., Elahi, M., Opdahl, A. L., Tessem, B., Borch, N., Fjeld, M., Øvrelid, L., De Smedt, K., & Moe, H. (2022). Responsible media technology and AI: Challenges and research directions. *AI and Ethics, 2*(4), 585–594. https://doi.org/10.1007/s43681-021-00126-4

Troshani, I., Rao Hill, S., Sherman, C., & Arthur, D. (2021). Do we trust in AI? Role of anthropomorphism and intelligence. *Journal of Computer Information Systems, 61*(5), 481–491. https://doi.org/10.1080/08874417.2020.1788473

Tsfati, Y., & Cappella, J. N. (2003). Do people watch what they do not trust?: Exploring the association between news media skepticism and exposure. *Communication Research, 30*(5), 504–529. https://doi.org/10.1177/0093650203253371

Tsfati, Y., & Cappella, J. N. (2005). Why do people watch news they do not trust? The need for cognition as a moderator in the association between news media skepticism and exposure. *Media Psychology, 7*(3), 251–271. https://doi.org/10.1207/S1532785XMEP0703_2

Van Aelst, P., Strömbäck, J., Aalberg, T., Esser, F., De Vreese, C., Matthes, J., Hopmann, D., Salgado, S., Hubé, N., Stępińska, A., Papathanassopoulos, S., Berganza, R., Legnante, G., Reinemann, C., Sheafer, T., & Stanyer, J. (2017). Political communication in a high-choice media environment: A challenge for democracy? *Annals of the International Communication Association, 41*(1), 3–27. https://doi.org/10.1080/23808985.2017.1288551

Weikmann, T., Greber, H., & Nikolaou, A. (2024). After deception: How falling for a Deepfake affects the way we see, hear, and experience media. *The International Journal of Press/Politics, 19401612241233539*. https://doi.org/10.1177/19401612241233539

Weitz, K., Schiller, D., Schlagowski, R., Huber, T., & André, E. (2019). "Do you trust me?": Increasing user-trust by integrating virtual agents in explainable AI interaction design. In *Proceedings of the 19th ACM international conference on intelligent virtual agents* (pp. 7–9). https://doi.org/10.1145/3308532.3329441

West, M. D. (1994). Validating a scale for the measurement of credibility: A covariance structure modeling approach. *Journalism Quarterly, 71*(1), 159–168. https://doi.org/10.1177/107769909407100115

Yang, R., & Wibowo, S. (2022). User trust in artificial intelligence: A comprehensive conceptual framework. *Electronic Markets, 32*, 2033–2057. https://doi.org/10.1007/s12525-022-00592-6

Zuboff, S. (2023). The age of surveillance capitalism. In *Social theory re-wired* (pp. 203–213). Routledge.

Castulus Kolo is the President of the Macromedia University of Applied Sciences, where he is also a professor of media management. He holds a doctorate in physics, earned through research at CERN, Geneva, and an additional doctorate in social anthropology from the Ludwig Maximilian University of Munich. After extensive practice in applied research with the Fraunhofer Society, he gained management experience in strategy consulting and as a board member of a publisher's digital venture. Generally, his publications are focused on preconditions, diffusion, and effects of media innovations. His current research focuses on the impact of artificial intelligence on the creative industries. He was President of the European Media Management Association from 2023 to 2025 and of the International Media Management Academic Association from 2019 to 2022 where he still serves as a board member.

Joschka Mütterlein is professor of management and vice president of teaching and faculty at Macromedia University of Applied Sciences. His research focuses on the effects of innovations on organizations and individuals and has been featured in journals like Technological Forecasting and Social Change, AIS Transactions on Human-Computer Interaction, and Journal of Media Business Studies.

Sarah Anna Schmid is a doctoral researcher investigating user interaction, identity, and engagement within extended reality (XR) environments. Her research further encompasses the role of artificial intelligence in digital communication, with a focus on AI-generated content, media trust, and virtual representations. She holds a Master's degree in Media and Communication Management and a Bachelor's degree in Business Informatics. Her professional background includes positions in innovation management and strategic development in higher education. Her work integrates theoretical and applied perspectives on emerging technologies in media and communication.

Ethical Limits of AI Use in the Media Sector

9

Jonas Schützeneder

Abstract

The present and future of the media industry are intensively influenced by groundbreaking developments in the field of automation and artificial intelligence (AI). The debates from science and practice largely trade off the opportunities and risks against each other. Regardless of this, one thing is certain: the AI innovation cycle has only just begun. As a "mediating authority," media ethics organizes and structures the various ideas, balances between philosophy and the reality of life in general and thus provides orientation, boundaries, and recommendations. This chapter takes up the idea of ethics as a "mediating authority" and asks specifically about the ethical limits of AI use in the media sector.

What does the current state of research and practice say about the ethical limits of AI use in the media industry? And: Where is there (nevertheless) a need for action, and how can the future of media products and productions be shaped in the medium term on the basis of ethical dimensions? Based on studies and documents from media policy, media-related institutions, and media companies, a broader picture of current efforts and media ethical boundaries emerges. Three central dimensions of ethical boundaries become particularly clear in the media companies: human and machine control, safeguarding quality standards, and free opinion-forming as well as limits in the function and use of "social scoring." These are not the only examples: AI provides completely changed possibilities for obtaining and disseminating information. This gives rise to new tasks and questions for media ethics in an AI-influenced media world.

J. Schützeneder (✉)
University of the Bundeswehr Munich, Munich, Germany
e-mail: jonas.schuetzeneder@unibw.de

S. Böhm et al. (eds.), *Handbook of AI-based Media Disruption*, Future of Business and Finance, https://doi.org/10.1007/978-3-032-07605-2_9

9.1 Introduction to the Topic

Every technological development has always been accompanied by joy and skepticism. This process is a typical negotiation of arguments, concerns, and hopes—a very human instinct. The broad field of research and application of AI in the media industry is an excellent example and illustrative material at the same time.

Since the early 2010s at the latest, the terms automation and machine learning have left the hitherto almost exclusive realm of computer science and have gradually become much-discussed buzzwords in business and society. From the very beginning, the enormous potential (acceleration, knowledge gain, participation)—but also the risks (control and loss of control, ethical dimensions, and responsibility)—were emphasized (Katzenbach & Pentzold, 2024, p. 4925). Looking back on these early years, it can be said that it was only with great difficulty that a decisive change in perspective was achieved (Baum & Owe, 2022, p. 141):

- From the very beginning, the development thrusts and public and corporate communication about automation and AI were strongly influenced and driven by the business interests of participating or dependent companies.
- The potentials and risks of this transformation were gradually taken up, discussed and further developed by all areas of society and academic disciplines, including the media industry and the disciplines of media studies and journalism studies (Hill & Hargis, 2024).
- It is only with great difficulty that those approaches in research and practice that take the common good-oriented perspective of society and ask about the "interests of the broader public" (ibid., p. 141) have found and continue to find a hearing.

This interest on the part of society is particularly justified by the fact that automation and AI have several highly relevant points of influence on our lives together. It is therefore far more than just a technological development or innovation, but a highly relevant driver of social disruption and transformation. We can differentiate between three important spheres of influence on this disruption and transformation (Schneider-Kamp, 2024):

1. **AI-influence on consumption:** Intelligent and learning recommendation systems are increasingly influencing consumer decisions algorithmically. These "smart objects" (Hoffman & Novak, 2018) are not only driving new decision-making processes but are also constantly creating new networks between consumers and companies. This is also associated with a complete realignment of the advertising market, particularly in the online sector.
2. **AI-influence on information:** These findings can be transferred almost congruently to the consumption of information, news, and media entertainment: Here too, AI is influencing the way in which society becomes aware of media offerings, what exact content is used via which devices. This development may be worrying for media management (Gundlach & Hofmann, 2020). Search engines

and their news preparation are entering into direct competition with media companies and not only have the advantage of reach, but also direct access to global sources Media providers who have become dependent on the large intermediaries.

3. **AI-influence on politics:** Based on consumption and information, developments in the field of automation and AI inevitably have a direct influence on politics. There are questions about political framework conditions and legal dimensions. The area is also a policy field in its own right, for example, in economic and security policy (Hunter et al., 2024). In the context of education policy, governments around the world are being asked to organize the challenges and required skills for schools, universities, and other training units (Knox, 2020). And last but not least, these developments are bringing about a change in the direct pattern of action of active politicians: they recognize that consumption and information (see above) are gradually and increasingly shaped by automation and AI and that this influences opinion-forming processes in society. Political action and political communication are being adapted accordingly (Thiel & Kailitz, 2024).

This initial approach to the topic makes it clear how crucial developments in the media market are for politics and society. When it comes to the question of solutions and orientation, reference is often made to the possibilities of media and ethics as a "mediating authority" (Münker, 2016). This mediation between different ideas, but also between philosophy and the reality of life in general, gives us orientation, limits, and recommendations. In the following, the chapter takes up the idea of ethics as a "mediating authority" and asks specifically about the ethical limits of AI use in the media sector. The central questions are therefore:

- What does the current state of research and practice say about the ethical limits of AI use in the media industry?
- Where is there (nevertheless) a need for action, and how can the future of media products and productions be shaped in the medium term on the basis of ethical dimensions?

The chapter begins with a brief review of current and relevant studies and publications and also specifies which areas of the media sector need to be differentiated in the context of AI use. This is followed by current developments and observations from the field as well as a compilation of theses and recommendations for the future.

9.2 Disruption in the Media Industry

This chapter focuses on the changing environment of the media industry, which has been intensively influenced by two key factors in recent years. Disruption in the media world has been driven in particular by

(a) The global corona pandemic, which has abruptly changed production routines (technology, organization, hybrid work) across national and cultural borders and has resulted in new practices of media production and media products (Chibuwe et al., 2022). In some cases, this is accompanied by significant changes in media usage habits (Jurkowitz & Mitchell, 2020; Mitchell et al., 2020).
(b) The transformative development spurts brought about by AI since 2017 at the latest. Emerging applications in various main areas (Chan-Olmsted, 2019) have gradually triggered further spurts of disruption. This applies not only to journalistic productions and brands—for example in the context of research, presentation and user interaction—but much more broadly in the area of general media communication by companies, institutions or individuals. AI is revolutionizing media communication and enabling (for better or worse) everyone to use simple production tools for media content of all kinds; "different emphases on societal threat and societal efficacy of AI" are constantly emerging (Schwarz, 2024).

An important distinction and clarification are necessary at this point. It is crucial to emphasize again and again: Journalism is not the same as media. Journalism is a sub-sector of the ever-growing media world that can be separated in terms of function, content, and organization, although the boundaries are becoming increasingly blurred, the so-called "Blurring Boundaries of Journalism in Digital Media" (Negreia-Rey et al., 2023). Journalism is a systemically relevant profession in democracies that produces content that is transported to an audience via the media. The activities (especially the focus on independent and critical research) of this profession guarantee democratic processes, provide criticism, information, and control on as objective and fair a basis as possible. Journalism pursues the goal of researching, selecting, and presenting topics that are new, real, and important (Meier et al., 2025).

Due to the enormous importance and unique constitutional position of journalism (in almost all democracies), the differentiation of journalistic content from forms of strategic communication is highly relevant. The media disruption of the recent past, in particular the transformation of the (media) world through social media (Graßl et al., 2023), has given rise to complex areas of discussion. In science, practice, and politics, it has long been about much more than platforms that use content to compete for the time of as many users as possible. Studies and experts are discussing the general influence and further development of a mediatized society (Hadzi, 2022; Hauer, 2022).

According to this, we are currently only in an intermediate stage with a short preparation time for another complete upheaval that will bring about completely new media content, production processes, and players. All of this will (be) largely driven by technology, by AI systems. Media ethics acts as an observer at the interface of these lines of development, potentials, and risks. We will therefore first take a look at relevant literature and studies on the ethics of AI use in the media industry before using current practical examples to compile the need for action and possible solutions.

9.3 Review of Relevant Literature and Existing Studies

In recent years, numerous publications and empirical studies have been produced on the topic. However, in relation to the extremely broad topic of AI and automation, media ethics approaches are clearly in the minority. The focus is on the effects on consumption, possibilities and current tools (in particular ChatGPT and DeepSeek at the beginning of 2025) and the legal framework. Almost omnipresent in all publications, regardless of subject, country and methodological approach, is the juxtaposition of the two poles of opportunities and risks. Almost all recent international studies support this impression.

For example, Diakopoulos et al. (2024) show that the biggest concerns with regard to the development of journalistic AI are the loss of human control, the susceptibility to errors/inaccuracies and the influence of bias. The study was conducted at the end of 2023 on the basis of almost 300 respondents in the media industry and adds the following statement: "Overall, editors, managers, and executives (rather than technologists) were the roles that respondents thought should be more responsible for ensuring effective and ethical uses of generative AI" (p. 7).

In another publication, Diakopoulos (2025) picks up on this preliminary work and approaches the topic from a more theoretical perspective and with the help of the concept of responsibility. The author notes that the responsibility surrounding algorithms, automation and AI has long been thought of and practiced retrospectively. His conclusion calls on individuals and media brands alike to take action: Everyone who distributes media content is asked to participate in the development of (new) norms for responsible media content and to implement them: "This includes norms for answerability, norms for establishing what is harmful and impactful that society may want to avoid, and norms for assigning responsibility to particular actors for mitigating those potential states of affair."

This is supplemented by the results of a media policy document analysis by Porlezza (2023): Whether and to what extent the use of AI tools in news media and journalism is currently regulated and discussed within the European Union and the Council of Europe. The study shows that the political, legal and ethical frameworks for AI in the media can at best be categorized as individual frameworks. There is also a lack of specific studies and templates that deal more specifically with the key areas of conflict between AI and the media. Porlezza mentions disinformation, diversity and social responsibility in particular.

Cheng and Lee (2024) take a partial view of the areas of conflict outlined by Porlezza in their approach to media ethics. The authors focus on training and skills at universities. They note that the fundamental awareness of ethical and legal dimensions of the media industry has long been a marginal aspect of education and studies. Their survey of students provides several important indications in the context of the topic. The interviewees argue that ethical guidelines and problems in the field of

AI and automation can be experienced and trained more intensively and better through on-site and live conditions in the context of internships in the media. The discussion and knowledge transfer of new technology is therefore always shifted in time and thus presents trainers and trainees with permanent challenges in terms of content and time. In addition, there are numerous studies that discuss the opportunities of AI as a challenge for the integrity of science and also of study and examination performance at universities (e.g., Malik et al., 2024; Yan et al., 2024).

Thomaß (2024) opens up the conceptual work more fundamentally and broadly in her basic contribution and acts here from the perspective of journalism research. The author begins by stating that the completely changed possibilities of "information procurement, processing and dissemination" created by AI create a wealth of new challenges for which it must be examined whether "they require a 'new' journalistic ethics or whether the previous norms and approaches remain valid" (p. 673). Under these conditions, the basic question of (media) ethics—"What should we do"—must be discussed anew and supplemented in relation to journalism to: "How can we create orientation globally and under new conditions, opportunities and risks in order to arrive at decisions for actions on this basis?"

From a technical perspective, Funk (2023) supplements the state of research and, with the support of computer science, also provides a valuable impetus in the context of the terms. The publication notes that AI ethics as a term has been appearing more frequently in journals and specialist publications since the 2010s. Funk shows historical lines of development in computer and information ethics and places AI ethics as part of these larger dimensions. He describes AI as a "generic term for all relevant cross-sectional technologies" and mentions big data (data ethics), digital media (digital ethics), and robotics (technology ethics).

Further conceptual groundwork is provided by Filipović and Lamers (2022), who approach the issue along ethical and media policy dimensions. They begin by noting that the growing importance of AI in business, media, and society has only gradually become a political challenge in the German parliament. The authors bundle the discourses on AI and ethics conducted there and beyond along three central normative conflicts (p. 142): Opportunities versus risks posed by algorithms in terms of precision, facticity and fairness (1), optimization and maximization versus privacy and data protection (2), and efficiency and quality of life versus fear of loss of control and jobs due to increasing AI deployments (3).

Sarısakaloğlu (2022) provides a further compilation of current studies and media policy examples. She first differentiates the most important fields of application and possibilities of AI in media production and then goes into more detail on the ethical challenges (p. 314). When analyzing current guidelines from politics and media companies, it is noticeable that respect for human autonomy and control, harm prevention, fairness, and explainability are understood and mentioned as central media ethical guidelines. From this, the demand for a human-centered approach can be derived, so that technology should be integrated into the processes in a supportive but not dominant way. Above all these debates, human dignity is the overriding principle and thus also a cautionary guideline. It is clear that algorithm-driven journalism faces a central challenge: Algorithmic distortions and risks of discrimination as a result of erroneous, incomplete, or biased source data must be weighed up, permanently checked and prevented.

This compilation of selected studies and publications represents a current selection of approaches, conceptual differentiations, and current examples. However, the particular challenge of the topic of ethics and ethical boundaries in the context of AI in the media world is also very clear here: the individual publications and ethical guidelines from politics and media companies are highly fragmented and fragmentary.

So far, there is only an overview with individual examples from media policy or the media companies themselves as well as smaller summaries. Following the contribution by Hauer (2022), the following section therefore looks for a way in which the further development of the field of AI ethics can be pushed and described in order to better prepare and model what possible effects new phenomena will have on the current concept of moral responsibility and on the concept of trustworthy AI. To this end, a few examples from politics and media practice will first follow, which usefully complement the studies presented, in order to then be able to clearly present the key questions and future research dimensions along a separate system.

9.4 Current Developments and Debates: Ethical Limits of AI Use

A look at current developments in politics and the media shows that the topic of ethics and AI is highly dynamic and increasingly relevant on a daily basis. Research in common databases, the specialist press, and news aggregators confirms this: almost daily, new publications, press releases, and case studies on the implementation of AI tools as well as corresponding AI guidelines are being released. When examining the various instruments and their effects, a more precise differentiation is therefore helpful. Following Winterthaler and Marquardt (2020, p. 5), different hierarchical levels of rules can be distinguished (Fig. 9.1):

Within companies and organizations, there are specific standards, work norms, and routines that correspond to their production processes and are usually only communicated internally. Company norms are a level above these and are typically also communicated externally. They serve as a guideline for the general working environment and the fundamental orientation of the company. At the state level, regulations *and* decrees can provide general directives for the entire economy or specific industries. Above these are the laws. These two levels are publicly accessible, carry the highest degree of liability force, and can be enforced legally.

The following section provides an overview of current standards, norms, regulations, and laws concerning AI and ethics in the media industry. An initial simple search using the above-mentioned approaches quickly yielded over 100 well-known examples. A similarly comprehensive overview was also compiled by de Lima Santos et al. (2024). This collection is expanded below on the basis of current developments (as of January 2025) and is initially structured along three dimensions for

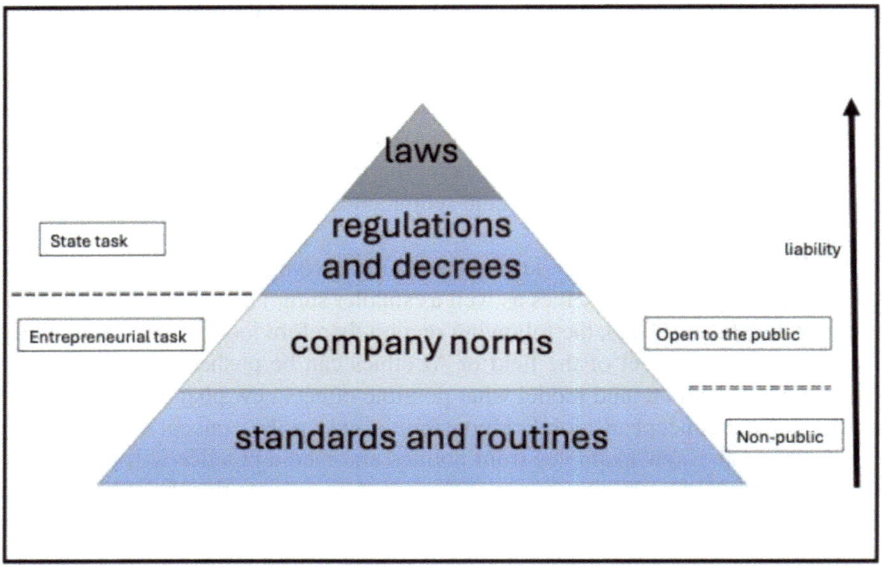

Fig. 9.1 Hierarchy levels of standards and laws (Source: Own representation based on Winterthaler & Marquardt, 2020)

clarity. Accordingly, examples of ethical guidelines for the use of AI in the media industry can be grouped into three distinct clusters:

(a) **Political Framework and (draft) Laws**

Compared to the other dimensions, this dimension is politically created and attempts to create a legally valid basis that is ultimately enforceable in court. Developments in this area are still very limited in most countries, with draft legislation or parliamentary working groups in the early stages at most. However, the European Union is going one step further with the so-called AI Act of 2024, which states at the outset (under 1):

> The purpose of this Regulation is to improve the functioning of the internal market by laying down a uniform legal framework in particular for the development, the placing on the market, the putting into service and the use of artificial intelligence systems (AI systems) in the Union, in accordance with Union values, to promote the uptake of human centric and trustworthy artificial intelligence (AI) while ensuring a high level of protection of health, safety, fundamental rights as enshrined in the Charter of Fundamental Rights of the European Union (the 'Charter'), including democracy, the rule of law and environmental protection, to protect against the harmful effects of AI systems in the Union, and to support innovation.

The great ambition of the project is already clear here: the AI Act is intended to comprehensively cover all areas of AI and AI effects and provide legal guidance throughout Europe. The reference to democracy and human rights is paramount. The bill has been taken up in many ways since its publication. However, from the perspective of media and journalism, the relevance of the AI Act is limited: media and journalism only appear as examples in a few places, but are not specifically targeted in the regulations. Instead, in terms of risk management, a template is created along a four-level scale (very low risk—too high risk), which can be used to classify AI tools in future. Here, too, it remains unclear how exactly (and who exactly) such classifications can be made and on what basis.

Nevertheless, the AI Act is an important template at the level of individual countries in Europe. Specifically, it calls on each EU member state to create a supervisory body for the national implementation of the AI Act in order to regulate the use of AI in various sectors more specifically at country level. In Germany, there has so far only been one question to the federal government (SPD/Greens/FDP) from September 2024, which failed shortly afterwards, asking for more detailed plans for implementation. In addition, there are legal and ethical questions about AI-based scoring mechanisms in the context of financial policy, for example using "credit scoring" to assess a person's creditworthiness (Spindler, 2021).

The Council of Europe's Guidelines on the responsible Implementation of Artificial Intelligence Systems in Journalism (2023) are more specific with regard to media and journalism. These guidelines begin with the demand that AI initiatives "should not be purely technology or commercially-driven, but also mission-driven." This is also followed by sections on transparency, data security, and responsible management of AI tools.

In the U.S., the envisaged "AI Bill of Rights" is also a proposal that can be seen as an initial basis for further legal work. This is also a cross-societal approach, so there are no direct references to the media industry. Nevertheless, the overview published as a blueprint (October 2022) contains several references to current debates on media ethics (see Chap. 4): With the help of the "AI Bill of Rights," safe, and effective AI tools are to be guaranteed (1). Discriminatory algorithms should also be prevented (2). Data protection must be guaranteed (3), the functioning, purposes and further development of AI systems should be transparent for everyone (4), and human control and responsibility must safeguard the automated systems (5).

(b) **Media-Related Institutions and Initiatives**

At the intersection of politics and media organizations, numerous initiatives and collaborations exist that have also formulated proposals or guidelines for the use of AI in the media industry. The following is merely a representative excerpt, supplemented by more recent examples based on Becker's publication (2023). Various initiatives from regulatory institutions are frequently mentioned: In Germany, the DJV (German Journalists Association) emphasized in 2023 that the responsibility for AI-generated content remains with the media brands and responsible individuals. Consequently, AI tools are not considered accountability bearers in terms of media ethics, and journalists must therefore retain and actively develop a control function (cf. DJV, 2023). The association also calls for legal regulations to "introduce a remuneration obligation for text and data mining, so that journalists can participate in the development and use of AI systems."

Two years earlier, the Catalan Press Council (Ventura Pocino, 2021) conducted a review based on a transfer-oriented study from Spain and derived eight central recommendations for action. Similar to the AI Bill of Rights (U.S.), measures for data security, data protection, and against discrimination through automation and algorithms are demanded. Additionally, it is asserted that the introduction, control, and further development of AI in the media represent an interdisciplinary task, necessitating the development of diverse competencies within editorial teams. The Catalan Press Council also concludes by emphasizing human responsibility: "Never forget that people can make ethical assessments that machines cannot."

In the U.S., there are numerous initiatives on this topic that have been established in recent years. A notable example is the often-cited Partnership on AI (PAI). It describes itself as "a nonprofit partnership of academic, civil society, industry, and media organizations creating solutions so that AI advances positive outcomes for people and society." The "AI and Media Integrity Steering Committee" of the initiative includes prominent figures from media companies and research institutions. Meta, Microsoft, Google, and *The New York Times* are also involved. A recent guideline emphasizes the importance of user research and the overall significance of constructive and trustworthy collaboration between science and practice. The general focus of the initiative is less on media ethics and more on media development and media policy.

More journalistically focused in the U.S. is the News Media Alliance, which promotes itself as "the leading voice for the news and magazine media industries." The Alliance also acts politically but aims to advocate more strongly for the protection of intellectual property (see also the case study from Germany). This aligns with the paper (News Media Alliance, 2023) based on a study, "that demonstrated how many large language models retain and often reproduce whole passages of copyrighted news articles. When AI companies can reproduce the work of publishers to provide users the information that they are seeking, without compensating publishers, this irreparably damages publishers' businesses, which depend on relationships with their readers, web traffic, and the trustworthiness of brands built over decades."

There is international consensus regarding transparency in the integration of AI tools. The Belgian "Raad voor de Journalistiek" was one of the first institutional players to demand a clear labeling requirement for AI content in the media industry (Article 12 in the Code van de Raad voor de Journalistiek). In Great Britain, Ofcom is a central player in the media market. As the regulator and competition authority for the UK communications industries, it has been providing concrete impulses for the development of AI tools in the media sector for some time. The latest Ofcom publication collects individual examples and arguments, concluding with key questions for the future (Ofcom, 2024, p. 18):

(i) If generative AI opens up the possibility of more accessible and inclusive interactions, how do we ensure this technology can be accessed by those who may benefit the most?
(ii) What will generative AI mean for human-to-human interaction, and how will this impact how we engage with the online and offline world?
(iii) What are users' attitudes toward generative AI? To what extent are users critically engaging with generative AI, and does that differ across age, gender, and socio-economic backgrounds?
(iv) What is it reasonable to expect of users, and where are the boundaries of media literacy compared to technological innovation and regulation?

(c) **Traditional Media Houses**

These questions also largely appear in the guidelines of various media houses. For this third group, a representative compilation of international examples follows. The research exclusively considers publications that are actively and transparently issued by the respective media organizations themselves and are accessible there. Other sources (e.g., social media posts or blog entries) were not taken into account. Nevertheless, a clear picture emerges that shows different approaches taken by various countries and media houses.

Example 1 The guidelines of the British BBC (BBC, 2024) are frequently cited and serve as a reference worldwide. Based in London, the BBC is one of the most important public service broadcasters globally and most recently revised its *Guidance for the Use of Artificial Intelligence* in February 2024. In this document, the BBC assumes responsibility for AI-generated content published on its own platforms. It takes a clear stance against purely automated text generation and also pledges to take responsibility for third-party content (Sect. 9.4). These and other elements go significantly further than the guidelines of many other media organizations in certain respects. As an overarching principle in the context of AI and ethics, the BBC states (Sect. 1):

> BBC use of AI must
> - never undermine the trust of audiences.
> - always be transparent and accountable with effective and informed human oversight.
> - always be used in a manner consistent with BBC editorial values, particularly of accuracy, impartiality, fairness, and privacy.

Example 2 The New York-based news agency Associated Press (AP) follows a different approach. It is one of the leading international news agencies. At AP (see AP, 2025), there is only a very brief guideline on the potential of AI in journalism. Here—just as in the following cases—a clearly technology-optimistic perspective dominates, while ethical aspects (responsibility for content, transparency, and security) are only briefly mentioned (see also Becker, 2023, p. 136 ff.). The focus is on AP's *Local News AI Initiative*. This cooperative project aims to provide local media organizations in the U.S. with easy, secure, and cost-effective access to AI tools. The project leaders describe it as follows: "Based on the scorecard results, AP wrote a report and designed an online course to share best practices and techniques on AI with local newsrooms. The initiative's third phase will be a consultancy program with 15 news operations."

Example 3 To gain a broader picture, it is also useful to take a look at the world of radio. This sector faces particular opportunities and risks—especially in the area of automated audio production (Bergin & Oppegaard, 2024). Sveriges Radio ("Sweden's Radio") is the national publicly funded broadcaster and provided insights into its AI guidelines in July 2023 (see Sveriges Radio, 2023). There, a specially established AI committee—composed of representatives from various fields—is intended to serve as the central authority and interface between the media brand and the audience. According to the committee, the highest importance is placed on journalistic quality of the overall offering, legal requirements, and security-related issues for both the organization and the public. This case study also emphasizes that AI-generated content must be approved by the responsible editorial team. In addition, there is a stated goal of openly and educationally communicating where and how AI is used. In Scandinavia, public trust in the media is traditionally particularly high, and this trust—as well as the importance of fair engagement with the audience—is repeatedly highlighted. Compared to other guidelines, the example from Sweden is less precise and rarely formulated on the basis of concrete cases.

Example 4 In Germany, the public service broadcaster ZDF has made its *Guiding Principles for the Use of Generative AI* publicly available since October 2023 (ZDF, 2023). The television and online provider begins by weighing opportunities and risks, committing itself to transparency and human oversight (Sects. 1–3). At ZDF, this oversight is also ensured by the well-established two-source principle: "Generative AI tools may be used in editorial and journalistic contexts. The two-source principle applies, whereby generative AI itself is not considered a source" (Sect. 4). This aspect is particularly interesting, as the question of AI's source quality has been addressed only marginally—if at all—in previous studies and in the document analysis of this chapter. In addition, ZDF—like many other media organizations—emphasizes the importance of data protection (Sect. 7) and concludes with a self-imposed commitment to transparently inform the public about any newly implemented or further developed forms of AI (Sect. 9).

This exemplary overview of international media organizations provides insight into commonly adopted policy frameworks. At the same time, it confirms Becker's summary (2023, p. 159): Almost all of the reviewed guidelines promise transparent labeling of AI-generated elements in media offerings. The same applies to the principle that human oversight must always have the final and overriding authority over machine control. Most of the analyzed guidelines also emphasize journalistic values (especially credibility, objectivity, fairness, and transparency) and underline their own responsibility.

In individual cases (such as the BBC), specific dimensions and areas of application are described in more detail. However, clear boundaries or limitations are rarely found in these guiding principles. This is partly due to the fact that they are generally formulated in very broad terms rather than argued using concrete examples. This gap will therefore be addressed in the following chapter through a summarizing discussion and structured analysis.

9.5 Discussion and Areas for Future Research

The review reveals a variety of initiatives and proposals for the media-ethical use of AI tools in the media industry. However, a systematic approach is still lacking; much of the discourse remains fragmented and is described in a practical, example-based manner. Additionally, studies clearly indicate that we are only in the early stages of a new era of media production. Many insights are therefore time-sensitive, and significant further developments can be expected. As is often the case, scientific observation, classification, and critique will follow these developments with some delay.

Nevertheless, for a clearer overview, it makes sense to compile a current summary of key guidelines on ethics, ethical boundaries, and the technical possibilities of AI tools. As of early 2025, the following overview—based on the examined studies and practical media examples—can be useful. To achieve this, the intersections of various media ethics areas according to Loretan (1994, p. 61) will be related to the individual steps of journalistic and media production processes (Schützeneder et al., 2024, p. 3) (Table 9.1).

Along the three areas of media policy, media organizations, and the individual level, various tasks and boundaries of media-ethical dimensions emerge. Given the constantly changing technological environments, concrete bodies of knowledge are highly fragile (Pentzold & Fechner, 2021, p. 715). Nevertheless, the current overview reveals clear and multifaceted boundaries and tasks in the context of media ethics:

Media Policy Level: At the national and international legal levels, some initial key milestones have already been set: AI tools should and must not develop an "autonomous life"; they operate based on human initiative and remain under human control in monitoring and further development. Initiatives regarding copyright have just begun, and it remains unclear how such regulations will be structured. The same applies to data protection and data security. There are still no concrete regulations governing AI-based data analysis and user statistics. This is particularly true for the dimension of "social scoring": When individuals are ranked based on data (e.g., in job applications), the data-driven power of these tools can have severe consequences for those affected. Regarding power concentration, it is also unclear how the data

Table 9.1 Boundaries and tasks of media-ethical dimensions in the production process of media content (Source: Own Representation)

	Research/ verification	Production	Distribution	Analysis	Archiving
Media Policy Level	Media policy and regulatory boundary: No complete delegation of control (fact-checking) and research to AI tools.	Regulation and legal framework for AI in production. Media policy initiatives for research, networking, and training.	Regulation and legal framework for distribution rules, particularly in the context of algorithmic fairness. Initiative against discriminatory AI. Regulations for copyright.	Regulation and legal framework for analysis and data processing of user figures. Measures for data security and privacy. Prevention of 'social scoring'.	Regulation and legal framework for user data protection. Special focus on transparency and retrospective access to AI-based media productions. Regulation and legal framework for user data protection. Special focus on transparency and retrospective access to AI-based media productions.
Media Organization Level	Establish workflows and control systems, no autonomous research and verification by AI tools. Review of raw material.	No AI elements in opinion-forming publications. Workflows and control systems for AI-assisted publications. Prevent AI from developing an "autonomous life."	No full-scale distribution and full automation through AI tools. Safeguards against potential distortions and external access.	Measures for data protection and security. Review of the impact of already published content in the context of society and the environment. Emergency plans and worst-case scenarios.	Measures for data protection and security. Accountability, transparency, and access to completed productions. Assignment of responsibility and roles.
Personal Level	Understand AI as a support tool, maintain human oversight. Individual training, adherence to guidelines, and workflows. Focus on copyright and potential biases.	Understand and actively control AI's limitations in interpretation, context, and moral evaluation. Ensure a balance between complexity and comprehensibility.	Recognize originality and copyright as critical issues. Maintain a distinction between technical and content-related AI support. Verify factual accuracy and potential discrimination.	Question the generalizability of processes. Apply insights from previously published content and experiences to new decision-making processes.	Compliance with data protection and security. Continuous review of archived content for legal and human rights compliance. Ensuring transparency and further development of existing processes.

dominance of major and dominant platforms in the AI context (Google, Microsoft, OpenAI/ChatGPT) can be effectively regulated and how fair competition can be ensured.

Media Organization Level: The examples from media practice reveal a relatively unified approach in the areas of research and production. Media organizations define human responsibility as the ultimate boundary of all AI capabilities. To this end, they have established workflows and internal control mechanisms. The frequently mentioned goal: AI must not determine opinion-forming publications (such as commentaries and essays); it must not condemn or insult individuals, or disadvantage them through false or misleading statements. Special attention is also given to data security and transparency toward the audience and institutions.

Personal Level: Individuals in media organizations take responsibility for the content they generate and publish through their use of AI (prompting). Here too, the boundary of AI as merely a supportive tool is emphasized. At the personal level, copyright, originality, and the associated transparency play a crucial role. Large portions of existing media law and media control guidelines apply to final media products and are therefore also useful in the context of AI-assisted productions. Regardless, new skills in handling AI are indispensable at the individual level, making personal and professional development across all mentioned levels essential for a responsible approach to tools and tasks.

This compilation synthesizes findings from media research, media practice, and media policy. However, several open questions and tasks remain, which, as of early 2025, have only been considered in a preliminary manner:

1. Where exactly is the boundary between a supportive and an autonomous AI?
2. Where is the line between an AI-assisted illustration that enhances understanding and an unlawful fabrication?
3. Where does the boundary lie between AI-assisted audience analysis, user typology, and a ranking or scoring system?
4. How can the practice of "social scoring" based on data and AI be effectively restricted to protect societal values and individual rights?
5. (How exactly) can a legally secure copyright system for intellectual creations be developed?
6. Where are the boundaries between individual responsibility and liability versus corporate responsibility and liability?
7. What specific new normative demands on journalistic practices and journalistic contributions can be derived from this?

9.6 Conclusion

"Where is action needed, and how can the future of media products and productions be shaped in the medium term based on ethical dimensions?" Based on this initial question, this article first attempted to compile current dimensions of academic discourse based on studies. This was then supplemented with numerous documents from media policy, media-related institutions, and media organizations. One thing is clear: AI and AI tools are the central drivers of a massive innovation cycle that has only just begun. As is often the case, this development is generating new business fields, processes, and products. It is the role of ethics to anticipate the societal consequences early on, to discuss and publish guidelines. Moreover, it is the role of media ethics to closely examine the interface between technology, media policy, media companies, and the public, and to take timely action in this regard. Application-oriented research plays a crucial role here, bridging the gap between developments in practice and established scientific insights.

The analysis of academic studies, documents from media policy, media-related institutions, and media organizations shows that in recent years, numerous attempts have been made to specify the tasks and opportunities surrounding AI in the media industry at the three identified levels. Across all examined materials, three central limitations accompany the overall rather technology-positive sentiment:

A widely shared principle is that AI should only serve as a support tool and must never gain independent momentum or operate without human control and influence (1). AI-driven productions must not actively contribute to opinion formation—either directly or based on incorrect data/information—such as through commentaries or explicit calls to action (see AI bots and chats, especially in the context of youth protection) (2). The practice of "social scoring" is a major ethical boundary and challenge in societal debates. Unlike in authoritarian systems, there is near consensus in Western states and social sciences that comprehensive ranking systems for evaluating people are incompatible with overarching values and individual rights, marking a clear limit for AI usage (3).

The efforts of the examined media organizations confirm these trend lines. Almost all reviewed guidelines from practice emphasize the importance of transparently labeling AI-generated elements in media content. Most of these guidelines also highlight journalistic values—particularly credibility, objectivity, fairness, and transparency—while emphasizing media organizations' responsibility. However, in most cases, the concretization of this responsibility or its precise implementation remains vague. This gap will likely only be filled gradually. In many cases, concrete case studies are still lacking. The academic assessment as of January 2025 also shows that studies and publications remain highly fragmented and incomplete. There are tentative efforts to define concepts, dimensions, and ethical limitations. The latter applies particularly to transparency and the risk of distortion and bias. A symbolic example is Thomaß (2024), who states that AI's fundamentally transformed capabilities for "information acquisition, processing, and dissemination" create numerous new challenges, "which must be examined to determine whether they require a 'new' journalistic ethic or whether existing norms and approaches remain valid" (p. 673). So far, the only available resources are an overview with selected examples from media policy and media companies themselves, along with smaller summaries. From the perspective of predictive journalism and media studies, both academia and practice are equally called upon: More research is urgently needed on the possibilities and limitations of AI in the media industry. By doing so, we are not only shaping the future of media but ultimately contributing to the development of society as a whole.

Literature

AP. (2025). *Artificial intelligence*. https://www.ap.org/solutions/artificial-intelligence/

Baum, S. D., & Owe, A. (2022). Artificial intelligence needs environmental ethics. *Ethics, Policy and Environment, 26*(1), 139–143. https://doi.org/10.1080/21550085.2022.2076538

BBC. (2024). *Editorial guidance on the use of artificial intelligence*. https://www.bbc.co.uk/editorialguidelines/documents/guidance-use-of-of-artificial-intelligence.pdf

Becker, K. B. (2023). New game, new rules. An investigation into editorial guidelines for dealing with artificial intelligence in the newsroom. *Journalism Research, 6*(2), 133–152. https://doi.org/10.1453/2569-152X-22023-13404-en

Bergin, D., & Oppegaard, B. (2024). Automating media accessibility: An approach for analyzing audio description across generative artificial intelligence algorithms. *Technical Communication Quarterly, 1–16*. https://doi.org/10.1080/10572252.2024.2372771

Chan-Olmsted, S. M. (2019). A review of artificial intelligence adoptions in the media industry. *International Journal on Media Management, 21*(3–4), 193–215. https://doi.org/10.1080/14241277.2019.1695619

Cheng, I., & Lee, S. T. (2024). The impact of ethics instruction and internship on students' ethical perceptions about social media, artificial intelligence, and ChatGPT. *Journal of Media Ethics, 39*(2), 114–129. https://doi.org/10.1080/23736992.2024.2333486

Chibuwe, A., Munoriyarwa, A., Motsaathebe, G., Chiumbu, S., & Lesitaokana, W. (2022). Newsroom disruptions and opportunities in times of crisis: Analysing Southern African media during the COVID-19 crisis. *African Journalism Studies, 43*(2), 53–70. https://doi.org/10.1080/23743670.2022.2071961

De Lima Santos, M. F., Yeung, W. N., & Dodds, T. (2024). Guiding the way: A comprehensive examination of AI guidelines in global media. *AI and Society*. https://doi.org/10.1007/s00146-024-01973-5

Diakopoulos, N. (2025). Prospective algorithmic accountability and the role of the news media. In M. Noorman & M. Verdicchio (Eds.), *Computer ethics across disciplines: Deborah G. Johnson and Algorithmic Accountability*. Springer VS. https://doi.org/10.2139/ssrn.5022167

Diakopoulos, N., Cooles, H., Li, C., Helberger, N., Kung, E., & Rinehart, A. (2024). *Generative AI in journalism: The evolution of newswork and ethics in a generative information ecosystem*. Associated Press Report.

DJV. (2023). *Positionspapier bezüglich des Einsatzes Künstlicher Intelligenz im Journalismus*. https://www.djv.de/fileadmin/user_upload/DJV/INFORMATIONEN/medienpolitik/DJV-Positionspapier_KI_2023-04.pdf

Filipović, A. & Lamers, J. (2022). Die ethische Relevanz von KI-Diskursen: Das Verhältnis von Diskursanalyse und Angewandter Ethik im Feld der Künstlichen Intelligenz. In: van Oorschot, F. & Fucker, S. (eds). *Framing KI: Narrative, Metaphern und Frames in Debatten über Künstliche Intelligenz* (pp. 137–154). heiBOOKS.

Funk, M. (2023). *Ethik künstlicher Intelligenz. Eine Topographie zur praktischen Orientierung*. Springer VS.

Graßl, M., Planer, R., Schützeneder, J., & Klinghardt, K. (2023). Dependent on the platform? Discussing journalistic transformation levels on and through Instagram. In A. Godulla & S. Böhm (Eds.), *Digital disruption and media transformation. How technological innovation shapes the future of communication* (pp. 205–215). Springer VS.

Gundlach, H., & Hofmann, U. (2020). Information search, behavioural economics, and relevance decisions in the online media industry: How strongly do the algorithms of intermediaries

influence the relevance evaluation of information? *Journal of Media Business Studies, 18*(3), 179–198. https://doi.org/10.1080/16522354.2020.1854602
Hadzi, A. (2022). Algorithms, ethics and justice. In A. Dingli, A. Pfeiffer, A. Serada, M. Bugeja, & S. Bezzina (Eds.), *Disruptive technologies in media, arts and design. ICISN 2021* (Lecture notes in networks and systems) (Vol. 382). Springer VS. https://doi.org/10.1007/978-3-030-93780-5_9
Hauer, T. (2022). Importance and limitations of AI ethics in contemporary society. *Humanities and Social Science Communication, 272*(9). https://doi.org/10.1057/s41599-022-01300-7
Hill, C., & Hargis, J. (2024). An ethics module on academic integrity and generative AI. *New Directions for Teaching and Learning*. https://doi.org/10.1002/tl.20626.
Hoffman, D. L., & Novak, T. P. (2018). Consumer and object experience in the Internet of things: An assemblage theory approach. *Journal of Consumer Research, 44*(6), 1178–1204. https://doi.org/10.1093/jcr/ucx105
Hunter, L. Y., Albert, C. D., Rutland, J., Topping, K., & Hennigan, C. (2024). Artificial intelligence and information warfare in major power states: How the US, China, and Russia are using artificial intelligence in their information warfare and influence operations. *Defense and Security Analysis, 40*(2), 235–269. https://doi.org/10.1080/14751798.2024.2321736
Jurkowitz, M., & Mitchell, A. (2020). Cable TV and COVID 19: How Americans perceive the outbreak and view media coverage differ by the main news source. *Journalism and Media*, 1–8.
Katzenbach, C., & Pentzold, C. (2024). Automating communication in the digital society Editorial to the special issue. *New Media and Society, 26*(9), 4925–4937. https://doi.org/10.1177/14614448241265655
Knox, J. (2020). Artificial intelligence and education in China. *Learning, Media and Technology, 45*(3), 298–311. https://doi.org/10.1080/17439884.2020.1754236
Loretan, M. (1994). Grundrisse der Medienethik. Eine "Ethik des Öffentlichen" als Theorie kommunikativen Handelns. *Zoom Kommunikation und Medien, 2*(4), 56–63.
Malik, A., Khan, M. L., Hussain, K., Qadir, J., & Tarhini, A. (2024). AI in higher education: Unveiling academicians' perspectives on teaching, research, and ethics in the age of ChatGPT. *Interactive Learning Environments*. https://doi.org/10.1080/10494820.2024.2409407
Meier, K., Graßl, M., Klinghardt, K., Körner, M., & Schützeneder, J. (2025). *Die Zukunft des Journalismus. Zehn Szenarien für das neue Jahrzehnt*. Springer VS.
Mitchell, A., Jurkowitz, M., Oliphant, J. B. & Shearer, E. (2020). *Americans' attention to news about the coronavirus pandemic remains steady in November as cases surge*. Pew Research Center, Journalism and Media.
Münker, S. (2016). Medienphilosophie. In: Heesen, J. (Ed.). *Handbuch Medien- und Informationsethik* (pp. 10–17). Metzler.
Negreia-Rey, M. C., Vázquez-Herrero, J., Sixto-García, J., & López-García, X. (Eds.). (2023). *Blurring boundaries of journalism in digital media: New actors, models and practices*. Springer VS.
News Media Alliance. (2023). *White Paper: How the pervasive copying of expressive works to train and fuel generative artificial intelligence systems is copyright infringement and not a fair use*. http://www.newsmediaalliance.org/wp-content/uploads/2023/10/AI-White-Paper-with-Technical-Analysis.pdf
Ofcom. (2024). *Future technology and media literacy: Applications of generative AI*. https://www.ofcom.org.uk/siteassets/resources/documents/research-and-data/media-literacy-research/making-sense-of-media/future-technology-trends-and-media-literacy/future-technology-and-media-lit-applications-of-generative-ai.pdf?v=384879
Pentzold, C. & Fechner, D. (2021). Probabilistic storytelling and temporal exigencies in predictive data journalism. *Digital Journalism, 9*(6), 715–736. https://doi.org/10.1080/21670811.2021.1878920
Porlezza, C. (2023). Promoting responsible AI: A European perspective on the governance of artificial intelligence in media and journalism. *Communications, 48*(3), 370–394.

Sarısakaloğlu, A. (2022). Algorithmisierung des Journalismus. Chancen und Herausforderungen künstlicher Intelligenzsysteme in sozio-technischen Newsrooms. *Communicatio Socialis, 55*(3), 308–319. https://doi.org/10.5771/0010-3497-2022-3-308
Schneider-Kamp, A. (2024). Can ethics be assembled? Consumer ethics in the age of artificial intelligence and smart objects. *Consumption Markets and Culture, 27*(1), 59–70. https://doi.org/10.1080/10253866.2024.2302598
Schützeneder, J., Graßl, M. & Meier, K. (2024). Grenzen überwinden, Chancen gestalten: KI im journalistischen Newsroom – Bestandsaufnahme, Perspektiven und Empfehlungen für Journalismus und Politik. In: *Friedrich Ebert Stiftung – FES Impuls*, ISBN 978-3-98628-512-8.
Schwarz, A. (2024). The mediated amplification of societal risk and risk governance of artificial intelligence: Technological risk frames on YouTube and their impact before and after ChatGPT. *Journal of Risk Research, 1–23*. https://doi.org/10.1080/13669877.2024.2437629
Spindler, G. (2021). Algorithms, credit scoring, and the new proposals of the EU for an AI Act and on a Consumer Credit Directive. *Law and Financial Markets Review, 15*(3–4), 239–261. https://doi.org/10.1080/17521440.2023.2168940
Sveriges Radio. (2023). *Därför publicerar Sveriges Radio en policy för generativ AI*. https://www.sverigesradio.se/artikel/darfor-publicerar-sveriges-radio-en-policy-for-generativ-ai
Thiel, T. & Kailitz, S. (2024). Generative artificial intelligence and political will-formation. *Upgrade democracy visions: Democracy and technology*, Part 1, 1–8.
Thomaß, B. (2024). Ethik des Journalismus. In M. Löffelholz & L. Rothenberger (Eds.), *Handbuch Journalismustheorien* (pp. 665–667). Springer VS.
Ventura Pocino, P. (2021). *Algorithms in the newsrooms. Challenges and recommendations for artificial intelligence with the ethical values of Journalism*. Catalan Press Council.
Winterthaler, C., & Marquardt, R. (2020). Normung und Standardisierung. In M. Hennecke & B. Skrotzki(Eds.),*HÜTTE –DasIngenieurwissen*.SpringerVS.https://doi.org/10.1007/978-3-662-57492-8_81-1
Yan, L., Sha, L., Zhao, L., Li, Y., Martinez-Maldonado, R., & Chen, G. (2024). Practical and ethical challenges of large language models in education: A systematic scoping review. *British Journal of Educational Technology, 55*(1), 90–112.
ZDF. (2023). *Guiding principles for the use of Generative AI*. https://www.zdf.de/zdfunternehmen/guiding-principles-generative-ai-100.html

Jonas Schützeneder is professor of digital journalism at the University of the Bundeswehr in Munich. His research focuses on social media, AI and innovations in the media industry.

Impact of AI Use on Creativity and Diversity in Media

10

Petri Honkanen and Mats Nylund

Abstract

Artificial intelligence (AI) is profoundly reshaping media production, consumption, and representation. This chapter examines AI's dual role as both a facilitator of creative expression and a potential homogenizing force, affecting the diversity of voices and perspectives in contemporary media. AI technologies, including generative models, enhance creative productivity by lowering technical barriers and enabling new forms of artistic experimentation. However, they also risk reinforcing biases and reducing novelty by drawing on existing patterns in training data.

Empirical studies suggest that AI tools enhance individual creativity but may reduce collective diversity by promoting stylistic convergence. While AI-driven content generation broadens access to creative opportunities, it may also lead to "synthetic tokenism," where superficial representation masks deeper systemic inequalities. Furthermore, AI's integration into journalism and entertainment raises ethical concerns regarding authorship, authenticity, and the role of human agency in storytelling.

This chapter explores the complex interplay between AI, creativity, and media diversity, assessing the broader cultural and societal implications. It argues that the future of AI-driven media requires a recalibration of how creativity is defined and valued. A balanced approach, incorporating regulatory oversight and ethical AI development, is necessary to ensure that AI serves as a tool for innovation without undermining originality and genuine inclusivity.

P. Honkanen · M. Nylund (✉)
Arcada University of Applied Sciences, Helsinki, Finland
e-mail: petri.honkanen@meiliboxi.fi; mats.nylund@folkhalsan.fi

S. Böhm et al. (eds.), *Handbook of AI-based Media Disruption*, Future of Business and Finance, https://doi.org/10.1007/978-3-032-07605-2_10

10.1 Introduction

Artificial intelligence (AI) represents a transformative force in contemporary society, reshaping industries, behaviors, and cultural landscapes. Among its many applications, the role of AI in media stands out due to its profound influence on creativity and diversity. This chapter explores these dimensions, providing a foundation for understanding AI's impact on creative expression and inclusivity within media ecosystems. Below is presented a detailed justification for why examining AI's role in media—with a focus on creativity and diversity—is both timely and essential.

AI technologies are increasingly embedded in media production, distribution, and consumption. They enable unprecedented capabilities, such as automating routine tasks, generating creative content, analyzing vast datasets for audience insights, and personalizing user experiences. As a result, AI is not merely a tool for efficiency; it is an active participant in shaping the narratives, visuals, and voices that populate contemporary media. Understanding this dual role—as both a creative enabler and a potential disruptor—is critical for appreciating its broader implications.

AI has the potential to augment creativity in media by providing tools that extend human capabilities. Generative AI models, such as GPT and DALL-E, can produce text, images, music, and video content, enabling creators to experiment with new forms of expression. These tools democratize creativity by lowering technical barriers, allowing more people to engage in artistic and content-creation processes (Tang et al., 2024). For example, a nontechnical individual can now create professional-quality visuals or music compositions with minimal training, expanding the pool of creators globally. Similarly, Huang and Rust (2024) have discussed how generative AI can automate aspects of creativity, providing tools that extend human capabilities in content generation. These advancements enable creators to experiment with new forms of expression, expanding the pool of global creators.

Moreover, AI can analyze trends and audience preferences, guiding creators toward innovative ideas that resonate with diverse audiences. For instance, AI can suggest storylines, visual styles, or music arrangements that are likely to appeal to specific demographic groups. This symbiotic relationship between AI and human creativity enhances the scope and reach of media content. Empirical studies, such as the work by Doshi and Hauser (2024), demonstrate that generative AI significantly enhances individual creativity, particularly for less experienced creators. Their study revealed that access to AI-generated ideas results in stories that are perceived as more creative, enjoyable, and better written. However, they also noted that while AI boosts individual creativity, it reduces collective diversity, as AI-generated outputs often exhibit similarities that limit novel content at the aggregate level (Doshi & Hauser, 2024). However, as Esmaeili et al. (2024) point out, generative AI depends on human-created content for training and refinement, creating a cyclical relationship where a lack of human input could degrade AI-generated outputs, reinforcing the ongoing need for human creativity to maintain quality and user satisfaction.

In a complementary study, Ashkinaze et al. (2024) explored how exposure to AI-generated ideas affects human creativity and diversity within a global experiment. Their findings suggest that while high exposure to AI-generated examples did not significantly impact individual creativity, it increased the collective diversity and rate of change in idea generation. This indicates that AI exposure can lead to a more dynamic and varied pool of collective ideas, although its influence on individual creative outputs may be limited (Ashkinaze et al., 2024).

The study of Spangher et al. (2024) highlights that AI lacks the depth of creativity demonstrated by human journalists. While AI can identify narrative structures and align moderately with human decisions, they struggle to provide novel or insightful angles and rely on fewer informational sources. These findings suggest that AI systems, while useful for basic planning and cognitive support, require significant enhancements to align with human creativity and decision-making processes in journalism.

Unlike other sectors, the creative industries rely uniquely on originality and human expression, making the balance between automation and authenticity crucial. While its potential is vast, challenges like intellectual property risks and ethical concerns require robust safeguards. Education is key to responsible adoption, empowering professionals to navigate these complexities. By integrating AI thoughtfully, the creative sector can thrive while preserving its essence and fostering innovation (Amankwah-Amoah et al., 2024).

Media diversity encompasses the representation of varied voices, identities, and perspectives. AI can serve as a catalyst for enhancing diversity by identifying gaps in representation, curating inclusive content, and enabling underrepresented creators to access global platforms. For instance, algorithms can analyze large datasets to detect patterns of underrepresentation in film, music, or journalism, prompting the creation of more equitable content strategies. AI-driven tools can also assist creators from marginalized backgrounds by providing resources and platforms that amplify their voices.

Yet, the potential of AI to foster diversity is tempered by the risks of perpetuating or amplifying existing biases. If AI systems are trained on historical data that reflects societal inequities, they may inadvertently reproduce those inequities. For example, an AI model trained on biased hiring data might recommend stereotypical representations in casting decisions for films or advertisements. Additionally, the opacity of AI decision-making processes can obscure accountability for biased outcomes, making it crucial to address these issues in both research and practice. Research by Noble (2018) highlights how algorithmic systems can reinforce systemic biases, calling for a more ethical approach to AI development. Furthermore, findings from recent studies emphasize the importance of using diverse datasets to train AI models, ensuring they promote equitable representation and do not exacerbate existing disparities (Esmaeili et al., 2024).

Das and Mitra (2024) bring another layer to this discussion, suggesting that AI can expand diversity by amplifying underrepresented voices. However, there is a risk of "synthetic tokenism," where representation exists superficially without addressing deeper systemic inequities.

Popular media outlets have highlighted both the promise and pitfalls of AI in creativity and diversity. Publications like Wired and The Atlantic have noted how AI democratizes creative tools but also warned about potential overreliance on these technologies. For example, The Atlantic reported on the homogenizing effects of AI in music creation, where algorithms may favor patterns that conform to existing popular genres, potentially stifling originality.

Conversely, business and technology magazines, such as Business Insider, have showcased the potential of AI to open new avenues in filmmaking and special effects, enabling small-scale creators to achieve results previously reserved for major studios. This dual narrative—highlighting both opportunities and challenges—reflects the nuanced role of AI in modern media.

The implications of AI's influence on creativity and diversity extend beyond media. They touch on fundamental questions about human agency, cultural heritage, and ethical responsibility. By examining these dynamics, this chapter contributes to a broader understanding of how AI shapes our shared narratives and the values they reflect.

In the following sections, we will define key concepts, delve into central themes, review existing research, debates, and propose avenues for future exploration. Together, these discussions aim to provide a comprehensive framework for understanding AI's dual impact as a driver of innovation and a source of critical challenges in media creativity and diversity.

10.2 Complex Impact of AI on Creativity and Diversity in Media

In this chapter, the term Artificial Intelligence (AI) denotes computer systems that are designed to carry out tasks typically requiring human intelligence, including learning, reasoning, and problem-solving.

Artificial General Intelligence (AGI) is a theoretical form of AI that possesses the ability to understand, learn, and apply knowledge across a wide range of tasks, similar to human cognitive capabilities.

Generative AI is a subset of AI focused on creating new content—such as text, images, or audio—by learning patterns from existing data and generating outputs that resemble the training data.

In the history of creativity research, two key characteristics of creativity have been identified: novelty (originality) and usefulness. These characteristics have a long history dating back to the mid-twentieth century (Runco & Jaeger, 2012). Creativity is commonly defined as the ability to generate ideas, solutions, or products that are both novel and useful. This dual criterion emphasizes originality and appropriateness within a given context.

Efforts to expand the definition of creativity have continued in various ways over the past decade, for instance, by conceptualizing it through five different dimensions (Wingström et al., 2022).

In media, diversity refers to the representation of varied voices, perspectives, and identities, reflecting the richness of human experience.

The relationship between AI, creativity, and diversity appears complex. AI tools democratize creativity by lowering technical barriers but can homogenize outputs due to reliance on existing patterns. Diversity, while potentially enhanced by AI's ability to amplify underrepresented voices, is contingent on addressing biases in AI systems.

10.2.1 The History of Artificial Intelligence in Content Creation and Consumption in Media

This section explores the historical trajectory of AI in media production, audience engagement, and organizational practices, with an emphasis on global trends and key milestones.

AI's incorporation into media production began as early as the 1960s with rudimentary experiments in computer-generated art and text. By the 1980s and 1990s, computational tools such as Adobe Photoshop and video editing software became integral to content creation, marking an era where automation enhanced creative workflows. These tools laid the groundwork for contemporary AI-driven systems, such as natural language generation (NLG) and computer vision technologies (Diakopoulos, 2019).

The twenty-first century witnessed a paradigm shift with the advent of machine learning algorithms, enabling AI to autonomously perform tasks previously dependent on human expertise. For example, algorithms developed by OpenAI and Google DeepMind have been employed to generate realistic audio and video content. AI tools such as DeepArt and Runway have empowered artists and filmmakers to explore novel aesthetic possibilities (Gunkel, 2018). Furthermore, AI-generated journalism, pioneered by outlets like the Associated Press and Reuters, has enabled the production of real-time, data-driven news articles (Clerwall, 2014).

Recent studies highlight AI's growing role in media production. In his analysis, Simon (2024) explores AI's influence on journalistic practices, highlighting efficiency and ethical challenges. In a related vein, Huang and Rust (2024) discuss the use of generative AI to enhance creative outputs in advertising and content marketing.

AI has reshaped media consumption patterns through personalized recommendation systems. Beginning with early internet-based algorithms in the 1990s, platforms like Amazon and Netflix used collaborative filtering to tailor recommendations to users. By the 2010s, deep learning techniques significantly improved these systems' accuracy and scope. Today, platforms such as Spotify, YouTube, and TikTok utilize AI to predict user preferences and curate highly individualized content streams (Smith & Telang, 2016).

Moreover, natural language processing (NLP) has enabled the proliferation of voice-activated virtual assistants like Amazon Alexa and Google Assistant, which serve as mediators between users and digital content. These systems exemplify the convergence of AI with media consumption, as they not only facilitate access to information but also shape how audiences engage with media environments (Napoli, 2019).

A study by Park et al. (2024) examines the role of AI-generated content on Instagram, revealing significant changes in audience behavior. The study found that participants struggled to differentiate between AI and human social media accounts, rated AI and influencer accounts as equally attractive and higher quality than public accounts, suggesting generative AI could transform social media and raise ethical concerns. The study of Lyu et al. (2024) found that YouTubers widely use generative AI (Gen-AI) across various domains, including marketing, career development, arts, entertainment, programming, and education, with a significant focus on content creation and monetization. The results indicate that Gen-AI tools, particularly large language models and image/video processors, are employed for generating, enhancing, and structuring content, which influences user-generated content platforms and raises concerns about authenticity and creativity.

Media organizations have increasingly integrated AI to optimize operations and decision-making. Newsrooms, for instance, have adopted AI-driven analytics to monitor audience engagement and forecast content performance. This approach, termed "computational journalism," enables media firms to allocate resources more effectively and address audience preferences (Diakopoulos, 2019).

Furthermore, AI has been instrumental in combating challenges such as misinformation (Dierickx et al., 2024). Initiatives like Facebook's AI-based fact-checking tools demonstrate the technology's potential to enhance media credibility. However, ethical concerns persist regarding transparency and algorithmic bias, which may influence editorial decisions and audience perceptions (Gillespie, 2018).

10.2.2 The Rise of Generative AI and Its Impact on Creativity and Diversity

In media production, generative AI has streamlined workflows, allowing creators to prototype ideas rapidly and automate repetitive tasks. For instance, filmmakers now utilize AI tools to generate storyboards, special effects, and postproduction elements, significantly reducing production times. In journalism, generative AI facilitates the creation of tailored news content for specific demographics, thereby enhancing audience engagement (Floridi, 2019).

In media consumption, the integration of generative AI into platforms has enabled unprecedented levels of personalization. AI-driven chatbots and virtual influencers, powered by generative algorithms, interact with users in highly realistic and context-aware ways, blurring the boundaries between human and machine-mediated communication. This phenomenon has given rise to new forms of entertainment and marketing strategies (Wardle & Derakhshan, 2017).

However, the proliferation of generative AI also poses significant challenges. The ability to produce convincing deepfakes and synthetic media has raised concerns about misinformation, copyright infringement, and ethical usage. As a result, media organizations are increasingly investing in AI-based detection tools to mitigate these risks while advocating for robust regulatory frameworks.

The historical development of AI in media highlights its transformative impact across production, consumption, and organizational practices. While AI has unlocked unprecedented efficiencies and creative possibilities, it has also introduced complex ethical challenges that necessitate ongoing scholarly and industrial scrutiny.

AI has significantly enhanced individual creativity by democratizing creative tools and lowering technical barriers. Nontechnical individuals can now create professional-quality content without extensive training, with research showing AI-assisted content is perceived as more creative and better written, particularly for less experienced creators. Generative AI models like GPT and DALL-E enable experimentation with new forms of expression while helping creators identify audience preferences and innovative ideas.

However, AI also presents challenges to creativity. While boosting individual output, it reduces collective diversity by producing similar content that limits novelty at the aggregate level. AI demonstrates limited depth compared to human creators, especially in journalism, where it struggles with novel insights and relies on fewer information sources. There is also a risk of homogenization as AI may favor existing popular patterns, potentially stifling originality.

AI shows promise for enhancing diversity through its ability to analyze large datasets and detect underrepresentation patterns in media, leading to more equitable content strategies. It provides platforms and resources that amplify marginalized voices and assists in creating inclusive content across various media formats.

However, significant risks accompany these benefits. AI systems trained on historical data may reproduce existing societal inequities and stereotypes rather than eliminating them. The concept of "synthetic tokenism" emerges, where representation exists superficially without addressing deeper systemic issues. The opacity of AI decision-making processes makes it difficult to identify and address biased outcomes, creating accountability challenges.

The research indicates that while AI offers substantial opportunities for enhancing creativity and diversity in media, careful implementation with robust safeguards is essential to maximize benefits while mitigating associated risks.

10.3 Expanding Activities Concerning Unknown Consequences of AI

Although AI has ushered in transformative changes across the media landscape, the impact of AI on creativity and diversity within the media field remains an underexplored area of research. While AI offers the potential to democratize content creation and amplify underrepresented voices, it also risks reinforcing existing biases and homogenizing cultural outputs. In an era marked by rapid technological advancements, there is a pressing need to critically examine how AI influences creative processes and the representation of diverse perspectives, ensuring that media systems align with society's evolving expectations of equity and cultural richness.

10.3.1 Current Research

Recent studies highlight the dual impact of AI on creativity. Zhou and Lee (2024) found that text-to-image generative AI enhances human creative productivity by 25%, boosting the quantity and peer evaluation of artworks. However, this increase is coupled with a decline in average content novelty, suggesting that while peak creativity rises, overall diversity of ideas may narrow (Zhou & Lee, 2024). Similarly, Zhu et al. (2024) indicate that AI tools democratize digital art creation but can lead to homogenization of visual styles. Haase and Hanel (2023) found that AI can generate creative ideas comparable to humans, but the diversity and originality depend heavily on user input prompts (Haase & Hanel, 2023).

AI's influence on media diversity is complex. AI democratizes content creation, lowering barriers and allowing more individuals to contribute, potentially enhancing media diversity by incorporating a wider range of voices. However, biases in AI training datasets can perpetuate stereotypes and reduce minority representation. This is particularly concerning in journalism, where AI-generated content can reflect and amplify societal biases (Breazu & Katson, 2024; Dutkiewicz et al., 2024).

Generative AI's role in journalism showcases its potential and challenges. AI can automate routine journalistic tasks, freeing journalists for in-depth analysis and investigative reporting. Tools like Reuters' News Tracer can identify emerging news stories, potentially uncovering stories missed by human reporters (Simon, 2024). However, the rise of AI-generated news raises ethical concerns about authenticity, reliability, and misinformation (Simon, 2024). ChatGPT demonstrates the balance AI can strike between automation and human oversight. Studies show that ChatGPT avoids sensationalism and inflammatory content, suggesting a role for AI in maintaining journalistic integrity while expanding content diversity (Breazu & Katson, 2024).

The relationship between AI, creativity, and diversity in media is evolving. While AI enhances creative productivity and democratizes content creation, it also risks homogenizing outputs and perpetuating biases. Future research should focus on mitigating these biases and ensuring diverse representation in AI-generated content (Zhou & Lee, 2024). Additionally, exploring the long-term impacts of AI on creative diversity and public trust in media is crucial. Understanding how AI influences cultural narratives and societal perceptions will be vital in shaping policies and practices for AI integration in media (Simon, 2024).

In conclusion, while generative AI holds immense potential to transform media production and consumption, its deployment must be managed carefully to foster creativity and ensure diversity. As AI evolves, it is essential to balance leveraging its capabilities and addressing its limitations to maintain a vibrant and inclusive media landscape.

10.3.2 Research Gaps and Future Directions

Despite the growing body of research on AI in media, significant gaps remain. There is a need for empirical studies examining the long-term effects of AI-generated content on audience perceptions of creativity and diversity. Additionally, future research should investigate how AI can be designed to proactively counteract biases and promote equitable representation.

For example, research could explore how algorithms might be adjusted to prioritize novelty over predictability, encouraging the emergence of unique creative outputs. Another important area of study involves understanding how AI tools can support collaborative creativity, where human and AI contributions are integrated to achieve innovative results. Studies like that of McCormack et al. (2019) on human-AI co-creativity and the findings of Doshi and Hauser (2024) regarding diversity in content creation offer valuable insights into these collaborative dynamics.

Advances in AI technologies, such as multimodal systems combining text, image, and video generation, are poised to revolutionize creative practices. For instance, tools capable of integrating multiple media formats could enable entirely new forms of storytelling. Similarly, AI-driven virtual reality (VR) environments promise immersive experiences that blend creativity with interactivity. However, these innovations also raise ethical questions. Overreliance on AI-generated content risks diminishing human contributions, while the proprietary nature of many AI tools limits accessibility for underrepresented creators.

Future Research Needs To navigate the complex interplay between AI, creativity, and diversity, future research should focus on:

Cultural Narratives: Analyzing how AI influences cultural narratives and societal perceptions, particularly in shaping public discourse around identity and representation.
Bias Mitigation: Developing strategies to identify and mitigate biases in AI systems, ensuring equitable and inclusive outputs.
Global Equity: Investigating the implications of AI on global media equity, particularly in terms of access and representation for creators from diverse socioeconomic backgrounds.
Ethical Frameworks: Establishing comprehensive ethical guidelines for AI use in media, encompassing transparency, accountability, and inclusivity.
Policy Implications: Examining regulatory approaches to AI in media to balance innovation with ethical considerations, protecting creators and audiences alike.

In conclusion, while AI holds immense potential to transform media, its integration must balance innovation with ethical responsibility. By addressing these challenges, we can harness AI's capabilities to foster a more inclusive and dynamic media landscape.

10.4 Toward New Definitions of Creativity and Diversity

The seemingly contradictory research findings about AI's impact on creativity and diversity can be explained through several fundamental tensions in how we measure and understand these concepts. At the individual level, studies like Zhou and Lee (2024) show that AI tools enhance creative productivity and technical capabilities, leading to a 25% increase in creative output. However, at the collective level, this increased productivity often comes with a risk of homogenization and reduced novelty in aggregate content. This creates what we might call a scale versus uniqueness paradox.

This paradox points to a deeper issue in how we conceptualize creativity in the age of AI. Traditional definitions focusing on novelty and usefulness (Runco & Jaeger, 2012) may no longer be sufficient when AI can rapidly generate vast quantities of technically proficient content. The emphasis on measurable outputs rather than creative process or human experience has led to a situation where increased production does not necessarily translate to meaningful creative advancement.

The relationship between creativity and diversity is particularly complex in this context. While AI democratizes content creation by lowering technical barriers to entry, it simultaneously risks creating what is termed "synthetic tokenism"—surface-level diversity without authentic representation or cultural depth. This suggests that we may need to decouple our understanding of technical creativity from cultural diversity, as they may no longer be as directly linked as in pre-AI media production.

10.4.1 Three Arguments to Elucidate Complexity of Concepts of Creativity and Diversity

In the following is analyzed the evidence and arguments for three claims based on the material we have discussed, highlighting key points and contradictions.

1. **Generative AI Enhances Creativity and Diversity in Media.** Justification comes from several key findings:

    - Democratization of creative tools enables more people to participate in content creation.
    - AI increases creative productivity.
    - Technical barriers to entry are lowered, allowing underrepresented voices to potentially reach wider audiences.
    - AI tools can help identify gaps in representation and promote inclusive content.
    - Automation of routine tasks frees human creators to focus on higher-level creative work.
    - AI can generate numerous variations and possibilities that humans might not consider.

However, these enhancements often focus on quantitative metrics rather than qualitative improvements, which leads us to the counterargument.

2. **Generative AI Diminishes Creativity and Diversity in Media.** Evidence supporting this claim includes:

    - Research showing decline in average content novelty despite increased production.
    - Risk of homogenization due to AI systems training on similar datasets.
    - "Synthetic tokenism" where surface-level diversity masks lack of authentic representation
    - Potential loss of human creative experience and personal meaning in the creative process.
    - AI systems can perpetuate existing biases and stereotypes.
    - Standardization of creative outputs due to algorithmic optimization.
    - Risk of creative dependency on AI tools reducing human initiative.

3. **Effects of Generative AI Require Broader Conceptualization of Creativity and Diversity.** This more nuanced perspective is supported by the following:

    - Traditional definitions of creativity (novelty and usefulness) prove insufficient in the AI era.
    - Need to consider both process and output in evaluating creative work.
    - Distinction between technical creativity and cultural-emotional creativity.
    - Evolution of creative roles from production to curation and direction.
    - Emergence of new hybrid forms of human–AI creativity.
    - Recognition that quantity of creative output does not necessarily correlate with meaningful diversity.
    - Importance of considering cultural context and authentic representation.

The evidence suggests that the third perspective offers the most productive framework for understanding AI's impact. Rather than viewing AI's effect on creativity and diversity as simply positive or negative, we need to recognize how it fundamentally transforms these concepts. This transformation requires new frameworks for evaluation that consider:

- The distinction between individual and collective creativity.
- The relationship between technical execution and cultural meaning.
- The role of human intention and experience in creative processes.
- The difference between surface-level and authentic diversity.
- The evolution of creative professional roles.
- The changing nature of audience engagement with creative works.

In conclusion, while the first two claims each capture important aspects of AI's impact, the third perspective provides a more comprehensive framework for understanding these changes. It suggests that rather than asking whether AI enhances or diminishes creativity and diversity, we should focus on how it transforms our understanding of these concepts and what that means for the future of media.

This analysis highlights the importance of developing new metrics and frameworks that can capture both the quantitative and qualitative dimensions of creativity and diversity in an AI-augmented media landscape. It also suggests that successful integration of AI in media will require careful attention to preserving authentic human creative expression while leveraging the technical capabilities that AI provides.

10.4.2 A Review of Possible Futures

Looking to the near future, several scenarios seem possible. In one potential future, we might see a creative bifurcation where AI handles routine content creation while human creativity focuses on high-value, unique experiences. This could lead to a premium being placed on "human-certified" creative works and the emergence of new creative roles that combine human insight with AI capabilities. Another possibility is the development of sophisticated human–AI collaborative frameworks that give rise to entirely new forms of creativity.

The impact on media organizations and creative professionals will likely be profound. Traditional creative roles may evolve from focusing on technical execution to emphasizing creative direction and meaningful curation. This shift raises important questions about worker motivation and satisfaction in creative industries. Will creative professionals find fulfillment in directing AI tools rather than hands-on creation? The research suggests this may depend on how we redefine creativity itself.

The role of audiences is relevant as well, because audiences might grow tired of AI-generated content. Early research indicates that while audiences may not always distinguish between AI and human-created content, there's growing awareness and potential fatigue with algorithmic homogeneity. This could lead to what we might call a creative renaissance, where human imperfection and authenticity become increasingly valued.

The concept of uniquely human creativity appears to be evolving in response to AI capabilities. As AI excels at pattern recognition and recombination, human creativity may become more associated with emotional resonance, cultural understanding, and intentional meaning-making. This suggests that the concept of creativity is not simply changing—it is bifurcating into technical creativity (where AI excels) and emotional-cultural creativity (where humans maintain advantage).

For the media industry, this evolution presents both challenges and opportunities. Organizations will need to balance efficiency with authenticity, developing new frameworks for evaluating both creative and diverse outputs. The research suggests successful adaptation will require new organizational structures that preserve human creative agency while leveraging AI capabilities.

Regarding a discussion about whether creativity and diversity remain interrelated, the evidence suggests a complex relationship. While AI might increase certain forms of creativity (particularly technical execution and production volume), this does not automatically translate to increased diversity. In fact, without careful attention to training data and implementation, AI systems might increase creative output while inadvertently reducing cultural diversity through algorithmic homogenization.

Looking forward, several research priorities emerge. We need better understanding of the long-term effects of AI on creative processes, impact on cultural diversity and representation, and frameworks for human–AI creative collaboration. Policy considerations should include protecting human creative rights, supporting cultural diversity, and developing ethical guidelines for AI in creative industries.

The future of creativity and diversity in media will likely depend on how well we navigate these challenges. Success may require developing new metrics that value both technical proficiency and human elements like cultural authenticity and emotional resonance. As AI capabilities continue to evolve, the media industry's relationship with creativity may indeed shift from pure production to a greater emphasis on curation, meaning-making, and cultural preservation.

10.5 Discussion

The impact of artificial intelligence (AI) on creativity and diversity in media presents a complex and evolving landscape. While AI has undoubtedly introduced new possibilities for content creation, its influence on the foundational concepts of creativity and diversity requires further examination. This discussion critically reflects on the previous sections, exploring whether existing definitions of these terms remain adequate in the AI era and considering broader implications for media and society.

10.5.1 Rethinking Creativity and Diversity in an AI-Driven Context

The rapid integration of AI into media production necessitates a reconsideration of the fundamental concepts of creativity and diversity. Traditionally, creativity has been defined through the dual criteria of novelty and usefulness, while diversity pertains to the representation of varied perspectives and voices. However, in an AI-driven media landscape, these definitions may require revision. AI-generated content often operates within preexisting patterns, raising the question: Does it truly create, or does it merely remix? If the latter, should our understanding of creativity account for AI's capability to augment, rather than originate, novel ideas? Furthermore, AI's role in content diversification is paradoxical—it has the potential to enhance inclusivity by enabling broader participation, yet it risks homogenizing creative outputs due to reliance on historically biased training data. Addressing these definitional challenges is essential to ensuring that AI-driven media continues to foster genuine innovation and representation.

10.5.2 From Production to Experience: A Shift in Perspective

Much of the preceding analysis has framed creativity and diversity in media as characteristics of production. However, an alternative perspective considers these concepts from the viewpoint of experience. If creativity is defined not just by what is produced but by how it is received and interpreted, AI's role becomes more intricate. For instance, the experiences of content creators, audiences, and cultural critics may shape new conceptual models of creativity. Should diversity be measured purely by the number of distinct perspectives represented, or should it also consider the depth of engagement and emotional resonance of content? These questions challenge existing theoretical frameworks and suggest the need for an expanded discourse that incorporates phenomenological and sociocultural dimensions.

10.5.3 Human–GAI Co-Creation: Implications for the Creative Process

The emergence of AI as a collaborative tool in creative processes has significant implications for human agency and authorship. The concept of *Human–GAI Co-Creation*—where human ingenuity and AI-driven capabilities intersect—raises philosophical and practical questions. If AI-assisted content generation becomes ubiquitous, does human authorship retain its distinct value, or does it become diluted? Furthermore, does AI-assisted creativity redefine artistic skill, shifting emphasis from technical execution to conceptual vision and curation? Some argue that AI-generated outputs, despite their sophistication, lack true creative depth as they derive from statistical probabilities rather than intentional meaning-making. If this argument holds, human creators may retain a unique role in guiding, refining, and adding emotive significance to AI-generated media.

10.5.4 The Boundaries of AI-Generated Creativity: Authenticity, Saturation, and Fatigue

As AI-generated content becomes increasingly pervasive, it is crucial to consider the potential limitations and consequences of an oversaturated media environment. With content production exponentially increasing, a critical issue emerges: will audiences eventually reach a saturation point where AI-generated material feels formulaic and uninspiring? If so, what distinguishes "authentic" human creativity from AI-driven imitation? There is an ongoing debate regarding whether AI can ever truly replicate the intangible qualities of human artistry—such as emotional depth, spontaneity, and subjective intentionality. Moreover, if audience begin to prioritize works with perceived authenticity, could a new form of *human-centric creativity* emerge as a response to AI's ubiquity?

10.5.5 Political and Ethical Dimensions: AI, Media, and Societal Shifts

Recent political and corporate developments, particularly in regions such as the United States and within major tech firms (e.g., Meta, Google, X), have influenced global discourses on freedom of expression, inclusivity, and equality. AI-driven content moderation, recommendation algorithms, and automated media curation shape public narratives and influence cultural representation. This raises critical questions: Is AI reinforcing dominant ideologies, or does it democratize access to diverse perspectives? Additionally, is the evolution of AI in media following a dialectical trajectory, where initial enthusiasm for AI-driven creativity (thesis) is met with concerns over bias and homogenization (antithesis), ultimately leading to a more balanced synthesis? If such a trajectory exists, its resolution remains uncertain and warrants ongoing scrutiny.

10.5.6 AI, Human Labor, and the Future of Creativity

A widely discussed argument is that AI liberates humans from repetitive tasks, allowing them to focus on inherently human-centric roles. However, if AI also assumes creative functions—traditionally considered a uniquely human domain—what roles remain distinctly human? While AI's capacity for automating routine creative processes is evident, it remains uncertain whether it can replace the broader cognitive, cultural, and ethical dimensions of human-led creativity. The future of creative professions may involve a shift toward curatorial and strategic roles, where human creators act as directors of AI-generated content rather than its primary producers. Yet, this transition prompts a deeper philosophical question: If AI is increasingly embedded in creative workflows, does the human touch become a luxury, a necessity, or an afterthought?

10.6 Conclusion: Navigating the AI-Creativity Nexus

The interplay between AI, creativity, and diversity in media remains dynamic and unresolved. While AI enhances accessibility and efficiency, it also challenges foundational notions of originality, representation, and artistic intent. This discussion highlights the need for continued theoretical refinement, policy intervention, and ethical reflection. Rather than viewing AI as a binary force—either as an enhancer or inhibitor of creativity—scholars and practitioners should approach it as a transformative agent that necessitates a reconfiguration of creative and cultural paradigms. As media industries adapt to AI's expanding role, the future of creativity will likely be shaped not by AI alone, but by the ways in which humans choose to engage with, resist, and redefine its capabilities.

Literature

Amankwah-Amoah, J., Abdalla, S., Mogaji, E., Elbanna, A., & Dwivedi, Y. K. (2024). The impending disruption of creative industries by generative AI: Opportunities, challenges, and research agenda. *International Journal of Information Management, 79*(2), 102759. https://doi.org/10.1016/j.ijinfomgt.2024.102759

Ashkinaze, J., Mendelsohn, J., Li, Q., Budak, C., & Gilbert, E. (2024). How AI ideas affect the creativity, diversity, and evolution of human ideas: Evidence from a large, dynamic experiment. Preprint retrieved from https://arxiv.org/abs/2401.13481.

Breazu, P., & Katson, N. (2024). ChatGPT-4 as a journalist: Whose perspectives is it reproducing? *Discourse & Society*. https://journals.sagepub.com/doi/10.1177/09579265241251479.

Clerwall, C. (2014). Enter the robot journalist: Users' perceptions of automated content. *Journalism Practice, 8*(5), 519–531. https://doi.org/10.1080/17512786.2014.883116

Das, S. & Mitra, A. (2024). Artificial intelligence and the evolution of creativity: An in-depth analysis of AI's role in modern content creation. J.U. Journal for Communication, Society and Outreach, 1(1). https://www.researchgate.net/publication/378739739_Artificial_Intelligence_and_the_Evolution_of_Creativity_An_In-Depth_Analysis_of_AI's_Role_in_Modern_Content_Creation.

Diakopoulos, N. (2019). *Automating the news: How algorithms are rewriting the media.* Harvard University Press. https://www.hup.harvard.edu/books/9780674976986.

Dierickx, L., Sirén-Heikel, S., & Lindén, C.-G. (2024). Outsourcing, augmenting, or complicating: The dynamics of AI in fact-checking practices in the Nordics. *Emerging Media, 2*(3), 449–473. https://doi.org/10.1177/27523543241288846

Doshi, A. R., & Hauser, O. P. (2024). Generative AI enhances individual creativity but reduces the collective diversity of novel content. *Science Advances, 10*(28), eadn5290. https://doi.org/10.1126/sciadv.adn5290

Dutkiewicz, L., Krack, N., Kuczerawy, A., & Valcke, P. (2024). AI and media. In N. A. Smuha (Ed.), Cambridge handbook on the law, ethics and policy of artificial intelligence. Cambridge University Press. https://www.cambridge.org/core/books/cambridge-handbook-of-the-law-ethics-and-policy-of-artificial-intelligence/artificial-intelligence-and-media/71A837E399E62C18438F937C7933857D.

Esmaeili, S. A., Bhawalkar, K., Feng, Z., Wang, D., & Xu, H. (2024). How to strategize human content creation in the era of GenAI? Preprint retrieved from. https://doi.org/10.48550/arXiv.2406.05187.

Floridi, L. (2019). *The logic of information: A theory of philosophy as conceptual design.* Oxford University Press.

Gillespie, T. (2018). *Custodians of the internet: Platforms, content moderation, and the hidden decisions that shape social media.* Yale University Press.

Gunkel, D. J. (2018). *Of remixology: Ethics and aesthetics after remix.* MIT Press.

Haase, J. & Hanel, P. (2023). Artificial muses: Generative artificial intelligence Chatbots have risen to human-level creativity Journal of Creativity. 33. https://www.sciencedirect.com/science/article/pii/S2713374523000250.

Huang, M.-H., & Rust, R. T. (2024). Automating creativity. Preprint retrieved from https://doi.org/10.48550/arXiv.2405.06915.

Lyu, Y., Zhang, H., Niu, S., & Cai, J. (2024). A preliminary exploration of YouTubers' use of generative-AI in content creation. In *Extended abstracts of the CHI conference on human factors in computing systems (CHI EA '24)* (pp. 1–7). ACM. https://doi.org/10.1145/3613905.3651057

McCormack, J., Gifford, T., Hutchings, P., Teresa Llano Rodriguez, M., Yee-King, M., & D'Inverno, M. (2019). In a silent way: communication between AI and improvising musicians beyond sound. In A. Cox, & V. Kostakos (Eds.), *Proceedings of the 2019 CHI Conference on Human Factors in Computing Systems Article 38 Association for Computing Machinery (ACM).* https://dl.acm.org/doi/10.1145/3290605.3300268.

Napoli, P. M. (2019). *Social media and the public interest: Media regulation in the disinformation age*. Columbia University Press.
Noble, S. U. (2018). *Algorithms of oppression: How search engines reinforce racism.* New York University Press.
Park, J., Oh, C., & Kim, H. Y. (2024). AI vs. human-generated content and accounts on Instagram: User preferences, evaluations, and ethical considerations. *Technology in Society, 79*, 102705. https://doi.org/10.1016/j.techsoc.2024.102705
Runco, M. A., & Jaeger, G. J. (2012). The standard definition of creativity. *Creativity Research Journal, 24*(1), 92–96. https://doi.org/10.1080/10400419.2012.650092
Simon, F. M. (2024). *Artificial intelligence in the news: How AI retools, rationalizes, and reshapes journalism and the public arena.* Tow Center for Digital Journalism, Columbia University. https://www.cjr.org/tow_center_reports/artificial-intelligence-in-the-news.php.
Smith, M. D., & Telang, R. (2016). *Streaming, sharing, stealing: Big data and the future of entertainment.* MIT Press.
Spangher, A., Peng, N., Gehrmann, S., & Dredze, M. (2024). Do LLMs plan like human writers? Comparing journalist coverage of press releases with LLMs. *Proceedings of the 2024 conference on empirical methods in natural language processing* (pp. 21814–21828). Retrieved from https://aclanthology.org/2024.emnlp-main.1216.pdf.
Tang, Y., Zhang, N., Ciancia, M., & Wang, Z. (2024). Exploring the impact of AI-generated image tools on professional and non-professional users in the art and design fields. Preprint retrieved from https://doi.org/10.48550/arXiv.2406.10640.
Wardle, C., & Derakhshan, H. (2017). Information disorder: Toward an interdisciplinary framework for research and policymaking. Council of Europe. https://edoc.coe.int/en/media/7495-information-disorder-toward-an-interdisciplinary-framework-for-research-and-policy-making.html.
Wingström, R., Hautala, J., & Lundman, R. (2022). Redefining creativity in the era of AI? Perspectives of computer scientists and new media artists. *Creativity Research Journal, 34*(2), 177–193. https://doi.org/10.1080/10400419.2022.2107850
Zhou, E., & Lee, D. (2024). Generative artificial intelligence, human creativity, and art. *PNAS Nexus, 3*, 1–8. https://doi.org/10.1093/pnasnexus/pgae052
Zhu, S., Wang, Z., Zhuang, Y., Jiang, Y., Guo, M., Zhang, X., & Gao, Z. (2024). Exploring the impact of ChatGPT on art creation and collaboration. *Telematics and Informatics Reports, 14*, 100138. https://www.sciencedirect.com/science/article/pii/S2772503024000240.

Petri Honkanen 's profile combines long-standing expertise in innovation policy, education, and the societal impacts of technology with a current focus on the societal role of generative AI, its ethical challenges, and its influence on media, creativity, and diversity—emphasizing responsible AI development and the broader societal implications of emerging technologies.

Dr. Mats Nylund has been doing media research for 30 years. He has lead a master's degree education in media management since 2012, and conducted research in emerging technologies. In 2025 he started a project on digital disconnection.

Impacts of AI on US Copyright Law

11

Steve Collins and Sarah Keith

Abstract

This chapter provides an overview of the clash between copyright and generative AI, exploring the tensions and possible solutions. Although this is a global issue and implicates multiple legal jurisdictions and traditions, this chapter will primarily focus on US copyright law. We begin with an overview of copyright itself and, importantly, illustrate that copyright has not remained static since its inception. We move on to introduce fair use, which ostensibly exists to act as a safety valve that prevents copyright monopolies from stifling future creativity, and is the main provision that supports training AI models on copyrighted material. The discussion section follows to interrogate the two key copyright issues raised by generative AI. First, we look at the authorship requirement of copyright: whether generative AI outputs are themselves copyrightable, and how the current stance affects the market value of these works. Second, we discuss the tensions in training generative AI models on copyrighted works. In assessing the claims for training as infringement and training as fair use, we will illustrate the culturally deterministic role played by copyright. As Goldstein (*Copyright's highway: The law and Lore of copyright from Gutenberg to the celestial jukebox*. Hill and Wang, 1994, p. 35) reminds us, "Other more familiar bodies of law—contracts, torts, and crimes—have an even longer history, but none occupies this special place in ordering a nation's culture, high and low." We finish this section with a discussion of possible solutions, some of which are beginning to emerge at the time of writing. The chapter concludes by affirming the crucial questions before judges and legislators as they decide whether copyright is a facilitator of or hurdle for generative AI. These are decisions that will carry significant ramifications

S. Collins (✉) · S. Keith
Macquarie University, Sydney, NSW, Australia
e-mail: stephen.collins@mq.edu.au; sarah.keith@mq.edu.au

S. Böhm et al. (eds.), *Handbook of AI-based Media Disruption*, Future of Business and Finance, https://doi.org/10.1007/978-3-032-07605-2_11

for concepts of authorship and ownership, as well as creativity and culture more broadly.

11.1 Introduction

Generative Artificial Intelligence (AI), like many other disruptive technologies before it (for example, streaming, MP3 players, file-sharing networks, home taping with cassettes and the VCR, the Pianola, the printing press, *inter alia*), has thrown copyright under a spotlight. Why? Generative AI raises questions about and challenges the contours of authorship, creativity, and crucially, ownership. Generative AI models like ChatGPT, Midjourney, and Suno require training on vast amounts of existing data, which is scraped from media that is usually copyrighted. Thus, there are immediate tensions between the AI technology industry and numerous parties involved with the creative and cultural industries: copyright owners including publishers, record labels, and individual authors, artists, and musicians, advocacy and representative groups like the Authors Guild, Recording Industry Association of America (RIAA), Screen Actors Guild and the American Federation of Television and Radio Artists (SAG-AFTRA). Many fans, audiences, and commentators also express concern over the potential impacts of generative AI on creativity and culture. These parties claim that AI companies are building billion-dollar enterprises off the back of intellectual properties owned by others without any compensation. Advocates for generative AI, on the other hand, claim that although copying is involved in training, the use of copyrighted material is fair because it is transformative; models are not directly reproducing inputs in their outputs (even though there is some evidence rebutting claims that guardrails exist to prevent this form of reproduction). Interventions along the way by commentators, judges, and legislators muddy the waters with support for claims of copyright infringement and support for claims of fair use. Question marks have been placed over whether copyright owners even hold a right to license works for AI training, or whether copyright is the appropriate legal mechanism to manage the issues raised by AI (Craig, 2025).

This chapter provides an overview of the clash between copyright and generative AI, exploring the tensions and possible solutions. Although this is a global issue and implicates multiple legal jurisdictions and traditions, this chapter will primarily focus on US copyright law. We begin with an overview of copyright itself and, importantly, illustrate that copyright has not remained static since its inception. We move on to introduce fair use, which ostensibly exists to act as a safety valve that prevents copyright monopolies from stifling future creativity, and is the main provision that supports training AI models on copyrighted material. The discussion section follows to interrogate the two key copyright issues raised by generative AI. First, we look at the authorship requirement of copyright: whether generative AI outputs are themselves copyrightable, and how the current stance affects the market value of these works. Second, we discuss the tensions in training generative AI models on copyrighted works. In assessing the claims for training as infringement and training as fair use, we will illustrate the culturally deterministic role played by copyright.

As Goldstein (1994, p. 35) reminds us, "Other more familiar bodies of law—contracts, torts, and crimes—have an even longer history, but none occupies this special place in ordering a nation's culture, high and low." We finish this section with a discussion of possible solutions, some of which are beginning to emerge at the time of writing. The chapter concludes by affirming the crucial questions before judges and legislators as they decide whether copyright is a facilitator of or hurdle for generative AI. These are decisions that will carry significant ramifications for concepts of authorship and ownership, as well as creativity and culture more broadly.

11.2 Fundamentals of Copyright

The history and development of copyright is entwined with disruptive technologies. Copyright itself was initially a response to a socially and politically disruptive technology; the printing press. Since then, copyright has responded to the disruptions caused by emerging technologies, but also disruptions to its own parameters and operations.

Copyright is often presented in the singular, but in the majority of scenarios, we are actually referring to a bundle of rights that includes reproduction, distribution, adaptation, performance, and communication to the public. These rights initially vest in the author (which in this context refers to all forms of creatives: writers, musicians, artists, etc.), but can be individually or wholly assigned to another party. Assignation is the bedrock of some industries. For example, the recording industry is a copyright industry; its prosperity is dependent on the acquisition and exploitation of copyrights that initially vest in musicians (Osborne, 2023). This separation of ownership from authorship plays a key role in the creative industries and was set in motion long before the first copyright law existed. The following section places a heavy emphasis on the history of copyright because it provides an understanding of how seeds planted hundreds of years ago germinated contemporary tensions.

11.2.1 History of Copyright

In the early fifteenth century, a group of booksellers in London called the Stationers' Company dominated the small English market for books. The arrangement with authors was simple. Manuscripts were purchased outright by Stationers and treated like any other piece of property. The concept of ongoing royalty payments did not exist. At this point in history, copyright did not exist and as Feather (1994, p. 10) asserts, there was no need for it to have developed as the concept of book piracy did not exist; books were individually made to order and labor-intensive to produce. The manuscript-book trade was based around specific orders for copies, thus there was no manuscript stock held and therefore no need to protect a long-term investment made in securing a manuscript for mass production (Feather, 1994). The investment made by Stationers in making copies of manuscripts would have been returned as soon as the copy was sold.

The introduction of the printing press caused fundamental changes to the economy of the book trade. While Caxton's press revolutionized the process of book production, it also placed new economic pressures on the trade as printing became the dominant process of book production. The costs of purchasing a printing press, maintenance, and sustaining a supply of ink and paper introduced new financial burdens. "This represented a substantial capital investment, on which the return was necessarily slow" (Feather, 1994, p. 11). This capital investment was a financial risk and as a result, protection for printed works was sought. By the early sixteenth century, printers joined the Stationers' Company, which resulted in the subsequent decline of a manuscript trade, rendered obsolete by the new technology.

Over the next 50 years, forms of protection for printing rights emerged: privileges bestowed by the Crown and letters patents offered exclusive rights to print specific texts, but as production increased in response to rising literacy rates, the majority of books were left without any legal protection against copying. In 1557, the last year of her reign, Queen Mary I granted the Stationers' Company a royal charter of incorporation. The objectives of the trade and the Crown had coincided. The Stationers needed to impose economic order on the trade and the Crown wanted to ensure that undesirable literature was not disseminated. The Stationers gained the exclusive right to print and sell books in England, effectively establishing an elite publishing caste that prevented those outside the Company from competing against them. A registration system was established to record all books authorized to be published. Publishing non-registered works would result in burning of books and fines. Further, registration of books was conducted with political acumen. Great care was taken to not register anything that might offend the religious persuasion of the reigning monarch. This operation continued until the early eighteenth century when political movements became unsympathetic to monopolies; 15 consecutive Bills attempted to change the status quo and break the Stationers' monopoly. The Statute of Anne, an Act for the encouragement of learning, was enacted in 1710 and introduced, for the first time, a copyright granted to authors—a monopoly over the reproduction of a text that was limited in duration to 14 years. The copyright could be assigned to another, for example, a Stationer, but if the author were still alive at the end of those 14 years, ownership would revert to him for a second, and final, period of 14 years. Ostensibly, the author could reassign ownership to the same Stationer or negotiate with a different one for a better deal. Books already in circulation when the Statute of Anne was enacted were protected for 21 years. Whether after 14, 21, or 28 years, at expiration, the book would fall into the public domain where it could be reprinted by anyone. This was a dramatic change to the perpetual ownership previously enjoyed by the Stationers. The Statute of Anne also established controls over exorbitantly priced books and mandated that nine copies of every book be deposited in the nation's libraries. Naturally, the Stationers were not happy with this arrangement. A library collection based on free legal deposits would affect the revenue from sales.

While this brief overview of how copyright came to be seemingly has little bearing on the issues raised by generative AI, it provides the important message that copyright was designed to enhance civil society by making information more accessible. Copyright was a means to an end to incentivize the production of new work to inform and advance society, but limited to ensure against perpetual monopolies over information. Naturally, the Stationers did not see it that way. As Young (2015, p. 45) argues, this was "a clash between those who demanded better access to reading material, and incumbent businesses hellbent on protecting their monopolies." They attempted to continue operating as if the Statute of Anne did not exist—that is until Alexander Donaldson, a Scottish bookseller, opened a store in London selling cheap prints of public domain works. Rose (1993) reports that Donaldson was undercutting the Stationers by 30–50%. The Stationers launched a battery of lawsuits, and even attempted purchasing all Donaldson's stock, but ultimately ended up in court, where they lost. The case of Donaldson v. Becket [1774] was fought over the authority for ownership of literary works. The Stationers, aided by William Blackstone's interpretation of Locke's labor theory,[1] argued that the Statute of Anne simply offered extra protection to an extant natural right in property, which by its very nature was perpetual, inalienable, and inviolable. Therefore, Donaldson was trespassing against their property with his reprints. The House of Lords disagreed and dismissed that a natural right in literary property ever existed. The only authority to the right to reproduce a book was granted by the Statute of Anne, limitations and all. This decision may have won the battle, but it set the rules of engagement for the war. If copyright was contingent on policy and politics, then *influence*—over legislators, judges, and politicians—would be the tool to increase the boundaries of ownership.

This outline of copyright's historical basis may seem distant from contemporary questions posed by AI. However, it demonstrates that copyright is a living and reactive framework that adapts to new technologies by (re)defining authorship, ownership, and market exploitation rights. Much as the Stationers' Company was forced to redefine its definition of authorship and ownership in response to the advent of the printing press, generative AI now compels legislators and industry stakeholders to redefine these fundamental relationships. AI companies including OpenAI, Anthropic, and Meta are arguing for transformative uses of copyright content, reviving historical tensions between innovation, economic order, and cultural growth. Today, disputes over training data, authorship, and remuneration are the center of discussions around AI and copyright.

11.2.2 Disruptions Across the Atlantic

The first federal copyright law in the USA was closely modeled on the Statute of Anne, but over the following 200 years, copyright expanded its scope and duration.

[1] John Locke's labor theory of property argues that individuals gain ownership of natural resources by mixing their labor with them. In his view property becomes private when a person applies their labor to something in the commons (like land or fruit), making it their own. William Blackstone reframed Locke's theory through a positivist lens to argue for property rights in literature in the case of Millar v. Taylor (1769).

Until the early twentieth century, copyright law only protected the right to reproduce a work. Translations, annotated copies, and abridgments were seen as socially useful and protected as noninfringing uses of copyrighted works as long as they advanced on the original work (Patry, 1985). (This ancestor of fair use was known as fair abridgment.) The right to control derivative works (including translations, annotated copies, and abridgments) was introduced in the Copyright Act 1909 to allow copyright owners to more fully exploit the value of works across the gamut of media forms (Odom, 2022). This coincided with the advent of motion pictures, and thus we observe copyright being adapted to emerging technologies. Copyright has had to repeatedly cope with many challenges brought by new technologies. Mechanical pianos and wax cylinders, for example, introduced new forms of copying music. While the Copyright Act 1897 introduced a right to control public performances of music, this did not apply to reproduction via format-shifting to piano rolls and recording, as there was no copyright in the underlying composition. At this time, "performance" could occur in three ways. First, music might be performed in a live context by an orchestra, band, or solo musician like a hotel pianist. Second, "performing" mechanical pianos emerged in the late 1800s when the Aeolian Corporation commenced mass production of Edward Votey's Pianola in 1898. The Pianola and rival player pianos performed music recorded into special rolls of paper that were punctuated with note data. Third, performances were captured by early audio recording technology, and reproduced on wax cylinders and discs as phonograph companies emerged in the early 1900s. Only the first instance here required payment to the copyright owner. A solution was forthcoming by virtue of the Copyright Act 1909, which introduced a "mechanical" right (Osborne, 2023). For the first time, protection was granted to the underlying composition, which meant that any reproduction method that captured the performance of a composition (such as piano rolls or recordings) required the permission of the copyright owner. Since then, copyright has responded to new technologies such as broadcasting, audiovisual works, intermittent copies (made by the internet), and streaming. This has necessitated the creation of new rights, expansion of copyright, and global harmonization of key principles. This harmonization allows intellectual property and creative work in myriad formats to circulate internationally, underpinning the global media industries.

Today, copyright is the backbone of contemporary cultural and economic exchange; without this robust framework, global media companies could not effectively distribute, monetize, or protect their creative assets. In the USA, copyright now lasts for the author's life plus 70 years, a far cry from the 14 years provided by the Statute of Anne. Many commentators argue that copyright has transitioned from shield to sword, acting as a censor and stifling free expression. Netanel (1996, p. 286) identifies neoclassical institutional economic property theory as the driving force behind contemporary policy, dictating that copyright "serves as a vehicle for directing investment in existing works." This goes further than the traditional utilitarian approach that views copyright as providing an incentive to create. Proponents of neoclassical institutional economic property theory treat works as commodities and copyright as the means for maximizing their market value. Netanel offers a countervailing democratic approach in which copyright is vital to democratic societies because it facilitates creative expression through its limited monopoly, which also fosters a vibrant public domain. He stresses that "while copyright may operate in the market, copyright's fundamental goals are not of the market" (Netanel, 1996, p. 341). Advocating for a "thin" copyright that does not go beyond preventing piracy, Netanel (2008, p6) argues that fair use is essential in providing a safety valve against copyright's capacity to monopolize content and stifle creativity and innovation by building on previous works. This defense is particularly significant today, as generative AI companies invoke fair use for the mass use of copyrighted works to train AI models.

11.2.3 Fair Use

The doctrine of fair use has a history almost as old as that of copyright itself. It can be traced back to the defense of fair abridgment, which was established in the English case of Gyles v. Wilcox in, 1740. Here, the core principle is that abridgments could be transformative and socially useful as long as they did not act as a substitute for the original work. This idea of transformative use remains central today, and informs contemporary debates around generative AI. There is continuity between fair abridgment and modern fair use that traveled through case law and across the Atlantic Ocean. Today, fair use is codified in s.107, Copyright Act 1976. Its purpose is to permit copying in certain circumstances such as commentary, criticism, news reporting, parody, and satire. The activities that qualify as fair use are not set in stone though. The Act offers guidance for judges to expand its application by considering factors such as how the copied portions are used, whether the copied content was factual or fictitious, the amount copied, and the effect on the market value of the source content. This section provides an overview of fair use in operation through the lens of two key cases—the "Betamax case" and Authors Guild v. Google—that will indubitably play roles in pending copyright infringement lawsuits and legislation concerning generative AI.

We set out earlier how new copyrights accompanied the emergence of new technologies and practices. Similarly, new uses of copyrighted works (usually catalyzed by new technologies) have been protected as fair. For example, after nearly a decade in court, in 1984, the Supreme Court delivered its judgment in Sony Corp. of America v. Universal City Studios, Inc. The case centered on the Betamax video cassette recorder (VCR) developed by Sony in the 1970s. The Betamax VCR was designed to facilitate time-shifting—recording shows and movies broadcast on television for later watching. An advertising slogan read, "Watch Whatever Whenever … For years you've watched TV shows at the times you've had to. Now you can watch them at the times you want to" (Sony, 1978). Universal City Studios took the VCR at face value—seeing it as a machine made for copying—and launched legal action for contributory copyright infringement, arguing that Sony was liable for the infringing activities of VCR users. The next decade saw an initial trial and two appeals. The initial decision by the US District Court for the Central District of California was that noncommercial home videotaping was a fair use. A Ninth Circuit Court reversed the decision on appeal and held Sony liable. The Supreme Court heard Sony's appeal and decided that noncommercial home videotaping was a fair use of copyrighted works, and thus Sony was not liable for contributorily infringing the entertainment industry's copyrights. The decision was heavily influenced by arguments that the VCR had substantial noninfringing uses. While the case was being argued, "consumer electronics manufacturers, retailers and consumers were successful in explaining to Congress that the payment of royalties to the motion picture industry would be unnecessary because VCRs create enormous income streams for the creative community and that, indeed, home taping would expand the audience for a work, and not diminish it" (Cunard, 1996, p. 246). Following the decision, movie studios unsuccessfully lobbied for a levy on VCRs, blank cassettes, and a video rental right (Menell & Nimmer, 2007), but Congress was unswayed given the mass adoption of VCR technology and (perhaps of relevance to current generative AI issues) the politics of attempting regulation after years of unrestricted use.

The "Betamax case" illustrates how copyright protections can rub up against new practices and new technologies, and that ownership has its limits. It shows that technologies capable of copying can qualify for protection under fair use. Just as the Betamax VCR allowed home users to produce transformative, noncommercial time-shifted copies for home use, AI companies argue that their systems produce transformative work and do not make original copyrighted works "accessible to a public for which it may serve as a competing substitute," thus should be protected under fair use (OpenAI, 2020, p. 6). Moreover, the decision also highlights the influence of individual jurisprudential persuasions. For example, Samuelson argues that Justice Stevens (delivering the verdict for the majority of the judges) is aligned with Netanel's democratic approach to copyright. She writes, "Justice Stevens views IP law as a limited statutory monopoly that must serve the public interest. He is skeptical of efforts by rights holders to extend their monopolies beyond the bounds set by the legislature. He takes seriously public policy limitations on the scope of IP rights and invokes constitutional values such as promoting public access to knowledge in explaining why IP rights should be limited in scope and breadth" (Samuelson, 2006, p. 1832). We will return to this point later as we speculate on possible outcomes of pending legal actions against generative AI companies.

In 2003, Google Books (originally named Google Print) was launched, and thus began a near-decade long legal battle between the tech giant and the Authors Guild (representing the publishing industry and its authors). The Authors Guild accused Google of mass copyright infringement, whereas Google responded with a defense of fair use. Google had produced a full-text searchable database of at least 25 million scanned print books, many of which were still protected by copyright—could this possibly be defensible as a fair use? The case hinged on whether the Google Books project was transformative or amounted to the production of derivative works, a right reserved to the copyright owner.

Much like Justice Stevens in the "Betamax case," the appeals court emphasized the constitutional values underpinning copyright, that "the ultimate goal of copyright is to expand public knowledge and understanding, which copyright seeks to achieve by giving potential creators exclusive control over copying of their works, thus giving them a financial incentive to create informative, intellectually enriching works for public consumption … while authors are undoubtedly important intended beneficiaries of copyright, the ultimate, primary intended beneficiary is the public, whose access to knowledge copyright seeks to advance by providing rewards for authorship" (Authors Guild v. Google, 2015, pp. 12–13). Ultimately, the court distinguished between transformation of *purpose* (fair use) and transformation of *form* (derivative work):

> Google's making of a digital copy to provide a search function is a transformative use, which augments public knowledge by making available information about Plaintiffs' books without providing the public with a substantial substitute for matter protected by the Plaintiffs' copyright interests in the original works or derivatives of them. (Authors Guild v. Google, 2015, p. 4)

Both the District Court and the Second Circuit Court of Appeal upheld Google's fair use defense, finding the digitization project to be transformative. The Supreme Court denied a writ of certiorari. Today, an identical argument is mounted by generative AI companies, who claim that using copyrighted materials in training AI models produces fundamentally transformative works such as literature analyses, reports, and generative art with "enormous potential societal benefits" (OpenAI, 2020, p. 10). In both cases, fair use hinges on transformative works expanding access to knowledge without competing with or substituting for the original copyrighted material.

Neoclassical institutional economic property theory emphasizes the right to exploit copyrighted works across all (actual and potential) markets, but fair use remains an essential part of the corpus of copyright law: "The doctrine of fair use need not be so mysterious or dependent on intuitive judgments. Fair use should be perceived not as a disorderly basket of exceptions to the rules of copyright, nor as a departure from the principles governing that body of law, but rather as a rational, integral part of copyright, whose observance is necessary to achieve the objectives of that law" (Leval, 1990, p. 1107). Commentators such as Lessig (2004, pp. 95–99), Heins and Beckles (2005, p. 54), and Netanel (2008, pp. 13–28) rightly argue that the efficacy of fair use is challenged by excessive emphasis on market values, but cases such as *Sony Corp. of America v. Universal City Studios, Inc.* and *Authors Guild v. Google, Inc.* remind us that the boundaries of ownership are determined by a politically appointed judiciary (Bazelon, 1963, p. 64). Whether fair use can succeed as a defense in infringement cases against generative AI companies remains to be seen, but any decision is likely to be as politically motivated as it is legally.

11.3 Discussion: AI Key Issues

Generative AI raises many questions around authorship, creativity, ethics, and ownership. The two key questions for copyright law are: First, is it possible for generative AI works to attract copyright protection? Second, does training an AI model infringe the copyrights of source material? This section explores both questions, but is also conscious that there are pending lawsuits, especially in the context of training as infringement.

11.3.1 Copyrighting AI-Generated Work

Artificial intelligence has existed in our imaginations for longer than in our computers and personal devices. Writers dreamt up robots with human-like intelligence as far back as 1872. Samuel Butler's *Erewhon: or, Over the Range* describes a society where machinery has been abolished. The protagonist, Higgs, finds *The Book of the Machines*, a set of documents describing a crisis thousands of years previously, when rapid technological evolution led to fears that machines would eventually enslave, or supersede, humanity. Since Butler, we have created countless other examples that take the concept of intelligent machines to new levels: For example, there is HAL 9000 in Stanley Kubrick's *2001: A Space Odyssey*, the more benign R2-D2 and C-3PO in *Star Wars*, The Terminator, Max Headroom, WALL-E, etc. Artificial intelligence is now all around us: spam filters, personalized recommendation systems, facial recognition, GPS and navigational technologies, robotics, healthcare, agriculture, investment and banking. Where it has *not* been is in the hands of the everyday user, but that changed on the 30th November 2022, with the public release of OpenAI's ChatGPT. Today, generative AI can "create" lots of things for us: poetry, prose, essays, haiku, code, music, voices, images, animations, and video. But can these works attract copyright protection?

At present, in the USA at least, works produced by generative AI cannot be copyrighted. The reasoning here is simple; only works created by a human attract copyright protection. This principle is neatly demonstrated through the "monkey-selfie" case, in which a Celebes macaque took a selfie and a whole copyright debacle unfolded. British wildlife photographer David J. Slater journeyed to Indonesia and befriended a group of wild macaques. Newspapers reported at the time that a macaque had run off with Slater's camera and taken numerous selfies. Slater claimed that this was not the case; it just made for a good tale. He actually set up his equipment in a way to encourage the macaques to get close to the lens and trigger the remote to take photos. In 2011, he licensed several images to the Caters News Agency who released them, along with a written promotional press release with quotes from Slater, for publication in the British media. On the fourth July 2011 several publications, including *Daily Mail*, *The Telegraph*, and *The Guardian*, picked up the story and published the pictures. The images were copied from *Daily Mail* and uploaded to the Wikimedia Commons image library. Upon discovery, Slater objected. The photos were briefly removed from the library, before being reinstated following a discussion about their copyright status. It was the opinion of Wikimedia that the photos were in the public domain, as "copyright cannot vest in non-human authors" and "when a work's copyright cannot vest in a human, it falls into the public domain" (Stewart, 2014). *Techdirt* then got involved by reporting on the dispute and reproducing the photos on its site.

The US Copyright Office (USCO) issued a statement clarifying that "only works created by a human can be copyrighted under United States law, which excludes photographs and artwork created by animals or by machines without human intervention" and that "Because copyright law is limited to 'original intellectual conceptions of the author,' the [copyright] office will refuse to register a claim if it determines that a human being did not create the work ... The Office will not register works produced by nature, animals, or plants" (United States Copyright Office, 2014, Chap. 300, p. 8, p. 22). Stressing the point, a list of examples of work that cannot be copyrighted expressly includes, "A photograph taken by a monkey."

The position that works of nonhuman authorship cannot attract copyright protection extends to works produced by machines: "Similarly, the Office will not register works produced by a machine or mere mechanical process that operates randomly or automatically without any creative input or intervention from a human author" (United States Copyright Office, 2014, Chap. 300, p. 22). To date, the USCO has refused to register work produced by generative AI systems. For example, it revoked copyright protection for *Zarya of the Dawn*, a graphic novel by Kris Kashtanova. Kashtanova's story was original, but the artwork was generated using Midjourney. Initially omitting to disclose Midjourney's use in the registration application, *Zarya of the Dawn* was granted copyright protection. However, the USCO reviewed the registration upon learning via statements on social media that Midjourney was used (United States Copyright Office, 2023a, p. 2). Despite Kastanova's claim that Midjourney merely served as "an assistive tool," copyright protection was revoked for the images, but she retained ownership of other copyrightable elements such as the text and arrangement of the images on the pages.

The USCO opined that there was too much "*distance* [emphasis added] between what a user may direct Midjourney to create and the visual material Midjourney actually produces" (United States Copyright Office, 2023a, p. 9). This leaves open the question of how much control a human must exert over generative AI to produce a copyrightable output. Currently, generative AI systems allow for iterative refinement of outputs. Perhaps, in future, interactions between humans and generative AI systems will be nuanced enough to meet the standards of the USCO, but current indications are not promising. For example, Jason Allen's artwork *Théâtre d'Opéra Spatial* won the digital art category in the 2022 Colorado State Fair's annual fine art competition. The revelation that the artwork was produced with Midjourney did not cost him the award, but did upset other artists and led the USCO to refuse registration. In an appeal, Allen argued that he had "closed the distance" through more than 620 prompts that adjusted the scene, selected portions to focus on, and dictated the tone of the image (Helmore, 2023). He subsequently edited and added to the image using Photoshop, before upscaling it with Gigapixel. The USCO Review Board held its position, stating "the steps in that process were ultimately dependent on how the Midjourney system processed Mr. Allen's prompts" and reiterated "the 'traditional elements of authorship' are determined and executed by the technology—not the human user" (United States Copyright Office, 2023b, pp. 6–7).

It appears that generative AI companies are content with this unresolved state of affairs, in which machine-produced work cannot attract copyright protection. In emphasizing the fair use defense, OpenAI has argued that existing copyright law is sufficient to deal with any infringements of AI systems, stating, "Generative AI systems might generate output media that infringes on existing copyrighted works … the proper solution is to entertain infringement suits for the outputs (with appropriate defenses, including fair use, available) as a court would for human-generated works" (OpenAI, 2020, p. 12). It is therefore beneficial to generative AI companies that AI models themselves cannot own copyright in, or bear responsibility for, works produced by generative AI. Human creators must be the party attracting copyright protections for AI-generated output (if any are granted), and deal with any resulting infringement suits.

In the USA, for now at least, the door seems closed to copyright protection for works produced by generative AI, but many questions remain open: Would the position be different if the "distance" was closed? For example, if instead of text prompts, users submitted draft artworks for enhancement? How do AI services like Vidu that animate static images fit in here? Is the "distance" caused by the differences in media form? It has been established that remastered audio can attract new copyright (Osborne, 2023, pp. 189–190), so how do automated mastering systems like LANDR problematize the situation (Collins et al., 2021)?

Further questions exist for how generative AI companies and their users can monetize outputs if anyone can freely copy and use them. For generative AI companies, revenue is generated by monetizing their services, not outputs. Midjourney, for example, offers subscriptions ranging from $10 to $120 per month. For users, the answer is more complex. Some users are not interested in monetizing the works produced; prompts may be input for amusement, curiosity, and personal interests. Other users, however, are making money from generative AI works. Jordan (2024) uncovered that 98% of the 560 top songs on Suno are being monetized across multiple streaming services. A substantive issue in monetizing generative AI works lies in the lack of copyright protection—how does one prevent others from exploiting the work for their own financial gain? Jason Allen claims that others are "blatantly and repeatedly stealing" his *Théâtre d'Opéra Spatial* artwork as copies are sold on sites such as Etsy and OpenSea (Prada, 2024). He claims that unauthorized use of the artwork has lost him "several million dollars." This claim, however, is vastly contentious as current copyright law does not attribute him authorship let alone a marketable right. Finally, it is entirely possible that generative AI works may be used to circumvent other licensable activities. For example, café owners require a license to play music in their establishments. Music generated from sites like Suno and Udio may allow business owners to circumvent the need to license copyrighted music. Generative AI companies have acknowledged this issue, and disclaim responsibility for its effects on the value of creative work. OpenAI argues, "We note that this concern falls into a broader category of concerns about the relationship between automation, labor, and economic growth. While we agree with the importance of addressing these distributive concerns, we feel strongly that copyright doctrine is not the proper means for doing so" (OpenAI, 2020, p. 12). Somewhat surprisingly, the company proposes that "such distributive claims are most efficiently addressed through taxation and redistribution" (ibid), shifting responsibility for generative AI's market effects to broader cultural policy and government legislation.

11.3.2 Training: Infringement or Fair Use?

Possibly the most disputed facet of generative AI is whether training models infringes copyrights. Generative AI systems such as large language models and diffusion are trained on vast amounts of data, much of which is copyrighted. The full extent of copyrighted works that have been "consumed" in training processes is unknown, but a number of lawsuits have been filed for copyright infringement—29 in total (Chat GPT Is Eating the World, 2024). This section focuses on some prominent complaints.

In December 2023, *The New York Times* (hereafter, *The Times*) filed suit against Microsoft and OpenAI. The key complaint being that the defendants infringed millions of copyrights when their generative AI models were trained on works owned by *The Times*. As Pope (2024) notes, the problem is "amplified" in two ways: First, the *The Times* has been able to prompt ChatGPT to reproduce its intellectual property, thus circumventing any guardrails against generating infringing content. Second, services like Copilot, which are essentially search engines blended with generative AI models, produce synthetic search results that display "significantly more expressive content from the original article than what would traditionally be displayed in a Bing search result for the same article … Unlike a traditional search result, the synthetic output also does not include a prominent hyperlink that sends users to [*The Times*]'s website" (The New York Times, 2023, p. 40). Together, these points argue that ChatGPT competes against the *The Times* (because ChatGPT is trained on, and can reproduce *The Times*'s copyrighted works) and Copilot's synthetic search results effectively allow readers to bypass the *The Times*'s paywall, which further means that readers are not exposed to revenue-generating advertising embedded on the *The Times* site. Astutely, the complaint was framed in the context of constitutional protectionism, emphasizing the importance of journalism in a democracy and decrying OpenAI as a threat (The New York Times, 2023, pp. 1–2); if readers can use ChatGPT to summarize *The Times*'s works, then it will "obviate the need" to subscribe to *The Times* itself and undermine its ability to fund the high-quality journalism that supports democratic society (The New York Times, 2023, pp. 22).

As we have shown, a key component of the fair use defense is that generative AI produces work that is transformative, not derivative; and that it does not reproduce copyrighted content. Increasingly, AI platforms deploy guardrails specifically to prevent infringing output; for instance Anthropic's generative AI Claude is no longer able to reproduce copyrighted song lyrics (Ferguson, 2025). It remains to be seen how other elements of work, such as style or likeness, may eventually also be protected against infringement as a matter of course. Style is not protected by copyright, however, Williams v. Gaye—in which Marvin Gaye's estate successfully claimed that the hit song "Blurred Lines" infringed on the copyright of Gaye's 1977 song "Got to Give It Up"—shows that "feel" can be protected by copyright. Likewise, generative AI outputs that mimic a recognizable artistic style may not infringe copyright, but may infringe trade dress, a form of trademark that protects distinctive visual identity in commerce (Justia, 2025). In the landmark case *Andersen v. Stability AI*, brought by visual artists against Stability AI and others, the court allowed the plaintiffs' claim of copyright infringement to proceed, on the basis that "their works were not only used in the training process but that the resulting AI models retained and reproduced elements of those works" (Sookman, 2024). There is also significant attention to the protection of personal likenesses, as shown by initiatives such as the ELVIS Act and the NO FAKES Act which aim to safeguard artists, particularly musicians, from unauthorized AI-generated reproductions of their voice and likeness. Each of these examples shows that copyright's separation of transformative from derivative work, and the boundaries of fair use for training, is increasingly unclear in the context of AI-generated outputs.

The companies behind generative AI systems argue that use of copyrighted works is a necessity, that "it would be impossible to train today's leading AI models without using copyrighted materials. Limiting training data to public domain books and drawings created more than a century ago might yield an interesting experiment, but would not provide AI systems that meet the needs of today's citizens" (OpenAI, 2024a, p. 4). In its defense against *The New York Times*, OpenAI is relying on fair use, arguing that although copying occurred, it was for a transformative purpose, much like the Google Books project—and fair use does not require the authorization of the copyright owner. OpenAI is not the only generative AI company asserting a defense of fair use. Anthropic, developers of Claude, are the defendants in two lawsuits brought by music publishers and authors, respectively. In the second complaint, filed in August 2024, Andrea Bartz, Charles Graeber, and Kirk Wallace Johnson alleged that Claude was trained on pirated copies of their works. Anthropic responded with a motion for summary judgment on the assertion of fair use. The motion begins by emphasizing how Claude has been used to advance human knowledge, how it is "a radically transformational tool" (Anthropic, 2025, p. 10). The plaintiffs argue that mere use of copyrighted works amounts to infringement, but Anthropic refutes this, responding that its use is fair because it is transformative: Claude is incapable of reproducing the materials on which it has been trained, and the transformative use of copyrighted works imposes no economic harm on copyrights owners. Further, Anthropic dismisses the plaintiffs' argument that it ought to have licensed its use of copyrighted works and has in fact deprived copyright owners of licensing revenue. Instead, Anthropic (2025, p. 2) asserts that "given the breadth and size of the necessary training corpus, comprising trillions of data points reflecting billions of works" there is no marketable right to license works for AI training. (Anthropic made the same point in its defense against music publishers UMG, Concord Music, and ABKCO.) Similarly to OpenAI and Anthropic, Meta is also relying on a fair use defense to copyright infringement claims from multiple authors over its generative AI model, Llama. Echoing Anthropic, Meta argues that Llama does not substitute for the books on which it was trained, or interfere with their usual financial exploitation. Again, the claim is made that there is no marketable right to license copyrighted works for AI training (Meta, 2025). It has furthermore been alleged, according to court papers filed by a group of authors, that Meta's AI models are trained on pirated material—namely, LibGen, the largest extant repository of pirated books (Brittain, 2025).

Licensing, permission, and attribution continues to be a hotly debated issue, and one that is not completely refuted by AI companies. For example, OpenAI—despite strongly arguing that fair use covers copyrighted training data—has announced the development of Media Manager, "a tool that will enable creators and content owners to tell us what they own and specify how they want their works to be included or excluded from machine learning research and training" (OpenAI, 2024b). Similarly, major music labels have warned AI companies that they must obtain an express license to "ingest creative works in connection with the creation of datasets, as inputs for any machine learning or AI technologies, or to train or develop any machine learning or AI technologies" (Tencer, 2024), following the European Parliament's landmark Artificial Intelligence Act (European Parliament, 2024). This has resulted in subsequent AI-focused licensing agreements between media companies and tech companies, including a late-2024 agreement between Warner Music Group and Meta (Stassen, 2024).

Whether the fair use defense is successful remains to be seen, but the Betamax and Google Books cases illustrate that mass copying combined with a profit motive is not a bar to a finding of fair use. However, there is a long line of commentators lamenting the unpredictability of fair use, including the eminent copyright law authority William F. Patry, who predicted that Google's reliance on fair use was unlikely to be successful (Liu, 2019). The unpredictability of fair use stems from the individuality of each case, and as Rajan (2024) notes, fair use decisions can "reflect a broader zeitgeist surrounding copyright. Court decisions fluctuate according to the social mood of the times." It may well be this latter point that proves influential in decisions. Indeed, recent events have shown the highly political nature of copyright law in relation to AI. In May 2025, the US Copyright Office published a draft report on Copyright and Artificial Intelligence, a lengthy document informed by over 10,000 submissions from AI companies, media companies, legislators, and the public. The report considers commerciality as a factor determining fair use, arguing that "making commercial use of vast troves of copyrighted works to produce expressive content that competes with them in existing markets, especially where this is accomplished through illegal access, goes beyond established fair use boundaries" (US Copyright Office, 2025, p. 107). As a solution, the report proposes that "effective licensing options can ensure that innovation continues to advance without undermining intellectual property rights" (US Copyright Office, 2025, p. 107). Days after the final draft section of the report was released, President Trump fired the head of the Library of Congress (which oversees the US Copyright Office) and reportedly also fired the head of the US Copyright Office. Observers have interpreted this as an attempt to weaken intellectual property laws to benefit AI companies, including X, owned by Trump ally, Elon Musk (Olivares, 2025).

Aligning with the US Copyright Office's recommendation, many copyright owners and creators have called for the negotiation of licensing agreements authorizing the use of their work in training generative AI models. Alongside pursuit of such agreements, technological solutions are being turned to in the emerging field of attribution technologies that are baked into generative AI tools. For example, ProRata.ai is designed to

> fractionally attribute and compensate content owners ... ProRata's technology analyzes AI output, measures the value of contributing content and calculates proportional compensation. The company uses a proprietary algorithmic approach to score and determine attribution. This attribution method enables copyright holders to share in the upside of generative AI by being credited and compensated for their material on a per-use basis. Unlike music or video streaming, generative AI pay-per-use requires fractional attribution as responses are generated using multiple content sources. (UMG, 2024).

This is somewhat reminiscent of the micropayment system factored into Ted Nelson's[2] (unrealized) Project Xanadu, a hypertext, digital repository for all literature conceptualized in the 1960s (Barnet, 2013). Licensing may be a possible solution to the urgent imperative to align AI services with content producers and copyright owners, but the question remains whether copyright owners actually possess a right to license their works for AI training. This line of reasoning goes beyond the fair use defense to attack the scope of ownership enjoyed by copyright holders. This reminds us that copyright is not a natural right, but a grant of statutory privilege and, in the US tradition at least, must be balanced against its constitutional mandate to "promote the progress of science and the useful arts"; it is a "deal" (Vaidhyanathan, 2001, p. 21). Citing *Cambridge University Press v. Patton* (2014, p. 1276), Tushnet (2025) in an amicus brief for Meta, argues that "[t]he goal of copyright is to stimulate the creation of new works, not to furnish copyright holders with control over all markets." And so, it is possible that AI training will be a "monopoly free zone."

This is an interesting inversion of Netanel's depiction of neoclassical institutional economic property theory in action that usually sees large companies seeking to exploit copyrights across all markets with contempt for fair use, which after all, is synonymous with "free use" (Collins, 2016). In these scenarios, the copyright owner is usually a large company or conglomerate wielding copyright against a smaller party. The present situation, however, is different and more complex. Some cases find copyright owners embroiled in lawsuits against similarly large and well-resourced opponents. It is important to remember our lessons from copyright history here: copyright industries separate ownership from authorship. Some parties to these disputes may not be acting in the best interests of their authors, artists, or musicians; they are fighting for a slice of the newest pie on the scene—another way to exploit the copyrights they have acquired. But, in other cases, we see authors, artists, and musicians battling another form of corporate expropriation without adequate compensation. For instance, an online "Statement on AI training"—that "the unlicensed use of creative works for training generative AI is a major, unjust threat

[2] Ted Nelson was a pioneer of information technology. He coined the terms "hypertext" and "hypermedia" in the early 1960s, and conceptualized an alternative to Tim Berners-Lee's World Wide Web called Xanadu.

to the livelihoods of the people behind those works, and must not be permitted"—has attracted tens of thousands of public signatories, including major writers, actors, musicians, and artists (Statement on AI training, 2025). The AI industry was worth USD $189 billion in 2023 and is predicted to increase in value to USD $4.8 trillion in a decade (UN Trade and Development, 2025). Its value cannot be separated from the extraction of creative labor, much of which is already poorly compensated. AI training questions the contours of ownership and perhaps reminds us that copyright is not a property (with all the entitlements that come along with it), but a statutory privilege designed to use private rights to enhance a public good. At the same time, however, copyright is supposed to provide an incentive to create. That incentive may be sorely damaged as creative works are drawn into generative AI models capable of providing market competition.

11.4 Conclusion

From the above, it is obvious that the implications of generative AI for copyright are plentiful and complex. The potential for further complexity will arise from jurisdictional differences both internationally and within the US domestic court system. But while court cases are pending, and legislators deliberate, the technology marches on. Will this be like the Betamax case where the technology becomes so ubiquitous by the time a court makes a decision that the prospect of reigning it back in is politically and socially untenable? If so, how will such a decision be justified? Will courts deny that copyright owners possess a right to license their works for training or find that training is protected as fair use? What would be the implications of such a decision? Copyright policy has always had the difficult charge of balancing competing interests for the ultimate benefit of society. If courts and legislators favor generative AI companies, there is a risk that copyright is likely "to function not as a safeguard for our culture, but as a tool to advance corporate power" (Craig in Kelly, 2025). Yet denying fair use would allow copyright law to be used in stifling the very creativity and innovation it was intended to foster. Should works generated by AI systems attract copyright protection or remain in the public domain? Ostensibly, copyright protects and incentivizes creativity as a product of human exceptionalism. If extended to generative AI, it could incentivize near-limitless automated works that flood our current media distribution systems, dominating the revenue systems of services like Spotify and marginalizing revenue opportunities for many human creators. This is a real risk, but on the other hand, the "distance" between human intention (the "prompt") and generated work may reduce in time. Already, the delineations are complicated: For example, the digital artist who uses Firefly in Adobe Photoshop to make minor contributions to a work that is then filtered and edited by hand, or the musician using SynthGPT to generate a sound that is further manipulated by EQ and effects in an Ableton Live session. Who will or even can police this? Do we want a world in which artists have to prove the human origin of their work? Ultimately, copyright was designed to harness private rights for a public good. Generative AI problematizes that position and leads us to a strange conclusion that *more* copyright is needed to save our cultural works from exploitation by tech companies.

References

Anthropic. (2025, March 25). Defendant anthropic PBC's notice of motion and motion for summary judgment. *Court Listener*. https://storage.courtlistener.com/recap/gov.uscourts.cand.434709/gov.uscourts.cand.434709.130.0.pdf

Authors Guild v. Google, Inc. (2015). *Justia*. https://law.justia.com/cases/federal/appellate-courts/ca2/13-4829/13-4829-2015-10-16.html

Barnet, B. (2013). *Memory machines: The evolution of hypertext*. Anthem Press.

Bazelon, D. (1963). *The paper economy*. Random House.

Brittain, B. (2025, January 9). Meta knew it used pirated books to train AI, authors say. *Reuters*. https://www.reuters.com/technology/artificial-intelligence/meta-knew-it-used-pirated-books-train-ai-authors-say-2025-01-09/

Chat GPT Is Eating the World. (2024, August 25). Map of all 29 copyright lawsuits v. AI. https://chatgptiseatingtheworld.com/2024/08/25/map-of-all-29-copyright-lawsuits-v-ai-includes-bartz-v-anthropic/

Collins, S. (2016). "They're creepy and they're kooky" and they're copyrighted: How copyright is used to dampen the (re-)imagination. *M/C Journal, 18*(6). https://doi.org/10.5204/mcj.982

Collins, S., Keith, S., Renzo, A., & Mesker, A. (2021). Transformations and continuities in the mastering sector. In J. P. Braddock, R. Hepworth-Sawyer, J. Hodgson, M. Shelvock, & R. Toulson (Eds.), *Mastering in music* (pp. 249–263). Routledge.

Craig, C. (2025). The AI-copyright trap. *Osgoode Digital Commons*. https://digitalcommons.osgoode.yorku.ca/context/all_papers/article/1400/viewcontent/The_AI_Copyright_Trap_CJ_Craig__31_01_25_pdf

Cunard, J. (1996). Past as precedent: Some thoughts on novel approaches to the nexus of digital technologies and the arts. *Leonardo, 29*(3), 245–247. https://doi.org/10.2307/1576263

Donaldson v. Becket (1774). 1 Cobbett Parliamentary History, col. 953.

European Parliament. (2024, March 13). Artificial Intelligence Act: MEPs adopt landmark law | News | European Parliament. *Europa.eu*. https://www.europarl.europa.eu/news/en/press-room/20240308IPR19015/artificial-intelligence-act-meps-adopt-landmark-law

Feather, J. (1994). *Publishing, piracy and politics: An historical study of copyright in Britain*. Mansell.

Ferguson, M. (2025, January 17). Anthropic reaches landmark settlement with music publishers over AI-generated lyrics. *OpenTools*. https://opentools.ai/news/anthropic-reaches-landmark-settlement-with-music-publishers-over-ai-generated-lyrics

Goldstein, P. (1994). *Copyright's highway: The law and Lore of copyright from Gutenberg to the celestial jukebox*. Hill and Wang.

Gyles v. Wilcox 2 Atk. 141 (1740).

Heins, M., & Beckles, T. (2005). *Will fair use survive. Free expression in the age of copyright control*. Brennan Center for Justice.

Helmore, E. (2023, September 24). An old master? No, it's an image AI just knocked up … and it can't be copyrighted. *The Guardian*. https://www.theguardian.com/technology/2023/sep/24/an-old-master-no-its-an-image-ai-just-knocked-up-and-it-cant-be-copyrighted

Jordan, B. (2024). Using AI To detect AI music (and other music industry data-porn). *YouTube*. https://www.youtube.com/watch?v=QVXfcIb3OKo&t=112s.

Justia. (2025). Trade dress under the law. (2018, April 25). *Justia*. https://www.justia.com/intellectual-property/trademarks/trade-dress/

Kelly, D. (2025, March 19). AI and copyright law: Osgoode expert describes what's at stake. *YFile*. https://www.yorku.ca/yfile/2025/03/19/ai-and-copyright-law-osgoode-expert-describes-whats-at-stake/
Lessig, L. (2004). *Free culture. How big media uses technology and the law to lock down culture and control creativity*. The Penguin Press.
Leval, P. (1990). Toward a fair use standard. *Harvard Law Review, 103*(5), 1105–1136.
Liu, J. (2019). An empirical study of transformative use in copyright law. *Stanford Technology Law Review, 22*(1), 163–241.
Menell, P., & Nimmer, D. (2007). Legal realism in action: Indirect copyright liability's continuing tort framework and Sony's De facto demise. *UCLA Law Review, 55*, 143–204.
Meta. (2025, March 24). Defendant Meta Platforms, Inc's: (1) Notice of motion and motion for partial summary judgment; and (2) opposition to plaintiffs' motion for partial summary judgment. *Court Listener*. https://storage.courtlistener.com/recap/gov.uscourts.cand.415175/gov.uscourts.cand.415175.489.0.pdf
Millar v. Taylor 4 Burr. 2303 (1769).
Netanel, N. (1996). Copyright and a democratic civil society. *The Yale Law Journal, 106*, 283–387.
Netanel, N. (2008). *Copyright's paradox*. Oxford University Press.
New York Times, The. (2023). Complaint. *The New York Times*. https://nytco-assets.nytimes.com/2023/12/NYT_Complaint_Dec2023.pdf
Odom, R. (2022). Caught by the act: Does the copyright act of 1909 pose legal disasters for modern music? *UIC Review of Intellectual Property Law, 21*(3), 292–306.
Olivares, J. (2025, May 12). Trump reportedly fires head of US copyright office after release of AI report. *The Guardian*. https://www.theguardian.com/us-news/2025/may/12/trump-fires-copyright-office-shira-perlmutter
OpenAI. (2020, January 10). Comment regarding request for comments on intellectual property protection for artificial intelligence innovation (US Patent and Trademark Office Dkt 2019) No. PTO-C-2019-0038. https://www.uspto.gov/sites/default/files/documents/OpenAI_RFC-84-FR-58141.pdf
OpenAI. (2024a, January 4). OpenAI—written evidence (LLM0113). *UK Parliament: Communications and Digital Committee*. https://committees.parliament.uk/writtenevidence/126981/pdf/
OpenAI. (2024b, June 7). Our approach to data and AI. (2024). *OpenAI.com*. https://openai.com/index/approach-to-data-and-ai/
Osborne, R. (2023). *Owning the masters. A history of sound recording copyright*. Bloomsbury Academic.
Patry, W. (1985). *The fair use privilege in copyright law*. Bureau of National Affairs.
Pope, A. (2024, April 10). NYT v. OpenAI: The times's about-face. *Harvard Law Review*. https://harvardlawreview.org/blog/2024/04/nyt-v-openai-the-timess-about-face/
Prada, L. (2024, October 4). AI artist is unironically mad that people are stealing his AI artwork. *Vice*. https://www.vice.com/en/article/ai-artist-copyright-lawsuit/
Rajan, M. (2024, February 29). Is generative AI fair use of copyright works? NYT v. OpenAI. *Kluwer Copyright Blog*. https://copyrightblog.kluweriplaw.com/2024/02/29/is-generative-ai-fair-use-of-copyright-works-nyt-v-openai/
Rose, M. (1993). *Authors and owners: The invention of copyright*. Harvard University Press.
Samuelson, P. (2006). The generativity of Sony v. Universal: The intellectual property legacy of justice Stevens. *Fordham Law Review, 74*(4), 1831–1876.
Sony. (1978). *Sony betamax SL-8600—Watch whenever*. https://archive.org/details/991831
Sookman, B. B. (2024, August 19). AI models and copyright infringement, Andersen v. Stability AI. *Lexology; McCarthy Tétrault LLP.*. https://www.lexology.com/library/detail.aspx?g=638f4e7a-0785-489d-9222-3864d7bcea67
Stassen, M. (2024, October 7). Warner and Meta strike multi-year licensing deal covering Instagram, Facebook and for the first time… WhatsApp. *Music Business Worldwide*. https://www.musicbusinessworldwide.com/warner-music-group-and-meta-strike-multi-year-licensing-deal/
Statement on AI training. (2025). *Statement on AI training.*. https://www.aitrainingstatement.org/

Stewart. L. (2014, August 21). Wikimedia says when a monkey takes a selfie, no one owns it. *Newsweek.* https://www.newsweek.com/lawyers-dispute-wikimedias-claims-about-monkey-selfie-copyright-265961
Tencer, D. (2024, July 3). Warner music notifies tech firms that they need permission to use WMG content to train their AI models. *Music Business Worldwide.* https://www.musicbusinessworldwide.com/warner-music-group-ai-developers-they-need-permission-to-use-its-content1/
Tushnet, R. (2025, March 31). *Amicus brief of intellectual property law professors.* https://chatgptiseatingtheworld.com/wp-content/uploads/2025/04/Tushnet-Amici-Brief-in-support-of-Meta-fair-use-Apr.-1-2025.pdf
UMG. (2024, August 6). ProRata invents generative AI attribution technology to compensate and credit content owners while facilitating fairness and fact, with support from Universal Music Group. *UMG.* https://www.universalmusic.com/prorata-invents-generative-ai-attribution-technology-to-compensate-and-credit-content-owners-while-facilitating-fairness-and-fact/
UN Trade and Development. (2025, April 7). AI market projected to hit $4.8 trillion by 2033, emerging as dominant frontier technology. *UN Trade and Development.* https://unctad.org/news/ai-market-projected-hit-48-trillion-2033-emerging-dominant-frontier-technology
United States Copyright Office. (2014). *Compendium of U.S. Copyright Office Practices.*
United States Copyright Office. (2023a, February 21). *Zarya of the dawn letter.* https://www.copyright.gov/docs/zarya-of-the-dawn.pdf
United States Copyright Office. (2023b, September 5). *Théâtre D'opéra spatial review board decision letter.* https://www.copyright.gov/rulings-filings/review-board/docs/Theatre-Dopera-Spatial.pdf
United States Copyright Office. (2025, May). *Copyright and artificial intelligence. Part 3: Generative AI training.* https://www.copyright.gov/ai/Copyright-and-Artificial-Intelligence-Part-3-Generative-AI-Training-Report-Pre-Publication-Version.pdf
Vaidhyanathan, S. (2001). *Copyrights and Copywrongs: The rise of intellectual property and how it threatens creativity.* New York University Press.
Williams v. Gaye, No. 15-56880 (9th Cir. 2018)
Young, S. (2015). A hack for the encouragement of learning. In J. McGuinness (Ed.), *Copyfight* (pp. 35–48). NewSouth Publishing.

Steve Collins is Discipline Chair of Media and Communications in the School of Communication, Society and Culture at Macquarie University in Sydney, Australia. His research focuses on disruptions in the creative industries, copyright law, music industries and music production. He is the co-author of Music 2.0: The Future of Music. Steve is also a music producer and remixer.

Sarah Keith is Senior Lecturer in Media in the School of Communication, Society and Culture at Macquarie University in Sydney, Australia. Sarah's research areas include media technology and platforms, East Asian popular culture, diplomacy and soft power, and the music industries. Recent research has explored AI in the music industries, online fandom platforms, K-pop and multicultural understanding in Australia and digital disruption.

Workforce Impact of AI-Based Automation in Media

12

Paul Heß and Stephan Böhm

Abstract

This chapter explores the labor market transformation in the media industry, with a focus on the rise of Artificial Intelligence (AI)-based automation. The rapid development of AI, especially since the introduction of Generative AI (GenAI) applications, such as ChatGPT, Midjourney, or Adobe Firefly, represents a significant change in the media sector. Here, the integration of AI impacts several fields in the value chain, with corresponding transformative effects on the related workforce and occupational fields. The focus of our analysis is on the interaction between AI as a technological innovation and its workforce transformation. AI-based automation will impact two fundamental directions: On the one hand, productivity increases are to be expected. On the other hand, AI automation can lead to job replacements. By integrating theoretical models and literature-based insights, this chapter structures frameworks for analyzing the effects of AI-based automation on the media workforce. In addition, this chapter comprises an empirical contribution in the form of a pre-study conducted among media professionals in Germany. This quantitative survey provides first-hand insights into how AI-based automation is currently perceived, adopted, and expected to affect employment and productivity across various segments of the media value chain. The findings from the pre-study underscore that AI tools such as ChatGPT and other generative technologies are already widely in use and are perceived to significantly impact both, the media industry structures and workforce. Respondents see a high potential for task substitution and time savings, while simultaneously anticipating a shift toward Human-AI Collaboration (HAIC), particularly in creative and editorial roles. The analysis identifies key trends in productivity gains,

P. Heß (✉) · S. Böhm
RheinMain University of Applied Sciences, Wiesbaden, Germany
e-mail: paul.hess@h-da.de; stephan.boehm@hs-rm.de

S. Böhm et al. (eds.), *Handbook of AI-based Media Disruption*, Future of Business and Finance, https://doi.org/10.1007/978-3-032-07605-2_12

task displacement, and skill transformation, while outlining avenues for future research and practical implications for workforce planning in the media sector.

12.1 Introduction to AI-Based Automation in the Media Industry

AI has become a topic widely discussed in recent years, both in general and within the media industry, especially since the launch of ChatGPT. One area of discussion is the labor sector. For example, The New York Times asked whether the end of knowledge work has begun due to AI automating knowledge work tasks previously not automatable (Scheiber, 2025). Additionally, Forbes predicted a significant shift in the media industry due to the implementation of AI in media companies, leading to increased efficiency and improved products (Granados, 2024).

To understand AI-based automation in the media industry, its three key terms—automation, AI, and media—need to be defined. Bainbridge defines the aim of automation as to "replace human manual control, planning and problem-solving by automatic devices and computers." (1983, p. 129). Here, he already sets out the core themes tackled in this chapter, including tasks, manual and cognitive skills, and the concept of human-computer collaboration. More recently, Groover (2010) defines automation as a technology that enables the performance of a process or procedure with minimum human assistance. With advancements in computer technology, the topic of AI emerged. For a definition of AI, this chapter refers to Khan, who defines AI as "a machine-based system that can, for a given set of human-defined objectives, make predictions, recommendations, or decisions influencing real or virtual environments" (2024, p. 2). Media companies are defined by Beck as "companies that deal with the procurement, selection, processing, utilization, bundling, and distribution of information or entertainment" (2022, p. 4, own translation). Although contrasting definitions exist, the stated definitions serve as a foundation for exploring the topic.

AI is a prominent point of discussion in public discourse. Despite the topicality of the subject, there are only a few publications and industry studies that deal specifically with the workforce impact of AI on the media sector. Willbold et al. (2023) explored the usage of AI in the top ten German media companies. They found that AI is used by all top ten media companies, primarily for read-aloud functions, voice assistants, and chatbots, utilizing underlying technologies such as natural language processing, speech assistants, and speech recognition. Bertelsmann and Arthur D. Little (2023) present several practical examples of AI use within the media value chain, such as Netflix utilizing AI for voice modification or Reuters implementing an automated news summary system. In her literature review, Chan-Olmsted (2019) finds potential for AI along the media value chain, like comment moderation for The New York Times or the Netflix Algorithm. These articles from the public discourse indicate that AI applications are already being implemented in media companies beyond prototypes or test cases.

Against this background, the chapter is structured as follows: First, the effects on workforce productivity and substitution are delineated and the corresponding fundamentals explained. This is followed by a comprehensive literature analysis of the state of research on the workforce impact of AI automation. Due to the novelty of the topic, research on general literature on the employment-relevant effects of automation is narrowed down to the specific impact of AI. Finally, the state of research in scientific literature specifically on the impact of AI on workforce automation in the media sector is presented. In a further section, existing approaches to quantifying the effects of automation through AI in a general context, as well as specifically in the media sector, are presented with corresponding findings. Subsequently, basic process models are systemized and the corresponding research needs and a research agenda are outlined. The chapter concludes with a preliminary study conducted in Germany on the effects of AI automation in the media sector.

12.2 Fundamental Effects of AI-Based Automation on the Media Workforce

In the working environment, AI can be seen as one of many technologies that are used to produce goods and services. A technology generally is socially shaped by the application of human knowledge to the practical aims of society or, as it is sometimes phrased, to the change and manipulation of the human environment (Williams & Edge, 1996). AI in general deals with computer-based processes that enable automated problem-solving modeled on human intelligence. This defines a very broad field of application (Khan, 2024).

In principle, AI is not a completely new technology, but its technical principles and application potential have been under discussion for a long time. The current breakthroughs are due to, for example, advances in algorithms, higher performance of computer systems, and better availability of large amounts of data for training corresponding AI models. After several epochs of rising and disappointed expectations, which led to a retreat and stagnation of further development in AI winters (Hirsch-Kreinsen, 2024), AI now seems to have reached the level of productive usability. Due to the currently discussed effects on a wide range of industries, AI also has the potential to develop into a basic innovation that will bring about far-reaching economic and social changes. This is in the sense of Kondratieff cycles, a proposed phenomenon where capitalist economies experience long economic cycles. These waves of economic growth and decline have a length of approximately 50 years. They are marked by systematic changes in economic growth indicators (Rostow, 1975). AI could therefore also be at the beginning of correspondingly long waves of economic cycles. This would be accompanied by significant upheavals in production methods and corresponding effects on the workforce.

More pragmatically, AI in the working environment and in an applicable form can be understood as a new type of production resource or tool. Tools are generally used to support humans in their work so that fewer resources have to be used or tasks can be completed in less time or with better quality (Graglia & von Huelsen,

2020). If AI is used as a new type of tool in production processes, the question of its effect on human work processes arises immediately. If the use of AI improves the ratio of resources used to work results, this will lead to an increase in productivity. As a result, either more goods and services can be produced with the same resources or resources such as human labor can be saved while output remains the same. The latter case describes the effect of workforce substitution. In addition to gradual improvements to existing production methods, the use of innovative technologies such as AI can also eliminate and substitute entire work steps or areas. The previously stated implications can be considered not only at the level of individual workers or institutions, such as companies, but also for entire sectors, societies, and economies. Before the state of research on AI-based automation is explored more systematically, the two aforementioned effects of AI workforce productivity and substitution are introduced.

12.2.1 AI Impact on Workforce Productivity

In his foundational work, Brynjolfsson examines the relationship between information technology and productivity. Here, he defines productivity as "the fundamental economic measure of a technology's contribution" (1993, p. 67). Brynjolfsson specifically examines the paradox that, while computing power increased from 1970 to the present time, productivity did not increase by the same amount, especially in the service sector (Brynjolfsson, 1993). He links this, among other things, to an error in measurement. For example, not waiting for the effects of the technology to settle or not measuring new effects, such as improved service quality. This is why he proposes the development of new forms of productivity measurements.

With the rise of AI, Brynjolfsson et al. (2017) revisited this paradox, finding the same decline in productivity growth. This is due to the slow and costly implementation of AI into the company, as well as too high expectations. In this research, productivity is measured mostly through Total Factor Productivity (TFP). This measurement considers all inputs, such as labor costs, required to produce the examined output (mostly Gross Domestic Product, GDP). Acemoglu and Restrepo (2018) describe a similar framework for measuring the impact of automation and AI on labor. Here, productivity is defined as the average output per worker, measured in relation to total production. This is done in a logarithmic measurement. They find that automation increases productivity and, in turn, GDP by reducing production costs. Regarding wage development, the paper has an ambivalent view. Examining the impact of AI on productivity, Brynjolfsson et al. (2017) present an ambivalent view as well, noting no clear implication for productivity increase but potential for future improvements. Zarifhonarvar (2024) finds increased productivity resulting from the implementation of ChatGPT in companies. Similarly, Manyika et al. (2017) find productivity increases due to AI. For businesses, these increases are reflected in faster innovation, improved performance, and enhanced safety. For economies and society, it is shown in increased GDP.

12.2.2 AI-Based Workforce Substitution

In his exploration of the future and history of workplace automation, Autor (2015) explores the question of why human labor has not become obsolete despite increasing automation and technological progress. As an answer, it is proposed that certain tasks and jobs due to automation are replaced (low skill) while demand for other tasks and jobs (high skill) rises. Here, training can help to prevent unemployment. Frey and Osborne (2017) expand upon this task-based approach to computer substitution. Here, they develop a model to measure substitution effects related to tasks replaced due to automation. Based on their research, substitution can be defined as tasks and jobs formerly performed by humans that are now being automated, for example, through AI. In their literature review on the topic, Montobbio et al. (2022) find a coherent view that tasks, including many standardized processes, can be replaced by innovations while they complement non-standardized tasks.

Besides jobs and skills being replaced, an option for collaboration with automation technology, in this case AI, exists. As an early term describing this phenomenon, Man–Computer Symbiosis was defined by Licklider (1960), and it has evolved over time with various versions. One term increasingly used in conjunction with the emergence of AI is Human-AI Collaboration (HAIC). In their research, Wilson and Daugherty (2018) could prove a relationship between the adoption of human–machine collaboration principles and performance improvement. They identify five elements of business processes that can be enhanced through HAIC: flexibility, speed, scale, decision-making, and personalization. Exploring this Human-AI Interaction (HAII) in relation to the previously mentioned productivity, Hemmer et al. (2023) analyzed the effect of AI delegation on the performance of human tasks and task satisfaction. Here, the indirect and direct effects on performance and satisfaction were measured using an experimental design, which found that task performance, as well as task satisfaction, is increased by AI delegation.

To ensure this productivity, Amershi et al. (2019) propose design guidelines for HAII. Similarly, Rezwana and Maher (2023) propose a Co-Creative Framework for Interaction Design (COFI) to explore HAIC. This model is divided into interactions between collaborators and with the shared product. Collaborator interaction is further divided into collaboration style and communication style. In contrast, interaction with the shared product is categorized into clusters, types of AI, creative products, and creative processes. Looking at the media industry, Doyle and Baumann (2024) discuss the notion of Baumol's disease, according to which creative labor within the media industry previously was deemed not automatable. Here, they conclude, that while AI has increased productivity and reduced cost, humans are still needed for creative work, resulting also in HAIC.

As shown, tasks and jobs can be substituted due to automation. However, human labor has not yet been replaced. This could be due to the introduced HAIC, which needs high-skill workers to interact with AI to ensure productivity. Presented frameworks for HAII show that a systematic basis for interaction exists.

12.3 State of Research on the AI Impact on Media Workforce

The impact of AI on the media industry has rarely been researched so far. This might be due to the fact that only the latest technical developments in generative AI, which can be used to generate content such as text, images, audio or video content, have attracted greater attention in the media industry and related research. As mentioned earlier, ChatGPT, as the most popular generative AI solution, was launched in 2022, just three years before this chapter was composed. However, the use of AI for optimization and automation tasks is not actually a completely new topic—neither in industry in general nor in the media sector. AI use has so far tended to take place less as a productive tool but embedded in media applications and solutions. Moreover, research into the effects of automation on workforces has a longer tradition, e.g., driven by technologies such as computers or robots.

In this context, a two-stage approach was chosen for the research of the literature and for the identification of relevant explanatory approaches as presented in Fig. 12.1. In a first phase, a search in the scholarly databases Google Scholar, Web of Science, and ResearchGate was conducted. These results were reconciled with the results of AI-based research assistants such as the Deep Research function of ChatGPT and Scite. This literature search and prompting were done through the predefined keywords as shown in Fig. 12.1. Due to the expectation that there is not yet much specific literature on the impact of AI on the media workforce, the search queries were carried out in stages. Initially, terms were used to search for literature on general automation effects on the workforce. This search was then narrowed down by adding terms related to AI and, finally, terms relevant to media. In a second phase, the found or proposed literature was screened for relevance by the title, the abstract, and the number of citations. Based on the literature cited in relevant papers, additional work was identified for further exploration. Papers deemed not relevant or beneficial in the screening were filtered out or examined with less intensity. In a last step, the resulting literature was clustered to the research funnel and reviewed in depth to identify a comprehensive state of research.

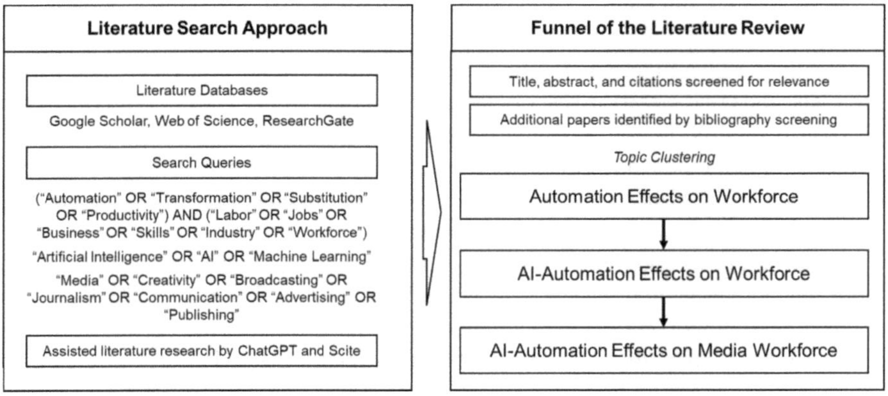

Fig. 12.1 Literature research approach

The papers identified in this procedure are shown in Table 12.1. It is immediately apparent that only a limited number of publications were found to be relevant after screening. Table 12.1 provides an overview of the research methods and specific automation aspects examined in each paper. Here, it can be seen that both cohesive content analysis and economic models exist in the three papers identified for the topic of labor automation. Research work on the effects of AI-based automation is already represented in somewhat greater numbers, with seven relevant studies. Research on media labor automation due to AI is currently limited to four qualitative studies only, including initial interviews and literature reviews. As a conclusion, it can be stated that there is a research gap in identifying the impact of AI on the media workforce. In particular, the authors have not yet been able to identify any approaches for quantifying the effects in the scientific literature.

Table 12.1 Overview on automation studies from literature review

Study subject	Method/approach	Automation aspects investigated
Automation		
Acemoglu and Restrepo (2020)	Quantitative economic modeling	Employment, wages, labor displacement due to automation
Arntz et al. (2016)	Quantitative content analysis	Automation risk, job displacement, labor market polarization
Frey and Osborne (2017)	Quantitative economic Modeling	Job automation risk, labor market, wage inequality
AI automation		
Babashahi et al. (2024)	Literature review	Skill transformation, workforce adaptation, AI integration in industry
Badet (2021)	Theoretical Modeling, literature review	Job displacement, skill transformation, new job creation through automation
Ellingrud et al. (2023)	Quantitative economic modeling	Job displacement, generative AI impact, labor market transitions
Enholm et al. (2022)	Literature review	AI business value, adoption challenges, organizational impact
Lu (2022)	Quantitative economic modeling	AI impact on employment, labor force participation, skill differentiation
Manyika et al. (2017)	Quantitative economic modeling	Job displacement, automation potential, productivity growth, labor market transformation
Zarifhonarvar (2024)	Quantitative content analysis	Occupational disruption, job displacement, AI labor impact
AI media automation		
Bailer et al. (2022)	Qualitative interviews, quantitative survey	AI automation levels, HAIC, media industry transformation
Belinskaya et al. (2024)	Qualitative interviews	AI automation in media, ethical concerns, regulatory challenges
Horska (2020)	Qualitative interviews	AI integration in media, job displacement, editorial process automation
Simon (2024)	Qualitative interviews	AI in journalism, editorial automation, news industry dependence on tech companies

In addition to the presented overview, the following three sections will present the identified research work in more detail with regard to their methodology and key findings. Moreover, the quantitative papers are described with the aim of identifying key procedural patterns to derive points of reference for applying corresponding approaches in the media sector. However, given the small number of relevant papers and the very different research, it can already be concluded that there is no established procedure for estimating AI-based workforce effects suitable to be directly adapted to the media sector.

12.3.1 Research on General Automation Effects on the Workforce

One of the key papers on transformation within the job market is the research of Frey and Osborne (2017) on how susceptible jobs are to computerization. In this research, Frey and Osborne employ a probability classification methodology to evaluate a dataset based on occupational characteristics (characteristics that can be attributed to a job) from O*NET data, a service from the US Department of Labor. Ultimately, 702 occupations were automatically examined using trained Gaussian process classifiers, an algorithmic method. As a result, approximately 47% of total US employment was identified as being at high risk of computerization in the next decade or two (counting from the time of the research). Additionally, a relationship was found between occupations involving lower wages or lower education and susceptibility to automation. Regarding skills, an increase in relevance for analytical, social, and STEM (science, technology, engineering, and mathematics) skills is predicted.

In another key paper, Arntz et al. (2016) similarly examine the risk of automation for jobs in OECD Countries. The study follows a task-based approach to estimate the risk of automation. For this, data from the Programme for the International Assessment of Adult Competencies (PIAAC) serve as the basis, providing information on socioeconomic characteristics, skills, job-related information, job tasks, and competencies. A generalized linear model is implemented to measure automatability. Key takeaways are that 9% of tasks in OECD countries are at risk of automation. A significantly lower estimation than the one proposed by Frey and Osborne. Arntz et al. (2016) see low skills at risk of automation, while cognitive and social skills are predicted to increase in relevance. A sentiment shared in other studies (Badet, 2021).

In a more recent study, Acemoglu and Restrepo (2020) examine the impact of industrial robots on US labor markets from 1990 to 2007. Here, an analysis is conducted using Instrumental Variable (IV) estimation, with key components of displacement and productivity effects, highlighting the relevance of the question of productivity versus substitution. The IV method is used when investigating a causal relationship between two variables and hidden factors could distort the results. As a result, Acemoglu and Restrepo estimate a negative impact on employment and wages with no complementation effects.

The summary of the findings from the literature analysis in Table 12.2 shows that the effects of automation at the job level are primarily substitution effects in

Table 12.2 Predicted automation effect on jobs and skills in general

Literature	Automation effects
Effects on jobs	
Acemoglu and Restrepo (2020)	Industrial robots reduced employment and wages in the USA; one robot per 1000 workers lowered employment by 0.2% and wages by 0.42%
Arntz et al. (2016)	9% of jobs in OECD countries are at high risk; automation changes job structures more than replacing them
Badet (2021)	Repetitive jobs displaced, but complex jobs created; outcomes depend on automation speed and national context
Frey and Osborne (2017)	47% of US jobs at risk; routine tasks most vulnerable; creative/social jobs safer; polarization increases
Effects on skills	
Arntz et al. (2016)	Low-skilled workers are at risk; cognitive and social skills gain importance; training/reskilling is essential
Badet (2021)	Future work needs digital skills and education; low-skilled workers at risk; lifelong learning is crucial
Frey and Osborne (2017)	Analytical, social, and STEM skills gain value; adaptability and lifelong learning essential

Note: Literature not listed here did not provide statements on the presented topic

repetitive and routine tasks. The quantitative effects vary greatly, up to a job substitution rate of 47%. However, these differences are also due to the specific study assumptions (e.g., effects of one robot per 1000 workers) and different automation technologies investigated. In qualitative terms, the effects are mainly limited to low-skilled workers, and the need for lifelong learning to retain jobs is highlighted.

From a methodological perspective, research providing a general overview of automation has shown that the use of different job or task databases is a productive way of assessing the impact on the workforce. For all the examined papers, predictive statistical models are used to examine the data. However, the results vary greatly and tend to reflect more general and aggregated trends. The research does not reveal how the specific characteristics of AI and the particularities of the media sector can be reflected and integrated in order to generate more specific insights or estimates on AI-based effects and the media sector.

12.3.2 Research on AI-Based Automation Effects on the Workforce

In the McKinsey Global report on AI, automation, employment, and productivity, Manyika et al. (2017) distinguish between occupations (e.g., retail workers) and activities (e.g., greeting customers). During the study's conduct, time spent on activities in occupations was primarily allocated to collecting, processing, and predicting physical activities. This concept of measurements, based on activities and professions, is further developed in a recent study by Ellingrud et al. (2023). Here, based on labor force data from the Current Population Survey (CPS) by the US Bureau of Labor Statistics (BLS) and O*NET, productivity was measured by GDP per Full-Time Employee (FTE). The automation impact was then calculated by multiplying the FTE by the predicted rate of automation based on the current and estimated growth rates of employment from the Occupational Employment Statistics data. This is illustrated in the formula measuring the Additional GDP impact of automation, which is calculated by multiplying the FTE impact of automation by productivity. This view of productivity measures the US economy but could be adapted. The study predicts that automation will account for 30% of hours worked today by 2030, with production work, food services, customer service, sales, and office support expected to decline, while healthcare and STEM are projected to increase labor demand. A clear shift in replacing white-collar workers, which would have been a distinguishing feature of Frey and Osborne's work, is not found; instead, a mix of different occupations is changing labor demand as well as work activities. To balance this, trainings are recommended. With such training, Ellingrud opens the possibility for low-wage workers to transition into higher-pay positions.

Examining the impact of AI on industry transformation, the research by Zarifhonarvar (2024) investigates the effects of artificial intelligence on the labor market and its occupational implications. Here, the International Standard Occupation Classification is structured through text mining of descriptions of occupational roles and responsibilities. The chosen technology example is ChatGPT. Zarifhonarvar first classifies two main categories of labor-saving technologies: robot-based automation and AI. Here, robot-based automation mostly affects workers in routine tasks, while AI affects the stated areas even faster, as well as areas beyond that. To measure the impact, the paper classifies the effects on the labor market into short-run and long-run impacts. These categories are combined with ten major occupational categories and subgroups from the International Standard Classification of Occupations (ISCO), as established by the International Labour Organization (ILO). The results of text-mined occupational roles and responsibilities are clustered in full impact, partial impact, and no impact, based on keywords indicative of generative AI capabilities, like data processing and summarizing, in the corresponding tasks in the ISCO (Zarifhonarvar, 2024). As a result, the impact of AI is linked to a mismatch in skills between jobs that are replaced and employees who lose their employment, with approximately one-third of jobs expected to experience full impact, one-third partial impact, and one-third no impact from ChatGPT.

Enholm et al. (2022) conduct a study focused on business value and AI impacts. The impact is clustered into first-order effects (process efficiency, insight generation, business process transformation) and second-order effects (operational performance, financial performance, market-based performance, sustainability performance, and unintended consequences and negative impacts). AI can impact through automation and augmentation based on technical, organizational, and environmental enablers or inhibitors. Lu (2022) examines the topic of AI replacing human jobs through a comparative static analysis, predicting developments similar to those explored in previous works. According to the results, a decline in labor is predicted for high-skilled workers, accompanied by an increase for low-skilled workers (Lu, 2022). This is contrary to trends predicted prior, where highly skilled work was deemed less automatable.

Babashahi et al. (2024) explore the impact of AI through the lens of skill change. Based on a Rapid Review (RR) literature review, they define two categories of skills: technical or hard skills and soft skills. Due to the impact of AI, future skills within these categories are being defined, including technical or hard skills such as programming, data analytics, and cybersecurity, as well as soft skills like lifelong learning, creativity, and emotional intelligence. In a brief deep dive into several industries, Babashahi et al. also define challenges in job obsolescence, resistance to change, and privacy issues of data for the media industry. Badet (2021), in his analysis of theoretical models, distinguishes between technologically stagnant economies with no automation and technologically advanced economies where jobs are replaced due to automation but also new ones are created, leading to a displacement of low-skill jobs but the creation of new ones, focusing on HAIC. Badet uses an algorithmic formula to examine the output of labor with a statistical measurement, like Frey and Osborne (2017) or Arntz et al. (2016).

A comparison of the results at the job level in Table 12.3 shows that the studies report substitution rates between 5% and around 37% for complete automation. The variations here can be explained by the different occupational groups included in the studies and the different AI technologies investigated. In contrast to general automation, the results on skill impact highlight the need to collaborate with the automation

Table 12.3 Predicted AI automation effect on jobs and skills in general

Literature	AI automation effects
Effects on jobs	
Lu (2022)	AI reduces vacancies and participation; mixed effects: Negative for skilled, positive for unskilled workers
Manyika et al. (2017)	5% of jobs fully automatable; 60% have 30% of tasks automatable; routine tasks most affected
Ellingrud et al. (2023)	Up to 30% of hours may be automated by 2030; job losses in services, gains in STEM, healthcare, legal; major occupation shifts
Enholm et al. (2022)	AI augments decision-making rather than fully replacing jobs; job roles are evolving
Zarifhonarvar (2024)	ChatGPT impacts 32.8% of jobs fully, 36.5% partially; journalism at high risk; new jobs in digital media emerge
Effects on skills	
Lu (2022)	Workers must upskill to collaborate with AI; reskilling and education in AI are required
Manyika et al. (2017)	Physical, predictable tasks most automatable; investment in workforce reskilling is needed
Ellingrud et al. (2023)	Increased demand for STEM, creativity, and adaptability; routine tasks decline; skills over degrees; reskilling needed
Enholm et al. (2022)	Data literacy, analytical and ethical skills are in demand; continuous workforce learning is key
Babashahi et al. (2024)	AI reshapes skill needs; demand for technical and soft skills rises; skill gap is growing; businesses adapt through training
Zarifhonarvar (2024)	AI literacy, prompt engineering, and soft skills (emotional intelligence, communication) remain essential; HAIC emphasized

Note: Literature not listed here did not provide statements on the presented topic technology AI. In addition, several studies point to the need for reskilling or that soft skills and ethical judgment are becoming more important.

From a methodological perspective, research on AI-based automation provides further data sources for labor data with CPS, BLS, and O*NET, as well as measurements and classification options with ISCO and the broader classification into technical, hard, or soft skills. Approaches to estimating the effects of AI automation vary between calculating the quantitative impact on economic indicators (e.g., GDP per FTE) and classifications schemes on the extent (e.g., full impact, partial impact, and no impact), or the relationship and hierarchy of effects (e.g., first-order and second-order effects). Automation and augmentation are found to provide these effects with organizational and environmental enablers or inhibitors. As a result, the studies predict further automation driven by AI, with mixed views on the impact on low- and high-skilled workers. An important finding is that the impact of AI is reflected in particular by the fact that the type of tasks and workers to be replaced is given greater prominence than in general studies. The effects of AI-based automation on the skill sets of workers and their classification are also considered more comprehensively than in the general automatization studies.

12.3.3 Research on AI-Based Automation Effects on the Media Workforce

To explore the impact of AI on the media sector, Simon (2024) examines the topic of automation and efficiency, along with other areas. For the comprehensive study, which also explored AI use cases and implementation motivations, 170 qualitative, semi-structured interviews were conducted with news workers and experts. The topic of efficiency (or productivity, as Simon uses both terms), which involves maximizing the use of journalistic talent within limited time and resources, was identified as one of the core motivations for AI implementation in media industries. This study does not present an approach for quantifying the effects of AI automation, related to the fact that measuring efficiency in journalistic work is already difficult to determine. Also, there is not one AI, but rather different AI technologies to measure. One important finding, however, is that AI may decrease efficiency if human oversight takes too much time.

Belinskaya et al. (2024) utilize the structure of the media value chain, encompassing sources or ideation, editorial, production or postproduction, multichannel distribution, and engagement, to measure the impact of AI on the media industry. To analyze the AI impact, a SWOT analysis is used as a structure for expert interviews. The potential of AI is being analyzed from various perspectives across the different stages of the value chain. For example, reference is made not only to the automation of repetitive tasks, but also to problems associated with AI, such as the risk of misinformation or dependence on high-quality, unbiased data. Yet no concrete predictions for jobs or skills are provided.

Bailer et al. (2022) employ a classification scheme to assess the impact of AI automation along the media value chain. The classification is based on established levels of automation in the autonomous driving field and was adapted to the media industry. The AI-automation levels for media tasks are clustered into AI-enhanced tools, AI-based assistance, conditional automation, high automation, and full automation. This classification scheme is then applied along the value chain to assess the levels of AI automation. Bailer et al. emphasize the HAIC aspect in their research, e.g., when stating that "while in low automation levels, AI is rather an isolated background component, in particular, the mid-to-high automation levels require tight human interaction" (Bailer et al., 2022, p. 9). Bailer et al. also do not provide predictions regarding job or skill impact.

Horska (2020) reviews the benefits and threats of AI in the media industry for journalists, as well as the balance of human work and AI. For this, semi-structured interviews provide use cases of AI that are then structured into fields of work. Here, most interviewed media representatives proclaim a new style of work instead of a complete substitution of journalism.

As shown in Table 12.4, results from the examined studies show that, as in the general job market, repetitive tasks in the media industry are at risk of automation. However, the studies emphasize the importance of HAIC and human-in-the-loop for quality assurance. Such a limitation is a special characteristic of the media sector that is evident from these studies. Because media professionals have a special responsibility toward society in the area of information provision and public opinion formation, for example, there are limits to job substitution and journalists are seen to remain vital for creativity, investigation, judgment, and storytelling. In terms of the impact on skills, AI literacy is introduced as a new skill that describes specific qualifications in dealing with AI. Other skills that are becoming increasingly important due to AI automation in the media sector include data analysis and the curation and critical reflection of AI results. This is related to the fact that content-generating GenAI was the focus of the analysis.

From a methodological perspective, the additional insights gained from the media-specific studies are limited. As mentioned above, these are exclusively qualitative studies. The reference to the media sector and the specific characteristic of this industry is established via the value chain and a further differentiation between

Table 12.4 Predicted AI automation effect on media jobs and skills

Literature	AI automation effects
Effects on jobs	
Horska (2020)	AI automates journalistic tasks, but journalists remain vital for creativity and investigation
Simon (2024)	AI automates reporting tasks, but does not replace journalists; judgment and storytelling remain human domains
Effects on skills	
Horska (2020)	Journalists need AI literacy, data skills, and digital curation capabilities; oversight remains key
Simon (2024)	AI literacy and data skills essential; adaptability and critical thinking needed in journalism

Note: Literature not listed here did not provide statements on the presented topic subsectors or products. As is partly the case in the other studies, a detailed analysis of the effects is then broken down into occupational groups or corresponding skills.

12.4 Implications for Analyzing the AI-Automation Impact on the Media Workforce

The review of existing research on the effects of automation on the workforce shows that there are very diverse methodological approaches. Especially when it comes to quantifying effects, there is a gap in research in the media sector. There is also no established methodological approach in the existing scientific literature from general or other industry-specific studies that can be directly transferred to the analysis of quantitative effects in the media sector. Due to the heterogeneity of the media industry, we must assume that the respective approach will have to be tailored to the specific research question in relation to the media subsector and the AI solution under consideration. Despite these limited findings, the literature analysis provides some initial recommendations for the design of corresponding studies. The findings can be broken down into three levels: (1) systematization approach for industry-specific aggregation and disaggregation of workforce impact, (2) databases with supporting classification schemes, and (3) approaches for qualitative or quantitative assessment of AI-automation impact. The findings identified in the literature analysis for these three areas are briefly described and summarized in the following subsections.

12.4.1 Systematization Approach

The object of investigation in this study is initially limited to the rather abstract concept of the workforce. According to a definition by the International Labour Organization (ILO), the workforce or labor force is defined as follows: "the labour force is the sum of persons in employment plus persons in unemployment. Together these two groups of the population represent the current supply of labour for the production of goods and services taking place in a country through market transactions in exchange for remuneration" (International Labour Organization, 2016). In economic studies, this definition generally includes both the employed and unemployed population of working age. This approach is also useful when analyzing the impact of AI because, for example, it allows for the analysis of effects in the area of skilled labor shortages, where suitable AI tools could be used as enablers to deploy insufficiently qualified personnel with AI support. However, the effects of substitution or productivity gains discussed above generally refer to the portion of the workforce that is employed during the period under review.

The workforce here is limited to a specific industry, namely, the media sector. According to the North American Industry Classification System (NAICS) of the US Bureau of Labor Statistics, an industry is "… a group of establishments engaged in the same or similar kinds of economic activities, primarily based on the production of goods or services" (US Bureau of Labor Statistics, 2023). As already mentioned, the media industry is characterized by very heterogeneous and constantly evolving subsectors. In many cases, subsectors are distinguished by the form of media distribution, e.g., print, TV, radio, online, but also by the type of content, such as entertainment, advertising, and games. The problem of differentiation is described in detail for the term media company by Voci et al. (2019, p. 46), who define "media companies as companies that produce and/or trade media content." Against this background, the media workforce can be defined as those workers in the population who are employed in media companies and are involved in the production or distribution of media content. This raises the question of how the impact of AI can be viewed in a more differentiated way. Media subsectors are only of limited use for defining an industry-specific workforce and an analytical framework for determining the workforce impact. In principle, individual products or distribution channels can of course be selected for analysis. Value chain approaches are also commonly used to further break down subareas of the media industry. To assess AI impact, Bailer et al. (2022), for example, structure the media industry through the media value chain areas of sourcing, production, and distribution. However, different approaches in defining the media value chain exist. Wirtz (2011) describes the value chain as a sequence of processes and activities through which media content is created, collected, prepared, produced, distributed, and finally transmitted to the target group. This then is divided into the steps of creation, aggregation and packaging, production, and marketing, which is illustrated in Fig. 12.2.

The individual value creation steps can then be further subdivided into tasks. The accuracy and differentiation of statements on AI impact increase with the degree to which corresponding tasks are broken down into elementary subtasks and work steps. Overall effects are determined in reverse by aggregating the elementary effects. This procedure is very time-consuming, partly because there are no standardized process and task descriptions. It is therefore more likely that such approaches are suitable for pre-studies and rough estimates of overall effects and qualitative analyses.

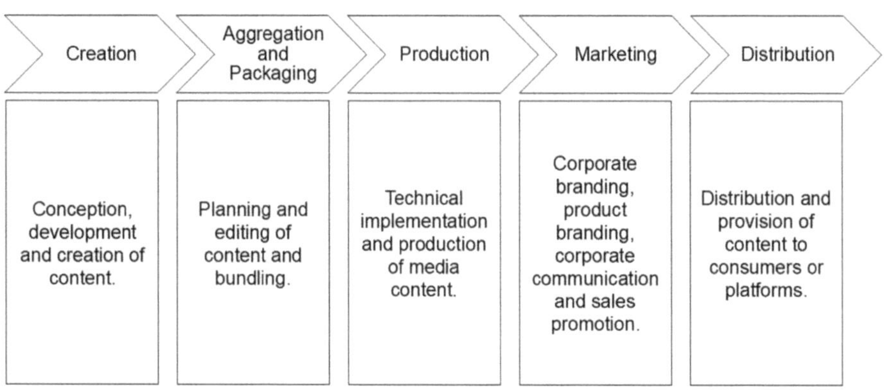

Fig. 12.2 Value chain approach, based on Wirtz (2011)

In addition to the literature discussed on workforce impact, there are also studies that initially investigated the areas of the media value chain in which AI is actually used. One such study, which was conducted using ten media companies in Germany as examples, is the study mentioned at the beginning of this chapter by Willbold et al. (2023). Based on a survey among the employees (n = 106) of the ten German media companies they identified the following distribution of AI usage along the value chain steps: acquisition of information and content (23%), acquisition of advertising (8%), production and aggregation of content (0%), placement of advertising (15%), packaging of products (9%), technical production (2%), distribution (24%), and marketing and service (4%). In her research, Chan-Olmsted (2019) utilizes Porter's value chain. Under the assumption that value creation activities are structured into primary and secondary categories, the review reveals that AI applications used in media companies can enhance value in product creation, marketing, distribution, and service. Thus, all phases. This is demonstrated in practical examples, such as identifying and storing raw materials (images, videos, sounds) and engaging with audiences. Most value is predicted to be generated within operations, outbound logistics, and marketing or sales. Regarding support value-generating activities, AI offers support in managing and processing the overall information and knowledge base of media companies. Overall, most value creation is seen in primary activities (Chan-Olmsted, 2019). These two studies demonstrate that AI is already being utilized in most areas of the value chain, with a primary focus on information and content work, as well as distribution and advertising.

Another approach to systematization, which can be pursued alternatively or in combination with a process-based approach, focuses on the individual workers in the media industry, who as a whole make up the workforce. From this perspective, the media workforce consists of a distinct group of employees who can be further broken down according to specific qualification profiles, occupational groups, or characteristics. In this respect, an occupation is a "set of jobs whose main tasks and duties are characterized by a high degree of similarity" (International Labour Organization, 2023). Corresponding qualification profiles or occupational groups can be further broken down into skills, which are then analyzed in terms of their AI impact. According to Autor et al. (2003), skills are the capacities to perform job-related tasks, shaped by education, training, or experience. A task is a unit of work activity that produces output and can, in principle, be performed either by a human or a machine. The advantage of this approach is that there are statistical and public databases where, for example, the number of employees in certain industries or the skills associated with an occupational profile can be found according to standardized definitions. The AI impact can be assessed at the skill level for detailed analysis and then aggregated from the bottom up to consolidate the findings. This approach is also effortful but offers advantages due to better availability and the resulting possibility of using standardized classification and databases.

12.4.2 Databases and Supporting Classification Schemes

The examined studies provide several sources on classification schemes and supporting data for AI-impact analysis as shown in Table 12.5. These databases should only be viewed as a selection and examples based on the literature analysis. It can be assumed that, depending on the analytical focus and regional focus of a study, there are other relevant databases and statistical sources that are not listed here. The databases O*NET (Occupational Information Network), ISCO, and ESCO mostly focus on occupational characteristics. ISCO (International Standard Classification of Occupations) and ESCO (European Skills, Competences, Qualifications and Occupations) provide an internationally standardized classification of jobs and corresponding subgroups. Moreover, detailed skill sets for several skill categories are provided. As the skills are standardized across jobs, the AI impact can be assessed once and reused when the effects are aggregated for different job profiles with the corresponding skill. A second type of databases, like PIAAC (Programme for the International Assessment of Adult Competencies), CPS (Current Population Survey), and Microcensus (Mikrozensus) contain statistical labor force data such as

Table 12.5 Databases used in literature on automation effects

Database	Type of data	Database contents	Media occupations and skills	Regional coverage
O*NET	Occupational characteristics	Type of job, wage, related industry. Media jobs included	Ca. 34 occupations/70 soft skills	United States
ISCO	Occupational characteristics	Ten major groups, divided into subgroups and related skills. Media jobs included	Ca. 37 occupations/88 skills	International
ESCO	Occupational characteristics	Ten major groups, divided into subgroups and related skills. Media jobs included	Ca. 88 occupations/ skills have to be picked manually	Europe
PIAAC	Labor force data	Income, productivity, socioeconomic data	No clear media link	OECD
CPS	Labor force data	Productivity, produced outcome (GDP)	Ca. 13 occupations/no skills	United States
Microcensus	Labor force data	Income, productivity, socioeconomic data	Ca. 10 occupations in GENESIS/no skills	Germany

income, productivity, produced outcome, or other socioeconomic data. This data is particularly useful when assessing and estimating the overall economic effects of AI.

The procedure described for assessing the impact of AI on the basis of job-specific skill sets is very complex, depending on the level of analysis, as described above. This is clearly illustrated in Table 12.6, which shows an excerpt from the skill set for the job profile of a graphic designer from the ESCO database. The database distinguishes between essential and optional skills, competencies and knowledge. On this basis, highly differentiated analyses of the AI impact for individual job profiles can be carried out. However, as a total of 88 estimated media professions are included in the ESCO database, an industry-wide analysis would be very laborious.

12.4.3 Qualitative and Quantitative Assessment of AI-Automation Impact

The final aspect of the analysis is to evaluate the AI impact at the defined analysis level using appropriate data sources and classification approaches. The literature review has shown that a fundamental distinction can be made between qualitative and quantitative evaluation of the effects. Qualitative studies describe, for example, how processes and tasks change at different levels from a procedural perspective

Table 12.6 ESCO skill set for graphic designers (European Commission, 2024)

Category	Skills and competences/knowledge
Essential skills and competences	Adapt to type of media; convert scribbles into virtual sketches; design graphics; design prototypes; develop an artistic framework; develop creative ideas; develop digital content; finish project within budget; follow a brief; identify customer's needs; perform market research; respect; publication formats; translate requirements into visual design; use creative suite software
Essential knowledge	Adobe creative suite; copyright legislation; desktop publishing; digital; media; graphic design
Optional skills and competences	Apply 3D imaging techniques; apply desktop publishing techniques; brainstorm ideas; create 3D characters; create 3D environments; create; advertisements; create animated narratives; create moving images; design; greeting cards; develop animations; draw design sketches Edit digital moving images; edit negatives; edit photographs; manage contracts; meet expectations of target audience; operate 3D computer; graphics software; perform ideation activities; select artwork developed by staff members; use CAD software; use digital illustration techniques; use photographic equipment; use presentation software; use traditional illustration techniques Use word processing software
Optional knowledge	3D lighting; 3D modeling; Adobe Illustrator; Adobe Photoshop; Adobe Lightroom; capture one; GIMP (graphics editor software); Microsoft Visio; SketchBook pro; Synfig; advertising techniques; aesthetics; computer graphics; design management; digital compositing; graphics editor software; interactive media; motion graphics; photography; publishing industry

Table 12.7 Automation levels for AI in the media domain

Level		Explanation
0	No automation	Humans control non-AI-based tools; topics monitored, analyzed, and verified by humans
1	AI-enhanced tools	Humans use AI tools for specific tasks (e.g., content quality, similarity, model fitting)
2	AI-based assistance	AI generates information used in later steps; humans verify; no AI decisions
3	Conditional automation	AI makes decisions; human intervention required at some steps
4	High automation	Fully AI-based process under human supervision
5	Full automation	Fully AI-based process without human supervision

Based on Bailer et al. (2022)

when AI is used. The impact on job profiles or skills can also be considered. Examples of such approaches have been presented in the discussion of the literature. However, it is difficult to aggregate such statements to higher levels.

Quantitative studies, on the other hand, attempt to determine the extent to which the use of AI produces corresponding effects. This requires a reference value that is related to the use of resources. In a first approach, the current situation must be determined before the impact of AI can be measured. This can be done at the task or skill level. If, for example, "convert scribbles into virtual sketches" is selected from the ESCO database for graphic designers under "essential skills and competencies," it would be necessary to determine (1) what proportion of time is spent on corresponding activities and (2) what reduction is possible through AI. This reduction can be determined by surveying members of this occupational group and asking them to self-assess, and also by expert estimates. Semiquantitative studies can simplify this process. For example, Bailer et al. (2022) adapted the established automation levels for autonomous driving to the media domain, as shown in Table 12.7. This scale ranges from no automation (0) to full automation (5) with several levels of HAIC in between. These automation levels could provide a basis for questioning media workers on the impact of AI on their area of work. However, this again leads to limitations in the possible aggregation of the findings. This is possible, however, if, for example, all full automation tasks are identified in a first step and then evaluated in terms of time in order to determine the corresponding savings.

The above remarks do not define a complete methodological framework. However, they do provide an initial systematization of basic design options for future studies. Due to the complexity of the data basis and the effort required to estimate the impact of AI, it is not to be expected that scientific research will provide a complete assessment of the impact of AI automation on the media industry. However, research work can use these findings to either gradually increase the level of detail or, based on focused analyses, to promote the transferability and expansion of the findings.

12.5 Insights from a Pre-Study on the Impact of AI-Automation on the Media Workforce

Parallel to the analysis of the existing literature, an empirical preliminary study was conducted. Selected results are presented in the following sections. Since the survey could only be conducted in parallel with the literature analysis due to time constraints, the results of the previous sections are only partially reflected in the study's methodology. This pre-study addresses a gap identified in the preceding literature analysis, where most existing research on AI-based automation in the media sector remains qualitative in nature, relying primarily on expert interviews and case-based insights (Bailer et al., 2022; Belinskaya et al., 2024; Horska, 2020; Simon, 2024). While these studies provide valuable depth and context, they often lack generalizability and do not quantify workforce-level effects. The present survey-based approach complements this body of work by offering broader empirical evidence and measurable indicators of AI's perceived impact across various media roles and value chain stages. In doing so, it helps translate theoretical insights into scalable, data-informed interpretations.

The pre-study among media workers in Germany was conducted to gain initial quantitative insights into the impact of AI on the media workforce. The survey was conducted through a panel service provider from December 17, 2024 to January 06, 2025, using the online survey platform Unipark. From a total sample of 723 study participants, 21% worked in the media industry, of whom 83% had experience with artificial intelligence, resulting in a sample of 128 participants. Most of the study participants are male (60%) young professionals with master's or bachelor's degrees (66%) and belong to the age group of 25–34 years. As shown in Table 12.8, most

Table 12.8 Demographics of panel study respondents

Question	Attributes	Percentage (%)
How large is the company you currently work for?	Up to 499 employees	52
	500 to 2999 employees	37
	From 3000 employees	10
How long have you been working in the media industry?	3 years and under	26
	4–6 years	36
	7–10 years	16
	Over 10 years	22
What is your current professional status?	Employed in a company	92
	Self-employed as an entrepreneur	5
	Freelance for other companies	2
	Other	1

study participants are employed in larger media companies and have been working for 4–6 years in the media industry.

Most respondents classify their own knowledge of AI solutions as very or rather comprehensive (57%), while 30% classify it as medium and only 13% as low or very low, indicating a broad arrival of AI solutions in media work. This trend shows itself in the stated AI use cases, shown in Fig. 12.3. Here, 57% state to use AI for automated text creation Very extensive or Rather Extensive. This is the most prominent use case, most likely due to the broad use of ChatGPT. Also, language processing and translation (48%), automated image creation (48%), personalization of content (46%), data analysis and visualization (46%), as well as predictions and forecasts (45%). Chatbots and virtual assistants (44%) and automated video creation (40%) are least utilized by media workers, possibly due to the technical state of existing solutions, not living up to expected standards.

Regarding the professional use of popular AI tools, ChatGPT is the most utilized tool, with 51% reporting that they use it regularly or very frequently. This is followed by Meta AI (34%), Microsoft Copilot (33%), and Google Gemini (32%). The least used tools, with under 30% indicating regular or very frequent use, are DeepL (29%), Microsoft Bing AI (27%), Adobe Firefly (27%), and Snapchat MyAI (25%). This still demonstrates the dominance of OpenAI and ChatGPT within the GenAI tools. The results regarding the impact of AI on the job situation, as shown in Fig. 12.4, are surprising given the novelty of AI solutions: 35% of respondents already experience job cuts and 40% state that they expect AI to (further) replace workers in their company. These job cuts are expected within the next year by over 57%, within the next 2 years by 25%, and by 18% beyond that time. The results show that media workers expect AI to have substantial effects on their job situation. However, it must be noted that these are only subjective assessments and that the extent and reasons for job vacancies or layoffs of media workers in their companies are probably not objectively verifiable.

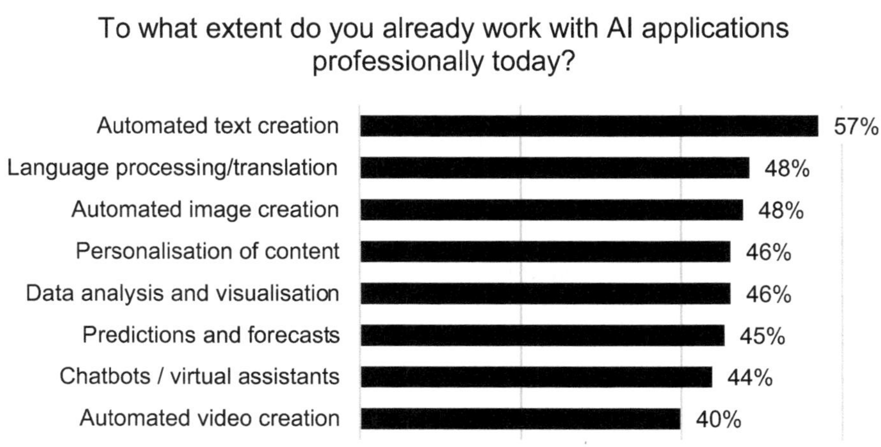

Fig. 12.3 AI usage by application area ($N = 128$). (Note: *Sum of "Very extensive" and "Rather Extensive" usage*)

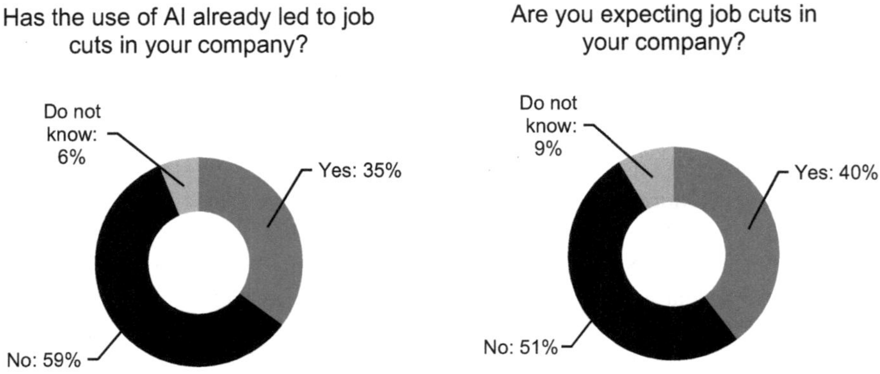

Fig. 12.4 Already perceived and expected AI-based job cuts ($N = 128$)

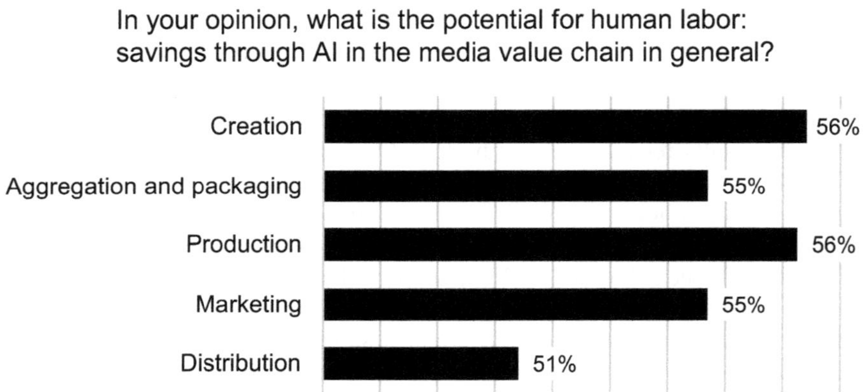

Fig. 12.5 Average percentage of expected AI job substitution along the media value chain ($N = 128$)

The expectations of respondents regarding the general savings potential of AI vary along the media value chain. In Fig. 12.5, creation and production exhibit the most potential for substituting human labor, while distribution is viewed as the least susceptible. This could relate to the most influenced use cases, which are in these value chain areas, such as image or text generation, whereas distribution would require more specific tools.

The vast majority of respondents believe that AI-based solutions lead to more productive work, as shown in Fig. 12.6. For example, most respondents believe that AI can achieve time savings of more than 50% in their own area of work. Only 21 of those surveyed believe that AI can reduce the time needed to complete their tasks by 25% or less.

With increased time-saving and quality of work, the question of substitution arises. Here, most media workers surveyed see the substitution of many of their own

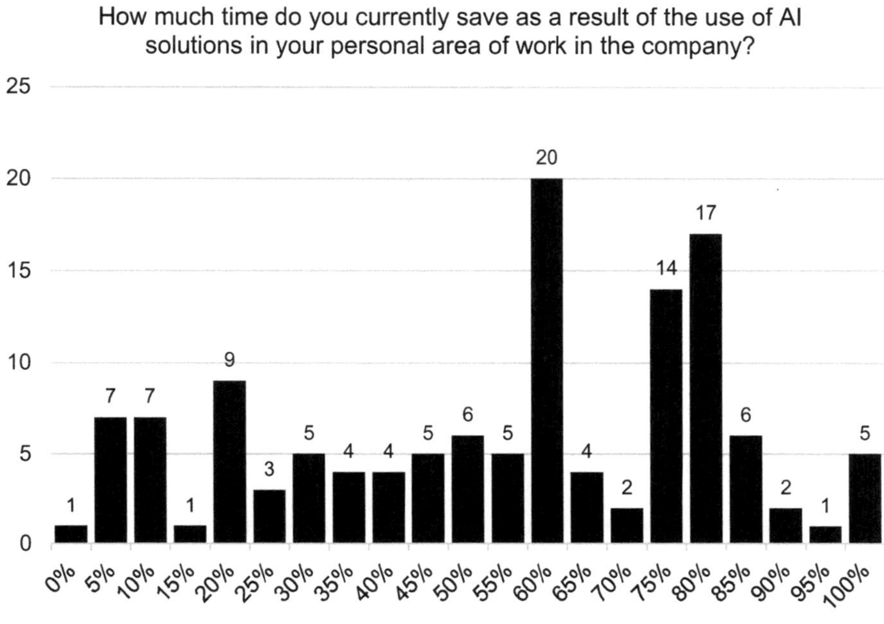

Fig. 12.6 Estimated personal time savings by AI solutions ($N = 128$)

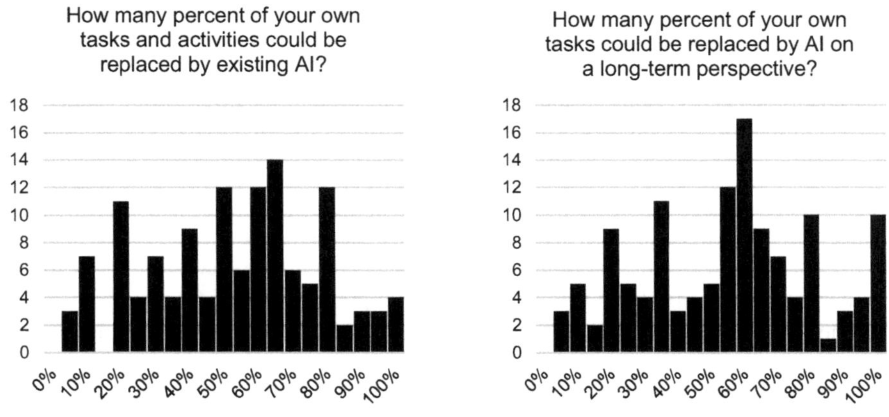

Fig. 12.7 Expected existing and long-term substitution potential of own tasks by AI ($N = 128$)

tasks as feasible in the future, as shown in Fig. 12.7. Surveyed media workers also perceive potential for substitution of most of their tasks in the future as well. On the one hand, this shows that a substantial portion of media work is already being substituted by AI and will continue to be substituted in the future.

As shown in Fig. 12.8, copywriting is seen as the activity with the expected highest potential for AI-based cost savings with a 64% substitution potential, followed by language processing and translation (62%). These high values could be explained

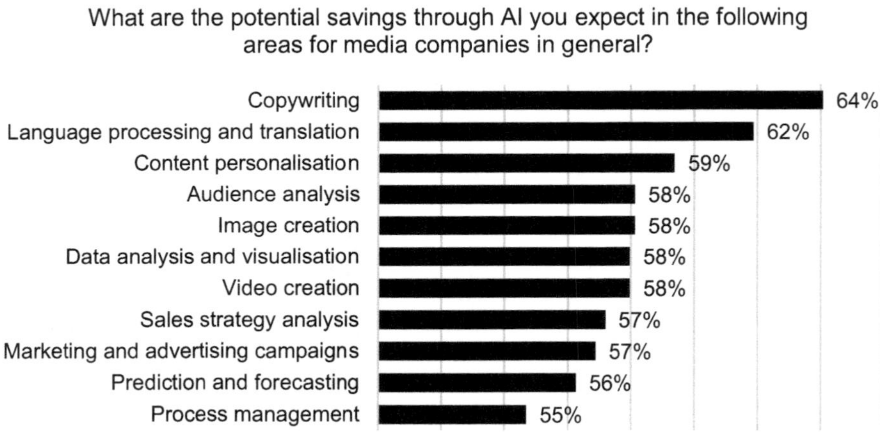

Fig. 12.8 Potential savings through AI by fields of activity ($N = 128$)

by the fact that corresponding tasks can be easily performed with popular AI solutions such as ChatGPT, where most of those surveyed already have experience and can assess their performance. Relevant experience with tools and a broad discussion of the possibilities of such GenAI solutions within the media community are also likely to contribute to the high ratings for the savings expected for the activities of image (58%) and video creation (58%). Content personalization (59%) and audience analysis (58%) also provide high potential for substitution according to respondents. This could be explained by the fact that at least simple tasks in this area can be performed by simple prompting with standard AI solutions. Data analysis and visualization (58%), sales strategy analysis, and prediction forecasting (56%) are predicted to have more than 50% saving due to AI. The least amount of substitution potential on average is seen with process management (55%). Such tasks require more specialized AI applications, which could explain the slightly lower, but still high, expected savings. However, every field of activity surveyed shows at least 50% expected substitution potential, which reflects the high expectations of respondents regarding the performance and application possibilities of AI.

The results about the participants' expectations on a future collaboration with or substitution by AI are shown in Fig. 12.9. According to our study, 38% (rather) expect their own tasks to be replaced, while 35% (rather) expect collaboration with AI, so a coexistence. However, with 27%, a larger proportion of respondents are still undecided about the expected effects.

The results of this panel study indicate a widespread adoption of AI tools in media work, with a majority of respondents reporting comprehensive knowledge and regular use, especially of ChatGPT. AI is already supporting various tasks such as text and image generation, language processing, and data analysis, which are perceived as highly susceptible to automation. At the same time, many media workers anticipate job cuts and task substitution in the near future, in their own area of work within their company.

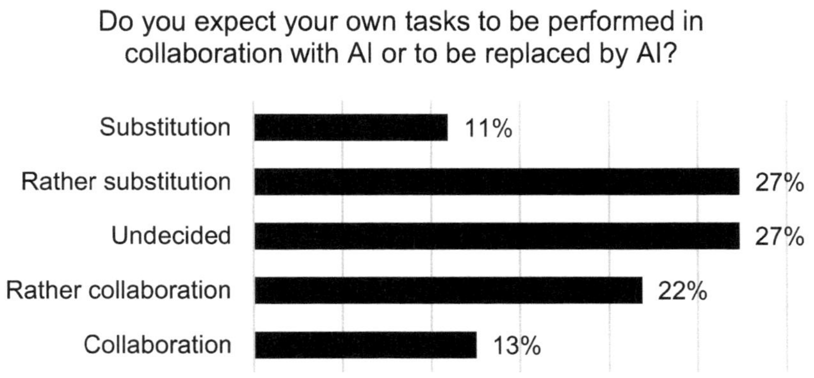

Fig. 12.9 Potential savings through AI by fields of activity ($N = 128$)

Various limitations must be taken into account when interpreting the results of this preliminary study. First, this is a panel study in which participants received an incentive to participate. This may have led participants to give rather arbitrary answers to questions that could not actually be answered in a well-founded manner in order to complete the survey. As already mentioned, the findings from the literature analysis were only incorporated into the study design to a very limited extent. This is a less systematic analysis of the impact than a snapshot survey of individual aspects of expectations and assessments. These expectations are also likely to be attributable to the current hype surrounding generative AI and the corresponding public debate. Despite the participants' extensive experience with AI solutions, the sometimes-exaggerated expectations and the endless reports about new and increasingly powerful AI solutions are also likely to have led to slightly exaggerated expectations of these new technologies. These have probably not yet been used by many or tried out productively on a broad scale.

12.6 Discussion

The results from the preliminary panel study imply that AI has arrived as a technology within the media industry and among media workers. The impact of this adoption on the media sector, based on existing research, needs to be discussed, as well as its effect on skills. Lastly, possible fields of research for future impact are examined.

12.6.1 Potential Job Displacement and Creation in the Media Sector

While studies on the workforce effects of automation in general and AI-based automation have already shown high rates of substitution potential—up to 60% of jobs are seen at least partially automatable due to AI (Ellingrud et al., 2023; Manyika et al., 2017; Zarifhonarvar, 2024)—such systematic analyses quantifying AI-based job substitution effects are still lacking for the media sector. However, in our preliminary panel study, one-third of media workers have witnessed displacement of jobs due to AI and 40% expect job cuts in the future. Across all areas of the value chain, the risk of substitution is evident. When the potential savings in certain areas of activity are assessed by the participants in the panel survey, between 55% and 64% of substitution potential is identified. The results of the pre-study are therefore well within the range of the general automation studies mentioned above. However, the few qualitative media-related studies by Bailer et al. (2022), Belinskaya et al. (2024), Horska (2020), and Simon (2024) also show that the media sector occupies a special position. Moreover, existing research often proposes that AI will create new jobs, leading to HAIC rather than substitution, which in turn creates new jobs that require new skills (Enholm et al., 2022). Since media also play an important role in providing information and shaping opinion in society, there will continue to be special requirements for a human-in-the-loop in the future, which will limit the technical and economic potential for automation. In the literature, this is also expressed by an emphasis on the importance of HAIC. Such expectations have also become evident in the pre-study. More than a third of those surveyed expect collaboration with AI in the future. Like the fundamental effects of AI on the media workforce in terms of substitution and productivity, such HAIC perspectives have hardly been systematically researched to date. There is a considerable need for research here, especially for research work in the field of media management.

12.6.2 Changes in Job Roles and Skill Requirements for Media Professionals

HAIC proposes a shift in job skills. While generally low skills were at risk for change with cognitive skills gaining importance (Arntz et al., 2016; Badet, 2021; Frey & Osborne, 2017), due to AI, these can be automated as well. However, physical tasks still are seen as most automatable (Manyika et al., 2017), with concrete technical and soft skills gaining importance due to AI in general (Babashahi et al., 2024; Zarifhonarvar, 2024) and the media industry (Horska, 2020; Simon, 2024). Yet, since media work encompasses these various aspects, ranging from routine and low-skill tasks to highly skilled and soft tasks, it seems likely that media work skills, although not completely replaced, will change due to AI-based automation. Also, surveyed media workers have already identified the relevance of technical AI-related skills, which are also proposed as relevant in prior research.

12.7 Conclusion

There is a growing relevance regarding the topic of AI and automation in the media industry. The results of this chapter can be considered pioneering work and have explored the transformative role of AI-based automation in the media industry, integrating theoretical frameworks, existing literature, and original empirical data. From a theoretical standpoint, the chapter highlights the impact of AI, boosting productivity while simultaneously posing risks of task substitution, even in high-skill, creative roles traditionally considered resistant to automation.

The review of existing studies revealed the research gap that most analyses of AI in media focus on qualitative insights, leaving a lack of quantifiable workforce impact assessments. To address this, this chapter introduced a preliminary empirical study of media professionals, which shows that AI tools are already widely adopted, particularly for tasks like text generation, translation, and data analysis. The findings show both the perceived productivity gains and the growing concern over job replacement, alongside optimism for new forms of HAIC.

The study implies an urgent need for media organizations to be aware of workforce development. As AI reshapes job roles, the demand for hybrid skill sets, combining technical literacy with creativity, adaptability, and critical thinking, will grow. A more systematic, quantitative analysis of automation across the media value chain is essential to guide reskilling efforts, curriculum reform, and ethical governance of AI deployment. In sum, the chapter lays a conceptual and empirical foundation for understanding AI's impact on the media workforce and offers a methodological strategy for future research. This contributes not only to academic discourse but also to practical decision-making in managing the ongoing digital transformation of the media sector.

References

Acemoglu, D., & Restrepo, P. (2018). *Artificial intelligence, automation and work* (pp. 197–236). University of Chicago Press.

Acemoglu, D., & Restrepo, P. (2020). Robots and jobs: Evidence from US labor markets. *Journal of Political Economy, 128*(6), 2188–2244. https://doi.org/10.1086/705716

Amershi, S., Weld, D., Vorvoreanu, M., Fourney, A., Nushi, B., Collisson, P., Suh, J., Iqbal, S., Bennett, P. N., Inkpen, K., Teevan, J., Kikin-Gil, R., & Horvitz, E. (2019). Guidelines for human-AI interaction. In *Proceedings of the 2019 CHI conference on human factors in computing systems*.

Arntz, M., Gregory, T., & Zierahn, U. (2016). *The risk of automation for jobs in OECD countries: A comparative analysis* (OECD Social, Employment and Migration Working Papers No. 189). OECD. https://www.oecd.org/en/publications/the-risk-of-automation-for-jobs-in-oecd-countries_5jlz9h56dvq7-en.html

Autor, D. H. (2015). Why are there still so many jobs? The history and future of workplace automation. *Journal of Economic Perspectives, 29*(3), 3–30. https://doi.org/10.1257/jep.29.3.3

Autor, D. H., Levy, F., & Murnane, R. J. (2003). The skill content of recent technological change: An empirical exploration. *The Quarterly Journal of Economics, 118*(4), 1279–1333. https://doi.org/10.1162/003355303322552801

Babashahi, L., Barbosa, C. E., Lima, Y., Lyra, A., Salazar, H., Argôlo, M., Almeida, M. A. D., & Souza, J. M. D. (2024). AI in the workplace: A systematic review of skill transformation in the industry. *Administrative Sciences, 14*(6), 127. https://doi.org/10.3390/admsci14060127

Badet, J. (2021). AI, automation and new jobs. *Open Journal of Business and Management, 9*(5), 2452–2463. https://doi.org/10.4236/ojbm.2021.95132

Bailer, W., Thallinger, G., Krawarik, V., Schell, K., & Ertelthalner, V. (2022). AI for the media industry: Application potential and automation levels. In *MultiMedia modeling* (pp. 109–118). Springer International Publishing.

Bainbridge, L. (1983). Ironies of automation. In *Analysis, design and evaluation of man-machine systems* (pp. 129–135). Elsevier. https://linkinghub.elsevier.com/retrieve/pii/B9780080293486500269

Beck, H. (2022). *Medienökonomie*. Springer Fachmedien Wiesbaden. https://doi.org/10.1007/978-3-658-36533-2

Belinskaya, Y., Krone, J., Litschka, M., & Roither, M. (2024). *KI in der Medienwirtschaft* (Studienreihe zu Künstlicher Intelligenz). https://www.rtr.at/medien/aktuelles/publikationen/Publikationen/Kuenstliche_Intelligenz_in_der_Medienwirtschaft.de.html

Bertelsmann, & Arthur D. Little (2023). *State of play: Exploring generative AI's Transformative Effects on the Media & Entertainment Industry*. https://www.bertelsmann.com

Brynjolfsson, E. (1993). The productivity paradox of information technology. *Communications of the ACM, 36*(12), 66–77. https://doi.org/10.1145/163298.163309

Brynjolfsson, E., Rock, D., & Syverson, C. (2017). *Artificial Intelligence and the Modern Productivity Paradox: A Clash of Expectations and Statistics* (w24001). National Bureau of Economic Research. http://www.nber.org/papers/w24001.pdf. https://doi.org/10.3386/w24001

Chan-Olmsted, S. M. (2019). A review of artificial intelligence adoptions in the media industry. *International Journal on Media Management, 21*(3–4), 193–215. https://doi.org/10.1080/14241277.2019.1695619

Doyle, G., & Baumann, S. (2024). *AI: A cure for Baumol's disease?* https://doi.org/10.5281/ZENODO.13167298

Ellingrud, K., Sanghvi, S., Madgavkar, A., Dandona, G. S., Chui, M., White, O., & Hasebe, P. (2023). *Generative AI and the future of work in America*. McKinsey Global Institute.

Enholm, I. M., Papagiannidis, E., Mikalef, P., & Krogstie, J. (2022). Artificial intelligence and business value: A literature review. *Information Systems Frontiers, 24*(5), 1709–1734. https://doi.org/10.1007/s10796-021-10186-w

European Commission. (2024). *ESCO occupations classification*. Directorate-General for Employment, Social Affairs and Inclusion. https://esco.ec.europa.eu/sites/default/files/graphic%20designer.pdf

Frey, C. B., & Osborne, M. A. (2017). The future of employment: How susceptible are jobs to computerisation? *Technological Forecasting and Social Change, 114*, 254–280. https://doi.org/10.1016/j.techfore.2016.08.019

Graglia, M. A. V., & von Huelsen, P. G. (2020). The sixth wave of innovation: Artificial intelligence and the impacts on employment. *Journal on Innovation and Sustainability RISUS, 11*(1), 3–17. https://doi.org/10.23925/2179-3565.2020v11i1p3-17

Granados, N. (2024). How artificial intelligence is shaping the new media and entertainment economy. *Forbes*. https://www.forbes.com/sites/nelsongranados/2024/05/31/how-artificial-intelligence-is-shaping-the-new-media-and-entertainment-economy/

Groover, M. P. (2010). *Fundamentals of modern manufacturing: Materials, processes, and systems*. Wiley.

Hemmer, P., Westphal, M., Schemmer, M., Vetter, S., Vössing, M., & Satzger, G. (2023). Human-AI collaboration: The effect of AI delegation on human task performance and task satisfaction. In *Proceedings of the 28th international conference on intelligent user interfaces*.

Hirsch-Kreinsen, H. (2024). Artificial intelligence: A "promising technology". *AI & SOCIETY, 39*(4), 1641–1652. https://doi.org/10.1007/s00146-023-01629-w

Horska, K. (2020). A new test of artificial intelligence: Should the media industry be afraid? *Science and Education a New Dimension, VIII*(231(39)), 26–29. https://doi.org/10.31174/SEND-HS2020-231VIII39-06

International Labour Organization. (2016). *Labour force*. International Labour Organization. https://www.ilo.org/resource/labour-force

International Labour Organization. (2023). *International Standard Classification of Occupations (ISCO-08)*. International Labour Organization. https://ilostat.ilo.org/methods/concepts-and-definitions/classification-occupation/
Khan, A. (2024). *Artificial intelligence: A guide for everyone*. Springer Nature. https://doi.org/10.1007/978-3-031-56713-1
Licklider, J. C. R. (1960). Man-computer symbiosis. *IRE Transactions on Human Factors in Electronics, HFE, 1*(1), 4–11. https://doi.org/10.1109/THFE2.1960.4503259
Lu, C.-H. (2022). Artificial intelligence and human jobs. *Macroeconomic Dynamics, 26*(5), 1162–1201. https://doi.org/10.1017/S1365100520000528
Manyika, J., Chui, M., Miremadi, M., Bughin, J., George, K., Willmott, P., & Dewhurst, M. (2017). *A future that works: AI, automation, employment, and productivity (No. 60)*. McKinsey Global Institute.
Montobbio, F., Staccioli, J., Virgillito, M., & Vivarelli, M. (2022). The empirics of technology, employment and occupations, lessons learned and challenges ahead. *SSRN Electronic Journal*. https://doi.org/10.2139/ssrn.4281286
Rezwana, J., & Maher, M. L. (2023). Designing creative AI partners with COFI: A framework for modeling interaction in human-AI co-creative systems. *ACM Transactions on Computer-Human Interaction, 30*(5), 1–28. https://doi.org/10.1145/3519026
Rostow, W. W. (1975). Kondratieff, Schumpeter, and Kuznets: Trend periods revisited. *The Journal of Economic History, 35*(4), 719–753. https://doi.org/10.1017/S0022050700073745
Scheiber, N. (2025). *Has the decline of knowledge work begun? New York Times*. https://www.nytimes.com/2025/03/25/business/economy/white-collar-layoffs.html
Simon, F. M. (2024). *Artificial Intelligence in the News: How AI retools, rationalizes, and reshapes journalism and the public arena*. Tow Center for Digital Journalism, Columbia University. https://ora.ox.ac.uk/objects/uuid:aeb25013-1d17-40b2-b471-5bdca309db87
U.S. Bureau of Labor Statistics. (2023). *North American Industry Classification System (NAICS)*. U.S. Department of Labor. https://www.bls.gov/bls/naics.htm
Voci, D., Karmasin, M., Nölleke-Przybylski, P., Altmeppen, K.-D., Möller, J., & von Rimscha, M. B. (2019). What is a media company today? Rethinking theoretical and empirical definitions. *Studies in Communication and Media, 8*(1), 29–52. https://doi.org/10.5771/2192-4007-2019-1-29
Willbold, K., Eisenbeis, U., & Ciepluch, M. (2023). *Einsatzgebiete und Anwendungsfälle von Künstlicher Intelligenz in der Wertschöpfungskette der zehn größten Medienunternehmen Deutschlands*. https://doi.org/10.21241/SSOAR.90872
Williams, R., & Edge, D. (1996). The social shaping of technology. *Research Policy, 25*(6), 865–899. https://doi.org/10.1016/0048-7333(96)00885-2
Wilson, H. J., & Daugherty, P. R. (2018). Collaborative intelligence: Humans and AI are joining forces. *Harvard Business Review, 96*(4), 114–123.
Wirtz, B. W. (2011). *Media and Internet Management* (1st ed.). Gabler.
Zarifhonarvar, A. (2024). Economics of ChatGPT: A labor market view on the occupational impact of artificial intelligence. *Journal of Electronic Business & Digital Economics, 3*(2), 100–116. https://doi.org/10.1108/JEBDE-10-2023-0021

Paul Heß is currently a Scholarship Holder at the Doctoral Center for Sustainability Sciences at Darmstadt University of Applied Sciences focusing on AI & sustainability. The work on this paper, however, was conducted while he was a Research Associate at the Center for Advanced E-Business Studies (CAEBUS) at RheinMain University of Applied Sciences in the field of AI and media.

Stephan Böhm is a Professor of Telecommunications and Mobile Media in the Media Management department of the RheinMain University of Applied Sciences in Wiesbaden, Germany. His research interests lie at the intersection of media technology and media management from an applied sciences perspective. Stephan's current research focuses on interactive media innovations, AI-based media disruption, technology acceptance research, and human-computer interaction (HCI).

New Skills and Educational Challenges by AI in Media

13

Sherman Young and Hilary Sarah Wheaton

Abstract

Knee-jerk reactions by Education to the rise of generative artificial intelligence (genAI) has clouded the discourse opportunities for critically evolving the practice and profession of learning and teaching. However, the rise and continued proliferation of AI capabilities have lent weight to existing reform narratives in the tertiary sector to ensure a future-ready society and workforce, and to safeguard the rights and privileges of expanding digital citizenship. By approaching this identity crisis inflection point using three lenses, a pivotal reimagining of the education experience can occur. These lenses include two that are already well-established, that of AI literacy and fluency, arguing for their place as transdisciplinary curriculum, integrated across academic and professional services. The third lens, that of AI relevancy, has been more poorly defined and absent as a critical provocation but is no less important. AI relevancy argues and invites critical reflection on the changes educational institutions should undertake in anticipating the future, consequently shaping and developing students for the complex human–AI ecosystem and rectifying the missed opportunities of the past.

13.1 Introduction

When ChatGPT 3 was released in late 2022 making generative AI accessible and useful for many, the initial response from some educators was a knee-jerk one. Their primary concern was that students could generate a fully formed assessment task simply by entering a simple prompt. The question many asked was how schools and universities could guarantee the integrity of their qualifications if they could not guarantee that

S. Young (✉) · H. S. Wheaton
RMIT University, Melbourne, VIC, Australia
e-mail: sherman.young@rmit.edu.au; hilary.wheaton@rmit.edu.au

S. Böhm et al. (eds.), *Handbook of AI-based Media Disruption*, Future of Business and Finance, https://doi.org/10.1007/978-3-032-07605-2_13

the work submitted for assessment was not created by an AI tool. This discourse extended existing concerns around academic integrity—notions of "cheating" that have always existed, accelerated with the expansion of the Internet, and the ability for assessment tasks to be easily pulled together from non-original material, or subcontracted to unknown authors from services provided somewhere in the world.

Nearly 3 years on, it is now broadly acknowledged that seeing AI as a threat to academic integrity in existing assessments is a futile game of Whack-A-Mole. Instead, while assurance of learning remains a priority, many consider that we should use this moment to consider what assessment and education more broadly should look like in a world where generative AI tools are as commonplace as Google search.

Educators, universities, schools, employers, and professions are coming to understand that artificial intelligence has become normalized that all our activities will incorporate AI tools in some way, shape, or form. In that context, the relationship between Education and AI needs deep examination.

What is also clear is that this AI moment is one of consumerization and mass adoption. Unlike other recent AI moments (Alpha Go, self-driving cars, and medical research) the ChatGPT moment of late 2022 was akin to the introduction of Mosaic, when that graphic web browser brought the World Wide Web and eventually the broader Internet to the rest of us. With the benefit of that experience (and the failure of our educational systems to properly prepare a citizenry for an Internet-dependent world), what are the lessons for education and AI in 2025? Of course, AI technologies and their adoption are far from static, and there is every chance that a post-2025 reader might find this chapter's observations from their past wryly amusing as they fail to accurately foresee the future.

Notwithstanding that caveat, our starting point is the different lenses through which AI and education need to be understood. When new technologies are introduced, there is a natural tendency for experts in components of those technologies to claim ownership of the debates. While experts such as technologists and data scientists have a rightful claim over some aspects of AI discourse, to fully understand its impact requires interdisciplinary academic interrogation. Looking back to the emergence of Web 2.0, debates across disciplines considered the impact of rising participatory culture across journalism, law, gender, authorship, intellectual property, print, and broadcast media. These were often isolated to their discipline narratives and failed to penetrate the divide of technology development to prepare society for the ramifications to come of social media, influencers, misinformation, NFTs, and aggressive data harvesting by private businesses.

13.2 Our Framework

We propose three lenses to frame this interdisciplinary approach to debate the impacts of AI. Two of the three lenses (AI literacy and AI fluency) are arguably noncontentious as they have been articulated well by others (e.g., Lui & Wang, 2024; DiPietro & Luckin, 2024).

The third lens—termed AI relevancy—is perhaps more contested. Here we argue that while literacy and fluency are necessary, they are not sufficient. To properly and critically engage with AI, not only do we need to be able to develop a range of attributes and skills in our students to prepare them for a world in which they coexist with intelligent technologies, but our approach to education needs to inform and reflect that reality. We must understand, and anticipate, the impact AI will have on everyday life to ensure what and how we teach empowers us to critically shape the world ahead.

13.3 Current State of Research in Education and Generative AI

There is a growing body of relevant research, some of which predates the ChatGPT moment. As with much academic writing that covers fast-moving technologies, the literature (while still useful) can date very quickly. As a relatively recent example, Crompton and Burke's (2025) edited collection covers theoretical foundations and ethics as well as providing case studies of AI use in particular educational settings. Its contents align with the most common research themes that include the following:

- Integration of AI in Education: Focusing on how generative AI might be integrated into educational settings to enhance teaching and learning. This includes both implementing and evaluating AI-powered tools for personalized learning experiences and support. For example, Deng et al. (2025) undertake a meta-analysis of the use of ChatGPT in student learning.
- AI Literacy and Competencies: Defining AI literacy and exploring how students and educators can understand AI's mechanisms, ethical implications, and its role in society. For example, Mah and Groß (2024) look at faculty use, Bond et al. (2024) provide a meta review of AI usage in higher education, and Liu and Wang (2024) propose a framework for understanding AI literacy.
- Pedagogies and Learning Design: Practical guidance for educators on how to leverage GenAI tools in their teaching, grounded in theoretical frameworks canvassed above. For example, Pratschke (2024) provides a comprehensive framework for approaching the use of Gen AI in education and Di Pietro and Luckin (2024) explore using AI as a collaborative pedagogical partner.
- Assessment and Evaluation: Panics over assurance of learning aside, generative AI challenges traditional assessment methods. As well as reflecting on the impact of GenAI on existing assessment types (Perkins et al., 2024), research is exploring new approaches that focus on higher-order skills like critical thinking, creativity, and ethical judgment, rather than rote memorization and recall (Xia et al., 2024).

Some older texts published prior to the ChatGPT inflection point include Zimmerman (2019), which focuses on practical applications and implications of AI in educational settings, and Fadel et al. (2019), which provides an older but comprehensive overview of AI applications in education, including ethical considerations and challenges in implementing AI in classrooms. Also worth noting, with a broader focus, is Kate Crawford's *Atlas of AI* (2022), which also predates the ChatGPT moment but provides an in-depth contextual understanding with a focus on the materiality of AI.

13.3.1 Lens 1: Education About AI (Literacy)

Education about AI (or AI literacy) is about ensuring that learners understand what artificial intelligence is, and how it works. Liu and Wang (2024, p. 4) suggest that AI literacy must now encompass three distinct but interconnected domains:

> Traditional AI literacy focused on technical understanding. Today's AI literacy requires equal attention to three domains: technical comprehension, critical evaluation, and ethical awareness. Students must understand not just how AI works, but how it shapes knowledge creation and influences social dynamics.

AI literacy is about the mechanics of AI, explaining the different approaches to artificial intelligence, their strengths and weaknesses, and interrogating our relationship with technologies. AI emerges from the foundations of math and data, the deep research into models, and the programming skills required to develop them. Education about AI also unpacks its materiality (Crawford, 2022). This includes the costs of AI, the economics, environmental impact and power dynamics involved, the ethical choices that underpin the models, and the impact of those choices on the outputs. Education about AI asks questions around how we do AI? and why? This conversation must be articulated through any number of disciplines across the humanities, social and political sciences, business and economics, as well as in the STEM disciplines. Each offers an important contribution to our critical engagement.

Given the growing impact of artificial intelligence on the world in which we live and work, we need a broad understanding that is not solely a technical one. While it is important to understand how AI works (and there are many ways in which it can and does work), it is just as important to understand AI from a multitude of perspectives. AI does not merely pose a math challenge or a programming challenge or just a challenge in processing power from GPUs. Rather, AI, like any other technological development, poses a range of challenges: ethical, material, political, economic, social, and cultural. These challenges are fundamentally wicked problems, interconnected and with unintended consequences from any solutions we seek to implement; thus, to address them requires an interdisciplinary mindset, drawing critically on cooperative methodologies that are effective at local, national, and global levels.

But just as everybody who drives a car does not need to understand the mechanics of their vehicle, they do need to be aware of the fundamentals required to drive the car, as well as its context—the road rules and what some might term a driving culture. Similarly, a more recent analogy is the introduction of the Internet. Early users were limited to those in technical roles—within organizations such as the military or universities. Access later expanded to allow the broader public to connect through "dial up" using commercial providers. Today, improvements in network technology and devices have defaulted users to "always online" via phones, tablets, and computers inside and outside the home. While these technical transitions simplified access to the Internet, a cultural shift evolved how the Internet was used, driving functionality and engagement, from basic communication and information sharing, to advertising, cocreation, e-commerce, virtual worlds and communities, to social media. For some, understanding the history of the Internet and its technical underpinnings is essential for their work, while for many others, it requires no further thought than opening a browser. However, this symbiotic relationship between technology and our interactions with those advances that shape their use, reveals the socio-technical paradigm necessary to frame Education About AI.

At this stage of AI development, there remains value in understanding what artificial intelligence is, how it works at a fundamental level, the thinking that drives and informs its decision-making processes, and the materiality of the technology. As an example, while the product of a ChatGPT conversation is of most relevance to users, it is still important to understand that ChatGPT works as a predictive text engine, using a large language model that was trained on a range of data. And that there remain concerns around that data—how it is sourced, its diversity and the ethics around its usage, and the human labor required to validate the model. Similarly, it remains useful to understand the training behind the model, including motivations and purposes; the rules and limitations used in its development is pivotal. This data, training, and nature of large language models (LLMs) contribute to the concerns and coverage of inaccuracies in outputs alongside missteps in implementations. Trends in accuracy and evolution of evaluation safeguards for implementation in industry will continue to be critical literacy requirements. It is also important to know that the processing power for generating an answer to a query is substantial. Understanding the *how's* of this implementation allows us to better assess our levels of comfort with particular use cases, better engage within its limitations, or look for supplementary information.

Education About AI also allows us to speculate on AI's development trajectory and develop scenarios that inform a longer-term vision about a future AI-intertwined world. Within those hypotheses, there should be robust debates around the opportunities and challenges properly shaped by the technical constraints so that we have a shared understanding of what AI is, how it works, and what are some of its possibilities. Education about artificial intelligence grounds the conversation with shared understandings so that the difficult questions can be asked, debated, and decided. Our researchers and learners may influence this trajectory at local, national, and international levels. In this regard, we should invest in developing this expertise, drawing from it, and ensuring its visibility for various benefits.

13.3.2 Lens 2: Education Using AI (Fluency)

Education Using AI (AI fluency) is about ensuring that educators themselves are fluent in using AI tools as part of their practice, enabling AI tools to help in learning design, the development of curriculum, learning activities, and assessment tasks.

Today's tools are already capable of crafting convincing drafts of each of these elements—writing and producing video artifacts, developing quizzes and question banks, helping to brainstorm classroom and online activities. We need to further explore the possibilities, uncover their (rapidly evolving) strengths and weaknesses, so that education staff can use them to their best advantage. This use of AI can help address some of the longstanding pressures on our educators in terms of workload, enhancing their capacity for innovation, engagement, and scholarly research. Considered in its use, AI can bridge the gap between academics who are masters of their discipline, and those who are born educators with a talent for translating research into rich learning experiences.

Additionally, we should not shy away from the potential for direct learner/AI engagement. AI tools can play an active role in supporting students, including academic support or mentoring. We are at the point where AI tools can teach and assess students. Universities are already exploring AI chatbots as teaching assistants in their courses. The University of Melbourne rolled out a 2024 pilot exploring the use of an AI learning assistant in their Canvas LMS (LMS Integration). It provides the opportunity for students to ask the tool questions about their subject or can act as a Socratic tutor guiding students through topics. As of the time of writing, the University has not published evaluations of its trial. As well, schools are exploring AI-based writing feedback. For example, a recent study of over 5000 Year 7 student assessments (Christodoulou & Wheadon, 2025) found that AI marking tools were as effective as humans in a comparative judging exercise. Education using AI will inevitably shift the relational elements of educator, learner, and content, giving way to new cooperative learning approaches. It is the role of academics and third space professionals to properly engage in shaping this practice to maximize the diverse, ethical, and inclusive benefits. There remain concerns around the accuracy of information provided by AI guides or tutors, but as well as working to constrain discourse to an accurate corpus of material, we should reflect on our very human desire for the perfect machine given our acceptance of already imperfect humans.

At the administrative level, AI tools have the potential to markedly improve the student experience. If we consider the typical experience for a university student—the entry process involves making an application to study that is then assessed against the relevant criteria. The student then enrolls in their chosen units of study, engages with the learning activities (both formal and informal), receives academic and well-being support as required, undertakes the relevant assessment tasks, and continues that cycle until sufficient credit is obtained and they graduate with their chosen qualification. The use of artificial intelligence to optimize the entirety of that journey is self-evident.

Designing, building, and delivering curriculum is core to the business of education and where there is already meaningful impact from artificial intelligence technologies. Generative AI can already build syllabi, construct reading lists, draft "lecture" material, draft visual presentation material, script and create videos, brainstorm assessment tasks, and help populate learning management systems. But doing it for individual courses of study only provides benefits for individual teaching staff, who would still need to quality assure the drafts and draw on their experience to mitigate risks of inappropriate material or narrative. Those individuals would need to be constantly aware of the possibilities and pitfalls, requiring significant development of their AI prompting and editing skills across a range of models and parameters.

AI could be used to supplement existing practice in that way, but the bigger impact would include rethinking how higher education curriculum is conceived of and thought through. Assurance of learning might be best delivered through a professionalized program design, development, and delivery process that assures consistency and quality. This should involve third space professional staff—learning designers and their colleagues who could complement existing skillsets to make effective use of artificial intelligence tools—negating the need for educators to integrate a further skill domain to their repertoire.

Take assessment for example. The appropriate response to the challenges of AI suggests that many of the tasks that are currently set for students are no longer appropriate. Not only are the generative AI tools capable of delivering more than reasonable submissions with the appropriate prompts, but there is little value in continuing with those tasks if they no longer reflect the capabilities that are required in broader life and work. This reflects the recent narrative response to "cheating," moving beyond academic integrity concerns and instead focusing on validity (Dawson et al., 2024). The better, but harder approach is to reconceive of assessment tasks to be contextualized for the "human x AI" continuum emerging. To (re) design for this continuum requires a shift away from binary thinking about AI and assessment methods. That is, the question educators and professionals must ask is not "Can AI do this?", but "What does it mean to demonstrate an outcome when an AI can do this?". Shifting mindset allows for a broader interpretation of "AI x human" relationships to demonstrate an outcome; yes, this naturally shifts focus to the process of a task *but it also changes that process*. An educator's learning outcomes will remain the same, but the role a student plays in the task to demonstrate the outcome shifts to assurer, curator, task owner, interrogator, conversationalist, discursive interlinker, and cooperative navigator. This requires evidence of the knowledge, skills, and behaviors traditionally defined—but in novel and authentic practices. The requirement to write a correct coding solution, for example, might require a shift *from* submitting correct code *to* generating code using different AI tools and evaluating their accuracy/format/efficiency, reverse engineering that code to trigger errors in the AI and articulating a process for verifying a workflow. These are instances where students still demonstrate foundational knowledge and skills required, but it is contextualized in a larger process that acknowledges AI's evolving capabilities. Is this not the "authentic assessment" that education has been searching for? Offering more meaningful interactions between educators and students? In short, traditional essays and term papers may no longer work, but this does not necessitate their complete abandonment and return to methods such as exams, instead we should face into the future.

In a collaborative, systemized approach, expertise in assessment design can be shared, with the ability to bring together diverse disciplines and approaches from our educators. The result, a well-documented process with several relevant assessment tasks, can be deployed across a program of study—allowing educators to capitalize on their different strengths and potentially offering opportunities for student choice in assessment. AI could be deployed systemically to help in the design, development, and delivery—including assistance in the marking—of those assessment tasks. Again, the tools should be deployed, but they will be most useful once the processes have been improved. True fluency in the use of AI in education demands a reconfiguration of systems and processes.

As part of the learner/student journey, we can also reimagine how students engage with curriculum in a more guided and directed manner. This will be contingent on smarter, and more relevant approaches to curriculum design. There is some instinctive over-indexing on personalization in this area with some pundits suggesting that artificial intelligence tools can provide unique learning pathways for individuals depending on their capabilities and requirements. While there is some truth in this proposition, it can often be oversimplified. Certainly, different cohorts of learners are positioned better for such personalization than others. Postgraduate cohorts looking for individual skills uplift, for example, would benefit enormously from being able to shape a program of study with greater flexibility, identifying only those areas that they require, and looking for direction and guidance toward targeted career outcomes.

While that general principle also applies to undergraduates, there is also immense value in exposing undergraduate students to a broader educational experience, to ensure that they have the ability for discovery outside of their comfort zones, and fellow learners outside of their focus discipline areas. The use of AI for undergraduates in this manner can help establish the lifelong and lifewide learner mindset, aiding in the development of curiosity and critical thinking required for inevitable career transitions or emergent industries.

Notwithstanding our need to reconsider assessment, there will continue to be the requirement to provide support for students who are struggling with their academic work and submissions. Historically, this has focused on academic writing and numeracy—and be in the form of human interventions with draft assignments, specific tutoring, or peer-assisted learning in particular subject areas. In addition to university provided support, third parties have emerged; some of these services are shifting their operating model to include generative AI approaches with a view to reducing costs and increasing efficiencies. For example, one of the largest providers of academic writing support has shifted its operating model from using subcontracted humans from around the world to using LLMs to provide instant and iterative writing support. Student feedback has been largely positive and there are significant advantages in the number of, and pace at which, students can be supported.

Surrounding the curriculum are notions of student engagement and belonging. Student support models acknowledge this with significant effort made to uplift the student experience, build a "sticky" campus, provide social opportunities, and generally create a vibrant campus life. This is useful for many, but being optional and self-selective, it does not cater for all—and it is not unusual for university life to seem particularly isolated and lonely for many. Young adults are particularly vulnerable, with 36% of Australians between the ages of 15 and 24 reporting mental or behavioral conditions (CYPEP, pp. 47), an age group that overlaps significantly with early tertiary study. Again, universities attempt to build networks, provide mentoring opportunities and friendships, and focus their pedagogies on smaller groups with greater opportunities for interaction. There are opportunities where the judicious use of intelligent teaching assistants, mentoring teams, and first-line support agents might provide a way forward.

Any AI approach would need to be a holistic one; in determining a solution that meets the needs of student engagement, belonging, and support, AI should complement and expand the possibilities available to fill gaps impossible to address by humans. Most current approaches take reasonable steps to gather available data associated with certain measures (e.g., lack of attendance, late submissions) and initiate automated triggers such as emails or text messages. However, analysis is lacking or simplistic, limiting the approach and reducing the potential synergy between human and AI support measures. Artificial intelligence may gather insights that lead to more nuanced, measured and meaningful support—building on information gleaned from conversations and interactions with an intelligent mentor, and there is anecdotal evidence that students may be more comfortable disclosing certain information to nonhuman agents.

There are already data points from learning management systems providing information about student engagement, and these are combined with data around class attendance, assignment submission, use of university resources etcetera indicating to universities when interventions are required to ensure that students are appropriately progressing. These are seldom as holistic and well-integrated as they could be, and there are certainly opportunities to incorporate signals from other systems—mentoring and placement data, engagement with clubs and societies, as well as (decidedly creepy) opportunities to learn from student social media threads.

A truly holistic approach would also factor in, anticipate, and look to address through support or change the existence of "critical moments" in the program. This is another data consideration that connects to institutionally contextualized curriculum architecture, signature pedagogy, and assessment aspirations. The "critical moments" are those where students may be inclined to seek support, see a dip in grades, make decisions about certain courses or majors/minors over others, and so forth. This is about understanding the relational elements of the learner experience, allowing support to inform actions and interventions for the student, but also actions and interventions that inform our curriculum design.

The use of AI in designing and delivering education and support are already being widely explored (Crompton and Burke, 2025) but there remain significant challenges in scaling the use of AI tools across institutions. Not only does this require a focus on cooperative professional development—involving technical competence, pedagogical understanding, and ethical awareness—but an understanding and acceptance of the cultural shift that the artificial intelligence tools are nudging us toward. This perspective is reinforced by DiPietro and Luckin (2024, p. 8), who argue:

> We must move beyond seeing AI as either a tool or a threat and instead recognize it as a collaborative partner in the educational process. This requires developing new pedagogical approaches that leverage AI's capabilities while cultivating distinctively human competencies.

13.3.3 Lens 3: AI Relevancy

While Education *About* AI and Education *Using* AI are arguably straightforward, the real challenge is how to educate for a world in which AI is normalized. This goes beyond AI literacy and requires consideration of how we teach, as well as what we teach.

Ensuring relevancy goes beyond literacy—is not merely about technical knowledge—teaching data science, statistical analysis, coding and direct engagement with the development of large language models. Nor is it only about understanding the impact of AI: teaching ethics, materiality, or appropriate application. True AI relevancy means that our students will emerge from their studies with the ability to critically engage with AI tools through all dimensions of their work and life. To do this requires a rethinking of our educational approaches, so that students understand that they are one part of a Deleuzian machinic assemblage (Deleuze and Guattari, 1987; Wise, 1997, pp. 91–102), which includes AI tools and other forms of information technology. That they are not merely familiar with the tools but have been equipped with ways of thinking critically with *and* through them. Arguably, this requires an education system, which understands and mirrors the modern information ecosystem and is not simply a continuation of practices built on previous ways of knowing and being.

Without delving into detailed discussions around the various forms of technological determinism (Levinson, 1997), the social shaping of technology (Wacjman, 1994), or actor network theory (Latour, 1997), the adoption of AI technologies mirrors the complexity of other technological implementations and is best described as a Deleuzian machinic assemblage. Such an assemblage is an apparatus that combines a particular "abstract machine" with specific material or physical implementations. The abstract machine does not exist materially. It exists only at a conceptual level—and is the idea that informs the shaping of a technology's components (both human and otherwise) (Deleuze & Guattari, 1987). The assemblage that we call the Internet provides a clear example. The early public Internet of the 1990s was informed by an abstract machine of openness, whereby both the builders of the enabling technologies and users were informed by an ideal of openness and social reconfiguration. Arguably, the key abstract machine was one of empowerment, which placed the tools of production into the hands of the end user. For example, Andrew Shapiro suggested a "control revolution"; the revolution being the relocation of the nexus of control from a remote central hierarchy into the hands of the individual user. Shapiro argued that Internet technologies allowed a devolution of cultural power, suggesting that end users were no longer subject to the dictates of authority or intermediary. Rather, the combination of computer and communication technologies allowed a shift in the locus of control. Of course, that abstract machine was contested—today's Internet has not seen that control revolution but rather a relocation of the locus of control to different actors—either in the form of authoritarian governments or megalomaniacal platform owners, both of whom have found mechanisms to exert forms of control over information flows. The ideals/abstract machine of early Internet adopters have not come to pass, and that, in part, is due to a failure to properly educate for the Internet—and equip citizens with the necessary thinking skills to actively shape its development.

In that context, Education *for* AI begins with questions. What *should* life and work look like into the future? How do we see the role of AI? Beyond developing the technical capabilities, how do we shape our engagement.

For example, the novelist Jeanette Winterson (2025) prefers the term "alternative" to "artificial" in an article praising OpenAI's efforts at creative writing. In a similar vein, Ethan Mollick suggests the term "co-intelligence" (2024) understanding our relationship with AI tools as either "centaurs" or "cyborgs." "Cyborgs blend machine and person integrating the two deeply… centaur work has a clear line between person and machine" (Mollick 2024, p. 18).

Both Winterson and Mollick's provocations suggest that there is work to be done to understand the place or role of AI into our future—the abstract machine for its development. This work is complicated by an assumed trajectory between current tools and the perceived existential threat of AGI (artificial general intelligence) polluted by historical Hollywood narratives from HAL through Terminator, which suggest dystopian futures. There is a long cultural history around artificial intelligence, which is both informed by, and informs, the actual technologies that are realized in the world.

Instinctively, Education *for* AI work sits broadly in the realm of a liberal arts education and, arguably, this conversation is best articulated through the humanities, ensuring that we all benefit and can build the necessary resilience through the lessons of history. Arguably, our education systems need to have greater emphasis on the traditional durable capabilities of creativity, critical thinking, communication, collaboration, and citizenship. If we agree that the role of education is to produce democratic citizens, and certainly in the Australian higher education sector, there is a shared understanding that as well as ensuring employability and skills outcomes, citizenship is a core aspiration. For example, The Australian Universities Accord (2024, p. 16) clearly states that the national objectives of the tertiary education system are to:

a. Underpin a strong, equitable and resilient democracy
b. Drive national, economic, and social development and environmental sustainability

While the AI literacy described earlier is necessary for this, literacy alone is not sufficient. There is little point in only having a theoretical understanding of AI when we all need to be able to live in a world that may be fundamentally different because of it. Our education needs to be applied and experiential AI must be an embedded part of learning outcomes, activities, and assessment. In short, both what we teach and how we teach need to be relevant to a world of AI.

Learning outcomes need adjustment and we need to reemphasize the so-called durable skills (Hutson et al., 2023). For example, students need the ability to apply critical thinking to broader social and political issues—whether the GenAI tools exist as either alternative intelligences or we inhabit cyborg/centaur frameworks. As alluded to earlier, the most instructive recent experience is the rapid emergence of the Internet, mobile computing, and social networks, and our collective failure as educational institutions to understand the nature and impact of those technologies within our approach to education. While academic research considered the spread and impact of social networks, universities did not adapt our required learning outcomes and graduate capabilities to properly equip our students for a world of uncontrolled social media. And we did very little to ensure that their proper usage was an integrated part of curriculum or delivery. Consequently, Internet usage generally, and social media usage specifically has been an activity largely external to formal education, diminishing the possibility of ensuring critical engagement with those information forms. The argument is straightforward. Reading and writing have long been the basis of necessary education. That reading and writing needs to evolve with and include the technologies and information ecosystems of our time. Students need to learn how to read and write *with and for* Internet; and now, read and write *with and for* AI. This requires a shift in both curriculum and pedagogy.

Our persistence with traditional passive pedagogies and formal print-focused artifacts does not properly prepare students with the ability to communicate, critique, or contribute productively to modern information fora outside of academia. While equipped to make a persuasive argument in academic language and structures, graduates often emerge underprepared and without the skills to translate any learned critical thinking to productively engage with the reality of a public for whom the formality of a well-argued essay is an elitist contrivance. To resolve this, we need to learn from our current failure in focusing on assessment artifact, and not the valuable process it taught; the essay is not the point, the analysis, argument, and logic required to produce it is, and this needs to be applied in a format relevant for the Internet and increasingly the pervasive allure of AI.

Education for AI requires us to reinvent what it means to educate, and for that we need educational expertise that properly understands that this is an inflection point on past and existing practices. Artificial Intelligence has both expanded and accelerated the need to reevaluate traditional approaches to learning and teaching. If AI tools can now create the artifacts of academic papers, reports, slide-decks, and videos, then what capabilities, and when, must humans bring into the process. Are the AI tools the equivalent of interns, assistants, or consultants? Do we then need to understand how best to edit and quality assure any final artifacts? How does that work if we are not creating artifacts but participatory environments? How do we totally reconfigure the idea of collaboration to include co-intelligent nonhuman team members (Dell'Acqua et al., 2025)?

Existing education culture is still firmly framed around analog (print) cultures and fails to properly address our digital reality. When the very notions of knowledge creation are contested, then our old-fashioned approach built on disseminating knowledge appears naive. The basis of traditional education assumes that access to information is curated by authoritative figures (e.g., experts) and distributed through formats that reinforce this (e.g., textbooks, academic publishing, lectures). Consequently, our methods align with this, focusing on disciplines and their related methodologies, scaffolding competence from remembering, understanding, and validating through exams or similar. However, information creation and access have shifted in the digital and AI age to be easily discoverable, generated, remixed, and reproduced by both humans and algorithms. This does not only apply to text, but various forms of multimedia which may take precedence as an authority, requiring a combination of literacies (e.g., academic, digital, visual, cultural, and AI). We need an increased focus on education methods that rethink how to engage with these vastly different information flows, and which emphasize evaluation of information sources and the ability to synthesize and create through collaborative and transdisciplinary approaches—all of which may involve AI tools.

13.4 Discussion

With the Internet, we live in a time where we can search for—and find—information from anywhere in the world, at any time of the day, and have it seemingly instantaneously presented to us in our language of choice. Not only is information ubiquitous, but it is also more easily discoverable than ever. Artificial intelligence adds two further dimensions. Firstly, it provides a way of searching for, synthesizing, and structuring that existing digital information rapidly and without human intervention. Secondly, generative AI tools allow the rapid creation of new information; but information does not equate to knowledge. Centuries ago, the printed book enabled a step away from information scarcity. Digital technologies allowed an enormous leap. AI takes it another step and reinforces the urgency to ensure that we engage with information differently. Whereas once it was sufficient to simply consume information uncritically from printed "expertise" to gain meaningful knowledge, critical reading skills are now essential—the ability to discern the value of information, to engage thoughtfully, and dissect reliability is a requirement of the modern citizen. AI requires us to continually interrogate what "critical reading" means. We now need to expand those critical skills to a world in which the content creator may not be human—but does not necessarily lack human motivation or bias.

Another provocation centers on the role of expertise and authorship. The basis of traditional approaches to learning and teaching (i.e., scarcity and authority) has given way to the expertise demonstrated by the amateur or genAI author to entice "spreadability" (see Jenkins & Green, 2013), achieving diffusion, distribution, recirculation, and repurposing of information in various media formats that validate consumption. As a result, authority is regularly contested and confused, held falsely equivalent to that of influence. Discerning this distinction in the plethora of information and creators is critical, and education systems need to rethink how to operate in this new value system. This cannot be achieved by ignoring digital and AI tools, instead they must be embedded in the education process to resolve this false equivalence, aiding students to work with them systematically and critically—enabling them to properly think digitally (and with AI).

In that context, concerns raised about AI accuracy rates (the so-called hallucinations) are valid and merit serious consideration. However, the landscape is more nuanced than initially feared, with significant advances in mitigation strategies and a growing understanding of how to responsibly integrate AI tools into educational settings.

Most importantly, understanding possible inaccuracies should shape our educational approach. Rather than viewing AI as an infallible source of information, we should position these tools as powerful but fallible resources that require critical evaluation—much like any other information source. This approach transforms the accuracy challenge into a pedagogical opportunity.

Students must learn to cross-reference AI outputs, understand probabilistic rather than deterministic information sources, and develop sophisticated information literacy skills. These competencies are not merely accommodations for AI limitations but essential capabilities for navigating an increasingly complex information landscape. Teaching students to identify, verify, and critically assess AI-generated content prepares them for workplaces where such skills will be fundamental.

The ultimate goal should be developing students' ability to work effectively with AI tools rather than avoiding them entirely. This means teaching verification strategies, encouraging multiple source consultation, and fostering healthy critical engagement toward any single information source—whether human or artificial.

Another dimension of the digital information age is a de-privileging of text. Already, the corporate world has embraced the slide-deck as the tool of persuasion, and an increasing proportion of information is communicated through graphics, photography, audio, and video. Not only do many students use YouTube as an alternative to lecture attendance, many use YouTube as a search engine; or default to video search results when looking for things. Video literacy is now as important as written literacy; the ubiquity of the smart phone with its ability to shoot, edit, and publish professional quality video has put the tools of video production into many, many hands. The required production skills are not as common; and we seldom have formal training in the grammar of video, or how to read video the way that school English classes are expected to teach critical reading, or critical writing. Education has overlooked McLuhan's most critical caution, that the medium is the message.

There should be the new expectation of literacy—medium literacy, the ability to communicate and engage critically in interchangeable media formats. As AI tools allow different media artifacts to be created, without needing the technical skills previously required, new challenges emerge. In that context, as AI seemingly simplifies the creation of reality from a vacuum, it enables the so-called deepfakes. At the most basic level, we need to ensure student ability to critically understand the authenticity of a source, to be able to triangulate and discern real from fake, fact from fiction, and truth from construct. But even then, such critical reading is not sufficient. Our long history of teaching writing is not underpinned by a belief it will produce generations of great writers, but in the acknowledgment that being able to write informs our ability to read; "writing is thinking." This should be enough to remind us that the "essay is not dead," but rather we should expand its demonstratable skills beyond textual elements. We need to expand the fundamentals of "writing" across media, including AI tools as part of the "writing" process.

Education systems need to reflect all the above. Not only in what we teach but in how we teach. To properly address the new information ecology, which embeds AI tools in a digital network, we need to consider evolving learning outcomes toward "thinking digitally"—critical information skills and multimedia reading and writing—and do so in ways which reflect the normality of artificial intelligence. Such learning outcomes must be supported through applied learning activities, involving cooperation, reflection, and embedded digital and AI tools. Add to this, development of capabilities inherent to AI, using approaches that differentiate and permeate our "human x AI" evolution.

13.5 Conclusion

The integration of AI into education represents not merely a technological evolution but a fundamental reconsideration of how we prepare learners for a world where the human cyborg/centaur is the norm. Through the three lenses discussed—AI literacy, AI fluency, and AI relevancy—we can chart a comprehensive approach that transforms education from its current reactive stance to one that proactively shapes the future. AI literacy ensures learners understand the transdisciplinary nature of artificial intelligence—its technical underpinnings, societal implications, and ethical considerations. AI fluency empowers educators to leverage these tools effectively in curriculum design, delivery, and student support. Lastly, it is AI relevancy that presents the most profound challenge, requiring us to reimagine education for a world where AI is ubiquitous.

The failures in responding to previous technological shifts—particularly the Internet and social media—serve as cautionary tales. By continuing to privilege traditional pedagogies and analogue information formats, we risk producing graduates ill-equipped for contemporary information ecosystems. Similarly, narrowing our discipline curriculum to learning outcomes that fail to encompass our transdisciplinary reality leaves us at the mercy of industries that reflect the economies of the past. True AI relevancy demands that we expand our conception of critical thinking, communication, and creativity to include cooperative work with AI tools. This shift necessitates moving beyond curricular adjustments to reimagine the very process of education. As generative AI increasingly handles information creation and curation, education must focus on developing distinctively human capabilities—contextual understanding, ethical judgment, and cross-disciplinary synthesis. We must teach learners not merely to use AI tools but to critically shape their development and application.

The fears that may hold educational institutions, and their communities, to reject AI due to beliefs that it leads to our redundancy may produce self-fulling prophecies. Instead, the path forward requires embracing AI as both subject matter and pedagogical partner, reconceptualizing assessment, redefining expertise, and fostering an educational culture that mirrors the emerging human–AI ecosystem. By doing so, we can prepare graduates not just to survive in an AI-driven world, but to actively influence societal progress by determining how these technologies evolve.

References

Australian Government. (2024). *Australian Universities Accord.*

Bond, M., Khosravi, H., De Laat, M., Lockyer, L., Agudelo, J., Rienties, B., Gasevic, D., Dawson, S., & Sheridan, L. (2024). A meta systematic review of artificial intelligence in higher education: A call for increased ethics, collaboration, and rigour. *International Journal of Educational Technology in Higher Education, 21*(4). https://doi.org/10.1186/s41239-023-00436-z

Christodoulou, D., & Wheadon, C. (2025). *So, can AI assess writing?* https://substack.nomoremarking.com/p/so-can-ai-assess-writing

Crawford, K. (2022). *Atlas of AI.* Yale University Press.

Crompton, H., & Burke, D. (Eds.). (2025). *Artificial applications in higher education*. Routledge.

Dawson, P., Bearman, M., Dollinger, M., & Boud, D. (2024). Validity matters more than cheating. *Assessment & Evaluation in Higher Education, 49*(7), 1005–1016. https://doi.org/10.1080/02602938.2024.2386662

Deleuze, G., & Guattari, F. (1987). A Thousand Plateaus (B Massumi Trans), University of Minnesota press, Minneapolis.

Dell'Acqua, F., Ayoubi, C., Lifshitz-Assaf, H., Sadun, R., Mollick, E. R., Mollick, L., Han, Y., Goldman, J., Nair, H., Taub, S., & Lakhani, K. R. (2025). *The cybernetic teammate: A field experiment on generative AI reshaping teamwork and expertise* (Harvard Business School Strategy Unit Working Paper No. 25-043). https://ssrn.com/abstract=5188231

Deng, R., Jiang, M., Yu, X., Lu, Y., & Liu, S. (2025). Does ChatGPT enhance student learning? A systematic review and meta-analysis of experimental studies. *Computers & Education, 227*, 105224. https://www.sciencedirect.com/science/article/pii/S0360131524002380

DiPietro, M., & Luckin, R. (2024). *Collaborative intelligence: Leveraging AI in education.*

Fadel, C., Holmes, W., & Bialik, M. (2019). *Artificial intelligence in education: Promises and implications for teaching and learning*. Centre for Curriculum Redesign.

Hutson, J., & Ceballos, J. (2023). Rethinking education in the age of AI: The importance of developing durable skills in the Industry 4.0. *Faculty Scholarship, 494.* https://digitalcommons.lindenwood.edu/faculty-research-papers/494

Jenkins, H., Ford, S., & Green, J. (2013). *Spreadable media: Creating value and meaning in a networked world.* NYU Press.

Latour, B. (1997). The trouble with actor-network theory. *Philosophia, 25*(3-4), 47–64. http://www.ensmp.fr/~latour/artpop/p67.html

Levinson, P. (1997). *The soft edge*. Routledge.

Liu, Y., & Wang, H. (2024). *Transforming education with AI: A framework for understanding AI literacy.*

Mah, D. K., & Groß, N. (2024). Artificial intelligence in higher education: Exploring faculty use, self-efficacy, distinct profiles, and professional development needs. *International Journal of Educational Technology in Higher Education, 21*(58). https://doi.org/10.1186/s41239-024-00490-1

Mollick, E. (2024). *Co-intelligence*. WH Allen.
Perkins, M., Roe, J., Vu, B. H., Phan, T., Lui, J., Johnson, C., & White, G. K. (2024). Simple techniques to bypass GenAI text detectors: Implications for inclusive education. *International Journal of Educational Technology in Higher Education, 21*(53). https://doi.org/10.1186/s41239-024-00487-w
Pratschke, B. M. (2024). *Generative AI and education*. Springer Nature.
Wajcman, J. (1994). Technological a/genders. In L. Green & R. Guinery (Eds.), *Framing technology*. Allen & Unwin.
Winterson, J. (2025, March 12). OpenAI's metafictional short story about grief is beautiful and moving. *The Guardian*. https://www.theguardian.com/books/2025/mar/12/jeanette-winterson-ai-alternative-intelligence-its-capacity-to-be-other-is-just-what-the-human-race-needs
Wise, J. M. (1997). Exploring Technology and Social Space, Sage, Thousand Oaks
Xia, Q., Weng, X., Ouyang, F., Jin, J., & Chen, X. (2024). A scoping review on how generative artificial intelligence transforms assessment in higher education. *International Journal of Educational Technology in Higher Education, 21*(40). https://doi.org/10.1186/s41239-024-00468-z
Zimmerman, M. (2019). *Teaching AI: Exploring new frontiers for learning*. International Society for Technology in Education.

Sherman Young is Deputy Vice-Chancellor (Education) and Vice-President of RMIT University where he is responsible for the strategic leadership of RMIT's learning, teaching and student experience.

Hilary Sarah Wheaton is Principal Advisor, Educational Practice Learning and Teaching, in the RMIT Education Portfolio. Her role focuses on supporting University-wide strategic initiatives, enabling their implementation with a focus on pedagogy. Her L&T research focuses on the intersection between technical and pedagogical practices and associated ideologies, while her discipline background includes internet/cultural studies, with publications on the themes of persona, celebrity, and computer games.

Part III

Case Studies and Selected Topics on AI in the Media Industry

Generative AI in Austrian News Media: Innovation Impact and Evidence on Path Dependence

14

Paul Clemens Murschetz, Maximilian Eder, and Bartosz Wilczek

Abstract

This study employs path dependence theory to study the impacts on changes in newsroom practices and strategic behavior of newsroom managers.

We use Sydow et al.'s (2012) organizational path dependence model and define AI innovation as (1) a dynamic process that is shaped by multiple factors of innovation; (2) causes path dependence when triggered by historical events leading to a critical juncture; (3) governed by a regime of positive, self-reinforcing feedback constituting a specific pattern of social practices, which gains more and more predominance against alternatives; and (4) leads, at least potentially, into an organizational lock-in, understood as a corridor of limited scope of action that is strategically inefficient; and (5) eventually leads to strategic action to break away from a chosen path and take strategic action to avoid any dismal dependence and thus inefficiency.

The empirical analysis follows a qualitative case study research design to account for emergent historical insights into path dependence in AI innovation gained over 3 years.

Two different groups of participants were interviewed about historical factors shaping and constraining AI innovation: (1) news media executives (n = *10*), including Austria's public service broadcasting corporation ORF, the country's

In honorable memory of Bartosz Wilczek (1979–2025).

P. C. Murschetz (✉)
Murschetz Media Consulting, Salzburg, Austria
e-mail: paul.murschetz@gmx.net

M. Eder · B. Wilczek
Department of Media and Communication, LMU Munich, Munich, Germany
e-mail: maximilian.eder@ifkw.lmu.de; bartosz.wilczek@ifkw.lmu.de

S. Böhm et al. (eds.), *Handbook of AI-based Media Disruption*, Future of Business and Finance, https://doi.org/10.1007/978-3-032-07605-2_14

national news media agency APA, managers of regional high-quality newspapers, and digital AI news media innovators; and (2) academic experts in the field ($n = 11$). Managerial perceptions were evaluated alongside four phases of path constitution practices (preformation, path creation, lock-in, and path release) and three path dependence mechanisms (historical events, critical juncture, and strategic action).

We found the evolution and constitution of an AI innovation path in news media to be an ambiguous concept and an overambitious practice. While AI raises opportunities for competitive advantage, it also leverages the complexity of challenges faced by journalists and newsroom executives. The analysis further proved that executives preferred the constitution of an idiosyncratic path and proposed AI innovation as a mindful strategy for breaking legacy paths. History mattered, but the actors also shaped it.

14.1 Introduction

The media landscape is currently undergoing a profound structural change that reshapes how information is produced, distributed, and consumed. This change is driven by the rapid development of artificial intelligence (AI) technologies that are revolutionizing every aspect of the media industry (Beckett & Yaseen, 2023). From content creation and curation to personalized recommendations and audience engagement, AI plays a critical role in defining how media content is created, distributed, and monetized.

The increasing quality of algorithmic communication is accompanied by the growing role of AI chatbots in receiving and fact-checking news (Kuznetsova et al., 2025). These disruptions put enormous pressure on journalistic newswork in that they largely reconfigure work processes and tasks (Grimme & Zabel, 2024). At the same time, they also leverage journalistic opportunities, empowering journalists and newsrooms to navigate technological change.

The introduction of AI technologies has greatly disrupted the principles and practicalities of journalism and news media. They violate many of the traditional principles of journalistic work, such as relying on trusted sources, as they allow publishing content directly without human oversight, while they also supplement workflow and augment newsgathering, content creation, and distribution.

Certainly, intensified scholarly attention has recently been given to explanations focusing on the challenges generative AI poses to the very essence of how journalism is perceived as an institution, its core creative processes, traditional norms of authorship, originality, and professional identity (Cools & Diakopoulos, in press; Dodds et al., in press; Guzman & Lewis, 2024; Lewis et al., 2025; Lindén, 2017; Túñez-López et al., 2021).

In the same vein, they have also urged news media managers to face the many other interrelated challenges, among which issues of designing effective business models and AI-based revenue strategies are essential for them to survive in a rapidly changing news media ecosystem (Chan-Olmsted, 2019; Sjøvaag, 2024).

Truly, the dominance of platforms to control access to audiences (Simon, 2024), the issue of "hallucinations" and biases in AI outputs to endanger trust (Wilczek et al., 2021), the spread of fake news sites and generative AI-induced disinformation campaigns (Vaccari & Chadwick, 2020), and the lack of proof on viable business models through workflow automation, personalized content, and deeper audience engagement (Belair-Gagnon & Steinke, 2020; Bodó, 2019; Broussard et al., 2019; Newman & Cherubini, 2025; Sirén-Heikel et al., 2023) are compromising the effectiveness of managerial decision-making as part of a generative AI news media innovation agenda, leading to potentially detrimental outcomes for news media.

This said, one might expect rich literature and ample empirical insights into the plethora of AI-induced factors influencing innovation in journalism and the news media domain. However, in our view, too little attention is given to the challenges these factors evoke for managerial decision-making from a media management perspective, particularly when stressing the importance of history as a salient historical factor for deciding about effective innovation paths and a future-fit AI news media innovation strategy, as they need to make the right managerial choices for change in a rational and thus historically conclusive manner.

Hence, the purpose of this study is twofold: First, it strives to improve our understanding of factors influencing generative AI innovation in news media by showing that "history matters" such that historical events are probably more likely to constitute an AI innovation path than more active strategic maneuvers of managers' appetite to innovate. To analyze this, we used Path Dependence Theory (henceforth PDT), a field which originated in historical and institutional economics, and especially in research on the evolution of technology, as a lens for studying the dynamics of organizational change and innovation in the news media domain, drawing from organizational path dependence literature (Dobusch & Kapeller, 2013; Dobusch & Schüßler, 2013; Koch, 2008, 2011; Rothmann & Koch, 2013; Schreyögg & Sydow, 2011; Sminia et al., 2024; Sydow et al., 2012, 2020).

We believe that reviewing these lineages of PDT is a useful exercise for answering questions surrounding the challenges that media managers are currently facing under the impact of AI-driven change, as well as the theoretical grounding PDT offers in understanding the breadth and complexity of these challenges, as it helps explain why news media can resist change over time and therefore fail to innovate, even when faced with new and potentially better approaches.

Second, in the empirical section, we aim to provide insights into AI-induced transformational change in newsroom management through a multi-case study analysis. For this, we conducted two waves of semi-structured interviews with media executives ($n = 10$) and academic experts ($n = 11$) in Austria from 2022 to 2025 (a list of interviewees is attached in the Appendix as Tables 14.2 and 14.3).

We study the impacts of innovation factors on the AI innovation path constitution across these 3 years. We asked two different groups of respondents—(1) news media executives ($n = 10$), including Austria's public service broadcasting corporation ORF, the country's national news media agency APA, managers of regional high-quality newspapers, and digital AI news media innovators; and (2) academic experts in the field (*n* = *11*)—questions about historical factors shaping and constraining AI innovation in the country. We further queried their perceptions on historical developments alongside four phases of path constitution practices (preformation, path creation, lock-in, and path release) and three consecutive path dependence mechanisms (historical events, critical juncture, and strategic action).

Therefore, we investigate the following research question: Which factors drive AI innovation in the news media and contribute to path dependence in innovation, and, if at all, does management have to break away from a chosen path and take strategic action in order to avoid any dismal dependence and thus inefficiency?

This chapter is structured as follows: in the following section, we review the PDT-related literature aligned to the field of AI news media and innovation management. In Sect. 14.3, we present the methodology, including the selected research strategy, data collection technique, and data procedure. In Sect. 14.4, we show the findings of our study. Following this, we discuss survey results by proposing a generative AI innovation strategy for breaking legacy paths (Sect. 14.5). Lastly, we present a conclusion and the implications of our research for research and practice (Sect. 14.6).

14.2 Path Dependence Theory

PDT originates in the historical studies by David (1985, 2001), who explored how an inferior and inefficient technological standard was established and is still maintained. Later, David (2007) argued that a chance decision or event can lock in an industry or technology on a particular path of subsequent development, whether that choice and path is in any sense the most desirable from an aggregate standpoint.

Analogously, Arthur (1989) found that path dependence is a property of "lock-in by historical events" (echoing the title of Arthur's influential paper), especially where those historical events are "insignificant" (i.e., they are probabilistic by nature, and happen incrementally, without much influence by managers). If such path dependence does occur, it means that marginal adjustments of individual agents may not offer the assurance of optimization or the revision of suboptimal outcomes. In turn, this implies that markets are failing. Although not all phenomena described as path dependence imply market failure, these normative concerns have been a prominent part of path dependence literature (Liebowitz & Margolis, 1995).

Path dependence describes how past decisions and events in the industry, such as initial choices in technology adoption, business models, or journalistic practices, constrain managerial choices by locking organizations into established ways of doing their business. Decision-makers may ultimately resist change because shifting to innovative systems would be too costly and burdensome (Garud et al., 2010; Garud & Karnøe, 2001; Sydow et al., 2009; Vergne & Durand, 2010).

14.2.1 Path Constitution Phases and News Media Applications

In what follows, we devise three emergent modes of path constitution (as part of path dependence) and one deliberate mode of path release as applied to AI innovation in news media. Hence, we distinguish between four consecutive phases of path development, whereby we integrate path release as a fourth phase. We thus follow Garud and Karnøe's notion of the importance of agency and institutional context (such as policy making) in defining organizational path innovation as part of an organizational-level strategy renewal process (Archambault Janvier et al., 2025; Fortwengel & Keller, 2020; Garud & Karnøe, 2001, 2003).

14.2.1.1 Phase I: Initial Conditions and Historical Events

In the first phase of path constitution (*preformation phase*), the range of strategic options is broad but simultaneously restricted by initial conditions. These initial conditions refer to the routines and practices, culture and competences, organizational structure, and resources that persist in an organization (Sydow et al., 2009). These are initially shaped by the founders, early employees, and the external conditions at the time of founding, and later by the emerging routines and institutions of the organization (Hannan & Freeman, 1984).

Thus, strategic choices do not start from scratch but "reflect, at least, partially, the rules and the culture making up the institution" (Schreyögg & Sydow, 2011, p. 324). In PDT, historical events are defined as those that set in motion a sequence of events or outcomes that shape future developments in difficult ways to reverse or deviate from. While initially contingent, these events create self-reinforcing mechanisms that lead to a specific outcome or path, making alternative outcomes less likely.

Although it is generally accepted that historical events are important in the emergence of a path-dependent process (Arthur, 1989; David, 1985), there are different perceptions on the influence of initial conditions and contingent historical events to create path dependence (Vergne & Durand, 2010, 2011).

Hence, in the news media, initial conditions determine how effectively news organizations can adopt AI tools and workflows. When newspapers build their business models around printed advertising and subscriptions, for example, they may struggle to switch to digital workflows due to reliance on legacy infrastructure, workflows, and revenue streams. Likewise, traditional news media that are (still) structured around editorial legacy workflows may face resistance to AI change from their journalists and workforce. Indeed, the launch of ChatGPT by OpenAI in November 2022 is such a contingent event, as it introduced generative AI as a potential new technology for news organizations. ChatGPT significantly impacted innovation in news media by accelerating automation, enhancing content creation, and reshaping audience engagement (Guzman & Lewis, 2024).

14.2.1.2 Phase II: Path Creation

The second phase (*path creation*) "commences with a critical juncture at the passage from Phase I to II," as Schreyögg and Sydow (2011, p. 324) state. A critical juncture occurs if a "decision made or an action taken in Phase I amounts to a trigger for the further development of the organization or an organizational subsystem" (Schreyögg & Sydow, 2011, p. 324). This suggests that, once news organizations have adopted specific technologies such as generative AI for specific use cases along their news value chains, these choices will set in motion their AI innovation path and determine, to some extent, their further trajectory.

During phase II, **self-reinforcing mechanisms**—which constitute any process of positive feedback and are often driven by increasing returns (Arthur, 1989)—will drive the formation of a dominant action pattern on an evolving innovation path and, thereby, reduce the range of possible strategic choices and actions even more (Schreyögg et al., 2003). The effects of these mechanisms as a cause for path dependence suggest that it is rational to follow that path, because the developed strategic pattern gains positive feedback. Thus, an innovation path implies both a successful strategic pattern, at least initially, and a diminished scope of strategic choice (Dobusch & Schüßler, 2013). Further self-reinforcing mechanisms in organizations involve coordination, complementarity, learning, and adaptive expectation effects (Dobusch & Schüßler, 2013; Schreyögg & Sydow, 2011). More specifically, the benefits of rule-guided behavior may lead to coordination effects, i.e., "the more actors adopt and apply a specific organizational rule or routine, the more efficient the interaction is among these actors" (Schreyögg & Sydow, 2011, p. 324). Coordination effects, however, make organizational rules and routines inflexible. Organizational inertia will follow.

In news organizations, ethical guidelines aimed at mitigating risks associated with AI use (Diakopoulos et al., 2024) relate to organizational rules shaping AI innovation and potentially reinforcing AI innovation paths. Complementarity, in turn, refers "to synergy resulting from the interaction of two or more separate but interrelated resources, rules or practices" (Schreyögg & Sydow, 2011, p. 324). This self-reinforcing mechanism occurs when "routines and/or practices are interconnected in such a way that it becomes ever more attractive to exploit the synergies" (Schreyögg & Sydow, 2011, pp. 324–325). In news organizations, editorial roles and routines, and the exploitation of legacy advertising and/or audience-based revenue models, may create complementarity effects, potentially constraining AI innovation paths. Learning effects occur as operations become more efficient with "decreasing average costs per unit of output" (Schreyögg & Sydow, 2011, p. 325), the more often they are performed. The adoption of AI in news organizations requires training of journalists and marketing specialists and IT or dedicated AI units depending on the use case along the news value chain. As acquiring new know-how or hiring specialists is costly, news organizations may be reluctant to shift their AI innovation path if such a shift will require a "switch to new learning sites" (Schreyögg & Sydow, 2011., p. 325). Furthermore, adaptive expectation effects occur due to the interactive building of preferences, i.e., the more customers prefer specific products or services, the more attractive they become (Schreyögg & Sydow, 2011). Such market constraints will also impact AI adoption in news organizations, as uncertain or lacking trust in and acceptance of AI-driven products and services among advertisers and audiences will hinder AI adoption in news organizations (Wilczek et al., 2021).

In sum, in addition to self-reinforcing mechanisms, defined as a regime of positive feedback loops constituting a specific pattern of social practices, which gains more and more predominance against alternatives, further factors may reinforce AI innovation paths in news organizations. For example, commitment effects occur when decision-makers allocate their resources to specific activities and, subsequently, are constrained "to pull out from the initial course of action" (Schreyögg & Sydow, 2011, p. 37). As AI technologies and the development and implementation of AI tools and products are (relatively) costly, initial investments in specific AI technologies and applications may reinforce AI innovation paths. There are further factors that may reinforce or constrain AI innovation paths. These refer to data availability as well as technical, cultural, and managerial challenges (Beckett & Yaseen, 2023) to the dependency on and the dominance of technology companies (Simon, 2024), and as well as to regulation (Helberger, 2024).

14.2.1.3 Phase III: Lock-In

As soon as the self-reinforcing mechanisms have crowded out all alternatives to a specific path, the organization enters a "lock-in," and the perception is that there are very few, if any, alternatives to this course of action (Schreyögg & Sydow, 2011). According to Vergne and Durand (2010), "lock-in characterizes a state of equilibrium with a very low potential for endogenous change" (p. 743). Thus, a specific technology, business model, or institutional practice becomes dominant, which can be difficult to shift away from, even if better alternatives emerge. This can both help and hinder innovation. Importantly, the limited option space does not necessarily negatively affect an organization's performance (Koch, 2011; Rothmann & Koch, 2013). Only when environmental changes (e.g., through the emergence of a novel technology or practice) lead to options outside the current path that an organization is locked into, path dependence poses a challenge (Schreyögg & Kliesch-Eberl, 2007).

In brief, a lock-in suggests that even if new AI technologies and applications emerge, which will open new and potentially better options to boost efficiency and revenues, news organizations that stick to their existing AI innovation path may, for instance, lock potentially inferior technologies in place, thereby possibly constraining AI innovation to the constitution of a technological path, while ignoring institutional practices and routines.

14.2.1.4 Phase IV: Unlocking and Path Release

However, lock-ins do not necessarily persist. Specific factors may enable decision-makers to overcome self-reinforcing mechanisms and further restrictions, thereby driving "unlocking" (Schreyögg et al., 2003, p. 277) of established innovation paths by taking strategic action. Individual, organizational, and contextual-level factors of innovation may enable such unlocking of an originally chosen path with the effect of ruling out that path and choosing a new one (Dobusch & Kapeller, 2013; Garud & Karnøe, 2001; Sminia et al., 2024).

News media often express a keen interest in leveraging the best of innovations on the market, improving the working lives of their editors and journalists, and enriching the experiences and products they can offer to audiences. If deemed necessary, news media follow specific trajectories of path dependence regarding innovation technologies and traditional organizational practices, such that it becomes possible to address issues of "structural inertia" (Hannan & Freeman, 1984) and "organizational resilience" toward change (Duschek, 2020) or even break away from dependence and reverse direction once some trajectory was followed to no avail (Sydow et al., 2009).

Still, as indicated above, deciding on the right innovation path is difficult. Cestino and Matthews (2016) examined why strategy innovation is difficult in regional news industry by examining the historic emergence, formation, and current lock-in of legacy regional newspapers. By integrating a knowledge-based view of a firm, path dependence theory and business model studies interpret the historic case of the provincial press in England to consider how, in an industrial context of relative simplicity and certainty, path-dependent formation processes are led by knowledge integration mechanisms. Rothmann and Koch (2013) analyzed how the key players in the quality-newspaper sector in Germany have tried to benefit from digitalization and why they have (mostly) failed so far. Using case study analysis, they found that, under specific conditions, organizations tend to use up all their creative potential to maintain problematic strategies rather than explore new ones (Rothmann, 2013). Wilczek (2019) found that managers of European legacy media are constantly striving to minimize their own complexity and uncertainty, which, in turn, drives change in their organization through different stages that are characterized by economization and integration or investment and specialization. Moreover, under lower external and internal complexity and uncertainty, managers are pushing news organizations toward more economization and integration. However, they invest and specialize if their external or internal complexity and uncertainty increase.

In sum, path dependence and a later path release consist of four phases (Fig. 14.1): (1) Phase I: *Preformation*, (2) Phase II: *Path creation*, (3) Phase III: *Lock-in*, and (4) Phase IV: *Unlocking and path release*. As indicated above, these phases are interlinked with several "causal mechanisms" (i.e., historical events, critical juncture, and strategic action) that link initial conditions with outcomes.

14.3 Methodology

Case study research is suitable when the scientific inquiry aims to investigate a contemporary phenomenon within its real-life context, especially when the boundaries between the context and phenomenon are not clear (Eisenhardt, 1989) and the relevant research domain and theories are in their early stages (Benbasat et al., 1987). Therefore, we conducted a multiple-case study analysis to examine factors of innovation that impact the constitution of path dependence in AI innovation of news media organizations in Austria.

We used the organization as unit of analysis to explain the dominant logic of path-dependent behavior in generative AI innovation, as well as specific cases of news media organizations to explore how AI innovation paths evolved and may

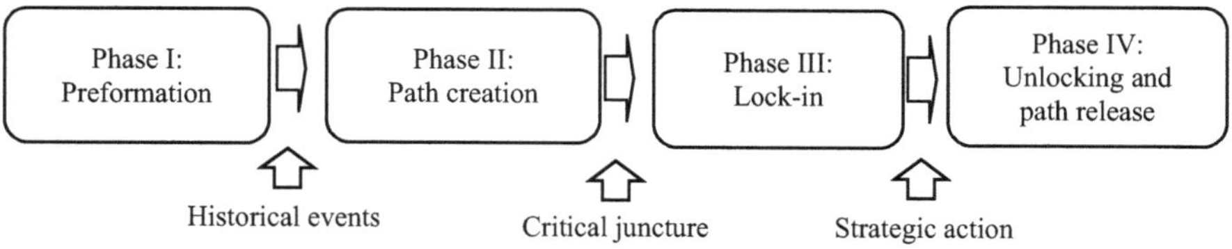

Fig. 14.1 Process model with path constitution phases (I–III) and release (IV) (Source: The authors)

eventually dissolve. Overall, the data collected enabled us to engage in a history-sensitive analysis of the processes of path dependence, and its logics and mechanisms toward path creation and later unwinding of the inscribed path-dependent pattern (Kipping & Üsdiken, 2014).

14.3.1 Sample

Data is drawn from two groups of respondents: (1) news media executives that included news media professionals at the managerial level, journalists, and technologists engaged in issues of AI innovation affiliated with these media; and (2) academic experts in the field analyzing issues of the digital transformation of news from their theoretical lenses. The selection of survey respondents aimed to cover a wide range of professional agents involved in the adoption and use of generative AI innovation research and practice within these media.

Austria was purposively selected as a case study country for the following reasons: First, the Austrian media market is characterized by several structural asymmetries that make it unique within the European context. Legacy media dominate the landscape, largely due to the de facto monopolies held by a few influential media organizations (Kaltenbrunner et al., 2024). Corporate-owned news media and media chains generally have greater financial resources to invest in AI (Simon, 2024). In these organizations, AI adoption and use are often driven by corporate priorities, such as enhancing operational efficiency and maximizing audience engagement across multiple outlets within the media network. Second, funding for AI technologies in Austrian media was recently introduced to support the digital transformation of newspapers and broadcasters, with a focus on workflow and newsroom automation, content moderation, and editorial processes (Kaltenbrunner & Luef, 2018). Additionally, AI tools for accessibility, such as automated transcription and subtitling, have been prioritized. While these initiatives may promote AI integration, challenges remain regarding resource distribution, particularly for digital-native media.

14.3.2 Data Collection

We collected various qualitative data from different sources. Following the example of previous case-based research on organizational path dependence (e.g., Koch, 2011; Wenzel, 2015), our main data source was a survey built on two questionnaires.[1] The survey design is particularly based on previous work by Sydow et al. (2009) to describe path dependencies. As such, the focus is on describing the identified causal mechanisms, such as historical events and initial conditions, lock-ins (i.e., economic, institutional, and technical), and strategic actions to overcome path dependence.

Executive managers were given a structured questionnaire containing a total of 22 questions. They were queried on their perception about current AI adoption and use in their newsrooms, with a focus on key factors influencing AI innovation (drivers and inhibitors) in their news media company, what goals were meant to be achieved, and what role specific features of path dependence played in overall innovation performance. They further had to answer questions related to the emergence and constitution of path dependence in their news media organization.

Academic experts had to answer 11 questions. They were queried about their impression of the factors that had contributed and were about to contribute the most to path dependence in AI. The experts were both asked about their perceptions of macro-environmental innovation drivers of industry change and ways to overcome them. All respondents provided informed consent for data collection and publication of the results before participating. An ethical review is not required because the data reported is not sensitive, and the study can generally be considered low risk.

14.3.3 Procedure

The questionnaires were sent out by email in two different time periods (Winter 2022 and Spring 2025) to the targeted respondents with personalized invitations. A total of 21 individuals completed the survey (Table 14.1).

In the first wave of data collection, the questionnaire was sent out to media executives in December 2022 to capture data on the emergence of path formation in a pre-ChatGPT era. In the first interview wave in 2022, all six media executives answered the invitation. In the second wave of collection in 2025, further questionnaires were sent out to media executives and academics to get hold of further insights on post-formation and lock-in practices in a post-ChatGPT era in February and March 2025. Another four media executives answered, supported by nine experts in the field. The sample selection process aimed to encompass a broad range of news media organizations involved in the adoption and use of AI innovation systems in practice. The 2022 sample included the Austrian Broadcasting Corporation

[1] The questionnaires used in this study are available on request from the corresponding author.

Table 14.1 Data collection method and data characteristics

Data collection method	Data characteristics		
	Date	Respondents	*N*
Qualitative survey I	December 2022	Media executives	$n = 6$
Qualitative survey I	February–March 2025	Media executives	$n = 4$
Qualitative survey II	February–March 2025	Academics	$n = 11$

(ORF), a private TV network, the country's news media agency APA, and a regional quality newspaper (*Kleine Zeitung*).

The 2025 sample was widened to include further regional newspapers, ad agencies, and AI innovators affiliated with the news media. The extended 2025 sample was recruited from the member network of experts participating in the *AI and the Media Industry* report (16 experts in total), published on behalf of Austria's Regulatory Authority for Broadcasting and Telecommunications (RTR) by Belinskaya et al. (2024). Further executives were added through personal contacts of the authors to key executive-rank news media professionals, news media journalists, as well as academic experts in the country.

14.4 Results

In the following section, the results of our study are presented alongside four phases of path constitution practices (i.e., preformation, path creation, lock-in, and path release) and three path dependence mechanisms (i.e., historical events, critical juncture, and strategic action). The respondents' initials are used to identify individual answers.

14.4.1 Phase I: Initial Conditions and Historical Events

Most survey respondents in both survey periods were not too consciously aware of the role and importance history plays in determining a specific innovation path. While the importance of audience data in understanding user needs and informing innovation strategies was acknowledged (FS), skepticism was expressed about the practical impact due to its lack of applicability. While conclusive data can support innovative projects, deriving actionable insights was considered complex and time-consuming. As a result, data were more frequently utilized in the daily newspaper domain "for optimizing and analyzing existing products or as a controlling instrument (KPIs, Business Intelligence)" (JD). Contrastingly, the respondent from the private broadcaster stated that data does not play a significant role in fostering innovation paths at all (ML).

Several historical events in the Austrian news media industry have prompted changes or shifts regarding AI adoption. For example, extensive reporting demanded during the COVID-19 pandemic led to the formation of new newsroom teams and the use of algorithms for data-driven reporting (CH). Similarly, the need for content recommendation, subscription models, and networking initiatives with other local media outlets in the German-speaking region, which facilitated knowledge transfer (JD), had influenced the adoption of AI. However, due to past factors, the process of AI implementation was not linear.

When media executives were asked in 2025 about their perceptions of what factors initially had set in motion a genuine AI innovation path in their organization, one practitioner mentioned that her media organization

> (...) has always been at the forefront of technological innovation and was the first media company to really embrace AI in Austria. While AI initiatives accelerated after the release of ChatGPT in November 2022, the company had already been integrating AI into editorial workflows, automation, and content strategies well before that. (IR)

Another executive stressed that no particular triggering event was needed to initiate the AI innovation journey (FJG). Rather, critically observing market developments and then deciding about the right moment to go live are crucial:

> Being a late adopter has been an advantage. We avoid many early mistakes made by others and benefit from significantly improved models. Our cautious approach has not put us at a disadvantage. (FJG)

And further

> The first time we successfully ran the pipeline from CMS through middleware to the LLM and back into production. That moment sparked many new ideas for future applications. (FJG)

In sum, the respondents highlight that AI innovation in Austrian media organizations is shaped by initial conditions (e.g., access to audience data), which was seen as more useful for optimizing existing products than driving innovation. While respondents often lacked awareness of history's role in shaping path dependency, events like the COVID-19 pandemic and cross-media collaborations undoubtedly influenced AI adoption. Ultimately, organizations differed in approach, with some being early adopters, and many others saw advantages in adopting AI later to avoid early pitfalls.

14.4.2 Phase II: Path Creation

When interviewed in 2022, several executives highlighted critical junctures in the innovation development process within their news media organization. However, by then, newsroom staff and data scientists were caught in a struggle between the conflicting demands of print and online media. As noted by a respondent:

> Print demands are getting defended until the last breath by (most) senior managers because, in their opinion, it is the better way to do journalism, and online media is more of a necessary evil. (JD)

Another critical juncture happens when an innovation project transitions from a temporary initiative to a standard business process (ML). This shift is important for the innovation process as it marks the point at which innovation was integrated into the media organization's ongoing workflow.

Regarding factors that lead the media organizations to choose one specific innovation path over another, existing research and development in the field of machine learning, as well as strong ethical values, were mentioned (KS).

Respondents further stressed the presence of positive feedback loops that reinforce existing practices and technologies. For example, print technologies and processes have been deeply ingrained in the organization for decades, a process which has led to a lock-in effect on print remaining the dominant focus of resources and innovation. Moreover, it was noted that

> [a]s long as print subscribers offer a better revenue stream than digital, resources will go to print; for example, weekend issues in print are growing extensively at the moment. (JD)

An agile working approach was also highlighted as a crucial factor in path creation. At least in theory, such organizational flexibility enables rapid experimentation with innovation in response to shifting audience needs (JD, MB). However, one respondent working for a private TV broadcaster stated that path dependence did not impact other strategic objectives (e.g., product development, organizational growth, or competition strategies) except for audience reach data (ML).

Path dependence in the media industry also led to a reliance on established business models, as was asserted:

> Media, in general, tend to make more of the same if something works, but less when it comes to news. (ML)

Lastly, data analysis and integration challenges hinder innovation as media companies struggle to leverage data-driven insights effectively (ML).

When interviewed in 2025, one practitioner stressed the challenge of "gaining acceptance within the team, especially with traditional journalistic working methods" (CN), suggesting that decision-makers at the executive level would rather stick to technological innovation paths. Therefore, a culture of innovation in news media organizations would be necessary, while market and customer needs would mainly drive innovation as well (KS).

The scholarly experts stressed the prevalence of ad-based revenue models shaping path dependencies, as content is increasingly optimized for advertising performance rather than journalistic or public interest values (RP, MK, GK, MG). This is further reinforced by algorithm-driven audience engagement (JL, ML, RP, MK, MG, CM, KS). Lastly, the concentration of cloud infrastructure within a few major organizations, alongside vertical integration strategies, strengthened the reliance on specific AI ecosystems, reducing flexibility and increasing dependency on existing technologies (JK).

Additionally, the standardization of AI tools and platforms further created path dependence, as widely adopted frameworks and software ecosystems encourage homogeneity in AI applications and discourage deviation from off-the-shelf solutions (JK, ML, RP, MK). Intellectual property laws and patents also played a significant role in path dependencies regarding AI innovation, as proprietary rights over such technologies create barriers to entry for new players and limit the open exchange of ideas necessary for diverse AI advancements (JK, RP, MK, CM, KS). Furthermore, government funding and policies contributed to path dependencies if not geared toward AI innovation funding (RP, MK, GK, CM).

Four respondents also mentioned public perception and societal trust in AI as influencing factors (MK, CM, JL, KS). Only four respondents stated that regulatory policies had little effect on AI innovation paths (MG, JL, MK, KS), with two respondents even concluding that they actively disrupted existing trends and fostered new paths (GT, JL).

Overall, there is a tension between news media organizations favoring print due to revenue dependence and emerging digital practices. As such, path dependencies are created by longstanding workflows and the standardization of AI tools, which limit flexibility and favor established technologies. Agile methods offer potential for innovation but (often) face organizational resistance, particularly from journalism staff. External factors like market needs, public trust in AI, and cloud infrastructure concentration also influence innovation paths, while regulatory impacts remain mixed.

14.4.3 Phase III: Lock-In

When media executives were asked in 2022 about the most important lock-in mechanisms during the formation of an innovation path, the fear of job losses emerged as a significant factor, as employees viewed innovation as a threat rather than an opportunity for growth (JD, SP).

However, while most respondents surprisingly did not experience any lock-in effects related to technology or organizational routine in practice, one respondent from the daily newspaper sector described the persistence of print-centric planning and formatting practices. (JD) This finding suggests that editorial decisions regarding length, layout, and content formats continue to be shaped by traditional print conventions, often without data-driven justification. Additionally, the organization of daily workflows (e.g., meeting schedules, deadlines, and topic selection) and editorial structures remained heavily focused on the needs of print production (CH), reinforcing habitual decision-making patterns that may slow down innovation.

At the same time, a lack of management competence, in which leadership fails to implement an effective innovation strategy, constituted another potential lock-in mechanism. Such a lack of managerial support for innovation would leave organizations petrified (JD, SP).

One further important lock-in feature was identified as originating on the market level, such as insufficient funding, declining political support for news media, and diminishing audience trust, which would divert resources away from innovation and place media organizations under significant financial and regulatory pressure (JD, SP, ML). A lack of financial resources further exacerbated these difficulties, limiting investment in new technologies and experimentation (SP, CH).

Interviews with scholarly experts found that several key factors contribute to lock-ins in AI development. Past organizational investments in AI are a significant mechanism, it was alleged, shaping the current adoption of AI in the news media, as most innovations follow past trends (RP, GT, JL), although new trends continue to emerge and drive innovation in unexpected directions (ML, MK, GK, CM). Only one respondent stated that current AI development is primarily independent of such investments (MG).

Moreover, the dominance of big platforms (e.g., Alphabet and Meta) and the overall media market structure played a crucial role (JK, ML, RP, MK, GK, MG, GT, CM, JL, MZ, KS). Such market conditions led to a self-reinforcing cycle in which smaller competitors struggle to challenge established players as they have created an ecosystem where AI tools and platforms were primarily controlled by a few influential players (JK, ML, RP, MK, MG), and high costs of alternative AI models create lock-ins (RP, MK, MG, CM).

Regarding lock-ins with technology or organizational routines in the context of AI adoption, the practitioners stated that they had not experienced any of those (IR, KS). However, surprisingly, self-reinforcing mechanisms constituted a specific pattern of practice:

> Yes, we experienced positive feedback loops in AI innovation, where specific choices have reinforced their own success and led to increasing returns. […] The more data it processes, the more accurate and useful it becomes, reinforcing its role in editorial workflows. (IR)

In the 2025 cohort, most scholarly experts interviewed agreed that lock-ins would significantly constrain future AI developments and innovation adoption in news media organizations (GK, MK, RP, ML, JK, MG, GT, CM).

However, from the point of view of one respondent,

> path dependence in AI is not inherently detrimental; in some contexts, it provides much-needed stability and accountability. However, the real challenge lies in discerning between productive continuity and innovation-inhibiting lock-in—a distinction that future AI research and policy must rigorously address. (MK)

Another respondent stated that lock-ins would inevitably constrain innovation,

> but in the long run, it will not hold up things, just a minor delay behind open models. Open innovation, like the science model, is ultimately superior to confidential/secret organization-internal proprietary R&D, [as it] do[s] not significantly constrain future AI development. (JL)

When asked about the strongest lock-in factor currently shaping AI innovation in Austria, the respondents first mentioned regulatory and ethical constraints, which can slow down AI adoption in sensitive areas such as data privacy and algorithmic decision-making (JK). Second, data availability and the reliance on large datasets were described as substantial challenges (ML, RP, MK, MG, GT, CM, JL, MK, KS). Since AI often requires vast training data, access limitations can hinder innovation for smaller media organizations that lack resources. Third, a dependency on specific technological infrastructure (e.g., reliance on 3D graphics technology) (ML, MG, GT, CM) and technologies (i.e., AI models and programming languages) (RP; MK, GK, GT, MZ, KS) contributed to technological lock-ins. One respondent also mentioned a "risk-averse European mindset" (JL), which relates to a "lack of ambition" and "parents instilling in their children the wish for 'safe' jobs, which do not exist anyway." (JL).

Regarding the experience of any lock-ins, one respondent stated:

> Yes. Our legacy subscription management software created a technological lock-in that required a long and expensive project to overcome. (FJG)

Moreover, path dependence has had an impact on other strategic objectives:

> Yes. We selected our new subscription and paywall system in part because it provides easy access to raw data, enabling data analysis and future automation—something not possible with the previous system. (FJG)

In summary, there are several key lock-in mechanisms that constrain AI innovation. Especially organizational inertia, such as print-centric routines or managerial reluctance to embrace change and market-level factors (e.g., limited funding, declining political support, and audience trust) relate to lock-ins. Technological lock-ins arise from prior investments, dependency on platform companies (e.g., Alphabet, Meta), and reliance on proprietary infrastructure, data, or software. While some respondents noted positive feedback loops that reinforce innovation success, most experts agreed that lock-ins would significantly constrain future developments. However, some respondents argued these constraints might provide stability or only cause minor delays, especially when open innovation models are embraced. Finally, regulatory constraints, data access issues, and risk-averse culture were also named as lock-in factors.

14.4.4 Phase IV: Unlocking and Path Release

Path dependence in news media can limit innovation, especially regarding AI adoption and integration toward digital transformation, and new business models. However, practitioners from the Austrian media testified to historical practices to break free from restrictive legacy systems and adapt to the changing landscape.

At the individual level, some stressed that fostering an environment where new ideas for applications can be pitched and discussed openly among individual team members and managerial staff had been stressed as important by the respondents to unlock established innovation paths (FS, JD). Other respondents mentioned the necessity of an open mindset in journalistic teams and individual journalists to drive innovation in news media and integrate technological advancements in their daily working processes as particularly relevant (IR, FJG). One respondent stated that:

> Many journalists try AI on their own because of personal interest or because they believe in the advantage. We had a couple of trainings, but to be honest, it is not a structured path. Some do, others don't. (CN)

Furthermore, the perception of one's job role within a news organization is important:

> Being editor-in-chief, I have to trigger discussion in AI, sort out what's reasonable and makes sense, get projects on the road, and monitor the process. (CN)

At the organizational level, the findings suggest that structural and cultural factors play the most critical role in unlocking established innovation paths. Several respondents stated that a strong culture of innovation is needed, and managerial strategies and implementation of innovation need to be aligned (FS, CH, IR). Within private broadcasting, "new technologies in combination with a desire for innovation within the company" (ML) were identified as primary catalysts. In this regard, data teams were described as particularly relevant in newspaper organizations. There, it was said they would serve as central hubs for innovation at the crossroads between customer marketing, the advertising department, and the newsrooms (JD).

One practitioner respondent mentioned a strong culture of innovation as a prerequisite to de-locking established innovation paths in the news media organization (IR). The process would be supported by decentralized decision-making and nonhierarchical organizational structures, which enable greater flexibility in adopting and implementing new technologies (IR).

Another important aspect was found in the role that the institutional context played in unlocking established innovation paths. While the respondent from the news magazine stated that the Austrian media environment is resistant to innovation—characterized by regulatory constraints and an industry culture that is not conducive to technological change (FS)—other respondents highlighted the importance of external pressures. It was confirmed that the hybrid media system necessitated integrating digital and print content management systems to unlock innovation paths to stay competitive in both business-to-business (B2B) and business-to-consumer (B2C) markets (JD). While regulatory frameworks can facilitate or hinder innovation depending on the degree of policy support for digital transformation, competitive market dynamics would push innovation in response to shifts in consumer behavior and media consumption trends (JD).

One practitioner confirmed that his news media organization was

> able to gain a strategic boost with an ongoing participation in the AI Launchpad of the Google News Initiative, run by the Financial Times. This enabled ideas, experiments, and innovations to be structured and the AI roadmap to be fleshed out. (CN)

Unlocking established innovation paths is further driven by both strategic initiatives and competitive pressures:

> Primarily contextual factors, especially competitive pressure. Due to economic constraints in the media industry, we focus on maintaining lean processes and structures to stay competitive. Innovation is a necessity rather than a luxury. (FJG)

One respondent noted that his news media organization was

> able to gain a strategic boost with an ongoing participation in the AI Launchpad of the Google News Initiative, run by the Financial Times. This enabled ideas, experiments, and innovations to be structured and the AI roadmap to be fleshed out. (CN)

When interviewed, scholarly experts, by and large, found breaking AI's path dependence as being a desirable feature:

> It is extremely important to quickly break through the current paths here, [as] the US and China now see AI as the new geopolitical wonder weapons and in the EU, we watch in surprise and are primarily concerned with regulation [...]. (GK)

> Overcoming path dependence in AI development is not only desirable but imperative from both an innovation economics and democratic theory standpoint. Technological lock-in—especially when reinforced by the dominance of specific market actors or standardized architectures (e.g., transformer models)—risks narrowing the space for innovation and concentrating power in ways that may perpetuate social biases. (MK)

> It is important as long as path dependence leads to lock-in effects with undesirable economic and societal consequences like monopolization tendencies, lacking AI competencies by consumers or entanglement of political power and enterprise power. (RP)

> If it helps to avoid being dependent on one or a very small number of suppliers, it definitely is. (GT)

Some scholars have highlighted strategies that could break AI's path dependence. First and foremost, the need for flexible regulatory policies would encourage experimentation with AI (JK, GK, CM, JL, KS), and cross-disciplinary AI research that combines AI with ethics and social sciences would stimulate its further development (GT, KS). For example, one respondent stated:

> AI should be developed with a strong ethical foundation. Aligning future progress with both established and emerging values—not just economic priorities—could provide a more sustainable and socially responsible path forward. (KS)

Another scholar emphasized the necessity of an ethically and legally secure framework to incentivize innovation, particularly in the media industry (ML, MK). Contrary to the argument that regulation stifled innovation, it was voiced that well-designed policies limiting AI monopolization in media can enhance entrepreneurial freedoms (ML, JL).

Additionally, there would be a strong call to prioritize European start-ups and firms to become "independent of developments in Asia and America" (ML), with "stricter usage limitations for non-European AI" (MZ). Moreover, established "AI Innovation Sandboxes" were mentioned. These would establish

> regulated experimental environments where novel models, data frameworks, and algorithmic methods can be tested without immediate full-scale compliance burdens. Similar to fintech sandboxes, these structured spaces enable risk-adjusted innovation, particularly for smaller enterprises and academic researchers. (MK).

At the same time, there is also a need for targeted (government) innovation funds to support AI adoption or tax incentives for venture capital for investments in tech start-ups (GK, MG, GT, CM, MZ, KS), which also relates to open-source AI development (ML, GT, CM, MZ, KS). Against this background, one respondent stated:

> When young start-ups or research groups gain access to resources and markets, the AI landscape can become more diversified and break established paths. (RP).

Additionally, policy or industry intervention can be effective in fostering more innovation in AI:

> Finally put an end to old solutions such as infrastructure investment only and increasingly transition from national states to awarding contracts to tech startups so that local, national and EU further players can emerge. (GK)

> Giving innovative companies an ethically and legally secured framework they can evolve in; reaching an agreement that regulation often enhances entrepreneurial freedoms instead of limiting them; focusing on European start-ups and firms, independent of developments in Asia and America. (RP)

> Clear legal regulations that both set limits and offer opportunities. (CM)

> The single best thing that the European Union can do is to provide special legal exemptions from copyright law, taxation, reporting duties and compliance for startups created in its jurisdictions that are less than 4 years old or earn less than € 250 k/year. (JL)

Overall, there are several factors regarding overcoming path dependencies. At the individual level, the respondents mentioned open-mindedness, decentralized decision-making, and informal experimentation by journalists. At the organizational level, a strong innovation culture, cross-departmental collaboration (e.g., involving data teams), and agile structures are essential enablers. External factors such as regulatory environments, market pressures, and participation in international initiatives (e.g., Google News Initiative) also play a key role in unlocking innovation paths. Scholars emphasized that breaking path dependence in AI is imperative to avoid lock-in effects and monopolization. They advocate flexible regulations and funding mechanisms with more support for open-source AI.

14.5 Discussion

In the present context, path dependence theory has emerged as a promising combination of two contrasting perspectives on technological innovation: path dependence, which focuses on historically embedded, contingent processes that are beyond the control of actors, and path creation or constitution, which emphasizes mindful contributions from powerful actors.

Certainly, path dependence may occur on all levels of strategizing innovation in a news media organization, and, when aligned to issues of AI, is brought about by a complex interplay of technologies, innovation management actions, and industrial and institutional structures, as well as social and cultural norms that shape and are shaped by innovation (Füller et al., 2024; Haefner et al., 2021). Still, decision-makers may stick to previous habits, decisions, and historically successful strategies rather than adopt present circumstances, even when better alternatives are available. This may prove a more cost-effective, less difficult, and hazardous historical approach to achieve similar outcomes as in the past. But while path dependence tends to reinforce existing trajectories, innovation can sometimes break free from established paths through radical technological shifts, paradigm changes, or external disruptions. Hence, news media managers may well consider proposing AI innovation as a strategy for breaking legacy paths by aligning it with core business objectives, yet fostering a culture of experimentation, and leveraging emerging technologies to disrupt traditional paradigms.

In his study of the strategic development of news media organizations in the market of national dailies that produce high-quality newspapers in Germany, Koch (2008) developed the concept of a "strategic path" and looked to the strategic trajectory of incumbent firms coping with path dependence and thus with a diminished range of strategic variety and choice. Koch argued that an organization's ability to act strategically under conditions of path dependence relies not only on the form of a developed strategic path but also on how this path is inscribed in an organization. Consequently, while historical events may by chance force organizations to follow a specific technological trajectory or stimulate organizational innovation from outside of the "organizational body," management may also identify and use paths that do not only depend on their history but also are reproduced, shaped, and created by human action (Brenner & zu Jeddeloh, 2023).

Again, while path dependence emphasizes the role of history and context, path creation in contrast emphasizes the active role of purposeful agency to ignite a manager's appetite to constitute a genuine, thus path-independent AI innovation strategy (Meyer & Schubert, 2007). Arguably, PDT helps explain some salient mechanisms for developing a genuine innovation path as part of an organizational strategy to safeguard organizational viability in the long run.

14.6 Conclusion

Research on AI increased with the dawn of generative AI in November 2022. However, while previous research has devoted considerable attention to how news organizations are using AI technologies along their news value chains, the drivers and barriers to AI innovation in journalism are underexplored. Therefore, the multi-case study of Austria retrieved what factors drive or constrain AI innovation in Austrian news organizations. More specifically, the core research question was: Which factors determine a news media's path dependence on AI innovation and, if at all, does management have to break away from a chosen path and take strategic action? To answer this, we conducted a small-scale survey with two types of respondents in 2022 and 2025 (2022: six executives; 2025: four executives; eleven academic experts).

Given the findings of our study, we can reasonably conclude the following: First, we found that AI innovation in the news media industry remains an ambiguous concept and overambitious practice. AI innovation may raise opportunities for competitive advantage, but also leverage the complexity of challenges for journalists and newsroom management.

More specifically, respondents revealed that AI innovation in news media path dependence is biased toward organizational stability and "structural inertia" (Schwarz, 2010). While established practices ensure consistency and credibility, thus stability, they also make it harder for news organizations to rapidly adapt to AI systems transformation, audience behavior changes, and new revenue models, thus unwanted inertia. The challenge is balancing tradition with innovation to remain relevant in a shifting media landscape.

Second, the investigation also indicates that executives preferred individualizing innovative paths to mindfully breaking away from an existing path. Strategizing on AI innovation ensured its successful adoption and integration into business (Brekke et al., 2024; Garud & Karnøe, 2001). History mattered, but the actors also shaped it actively. Case study evidence, however, revealed that such an effective AI innovation strategy is hard to come by. Identifying the right AI innovation path is tricky because of a plethora of factors that drive or inhibit AI innovation performance (rapidly evolving technology, unclear business impact, needs for organizational restructuring, data challenges, ethical and regulatory concerns, expertise gaps and workforce challenges, integration within existing value propositions and chains, etc.) To find out why and how the integration of AI innovation into an effective AI innovation strategy affects the path-dependent behavior of news media organizations, investigating the evolution of innovation models in the news media domain is a valuable context, as PDT validly explains how specific mechanisms constrain and potentially enable innovation during different phases—from preformation to formation and lock-in and later potential unlocking (Schreyögg et al., 2003). This makes PDT particularly useful to examine factors that shape AI innovation in news organizations over time.

Third, AI is reshaping the news media landscape, offering unprecedented opportunities for innovation and growth. From automating content creation to enhancing audience engagement, AI serves as a powerful tool for media organizations. However, its adoption also demands careful consideration of ethical and societal implications. As AI technology continues to evolve, future research should explore ways to balance the benefits of AI with potential risks, ensuring a sustainable and equitable media ecosystem.

And finally, of course, this study has one central limitation. While the empirical case for AI innovation is rough and ready, the persuasive parts are qualitative rather than rigorous and quantitative. Simply, evidencing contingencies of the emerging AI innovation ecosystem in Austria is still confined to qualitative evidence rather than rigorous academic inquiry. Although the strategic choices for an AI innovation strategy that were identified revealed some metaphoric quality, they nonetheless remained qualitative and, hence, laden with a great deal of uncertainty as to the general outcome of AI innovation in news media as such. More research that improves the validity of analysis by generating testable hypotheses is needed. This would imply establishing a conceptual model that postulates impacts between the technological, economic, and contextual determinants of AI innovation. Essentially, a more nuanced investigation needs to be made into the multilevel impacts of AI innovation in news media, since path dependence can become critical for overall business success.

Appendix: List of Interviewees (Tables 14.2 and 14.3)

Table 14.2 Overview of Executive Managers and Journalists

ID	Name	Position	Organization	Country
CH	Christian Haslacher	Journalist	Austrian Press Agency (APA)	Austria
CN	Christian Nusser	Editor-in-Chief	Newsflix	Austria
FJG	Florian Jungnikl-Gossy	Chief Product Officer	Falter Media Group	Austria
FS	Florian Skrabal	Editor-in-Chief	Dossier	Austria
IR	Isabel Russ	Managing Director	Vorarlberger Nachrichten	Austria
JD	Judith Denkmayr	Content Performance and Digital Strategy Manager	Kleine Zeitung	Austria
KS	Katharina Schell	Deputy Editor-in-Chief	Austria Press Agency (APA)	Austria
MB	Michael Brottrager	Head of Data	Kleine Zeitung	Austria
ML	Mario Lenz	CEO Newsroom, Sports & Production	Puls 4 TV	Austria
SP	Stefan Pollach	Head of Digital Media	Österreichischer Rundfunk (ORF)	Austria

Note. $n = 10$

Table 14.3 Overview of academic experts

ID	Name	Position	Organization	Country
CM	Christoph Moss	Professor of Digital Marketing	International School of Management	Germany
GK	Gerhard Kürner	Chief Executive Officer	506.ai	Austria
GT	Georg Thallinger	Research Manager	Joanneum Research	Austria
JK	Jan Krone	Professor of Media Business and Ethics	St. Pölten University of Applied Sciences	Austria
JL	Jochen Leidner	Professor of Explainable and Responsible Artificial Intelligence in Insurance	Coburg University of Applied Sciences and Arts	Germany
KS	Konstantin Schätz	Postdoctoral Researcher	University of Salzburg	Austria
MG	Michael Graßl	Interim Professor of Journalism & Digital Innovation	Magdeburg-Stendal University of Applied Sciences	Germany
MK	Manuela Klauser	Chief Executive Officer	Creative Agency voller Ideen	Austria
ML	Michael Litschka	Professor of Media Business and Ethics	St. Pölten University of Applied Sciences	Austria
MZ	Matthias Zeppelzauer	Professor for Computer Vision, Multimedia Retrieval, and Machine Learning	St. Pölten University of Applied Sciences	Austria
RP	Robert Pinzolits	Professor of Information Technology	University of Applied Sciences Burgenland	Austria

Note. $n = 11$

References

Archambault Janvier, C., Van Lent, W., & Sydow, J. (2025). Breaking organizational paths for strategic renewal: Towards a dialectical perspective. Long Range Planning, 58(4), Article No. 102560. https://doi.org/10.1016/j.lrp.2025.102560

Arthur, W. B. (1989). Competing technologies, increasing returns, and lock-in by historical events. *The Economic Journal, 99*(394), 116–131. https://doi.org/10.2307/2234208

Beckett, C., & Yaseen, M. (2023). *Generating change: A global survey of what news organisations are doing with AI*. London School of Economics and Political Science.

Belair-Gagnon, V., & Steinke, A. J. (2020). Capturing digital news innovation research in organizations, 1990–2018. *Journalism Studies, 21*(12), 1724–1743. https://doi.org/10.1080/1461670X.2020.1789496

Belinskaya, Y., Krone, J., Litschka, M., Roither, M., & Pinzolits, R. (2024). Künstliche Intelligenz in der Medienwirtschaft. *Rundfunk und Telekom Regulierungsbehörde*. https://www.rtr.at/medien/aktuelles/publikationen/Publikationen/Studie_KI_Medienwirtschaft_2024.pdf

Benbasat, I., Goldstein, D. K., & Mead, M. (1987). The case research strategy in studies of information systems. *MIS Quarterly, 11*(3), 369–386. https://doi.org/10.2307/248684

Bodó, B. (2019). Selling news to audiences: A qualitative inquiry into the emerging logics of algorithmic news personalization in European quality news media. *Digital Journalism, 7*(8), 1054–1075. https://doi.org/10.1080/21670811.2019.1624185

Brekke, T., Lenka, S., Kohtamäki, M., Parida, V., & Apenes Solem, B. A. (2024). Overcoming barriers to transformation in manufacturing firms: A path-dependence perspective of digital servitization. *Review of Managerial Science, 18*, 385–412. https://doi.org/10.1007/s11846-023-00641-0

Brenner, T., & zu Jeddeloh, S. (2023). Path dependence in an evolving system: A modeling perspective. *Cliometrica, 18*, 1–36. https://doi.org/10.1007/s11698-023-00266-z

Broussard, M., Diakopoulos, N., Guzman, A. L., Abebe, R., Dupagne, M., & Chuan, C.-H. (2019). Artificial intelligence and journalism. *Journalism & Mass Communication Quarterly, 96*(3), 673–695. https://doi.org/10.1177/1077699019859901

Cestino, J., & Matthews, R. (2016). A perspective on path dependence processes: The role of knowledge integration in business model persistence dynamics in the provincial press in England. *Journal of Media Business Studies, 13*(1), 22–44. https://doi.org/10.1080/16522354.2015.1133785

Chan-Olmsted, S. M. (2019). A review of artificial intelligence adoptions in the media industry. *International Journal on Media Management, 21*(3–4), 193–215. https://doi.org/10.1080/14241277.2019.1695619

Cools, H., & Diakopoulos, N. (in press). Uses of generative AI in the newsroom: Mapping journalists' perceptions of perils and possibilities. *Journalism Practice*. https://doi.org/10.1080/17512786.2024.2394558

David, P. A. (1985). Clio and the economics of QWERTY. *The American Economic Review, 75*(2), 332–337. https://www.jstor.org/stable/1805621

David, P. A. (2001). Path dependence, its critics and the quest for "historical economics". In P. Garrouste (Ed.), *Evolution and path dependence in economic ideas: Past and present* (pp. 15–40). Edgar Elgar.

David, P. A. (2007). Path dependence: A foundational concept for historical social science. *Cliometrica, 1*(2), 91–114.

Diakopoulos, N., Cools, H., Li, C., Helberger, N., Kung, E., & Rinehart, A. (2024). Generative AI in journalism: The evolution of newswork and ethics in a generative information ecosystem. *The Associated Press*. https://doi.org/10.13140/RG.2.2.31540.05765

Dobusch, L., & Kapeller, J. (2013). Breaking new paths: Theory and method in path dependence research. *Schmalenbach Business Review, 65*, 288–311. https://doi.org/10.1007/BF03396859

Dobusch, L., & Schüßler, E. (2013). Theorizing path dependence: A review of positive feedback mechanisms in technology markets, regional clusters, and organizations. *Industrial and Corporate Change, 22*(3), 617–647. https://doi.org/10.1093/icc/dts029

Dodds, T., Zamith, R., & Lewis, S. C. (in press). The AI turn in journalism: Disruption, adaptation, and democratic futures. *Journalism*. https://doi.org/10.1177/14648849251343518

Duschek, S. (2020). Organizational resilience: A capability-based conceptualization. *Business Research, 13*, 215–246. https://doi.org/10.1007/s40685-019-0085-7

Eisenhardt, K. M. (1989). Building theories from case study research. *Academy of Management Review, 14*(4), 532–550. https://doi.org/10.2307/258557

Fortwengel, J., & Keller, A. (2020). Agency in the face of path dependence: How organizations can regain scope for maneuver. *Business Research, 13*, 1169–1201. https://doi.org/10.1007/s40685-020-00118-w

Füller, J., Tekic, Z., & Hutter, K. (2024). Rethinking innovation management: How AI is changing the way we innovate. *The Journal of Applied Behavioral Science, 60*(4), 603–612. https://doi.org/10.1177/00218863241287323

Garud, R., & Karnøe, P. (2001). Path creation as a process of mindful deviation. In R. Garud & P. Karnøe (Eds.), *Path dependence and creation* (pp. 1–38). Lawrence Erlbaum Associates.

Garud, R., & Karnøe, P. (2003). Bricolage versus breakthrough: Distributed and embedded agency in technology entrepreneurship. *Research Policy, 32*(2), 277–300. https://doi.org/10.1016/S0048-7333(02)00100-2.

Garud, R., Kumaraswamy, A., & Karnoe, P. (2010). Path dependence or path creation. *Journal of Management Studies, 47*(4), 760–774. https://doi.org/10.1111/j.1467-6486.2009.00914.x

Grimme, M., & Zabel, C. (2024). AI in the newsroom: A collective case study about newsworker-AI collaboration in the German newspaper industry. *Journal of Media Business Studies, 22*(2), 118–142. https://doi.org/10.1080/16522354.2024.2380120

Guzman, A. L., & Lewis, S. (2024). What generative AI means for the media industries, and why it matters to study the collective consequences for advertising, journalism, and public relations. *Emerging Media, 2*(3), 347–355. https://doi.org/10.1177/27523543241289239

Haefner, N., Wincent, J., Parida, V., & Gassmann, O. (2021). Artificial intelligence and innovation management: A review, framework, and research agenda. *Technological Forecasting and Social Change, 162*, Article No. 120392. https://doi.org/10.1016/j.techfore.2020.120392

Hannan, M. T., & Freeman, J. (1984). Structural inertia and organizational change. *American Sociological Review, 49*(2), 149–164. https://doi.org/10.2307/2095567

Helberger, N. (2024). FutureNewsCorp, or how the AI Act changed the future of news. *Computer Law & Security Review, 52*, Article No. 105915. https://doi.org/10.1016/j.clsr.2023.105915

Kaltenbrunner, A., & Luef, S. (2018). Heimvorteil? Digitale Transition im Lokaljournalismus. Ausgewählte Ergebnisse der Studie zu Arbeitsbedingungen und digitalen Veränderungen in Österreichs Regionaljournalismus. *Medienhaus Wien*. https://www.mhw.at/uploads/1/4/5/2/145228725/heimvorteil_-_____digitale_transition_____im_lokaljournalismus.pdf

Kaltenbrunner, A., Lugschitz, R., & Karmasin, M. (2024). Country report Austria: Difficult departure from the comfort zone. In K. Meier, J. A. García-Avilés, A. Kaltenbrunner, C. Porlezza, V. Wyss, R. Lugschitz, & K. Klinghardt (Eds.), *Innovations in journalism: Comparative research in five European countries* (pp. 37–48). Routledge.

Kipping, M., & Üsdiken, B. (2014). History in organization and management theory: More than meets the eye. *The Academy of Management Annals, 8*(1), 535–588. https://doi.org/10.5465/19416520.2014.911579

Koch, J. (2008). Strategic paths and media management: A path dependency analysis of the German newspaper branch of high quality journalism. *Schmalenbach Business Review, 60*, 50–73. https://doi.org/10.1007/BF03396759

Koch, J. (2011). Inscribed strategies: Exploring the organizational nature of strategic lock-in. *Organization Studies, 32*(3), 337–363. https://doi.org/10.1177/0170840610397486

Kuznetsova, E., Makhortykh, M., Vziatysheva, V., Stolze, M., Baghumyan, A., & Urman, A. (2025). In generative AI we trust: Can chatbots effectively verify political information? *Journal of Computational Social Science, 8*(15). https://doi.org/10.1007/s42001-024-00338-8

Lewis, S., Guzman, A., Schmidt, T., & Lin, B. (2025). Generative AI and its disruptive challenge to journalism: An institutional analysis. *Communication and Change, 1*(9). https://doi.org/10.1007/s44382-025-00008-x

Liebowitz, S. J., & Margolis, S. E. (1995). Path dependence, lock-in, and history. *Journal of Law, Economics, & Organization, 11*(1), 205–226. https://doi.org/10.1093/oxfordjournals.jleo.a036867

Lindén, C.-G. (2017). Algorithms for journalism: The future of news work. *The Journal of Media Innovations, 4*(1), 60–76. https://doi.org/10.5617/jmi.v4i1.2420

Meyer, U., & Schubert, C. (2007). *Integrating path dependency and path creation in a general understanding of path constitution. The role of agency and institutions in the stabilisation of technological innovations* (pp. 23–44). STI Studies.

Newman, N., & Cherubini, F. (2025). *Journalism, media, and technology trends and predictions 2025*. Reuters Institute for the Study of Journalism. https://doi.org/10.60625/risj-vte1-x706

Rothmann, W. (2013). *Wahrnehmung des strategischen Handlungsspielraums: Die verlegerische Entwicklung deutscher Qualitätstageszeitungen seit 2001*. Springer VS.

Rothmann, W., & Koch, J. (2013). Creativity in strategic lock-ins: The newspaper industry and the digital revolution. *Technological Forecasting and Social Change, 83*, 66–83. https://doi.org/10.1016/j.techfore.2013.03.005

Schreyögg, G., & Kliesch-Eberl, M. (2007). How dynamic can organizational capabilities be? Towards a dual-process model of capability dynamization. *Strategic Management Journal, 28*(9), 913–933. https://doi.org/10.1002/smj.613

Schreyögg, G., & Sydow, J. (2011). Organizational path dependence: A process view. *Organization Studies, 32*(3), 321–335. https://doi.org/10.1177/0170840610397481
Schreyögg, G., Sydow, J., & Koch, J. (2003). Organisatorische Pfade: Von der Pfadabhängigkeit zur Pfadkreation? In G. Schreyögg & J. Sydow (Eds.), *Strategische Prozesse und Pfade* (pp. 257–294). Gabler.
Schwarz, G. M. (2010). The logic of deliberate structural inertia. *Journal of Management, 38*(2), 547–572. https://doi.org/10.1177/0149206309361206
Simon, F. M. (2024). Escape me if you can: How AI reshapes news organizations' dependency on platform companies. *Digital Journalism, 12*(2), 149–170. https://doi.org/10.1080/21670811.2023.2287464
Sirén-Heikel, S., Kjellman, M., & Lindén, C.-G. (2023). At the crossroads of logics: Automating newswork with artificial intelligence—(Re)defining journalistic logics from the perspective of technologists. *Journal of the Association for Information Science & Technology, 74*(3), 354–366. https://doi.org/10.1002/asi.24656
Sjøvaag, H. (2024). The business of news in the AI economy. *AI Magazine, 45*(2), 169–296. https://doi.org/10.1002/aaai.12172
Sminia, H., Bohn, S., & Sydow, J. (2024). Path release among practices in the process of path constitution: How the MP3-path appeared in the field of recorded music. *Research Policy, 53*(8), Article No. 105073. https://doi.org/10.1016/j.respol.2024.105073
Sydow, J., Schreyögg, G., & Koch, J. (2009). Organizational path dependence: Opening the black box. *Academy of Management Review, 34*(4), 689–709. https://doi.org/10.5465/amr.34.4.zok689
Sydow, J., Schreyögg, G., & Koch, J. (2020). On the theory of organizational path dependence: Clarifications, replies to objections, and extensions. *Academy of Management Review, 45*(4), 717–734. https://doi.org/10.5465/amr.2020.0163
Sydow, J., Windeler, A., Müller-Seitz, G., & Lange, K. (2012). Path constitution analysis: A methodology for understanding path dependence and path creation. *Business Research, 5*, 155–176. https://doi.org/10.1007/BF03342736
Túñez-López, J.-M., Fieiras-Ceide, C., & Vaz-Álvarez, M. (2021). Impact of artificial intelligence on journalism: Transformations in the company, products, contents and professional profile. *Communications Society, 34*(1), 177–193. https://doi.org/10.15581/003.34.1.177-193
Vaccari, C., & Chadwick, A. (2020). Deepfakes and disinformation: Exploring the impact of synthetic political video on deception, uncertainty, and trust in news. *Social Media + Society, 6*(1), 1–13. https://doi.org/10.1177/2056305120903408
Vergne, J., & Durand, R. (2010). The missing link between the theory and empirics of path dependence: Conceptual clarification, testability issue, and methodological implications. *Journal of Management Studies, 47*(4), 736–759. https://doi.org/10.1111/j.1467-6486.2009.00913.x
Vergne, J.-P., & Durand, R. (2011). The path of most persistence: An evolutionary perspective on path dependence and dynamic capabilities. *Organization Studies, 32*(3), 365–382. https://doi.org/10.1177/0170840610397485
Wenzel, M. (2015). Path dependence and the stabilization of strategic premises: How the funeral industry buries itself. *Business Research, 8*(2), 265–299. https://doi.org/10.1007/s40685-015-0021-4
Wilczek, B. (2019). Complexity, uncertainty, and change in news organizations. *International Journal of Media Management, 21*(2), 88–129. https://doi.org/10.1080/14241277.2019.1590839
Wilczek, B., Stanoevska-Slabeva, K., Kernbach, K., & Meckel, M. (2021). Unlocking strategic lock-ins of local media: An investigation of local media's preferences towards public support for strategic innovation. *Digital Journalism, 9*(3), 276–299. https://doi.org/10.1080/21670811.2021.1878382

Paul Clemens Murschetz (Ph.D. habil., Vienna University of Economics and Business), is Privatdozent of media management studies based in Austria. He applies media management, media economics, governance theory, and theories of the political economy of the media to address issues related to public service media, sustainable communication, and path dependence in media innovation. Paul graduated from the University of Klagenfurt (Habilitation thesis in the digital transformation of the media industry), the Vienna School of Economics and Business Administration (Ph.D. in Business Studies), and the LSE (MSc. in Media and Communications). Paul is author of Die digitale Transformation der Medien: Leitmedien im Wandel (Springer, 2022), The Handbook of State Aid for Film: Finance, Industries, Regulation (Springer, 2018), Digital Mediamorphosis (Springer, 2019), and State Aid for Newspapers: Theories, Cases, Actions (Springer, 2014).

Maximilian Eder is a Research Associate at the Department of Media and Communication, LMU Munich, focusing on artificial intelligence in local journalism. He is also an honorary Research Fellow of the Bundeswehr University Munich. His main research interests include (digital) journalism practice, political journalism, and scandalization dynamics in media.

Bartosz Wilczek is a PostDoc at the Department of Media and Communication at LMU Munich, Germany. His research and teaching interests focus on AI in journalism, digital journalism, and media management.

AI-Supported Corporate Content Production in the Newsroom: Insights from Literature and Practice

15

Cornelia Wolf

Abstract

This chapter investigates how artificial intelligence (AI) transforms corporate content production, with a focus on its integration into topic-based newsroom structures. Drawing on academic research and industry discourse, it develops a comprehensive framework for an AI-supported communication process, structured along the phases of communication management. The framework is then applied to a leading European IT service provider that has operated a corporate newsroom for over a decade. Based on qualitative interviews and workflow analyses, the study assesses current AI use and implementation priorities. The findings reveal that AI holds substantial potential to increase efficiency, creativity, and personalization—especially in content creation and workflow automation—while also highlighting structural and cultural challenges. This chapter provides a strategic blueprint for AI adoption in corporate communication and offers a prioritization logic for implementation. It contributes to both research and practice by outlining a process-oriented roadmap for AI integration.

15.1 Introduction: The Impact of AI in Corporate Content Production

Artificial intelligence (AI) is increasingly viewed as a disruptive force in public relations and marketing communication (Adi, 2023; Biswal, 2020; Swiatek & Galloway, 2022; Zerfass et al., 2020). Since the release of ChatGPT, debates around human–machine collaboration have intensified, as AI tools are now capable of

C. Wolf (✉)
Leipzig University, Leipzig, Germany
e-mail: cornelia.wolf@uni-leipzig.de

S. Böhm et al. (eds.), *Handbook of AI-based Media Disruption*, Future of Business and Finance, https://doi.org/10.1007/978-3-032-07605-2_15

performing tasks traditionally depending on human intelligence (Panda et al., 2019; Rettig & Mickeleit, 2023; Seidenglanz & Baier, 2023).

The transformation of corporate content production is particularly compelling, as many companies focus on topic-based strategic communication. Over the past decade, many organizations have implemented corporate newsrooms, enabling a digital, networked, multichannel production of corporate content for diverse internal and external stakeholders. Topic-based strategic communication facilitates "the management of narratives and media content that are critical to corporate strategy and that define the identity of the organization in stakeholders' perceptions" (Ninova-Solovykh et al., 2019, p. 4). As a result, a newsroom—especially when using specifically developed software—supports integrated corporate communication as a means of corporate management focused on analysis, planning, organization, execution, and evaluation of communication processes to achieve goals (Bruhn, 2008; Holtzhausen & Zerfass, 2013).

Despite extensive discussions on AI in academic and industry publications, a holistic understanding of its role for the communication management process and the corporate communications value chain remains limited. Hence, this chapter first focuses on the changes in corporate content production over the past decade. Afterwards, the potentials of AI referring to both academic and industry literature are systemized in a framework for AI-supported communication. Last, the framework is applied to one of the largest IT service companies in Europe. Based on qualitative interviews and workflow analyses, the study assesses current AI use and identifies priorities for implementation.

The empirical data were collected in a research project at Leipzig University led by Daniel Bendahan Bitton and the author. The project team included: Alexandra Grüber, Carl Krauß, Louisa Marko, Elise Mattheus, Jule Schepers, Lotta Wegner, Jessica Winkler, Hannes Witerspan, and Laura Zapke. The study was funded by the company under investigation.

15.2 Current Changes in Corporate Content Production

Digital technologies and the process of digital transformation have fundamentally changed corporate communication and content production. "Throughout the 20th century, the main audience of corporate communication was journalists who then spread the story to the public at large" (Seiffert-Brockmann et al., 2021, p. 129). This established system of public communication, in which journalism acted largely as a gatekeeper, has changed drastically due to disintermediation and the rise of platforms and channels of direct, dialogic, and co-created communication between companies and their stakeholders (Ninova-Solovykh et al., 2019, p. 8). In this fragmented communication environment, managing strategically important content, narratives, and stories, which shape the image and identity of an organization in the eyes of stakeholders and the public, has become increasingly important (Seiffert-Brockmann & Einwiller, 2020, p. 6). Moreover, organizations seek to position themselves as thought leaders in public discourse on relevant issues (Wiencierz et al., 2017). This has intensified in recent years, as organizations publicly address socially and politically controversial topics (van der Mer & Jonkman, 2021).

A key indicator of the changed media environment is the growing presence of owned media—content created and published by companies themselves (Baetzgen & Tropp, 2013; Savič, 2016; Seiffert-Brockmann et al., 2021). For instance, Bosch, a leading global supplier of technology and services in Germany, adopted an integrated approach to position itself as a digital publishing house as early as 2017 (Wiencierz et al., 2017). As a result, "the topics and the corresponding content are more than ever the center of organizational attention" (Ninova-Solovykh et al., 2019, p. 7). Content management thus plays a crucial role in building and maintaining relationships with key publics (Broom et al., 1997; Bruning & Ledingham, 1999; Ledingham, 2006).

To sum up, communication departments have evolved from reactive media relations units into strategic content producers that plan, create, and distribute on a regular basis. As a result of this transformation, the newsroom concept was adopted and adapted from journalism (Seiffert-Brockmann et al., 2021). This chapter understands corporate communication as a management function aimed at strategically controlling communication processes to achieve defined goals (Holtzhausen & Zerfass, 2013). From a holistic perspective, the corporate communication value chain follows a structured process: it defines objectives and allocates resources (input), develops and coordinates communication activities (analysis, planning, organization, execution, and evaluation), distributes these to target groups (output), achieves direct effects (outcomes), and creates organizational value by achieving its objectives (impacts) (AMEC, 2016; Bruhn, 2008).

Next, the newsroom model as a structural response to these changes is explored, focusing on developments in the DACH region (Germany, Austria, and Switzerland) since 2015. This chapter then addresses current developments related to artificial intelligence.

15.2.1 Establishment of Corporate Newsrooms

As stated above, the digital transformation has changed the media landscape and stakeholder expectations. Organizations today often use owned media to communicate directly with stakeholders. These shifts, "force organizations to think and work like media producers and to efficiently and effectively align their communication content" (Ninova-Solovykh et al., 2019, p. 3). Hence, storytelling has become a central element of corporate communications. In the past, companies primarily focused on qualities and benefits of products and services. Today, however, content must be embedded in broader narratives shaped by corporate vision, mission, and strategy (Moss & Stog, 2021; Ninova-Solovykh et al., 2019). To address this challenge, many organizations have adopted new structures and processes—most notably corporate newsrooms, adapted from journalistic practice. The newsroom serves as a central hub for strategic topic management and enables flexible collaboration structures and processes. From the mid-2010s onward, corporations increasingly adopted newsroom models into their communications departments, applying journalistic principles to plan, produce, and manage content (Seiffert-Brockmann et al., 2021; Seiffert-Brockmann & Einwiller, 2020).

Traditionally, corporate communications was organized by stakeholder groups, such as employees, journalists, customers, and investors, as well as media channels, such as employee magazines or websites. Marketing handled customer communication; finance oversaw investor relations. These siloed structures tend to lead to inefficiencies, misaligned messaging, and duplicated efforts (Ninova-Solovykh et al., 2019; Seiffert-Brockmann et al., 2021). As Moss and Stog (2021, p. 7) state: "Abandoning the silos for open, communicative structures, modern Corporate Newsroom concepts can help to break down the barriers between communication and marketing, between internal and external target groups or between product PR and media relations." By shifting from channel-based to topic-based structures, the corporate newsroom introduces new roles: topic managers and channel managers, coordinated by a managing editor (Moss, 2021a, p. 27). Thereby, topic-based strategic communication can be established: Topics are identified strategy-driven, presented by storytelling, and kept consistent by an integrated process (Ninova-Solovykh et al., 2019, p. 11). The implementation of topic-based strategic communication often requires restructuring, leading to either a "newsroom light" or a fully developed corporate newsroom (Ninova-Solovykh et al., 2019, p. 14).

As journalistic adaption, the corporate newsroom applies characteristic features and roles of editorial offices (Behrens et al., 2021). A corporate newsroom is more complex than a journalistic newsroom, among other things, due to a larger number of different stakeholders (Moss, 2021a, p. 47). Editorial conferences enable collaboration across departments. Like journalists, communication professionals gather and evaluate content from across the company in regular meetings (Seiffert-Brockmann & Einwiller, 2020). Strategic oversight is provided by a strategy team, while operational coordination rests with managing editors, who link topic desks and media desks. They oversee prioritization and task delegation and use planning tools to remain up to date. Topic desks are staffed by one or more topic managers—comparable to reporters—who liaise with subject-matter departments, conduct research, and produce content. They propose topics, ensure relevance and accuracy, and participate in editorial meetings. Topic desks are designed to align projects with the company's content strategy and may be structured around different business areas (Moss, 2021a, p. 31 f.).

Media desks, led by media managers, correspond to the company's communication channels (e.g., print, online, social media, audio, video). Like editors, media managers adapt and publish content, suggest topics for their channels, and work closely with managing editors. Their role is comparable to that of editors in journalism. Media desks are structured based on the company's chosen communication channels and target audiences, with potential desks including print, online, social media, audio, and video (Moss, 2021a, p. 32ff.). Thus, corporate newsroom routines center around the question: "How to get a topic into the right channels?" (Moss, 2021a, p. 38).

Literature shows an adoption of the newsroom models, especially in the DACH region (Germany, Austria, Switzerland) (Keel & Niederhäuser, 2016; Moss & Sadrowski, 2021; Seiffert-Brockmann et al., 2021). While initially rooted in Europe, the newsroom concept has since been adopted globally—by corporations and public institutions alike (Moss, 2021b). Since 2015, newsrooms have emerged in various sectors including technology, finance, transportation, consumer goods, and public services (Moss, 2021b; Seiffert-Brockmann et al., 2021). A 2019 survey of 172 communication managers in the DACH region found that more than half had implemented or were planning to implement newsroom structures (Moss & Sadrowski, 2021, p. 92).

Realizing newsroom principles entails significant organizational change: shifts in structures, power dynamics, spatial arrangements, working patterns, and editorial focus (Moss & Stog, 2021, p. 13). Models vary depending on organizational and national context, with considerable differences between individual implementations.

The adoption of corporate newsrooms marks a shift toward agile, integrated communication in fragmented digital landscapes supporting the consistent public representation of an organization (Seiffert-Brockmann et al., 2021; Seiffert-Brockmann & Einwiller, 2020). Despite its growing prominence, few authors have systematically analyzed newsroom implementation from both theoretical and empirical perspectives (Moss, 2021; Seiffert-Brockmann et al., 2021). To date, research on the use of AI in this context is still lacking.

15.2.2 The New Role of AI in Corporate Content Production

The influence and usage of artificial intelligence (AI) in corporate communications is widely discussed in both academic research and the practical field. Since the release of ChatGPT, discussions about human–machine interaction have intensified (Adi, 2023; Rettig & Mickeleit, 2023). Advances in hardware, faster networks, and more efficient algorithms (Alsheibani et al., 2020) have unlocked new potential, particularly in strategic communication and the communication management process.

Hancock et al. (2020) define AI communication as a process in which an AI agent processes, modifies, or independently generates messages on behalf of a human communicator to achieve communication goals. Weller and Lock (2024) highlight that the growing trend toward automation, AI, and algorithms is shaping strategic communication research, while revealing conceptual ambiguities in how automated communication is understood. In this context, AI may be described as the flexible decision-making processes and actions of software-driven agents. Within corporate communications, such agents interact with human or nonhuman actors by generating, transmitting, mediating, and receiving text, audio, or visual content to achieve communication objectives (Weller & Lock, 2024; Zerfass et al., 2020).

The majority of communication professionals see AI as a transformative force for the industry, with managers rating its influence higher than team members (Zerfass et al., 2020). Despite this, implementation at scale remains rare (Adi, 2023). This can be attributed to limited knowledge sharing, exchange of experiences, and dissemination of information in practice (Iaia et al., 2024). Key barriers include missing skills, inadequate structures, and a lack of support from top management (Zerfass et al., 2020).

Nonetheless, even partial integration offers benefits: professionals report that AI tools save time, simplify routine tasks, and support creative processes and personalized content creation (Cusnir & Neagu, 2024; Panda et al., 2019). Tools like ChatGPT and other platforms enable PR professionals to make data-informed decisions, design campaigns efficiently, and strengthen customer loyalty through tailored analyses and content. Yet questions of governance, accountability, and human oversight will remain critical in shaping the future use of AI in communication (Panda et al., 2019; Zerfass et al., 2020).

Existing research tends to focus on individual tools or specific communication subdomains (Cusnir & Neagu, 2024; Panda et al., 2019; Seidenglanz & Baier, 2023; Zerfass et al., 2020). Contributions address GPT-4 in internal communication (George et al., 2023), AI in marketing (Binlibdah, 2024; Kubovics, 2024) and organizational acceptance (Gabelaia et al., 2024; Kelm & Johann, 2024). Other studies provide early insights into AI's potential and limitations in strategic communication (Osei-Mensah, 2023; Weller & Lock, 2024).

However, a systematic overview of the entire communication management process remains absent. Consequently, a comprehensive understanding of how AI can be integrated into the process steps of corporate content production is still lacking. Hence, the question arises: How can an AI-supported communication value chain be designed?

15.3 Literature Analysis: The AI-Supported Communication Value Chain

Through a systematic literature analysis, academic studies and professional discourse were consolidated into a comprehensive framework for the use of AI in corporate communications. The findings were categorized using the AMEC (International association for the measurement and evaluation of communication) framework (AMEC, 2016), with particular attention given to AI's influence on the dimensions input, output, outcomes, and impact. Communication activities—represented as "activities" in the AMEC framework—were differentiated into the stages of analysis, planning, organization, execution, and evaluation, aligning with the understanding of corporate communications as a management process.

The analysis included literature from the scientific databases *Communication & Mass Media Complete, Business Source Complete* and *the Social Sciences Citation Index* of the *Web of Science* (published from 01.01.2017 to 28.10.2024). In addition, articles from the German-language industry publications *Kommunikationsmanager*,

Manager Magazin, *Horizont*, *PR Report*, *prmagazin* and *KOM* (published from 01.01.2023 to 28.10.2024).[1] Search terms focus on AI, corporate communications, and communication management.[2] Only texts that aligned with the conceptual understanding of AI and corporate communications as defined in this chapter were included.

The search in the scientific databases initially yielded 297 articles. To be included, articles had to address the phases of the classic communication management process (Buhmann & Volk, 2022) and/or explicitly refer to corporate communications, while referencing either the technological functionalities of AI, such as natural language processing, machine learning, predictive analytics, data retrieval, knowledge representation, or semantic reasoning (Schweyer, 2018; Tredinnick, 2017; Zerfass et al., 2020) or intelligent behavior of AI agents including perception, reasoning, learning, communicating, and acting in complex environments (Nilsson, 1998). In addition, there should be a reference to the creation and distribution of AI-generated content (sending, authoring, mediating) (Weller & Lock, 2024). After applying these criteria, 38 academic publications remained. From the 65 identified industry articles, 59 met the inclusion requirements. The final sample consisted of 97 documents. All materials were coded using MAXQDA 2024 by the trained team of master students.

15.3.1 Dimensions of the Framework

The following section presents an overview of the dimensions and categories of the framework. Table 15.1 summarizes the findings, illustrating—where supported by the literature—management process steps (mentioned in bold in the text), functional AI capabilities (mentioned in bold italics in the text), and specific applications as examples.

Input refers to how AI affects organizational **resources** and **objectives**. The sample primarily provides insights into resources, as strategic objectives are not yet addressed in either academic literature or industry discourse. Resources can be optimized through ***resource, budget, and personnel savings*** (Biebl et al., 2023; Kondak, 2023; Neuen, 2023a, 2024b). AI also enables ***new job profiles*** and ***new work models*** (Harms & Han, 2018; Schuster, 2023b).

Activities encompass the steps of communication management:

[1] The broader period for academic literature allows for a comprehensive inclusion of theoretical and empirical contributions to AI in corporate communication, particularly since the rise of data-driven and AI-assisted communication strategies. In contrast, the shorter period for industry publications captures recent discourse shifts and emerging practices following the public launch of generative AI tools such as ChatGPT in late 2022, which marked a turning point in the professional debate and adoption dynamics.

[2] The following search string was used: AI (artificial intelligence OR AI OR A.I.) and corporate communications (OR strategic communication OR internal communication OR communication management), and the process of communication management (Planning OR controlling OR measurement OR evaluation OR implementation OR organisation OR organization OR process management)

Table 15.1 AI-supported communication value chain

Input	Activities	Output	Outcomes	Impacts
Resources Resource savings Budget savings Personnel savings New job profiles New work models	**Analysis** Data analysis (*sentiment analysis, target group analysis)* Trend prediction **Planning** Idea generation and creativity (*topic extraction, text summarization)* Topic research Strategy and concept development (*scenario development, time planning, budget planning)* **Organization** Automation of workflows (*workflow design, document management, query sorting, schedule management)* **Execution** Content creation (*text creation and editing, image generation and editing, graphic and presentation design, layout design and editing, audio creation, video creation website creation, report generation)* Personalization Translation Transcription **Evaluation** Monitoring (*media monitoring, sentiment analysis, impact measurement)* Controlling Presentation evaluation Self-reflection Benchmarking	**Distribution** Content distribution Query response Knowledge management	**Satisfaction** Perception of human qualities Customer experience **Preference** Personalization Attention enhancement Entertainment **Learning and knowledge** **Trust** **Attitude change** **Endorsement**	**Organizational change** Efficiency improvement Effectiveness improvement Emergence of new tasks Quality Enhancement Strategic realignment Decision-making processes Increasing creativity Rationalization of job profiles AI as management Change in corporate culture Improved collaboration Skills development Profit Competitive advantages **Relationships** Customer Relationships

				Employee Relationships AI as colleague/ assistance Improved stakeholder understanding **Societal change** Reduction of discrimination Talent development AI representations Combating skilled labor shortages Loss of human expertise **Reputation** **Compliance**

- **Analysis**: AI supports large-scale data processing (***statistical data analysis***) (Neuen, 2023d), such as *sentiment analysis* and *target group analysis* (Biebl et al., 2023; Brune, 2023; Kondak, 2023; Laskin & D'Agostino, 2024) and enables data-driven decisions through ***trend forecasting*** *(*Durmus Şenyapar, 2024; Kondak, 2023).
- **Planning**: AI tools help with ***idea generation and creativity*** and ***topic research*** *(topic extraction, text summarization);* they support ***strategy and concept development,*** e.g., *scenario development* in areas such as crisis and change management, or social media campaigns (Appel & Biebl, 2023; Biebl et al., 2023; Cusnir & Neagu, 2024; Zerfass et al., 2020), but also *time or budget planning*. Thereby, AI enables to experiment with multiple content variations (Malthouse & Copulsky, 2023).
- **Organization:** AI serves the ***automation of workflows***, making recurring organizational tasks more efficient and reducing the human workload. AI optimizes *workflow design* (e.g., by creating agendas, schedules, or posting plans) (Cusnir & Neagu, 2024; Göke, 2023), *document management* (e.g., by making them searchable and preparing them for easy further processing) (Göke, 2024a), *query sorting* (e.g., by monitoring email inboxes or forms) (Biebl et al., 2023; Brune, 2023; Harms & Han, 2018), and *schedule management* (e.g., automated creation of invitations and reminders as well as calendar management) (Biebl et al., 2023; Cusnir & Neagu, 2024; Getchell et al., 2022; Göke, 2024b).
- **Execution:** ***Content creation*** is a major area (Cusnir & Neagu, 2024; Kondak, 2023; Neuen, 2023b). This includes *text creation and editing* (Cusnir & Neagu, 2024), such as SEO optimization (Brune, 2023), press release, and social media drafting (Göke, 2023; Schuster, 2023a). AI allows *report generation*, e.g., speeches (Schuster, 2023b) or entire reports (Cusnir & Neagu, 2024) and improves tonal and linguistic text optimization (Biebl et al., 2023; Haller, 2024). AI agents offer *image generation and editing*, *graphic and presentation design* (Biebl et al., 2023; Brune, 2023; Kyriasoglou & Rest, 2023; Schuster, 2023b), *layout design and editing* (Brune, 2023), and *website creation*. AI accelerates and personalizes the design process (Biebl et al., 2023). In addition, AI enables *audio creation* (e.g., composing, cutting, editing, voice cloning) (Biebl et al., 2023; Göke, 2023; Kyriasoglou & Rest, 2023; Schuster, 2023a) and *video creation,* e.g., with virtual characters (Sieber & Hoewner, 2024). There is also content ***personalization*** by AI using data on target group profiles (Kondak, 2023; Mickeleit & Tigges, 2023). ***Translation and transcription*** of media content (Biebl et al., 2023; Steck, 2024) supports customer meetings or interviews (Steck, 2024; Wiegand, 2023).
- **Evaluation:** AI is used for ***monitoring***, e.g. *media monitoring, sentiment analysis, and impact measurement* (Marell, 2023; Ta, 2023). Based on KPIs, AI can guide ***controlling*** (Appel & Biebl, 2023; Cusnir & Neagu, 2024; Ta, 2023), and also ***presentation evaluation*** (e.g., by using Natural Language Understanding, computer vision, and speech recognition) (Getchell et al., 2022; Paschen et al., 2020). AI agents support employee ***self-reflection***, promoting self-assessment

and well-being insights (Getchell et al., 2022). Another option is ***benchmarking*** (Neuen, 2024a).

Output refers to AI's influence on **distribution**. ***Content distribution*** encompasses, for example, the automatic creation and publication of social media posts (Neuen, 2023d) or advertisement playout (Schuster, 2023a). ***Query response*** includes automated answers to questions and concerns (chatbots, voicebots) (Dogan & Gurcan, 2024; Men, Qin, et al., 2023; Paschen et al., 2020; Steck, 2024). AI enables personalized email communication and enhanced service quality by optimizing sending times based on historical success data (Bajak & Majerczyk, 2022; Gentsch, 2023) and allows automatically composed and sent responses to press inquiries or costumer complaints (Biebl et al., 2023; Neuen, 2024a). ***Knowledge management*** refers to AI providing access to relevant information for internal and external target groups (Benz & Zerfaß, 2024; Schuster, 2023a), supporting learning processes (Biebl et al., 2023; Schuster, 2023a), and improving knowledge transfer (Hromatka, 2024; Neuen, 2024a).

Outcome includes user experience and relationship-level effects. AI enhances positive experiences for target groups and leads to **satisfaction.** ***Customer experiences*** improve through individualized services (Biebl et al., 2024; Gentsch, 2023), while customer loyalty benefits from the ***perception of human qualities***, e.g. human-like dialogue (Bergner et al., 2023). **Preference** refers to the choice of a brand, product, or service over others. By analyzing customer behavior, AI enables ***personalization*** (Paschen et al., 2020), e.g., suggesting suitable products, which increases customer loyalty and satisfaction (Kondak, 2023) and enables personalized user experiences (Neuen, 2023b). AI-supported analysis of visual patterns allows ***attention enhancement*** (Kondak, 2023), thereby increasing user interaction (Łaszkiewicz, 2024; Schuster, 2023a). AI also generates hybrid experiences and transforms how people learn and consume ***entertainment*** by enabling interactive and personalized content (Gentsch, 2023; Neuen, 2023b).

In addition, AI simplifies **learning and knowledge** processes: AI agents improve access to information, reduce workload, and accelerate knowledge flows by efficiently consolidating information (Benz & Zerfaß, 2024; Schaller, 2024).

Trust and acceptance are shaped by interface design—e.g. embodied AI agents are perceived as more trustworthy than purely text-based systems (Getchell et al., 2022; Men, Zhou, et al., 2023). Clear role communication (AI as tool, not substitute) fosters user confidence and **attitude change** (Van Quaquebeke & Gerpott, 2024).

AI can also strengthen self-efficacy and skills development (Poetz et al., 2024). Endorsement includes guidance, acceptance support, and the promotion of skills and self-efficacy through targeted and conscious AI use (Poetz et al., 2024).

Impacts refer to structural, cultural, and economic effects. These encompass aspects of **organizational transformation**. ***Efficiency improvement*** relates to time-saving through automation of routine tasks, freeing up capacities for strategic functions (Banasik & Pikiewicz, 2023; Mickeleit & Tigges, 2023). For example, AI facilitates ***decision-making processes*** by offering solution options (Von dem Bussche, 2023). The literature highlights ***effectiveness improvement*** across personnel decisions, workflows, marketing strategies, and communication measures (Brune, 2023; Cusnir & Neagu, 2024; Dogan & Gurcan, 2024; Kondak, 2023; Schaller, 2024). The ***emergence of new tasks*** leads to evolving roles, skills, and responsibilities, such as postediting AI outputs (Biebl et al., 2024; Göke, 2024c; Neuen, 2023a, 2024a, 2024b; Upadhyay & Khandelwal, 2018). AI contributes to ***quality enhancement***, e.g., improving text quality or ***increasing creativity*** through generated content (Bastian & Stoltenow, 2023; Biebl et al., 2024; Kondak, 2023; Marell, 2023).

AI also supports ***strategic realignment*** by enabling the redesign of organizations, processes, and communication strategies. This includes fostering new business models and reintegrating previously outsourced tasks (Behera et al., 2024; Neuen, 2023b, 2023c).

Another effect is the ***rationalization of job profiles***: The use of AI transforms (Neuen, 2024a), automates, or reduces existing occupational fields (Lee & Park, 2023; López-Garcia & Negreira-Rey, 2024; Mayer, 2024; Upadhyay & Khandelwal, 2018). There can be a shift toward ***AI management***, in which AI takes on leadership and management tasks (motivating, supporting, and developing employees and coordinating tasks) (Harms & Han, 2018).

AI may lead to ***improved collaboration*** (Wiegand, 2023), evoke a ***change in corporate culture*** (Biebl et al., 2024) and enable ***skills development*** by sharing *knowledge and skills* (Iaia et al., 2024). Effects on ***profit*** and ***competitive advantages*** include optimized sales, revenue growth, and increased efficiency (Paschen et al., 2020; Schuster, 2023a).

A second impact area is **relationships**. AI enhances ***customer relationships*** through personalized interactions, e.g. AI influencers can build communities and simulate emotional engagement (Malthouse & Copulsky, 2023; Men, Zhou, et al., 2023; Sieber & Hoewner, 2024). AI also improves ***employee relationship*** in the areas of communication, well-being, and engagement, e.g., by supporting onboarding, tailoring content for non-desk workers, or identifying emotional states (Harms & Han, 2018; Schuster, 2023a).

AI as a colleague/assistant includes support in everyday tasks such as scheduling, idea generation, or content optimization (Bernau, 2023; Getchell et al., 2022) and helps build ***improved stakeholder understanding*** (Cusnir & Neagu, 2024).

Societal change encompasses the ***reduction of discrimination***, e.g., by minimizing bias or language barriers and promoting inclusive data use (Getchell et al., 2022; Schuster, 2023a; Upadhyay & Khandelwal, 2018). AI contributes to ***talent development*** through automated recommendations for training (Brune, 2023; Kyriasoglou & Rest, 2023; Upadhyay & Khandelwal, 2018). ***AI representations*** involve creation of virtual agents such as voice avatars, image generators, or AI artists (Karst, 2023; Schuster, 2023a, 2023b). AI also helps ***combating skilled labor shortages*** by compensating resource gaps and automating workflows (Brune, 2023; Gentsch, 2023). In addition, a ***loss of human expertise*** by AI is possible, such as reduced problem-solving capacity (Lee & Park, 2023).

AI supports **reputation** by monitoring large amounts of data, identifying risks, and anticipating negative coverage (Cusnir & Neagu, 2024). However, without responsible use, AI itself can endanger corporate reputation (Pinter & Ihász, 2019). Finally, AI facilitates *compliance* by embedding regulations into development processes. This strengthens reputation, reduces legal risks, and supports foresight via predictive models and innovation ecosystems (Seibt, 2024).

To sum up, the analysis reveals that AI's influence on corporate communication extends across multiple dimensions (see Table 15.1), with particularly strong relevance in the areas of content implementation, data-driven analysis, and workflow automation. These dimensions not only reflect current application trends but also indicate where AI is most likely to reshape strategic and operational practices. For instance, the central role of AI in content creation highlights its potential to streamline production processes, personalize messaging, and improve linguistic precision. Similarly, the strong presence of AI in analytical tasks underscores its value in enabling real-time monitoring and informed decision-making. These findings suggest that organizations should prioritize the integration of AI tools in these areas to enhance communicative effectiveness and strategic responsiveness.

15.4 Implementing AI in the Newsroom: Industry Case

The analysis of the academic and professional discourse resulted in a framework that systematizes AI implementation options along the corporate communication value chain. It can serve as a blueprint or checklist for AI implementation and structure the analysis of AI effects in corporate newsrooms. Hence, in a second step, this chapter explores how AI can be integrated into the corporate communication value chain in a specific company and which organizational changes can be realized incrementally.

The case organization is one of the largest IT service providers in Europe, with over 9000 employees and a revenue of EUR 1.5 billion in 2024. AI is currently used selectively in corporate communication, mostly through exploratory use cases. The company aims to establish an AI-supported communication value chain within the next five years.

This chapter first introduces the current state of corporate content production at the case company, which has been based on a corporate newsroom model for over a decade. To analyze structures and workflows, corporate publications were reviewed, regular consultations with communication staff conducted, and qualitative interviews held. The findings inform how the framework developed earlier can be adapted to the organization's specific priorities.

15.4.1 Corporate Content Production at a German IT Service Company

The corporate communications unit comprises over 200 employees and oversees both digital and analog channels, including the website, internal screens, the intranet, a digital and print magazine, and the internal community. This study focuses on the newsroom-structured corporate content department, which includes most employees (approx. 130). Other areas such as press, brand management, and events were not included.

In the early 2010s, the company was one of the first in Germany to implement a corporate newsroom, initiating a fundamental change process. This not only transformed structures, but also job profiles and responsibilities. Since then, content production has followed a topic-based logic, with distribution channels selected afterward. There are no distinct responsibilities for specific communication areas such as internal communication. The newsroom model was designed to flexibly integrate new topics and media.

Since 2020, a transformation toward a data-driven newsroom has been underway, currently nearing completion. Digital channel analytics—such as for social media and podcasts—are visualized via newsroom dashboards. However, since the dashboard is supported externally, data is available only with a weekly delay. As a result, social media managers still use Excel-based reports for daily analysis. The long-term goal is to standardize daily analytics across all channels. Currently, the intranet is analyzed once per year; the website is evaluated separately and not yet integrated into the dashboard system.

According to the newsroom structure, topics and media are clearly separated: editors at topic desks develop content, while media desks adapt and publish it across channels. Topic owners are responsible for content regardless of the platform or audience. The managing editor plays a central role by coordinating across desks, setting priorities, and ensuring efficient workflows. Structurally, content and media teams are organized into separate departments. Cross-functional responsibilities, formerly handled by a chief of staff, are now assigned to an operations team. Weekly editorial meetings set the agenda and assign topics using internal software; daily departmental meetings coordinate follow-up and strategy.

At least one topic manager oversees content for each media channel, including social media. An exception is TikTok, which is currently managed by an external agency. The social media strategy includes LinkedIn, Instagram, Facebook, and TikTok, with some platforms running multiple channels targeting specific groups (e.g., members, young professionals). In 2023, the social media channels achieved 130 million impressions across over 5000 posts.

To analyze work processes and identify AI potentials, guided qualitative interviews were conducted. As a semi-standardized method, they enable comparability through a structured framework (Helfferich, 2022). A total of 25 employees from the corporate content unit participated: Five in leadership roles and twenty in operational functions across subdepartments (corporate communications, social media, multimedia, marketing, strategy, data analysis). The interviews lasted between 17 and 56 min (average age: 42), were recorded and transcribed using MAXQDA transcription software.

15.4.2 Company-Specific Priorities for an AI-Supported Communication Value Chain

Typical tasks mentioned in the interviews were systematically assigned to the five process steps: analysis, planning, organization, execution, and evaluation. Currently, in analysis, AI is primarily used for *data analysis* and *target group analysis* as well as identifying needs from specialist departments. Planning includes *creative work* and *topic extraction*, along with budget planning, and concept development. In organization, the only task mentioned was *coordination of stakeholders*, which are involved in a project, especially with agencies and service providers. AI tools might increase efficiency in decreasing the amount of software used to coordinate workflows by automizing team schedules. The strongest emphasis was on execution, particularly *content creation*, e.g. text creation and optimization, image generation and editing, report summarization, and presentation design and *personalization* of content. It also supports *transcription* and *translation*. Furthermore, AI has been incorporated into *creative tasks* (topic research, specifically topic extraction and text summarization, the development of communication concepts). One example is AI-supported *workshop planning*. Changes were also noted in self-reflection and collaborative learning. AI is also used *to investigate tool functionality* by asking questions about the tools. However, no tasks have been eliminated by AI. Evaluation involves *monitoring and controlling*, e.g. benchmarking. Additionally, interviewees highlighted the potential of AI in taking over *management and leadership tasks* that have traditionally been reserved for human leaders. These include motivating, supporting, and developing employees, as well as delegating tasks.

Interestingly, several tasks mentioned in relation to AI were not named as "typical tasks" earlier. For example, *image processing* was highlighted as an AI-affected task but not initially listed. This gap may result from differences in how respondents interpret "typical tasks" versus AI-related ones. It also suggests that AI may be applied to emerging or previously peripheral responsibilities by experimental usage.

Respondents identified several *organizational challenges*: structure, leadership support, readiness, infrastructure, and integration. At the same time, they see AI potential in *content personalization*, *task innovation*, *quality and creativity enhancement*, *decision support*, *customer relations*, and *AI as a colleague or assistant*. Desired benefits include better *meeting and email consolidation*, *reducing redundancies*, and *freeing time for creativity and reflection*.

When asked about their workflows and AI potential, respondents reported engagement across all five process steps, plus *management*. Emphasis lies on *concept creation* and *content production*, especially *text work*. While AI has already impacted *execution*, its use in *strategy and concept development* remains limited. Respondents also expressed interest in using AI to improve *organization*, identifying it as the process step with the greatest untapped potential.

A company-specific *prioritization* (see Table 15.2) of the AI-supported communication chain was derived by the researching team by combining, (a) actual task profiles and AI use cases in the organization stated in the interviews (assessment by the interviewees), (b) relevance in academic and industry literature revealed by the

Table 15.2 Prioritization of applications for the industry case

Application	Assessment by the interviewees	Application in research and practice	Feasibility	Overall potential
Analysis				
Data analysis	- Firmly embedded in daily tasks, particularly in target group analysis and the evaluation of large data sets - AI is used as a chatbot to answer questions about data, create personas, and support interpretation - Usage is experimental and unstructured - Strong interest in using AI for the evaluation of large data sets	- Development of target group profiles, stakeholder mapping, audience segmentation, and sentiment analysis is possible - Wide range of application options requires a strategic approach	- Data volume - Data access - Data quality - Data protection (audience-dependent)	High
Trend prediction	- Not used so far - Not expressed as a need - Potential for use may not yet have been recognized	- Consumer behavior and market trends can be analyzed based on current data and appear promising - Predictions are generated as the AI's own interpretation of the data	- Black box → AI competency development is necessary - Quality control - Data quality - Data volume	Medium
Planning				
Idea generation and creativity	- AI as a source of inspiration is a well-known use case - Desire to enhance creativity through AI	- AI as a source of inspiration - Development and validation of ideas	- AI functionality (lack of creativity and empathy) - AI literacy/ competence	Medium
Topic research	- AI is occasionally used to approach and explore topics - Desire for a virtual assistant to act as a sparring partner	- Development and validation of ideas	- Accuracy of results - Bias	Medium

Strategy and concept development	- Occasional use for developing communication concepts and workshops - AI provides impulses - There is a desire for support in planning work processes	- Experimental development of concepts by generating multiple variations	- Quality of results - AI competence	High
Organization				
Automation of workflows	- Not used so far - Strong desire to increase efficiency through the automated organization of daily tasks	- Numerous workflow management systems are capable of managing daily organizational tasks, including self-management and team coordination	- Integration of multiple tools - Vendor dependency - Strategic integration - Expectation management	High
Execution				
Content creation	- Firmly embedded in daily tasks: Creation and editing of text, presentations, audio, video, websites, and reports - AI is already being used - There is a wide range of possible AI applications, as content creation is a core aspect of typical tasks—Continued focus on AI is recommended	- Extensively mentioned in both research and practice - Wide range of possible applications; however, some use cases are complex - High level of dynamism and rapid development; significant efficiency gains can be expected	- Integration of multiple tools - Selection of suitable providers - Data protection - Technical infrastructure - Alignment with corporate values such as sustainability - Result quality - AI competence	High

(continued)

Table 15.2 (continued)

Application	Assessment by the interviewees	Application in research and practice	Feasibility	Overall potential
Personalization	- Not yet used - Expressed as a desire by interviewees and priority for AI project management	- Use of AI to personalize content for different target groups	- Data protection - AI training - Data access - Data quality	Medium
Translation	- Hardly used - Not expressed as a need	- Well established in practice		Low
Transcription	- Hardly used - Hardly expressed as a need	- Well established in practice	- Selection of a suitable provider - Data protection	Medium
Evaluation				
Monitoring	- No use of AI so far	- Media monitoring, sentiment analysis, and impact measurement	- Data volume - Data access - Data quality - Data protection (depending on the target audience)	High
Controlling	- AI is already used for measuring click rates, reach, KPIs, and performance evaluation - Further use of AI is desired	- Performance evaluation, performance measurement, data analysis	- Accuracy of results. - Data access	High
Presentation evaluation	- No application, no expressed need	- No established use of AI, only mentioned occasionally - Maturity of the technology is uncertain	- Accuracy of results - AI functionality: lack of empathy - Black-box nature	Low
Self-reflection	- No application, no expressed need	- No established use of AI, only mentioned occasionally - Maturity of the technology is uncertain	- AI functionality: lack of empathy	Low

Benchmarking	- AI-based benchmarking, analysis of historical data, and AI-generated benchmark suggestions (using an AI solution) - Further potential identified - Desire for support	- No established use of AI, only mentioned occasionally	- Data access - Data quality - Data volume	Low
Output				
Query response	- Previous use of AI not mentioned - Not expressed as a need	- Responding to inquiries from various stakeholder groups - Usable for a wide range of applications - Established use in chatbots; occasional use in email and phone inquiries	- AI functionality: lack of empathy - Transparency of use - Misuse	Medium
Content distribution	- No prior use of AI mentioned. - Wished for automation of work processes (e.g., newsletter distribution)	- Automated content delivery by AI - Applicable across various channels and formats	- Data access	Low
Knowledge management	- Desire for improved knowledge management to break down information silos - Priority for AI project management	- AI for employee training and as an internal knowledge base - AI as a knowledge base or wiki for external users	- Data access - Data volume - Data quality - AI training.	Medium

literature analysis (application in research and practice), and (c) organizational implementation challenges stated in the interviews (feasibility). The prioritization focuses on activities that can be directly managed operationally from within the communications department. The interview guide only explicitly addressed these phases, as the subsequent phases could not necessarily be answered by the employees.

Dimensions marked as *high priority* should be addressed first, as they combine strategic relevance with strong integration potential: They show high overall potential based on the literature analysis and can be transferred to the typical workflows at the industry case. *Medium priority* applies to partially implemented or less central processes. These typically involve tasks that have already been partially implemented experimentally using AI or consist of less common work steps, and therefore are not expected to require any major restructuring within the company or its workflows. *Low priority* includes areas with limited relevance or unresolved challenges—but these should still be considered over a five-year horizon.

1. **Analysis:** ***Statistical data analysis*** has high priority: Target group analyses and data processing are established. AI has so far been used experimentally to interpret data and create personas, but there is a desire to expand AI-supported data analysis. Data protection, data quality, and accessibility pose challenges. Medium priority can be asserted to ***trend prediction***: There is no current use, but AI offers huge potential.
2. **Planning:** AI-supported ***strategy and concept development*** has a high priority. AI is already being used for communication concepts, but its potential for the experimental creation of different variants remains largely untapped. As concepts are complex, their use requires greater AI expertise for reliable results. ***Idea generation and creativity*** is rated as medium priority. AI is already being used as a source of inspiration for creative work and there is a desire to further utilize it to increase creativity. As the creative understanding of AI is limited, AI skills are essential to ensure originality and quality. ***Topic research*** can also be seen as a medium priority: AI is occasionally used for topic research and is desired as an assistant. The selection of sources, bias, and correctness of results must be critically examined.
3. **Organization:** ***Automation of workflows*** is categorized as high priority. Most interviewees want to automate organizational tasks. There are numerous applications with high potential, but implementation poses strategic challenges. In addition, dependence on existing software providers makes external solutions more difficult.
4. **Execution:** Since ***content creation*** is the central activity of the corporate communications unit, it is ranked high priority. Today, AI is primarily used for texts. Science and practice show great potential for increasing efficiency, but challenges exist in tool integration, choice of provider, data protection, copyright, technical infrastructure, increasing computing power, sustainability, and the risk of generic content. AI is currently not used for ***personalization*** but is seen as useful for this. Greater individualization would be important for more effective

communication, but data protection, data quality, and data access pose challenges. Therefore, a medium priority is attributed. The need for ***translations*** is low. In addition, large language models (LLMs) deliver good results even without a high level of expertise. Therefore, low priority is noted. ***Transcription*** on the other hand, has a medium priority: It has hardly been used to date, but offers potential to increase efficiency, e.g., in meetings.

5. **Evaluation:** ***Monitoring*** should have a high priority. Although there is great potential in areas such as media monitoring, sentiment analysis, and impact measurement, the company has not yet used any of it. The selection of suitable sources and access to the necessary data are challenges. ***Controlling*** is also ranked high priority. AI is already used, but the application is not yet widespread in the company. Specialized tools are essential, as LLMs sometimes deliver unreliable results. In addition, access to various channels, APIs, and access tokens makes data analysis more difficult. AI-supported ***presentation evaluation*** as well as AI-based ***self-reflection*** is not used or desired; both are ranked low priority. The level of technological maturity is also unclear, as a lack of empathy and context dependency limit applicability. The organization already uses an AI solution for ***benchmarking***, but not comprehensively. Its use is also not established in the literature and challenges lie in data quality, quantity, and access. Hence, it is seen medium priority.
6. **Output:** Interviewees do not use AI for ***content distribution***, but there is interest in automation, for example, for sending newsletters. Challenges lie in accessing data and connection to existing systems; hence it is low priority. AI is neither used for ***query response*** nor seen as a need, nevertheless chatbots are considered a successful application in the literature. Challenges include a lack of empathy, cybersecurity risks and the labeling of bots, while advantages include a reduction in the workload of employees and better accessibility; hence level is medium priority. The same applies to ***knowledge management***. A reduction of information silos and an improvement in knowledge management would be desired. AI can avoid redundancies, facilitate access to information, and provide support through knowledge databases. Challenges lie in organizational silos, data-related problems, and the need for large, high-quality data volumes.

15.5 Discussion and Areas for Future Research

This chapter contributes a structured and comprehensive framework for AI adoption across all phases of the communication management process. While previous research has often focused on isolated tools or application areas, the AI-supported communication value chain developed offers a process-oriented, holistic perspective grounded in both academic and professional discourse.

Its central theoretical contribution lies in mapping AI functionalities onto established phases of communication management and aligning them with documented potentials. This conceptual structure supports a more integrated understanding of AI in strategic communication and offers a basis for empirical exploration across diverse organizational contexts. To maintain analytical and practical relevance, the framework should be continuously reviewed and refined, particularly as the weighting of individual process phases may shift over time.

The case study confirms that AI is already reshaping corporate communication—especially in execution, planning, and evaluation—while also revealing implementation gaps, notably in strategic development and organizational coordination. Interviewees identified potential in automating workflows and enhancing content production, while also highlighting structural, technical, and cultural barriers. Strategic AI adoption requires not only technological readiness but also clear alignment with communication goals, sufficient AI literacy, and integrated infrastructures such as dashboards or editorial systems. Overcoming organizational silos remains essential to enabling cross-functional collaboration and knowledge sharing.

AI should not be understood as a replacement for human expertise, but as a collaborative agent that augments creativity, accelerates workflows, and supports personalization. For communication professionals, this shift implies not redundancy, but a redefinition of roles and competences.

Future research should empirically examine the long-term effects of AI integration on communication strategy, organizational roles, and value creation. Particular attention should be given to ethical considerations, trust mechanisms, and regulatory frameworks as AI systems increasingly interact with stakeholders. Comparative and cross-sectoral studies may also reveal relevant institutional or cultural conditions. In addition, the evolving dynamics of human–machine collaboration—especially its emotional and cognitive implications for professionals—represent a largely underexplored area of inquiry.

15.6 Conclusion

Artificial intelligence is set to fundamentally transform corporate content production by enhancing strategic planning, automating workflows, and enabling more personalized and engaging communication. This chapter introduced a framework for understanding AI's role across all phases of the communication management process and demonstrated its applicability through a real-world case from the European IT sector.

The findings highlight both the transformative potential and the contextual limitations of AI. Successful implementation depends not only on technological capabilities but also on organizational readiness, cross-functional alignment, and a culture of continuous learning. In this regard, the corporate newsroom offers a strong foundation: its established workflows and digital infrastructure enhance readiness; its interdisciplinary setup fosters alignment; and its iterative, fast-paced working mode promotes learning and adaptability—key conditions for AI adoption. Rather than replacing communication professionals, AI is likely to shift their roles—augmenting creativity, accelerating processes, and enhancing strategic decision-making. Ultimately, the implementation of AI is not just a technical upgrade, but a comprehensive change process that affects structures, roles, and routines, which should be reflected in communication research.

By embracing AI as a collaborative agent and adopting a structured, phase-oriented approach to integration, communication departments can position themselves as agile, adaptive, and future-ready actors in a dynamic media landscape. Continued empirical research and critical reflection will be essential to ensure that AI-supported communication systems remain both effective and responsible.

References

Adi, A. (2023). *Artificial intelligence in public relations and communications: Cases, reflections and predictions*. Quadriga University of Applied Sciences. https://www.quadriga-hochschule.com/app/uploads/2023/09/QHS_Artificial_Intelligence_in_Public_Relations__Communications_2023-2.pdf

Alsheibani, S., Messom, D. C., Cheung, Y., & Alhosni, M. (2020). *Reimagining the strategic management of artificial intelligence: Five recommendations for business leaders*. AMCIS 2020 Proceedings. https://aisel.aisnet.org/amcis2020/is_leadership/is_leadership/4

AMEC. (2016). *Taxonomy. AMEC integrated evaluation framework*. https://amecorg.com/amecframework/home/supporting-material/taxonomy/

Appel, M., & Biebl, M. (2023). 99+ 2 nützliche Prompts für die PR. [99+2 useful prompts for PR.] *PR Report*, 5, 30–38.

Baetzgen, A., & Tropp, J. (2013). "Owned media": Developing a theory from the buzzword. *Studies in Media and Communication, 1*(2), 1–10. https://doi.org/10.11114/smc.v1i2.172

Bajak, M., & Majerczyk, P. (2022). Identification of areas for optimising marketing communications via AI systems. Scientific papers of Silesian university of technology. *Organization & Management, 160*(139), 25–38. https://doi.org/10.29119/1641-3466.2022.160.2

Banasik, A., & Pikiewicz, P. (2023). Application of AI in crisis management. Scientific papers of Silesian university of technology. *Organization & Management /Zeszyty Naukowe Politechniki Slaskiej. Seria Organizacji i Zarzadzanie, 186*, 9–19. bth. https://doi.org/10.29119/1641-3466.2023.186.1

Bastian, M., & Stoltenow, S. (2023). So verändert Sprach-KI die Arbeit mit Texten. [How language AI is changing the way we work with texts] *PR Report*, 4, 38–41.

Behera, R. K., Rehman, A., Islam, M. S., Abbasi, F. A., & Imtiaz, A. (2024). Intelligent machines as information and communication technology and their influence on sustainable marketing practices for beneficial impact on business performance: A conceptual framework. *Journal of Cleaner Production, 475*, 1–12. https://doi.org/10.1016/j.jclepro.2024.143676

Behrens, L., Moss, C., & Sadrowski, M. (2021). The journalistic newsroom as a blueprint for corporate communications. In C. Moss (Ed.), *The corporate newsroom. Steering companies efficiently through communication* (pp. 7–24). Springer. https://doi.org/10.1007/978-3-030-67642-1

Benz, L., & Zerfaß, A. (2024). Metaverse für die interne Unternehmenskommunikation. [Metaverse for internal communication.] *Kommunikationsmanager*, 21(1), 46–49.

Bergner, A. S., Hildebrand, C., & Häubl, G. (2023). Machine talk: How verbal embodiment in conversational AI shapes consumer–brand relationships. *Journal of Consumer Research, 50*(4), 742–764. https://doi.org/10.1093/jcr/ucad014

Bernau, P. (2023). Mehr Ideen durch chat GPT. [More ideas with chat GPT.] *PR Report*, 3, 34–35.

Biebl, M., Bindhammer, T., & Appel, M. (2024). Künstliche Intelligenz 2.0. [Artificial intelligence 2.0.] *PR Report*, 3, 2–15.

Biebl, M., Bindhammer, T., & Haberman, L. (2023). Künstliche Intelligenz: Wie PR-Profis chat GPT, Midjourney und co. smart und sicher als tägliche Arbeitshelfer einsetzen können.

[Artificial intelligence: How PR professionals can use ChatGPT, Midjourney & co. smartly and safely as everyday work tools] *PR Report,* 3, 2–15.

Binlibdah, S. (2024). Investigating the role of artificial intelligence to measure consumer efficiency: The use of strategic communication and personalized media content. *Journalism and Media, 5*(3), 1142–1161. https://doi.org/10.3390/journalmedia5030073

Biswal, S. K. (2020). The space of artificial intelligence in public relations: The way forward. In A. J. Kulkarni & S. C. Satapathy (Eds.), *Optimization in machine learning and applications* (pp. 169–176). Springer Singapore. https://doi.org/10.1007/978-981-15-0994-0_11

Broom, G. M., Casey, S., & Ritchey, J. (1997). Toward a concept and theory of organization-public relationships. *Journal of Public Relations Research, 9*(2), 83–98. https://doi.org/10.1207/s1532754xjprr0902_01

Bruhn, M. (2008). Planning integrated marketing communications. Communication and leadership in the 21st century: The difficult path from classical public relations to genuine modern communication management. In H. Sievert & D. Bell (Eds.), *Communication and leadership in the 21st century. The difficult path from classical public relations to genuine modern communication management* (pp. 13–34). Verlag Bertelsmann Stiftung.

Brune, G. (2023). Künstliche Intelligenz. [Artificial intelligence] *Kommunikationsmanager,* 1, 14–16.

Bruning, S. D., & Ledingham, J. A. (1999). *Public relations as relationship management: A relational approach to the study and practice of public relations.* Lawrence Erlbaum Associates.

Buhmann, A., & Volk, S. C. (2022). Measurement and evaluation: Framework, methods, and critique. In J. Falkheimer & M. Heide (Eds.), *Research handbook on strategic communication* (pp. 475–489). Edward Elgar Publishing. https://doi.org/10.4337/9781800379893.00039

Cusnir, C., & Neagu, A. N. (2024). Using generative artificial intelligence tools in public relations: Ethical concerns and the impact on the profession in the Romanian context. *Communications Society, 37*(4), 309–323. https://doi.org/10.15581/003.37.4.309-323

Dogan, O., & Gurcan, O. F. (2024). Enhancing e-business communication with a hybrid rule-based and extractive-based chatbot. *Journal of Theoretical & Applied Electronic Commerce Research, 19*(3), 1984–1999. https://doi.org/10.3390/jtaer19030097

Durmus Şenyapar, H. N. (2024). The digital transformation: The forty years of marketing communication research. *Dijital D.nüşüm: Pazarlama İletişimi Araştırmalarının Kırk Yılı., 14*(1), 197–229. https://doi.org/10.18074/ckuiibfd.1377357

Gabelaia, I., Bagočiūnaitė, R., & Navickienė, V. (2024). Exploring the intersections of artificial intelligence, organizational behavior, and communication dynamics in the modern workplace. *International Journal of Management, Knowledge and Learning, 13.* https://doi.org/10.53615/2232-5697.13.71-80

Gentsch, P. (2023). ChatGPT & co als business booster. [ChatGPT & co as business booster.] *Kommunikationsmanager,* 1, 18–21.

George, S., Hovan George, A. S., Baskar, T., & Gabrio Martin, A. S. (2023). Revolutionizing business communication: Exploring the potential of GPT-4 in corporate settings. *Partners Universal International Research Journal (PUIRJ), 2*(1), 149–157. https://doi.org/10.5281/ZENODO.7775900

Getchell, K. M., Carradini, S., Cardon, P. W., Fleischmann, C., Ma, H., Aritz, J., & Stapp, J. (2022). Artificial intelligence in business communication: The changing landscape of research and teaching. *Business & Professional Communication Quarterly, 85*(1), 7–33. https://doi.org/10.1177/23294906221074311

Göke, K. (2023). Hungriger Ideengeber. [Hungry idea generator] *KOM–Magazin für Kommunikation,* 1, 64–65.

Göke, K. (2024a). Das Auge denkt mit. [The eye thinks too] *KOM–Magazin für Kommunikation,* 3, 54–55.

Göke, K. (2024b). Einsteigen, bitte ![All aboard!] *KOM–Magazin für Kommunikation*, 4, 61.

Göke, K. (2024c). Memes leicht gemacht. [Memes easily done] *KOM–Magazin für Kommunikation,* 4, 65.

Haller, C. (2024). GWPR-Kolumne: Zeitalter der Effizienz. [GWPR column: The age of efficiency.] *PR Magazin*, 3, 27.

Hancock, J. T., Naaman, M., & Levy, K. (2020). AI-mediated communication: Definition, research agenda, and ethical considerations. *Journal of Computer-Mediated Communication, 25*(1), 89–100. https://doi.org/10.1093/jcmc/zmz022

Harms, P. D., & Han, G. (2018). Algorithmic leadership: The future is now. *Journal of Leadership Studies, 12*(4), 74–75. https://doi.org/10.1002/jls.21615

Helfferich, C. (2022). Leitfaden-und Experteninterviews. In N. Baur & J. Blasius (Eds.), *Handbuch Methoden der empirischen Sozialforschung [Handbook of methods of empirical social research]* (pp. 875–892). Springer VS.

Holtzhausen, D. R., & Zerfass, A. (2013). Strategic communication—Pillars and perspectives of an alternative paradigm. In A. Zerfaß, L. Rademacher, & S. Wehmeier (Eds.), *Organisationskommunikation und Public Relations* (pp. 73–94). Springer. https://doi.org/10.1007/978-3-531-18961-1_4

Hromatka, C. (2024). Das KI-Narrativ selbst bestimmen. [Taking control of the AI narrative.] *Kommunikationsmanager,* 2, 14–16.

Iaia, L., Nespoli, C., Vicentini, F., Pironti, M., & Genovino, C. (2024). Supporting the implementation of AI in business communication: The role of knowledge management. *Journal of Knowledge Management, 28*(1), 85–95. https://doi.org/10.1108/JKM-12-2022-0944

Karst, A. (2023). Wie KI den Bildermarkt verändert. [How AI changes the picture market.] *PR Report,* 4, 42–43.

Keel, G. and Niederhäuser, M. (2016). *Corporate Newsrooms in der Schweiz. Ergebnisse einer Befragung von Schweizer Unternehmen und Verwaltungen,* study report by IAM Institute of Applied Media Studies, Zürich University of Applied Sciences (ZHAW). https://blog.zhaw.ch/iam/files/2016/06/IAM_CorpNewsroomSchweiz_2016.pdf

Kelm, K., & Johann, M. (2024). Artificial intelligence in corporate communications: Determinants of acceptance and transformative processes. *Corporate Communications: An International Journal, 30*, 124. https://doi.org/10.1108/CCIJ-04-2024-0051

Kondak, A. (2023). The application of eye tracking and artificial intelligence in contemporary marketing communication management. Scientific papers of Silesian University of Technology. *Organization & Management, 186*, 239–253. https://doi.org/10.29119/1641-3466.2023.186.18

Kubovics, M. (2024). Innovative content production in marketing communication through AI. *European Conference on Innovation and Entrepreneurship, 19*(1), 377–383. https://doi.org/10.34190/ecie.19.1.2877

Kyriasoglou, C., & Rest, J. (2023). Kampf der Götter. [Battle of the Gods.] *manager magazin,* 4, 36–41.

Laskin, A. V., & D'Agostino, G. (2024). The Delphi panel investigation of artificial intelligence in investor relations. *Public Relations Review, 50*(4), 1–9. https://doi.org/10.1016/j.pubrev.2024.102489

Łaszkiewicz, A. (2024). Artificial intelligence (AI) influencers in influencer marketing. Scientific papers of Silesian University of Technology. *Organization & Management, 193*, 23–34. https://doi.org/10.29119/1641-3466.2024.193.2

Ledingham, J. A. (2006). Relationship management: A general theory of public relations. In C. H. Botan & V. Hazleton (Eds.), *LEA's communication series. Public relations theory II* (pp. 412–426). Lawrence Erlbaum Associates.

Lee, J., & Park, J. (2023). AI as "another I": Journey map of working with artificial intelligence from AI-phobia to AI-preparedness. *Organizational Dynamics, 52*(3), 1–10. https://doi.org/10.1016/j.orgdyn.2023.100994

López-Garcia, X., & Negreira-Rey, M.-C. (2024). A multi-perspective approach to AI integration in the communication sector: Strategies, uses, debates, and challenges. *Trípodos, 55*, 6–9. https://doi.org/10.51698/tripodos.2024.55.08

Malthouse, E., & Copulsky, J. (2023). Artificial intelligence ecosystems for marketing communications. *International Journal of Advertising, 42*(1), 128–140. https://doi.org/10.1080/02650487.2022.2122249

Marell, S. (2023). Mensch und Maschine: Ein starkes Duo in der Kommunikation? [Human and machine: A strong duo in communication?] *Kommunikationsmanager*, 3, 14–17.
Mayer, B. (2024). World economic forum 2024: KI im Fokus. [world economic forum 2024: AI in focus.] *PR Magazin,* 3, 6–8.
Men, L. R., Qin, Y. S., Mitson, R., & Thelen, P. (2023). Engaging employees via an inclusive climate: The role of organizational diversity communication and cultural intelligence. *Journal of Public Relations Research, 35*(5/6), 450–471. https://doi.org/10.1080/1062726X.2023.2222859
Men, L. R., Zhou, A., Jin, J., & Thelen, P. (2023). Shaping corporate character via chatbot social conversation: Impact on organization-public relational outcomes. *Public Relations Review, 49*(5), 102385. https://doi.org/10.1016/j.pubrev.2023.102385
Mickeleit, T., & Tigges, R. (2023). KOM fragt. [KOM asks.] *KOM—Magazin für Kommunikation,* 1, 66.
Moss, C. (2021a). The corporate newsroom model. In *The corporate newsroom. Steering companies efficiently through communication* (pp. 27–48). Springer. https://doi.org/10.1007/978-3-030-67642-1_4
Moss, C. (2021b). *The corporate newsroom. Steering companies efficiently through communication*. Springer. https://doi.org/10.1007/978-3-030-67642-1
Moss, C., & Sadrowski, M. (2021). The dissemination of corporate newsrooms in practice: Empirical studies. In *The corporate newsroom. Steering companies efficiently through communication* (pp. 91–100). Springer. https://doi.org/10.1007/978-3-030-67642-1
Moss, C., & Stog, N. (2021). Integrated communication in the corporate newsroom as a contribution to Enterprise value. In *The corporate newsroom. Steering companies efficiently through communication* (pp. 7–14). Springer. https://doi.org/10.1007/978-3-030-67642-1
Neuen, D. (2023a). Alle Jobprofile werden sich durch KI verändern. [All job profiles will be transformed by artificial intelligence.] *PR Report,* 2, 12–19.
Neuen, D. (2023b). KI führt hoffentlich zu einer Sinnkrise der PR. Hopefully, AI will trigger an identity crisis in PR.] *PR Report,* 4, 34–37.
Neuen, D. (2023c). Manchmal fühlt sich KI an wie ein super-absolvent. [Sometimes, AI feels like a super graduate.] *PR Report,* 6, 47–50.
Neuen, D. (2023d). Welche PR-jobs die KI bedroht: Sieben Thesen zur Zukunft der Arbeit in der Kommunikationsbranche. [Which PR jobs are threatened by AI: Seven theses on the future of work in the communications industry] *PR Report,* 4, 24–32.
Neuen, D. (2024a). Alle Kernprozesse in der PR Sind automatisierbar. [All core processes in PR can be automated.] *PR Report,* 3, 14–19.
Neuen, D. (2024b). Besser als die Maschine: Was Kommunikationsprofis im KI-Zeitalter können müssen. [Better than the machine: What communication professionals have to be able to do in the age of AI.] *PR Report,* 3, 24–28.
Nilsson, N. J. (1998). *Artificial intelligence: A new synthesis*. Elsevier. https://doi.org/10.1016/C2009-0-27773-7
Ninova-Solovykh, N., Seiffert-Brockmann, J., Einwiller, S., Wolfgruber, D., & Berger, K. (2019). It's all about content. Strategic topic management in agile organizations (Communication Insights, Issue 6). Academic Society for Management & Communication. www.academic-society.net
Osei-Mensah, B. (2023). Strategic communication and artificial intelligence: Reviewing emerging innovations and future directions. *Archives of Business Research, 11*(1), 85–102. https://doi.org/10.14738/abr.111.13616
Panda, G., Upadhyay, A. K., & Khandelwal, K. (2019). Artificial intelligence: A strategic disruption in public relations. *Journal of Creative Communications, 14*(3), 196–213. https://doi.org/10.1177/0973258619866585
Paschen, J., Wilson, M., & Ferreira, J. J. (2020). Collaborative intelligence: How human and artificial intelligence create value along the B2B sales funnel. *Business Horizons, 63*(3), 403–414. https://doi.org/10.1016/j.bushor.2020.01.003

Pinter, D. G., & Ihász, P. L. (2019). Bridging natural language processing AI technique and corporate communications. *Informàciós Tàrsadalom: Társadalomtudomány Folyóirat, 19*(4), 100. https://doi.org/10.22503/inftars.XIX.2019.4.7

Poetz, F., von Kroge, L., & Sternberg, L. (2024). KI: Gezeichnet vom Leben—Und vom Bildgenerator. [AI: Shaped by life—And by the image generator] *PR Report,* 1, 54–57.

Rettig, C., & Mickeleit, T. (2023). There is no shortcut to AI. Or is there? In A. Adi (Ed.), *Artificial intelligence in public relations and communications: Cases, reflections and predictions* (pp. 63–72). Quadriga University of Applied Sciences. https://www.quadriga-hochschule.com/app/uploads/2023/09/QHS_Artificial_Intelligence_in_Public_Relations__Communications_2023.pdf

Savič, I. (2016). Mediatization of companies as a factor of their communication power and the new role of public relations. *Public Relations Review, 42*(4), 607–615. https://doi.org/10.1016/j.pubrev.2016.03.017

Schaller, M. (2024). Der mensch zählt. [The human counts] *PR Magazin,* 9, 22.

Schuster, M. (2023a). 15 inspirierende KI-cases aus der praxis. [15 inspiring AI cases from practice.] *PR Report,* 6, 35–44.

Schuster, M. (2023b). Fenster in die Zukunft: Wie verändert chat GPT die Kommunikationsbranche? [A window into the future: How is ChatGPT changing the communications industry?] *PR Report,* 1, 32–36.

Schweyer, A. (2018). *Predictive analytics and artificial intelligence in people management.* https://theirf.org/research_post/predictive-analyticsand-artificial-intelligence-in-people-management/

Seibt, C. H. (2024). Warum die KI zur Pflicht wird. [Why AI is becoming mandatory.] *manager magazin,* 4, 67.

Seidenglanz, R., & Baier, M. (2023). The impact of artificial intelligence on the professional field of public relations/communications management: Recent developments and opportunities. In A. Adi (Ed.), *Artificial intelligence in public relations and communications: Cases, reflections and predictions* (pp. 14–25). Quadriga University of Applied Sciences.

Seiffert-Brockmann, J., & Einwiller, S. (2020). Content-Strategien in der Unternehmenskommunikation: Themensetzung, Storytelling und Newsrooms. [Content Strategies in Corporate Communications: Topics, Storytelling and Newsrooms.] In A. Zerfaß, M. Piwinger, & U. Röttger (Eds.), *Handbuch Unternehmenskommunikation: Strategie—Management–Wertschöpfung* (pp. 1–17). Springer. https://doi.org/10.1007/978-3-658-03894-6_24-1

Seiffert-Brockmann, J., Einwiller, S., Ninova-Solovykh, N., & Wolfgruber, D. (2021). Agile content management: Strategic communication in corporate newsrooms. *International Journal of Strategic Communication, 15*(2), 126–143. https://doi.org/10.1080/1553118X.2021.1910270

Sieber, A., & Hoewner, J. (2024). Frankensteins Töchter. [Frankenstein's daughters.]. *PR Magazin, 4*, 46–49.

Steck, V. (2024). Wie KI sinnvoll eingesetzt werden kann: Die Rolle der Kommunikation bei der Kundenzufriedenheit. [How AI can be used meaningfully: The role of communication in customer satisfaction.] *Kommunikationsmanager,* 3, 10–12.

Swiatek, L., & Galloway, C. (2022). Artificial intelligence and public relations. In D. Pompper, K. R. Place, & C. K. Weaver (Eds.), *The Routledge companion to public relations* (pp. 352–362). Routledge. https://doi.org/10.4324/9781003131700-32

Ta, B. (2023). KI in der Kommunikation: Assistenz oder Konkurrenz? [AI in communication: Assistant or competitor?] *Kommunikationsmanager,* 2, 34–37.

Tredinnick, L. (2017). Artificial intelligence and professional roles. *Business Information Review, 34*(1), 37–41. https://doi.org/10.1177/0266382117692621

Upadhyay, A. K., & Khandelwal, K. (2018). Applying artificial intelligence: Implications for recruitment. *Strategic HR Review, 17*(5), 255–258. https://doi.org/10.1108/SHR-07-2018-0051

van der Mer, T. G. L. A., & Jonkman, J. G. F. (2021). Politicization of corporations and their environment: Corporations' social license to operate in a polarized and mediatized society. *Public Relations Review, 47*(10), 101988. https://doi.org/10.1016/j.pubrev.2020.101988

Van Quaquebeke, N., & Gerpott, F. H. (2024). Artificial intelligence (AI) and workplace communication: Promises, perils, and recommended policy. *Journal of Leadership & Organizational Studies, 31*(4), 375–381. https://doi.org/10.1177/15480518241289644

Von dem Bussche, C. (2023). So erstellen Sie Bilder mit KI. [How to create images with AI.] *PR Report,* 3, 28–32.

Weller, T., & Lock, I. (2024). Automated communication's impact on strategic communication: Implications from a systematic review. *International Journal of Strategic Communication, 19*(1), 13–34. https://doi.org/10.1080/1553118X.2024.2379501

Wiegand, M. (2023). KI muss rein in die Führungsebene. [AI needs to make its way into the executive level.] *PR Report,* 3, 36–39.

Wiencierz, C., Berger, K., Röttger, U. & Wietholt, C. (2017). Startklar für Big Data. Chancen, Voraussetzungen und Anwendungen für die Unternehmenskommunikation. [Ready for big data. Opportunities, requirements and applications for corporate communications.] *Communication Insights*, 4. Akademische Gesellschaft für Unternehmensführung & Kommunikation.

Zerfass, A., Hagelstein, J., & Tench, R. (2020). Artificial intelligence in communication management: A cross-national study on adoption and knowledge, impact, challenges and risks. *Journal of Communication Management, 24*(4), 377–389. https://doi.org/10.1108/JCOM-10-2019-0137

Cornelia Wolf Full Professor of Online Communication at the Institute for Communication and Media Studies (IfKMW) at Leipzig University, Germany. Main research interests: Media transformation, institutionalization of digital media, cross-media strategies, nonprofit communication, innovation and science communication, start-up communication.

AI in the Audiovisual Industry: Perceptions, Practices, Challenges, and Opportunities

16

Catarina Duff Burnay, Paulo Nuno Vicente, and José Manuel Sotero

Abstract

The rapid infusion of Artificial Intelligence (AI) into the audiovisual industry marks a pivotal evolution in content creation and production methodologies. This transformation is prominently visible in Portugal, where AI's integration has sparked significant interest among production companies, particularly within SP Televisão, which was ranked seventh among Europe's top production companies in terms of fiction output in 2019. This chapter examines how AI technologies are reshaping the audiovisual sector through empirical analysis and original data collected from SP Televisão. The study encompasses an extensive empirical investigation involving a survey by online questionnaire and expert panels across various departments within the production house. The questionnaire, achieving a 95% confidence level, was distributed to employees to gauge their understanding and attitudes toward AI, revealing that while 51% of respondents possess basic AI knowledge, a significant 87% have never received specialised training in this area. Notably, 47% of the workforce anticipates a positive impact of AI on professional performance, particularly in automating repetitive tasks and enhancing operational efficiency. Further insights were derived from qualitative data collected during a series of five expert panels ($N = 31$), which discussed hypothetical scenarios involving generative AI tools, predictive analytics, and recommender systems. The findings indicate a curiosity and openness toward AI adoption, despite existing concerns about the digital transformation capabilities, AI literacy, and the suitability of AI technologies for specific production formats like

C. D. Burnay (✉)
Universidade Católica Portuguesa, CECC, LACS, Lisbon, Portugal
e-mail: cburnay@ucp.pt

P. N. Vicente · J. M. Sotero
Universidade Nova de Lisboa, ICNOVA, iNOVA Media Lab, Lisbon, Portugal
e-mail: pnvicente@fcsh.unl.pt; jmsotero@fcsh.unl.pt

S. Böhm et al. (eds.), *Handbook of AI-based Media Disruption*, Future of Business and Finance, https://doi.org/10.1007/978-3-032-07605-2_16

soap operas (*telenovelas*). The integration challenges identified include insufficient training and a general lack of comprehensive AI understanding, which hinders the full utilisation of AI in enhancing production processes. However, the interest in AI tools suggests a potential shift towards more technologically integrated production models, potentially leading to significant improvements in efficiency and creativity. This chapter highlights the dual aspects of AI in the audiovisual industry: the opportunities it presents for innovation and the practical challenges it poses in terms of workforce integration and acceptance. By analysing original data from one of Portugal's leading production companies, the study contributes to a deeper understanding of how AI is being incorporated into the industry and the broader implications for media production in Europe.

16.1 Introduction

The intersection between artificial intelligence (AI) and the audiovisual industry represents a rapidly transforming field, marked by substantial technological advances and disruptive potential across production, distribution, and media consumption processes. The increasing sophistication of machine learning algorithms, the exponential growth in computing power, and the availability of vast data sets have propelled AI into a central role in reshaping contemporary media ecosystems.

One of the most dynamic areas of this transformation is the rise of generative AI (Feuerriegel et al., 2024), which enables the automated production of high-quality textual, graphic, audio, and audiovisual content. Large language models (LLMs) can now draft scripts (Kumaran et al., 2023; Mirowski et al., 2023), while generative adversarial networks (GANs) and diffusion models make it possible to create images, graphics, and videos from text prompts (Jiang et al., 2024; Zhu et al., 2023). On the other hand, synthetic media generation exemplifies the power—and the risks—of realistically replicating human faces and voices (e.g. *deepfakes* (Gambín et al., 2024; Johnson & Diakopoulos, 2021)).

AI is also making significant inroads into editing and post-production workflows, with automated tools being increasingly used for organising, classifying, and manipulating raw footage. In parallel, personalised recommendation systems, based on techniques like transformer-based embeddings, have become central to curating digital media consumption and shaping audience behaviour (Vicente & Burnay, 2024).

It is against this backdrop of technological change that the present case study examines SP Televisão, one of Portugal's leading producers of television fiction and a European reference in the sector. Established in 2007 and based in Lisbon, SP Televisão employs around 300 professionals across specialised departments covering all phases of audiovisual production—from development and pre-production to final delivery for both linear television and digital platforms. The company consistently produces soap operas (*telenovelas*) and drama series, working with in-house teams dedicated to scriptwriting, directing, editing, sound design, subtitling, and other functions. This integrated production model enabled SP Televisão to rank seventh among the top fiction producers in the European Union in 2019 (European Audiovisual Observatory, 2020).

This chapter investigates how SP Televisão is engaging with the integration of AI technologies into its creative and operational workflows. To this end, an original mixed-methods research design was implemented. The quantitative component involved an online survey distributed among employees, conducted with a 95% confidence level and a margin of error of 5%. The questionnaire assessed levels of knowledge and attitudes towards AI. The qualitative component consisted of five expert panel discussions conducted with staff members from various departments, in which participants examined hypothetical scenarios involving generative AI tools, predictive analytics, and recommender systems. These discussions revealed both an openness to AI adoption and concerns related to internal digital literacy, the suitability of AI solutions for specific formats—such as long-running soap operas (*telenovelas*)—and broader organisational capacity for digital transformation.

Taken together, the findings highlight the dual impact of AI on the audiovisual sector: on the one hand, the opportunities for innovation through technological integration; on the other, the practical challenges of workforce adaptation, training needs, and organisational readiness. By providing an in-depth analysis of a leading Portuguese production company, this chapter contributes to a broader understanding of how AI is being integrated into media production across Europe, and of the implications this shift holds for the future of creative and technical labour in the industry.

16.2 Literature Review

The intersection between AI and the audiovisual industry represents a significant and ongoing transformation within contemporary media ecosystems. While it would be premature to describe this convergence as revolutionary in all its dimensions, the growing integration of AI—particularly generative models—has begun to reshape established workflows, influence aesthetic norms, and redefine the modalities of audience interaction and content distribution, as current AI tools tend to operate as augmentative systems, offering new possibilities for automation, experimentation, and scalability (Caballero et al., 2025; Caballero & Sora-Domenjó, 2024; Franganillo, 2023; Ufarte-Ruiz et al., 2024).

This section offers a brief overview of the current state of the art regarding AI's role in the audiovisual sector. To support this analysis, a literature review was conducted using the Web of Science Core Collection. The search strategy employed the following query: ("artificial intelligence" OR "generative AI") AND ("audiovisual" OR "television" OR "film" OR "cinema"), targeting documents published between 2020 and 2025. The search was restricted to publications in English and to the following document types: article, review article, and proceeding paper. To ensure disciplinary relevance, results were filtered by research areas such as Communication, Film, Radio, and Television, Cultural Studies, Sociology, Arts and Humanities, among others. AI technologies are progressively being integrated across multiple phases of audiovisual production, from the early stages of planning and script development to distribution and audience analytics. Commercially available tools such as Runway, Midjourney, and Stable Diffusion enable the creation of audiovisual content using relatively modest resources. This growing accessibility empowers independent artists and smaller studios to adopt techniques that were once the preserve of large-scale productions. As a result, AI may contribute to the diversification of the creative landscape, offering space for innovation beyond dominant commercial circuits (Bo, 2021; Wang et al., 2023).

Within content development, AI is increasingly functioning as a co-creative agent supporting script writing through the generation of draft dialogues and narrative outlines based on keywords or thematic inputs. It can visualise characters and environments described in text, and it can assist in building dynamic storyboards. Rather than replacing human authorship, such tools offer supplementary layers of input that may accelerate production and stimulate creative decision-making. In pre-production, AI has also proven useful in budget forecasting, logistical planning, and scene visualisation, contributing to a more efficient allocation of time and resources (e.g. Bo, 2021).

AI is likewise being embedded within virtual production environments, where it assists in the simulation of sets, lighting conditions, and camera movements. While particularly relevant to genres such as science fiction, fantasy and animation, these techniques are increasingly being adopted in more conventional film production and even theatrical and live performance contexts (Jungherr & Schlarb, 2022).

Post-production has emerged as a particularly fertile ground for AI applications. Machine learning tools are getting widely used to manage extensive audiovisual datasets, automating tasks such as scene classification, facial and object recognition, metadata extraction, and audio synchronisation. By reducing repetitive or time-consuming processes, these tools allow editors to focus on more creative aspects of their work (Kim & Lee, 2020; Song & Wook, 2020). Moreover, AI can function as an editorial assistant by proposing alternative sequences, pacing adjustments, or structural changes based on learned genre patterns or emotional arcs (Caballero & Sora-Domenjó, 2024).

Another prominent area of implementation is voice cloning. These systems are increasingly employed for reconstructing historical voices in documentaries or synchronising voiceovers across multiple languages. However, they also raise substantial ethical and legal concerns, particularly in relation to consent, authenticity, and the potential for misuse in disinformation campaigns. In some regions, notably in East Asia, AI-generated television presenters have already been trialled, prompting renewed debate about the role of synthetic performance in public communication and the implications for labour in the performance industries (Vizoso et al., 2021).

The growing integration of AI across the audiovisual production and distribution chain also includes film scoring, automated subtitling and machine translation, the generation of synthetic avatars, performing real-time facial motion capture, and executing background keying, thereby reducing production complexity and enabling greater creative flexibility (Liu, 2021; Tardel et al., 2021; Zhuang et al., 2022). On the reception side, recommendation engines powered by AI are now central to the user experience on streaming platforms, using behavioural data to personalise content offerings (Fulian Yin et al., 2015; Negrete-Yankelevich & Morales-Zaragoza, 2013).

16.3 Case Study

16.3.1 The Portuguese Audiovisual Sector and SP Televisão

The Portuguese audiovisual sector has developed from the sustained experience of telenovela production. As an industrial-scale format with its own distinctive characteristics, it has fostered the creation of short-serial formats, particularly by the public service broadcaster, owing to its specific remit and lower dependence on advertising revenue. Although this diversification of formats has been gaining traction over the past 5 years—enabling greater participation in international distribution circuits and the promotion of co-productions—the sector remains heavily reliant on the generalist channels and their rigid programming schedules. This has hindered independent production companies from taking the necessary "leap" towards sector consolidation. At the same time, this slow evolution has yet to provide the degree of certainty required to support the development of more ambitious public policies, akin to those being implemented in other European countries, where the audiovisual sector is increasingly recognised as a key asset for economic development.

In this context, the transposition of Directive (EU) 2018/1808 of the European Parliament and of the Council into national law through Law No. 74/2020 of 19 November brought a degree of hope to independent producers. The emerging digital ecosystem demanded not only regulatory adaptation but also the implementation of operational models capable of ensuring that foreign players with regular activity in Portugal contribute to the development of the national audiovisual industry. Although the outcomes of the legislative process fell short of the standards achieved in other jurisdictions—namely, Spain, France, and Italy—the entry into force of the new law nevertheless generated a sense of renewed optimism within the sector, particularly among independent production companies. In principle, the legal framework opened up additional opportunities for employment and exhibition of locally produced content.

These companies remain heavily dependent on broadcasters, particularly on the public service media, given its mission and funding structure. As such, they have been constrained by a horizontal programming model that has prioritised two telenovela strands in prime time, 5–6 days per week, for over two decades. While public funding has been progressively increased, it continues to be primarily allocated to cinema (70%) rather than audiovisual production (30%).

The limited investment obligations imposed on streaming platforms following the transposition of the directive have not resulted in a significant expansion of investment in national fiction production, nor have they facilitated the internationalisation of Portuguese series. Although data on co-productions and licensing agreements with international video-on-demand platforms are not publicly disclosed, available evidence suggests that the volume remains well below initial expectations.

According to the 2024 Annual Report of the Association of Independent Television Producers (APIT, 2023), over 90% of Portuguese independent production companies consider the new Cinema and Audiovisual Law to have had a predominantly "neutral impact". In open-ended responses, members expressed disappointment regarding the investment commitments foreseen in the legislation.

In this context, only a limited number of production companies possess the capacity to maintain a continuous production pipeline, and many continue to face significant technical and technological challenges, particularly due to insufficient resources to support a digital transition—an essential condition for remaining competitive in a rapidly evolving media landscape. In this regard, SP Televisão has distinguished itself through a proactive stance and has emerged as a key player within the contemporary Portuguese audiovisual sector.

SP Televisão is a Portuguese audiovisual production company based in Lisbon, established in 2007. The company employs approximately 300 professionals across various departments who regularly collaborate and operate throughout the entire spectrum of television fiction production, including development, pre-production, production, post-production, and delivery of scripted content such as telenovelas and drama series (SP Televisão, 2022). The company works predominantly with national broadcasters, and its production volume positions it among the highest producers of fiction hours in the European Union (Cardoso, 2021).

Organisationally, SP Televisão is structured into specialised departments corresponding to the main stages of the production process. These include units responsible for script development, technical planning, directing, filming, editing, sound design, colour correction, and subtitling (SP Televisão, 2022). The company maintains in-house facilities to support each of these functions, operating with dedicated teams assigned to specific phases of production.

The development of content is carried out internally by a team of writers and script editors, who work in collaboration with other departments to structure long-form fictional narratives. These narratives are then implemented through workflows that combine logistical coordination and technical execution, following the operational models established for serial television production.

In addition to national fiction projects, SP Televisão has been involved in co-productions and content distribution for other Portuguese-speaking markets. Its production model is designed to supply both linear television and digital distribution channels, incorporating delivery formats adapted to different broadcasting environments (Cardoso, 2021; SP Televisão, 2022).

16.4 Methods

16.4.1 Methodology

Considering the objectives of this study, a mixed-methods approach was adopted, combining quantitative and qualitative methods to explore perceptions, expectations, and potential impacts of AI-driven technologies within the organisational context of SP Televisão (Jensen, 2002). Data were gathered via an online survey (Ball, 2019; Slattery et al., 2011) and a series of expert panel discussions (Flick, 2018; Van Audenhove & Donders, 2019).

The online questionnaire consisted of 12 items organised into three thematic sections. The first section focused on participants' familiarity with AI, their predisposition towards its use, and anticipated impacts on daily work routines. The second section presented hypothetical scenarios involving the integration of AI into decision-making processes. The third and final section collected sociodemographic data. The survey was disseminated by the company's communication department and made available to 274 professionals who collaborate on a regular basis with the company. The data collection period extended from 31 May to 20 June 2023. A total of 167 responses were received, corresponding to a response rate of 61.95%. After data cleaning, which involved excluding 48 responses due to lack of consent for data processing and/or improper completion, the final sample consisted of 119 valid responses. Descriptive and inferential statistical analyses were applied to the data using a confidence level of 95% and a margin of error $\alpha = 0.05$. Statistical significance was considered for p-values below 0.05 (Agresti, 2018).

To complement the quantitative data, five expert panels were conducted with professionals from key departments involved in the audiovisual production pipeline (Flick, 2018; Van Audenhove & Donders, 2019). The structure of the expert panels was informed by the company's job description manual and production flow chart, ensuring alignment with organisational realities and processes. Participants were purposively selected to ensure representation across key departments involved in the audiovisual production pipeline at SP Televisão. Invitations were disseminated internally via the company's official communication channels, primarily through email, and participation was entirely voluntary. The recruitment aimed to capture a diverse range of professional perspectives, encompassing Pre-production, Production (including specialised teams such as set design, make-up, and props), Direction, Post-production, and Complementary Services. This approach facilitated a comprehensive understanding of the organisation's workflows, operational interdependencies, and internal communication dynamics.

The objective was to deepen understanding of work routines, data flows, interdepartmental dependencies, and potential reservations regarding the implementation of AI technologies. The sessions took place between 3 and 26 May 2023, with a total of 31 participants representing the departments of Pre-production, Production (including set design, make-up, and props), Direction, Post-production, and Complementary Services. Each session lasted approximately 90 min and was recorded with prior informed consent from participants.

16.4.2 Sample Characterisation

16.4.2.1 Online Survey

The sample comprises 119 professionals from SP Televisão who responded to the questionnaire. The average age of respondents is 42 years (mean [$\bar{x}$] = 41.47; standard deviation [s] = 9.65), with ages ranging from 18 to 64 years.

With regard to years of professional experience, participants report an average of approximately 15 years ($\bar{x}$ = 14.71; s = 9.45), with reported experience ranging from less than 1 year to a maximum of 40 years. In terms of educational qualifications, a significant proportion of the sample holds higher education degrees. Specifically, 59.72% of respondents possess a bachelor's degree, and a further 9.65% have completed a master's degree. In contrast, 37.63% of respondents have completed primary, secondary, or vocational/technical education. Regarding the roles held within the organisation, respondents are distributed across multiple departments, as defined in the SP Televisão Job Description Manual. The Head of Production and Post-production departments are the most represented, comprising 31.93% and 17.65% of the sample, respectively. These two areas alone account for nearly half of the total respondents, reflecting their centrality to the company's operational structure. Other departments with notable representation include Administration (7.56%), the Finance Department (7.56%), and Technical Direction (6.72%). Departments such as Communication and Marketing (0.84%) and Planning and Control (1.68%) are the least represented, which may reflect their relatively smaller size or lower response rates within the sample.

Overall, the data indicate a predominantly experienced and highly educated workforce, concentrated in core areas of production and post-production. A detailed breakdown of the sample's sociodemographic characteristics is presented in Table 16.1.

16.4.2.2 Expert Panels

A total of 31 professionals from SP Televisão took part in the expert panels, representing various key areas of the production process. The sample includes professionals from Pre-production, Production (including specific areas such as set design, make-up, and props), Direction, Post-production, and Complementary Services. The participants were distributed across five expert panel sessions conducted throughout May 2023.

The largest group of participants (n = 13) was drawn from the Pre-production and Production departments, highlighting the centrality of these phases in the audiovisual production workflow. Complementary Services—covering areas such as logistics and support functions—were represented by five individuals. An additional session focused on specialised production teams, including set design, make-up, and props, bringing together four participants.

The sample reflects a cross-section of operational roles and responsibilities within the company, providing a comprehensive view of daily routines, interdepartmental dynamics, and the internal flow of information throughout the production pipeline.

Table 16.1 Sample characteristics of the online survey

Factor	fr
Age	
18–27	8.40%
28–37	17.65%
38–47	44.54%
48–57	25.21%
58–67	2.52%
Did not answer	1.68%
Years of experience	
<1	0.84%
1-11	37.82%
11–21	32.77%
21–31	24.37%
31–41	4.20%
Education level	
Primary education	0.15%
Lower secondary education	0.31%
Upper secondary education	1.38%
High school	7.35%
Vocational or technical training	21.44%
Bachelor's degree	59.72%
Master's degree	9.65%
Role in the organisation	
Head of production	31.93%
Post-production	17.65%
Administration	7.56%
Finance department	7.56%
Other	7.56%
Technical direction	6.72%
Head of content	5.88%
General services management	5.88%
Artistic direction	4.20%
Planning and control	1.68%
Communication and marketing management	0.84%
Did not answer	2.52%

16.5 Results

16.5.1 Familiarity With, Predisposition Towards, and Anticipated Impact of AI Technologies

Analysis of the survey data indicates that most professionals at SP Televisão report either a basic understanding of AI (52.1%; 95% CI: 42.75%–61.34%) or a limited familiarity without in-depth knowledge (43.7%; 95% CI: 34.63%–53.09%). Only a small minority reported either never having heard of AI or possessing advanced knowledge of its applications, with both categories accounting for 4.2% of responses.

When examining potential associations between familiarity with AI and key sociodemographic variables—namely age, years of professional experience, and level of education—no statistically significant correlations of strong relevance were found. Nonetheless, some patterns emerged. Respondents who stated, "I have heard about AI but do not have in-depth knowledge", had the highest median age (47 years), while those claiming advanced knowledge of AI reported the lowest median age (42 years).

In terms of professional experience, the group with no knowledge of AI exhibited the highest median years of experience (26 years), while those with advanced knowledge reported the lowest. Educational background appears to be more strongly associated with familiarity: all respondents who claimed advanced knowledge of AI held a higher education degree (Bachelor's and/or Master's). Among those with basic knowledge, 56.76% had completed higher education. By contrast, none of the participants who reported no knowledge of AI had pursued higher education. Table 16.2 displays the distribution of professionals according to their self-reported level of familiarity with artificial intelligence (AI), disaggregated by age, years of professional experience, and educational level.

16.5.2 Integration of AI at SP Televisão

Emotional responses towards the integration of AI at SP Televisão appear to be predominantly positive, with 68.1% of professionals reporting feelings of curiosity

Table 16.2 Level of familiarity with AI by age, years of experience, and educational level

Level of familiarity	%	Mean age ($\bar{x}$) Median (M)	Years of experience ($\bar{x}$) Median (M)	Lower education (%)[a]	Superior education (%)[b]
I have no knowledge of AI	1.70	($\bar{x}$) 45.5 (M) 45.5	26.5 25.5	4.44	0
I have heard about AI, but do not have in-depth knowledge	43.70	45 47	13.77 12.5	51.11	39.19
I have basic knowledge of AI and its practices	52.10	41.82 44	15.5 17	44.44	56.76
I have advanced knowledge of AI and its applications	2.50	39.75 42	12.33 12	0	4.05
P-value	–	*0.5604*	*0.2709*	*0.0715*	

[a] *Group*: Primary Education, Lower Secondary Education, Upper Secondary Education, High School, Vocational or Technical Training

[b] *Group*: Bachelor's Degree, Master's Degree

and interest. Statistical inference suggests that the true proportion of respondents expressing such emotions lies between 58.07% and 76.31%.

When disaggregated by age, professionals who described themselves as excited and confident had the highest median age (45 years), whereas those reporting feelings of concern and insecurity exhibited the lowest median age (39 years). This trend is mirrored when the data are examined in relation to years of professional experience, with more experienced professionals tending to express greater confidence.

Among those who reported feeling excited and confident about AI integration, 13.51% had higher education, compared to 10.81% among those who reported feeling concerned and insecure. Respondents who described themselves as curious and interested made up the largest share of those with higher education (70.27%), while the indifferent group included the smallest proportion (5.41%). Although these differences suggest some variation across emotional response groups, statistical testing did not confirm a significant association between educational level and emotional orientation towards AI ($p = 0.3421$). Table 16.3 displays the reported emotions regarding the adoption of AI at SP Televisão by age, years of experience, and educational level.

16.5.3 Perceived Impact of AI on Daily Work Tasks at SP Televisão

Survey results reveal that 42% of professionals believe that the integration of AI will change the nature of certain jobs within the audiovisual sector, including those carried out at SP Televisão, while also creating new opportunities. The estimated

Table 16.3 Reported emotions regarding the adoption of AI at SP Televisão by age, years of experience, and educational level

Reported emotions regarding the adoption of AI at SP Televisão	%	Mean age ($\bar{x}$) Median (M)	Years of experience ($\bar{x}$) Median (M)	Lower education(%)[a]	Superior education(%)[b]
Concerned and insecure	10.1	($\bar{x}$) 37.17 (M) 38.5	13.5 14.5	8.89	10.81
Curious and interested	68.1	41.51 44	15.12 15	64.44	70.27
Indifferent	9.2	38.27 41	12.36 12	15.56	5.41
Excited and confident	10.1	43.8 45	16.33 16	11.11	13.51
P-value	–	*0.2709*	*0.6739*	*0.3421*	

[a] *Group*: Primary Education, Lower Secondary Education, Upper Secondary Education, High School, Vocational or Technical Training

[b] *Group*: Bachelor's Degree, Master's Degree

confidence interval for this response ranges between 33.03% and 51.41%, suggesting a prevailing view of AI as a transformative, though not necessarily threatening, force.

When responses were analysed by age, no meaningful differences emerged between groups. A slightly different pattern emerged in relation to years of professional experience, since those who expressed concern that AI might replace many jobs reported the highest median level of experience (17 years). However, statistical analysis suggests that differences in professional experience across the response categories are not significant.

Educational background also appears to influence perceptions. Among those who believed AI would alter the nature of certain roles while creating new opportunities, 51.35% had completed higher education. Table 16.4 presents the reported emotions regarding the adoption of AI at SP Televisão by age, years of experience, and educational level.

Table 16.4 Reported emotions regarding the adoption of AI at SP Televisão by age, years of experience, and educational level

						4.1. Automating repetitive and time-consuming tasks	
Reported emotions regarding the adoption of AI at SP Televisão	%	Mean age ($\bar{x}$) Median (M)	Years of experience ($\bar{x}$) Median (M)	Lower education (%)[a]	Superior education (%)[b]	Yes(%)	No(%)
Yes, AI will replace many jobs	10.1	($\bar{x}$) 39.41 (M) 40.5	16.25 16.5	11.11	9.46	7.14	12.7
Yes, AI will change the nature of some jobs, but new opportunities will emerge	42	40.9 44	13.28 13.5	26.67	51.35	57.14	28.57
No, AI will only have a limited impact on workers' tasks	21	40.44 44	15.25 15	26.67	15.57	17.86	23.81
I'm not sure	26.9	42.4 44	16.47 12	35.56	21.62	17.86	34.92
P-value	–	*0.6231*	*0.6005*	*0.0715*		*0.0156*	

[a] *Group*: Primary Education, Lower Secondary Education, Upper Secondary Education, High School, Vocational or Technical Training

[b] *Group*: Bachelor's Degree, Master's Degree

16.5.4 AI and Performance

Perceptions regarding the impact of AI on professional performance reveal a generally optimistic outlook. Nearly half of the respondents (46.56%) believe that their performance could benefit from the automation of repetitive and time-consuming tasks. An equal proportion (46.56%) expect AI to serve as a complement to creative work through the use of specialised software. Additionally, 32.06% foresee improvements in the optimisation and efficiency of information flows within the organisation.

When examined by age, the highest median age (48 years) was associated with respondents who indicated that AI would not contribute to improving their professional performance. A similar trend was observed in relation to years of experience, with this group reporting the highest median level of professional experience (17 years).

Among those who expressed confidence in AI's potential to enhance performance through task automation, 73.21% held a superiors' degree. This result indicates a substantial and statistically significant association between selecting the option "automating repetitive and time-consuming tasks" and holding a higher education qualification ($p < 0.05$). Table 16.5 presents the perceptions about how AI can enhance your performance at SP Televisão by age and years of experience.

16.5.5 Training on AI

Findings related to AI training indicate that none of the respondents reported having received advanced instruction in artificial intelligence. Despite this, interest in training is notably high: 86.6% of professionals expressed a willingness to engage in AI-related training, with the estimated true proportion ranging between 79.09% and 92.12%.

When analysed by age, the group reporting basic AI training had the highest median age (48 years), while those who had neither received training nor expressed interest in it had the lowest median age (42 years). However, statistical analysis did not reveal any significant differences across age groups. This pattern was similarly reflected when examining years of professional experience.

Educational background appears to show some variation across interest and experience in AI training. Among those who had not received training but expressed interest in doing so, 89.19% had higher education, compared to 10.81% in the group not interested in training. Notably, the proportion of professionals with only lower education was highest (8.89%) both among those with no interest in training and those who had received only basic training. No respondents with higher education reported having received basic training in AI. A statistically significant association was observed between educational attainment and AI training experience or interest ($p = 0.0404$), suggesting that educational level may play a role in shaping both exposure to and motivation for AI-related learning opportunities. Table 16.6 presents the reported feelings towards the hypothetical scenario where generative systems are used, considering age, years of experience, and education level variables.

Table 16.5 Perceptions about how AI can enhance your performance at SP Televisão by age and years of experience

Perceptions about how AI can enhance your performance at SP Televisão	Answer	%	Mean age ($\bar{x}$) Median (M)	Years of experience ($\bar{x}$) Median (M)
Automating repetitive and time-consuming tasks	Yes	46.56	($\bar{x}$) 39.66 (M) 42.5	15 15
	No	53.44	42.3 44	14.72 14
	P-value	–	*0.1259*	*0.5812*
Providing data-driven recommendations to support decision-making	Yes	22.9	41.79 45	15.18 16
	No	77.1	40.82 43	14.74 14
	P-value	–	*0.3637*	*0.5812*
Optimising operational efficiency related to information flows within the company	Yes	32.06	42.6 44.5	15.28 15
	No	67.94	40.28 43	16.64 13
	P-value	–	*0.398*	*0.5412*
Complementing my creative work through the use of specialised software	Yes	46.56	41.79 43.5	15.93 14
	No	53.44	40.79 44	15.45 15
	P-value	–	*0.6656*	*0.6656*
AI cannot help improve my professional performance	Yes	4.58	48.33 54.5	16.5 16
	No	95.42	40.67 43	14.76 15
	P-value	–	*0.1512*	*0.6227*
I'm not sure	Yes	19.9	37.95 41	14.09 12
	No	80.1	41.72 44	15.01 15
	P-value	–	*0.2394*	*0.6227*

16.5.6 AI Integration Scenarios

16.5.6.1 Generative Systems

When presented with a hypothetical scenario in which SP Televisão is producing a new telenovela using generative AI systems to draw on a video image database sourced from the Internet to automatically generate computer-composed sequences, 53.8% of professionals reported feeling curious and interested. Meanwhile, 29.4% expressed feelings of concern and insecurity.

In terms of age, those who reported feeling excited and confident had the highest median age (47 years). Across the different response groups, years of professional experience were relatively similar, with medians ranging between 15 and

Table 16.6 Training related to AI by age, years of experience, and educational level

Training related to AI	%	Mean age ($\bar{x}$) Median (M)	Years of experience ($\bar{x}$) Median (M)	Lower education (%)[a]	Superior education (%)[b]
Yes, I have received advanced training in AI	–	–	–	–	–
Yes, I have received basic training in AI	3.4	($\bar{x}$) 37.75 (M) 47.5	14.08 17	8.89	0
No, but I am interested in receiving AI training	86.6	41.29 44	15.32 15	82.22	89.19
No, and I am not interested in receiving AI training	3.4	40.17 41.5	11.08 12	8.89	10.81
P-value		*0.8127*	*0.8127*	*0.0404*	

[a] *Group*: Primary Education, Lower Secondary Education, Upper Secondary Education, High School, Vocational or Technical Training
[b] *Group*: Bachelor's Degree, Master's Degree

16 years—except for the group that reported feeling indifferent, which had a notably lower median of 7 years. However, these differences were not statistically significant.

Educational attainment was consistently high across all groups, with higher education qualifications dominating each category. The most pronounced variation was observed in the indifferent group (response option 3), which displayed greater heterogeneity in levels of education. These findings suggest that, while reactions to the use of generative AI in content creation vary, educational background remains a relatively stable factor across attitudes. Table 16.7 presents the reported feelings towards the hypothetical scenario where generative systems are used, considering age, years of experience, and education level variables.

16.5.6.2 Predictive Systems

As in the previous case, similar results were observed when participants were presented with a second hypothetical scenario involving the application of predictive AI. In this scenario, SP Televisão implements an AI-based analytics system designed to estimate the likelihood of success for specific productions by forecasting potential audience reach and return on investment. Among other production variables, the system evaluates narrative elements within scripts, identifying those most likely to enhance commercial performance. The creative team is then tasked with balancing the original, human-authored script with the optimisation recommendations generated by the AI system.

In response to this, 66.4% of professionals reported feeling curious and interested. The age distribution mirrored the previous scenario, with the highest median age (47 years) found among those who described themselves as excited and confident.

Table 16.7 Feelings towards scenarios by age, years of experience, and education level

Scenario	Feeling towards scenario	%	Mean age ($\bar{x}$) Median (M)	Years of experience ($\bar{x}$) Median (M)	Lower education (%)[a]	Superior education (%)[b]
Scenario 1: Generative systems	Concerned and insecure	29.4	($\bar{x}$) 40.17 (M) 43	16.09 16	37.78	24.32
	Curious and interested	53.8	41.3 44	14.66 15	51.11	55.41
	Indifferent	9.2	38.45 40	9.55 7	4.44	12.16
	Excited and confident	7.6	46 47	16 15	6.67	8.11
	P-value	–	*0.2472*	*0.3032*	*0.314*	
Scenario 2: Predictive systems	Concerned and insecure	19.3	40.17 43	16.09 16	11.11	24.32
	Curious and interested	66.4	41.3 44	14.66 15	73.33	62.16
	Indifferent	5	38.45 40	9.55 7	6.67	4.05
	Excited and confident	9.2	46 47	14.89 15	8.89	9.46
	P-value	–	*0.2472*	*0.3032*	*0.3161*	
Scenario 3: Recommendation systems	Concerned and insecure	32.8	41.18 43	15.64 15	33.33	32.43
	Curious and interested	47.9	42.86 44	16.16 17	48.89	47.3
	Indifferent	10.1	38.75 40	9.92 12	6.67	12.16
	Excited and confident	9.2	38.45 42	9.09 3	11.11	8.11
	P-value	–	*0.4102*	*0.0249 effect size = 0.0551*	*0.7952*	

A similar pattern was observed in relation to years of professional experience, with most response groups reporting medians between 15 and 16 years, while the group expressing indifference once again had the lowest median (7 years). As for educational background, the trend remained consistent with the previous case: higher education qualifications were dominant across all response groups, with no substantial shifts observed.

These findings suggest a stable pattern of emotional responses across different AI implementation scenarios, with levels of interest, concern, and indifference showing little variation, and demographic indicators maintaining a consistent distribution.

Table 16.7 presents the reported feelings towards the hypothetical scenario where predictive systems are used, considering age, years of experience, and education level variables.

16.5.6.3 Recommendation Systems

In a third hypothetical scenario, participants were asked to consider the implementation of an AI-supported casting system in SP Televisão's upcoming production. In this scenario, the system matches inputted criteria with potential cast members, providing computationally generated affinity scores to recommend the most suitable actors for each role.

In response to this scenario, 47.9% of professionals reported feeling curious and interested. Notably, this scenario elicited the highest proportion of concern and insecurity among all presented cases, with 32.8% of respondents expressing apprehension about the use of such a system.

Age distribution revealed that 59% of those who reported feeling curious and interested were aged 40 or older, whereas 58.3% of those who described themselves as indifferent were under the age of 40. A statistically significant association was also found between responses to this scenario and years of professional experience, with an effect size of 5.51% ($eta^2[H]$ between 0.01 and 0.06), indicating that 5.51% of the variation in responses is explained by professional experience. Specifically, professionals who reported feeling concerned and insecure tended to have more years of experience than those who reported feeling excited and confident. Similarly, those who felt curious and interested reported more years of experience than those who were indifferent.

With respect to educational background, 61.5% of those who expressed concern and insecurity held higher education qualifications. A nearly identical proportion (61.4%) was observed among those who reported feeling curious and interested when confronted with the idea of using AI-driven recommendation systems for casting decisions. Table 16.7 presents the reported feelings towards the hypothetical scenario where recommendation systems are used, considering age, years of experience, and education level variables.

These findings suggest that, while curiosity and openness remain prevalent, the application of AI to casting decisions raises comparatively higher levels of concern—particularly among the more experienced professionals—indicating that certain domains of creative judgement may provoke stronger reservations regarding the role of AI.

16.5.7 Expert Panels

The expert panels with SP Televisão professionals produced a set of concrete insights regarding the operational structure and data practices across the production pipeline. One of the main outcomes was the development of a comprehensive workflow diagram, detailing the circulation of tasks and information from the pre-production phase through to project completion. This diagram incorporates multiple layers of operational granularity, outlining specific actions, the types of artefacts produced, software tools employed, and the databases consulted and/or generated at each stage. This mapping allowed for a clearer visualisation of dependencies and critical handoffs between departments and production phases.

The expert panels also identified tangible needs for process digitalisation in several areas. These include the formalisation of data entry procedures, standardisation of file management systems, and the integration of metadata practices across departments. Such needs are viewed as foundational prerequisites for the future implementation of AI tools within the organisation. The findings suggest that, in order to enable the effective adoption of AI, a broader transition towards digitised workflows must first be prioritised.

Furthermore, participants provided input on existing points of friction or inefficiency in information flows, highlighting areas where automation or AI-driven support systems could add value. These include content cataloguing, scheduling coordination, and version control across departments. Regarding this, the expert panels allowed to map the current processes as well as to reveal strategic entry points for technological intervention, including AI tools, aligned with the real needs of each production phase.

16.6 Discussion

The integration of AI in the audiovisual industry has frequently been framed in terms of its disruptive potential. However, the findings of this study suggest a more nuanced reality. The case of SP Televisão—a company with a high degree of internal specialisation, long-standing operational routines, and substantial in-house technical capacity—reveals a complex interplay between openness to innovation, structural constraints, and varying degrees of digital readiness.

The survey results show that while a majority of professionals report basic familiarity with AI, there remains a significant gap in formal training. This asymmetry between interest and technical literacy is made explicit by the strong willingness to engage in AI-related training, despite the near-absence of prior advanced instruction. These findings suggest that the successful integration of AI depends not only on technological availability but also on the organisation's capacity to promote structured and continuous learning. The association between educational level and openness to AI-supported automation also reinforces the importance of tailored professional development initiatives that address both technical skills and broader conceptual understandings of AI's role in creative work.

On the other hand, attitudes towards AI integration were generally positive, with curiosity and interest emerging as dominant affective responses across all scenarios presented. However, emotional responses varied depending on the specific type of AI system involved. Generative systems and predictive analytics elicited greater enthusiasm, while AI-driven recommendation systems—particularly in relation to casting decisions—provoked higher levels of concern and resistance. This distinction suggests that the acceptability of AI is not uniform across all domains of the production process. Instead, it appears to be shaped by the perceived degree of creative autonomy at stake. Tasks considered routine or logistical are more readily associated with AI-assisted automation, whereas areas traditionally linked to artistic judgement—such as casting or directing—remain more sensitive to algorithmic intervention.

Moreover, the data show that professionals with greater experience or seniority tend to exhibit more cautious or ambivalent attitudes, especially when AI is framed as a replacement rather than a support tool. Conversely, respondents with fewer years of experience or higher levels of formal education are more inclined to view AI as a complement to their work. This generational and experiential gap may point to broader cultural dynamics within the organisation that could affect the pace and direction of technological adoption.

The qualitative data obtained from the expert panels contextualise these findings. Participants demonstrated a sophisticated awareness of the organisational realities shaping technological implementation. The workflow mapping exercise—which identified operational bottlenecks, artefact flows, and software usage across departments—served not only as a diagnostic tool but also as a platform for envisioning AI-supported improvements. Critically, however, the panels also exposed structural limitations that need to be addressed before AI can be meaningfully embedded into the company's production processes. These include the lack of formalised metadata practices, inconsistent file management protocols, and limited interoperability between departmental systems.

These panels confirmed that interest in AI is closely tied to concrete organisational needs. Rather than abstract enthusiasm for innovation, participants identified specific use cases—such as version control, content indexing, and scheduling coordination—where AI could offer clearer operational advantages. This alignment between perceived need and technological affordance seems a crucial precondition for effective implementation, yet it also requires that digital infrastructures and data practices be sufficiently mature to support such transitions.

16.7 Conclusion: A Roadmap for AI Integration in Production Companies

This chapter has examined how AI technologies are being perceived and integrated within the context of SP Televisão, a leading player in the Portuguese audiovisual sector. The findings suggest that while the discourse around AI is often dominated by narratives of disruption or replacement, the reality on the ground is marked by careful negotiation, contextual sensitivity, and gradual adaptation.

AI is seen by many professionals at SP Televisão as a promising set of tools capable of enhancing efficiency, supporting creativity, and reducing the burden of repetitive tasks. Yet its implementation is conditioned by structural, organisational, and educational variables that shape both its perceived usefulness and its potential impact. Training gaps, uneven digital practices, and resistance in areas associated with artistic autonomy constitute key challenges that must be addressed if AI is to be meaningfully integrated into production workflows.

Based on the original case study of SP Televisão, we outline a roadmap comprising a seven-phase strategy to support production companies in adopting a digital-first culture and integrating AI into their internal processes. Each phase includes actionable steps and is adaptable across organisational contexts:

Phase 1—Strategic planning and vision

1.1. Establish a permanent cross-departmental task force composed of representatives from key operational units. This team will lead the digital-first culture agenda and prepare the groundwork for future AI integration.

1.2. Conduct an internal audit to map the current levels of digitisation and datafication across production workflows and organisational processes.

1.3. Draft an internal position paper outlining the organisation's vision for adopting a digital-first culture. This document should include specific milestones for digitisation and the progressive adoption of AI technologies.

Phase 2—Knowledge building

2.1. Strengthen the task force by integrating departmental frontrunners with a proven interest or expertise in digital innovation.
2.2. Benchmark studies, partnerships, and sector-specific research regarding AI use in the sector.
2.3. Create internal communication channels (e.g. newsletters, forums, intranet spaces) for the regular dissemination of AI-related knowledge.
2.4. Identify and engage with external events, workshops, and conferences where staff can actively participate and report back.
2.5. Allocate a dedicated budget line to cover registration fees, travel, and accommodation for such external initiatives.

Phase 3—Datafication of internal processes

3.1. Organise training sessions and workshops on datafication, tailored to the specificities of the production company. Use case studies to support experiential learning.
3.2. Develop a procedural manual and organisational chart to guide the implementation of a data-first strategy.
3.3. Facilitate internal listening and clarification sessions to prepare teams for the rollout of the data-first implementation plan.
3.4. Draft a comprehensive Data Management Plan that outlines data governance protocols, responsibilities, and tools.
3.5. Introduce regular internal evaluations to measure the effectiveness and efficiency of the data-first implementation process.

Phase 4—Internal AI training and capacity building

4.1. Deliver foundational AI training programmes with the support of external trainers.
4.2. Identify department-specific AI training needs through interviews, surveys, or skills assessments.
4.3. Establish assessment moments to evaluate the impact and knowledge retention from each training initiative.

Phase 5—AI solutions integration

5.1. Design departmental roadmaps for automation and AI integration, based on strategic priorities and existing capacities.
5.2. Develop a formal AI Adoption Plan that includes timelines, risk assessment, and KPIs.
5.3. Conduct periodic internal reviews to assess the implementation success and identify areas for improvement.

Phase 6—Stakeholder engagement and compliance

6.1. Reassess the categories and structures of data collected for internal databases, with attention to relevance and ethical considerations.
6.2. Review third-party service contracts to ensure full compliance with applicable legislation.

Phase 7—Monitoring and impact evaluation

7.1. Create a monitoring and evaluation framework to measure the impact of digital transformation and AI integration on productivity and organisational culture.
7.2. Implement regular monitoring activities that track outcomes at both departmental and individual levels, ensuring continuous feedback and refinement of the strategy.

As the European audiovisual industry increasingly explores the potential of AI, the experience of SP Televisão illustrates both the opportunities for operational innovation and the critical importance of organisational preparedness, inclusive dialogue, and targeted capacity-building. The future of AI in media will not be determined by technology alone, but by the ways in which human professionals, institutions, and systems of meaning adapt to—and shape—its implementation.

Declaration of Generative AI and AI-Assisted Technologies in the Writing Process During the preparation of this work, the authors used ChatGPT in order to improve the readability and language of the manuscript. After using this tool, the authors reviewed and edited the content as needed and they take full responsibility for the content of the published chapter.

Acknowledgements This research was supported by national funds through the Fundação para a Ciência e a Tecnologia (FCT), under the project references UID/05021/2023 and UIDB/00126, Research Center for Communication and Culture.

References

Agresti, A. (2018). *Statistical methods for the social sciences (fifth edition, global edition)*. Pearson.

APIT. (2023). *Yearbook of the audiovisual production sector in Portugal 2023*. Association of Independent Television Producers. https://www.apitv.com/wp-content/uploads/2024/05/240506-ANUARIO-UCP-23-DIGITAL.pdf

Ball, H. L. (2019). Conducting online surveys. *Journal of Human Lactation, 35*(3), 413–417. https://doi.org/10.1177/0890334419848734

Bo, Y. (2021). Reflect on the application of human-machine cooperation Technology in Film art Creation in virtual production era. In *2021 IEEE 21st international conference on software quality, reliability and security companion (QRS-C)* (pp. 433–439). https://doi.org/10.1109/QRS-C55045.2021.00070

Caballero, J., & Sora-Domenjó, C. (2024). Automation and creativity in AI-driven film editing: The view from the professional documentary sector. *Communications Society*, 201–218. https://doi.org/10.15581/003.37.3.201-218

Caballero, J., Sora-Domenjó, C., & Codina, L. (2025). Implicaciones de la inteligencia artificial generativa en la narrativa y la estética cinematográfica: Un estudio sobre las convocatorias OpenDocs y +RAIN Film Festival. *Anàlisi, 71*, 55–76. https://doi.org/10.5565/rev/analisi.3773

Cardoso, J. A. (2021, April 8). *País da novela: Portugal e SP Televisão entre os maiores produtores de horas de ficção televisiva da UE*. PÚBLICO. https://www.publico.pt/2021/04/08/culturaipsilon/noticia/pais-novela-portugal-sp-televisao-maiores-produtores-horas-ficcao-televisiva-ue-1957670

European Audiovisual Observatory. (2020). *Audiovisual fiction production in the European Union*. https://rm.coe.int/european-fiction-production-2020-edition/1680a206c4

Feuerriegel, S., Hartmann, J., Janiesch, C., & Zschech, P. (2024). Generative AI. *Business & Information Systems Engineering, 66*(1), 111–126. https://doi.org/10.1007/s12599-023-00834-7

Flick, U. (2018). *An introduction to qualitative research* (6th ed.). SAGE Publications.

Franganillo, J. (2023). La inteligencia artificial generativa y su impacto en la creación de contenidos mediáticos. *methaodos revista de ciencias sociales, 11*(2), m231102a10. https://doi.org/10.17502/mrcs.v11i2.710

Fulian Yin, L. L., Li, Y., & Chai, J. (2015). Crowd mining system for TV program based on audience behavior analysis. *2015 Seventh International Conference on Advanced Computational Intelligence (ICACI)*, 48–51. https://doi.org/10.1109/ICACI.2015.7184747

Gambín, Á. F., Yazidi, A., Vasilakos, A., Haugerud, H., & Djenouri, Y. (2024). Deepfakes: Current and future trends. *Artificial Intelligence Review, 57*(3), 64. https://doi.org/10.1007/s10462-023-10679-x

Jensen, K. B. (2002). *A handbook of media and communication research: Qualitative and quantitative methodologies (Klaus Bruhn Jensen)*. Routledge.

Jiang, H., Wang, X., Christie, M., Liu, L., & Chen, B. (2024). *Cinematographic Camera Diffusion Model* (No. arXiv:2402.16143). arXiv. https://doi.org/10.48550/arXiv.2402.16143

Johnson, D. G., & Diakopoulos, N. (2021). What to do about deepfakes. *Communications of the ACM, 64*(3), 33–35. https://doi.org/10.1145/3447255

Jungherr, A., & Schlarb, D. B. (2022). The extended reach of game engine companies: How companies like epic games and Unity Technologies provide platforms for extended reality applications and the Metaverse. *Social Media + Society, 8*(2), 20563051221107641. https://doi.org/10.1177/20563051221107641

Kim, Y., & Lee, S. (2020). Exploration of the characteristics of emotion distribution in Korean TV series: Common pattern and statistical complexity. *IEEE Access, 8*, 69438–69447. https://doi.org/10.1109/ACCESS.2020.2985673

Kumaran, V., Rowe, J., Mott, B., & Lester, J. (2023). SCENECRAFT: Automating interactive narrative scene generation in digital games with large language models. *Proceedings of the Nineteenth AAAI Conference on Artificial Intelligence and Interactive Digital Entertainment, 19*, 86–96. https://doi.org/10.1609/aiide.v19i1.27504

Liu, Z. (2021). Research on subtitle translation from the perspective of computer-aided translation. In *2021 2nd international conference on artificial intelligence and information systems* (pp. 1–4). https://doi.org/10.1145/3469213.3471318

Mirowski, P., Mathewson, K. W., Pittman, J., & Evans, R. (2023). Co-writing screenplays and theatre scripts with language models: Evaluation by industry professionals. In *Proceedings of the 2023 CHI conference on human factors in computing systems* (pp. 1–34). https://doi.org/10.1145/3544548.3581225

Negrete-Yankelevich, S., & Morales-Zaragoza, N. (2013). E-motion: A system for the development of creative animatics. In *Proceedings of the fourth international conference on computational creativity 2013. Fourth international conference on computational creativity 2013*. https://www.computationalcreativity.net/iccc2013/download/iccc2013-negrete-yankelevich-morales-zaragoza.pdf

Slattery, E. L., Voelker, C. C. J., Nussenbaum, B., Rich, J. T., Paniello, R. C., & Neely, J. G. (2011). A practical guide to surveys and questionnaires. *Otolaryngology–Head and Neck Surgery, 144*(6), 831–837. https://doi.org/10.1177/0194599811399724

Song, Q., & Wook, Y. S. (2020). Exploration of the application of virtual reality and internet of things in film and television production mode. *Applied Sciences, 10*(10), 3450. https://doi.org/10.3390/app10103450

SP Televisão. (2022). *Sobre a SP TV*. https://www.sptelevisao.pt/pt/sobre-a-sp-tv/

Tardel, A., Hansen-Schirra, S., & Nitzke, J. (2021). Post-editing job profiles for Subtitlers. In M. Turchi & C. Fantinuoli (Eds.), *Proceedings of the 1st workshop on automatic spoken language translation in real-world settings (ASLTRW)* (pp. 13–22). Association for Machine Translation in the Americas. https://aclanthology.org/2021.mtsummit-asltrw.2/

Ufarte-Ruiz, M.-J., Borden, S.-L., & Codina, L. (2024). Introduction. The revolution driven by artificial intelligence continues: A journey through the media landscape. *Communications Society*, 197–199. https://doi.org/10.15581/003.37.3.197-199

Van Audenhove, L., & Donders, K. (2019). Talking to people III: Expert interviews and elite interviews. In H. Van Den Bulck, M. Puppis, K. Donders, & L. Van Audenhove (Eds.), *The Palgrave handbook of methods for media policy research* (pp. 179–197). Springer International Publishing. https://doi.org/10.1007/978-3-030-16065-4_10

Vicente, P. N., & Burnay, C. D. (2024). Recommender systems and over-the-top services: A systematic review study (2010–2022). *Journalism and Media, 5*(3), 1259–1278. https://doi.org/10.3390/journalmedia5030080

Vizoso, Á., Vaz-Álvarez, M., & López-García, X. (2021). Fighting Deepfakes: Media and internet giants' converging and diverging strategies against hi-tech misinformation. *Media and Communication, 9*(1), 291–300. https://doi.org/10.17645/mac.v9i1.3494

Wang, J., Huang, X., Yang, Z., & Zhao, W. (2023). Construction of artificial intelligence generated content in digital film production. In *2023 IEEE 22nd international conference on trust, security and privacy in computing and communications (TrustCom)* (pp. 2621–2628). https://doi.org/10.1109/TrustCom60117.2023.00366

Zhu, J., Yang, H., He, H., Wang, W., Tuo, Z., Cheng, W.-H., Gao, L., Song, J., & Fu, J. (2023). MovieFactory: Automatic movie creation from text using large generative models for language and images. In *Proceedings of the 31st ACM international conference on multimedia* (pp. 9313–9319). https://doi.org/10.1145/3581783.3612707

Zhuang, W., Qi, J., Zhang, P., Zhang, B., & Tan, P. (2022). *Text/Speech-Driven Full-Body Animation* (No. arXiv:2205.15573). arXiv. https://doi.org/10.48550/arXiv.2205.15573

Catarina Duff Burnay holds a post-doctorate in Communication Studies from the School of Communications and Arts, University of São Paulo and a PhD in the same area from the Faculty of Humas Sciences, Universidade Católica Portuguesa. Associate Professor at FCH/UCP, she is the Dean of the Faculty of Human Sciences and coordinates the Master in Communication Studies. She is a main researcher and member of the Board of Directors of the Research Centre for Communication and Culture (CECC) and founder and coordinator of LACS—Laboratory for Audiovisual Commuication Studies. She is the general co-coordinator of the Iberoamerican Observatory of Television Fiction (OBITEL) and coordinates the Portuguese team. She is a non-executive director of IMPRESA, a Portuguese media group. Her main research areas are media studies, media industries studies, AI and Audiovisual, fictional and entertainment content, production and programming strategies, media representations.

Paulo Nuno Vicente is an Associate Professor with Habilitation in Digital Media at the Faculty of Social and Human Sciences of NOVA University Lisbon, where he coordinates the NOVA Institute of Communication (ICNOVA). His research focuses on the social study of emerging technologies in their relationship with media, society, and culture.

José Manuel Sotero is a doctoral candidate in Digital Media at NOVA University Lisbon (FCSH), where he also earned a Master's in Communication Sciences. He is currently a visiting professor at NOVA FCT and NOVA FCSH. As a researcher, he is affiliated with the iNOVA Media Lab, OBI.Media, and is a founding member of the Social Observatory for Artificial Intelligence and Digital Data. In addition to his academic work, José serves as AI Integration Manager at the HAVAS Portugal Group and collaborates as a consultant in diagnosing and implementing AI tools in production workflows, particularly within the Cultural and Creative Industries.

AI Speech Generation: Balancing Disruption, Opportunity, and Performer Rights

17

Richard Savery

Abstract

Recent advances in artificial intelligence (AI) have led to text-to-speech and voice cloning systems that are nearly indistinguishable from human performances, causing both excitement and apprehension in the voice industry. While AI-generated voices offer unprecedented opportunities for scalability, efficiency, and creative experimentation, they also raise urgent concerns about consent, labor rights, and the erosion of artistic identity. Drawing on historical precedent, industry data, and firsthand interviews with practitioners on both sides of the technology, this chapter investigates the ethical and economic challenges arising from AI-based voice synthesis. By exploring the perspectives of a veteran voice actor and a CEO of an AI startup reputed for its ethical practices, we examine how these disruptive technologies can simultaneously threaten and transform professional voice work. Our findings highlight the growing importance of clear contractual boundaries, consent-based data acquisition, and fair compensation structures that treat performers as collaborators rather than expendable data sources. The discussion outlines possible pathways toward a sustainable AI ecosystem—one in which synthetic voices augment rather than replace human artistry, and where rights, revenue, and reputation remain securely in the hands of the people behind the microphone.

R. Savery (✉)
Faculty of Arts and Design, University of Canberra, Canberra, Australia
e-mail: richard.savery@canberra.edu.au

S. Böhm et al. (eds.), *Handbook of AI-based Media Disruption*, Future of Business and Finance, https://doi.org/10.1007/978-3-032-07605-2_17

17.1 Introduction

Artificial intelligence (AI) is rapidly reshaping the way voices are created, performed, and disseminated in modern media. With text-to-speech and voice cloning tools now capable of mimicking the nuances of human speech to a remarkable degree (Mehrish et al., 2023), content creators and production studios can integrate synthesized voices into everything from video game characters to virtual assistants. While these innovations expand creative possibilities and drive down costs, they also expose deep vulnerabilities for voice actors whose work can be appropriated, replicated, or replaced without adequate compensation or consent. Recent reports warn that unchecked voice cloning technologies may pose an "existential crisis" for performers, threatening both their livelihoods and sense of artistic agency (Huamani, 2025).

To understand these risks, it helps to recognize that AI speech now splits into two technological lineages. AI voice generation fabricates a non-identifiable synthetic timbre, essentially a "digital session actor" that producers can sculpt at will. AI voice imitation, by contrast, clones the spectral and prosodic fingerprint of a named individual, allowing entirely new lines to be spoken in that person's voice. Although this chapter focuses on the sharper ethical dilemmas raised by imitation, both lineages amplify economic disruption: generation removes human scarcity and drives prices toward zero, while imitation questions who owns, licenses, and profits from a recognizable vocal identity.

Against this backdrop, this chapter examines AI's impact on the voice industry through the experiences and insights of two central figures. First, we consider the perspective of Bonnie Bogovich, a seasoned voice actor who has long been proactive in updating her contracts with "No AI Clauses" to safeguard her vocal identity. Next, we explore the viewpoint of Brian Cook, CEO of WellSaid Labs, an AI voice company recognized for its commitment to transparency and fair treatment of the actors behind their synthesized products. Both Bogovich and Cook were interviewed by the author in March 2025, following a semi-structured format. Data from these interviews was then analyzed using the constant comparison method (Dye et al., 2000) to identify key themes and relationships. Drawing on the extended interviews and supported by resources from organizations such as the National Association of Voice Actors (NAVA), we situate their experiences within a broader historical context that highlights the recurring disruptions voice technology has introduced over the past century.

In doing so, this work contributes to a nuanced discussion of how AI-driven speech synthesis might coexist with and even enhance the craft of voice performance, rather than displacing it entirely. This chapter presents a balanced analysis of risk and opportunity, arguing that robust ethical frameworks, legal protections, and innovative business models are all vital to ensuring that humans remain at the core of a domain they have so long defined through talent, emotion, and creativity.

17.2 Historical Overview of Technological Disruption in Voice

Technological innovations have repeatedly disrupted voice-based creative fields over the last century, reshaping how voices are produced and consumed in media. From the emergence of radio to modern speech synthesis, each major advance has forced practitioners to adapt, even as it opened new opportunities. This section traces the evolution of these disruptions and highlights the continually shifting role of voice actors within them.

17.2.1 Radio, Talkies, and the Birth of Professional Voice Actors

Radio began its rise in the early twentieth century, creating a new broadcast medium for voice-only entertainment. Audiences could now experience dramas and news at home rather than attending live theater or vaudeville performances, which faced upheaval as a result. Voice performances on radio prompted the emergence of specialized talent, the first "voice actors," tasked with conveying character and emotion purely through vocal performance (Hilmes & Loviglio, 2002).

The introduction of sound in film around 1927 ("talkies") similarly upended silent cinema (Taylor, 2009). Actors were suddenly required to speak lines on screen, and some silent film stars could not transition to this new format, causing their careers to wane. At the same time, talking pictures created tremendous demand for actors with clear diction and expressive vocal presence, further establishing voice as a core element of cinematic storytelling.

17.2.2 Dubbing, Globalization, and the Expansion of Voice Work

By the mid-twentieth century, film dubbing technology allowed voices in a film to be replaced for different language markets, expanding the global reach of movies. This process could be seen as disruptive, as a single on-screen performance might be "re-voiced" by multiple actors, raising questions of authenticity. Yet dubbing fostered new employment for voice actors worldwide and consolidated their importance in media production (Bosseaux, 2018). Around the same time, voice acting took root in radio dramas and animation. Performers became central to bringing cartoon characters to life in theatrical shorts and later television programs (Cousins, 2025).

17.2.3 The Rise of Electronic Audio and Early Synthesis

In the latter half of the twentieth century, electronic audio technology developed to the point of encroaching on domains once entirely reliant on human vocalists. Early text-to-speech (TTS) and speech synthesis, while rudimentary, set the stage for today's AI-driven voices. As early as 1939, Bell Labs demonstrated the vocoder, an electromechanical voice synthesizer (Dudley, 1940), and by the 1980s, niche uses of electronic voices began appearing in entertainment. Some arcade video games used synthesized speech to save storage space. These robotic voices, however, lacked natural intonation and thus posed no real threat to professional human voices. They primarily served as novelties or special effects that hinted at future possibilities for synthetic voices (Story, 2019).

17.2.4 Video Games, Performance Capture, and the Broadening of Voice Acting

By the late twentieth century, technological advances in storage and processing (such as CD-ROMs and subsequent generations of consoles) allowed for more extensive spoken dialogue in video games. Early titles often made limited use of voice due to technical constraints, but landmark releases like *Fallout* (1997) and *Metal Gear Solid* (1998) demonstrated that skilled voice performances could significantly enhance interactive storytelling (Allison et al., 2020).

As games grew more ambitious, the role of voice actors expanded. Modern "AAA" titles feature tens of thousands of recorded lines delivered by professional casts, blurring lines between traditional screen acting and voice acting. Performance capture, which records voice, facial expressions, and movements simultaneously, allowed performers such as Andy Serkis and Troy Baker to infuse animated and game characters with lifelike detail that goes beyond traditional vocal work (Walton, 2020).

17.2.5 Remote Collaboration and the Globalization of Voice Talent

Advances in digital collaboration have further transformed how voice actors work. While performers once needed to record on-site with directors in professional studios, it became common, well before 2020, for actors to have home studios and connect remotely to clients via ISDN or internet tools like Source-Connect. These developments allowed a single actor to work with production teams on different continents, broadening access and reducing logistical barriers (Mandiberg, 2021).

17.3 AI-Generated Voices: Unique Disruption

AI-generated voices, particularly those created through deep learning techniques, represent a qualitatively new disruption in voice-based media. Unlike previous technological shifts, such as improved microphones or remote collaboration tools, AI voice synthesis allows speech to be generated without continuous human participation, raising fundamental questions about creativity, authenticity, ownership, and labor. Recent scholarly work explores these issues from ethical, legal, and labor-economic standpoints, reflecting a growing consensus that AI voice technology both promises new creative possibilities and poses serious risks for voice actors.

17.3.1 Why AI-Generated Voices Are Different

AI voice synthesis can closely mimic a human's voice, even when that human did not speak the recorded lines. Cloning technology now often requires only seconds of training audio (Li et al., 2022), enabling productions to generate new dialogue in the style of a specific actor, potentially without that actor's knowledge or consent. Unlike any previous innovation, this scenario shifts from using technology as a tool for human performance to technology acting *in place of* the human performer. The ethical dilemma is stark: a microphone cannot spontaneously impersonate someone, but an AI algorithm can, raising profound concerns about personal rights and creative agency.

Moreover, once an AI voice model is created, it can generate speech at massive scale with minimal additional cost. Producers see opportunities to accelerate workflows, revise dialogue at will, and cut expenses. Some studios already use AI voices for iterative "placeholder" recordings during pre-production (Carter, 2022), but the practice can quickly extend into final deliverables. This heightens the threat of displacement for voice actors, especially in lower-budget projects where cost pressures dominate. While past disruptions (e.g., remote studios) typically required actors to adapt their methods, AI voice generation could eliminate entire categories of work by obviating the need for human performance.

In creative terms, many directors and actors argue that AI-generated voices lack emotional nuance and spontaneity. Even sophisticated systems can produce a subtle sense of "artificiality" or the "uncanny valley" effect, potentially reducing audience engagement (Wang et al., 2024). Nevertheless, supporters view AI as a new tool akin to musical synthesizers, enabling novel vocal styles or real-time translation. These tensions underscore why AI voice technology has triggered deeper alarm than earlier changes: it can appropriate a performer's distinct identity, displace entire segments of the labor market, and alter the expressive nature of performance itself.

17.3.2 Emerging Ethical and Legal Debates

In response to these disruptions, scholars and practitioners have turned attention to ethical safeguards and new legal frameworks. The question "Who owns a voice?" is now a focal point in both media studies and intellectual property law, with many proposing that a vocal identity be treated akin to an image or likeness right (Paul, 2023). Scholars and advocacy groups call for tighter contracts and updated legislation, ensuring that any AI-generated performance involving a recognizable human voice is done with informed consent. In some jurisdictions, voice-likeness is now protected, such as the ELVIS act in Tennessee, USA (Fowler & Fowler, 2024). Unauthorized cloning has also sparked lawsuits and public outcry from high-profile voice actors whose voices were replicated without permission (Low, 2024).

Beyond legal structures, many researchers emphasize the importance of attribution and transparency: any synthetic voice that imitates a real person should clearly state its artificial nature and credit the original performer. Ethicists fear that without these measures, actors lose control not only of their earnings but also of the intangible essence of their craft, what Paul (2023) calls the erosion of "artistic identity."

17.3.3 Labor Dynamics and Economic Implications

Labor economists compare today's AI revolution in voice acting to prior waves of automation in entertainment. Though no consensus exists on the extent of potential job loss, multiple analyses predict a notable decline in traditional voice-over roles, especially in low-budget or entry-level categories with some estimating a 30–50% reduction in traditional voice acting jobs (Berger, 2024). Paradoxically, new "AI-adjacent" roles may emerge: actors might be hired to train or fine-tune AI models, or to provide emotional "finishing touches" that purely synthetic outputs cannot yet achieve. This scenario suggests a shift from performer to operator or collaborator, echoing how editing and CGI roles arose alongside new film technologies (Amba & Singh, 2023).

Unions and professional organizations, including the National Association of Voice Actors (NAVA), have begun to develop guidelines and best practices around the integration of AI in voice acting. According to NAVA's *Synth AI Info* resource (NAVA, 2025), key proposals include requiring a human in the loop for final performances, implementing minimum pay structures for AI-model training sessions, and mandating explicit consent for voice replication. Such measures could help preserve a more equitable landscape, especially for early-career talent who rely on smaller gigs to break into the industry (NAVA, 2025).

No-royalty AI voices exert downward pressure on rates by turning a human day-rate into a $0 software toggle. As quality gaps close, even ethically licensed clones must compete against a "good-enough-for-free" baseline. Scarcity therefore changes from actor minutes behind the microphone to intangible traits that generic synthesis cannot create, such as personality and recognizability. Actors who cultivate distinct vocal brands and negotiate transparent licenses can still command premiums, converting their voice into durable intellectual property rather than one-off labor.

17.3.4 Creative and Cultural Considerations

Scholars also point to the broader cultural and creative ramifications of ubiquitous AI voices. While synthetic speech can democratize content creation, allowing small teams or independent artists to access high-quality narration, there is concern about homogenization if studios converge on a few perfected AI voice models.

Representation and authenticity likewise come into play: AI could help performers transcend language barriers, or it could sideline diverse human talent by cheaply simulating accents and dialects (Paul, 2023). Conversely, in some contexts, such as Indian call centers, accents are intentionally neutralized, yielding a homogenized, mechanical voice that erases the richness of languages, dialects, and cultures (Chan, 2022). Furthermore, consumer reception remains an open question, with early advertising research indicating that audiences can be wary of synthetic voices (Wang et al., 2024). Yet younger demographics, accustomed to digital assistants and virtual influencers, may be more accepting of AI-driven performance (Zhang, 2023).

17.4 Bonnie Bogovich: Voice Artist's Perspective

Bonnie Bogovich is a seasoned voice actor and multimedia producer who has seen firsthand how swiftly AI voice technologies can alter the landscape. In her words, she has "been changing contracts based on this stuff" for years, well before she sensed that a "big AI scare" was dawning. According to Bogovich, the necessity of protective contract language became evident as far back as 2019, when she formally shifted her work into a freelance structure and began to notice early encroachments of synthetic voice in the projects around her. She recalled:

> Probably a couple years ago, starting before the big AI scare officially began, stuff was already feeling questionable, and I started seeing other colleagues like myself making legal clauses to paste into our contracts, clauses approved by their lawyers.

At first, her inclusion of what she calls a "No AI Clause" was fairly minimal. She explained that the earliest clauses simply forbade any use of her recorded speech to create non-fungible tokens (NFTs), which were surging in popularity around 2021. Over time, she expanded the scope of that restriction to cover "artificial voice technology" or "robot voices." Bogovich's rationale is clear: she has seen enough examples of voice data being repurposed in ways never intended or consented to by the original performer. Although she frames much of this as "protecting my voice," the subtext is also about ensuring fair compensation and preventing unauthorized usage that might harm her reputation or moral standing.

17.4.1 Evolving Contract Templates and "In Perpetuity" Clauses

Bogovich points out that voice actors commonly sign away usage rights "in perpetuity" when performing for a production, meaning the client can continue using the recorded material indefinitely and in multiple contexts. She says:

> Even before that, most template contracts say something like, 'may be used in all forms of media for all time.' When I first formed my LLC, I hired an attorney to help me write up some templates, and she was like, 'Let's limit that.'

The problem is magnified in the era of AI. If a company has raw recordings of her voice, it may be trivial, given today's machine-learning capabilities, to clone or fine-tune a voice model from that audio. Such a model could then generate new lines that Bogovich never recorded, effectively bypassing her control or additional payments. She argues that few voice actors, especially those starting out, are attuned to these hidden dangers. Many, she laments, "just sign," not realizing the potential scope of what "in perpetuity" means when combined with synthetic voice generation. To counter this, Bogovich and other experienced voice actors have begun inserting explicit prohibitions against AI training or cloning within their standard service agreements.

17.4.2 Unions, Industry Groups, and the Need for Solidarity

Though not currently unionized herself, Bogovich keeps a close watch on union-driven negotiations and guidelines. She references SAG-AFTRA's (Screen Actors Guild-American Federation of Television and Radio Artists) ongoing struggles to integrate AI clauses into its interactive media contracts, as well as the efforts of NAVA. NAVA, according to Bogovich, is "pushing for clarity" by circulating questionnaires and standard riders that require producers to state whether, and how, they intend to use a performer's recordings in AI contexts. In her experience, producers often assume they own the recordings outright and can do what they please with them:

> Producers often think, 'Oh, we own this in perpetuity.' But did they consider, for example, a scenario where your voice ends up somewhere you'd never approve of? That's part of why the SAG-AFTRA interactive contracts are still under negotiation, and NAVA has been pushing for clarity.

A key element of this clarity is setting boundaries around the possibility of "re-voicing" content. Bogovich emphasizes that such boundaries are not only about financial harm (e.g., losing out on future work), they are also about emotional well-being and brand alignment. Nobody wants to discover their voice attached to extremist material or explicit content. She points out that while this might sound hyperbolic, she is aware of colleagues who have had their voice data used without their knowledge.

17.4.3 AI As a Potential Opportunity, But Only with Guardrails

Despite her vigilance against unauthorized AI usage, Bogovich acknowledges the upside of AI voice cloning if it is governed by transparent, well-compensated agreements:

> It'd be great if I could license a 'Bonnie voice' for educational clients who regularly need me to record 20 hours of grammar scripts. If we set up a deal so they legally pay me for that

usage while I'm not in the booth constantly, that could be cool, especially if it's locked down so they can't just sell 'my voice' to third parties.

This concession highlights a nuanced stance: the core issue is not the technology itself but the labor relationships and control structures around it. Bogovich advocates a model in which AI is treated as a supplement to, rather than a replacement for, her creative contribution. She anticipates that ethical AI companies will likely adopt licensing frameworks akin to what the music industry has done for sample-based works, with detailed tracking of usage and corresponding royalties.

However, she also warns that "a lot of big studios don't want to handle that complexity." In her experience, some companies simply opt for a cheaper approach by hiring a voice actor who is unaware of these issues (or lacks the bargaining power to push back). This dynamic contributes to a "race to the bottom" environment, where unscrupulous entities exploit the least-informed or most desperate performers. Bogovich thus calls for industry-wide standards, accompanied by education for new and veteran voice actors alike, on reading contracts carefully.

17.4.4 Summarizing Bogovich's View

From Bogovich's perspective, the arrival of AI-generated voices is both a threat and an opportunity. On one hand, if not carefully regulated, it can erode basic ownership and compensation structures for voice work; on the other hand, it can expand a performer's reach and earnings if done ethically. The pivot point is contractual clarity. Her longtime insistence on adding "No AI Clauses" underscores her commitment to ensuring that the human talent behind the mic remains recognized, respected, and fairly paid, even when AI enters the picture.

17.5 Brian Cook: An AI Company's Ethical and Creative Vision

Brian Cook is the CEO of WellSaid Labs, a speech-synthesis company recognized for its commitment to ethical, high-quality AI voices. Coming from both a technology and an audio-production background, Cook built and sold multiple tech startups before focusing on AI. His interests in music recording and entrepreneurship converge at WellSaid Labs, where he aims to develop synthetic voices in partnership with voice actors rather than at their expense.

17.5.1 Core Ethical Distinction: Consent-Based Training

From its inception, WellSaid Labs made a deliberate decision to avoid large-scale audio scraping. According to Cook:

> The guys had an approach that said, you know, there's kind of two ways to start an AI business. You can get an ML engine, get some open source, point it at the Internet, feed it enough tokens and eventually you'll have a trained voice AI. But the issue …is how do you know what was used to train that AI? How can you grant copyright? All of those type of things.

Instead of amassing data from unknown or unauthorized sources, WellSaid relies on direct relationships with professional voice actors:

> From very early on we had a different approach which was let's only train on source content that we know and ideally we have a relationship with and we pay them a royalty and so forth. So all of WellSaid's actors are paid, known actors, they're paid a royalty. So as their voices [are] used they get a royalty. And so what we're able to do is grant to organizations copyright …we can really guarantee them that we know where the source comes from and how it's to be used.

By focusing on consent and clear contractual rights, WellSaid can assure enterprise clients, especially those sensitive to legal or reputational risks, that the synthesized voices are cleanly sourced. Cook believes this stance will become an even stronger market differentiator as legislation tightens in regions like the EU.

17.5.2 Embracing Slower Growth for Ethical Practice

Cook openly recognizes that a consent-based, carefully curated approach to data collection can hamper rapid scaling:

> Absolutely. Like, if we wanted to go faster and provide capability quicker, it's really easy. …Sometimes it's hard to tell the story because customers say, well, we've got, you know, your competitors out there …they're cheaper and they've just added this new capability. …But yeah, I, I think it'd be much easier to grow if you weren't ethical about it.

In other words, WellSaid deliberately turns down certain immediate gains to maintain an ethical standard. This discipline may slow short-term feature roll-outs, especially compared to companies building gargantuan "universal" voice models on scraped datasets. However, Cook believes that an ethical strategy best positions WellSaid for long-term sustainability and compliance:

> We move slower …but …that's really the difficulty …I'm betting that our approach will stand the test of time, especially as regulations catch up.

17.5.3 Cultivating Actor Partnerships and Royalty Streams

From the performer's standpoint, this ethically grounded approach translates into more than just formal consent. Cook emphasizes that WellSaid pays actors a fee upfront for recording sessions and then splits a share of profits based on usage:

> We want 300, 400 super high quality voices that we hand pick, curate ...We pay them a fee for doing the initial training and so they get a fee up front and then we have a royalty

He sees an attitudinal shift among voice actors, many of whom initially viewed AI with alarm:

> I think what's happened over the last two years is ...actors have gone from Voice AI is a bad thing and threatening me to Gen AI voice is inevitable. And I have the opportunity to ...make more money and ongoing, you know, potentially income for the rest of my life as opposed to this is a threat. And so what we're trying to do is appeal to those actors ...let's make sure that your voice is not used in an unethical way and bring them to our platform.

Far from replacing voice actors outright, Cook hopes that licensed AI voices will serve as an additional revenue stream for performers, especially for projects requiring large volumes of straightforward or repetitive reads.

17.5.4 Beyond the Studio: Moderation, API Integrations, and Client Vetting

WellSaid's philosophy extends beyond the recording booth. Once an actor's voice is turned into an AI model, the company must ensure it is not used irresponsibly. As Cook explains, WellSaid has two business lines: a "studio platform" where clients manually create voice content, and an "API business," where third-party developers integrate WellSaid's voices into larger products, such as AI video tools:

> So we sell our API to vendors ...A lot of the major AI video creators use WellSaid voices. ...One of the issues we have to manage is what if one of our partners is not as strict on ethics and moderation as we are, then something could slip through. So we spend a lot of time working with our partners to make sure that they have the right content moderation in place.

Such vigilance stands in contrast to a more laissez-faire model, where any paying customer can do what they wish with the AI voice. Cook notes that clients sometimes balk at these extra steps, but he maintains that brand safety and ethical integrity can spare WellSaid (and its actors) from damaging headlines or legal tangles later on.

17.5.5 Technical Approach: High-Quality Recording and Targeted Data Sets

Cook repeatedly underscores that WellSaid's success hinges on careful, professional-grade data collection. Rather than amassing random or low-fidelity recordings, the company has each actor read from a prepared script in a "well-treated home booth with a high-end mic" or a professional studio:

> We have a standard script we ask the actor to read, often in a professional studio or a well-treated home booth with a high-end mic. We want minimal background noise, consistent levels, and no weird artifacts. Then we carefully process that audio before ever passing it to our model. Some folks think you can just dump hours of Zoom recordings into an algorithm and get a perfect voice out. That's not how it works if you want top-quality output.

This devotion to "clean" data ties into what Cook calls WellSaid's "sharpen the spear" mentality: it is better to do less, but do it at a higher fidelity, than to attempt a one-size-fits-all approach. The company invests in rerecording sessions if earlier captures do not meet new internal standards:

> As our new model ...Caruso ...can do super high resolution, 96 kHz resolution, we're having to go back and say look, some of the recordings we have were recorded at 22 kHz or lower resolution. So we've got to go back and do them again ...so we've actually been going back through our library ...saying look, we've moved on, we need to do it again. So go and record high quality.

Cook believes that a meticulously curated dataset yields clearer, more authentic voices, providing an advantage over competitors who simply feed massive volumes of random audio into a machine-learning pipeline.

17.5.6 Actor Voices As Individual Brands

Another theme emerges in Cook's remarks: the idea that voices must remain individual, rather than merged into one "universal accent" or "generic style." He notes:

> 100% agree, yes. If you train voice off a whole lot of voices and so you take a whole lot of American voices from different regions and you blend it all together, you end up with this generic voice.

By treating each voice as a distinct brand, complete with dialect, range, and subtle expressive features, WellSaid can serve a wide range of corporate or creative markets. The ethos echoes concerns from voice actors like Bonnie Bogovich, who worry that giant AI models could flatten out uniqueness in the name of cost efficiency. Cook's refusal to homogenize data sets reflects a broader aspiration to preserve the humanity (and variety) in synthetic speech.

17.6 Discussion

17.6.1 The Necessity of Consent

A foundational commonality between Bogovich and Cook is the belief that AI voice models must be built on explicit, informed consent. Bogovich began adding clauses to her contracts in 2019, forbidding clients from creating or using AI-generated versions of her voice without her written permission. Her rationale was initially sparked by the rise of NFTs, but soon expanded to address the broader issue of voice cloning. She fears that once "in perpetuity" usage rights are granted for raw audio files, companies can, at minimal additional cost, feed that data into an AI system to generate unlimited lines of dialogue, robbing the original performer of both control and subsequent income.

From the AI-company side, Cook argues that ethical operations require consent-based data collection. WellSaid's founding principle was to form direct agreements with performers, rather than scrape audio from unauthorized or anonymous sources. While such an approach slows model development and raises upfront costs, Cook believes it safeguards WellSaid, and its clients, from legal and reputational risks. More importantly, it upholds the agency of the performers, who decide how and when their voices can be used. In this model, personal identity and professional reputation remain within the performer's purview, a radical departure from the more common "wild west" scenario in which an actor's voice might be appropriated without notice or compensation.

17.6.2 Fair Compensation and Royalties

Closely tied to questions of consent is the matter of equitable, ongoing payment. Bogovich laments the prevalence of "all media, in perpetuity" clauses in standard acting contracts, which often neglect any mention of AI usage. Such omissions open the door to companies extracting indefinite value from her recorded performances. Without legal protections, she cautions, many voice actors risk discovering that their voices have been cloned for derivative work without further payment or even notification.

By contrast, Cook's business model attempts to align AI-based synthesis with a sustained revenue stream for actors. WellSaid pays performers an upfront fee for the initial training recordings, followed by royalties when the synthesized voice is later used. In Cook's view, this arrangement frames AI as an extension of an actor's earning potential rather than a competitor. Ceding a one-time buyout to a tech company would, in his words, create a "race to the bottom," where performers relinquish not just control over their voice but also the financial benefits that accompany its successful deployment. Bogovich and Cook thus converge on the principle that if synthetic voices are to be ethically integrated into media production, the human originators must share in the profits.

17.6.3 Voice Identity and Authenticity

A further thread running through both interviews is the importance of preserving the uniqueness of an actor's vocal "brand." Bogovich refers to her voice as an extension of her creative persona, cautioning that AI threatens to replicate it for uses she would never endorse. Beyond the potential financial harm, she fears reputational damage should her voice be digitally manipulated to endorse political messages or appear in explicit content.

Cook's discussion of WellSaid's methodology underscores a similar respect for distinct vocal characteristics. Rather than pooling data into a massive, undifferentiated model, WellSaid curates individual voices, preserving dialectical nuances and emotional range. As discussed earlier in Section 17.5.6, WellSaid's brand-centric strategy preserves each performer's vocal signature.

17.6.4 Market Pressures and Ethical Differentiation

Even as both parties advocate consent and fair pay, they acknowledge the competitive hurdles. Bogovich observes that some studios and low-budget projects look for bargains, leading them to exploit loopholes or hire performers unaware of AI implications. Meanwhile, Cook concedes that WellSaid's dedication to careful data sourcing and royalty agreements can mean slower growth in a market propelled by cost savings and rapid innovation. This tension encapsulates a core risk: when an industry is in flux and regulations are still forming, actors and companies that uphold stricter ethical standards may find it harder to compete with players willing to compromise on consent or compensation.

Nonetheless, Cook views WellSaid's principles as a long-term advantage, especially given growing consumer and corporate awareness about the need for "clean" data. In an era of increasing scrutiny over deepfakes and unauthorized content, clients may prefer to partner with a company that can guarantee no hidden legal entanglements down the line. While Bogovich focuses on contract language to protect herself on a case-by-case basis, Cook's entire business model is rooted in stable, transparent relationships with talent. Both approaches, if adopted more broadly, could shift industry norms toward shared accountability.

17.6.5 Toward a Sustainable AI Ecosystem

The final concern bridging both perspectives is the ongoing stewardship of AI voices. For Bogovich, the fear is clear: once a model of her voice exists, how can she ensure it is not abused for hateful, fraudulent, or explicit projects? Cook underscores that moderation cannot end at the point of training, monitoring and vetting must extend throughout the product's lifecycle. WellSaid declines potential partners it deems questionable and periodically reviews existing users to ensure compliance with ethical guidelines. This is labor-intensive, but vital for protecting both the performer's reputation and WellSaid's brand credibility.

When taken together, Bogovich's individual protective measures and Cook's organizational policies form a template for sustainable AI deployment. In such a framework, voice actors wield contractual power, licensing their voice for AI usage under clearly defined terms, while AI platforms put in place robust oversight that curtails misuse. This model, however, hinges on collective buy-in. If voice actors, studios, and AI providers all accept a baseline standard of informed consent, fair compensation, and active moderation, the result could be an industry that captures the benefits of synthetic speech without sacrificing artistic identity or livelihood.

Ultimately, neither Bogovich nor Cook views AI-generated voices as inherently beneficial or detrimental. Rather, the outcome depends on the ethical scaffolding that shapes how these voices are produced, owned, and used. Bogovich's "No AI Clause" and Cook's royalty-based licensing stand as two sides of the same protective shield. They indicate that ethical AI voice practices can endure, perhaps even flourish, in a marketplace increasingly aware of the need for transparency and respect for creators. In an environment of intensifying competition, whether this model prevails over cheaper, less ethical alternatives may depend on evolving regulations, union advocacy, and a consumer base that prizes authenticity.

17.7 Conclusion

AI-driven voice synthesis is reshaping the creative and commercial landscape in ways that demand fresh thinking around consent, compensation, and authenticity. Bonnie Bogovich's experience as a freelance voice actor defending her vocal identity through contractual "No AI Clauses" intersects with Brian Cook's approach at WellSaid Labs, where consent-based model training and royalty-sharing serve as cornerstones of an ethical business strategy. Together, they paint a picture of an industry on the cusp of either a "race to the bottom" or a more principled evolution.

At the heart of these discussions is the recognition that a performer's voice is more than just raw data: it is a defining aspect of personal and artistic identity. When AI systems respect this fact, by securing explicit permission, compensating actors fairly, and preserving the individual qualities that make each voice unique, technology can augment rather than supplant human creativity. Such frameworks require careful design, including robust oversight to prevent misuse and ongoing negotiation to balance efficiency with respect for the people behind the voices.

Whether ethical AI speech generation can thrive depends on collective will. As Bogovich's contractual vigilance meets Cook's curated approach to voice modeling, we see the rudiments of an industry standard that safeguards both performers and companies. If more stakeholders adopt similar principles, AI voice technology could open new avenues of creativity and reach, all while fortifying, rather than undermining, the value and dignity of human performers.

References

Allison, F., Carter, M., & Gibbs, M. (2020). Word play: A history of voice interaction in digital games. *Games and Culture, 15*(2), 91–113.

Amba, R., & Singh, H. (2023). The influence of the artificial intelligence based CGI on the growth of the film industry. In *2023 Seventh International Conference on Image Information Processing (ICIIP)* (pp. 194–198).

Berger, V. (2024). *SAG-AFTRA's AI deal: A $5 billion gamble on the future of voice acting*. Forbes. https://www.forbes.com/sites/virginieberger/2024/08/21/sag-aftras-ai-deal-a-5-billion-gamble-on-the-future-of-voice-acting/
Bosseaux, C. (2018). Investigating dubbing: Learning from the past, looking to the future. In *The Routledge handbook of audiovisual translation* (pp. 48–63). Routledge.
Carter, J. (2022). *Ninja theory, other triple-a devs reportedly using AI voice acting tech over people*. Game Developer, https://www.gamedeveloper.com/business/ninja-theory-other-triple-a-devs-reportedly-using-ai-voice-acting-tech-over-people
Chan, W. (2022). *The AI startup erasing call center worker accents: Is it fighting bias—or perpetuating it? The Guardian*. https://www.theguardian.com/technology/2022/aug/23/voice-accent-technology-call-center-white-american
Cousins, R. (2025). "Bugs bunny? Why are you hanging around with these guys?": Celebrity hierarchy and voice characterization in Warner Brothers cartoon shorts 1930-1970. *Semiotic Review*.
Dudley, H. (1940). The vocoder—Electrical re-creation of speech. *Journal of the Society of Motion Picture Engineers, 34*(3), 272–278.
Dye, J. F., Schatz, I. M., Rosenberg, B. A., & Coleman, S. T. (2000). Constant comparison method: A kaleidoscope of data. *The Qualitative Report, 4*(1/2), 1–9.
Fowler, S. L., & Fowler, J. D. (2024). Why Tennessee's ELVIS act is the king of artificial intelligence protections. *Vanderbilt Journal of Entertainment and Technology Law, 27*, 259.
Hilmes, M., & Loviglio, J. (2002). *Radio reader: Essays in the cultural history of radio*. Psychology Press.
Huamani, K. (2025). Voice clones pose an 'existential crisis' for actors: 'It's a violation of our humanity'. *Los Angeles Times*. https://www.latimes.com/entertainment-arts/story/2025-03-24/ai-voice-clones-replication-voice-actors-job-loss-siri-tiktok
Li, R., Pu, D., Huang, M., & Huang, B. (2022). Unet-tts: Improving unseen speaker and style transfer in one-shot voice cloning. In *ICASSP 2022–2022 IEEE international conference on acoustics, speech and signal processing (ICASSP)* (pp. 8327–8331).
Low, S. (2024). *Voice actors from japan insist on tighter AI regulation*. Tokyo Weekender, https://www.tokyoweekender.com/entertainment/tech-trends/voice-actors-from-japan-insist-on-tighter-ai-regulation/
Mandiberg, S. (2021). Video games have never been global: Resituating video game localization history. In *Game history and the local* (pp. 177–198). Springer.
Mehrish, A., Majumder, N., Bharadwaj, R., Mihalcea, R., & Poria, S. (2023). A review of deep learning techniques for speech processing. *Information Fusion, 99*, 101869.
NAVA. (2025). *Synth/AI info*. https://navavoices.org/synth-ai-info/.
Paul, A. (2023). The voice actor and their double: Working as a voice actor and teaching voice acting in the age of AI voice cloning. *Tradition Innovations in Arts, Design, and Media Higher Education, 1*(1), Article 6. https://digitalscholarship.unlv.edu/tradition_innovations/vol1/iss1/6/
Story, B. H. (2019). History of speech synthesis. In *The Routledge handbook of phonetics* (pp. 9–33). Routledge.
Taylor, J. (2009). "Speaking shadows": A history of the voice in the transition from silent to sound film in the United States. *Journal of Linguistic Anthropology, 19*(1), 1–20.
Walton, M. (2020). Writing for AAA games: Playing in the big leagues. In *Professional techniques for video game writing* (pp. 105–120). CRC Press.
Wang, X., Zhang, Z., & Jiang, Q. (2024). The effectiveness of human vs. AI voice-over in short video advertisements: A cognitive load theory perspective. *Journal of Retailing and Consumer Services, 81*, 104005.
Zhang, X. (2023). *How does AI-generated voice affect online video creation?: Evidence from TikTok* [PhD thesis]. University of British Columbia.

Richard Savery is a developer of artificial intelligence and robotics, using music and creativity as a medium to program better interactions, understandings and models. He was a Senior Research

Scientist at Jen Music and a Macquarie University Research Fellow, developing ethically trained, high-fidelity text-to-music systems and a rapping, drumming interactive robot. He now holds an ARC DECRA fellowship (2025–2027) at the University of Canberra, focusing on robots and AI in long-term use and groups. His research has received $3.8 million in funding and significant industry partnerships. His work has been featured in Scientific American, BBC Radio and Disney+ with Jeff Goldblum. He completed a PhD in Music Technology (minor in Human–Computer Interaction) at the Georgia Institute of Technology.

Deepfakes: Threats and Media Impact 18

Daniel Bendahan Bitton, Alexander Godulla, and Christian P. Hoffmann

Abstract

Recent developments of generative artificial intelligence (AI) have gained significant interest in research and practice and are expected to profoundly transform the media landscape. Among new AI technologies, deepfakes—hyper-realistic, AI-generated media—stand out for their significant impacts. This chapter provides a comprehensive reflection of the emergence of deepfakes, their opportunities and risks across multiple areas as well as the state of research on the phenomenon. It provides an overview of deepfakes from a communication and media studies perspective, combining a conceptual examination of the technology's further development with empirical findings from 5 years of the authors' research. Drawing on original studies, this chapter discusses the role of deepfakes in the context of AI inequalities by focusing on Internet users' knowledge and attitudes toward the phenomenon and highlighting gender-related differences. Furthermore, it investigates the impacts of the technology for journalistic practice by discussing changing routines and the need for guidelines in order to exploit the potential for innovation of the technology while maintaining journalistic norms, the audiences' trust, and mitigating harmful uses of the technology. Finally, this chapter discusses a multidimensional framework for future research, emphasizing the need to address deepfakes across an individual, organizational, and sociopolitical level. The rise of the novel technology calls for an integrative approach that considers (ethical) regulations, technological solutions, and audience-centered perspective in order to responsibly shape communication in the age of synthetic realities.

D. Bendahan Bitton (✉) · A. Godulla · C. P. Hoffmann
Leipzig University, Leipzig, Germany
e-mail: daniel.bendahan@uni-leipzig.de; alexander.godulla@uni-leipzig.de; christian.hoffmann@uni-leipzig.de

S. Böhm et al. (eds.), *Handbook of AI-based Media Disruption*, Future of Business and Finance, https://doi.org/10.1007/978-3-032-07605-2_18

18.1 The Emergence of Deepfake Technology

The term "deepfake" finds its origin in 2017 with an anonymous Reddit user known by the pseudonym "deepfake." This user promoted the use of generative AI technology by creating a forum for sharing artificially manipulated pornographic videos (Somers, 2020). The videos were created using the faces of female celebrities that were then projected onto existing pornographic videos using Generative Adversarial Networks (GANs). Hence, the term "deepfake" combines the underlying deep-learning technology and an admission of manipulation—"fake" (Block, 2023; Kietzmann et al., 2020). Deepfakes are a form of synthetic media that imitate faces, voices, and change the portrayal of an individual (e.g., Bateman, 2022; Kietzmann et al., 2020; Pawelec, 2024a). Deepfake images, videos, and audio can be created based on AI tools. Elaborate deepfakes enable lip syncs by "manipulat[ing] mouth movements and facial expressions alongside audio materials" and can be used "to have someone convincingly say things which they have never said" (Whittaker et al., 2020, p. 91 f.).

Deepfakes are frequently malicious in nature (Hameleers & Marquart, 2023), and aim to deceive the audience. Thus, deepfakes are often approached as a new form of visual disinformation in public discourse and research (Hameleers, 2024; Hameleers & Marquart, 2023; Vincent, 2018; Weikmann & Lecheler, 2023). The technology can be used to spread false information in the context of elections or in times of crisis and war (Citron & Chesney, 2018). In contrast, deep-learning technologies can also be used for beneficial applications such as entertainment, advertising, gaming and film, education and journalism (e.g., Godulla et al., 2021; Seibert, 2023). Consequently, deepfake technology is not inherently unethical but requires compliance with certain criteria, for example: consent of the depicted person, context of use, intention behind the creation (De Ruiter, 2021). Further, while some researchers also refer to these applications as "deepfakes," others use the less negatively connoted term "synthetic media" or refer more generally to the use of AI in the creation of artificial media (e.g., Bateman, 2022; McCammon, 2021).

This chapter discusses the challenges and impacts of deepfakes for media organizations by reflecting on key findings of 5 years of research by the authors from the perspective of communication and media studies. After highlighting the technological disruption caused by deepfakes, this chapter presents findings on (1) the state of research on deepfakes, (2) the awareness and perception of deepfakes by Internet users, and (3) the perspective of journalism and innovation experts on the implications of the technology such as for detection processes (fact-checking) but also regarding beneficial uses (e.g., content creation, new journalistic formats). Based on the reflection of these insights, the chapter discusses future impacts of deepfakes for media and audiences, and formulates areas for future research.

18.2 Disruption Caused by Deepfakes

The manipulation of media is not a new phenomenon. Retouching photographs, editing footage, and misleading representations have long been part of public communication (Habgood-Coote, 2023; Mahony & Chen, 2024). Historical cases of media manipulation illustrate that photographs have been altered to serve political and ideological purposes, long before the development of digital tools. Stalin's regime, for example, systematically edited photographs to erase political opponents (Kruse, 2014). With the development of digital image editing software such as Photoshop, the manipulation of media has been revolutionized and became accessible to a broad public of users (Manovich, 2001; Mitchell, 2001). Media that are manipulated using digital tools that are not based on AI are also referred to as "cheap fakes" or "shallow fakes." Cheap fakes are characterized by rather little technological sophistication and depict content that was cut, edited, slowed down, sped up, or presented in a different context (Brady & Meyer-Resende, 2020). While such non-AI-based computer generated or manipulated images might blur their viewers' perception of reality and fiction (e.g., Farid & Bravo, 2012), they still require a significant amount of time and expertise for their creation. In contrast, AI-based technology enables users to create or manipulate images, videos, and audio with comparatively little knowledge and within a short period of time. Therefore, with the rise of AI-driven technologies, manipulation has reached a high level of sophistication and accessibility. Synthetic media such as deepfakes make it increasingly difficult for both media professionals and Internet users to distinguish between real and artificially generated media (Weikmann & Lecheler, 2023).

Advances in the development of deep-learning technology have resulted in a high degree of realism and persuasiveness of deepfakes (Lee & Shin, 2022). The latter is at the heart of the risks posed by the technology: For a long time, audiovisual media have enjoyed a high level of trust and credibility among audiences (Fehrensen & Täubner, 2019). While the public already has been increasingly confronted with visual manipulation (such as cheap fakes) through, for example, Photoshop or computer-generated imagery (CGI), deepfakes represent a novel form of media manipulation (Pawelec, 2022). This is due to the higher technological sophistication of deepfakes as well as their increasing realism and persuasiveness (Fehrensen & Täubner, 2019; Lee & Shin, 2022). Unlike manual media manipulations, that have mostly been limited to static images and the manipulation of existing visual material, technologically sophisticated deepfakes are entirely new media that replicate facial expressions, body movements, and speech in a way that mimics real persons and change their whole appearance (movements, gestures, and what is said). This multilayered manipulation of not only visual but also auditive content increases the illusion of reality (Kietzmann et al., 2020). Consequently, deepfakes challenge the perception of audiovisual truth to an unprecedented extent. In the context of disinformation, the persuasiveness and impact of deepfakes might be amplified if the manipulated content resonates with the audiences' ideological beliefs. Hence, targeted deepfakes that are tailored to specific audiences (e.g., based on political orientation) can reinforce their effects and might destabilize public (political) discourses (Citron & Chesney, 2018; Dobber et al., 2020).

18.3 State of Research on Deepfakes

Since the emergence of deepfakes in 2017, the phenomenon has received increasing interest from the public and researchers. Therefore, in 2021, Godulla et al. examined the state of research on deepfakes. Their article "Dealing with deepfakes" examines the interdisciplinary research landscape on deepfakes and highlights gaps in research. Focusing on implications for communication, the authors discuss how communication and media studies can contribute to the discourse on deepfakes. The authors conducted a systematic literature analysis on (peer-reviewed) journal articles and conference papers published between 2018 and 2020. In total, 37 studies were considered in the literature analysis. The findings indicate that, at the time, the majority of research on deepfakes had its origin in computer science and law while only few studies from the social sciences were focusing on the societal and communicative impacts of the emergence and increasing use of deepfakes. The authors developed the *model of dealing with deepfakes* as a method for mapping their findings (Godulla et al., 2021, p. 89, see Fig. 18.1).

The model initially summarizes opportunities and risks associated with deepfakes. Opportunities discussed in the analyzed literature focus, for example, on the use of the technology for virtual reality applications (fashion), advertising and entertainment (stunt doubles), and art (creation of new art works) and education. In contrast, risks associated with the technology include financial fraud, damages to a person's or organization's reputation, deception of law enforcement, and humiliation through deepfake pornography. Further, harmful uses of the technology are associated with negative influences on political campaigns and the public opinion, which in turn could result in declining trust in media and institutions (Godulla et al., 2021).

Godulla et al. (2021) further differentiate approaches to combat and to regulate deepfakes in order to deal with this phenomenon. Prior research frequently discusses the need for automatic deepfake detection. These methods are based on audiovisual inconsistencies such as unnatural eye-blinking patterns, irregular lip and mouth movements, or inconsistencies in lighting and contrast—characteristics that can be noticeable through human observation and that are integrated in the development of detection tools using machine learning techniques (e.g., analysis of eye-blinking rate; Sunil et al., 2025). In addition, findings of the literature analysis point to the need for establishing new law enforcement agencies and developing policies to handle negative applications of deepfakes. This includes working on international legal regulations and introducing economic sanctions as well as legal consequences in the event of harmful uses of deepfakes (e.g., privacy violations).

Finally, Godulla et al. (2021) highlight opportunities for future research, specifically for communication and media studies, to address the technology's implications. Deepfakes are considered a growing threat to audiences and media

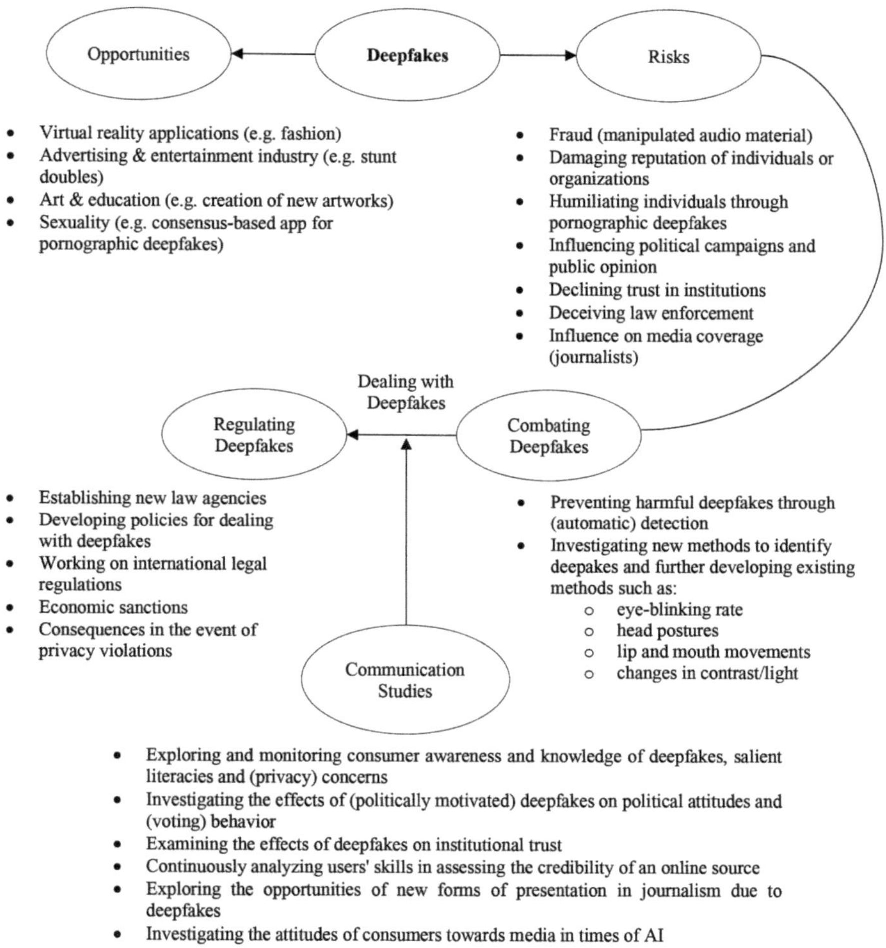

Fig. 18.1 Model of dealing with deepfakes [reprinted from Godulla et al., 2021, p. 89]

professionals as they make it increasingly difficult to verify the authenticity and source of audiovisual media. Also, existing laws struggle to address the impact of the harmful use of deepfakes. While the tools to detect deepfakes are improving, the forensic examination of audiovisual media is always one step behind the methods used to create such synthetic media. Hence, as technological solutions might fail, the authors emphasize the need for examining the audiences and journalists' skills and perceptions of the technology. They propose several areas that require further investigation, including studies on Internet users' awareness and knowledge of deepfakes and the role of media literacy in their identification. Further, they highlight the relevance of examining the impacts of politically motivated deepfakes on attitudes and voting behavior, as well as analyzing their impacts on institutional trust. The authors also point out the need to consider attitudes toward AI, which might relate to potential beneficial uses of the technology, for example, in education or journalism (e.g., new opportunities for journalistic storytelling).

Since the examination of the state of research on deepfakes by Godulla et al. (2021), the corpus of literature from social sciences and communication studies has increased significantly and often centers on implications of the technology for audiences and journalists. Some of these recent insights are discussed in the following. Research focusing on audiences, for example, has begun examining their skills and relevant factors for identifying deepfakes. Empirical studies demonstrate that audiences struggle to differentiate between deepfakes and real media (Hameleers, 2024; Lewis et al., 2022). Further, research indicates that while individuals express confidence in their ability to detect deepfakes, they are often unable to correctly identify manipulated media (Bray et al., 2023; Hashmi et al., 2024; Köbis et al., 2021).

In this context, ethical implications of deepfakes such as the spread of disinformation and reputational harms for the individuals depicted in deepfakes are increasingly discussed (Pawelec, 2024a). A study by Gehringer et al. (2024) demonstrates that while deepfake technology is still most frequently used for fraud and nonconsensual pornography, cases of political deepfakes are increasing. To counter audience deception by the content of harmful deepfakes, research examines the role of content warnings and educational interventions. For example, Lewis et al. (2022) show that providing content warnings might increase the likelihood of correctly deciding whether media is a deepfake or not. In contrast, initial studies indicate that educational interventions such as repeated exposure or training often fail to significantly improve audiences' detection accuracy (Bray et al., 2023; Doss et al., 2023).

Murillo-Ligorred et al. (2023) found that (among students) there is only low general awareness of the existence of deepfakes. These results stand in line with the study by Bendahan Bitton et al. (2024) who examined the awareness of and attitudes toward deepfake among German Internet users. The authors conclude that most participants had no or only little knowledge of the emergence of the technology and its associated societal implications. In this context, however, the need to educate the public about deepfakes should be addressed with caution: The study of Wahl-Jorgensen and Carlson (2021) revealed that journalists tend to report on worst-case scenarios emerging due to deepfakes. This in turn, might distort the audiences' perceptions of the prevalence and dangers of deepfakes, thus potentially reinforcing public concerns that contrast with limited actual negative consequences of harmful uses of the technology. Hence, raising awareness of deepfakes could perhaps strengthen the public's ability to identify them in the long term, but it might also lead to an exaggerated sense of threat (Gregory, 2022). More recent studies demonstrate that exposure to deepfakes fosters skepticism and mistrust toward audiovisual media and (online) news sources (Bray et al., 2023; Ternovski et al., 2022). A study by Hameleers and Marquart (2023) investigated the effects of deepfake labels in this context. Results show, however, that labeling a video as a deepfake—regardless of the label's accuracy—reduces the audiences' credibility of the media under consideration. Hence, the mere awareness of the existence of the technology might generally lower trust in legitimate audiovisual media.

In addition to the focus on impacts of deepfakes on audiences, journalism and challenges for fact-checking routines are at the center of a number of recent studies (e.g., Bendahan Bitton et al., 2026; Ritchie, 2023). Results indicate that journalists demonstrate a high level of openness toward the implementation of deepfake detection tools into their verification process (Sohrawardi et al., 2024). In contrast, the study by Weikmann and Lecheler (2023), demonstrates that (so far) traditional fact-checking such as checking the accuracy and authenticity of information is considered the most effective tool for identifying deepfakes. This is because, while detection technologies are being introduced in practice, their accuracy remains unreliable, thus limiting their integration into newsrooms and journalistic workflows (Weikmann & Lecheler, 2023). Additionally, the integration of detection tools in journalistic practice requires AI literacy among its users and calls for training programs (Bendahan Bitton et al., 2026; Sohrawardi et al., 2024). This is particularly relevant to avoid an overreliance on the outputs of these tools (Sohrawardi et al., 2024).

Despite the focus of most studies on risks of deepfakes, some authors focus on opportunities of the technology for journalism (e.g., automated news production, personalized storytelling, and new formats; Bendahan Bitton et al., 2026; Ritchie, 2023; WDR Innovation Hub, 2021). The implementation of deepfake technology in journalism, however, calls for guidelines to ensure their responsible and ethical use (e.g., transparency).

18.4 Insights on Internet Users' and Media Professionals' Perception of Deepfakes

In the following section, two studies that were conducted as part of a research project on deepfakes (Deepfake Project, n.d.) are presented to highlight current debates on the impacts of the technology. First, the role of deepfakes is discussed regarding inequalities arising from the use of AI (Bendahan Bitton et al., 2024). Second, the implications of the technology on journalism are investigated, taking into account impacts emerging at the level of individual journalists, news organizations, and the journalistic system in general (Bendahan Bitton et al., 2026).

18.4.1 Study I: Deepfakes in the Context of AI Inequalities

So far, there is only a little research on AI-related inequalities (e.g., Cardenuto et al., 2023; Carter et al., 2020; Kurpicz-Briki et al., 2023). While the digital divide originally referred to inequalities in Internet and technology access, it has evolved into a multidimensional concept that also considers sociodemographic, motivational, and skill-based disparities (Van Deursen et al., 2017; Van Dijk, 2013). Hence, factors such as age, gender, educational attainment, and income as well as digital skills and attitudes (e.g., trust in or fear of new technology) are considered relevant factors influencing Internet user's digital inclusion (Bozic, 2023; Kitsara, 2022; Yu, 2020;

Reisdorf & Groselj, 2017). In this context, knowledge of a technology can be considered a further factor in shaping users' attitudes and in turn also their motivation to use new technology (Eichhorn et al., 2022).

On the one hand, the rise of and access to AI may ameliorate inequalities, for example, through improved and personalized learning environments or opportunities for establishing new businesses and economic growth (Bozic, 2023; Kitsara, 2022; Lainjo, 2023). Deepfakes, in particular, might be an opportunity for education by transferring knowledge in a personalized way, for example, through synthetic historical scientists that provide testimonials and interact with users (Pawelec, 2024b). This way, the technology can be used as a form of artificial pedagogical agent and could help improve cognitive performance by enhancing engagement and creating an immersive, satisfying learning experience in online environments (Herbert & Dołżycka, 2024).

On the other hand, utilizing the potentials of AI assumes that Internet users are aware of and have the necessary digital skills to make use of AI-based technologies (Kitsara, 2022; Yu, 2020). Hence, AI may further deepen socioeconomic inequalities if gaps in users' abilities to benefit from these economic opportunities are widening (Lainjo, 2023). Focusing on deepfakes, digital inequalities in knowledge and perception of the technology as well as skills in handling its impacts might prevail. Certain users could be more susceptible to being deceived by deepfakes and thus, for example, become victims of financial fraud (Citron & Chesney, 2018). While there may already be a high number of unreported cases of financial fraud in the private sector, employees in companies have demonstrably been victims of cases of deepfake fraud. For example, in Hong Kong, deepfakes were used to simulate a video conference in which scammers, posing as company executives, convinced an employee to transfer approximately 24 million euros to an external bank account (Hurtz, 2024). Furthermore, harmful uses of the technology relate to inequalities among marginalized groups: Deepfakes are frequently used to harass, silence, and harm individuals (women, LGBTQ individuals, people of color), for example, by depicting them in pornographic content (Paris, 2021). The malicious use of the deepfake technology could therefore reinforce inequality in visual representations and can lead to negative psychological implications for the victims.

While prior research has frequently examined audiences' ability to recognize deepfakes (e.g., Bray et al., 2023; Ternovski et al., 2022; Vaccari & Chadwick, 2020), the public's knowledge of and attitudes toward deepfakes have so far rarely been in focus. The study by Bendahan Bitton et al. (2024) addresses this lacuna and examines deepfakes in the context of the AI divide. By conducting a survey of 1421 German Internet users, the authors examine how sociodemographic factors (age, gender, education, income), digital skills, and personal innovativeness shape knowledge and attitudes toward deepfake technology. Furthermore, the study explores whether higher deepfake knowledge relates to Internet users' perception of the technology's risks and opportunities. In doing so, participants of the study were asked about their familiarity with deepfakes and tested on their knowledge. To ensure that all participants understand what deepfakes are, they were provided with a definition and a deepfake video example depicting Morgan Freeman, which was created by voice actor Boet Schouwink (Diep Nep, 2021). Afterward, participants evaluated statements toward potential use cases of the technology (associated risks and opportunities) and were asked to provide an overall assessment of the technology ranging from dangerous (0) to promising (100).

The study revealed that the majority of respondents had little or no prior knowledge of the existence and characteristics deepfakes (see Table 18.1). Further,

Table 18.1 Knowledge and attitudes toward deepfakes

Variable		All participants	Male participants	Female participants
Knowledge	No/low knowledge	1115 (78.5%)	500 (71.5%)	614 (85.4%)
	Medium knowledge	247 (17.4%)	158 (22.5%)	89 (12.4%)
	High knowledge	59 (4.2%)	42 (6%)	16 (2.2%)
Risk perception	I have concerns that detecting deepfakes will become increasingly difficult	1199 (86.6%)	561 (82.7%)	638 (90.2%)
	I have concerns about deepfakes influencing public opinion	1088 (79.5%)	509 (76.1%)	579 (82.8%)
	I have concerns that soon I won't be able to trust any video content	918 (67.5%)	409 (61.8%)	509 (73%)
	I have concerns that manipulation of personal data will become easier	1000 (73.3%)	464 (69.4%)	536 (77.1%)
	I have concerns about falling for a deepfake	915 (67.3)	410 (61.6%)	505 (72.8%)
	I have concerns about becoming a victim of a harmful deepfake	632 (50.8%)	259 (43.2%)	373 (57.8%)
Opportunity perception	Deepfakes provide benefits to the film industry	817 (63%)	419 (64.3%)	398 (61.7%)
	Deepfakes provide benefits to the video game industry	705 (55.4%)	371 (57.7%)	334 (53%)
	Deepfakes can also be used for beneficial purposes	542 (44.7%)	300 (49.1%)	242 (40.3%)
	Deepfakes foster creativity in media content production	452 (38%)	261 (42.7%)	191 (33.1%)
	Deepfakes provide me with benefits	349 (32.9%)	215 (38.7%)	134 (26.5%)
	Deepfakes also benefit the creation of pornographic content with the consent of those involved	235 (28%)	159 (34%)	76 (20.5%)

Note: N is varying. The frequencies and percentages shown in the table regarding the perceived risks and opportunities of deepfakes relate to the participants' agreement with formulated statements and examples on potential risks and opportunities (rather or full agreement on these statements)

significant disparities in knowledge of deepfakes and attitudes toward associated risks and opportunities of the technology prevail. Focusing on predictors of knowledge of deepfakes, a linear regression using the software SPSS Statistics 2021 was carried out. The results show that age, educational attainment, gender, digital skills, and usage of social media stood out as significant predictors of deepfake knowledge. Hence, younger, more educated, male, digitally equipped and social media proficient individuals exhibit a higher familiarity with deepfake technology. Contrary to the authors' expectations, deepfake knowledge only had a limited influence on attitudes toward the technology. Linear regressions were conducted to examine predictors of opportunity and risk perceptions. Results show that higher knowledge is associated with higher agreement with beneficial areas of application (opportunities of deepfakes). In addition, the results revealed that the perception of opportunities is influenced by the participants' degree of personal innovativeness, i.e. their willingness to experiment with and adopt new technologies. While participants' age played a subordinate role in the perception of risks and opportunities of deepfake technology, the study reveals strong effects regarding gender (see Table 18.1).

Overall, deepfakes are strongly associated with risks. Participants fear that detecting deepfakes is becoming increasingly difficult and that the technology is used to manipulate public opinion. Further, they fear that, in the future, they can no longer trust audiovisual media. Finally, participants express the fear that their personal data could be misused to create deepfakes, that they could be deceived by a deepfake, and that they could fall victim to a harmful deepfake. Overall approval of the technology's opportunities is significantly lower. Participants see potential benefits in the use of deepfake technology in the film and gaming industry. The possibility that deepfake technology promotes creativity also receives approval. Few respondents, however, see personal benefits from using the technology (e.g., for entertainment, education) or agree to the potential that the technology might be used to create pornographic content that is based on the depicted individuals' consent.

Furthermore, the perceived risks and opportunities of the technology were analyzed separately for the gender of the participants using t-tests on overall perception of the technology (from dangerous to promising) and Chi-squared tests and Cramér's V measures on individual statements on risks and opportunities of the technology. Significant differences were shown that are pointing to a gender divide. Gender emerged as the strongest predictor of concerns toward deepfake technology. Female participants, for example, express stronger concerns about being deceived by a deepfake, falling victim to a harmful deepfake, and personal data being manipulated. The findings further indicate that female respondents appear to be more skeptical about the technology, regardless of their prior knowledge about deepfakes. In contrast, male participants not only show higher familiarity with the phenomenon, they also express less concerns and evaluate the opportunities associated with the technology to be more promising. On the one hand, this divide may be intensified due to the gendered impact of AI technology in general. On the other hand, it could also relate to particular challenges posed by deepfake technology: Women are disproportionately often depicted in nonconsensual and objectifying (pornographic) deepfakes. This poses the risk of further reinforcing gender-specific inequalities in visual information (Raffaghello et al., 2019; Wagner & Blewer, 2019).

18.4.2 Study II: Implications of Deepfake Technology for Journalistic Practice

While the technology's impacts on journalists' fact-checking routines in practice have been initially examined by Weikmann and Lecheler (2023), there is still a lack of research examining journalists' knowledge and perception of both the risks as well as the opportunities the deepfake technology poses for journalistic practice. In academic and public discourse, so far, there has been a clear emphasis on the dangers of deepfakes (Godulla et al., 2021). In contrast, however, uses of the technology might also pose opportunities for content creation, visualization, personalization, and automation as well as the development of new formats and business models (e.g., Ritchie, 2023; WDR Innovation Hub, 2021).

Bendahan Bitton et al. (2026) address this gap and investigate the implications of deepfakes for media outlets and journalistic practice focusing on the effects at three levels: individual journalists (micro-level), news organizations (meso-level), and journalism as a whole (macro-level). The authors conducted 20 qualitative interviews with journalism and innovation experts from Germany. The interviews followed a structured guideline covering awareness of deepfakes, opportunities and risks the technology holds for journalism, verification practices, and future implications for journalism (e.g., training). The data was analyzed conducting a qualitative content analysis and the findings are summarized in Table 18.2.

On the micro-level, Bendahan Bitton et al. (2025) find that journalists need to develop competencies in identifying audiovisual deepfake media. This finding ties in with previous studies that provide similar insights into how journalists deal with deepfakes (AI literacy, developing advanced verification skills; e.g., Walker, 2019; Weikmann & Lecheler, 2023; Westerlund, 2019). With regard to the role of detection tools, the authors state that these tools remain complex, thus requiring additional training and knowledge for journalists to interpret their outputs accurately. Further, the authors also argue that journalists need digital skills to integrate

Table 18.2 Summary of main impacts of deepfake technology for journalism

Level	Implications
Micro-level (individual journalists)	Journalists need to develop competencies in using deepfake technology and also in identifying audiovisual deepfake media
Meso-level (newsrooms)	Newsrooms will need to develop new guidelines for weighing the risks (fact-checking) and opportunities (new financing potentials) of deepfake technology
Macro-level (journalism, quality, audience–media relationship)	Deepfake technology could facilitate a trend toward personalization but might also harm journalistic quality

deepfake technology into media production. This also requires understanding of the functioning of machine learning and data-driven applications.

On the meso-level, Bendahan Bitton et al. (2026) state that newsrooms need to develop new guidelines for weighing the risks and opportunities of deepfake technology. In this context, their interviews point to the relevance of ensuring transparency to maintain the audiences' trust. Hence, guidelines should serve to ensure ethical use of deepfake technology regardless of whether generated media will be labeled as "deepfake," "synthetic media," or "AI-generated media." The findings suggest that newsrooms will need to adapt their production workflows in the future if they chose to incorporate the technology (e.g., reconstructing historical events, creating easy-access and personalized formats). Additionally, guidelines are needed as a foundation for standardized procedures for fact-checking (deepfake identification). The results reflect the claim that deepfake detection and thus fact-checking is becoming increasingly complex (e.g., Weikmann & Lecheler, 2023). The authors add that the verification of deepfakes must be seen as an ongoing challenge, as improvements in AI-generated media require constant adaptation of fact-checking strategies. Finally, the findings demonstrate that the technology might pose both economic risks and opportunities. For example, personalized media (e.g., new formats, synthetic news anchors, podcast translations) could expand audience reach and generate new revenue streams. In contrast, the audiences might reject the use of the technology and new formats. Hence investments in deepfake-based innovations could fail.

On the macro-level, the authors conclude that deepfake technology could facilitate a trend toward personalization but might also harm journalistic quality. In this context, the authors describe an ongoing tension between innovation and ethical considerations. While personalization through deepfake technology holds the potential to attract younger audiences and increase accessibility (customized avatars, tailored news formats), concerns persist that it could lead to journalism becoming too entertainment-driven rather than maintaining its democratic function of informing the public. Further, the authors discuss the audience-media relationship: While journalists' effective detection of deepfakes could strengthen media outlets' credibility by ensuring reliable fact-checked information, the mishandling of the technology could heighten skepticism toward those media outlets (e.g., in the event of mislabeled AI-generated media or the accidental spread of a deepfake).

In summary, the study concludes that deepfakes challenge traditional journalistic production and verification processes. Hence, journalists must develop new competencies in detecting deepfake content, while newsrooms experiment with detection tools and need to establish guidelines to manage the technology's negative implications. Further, media professionals must also adapt to new realities where synthetic media can be produced at scale, thus affecting traditional business models and content production processes. The proliferation of deepfakes hence necessitates regulatory frameworks that address new challenges while balancing beneficial implementations of the technology and ensuring journalistic quality.

18.5 Responding to the Rise of Deepfakes: Areas for Future Research

AI is a highly disruptive technology that touches and permeates every area of society. At the same time, it is an entirely digital technology: its algorithms, training data, and products are all immaterial. It is therefore obvious that it is changing the World Wide Web and the communication that takes place online, in particular. Deepfakes should therefore be interpreted as a symptom of a larger development: Since AI is excellent at recognizing, interpreting, reproducing, and varying patterns, all of this naturally applies to its representation of people and their behavior. In other words, deepfakes are just one of many varieties of AI. If we want to extend the scope of the term, we need to talk about synthetic media, for example. As is so often the case in communication science, however, this is accompanied by a fundamental problem: Synthetic media as a term is not necessarily any sharper than media per se. The material object of research is thus delimited by such decisions. In any case, digital media exist in a highly convergent environment in which they are continuously moving toward each other morphologically.

This results in important key areas for further research on the topic. The idea that research should generally focus on the automated detection of deepfakes is obvious. However, this approach falls short for various reasons. Firstly, detection usually must be based on similar models that are also used to create deepfakes. This inevitably results in a discrepancy that is accompanied by technological uncertainty: As soon as the deepfake software improves, the detection software has to reach the same level again. Secondly, the technological advances in the field of deepfakes are so enormous that it will no longer be possible to distinguish them from real media content on a visual and auditory level in the foreseeable future. In this context, however, some people already share obviously false content on social media if they see their world view and prejudices confirmed in it. The explosive nature of deepfakes is therefore not necessarily limited to their quality. Nevertheless, it is not possible and, from a normative perspective, not desirable to suppress deepfakes in general. After all, they can also serve legitimate purposes and be covered by the right to freedom of expression and freedom of art.

Seibert (2023) further expanded the model of dealing with deepfakes by Godulla et al. (2021) and proposes a classification of risks and potentials of deepfakes at the micro-, meso-, and macro-level that enables the localization of future research projects on the topic (see Fig. 18.2). Accompanying research in all relevant communication professions and industries is necessary, as they are all affected by deepfakes without exception and must develop professional routines to be able to react sensibly to the changing requirements.

The author demonstrates that the quality and realism of deepfakes is constantly increasing and that deepfakes are already entering new fields of application. At the micro-level this means that individuals, on the one hand, will increasingly get into contact with beneficial applications of the technology, for example, in the context of entertainment, education, and film. On the other hand, individuals could fall victim to deepfakes more frequently in the future (identity theft, fraud). Based on the

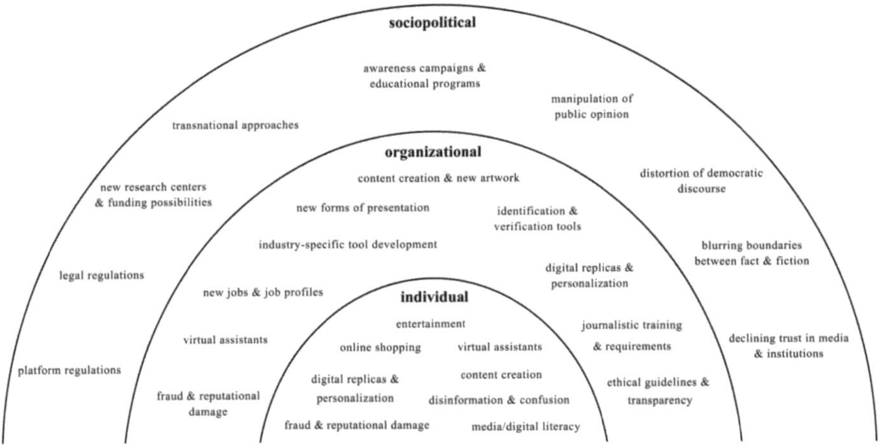

Fig. 18.2 Key aspects of deepfake research on an individual, organizational, and sociopolitical level [reprinted from Seibert, 2023, p. 148)

identified gender divide in the study of Bendahan Bitton et al. (2024), future studies should investigate how knowledge and attitudes toward deepfakes are related to gender-specific perceptions and motives for use (e.g., in the context of pornography). In this context, the question of whether feminist attitudes go hand in hand with increased sensitivity toward pornographic deepfakes or data protection concerns might be considered particularly interesting. Further studies should investigate who is particularly worried about the blurring of reality and fiction by deepfakes. Potential influencing factors such as personality traits, political interest, or "need for chaos" could provide differentiating insights here. In this context, it would also be useful to investigate the connection between conspiratorial thinking and the reaction to deepfakes. People with a high level of conspiratorial thinking could interpret deepfakes as evidence of their worldview and thus fall more strongly into cynical or suspicious thought patterns. Finally, to date, there are no insights into questions such as how and why do people create and spread deepfakes. Hence, future studies should investigate the patterns of creating and consuming deepfake content.

At the meso-level, Seibert (2023) concludes that companies continue to develop, test, and implement detection tools to guard against harmful uses of the technology. Additionally, companies have already begun to explore beneficial applications of the technology, for example, in media and marketing. In this context, future research should investigate how companies use deepfake technology (or the less negatively connoted term: synthetic media) specifically for marketing, customer interaction, or brand staging, for example, through virtual spokespersons, personalized advertising, or storytelling formats. In this context, opportunities, limitations, ethical implications, and the perceptions of their audiences toward new forms of presentation should be analyzed: How do consumers react to synthetically generated brand ambassadors or avatars? What roles do authenticity, perception of reality, and trust play in this context? And more generally: Which intentions for the use of deepfakes are more likely to be accepted or rejected by the audiences?

Finally, on the macro-level, the author argues that while the existing legal framework still needs improvement to keep up with the rapid progress and spread of the technology, requirements for legal and ethical uses of the technology are needed to maintain Internet users' trust in media and institutions. While the question of regulation is of particular interest to the legal sciences, there are also implications in other fields such as politics. Future studies should examine, for example, the impact of deepfakes on political debates. In this context, interventions should be considered to analyze which resilience mechanisms might prove effective to counter deepfake disinformation. Additionally, the role and responsibility of platforms in dealing with deepfakes (and synthetic media) without jeopardizing freedom of expression should be considered. Hence research should focus on moderation strategies and automated identification and labeling mechanisms. The labeling of deepfakes seems to represent a conceivable compromise between the public's legitimate interest in information on the one hand and the protection of the freedom of public communication on the other. In a nutshell, research into deepfakes should and must be considered holistically, taking into account sociopolitical interests as well as needs and requirements of the public and economic players, in order to be able to meet the increasing demands appropriately.

18.6 Conclusion

Deepfakes are exemplary of a technological caesura that is shaking the media ecosystem to its very foundations. Their ability to generate highly realistic audiovisual content not only calls into question the distinction between fact and fiction but also undermines the central epistemological foundations of public communication: visibility, authenticity, and verifiability. As products of generative AI, deepfakes have an impact far beyond their technical origin—they materialize a deeper shift within the communication logic of digital public spheres. The studies discussed in this chapter demonstrate that this technology is not only a technical challenge, but also a sociocultural and normative imposition. At an individual level, asymmetrical levels of knowledge, differentiated risk perceptions, and divergent assessments of the technology's potential are revealed. In particular, the pronounced gender divergence in the assessment of deepfakes points to existing digital inequalities that are not only reproduced by the technology but can even be exacerbated in certain fields of application—for example, in the area of nonconsensual deepfake pornography.

Journalistic practice is at a neuralgic point: on the one hand, it is itself affected by the risks of manipulative deepfakes—for example, through deception or loss of trust—on the other hand, it has the potential to contribute to clarification and de-escalation. Interviews with experts show that the strategic integration of deepfake technology into journalistic formats opens up innovative opportunities for design, but requires binding normative guidelines, new skills, and sensitive risk assessment. In this context, the core journalistic task of verification becomes more complex and important. At the same time, the results make it clear that a one-sided focus on technical detection solutions is not enough. Technological progress in the field of deepfake generation will inevitably overtake detection—a structural race with no foreseeable winner. As a result, a broader understanding of research is needed: Deepfake research must be interdisciplinary, multidimensional, and practice oriented. In addition to technical issues, it should also systematically cover social, psychological, economic, ethical, and legal implications.

In their ambivalence, deepfakes are both a challenge and a catalyst: they force new forms of media literacy and highlight the need for media education, ethical AI governance, and transparent communication structures. At the same time, they jeopardize the foundations of a democratic public sphere if truth claims can be substituted at will. Between disinformation and the promise of creativity, between loss of control and innovative power, between enlightenment and abuse, a field of tension arises that can only be addressed through integrative, reflective, and responsible research. The central conclusion is therefore: Deepfakes do not mark a singular media change, but rather a symptom of profound transformations in the relationship between technology, communication, and society. Researching them requires a holistic understanding that takes technological dynamics just as seriously as social practices, institutional structures, and individual skills. This is the only way to master the double challenge posed by deepfakes: maintaining trust in a mediatized world and shaping the future under the conditions of synthetic realities.

References

Bateman, J. (2022). *Deepfakes and synthetic media in the financial system: Assessing threat scenarios*. Carnegie Endowment for International Peace.

Bendahan Bitton, D., Hoffmann, C. P., & Godulla, A. (2024). Deepfakes in the context of AI inequalities: Analysing disparities in knowledge and attitudes. *Information, Communication & Society, 28*(2), 1–21. https://doi.org/10.1080/1369118X.2024.2420037

Bendahan Bitton, D., Ötting, H. L., Godulla, A. & Hoffmann, C. P. (2026). Implications of deepfake technology for journalistic practice: A technology at the crossroads of challenges and opportunities [Manuscript in preparation]. *Journalism*.

Block, M. (2023). *Deepfakes und Recht: Einführung in den deutschen Rechtsrahmen für synthetische Medien*. Springer.

Bozic, V. (2023). Strengthening EFL learners' autonomy: Exploring the Voscreen app and its impact on encouragement and engagement in technology-based language learning. *Language Education & Technology (LET Journal), 3*(2), 96–109. http://www.langedutech.com/letjournal/index.php/let

Brady, M., & Meyer-Resende, M. (2020). *Deepfakes: a new disinformation threat*. Democracy Reporting International.

Bray, S. D., Johnson, S. D., & Kleinberg, B. (2023). Testing human ability to detect 'deepfake' images of human faces. *Journal of Cybersecurity, 9*(1), 1–18. https://doi.org/10.1093/cybsec/tyad011

Cardenuto, J. P., Yang, J., Padilha, R., Wan, R., Moreira, D., Li, H., & Rocha, A. (2023). The Age of Synthetic Realities: Challenges and Opportunities. *arXiv preprint*, 1–27. https://arxiv.org/pdf/2306.11503.pdf

Carter, L., Liu, D., & Cantrell, C. (2020). Exploring the intersection of the digital divide and artificial intelligence: A hermeneutic literature review. *AIS Transactions on Human-Computer Interaction, 12*(4), 253–275. https://doi.org/10.17705/1thci.00138

Citron, D. K., & Chesney, R. (2018). Deep fakes: A looming challenge for privacy, democracy, and national security. *California Law Review, 107*, 1753–1820. https://scholarship.law.bu.edu/faculty_scholarship/640

de Ruiter, A. (2021). The distinct wrong of deepfakes. *Philosophy & Technology, 34*(4), 1311–1332. https://doi.org/10.1007/s13347-021-00459-2

Deepfake Project. (n.d.). *The Deepfake Project*. Retrieved March 12, 2025, from https://deepfake-project.com/en/

Diep Nep. (2021, July 29). *This is not Morgan Freeman—A look behind the Deepfake Singularity[video]*. YouTube. https://www.youtube.com/watch?v=F4G6GNFz0O8

Dobber, T., Metoui, N., Trilling, D., Helberger, N., & de Vreese, C. (2020). Do (microtargeted) deepfakes have real effects on political attitudes? *The International Journal of Press/Politics, 26*(1), 69–91. https://doi.org/10.1177/1940161220944364

Doss, C., Mondschein, J., Shu, D., Wolfson, T., Kopecky, D., Fitton-Kane, V. A., & Tucker, C. (2023). Deepfakes and scientific knowledge dissemination. *Scientific Reports, 13*(1), 1–12. https://doi.org/10.1038/s41598-023-39944-3

Eichhorn, T., Jürss, S., & Hoffmann, C. P. (2022). Dimensions of digital inequality in the sharing economy. *Information, Communication & Society, 25*(3), 395–412.

Farid, H., & Bravo, M. J. (2012). Perceptual discrimination of computer-generated and photographic faces. *Digital Investigation, 8*(3–4), 226–235. https://doi.org/10.1016/j.diin.2011.06.003

Fehrensen, M. & Täubner, M. (2019, March). Social Media: Warum wir nicht glauben sollten, was wir sehen [Social Media: Why we should not believe what we see]. *brand eins*. https://www.brandeins.de/magazine/brand-eins-wirtschaftsmagazin/2019/gefuehle/social-media-warum-wir-nicht-glauben-sollten-was-wir-sehen

Gehringer, F., Nehring, C., & Łabuz, M. (2024). *The influence of deep fakes one elections: Legitimate concern or mere alarmism? Monitor security*. Konrad Adenauer Stiftung. https://www.kas.de/documents/d/guest/the-influence-of-deep-fakes-on-elections

Godulla, A., Hoffmann, C. P., & Seibert, D. (2021). Dealing with deepfakes—An interdisciplinary examination of the state of research and implications for communication studies. *SCM Studies in Communication and Media, 10*(1), 72–96. https://doi.org/10.5771/2192-4007-2021-1-72

Gregory, S. (2022). Deepfakes, misinformation and disinformation and authenticity infrastructure responses: Impacts on frontline witnessing, distant witnessing, and civic journalism. *Journalism, 23*(3), 708–729.

Habgood-Coote, J. (2023). Deepfakes and the epistemic apocalypse. *Synthese, 201*(103), 1–23. https://doi.org/10.1007/s11229-023-04097-3

Hameleers, M. (2024). Cheap versus deep manipulation: The effects of Cheapfakes versus Deepfakes in a political setting. *International Journal of Public Opinion Research, 36*(1), 1–9. https://doi.org/10.1093/ijpor/edae004

Hameleers, M., & Marquart, F. (2023). It's nothing but a Deepfake! The effects of misinformation and Deepfake labels delegitimizing an authentic political speech. *International Journal of Communication, 17*, 6291–6311. https://ijoc.org/index.php/ijoc/article/view/20777/4351

Hashmi, A., Shahzad, S. A., Lin, C. W., Tsao, Y., & Wang, H. M. (2024). Unmasking illusions: Understanding human perception of audiovisual deepfakes (preprint). *arXiv*. https://arxiv.org/abs/2405.04097

Herbert, C., & Dołżycka, J. D. (2024). Teaching online with an artificial pedagogical agent as a teacher and visual avatars for self-other representation of the learners: Effects on the learning performance and the perception and satisfaction of the learners with online learning — previous and new findings. Frontiers in Education, 9. https://doi.org/10.3389/feduc.2024.1416033

Hurtz, S. (2024, August 15). Deepfake-Betrug: Angestellter überweist 24 Millionen Euro ins Nichts [Deepfake fraud: Employee transfers 24 million euros to nowhere]. *Süddeutsche Zeitung*. https://www.sueddeutsche.de/wirtschaft/deepfake-betrug-videokonferenz-hongkong-1.6344209

Kietzmann, J., Lee, L. W., McCarthy, I. P., & Kietzmann, T. C. (2020). Deepfakes: Trick or treat? *Business Horizons, 63*(2), 135–146. https://doi.org/10.1016/j.bushor.2019.11.006

Kitsara, I. (2022). Artificial intelligence and the digital divide: From an innovation perspective. In *A. Bounfour platforms and artificial intelligence: The next generation of competences* (pp. 245–265). Springer International Publishing.

Köbis, N. C., Doležalová, B., & Soraperra, I. (2021). Fooled twice: People cannot detect deepfakes but think they can. *iScience, 24*(11), 1–17.

Kruse, T. (2014, November 12). Ausradierte Genossen. *Fluter.* https://www.fluter.de/ausradierte-genossen

Kurpicz-Briki, M., Glauser, C., & Schmid, L. (2023). Vom "digital divide "zum" cyber divide". *HMD Praxis der Wirtschaftsinformatik, 61*, 555–571. https://doi.org/10.1365/s40702-023-00971-3

Lainjo, B. (2023). The global social dynamics and inequalities of artificial intelligence. *International Journal of Innovation Scientific Research and Review, 5*(8), 4966–4974. http://www.journalijisr.com/sites/default/files/issues-pdf/IJISRR-1306.pdf

Lee, J., & Shin, S. Y. (2022). Something that they never said: Multimodal disinformation and source vividness in understanding the power of AI-enabled deepfake news. *Media Psychology, 25*(4), 531–546. https://doi.org/10.1080/15213269.2021.2007489

Lewis, A., Vu, P., Duch, R. M., & Chowdhury, A. (2022). *Do content warnings help people spot a deepfake? Evidence from two experiments*. OSF Preprint.

Mahony, S., & Chen, Q. (2024). Concerns about the role of artificial intelligence in journalism, and media manipulation. *Journalism*, 1–19. https://doi.org/10.1177/14648849241263293

Manovich, L. (2001). *The language of new media*. MIT Press.

McCammon, M. N. (2021). The emerging threat of synthetic media. In L. Corredoira, I. B. Mallén, & R. C. Presuel (Eds.), *The handbook of communication rights, law, and ethics* (pp. 292–302). https://doi.org/10.1002/9781119719564.ch24

Mitchell, W. (2001). *The reconfigured eye: Visual truth in the post-photographic era*. MIT Press.

Murillo-Ligorred, V., Ramos-Vallecillo, N., Covaleda, I., & Fayos, L. (2023). Knowledge, integration and scope of deepfakes in arts education: The development of critical thinking in postgraduate students in primary education and master's degree in secondary education. *Education Sciences, 13*(11), 1–15. https://doi.org/10.3390/educsci13111073

Paris, B. (2021). Configuring fakes: Digitized bodies, the politics of evidence, and agency. *Social Media + Society, 7*(4), 1–13. https://doi.org/10.1177/20563051211062919

Pawelec, M. (2022). Deepfakes als Chance für die Demokratie? In *Digitalisierung und die Zukunft der Demokratie* (pp. 89–102). Nomos.

Pawelec, M. (2024a). Decent deepfakes? Professional deepfake developers' ethical considerations and their governance potential. *AI and Ethics*, 1–26. https://doi.org/10.1007/s43681-024-00542-2

Pawelec, M. (2024b, December 5). *Chancen für die Demokratie*. Bundeszentrale für politische Bildung. https://www.bpb.de/lernen/bewegtbild-und-politische-bildung/556803/chancen-fuer-die-demokratie/

Raffaghello, I., Kastalio, L., Kalf, S., & Paisley, E. (2019). What does a feminist approach to deepfake pornography look like? https://mastersofmedia.hum.uva.nl/blog/2019/10/24/what-does-a-feminist-approach-to-deepfake-pornography-look-like/

Reisdorf, B. C., & Groselj, D. (2017). Internet (non-)use types and motivational access: Implications for digital inequalities research. *New Media & Society, 19*(8), 1157–1176. https://doi.org/10.1177/1461444815621539

Ritchie, D. (2023). How Deepfakes Could Affect the Journalism Industry. *readwrite*.

Seibert, D. (2023). Deepfakes: Temporary hype or long-term innovation driver? In A. Godulla & S. Böhm (Eds.), *Digital disruption and media transformation: How technological innovation shapes the future of communication* (pp. 143–152). Springer International Publishing.

Sohrawardi, S. J., Wu, Y. K., Hickerson, A., & Wright, M. (2024). Dungeons & deepfakes: Using scenario-based role-play to study journalists' behavior towards using AI-based verification tools for video content. In *Proceedings of the 2024 CHI conference on human factors in computing systems* (pp. 1–17). https://doi.org/10.1145/3613904.3641973

Somers, M. (2020, July 21). Deepfakes explained. *MIT*. https://mitsloan.mit.edu/ideas-made-to-matter/deepfakes-explained
Sunil, R., Mer, P., Diwan, A., Mahadeva, R., & Sharma, A. (2025). Exploring autonomous methods for deepfake detection: A detailed survey on techniques and evaluation. *Heliyon, 11*, 1–28. https://doi.org/10.1016/j.heliyon.2025.e42273
Ternovski, J., Kalla, J., & Aronow, P. (2022). The negative consequences of informing voters about deepfakes: Evidence from two survey experiments. *Journal of Online Trust and Safety, 1*(2), 1–16. https://doi.org/10.54501/jots.v1i2.28
Vaccari, C., & Chadwick, A. (2020). Deepfakes and disinformation: Exploring the impact of synthetic political video on deception, uncertainty, and trust in news. *Social Media + Society, 6*(1), 1–13. https://doi.org/10.1177/2056305120903408
Van Deursen, A. J., Helsper, E. J., Eynon, R., & Van Dijk, J. A. (2017). The compoundness and sequentiality of digital inequality. *International Journal of Communication, 11*, 452–473.
Van Dijk, J. A. (2013). A theory of the digital divide. In M. Ragnedda & G. W. Muscher (Eds.), *The digital divide. The internet and social inequality in international perspective* (pp. 29–52). Routledge.
Vincent, J. (2018, May 22). Why we need a better definition of 'deepfake'. *The Verge*. https://www.theverge.com/2018/5/22/17380306/deepfake-definition-ai-manipulation-fake-news
Wagner, T. L., & Blewer, A. (2019). The word real is no longer real: Deepfakes, gender, and the challenges of AI-altered video. *Open Information Science, 3*(1), 32–46. https://doi.org/10.1515/opis-2019-0003
Wahl-Jorgensen, K., & Carlson, M. (2021). Conjecturing fearful futures: Journalistic discourses on deepfakes. *Journalism Practice, 15*(6), 803–820. https://doi.org/10.1080/17512786.2021.1908838
Walker, A. S. (2019). Preparing students for the fight against false information with visual verification and open source reporting. *Journalism & Mass Communication Educator, 74*(2), 227–239.
WDR Innovation Hub. (2021). *Synthetische Medien. Zukünfte der Medienproduktion mit Künstlicher Intelligenz [synthetic media. The future of media production with artificial intelligence]*. Westdeutscher Rundfunk Köln. https://bit.ly/3xQBirJ
Weikmann, T., & Lecheler, S. (2023). Cutting through the hype: Understanding the implications of Deepfakes for the fact-checking actor-network. *Digital Journalism, 11*(1), 1–18. https://doi.org/10.1080/21670811.2023.2194665
Westerlund, M. (2019). The emergence of deepfake technology: A review. *Technology Innovation Management Review, 9*(11), 39–52. https://doi.org/10.1080/13683500.2020.1738357
Whittaker, L., Kietzmann, T. C., Kietzmann, J., & Dabirian, A. (2020). "All around me are synthetic faces": The mad world of AI-generated media. *IT Professional, 22*(5), 90–99. https://doi.org/10.1109/MITP.2020.2985492
Yu, P. K. (2020). The algorithmic divide and equality in the age of artificial intelligence. *Florida Law Review, 72*(2), 331–390.

Daniel Bendahan Bitton is a research associate at the department of Empirical Communication and Media Research II at the Institute for Communication and Media Studies at Leipzig University. Since April 2022, Daniel is the coordinator of the SAB-funded project "Audiovisual media content based on artificial intelligence". In his dissertation, he investigates the impact of deepfakes on the audience's perception of online media content and also addresses future advantageous applications of deepfake technologies.

Alexander Godulla is a Professor of Empirical Communication and Media Research at the Institute for Communication and Media Studies (IfKMW) at Leipzig University, Germany. His research interests include AI in the media industry (deepfakes), innovations in digital journalism (virtual reality) and strategic communication (trend research), the transformation of public communication, cross-media and transmedia storytelling, denialism and the development of international photojournalism.

Christian Pieter Hoffmann is professor for Communication Management at Leipzig University's Institute of Communication and Media Studies. He is also associated with the Institute of Political Science, where he is responsible for research and teaching in Political Communication. Prof. Hoffmann is the academic director of the Center for Research in Financial Communication. His research portfolio encompasses strategic communication management, financial communication and political communication—with a focus on opportunities and challenges provided by new media.

“Limitless Computation on a Finite Planet?” The *Actually Existing* Ecology of Generative AI

19

Ian Collinson

Abstract

Despite all the published discourse on the topic, thinking about AI has not been critical enough (Lingren, *Handbook of Critical Studies of artificial Intelligence*. Edward Elgar, 2023). Researchers and scholars are now working to rectify this. When thinking about AI and ecology, researchers have examined the positive potential for these new technological assemblages to help deal with many environmental challenges. Unlike this important body of work, this chapter will focus not on the capacity for AI to intervene in environmental problems but on the ecological impact of AI itself. AI does not sit outside the ecological systems that it might be thought to improve. The growth of communication systems and computational power are part of the “great acceleration” that began in the aftermath of the Second World War. Following Lopez (*Ecomedia literacy: integrating ecology into media education*. Routledge, 2021), this chapter will frame AI as an *ecomedia object* within the *ecomediasphere*. This chapter can be framed as a contribution to the “material turn” in ecomedia research. This chapter focuses its discussion on the *ecomateriality* of AI and three particular disruptions: energy, raw materials, and e-waste. First, the AI assemblage is placing increasing demands on the electricity supply, demands that will only increase. Second, the AI assemblage is a product and a process dependent on supplies of raw materials that are used to construct, operate, and maintain its infrastructure and components. The expansion of AI means a growth in demand for all these materials. Third, AI explosion has implications for the afterlife of its components. As it increasingly colonizes the lifeworld, and with constant upgrades and developments, AI has the potential to accelerate the pace of obsolescence and therefore increase the already complex problem of e-waste. This chapter makes it clear

I. Collinson (✉)
Macquarie University, Sydney, NSW, Australia
e-mail: ian.collinson@mq.edu.au

S. Böhm et al. (eds.), *Handbook of AI-based Media Disruption*, Future of Business and Finance, https://doi.org/10.1007/978-3-032-07605-2_19

why any discussion about the future of AI must include consideration of the *actually existing* ecology of this transformative technology.

19.1 Introduction: AI, Media, and Ecology

In an editorial introduction to a special number of the journal *Sustainability,* Tan Yigitcanlar glosses some of the current critical work that has investigated the connection between AI and ecology. According to Yigitcanlar,

> AI is becoming an integral part of autonomous marine environmental monitoring…, wildlife monitoring…, environmental surveillance and flood protection…, water quality modeling …, biodiversity assessment …, detecting natural disasters, damage, and incidents in the wild …, and climate change modeling and preparedness …' (Yigitcanlar, 2021 p. 2).

This summary highlights the possibilities offered by AI to those who wish to respond to environmental challenges faced around the globe. However, none of the articles in this themed journal is focused on the ecological impact of AI itself.

For a long time, AI has been imagined as an agent of positive change. Since the 1950s, AI has been framed as a technological fix for our problems (Brevini, 2023). Much media about AI is driven by a utopian technophilia or an overly optimistic scientism, while its negative effects are cloaked in a "digital enchantment" (Maxwell & Miller, 2012). Despite such promise, both real and imagined, there is a need to think critically about the *environmentality* (Buell, 2005) of the AI assemblage. AI may have great potential for ameliorating environmental problems (Dauvergne, 2020) but at the same time it does not float outside the ecological systems that it might have the potential to improve. AI is not an agent from *outside* that can simply *intervene* and solve the problems that face us because ecologies have no outsides. Even as AI might mitigate ecological disasters, tackle environmental challenges, or help us "green the planet," it could simultaneously entrain ecological problems of its own, problems that are starting to become evident to those willing to think critically about its development. So, while it has been argued that AI might help mitigate bushfires, it also has the potential to supercharge fossil fuel extraction, which will increase greenhouse gas emissions that increase the frequency and intensity of such fires (Dauvergne, 2020, Crawford, 2021).

Lingren (2023) argues that despite all the published discourse about AI, our thinking about it has not been critical enough. As AI "seeps into ever more areas of society and culture," argues Lingren, "critical perspectives of the technology are more urgent than ever before" (Lingren, 2023, p. 1). Critical engagement with AI is necessary to counterbalance the viewpoints of the profit-driven and powerful tech industry whose interests are frequently elevated above those of others. Recent research has set out to investigate AI's position in the actually existing ecology (Brevinni, 2021, 2023, Crawford, 2021, Dauvergne, 2020 for example). This chapter is likewise concerned with the relationship between the actually existing ecology and AI, a relationship that will be framed via the disruptions that emerge from this new research. It is difficult to disagree with Yigitcanlar and Cugurullo when they assert that AI "is one of the most disruptive technologies of our time" (Yigitcanlar & Cugurullo, 2020). It might turn out to be the most disruptive technology of anyone's time.

The growth of communication systems and computational power are part of the "great acceleration" that began in the aftermath of the Second World War and shows little sign of braking. Just as we may investigate the ecological impact of music playback media, film processing technology, cathode-ray and LED TV production, or the Co2 emissions of media streaming platforms, so we can look at similar issues in the context of AI because "the effects of digital media technologies on the environment can be traced all along the production chain" (Lopez, 2021, p. 124). Drawing on Lopez (2021), this chapter frames AI as an "eco-media object" within the ecomediasphere. This chapter is a contribution to the "material turn" in ecomedia research, a label given to work that recognizes the material basis of all media "production, distribution, consumption" (Ziser, 2016, p. 75). Specifically, this chapter focuses its discussion on the *ecomaterality* of AI and three specific but broad material disruptions: to energy, materials, and e-waste. First, the AI assemblage is an energy-hungry technology that places increased and increasing demands on the electricity supply and has implications for climate change and countries' abilities to meet their emissions targets. Second, the AI assemblage is a product and a process dependent on supplies of raw materials that are used to construct, operate, and maintain its infrastructure and its components, from minerals like nickel and gold, to plastics, and even water. Growth in AI means a growth in demand for all these materials. Third, the growth of AI has implications for the afterlife of its components. As it increasingly colonizes the lifeworld, and with constant upgrades and developments, AI has the potential to accelerate the pace of obsolescence and therefore increase the already complex problem of e-waste.

19.2 AI, Ecomateriality, and the Ecomediasphere

The term AI appears everywhere in the mediasphere, but its ubiquity does not equal clarity. According to Brevini, "AI is a collection of technologies that combine data, algorithms and computing power" (Brevini, 2021, p. 40). AI is a constellation of singularities, an "assemblage of material devices and infrastructures" (Brevini & Doctor, 2023, p. 171)—assemblages being collections of relations between different collaborative entities (Muller & Schurr, 2016, p. 219). To frame AI as an ecomedia object, it is necessary to outline what Antonio Lopez has dubbed the "ecomediasphere" (Lopez, 2021). The ecomediasphere can be divided into quadrants, the ecomedia object itself being the point of convergence of these quadrants. The ecomedia object is a "boundary object" (Lopez, 2021) that sits at the center of four interconnected zones: eco-cultural (discourse, narrative, etc.), lifeworld (affects, emotions), ecopolitical (production, commodification, regulation), and ecomateriality (environmental entanglements and effects). Lopez notes that his formulation is influenced by Felix Guattari's "three ecologies" (1980), which recognizes that there are three different ecologies at play at any one time, ecologies *material*, *social*, and *mental* (Lopez, 2021, p. xvi).

Any analysis of AI must account for the ecomateriality of the medium. Lopez observes that "media technologies are [themselves] part of a vast network of ecological and material relations" (Lopez, 2021, p. 123). "Ecomateriality," writes Lopez, "...is the objective material conditions of the ecomaterial object and its technological apparatus" (Lopez, 2021, p. 150); "built environments, wireless footprints, semiconductor production, cables, pipes, ocean pings and acoustic ecology, cell towers and electromagnetic radiation, extraction, production, e-waste and energy" all fall within this ecomaterial zone (Lopez, 2021, p. 150). Similarly, in his chiasmic pair "images of ecology" and "ecology of images," Andrew Ross (1990), some three decades ago, drew a critical distinction between the media's representation of ecological issues and attendant concerns at the level of images and narrative on the one-hand—a concern that had dominated critical thinking about the relationship between the media and the environment—and the "actually existing ecology" in which media production, distribution, and consumption are entangled, on the other. Ross's distinction allows us to think of the ways in which all media is ecological, even if media content is not explicitly related to what we might consider to be environmental issues. Ross's distinction recognizes that all media has an "environmentality" (Buell, 2005). The "material turn" is used to describe this growing recognition of the material basis of all media; to think of the media ecologically we must thoroughly engage with its "production, distribution, consumption" (Ziser, 2016, p. 75). Ziser suggests that "there is a story worth telling about the environmental history of twentieth-century representational technologies—the toxic legacy of still and moving film processing, the production of cathode-ray televisions and transistor radios, the rapid obsolescence of computing technology" (Ziser, 2016, p. 75). Similarly, there is an emergent story to be told about AI as it creates "new opportunities to accelerate unsustainable production, [to] extract scarce resources, and supercharge consumerism" (Dauvergne, 2020, p. 149)—AI is the accelerator of the "great acceleration." This chapter tells just a small part of such a quickly unfolding tale, a tale that is harder to tell because "... many industries that make up the AI system chain conceal the ongoing cost of what they do" (Crawford, 2021, p. 49). The purpose here is to make visible the "double ground" (Citton, 2017) of AI that our overtaxed attentions miss. This "double-ground" of human action has been "rediscovered by ecological consciousness over the course of the twentieth century," an awareness that all human activity on this planet "always depends in the last resort on the constraint of the *eco*-, ... on the physico-chemical *oikos* on which our existence is based" (Citton, 2017, p. 197).

A decade ago, Maxwell and Miller (2012, p. 4) argued that "the enchantment with media technology certainly clouds much of the received history on the subject, making it hard to perceive its material connection to ecological decline." Thankfully, we are now more likely to see and critique these connections. For example, the powerful myth that the digital realm registers the dematerialization of media (signaled through euphemisms such as "the cloud" and the prefix "virtual") has been well and truly put to bed (Kirschenbaum, 2008, Casemajor, 2015, Crawford, 2021). The digital realm and the electronic devices on which it is founded is now regarded as material "all the way down" (Stone Short, 2014, p. 290). Rather than being intangible, "the effects of digital media technologies on the environment can be traced all along the production chain of our technological gadgets, which disproportionately and negatively impacts the global south by entailing inputs from Earth (mining, logging, drilling) and outputs into Earth (air, land, water)" (Lopez, 2021, p. 124). As we begin to think more critically about AI, its materiality begins to loom large, not just for scholars and researchers but for technologists and tech companies: material resources shape the future of AI as they enable and limit AI development. As AI has been developed within a capitalist media technoscape, the need to reconcile energy and hardware costs with profitability shapes its development. We will not get the "best" AI, in the broadest sense—we will get an AI that will be profitable. Here the ecomateriality of AI will be investigated from three perspectives: *energy*, *raw materials,* and *e-waste*.

19.3 AI: Three Disruptions

19.3.1 Disruption One: Energy

The first of the three disruptions is in energy production and consumption. As with technologies like cryptocurrency, AI is a very energy-hungry technology and therefore has a great capacity to disrupt global energy supplies. The availability of sufficient electricity at the right price, which means at a profitable price, is a clear restraint on AI development. The availability and cost of power will shape the development of AI and as tech companies look to continually increase computational power so the demand for energy will also grow.

Energy is required to both train and operate an AI. Training and operation consume different amounts of power; more power is supposedly used in training AI than in deployment, but exactly how much power AI uses is not always easy to discern. Tech companies are often secretive about power consumption in the training stage. One estimate suggests that training ChatGPT-3 required almost 1300 MWh of electricity, as much power used in a year by 130 US homes, or equivalent to the electricity required to watch over a million and half hours of Netflix (Vincent, 2024). In addition to the electricity used for training there is the energy used in its ongoing operation. According to some reports, in just 2 weeks an AI like ChatGPT-4 might use more electricity than in its entire training period (Heikkila, 2023). Certainly, using general purpose AI to perform tasks rather than task-specific software greatly increases energy use, as does building AI into common activities such as web searches that have no functional necessity for an AI component. Such are AI's power demands that using an AI to generate a single still image requires as much energy as fully charging a smartphone (Heikkila, 2023); after OpenAI released its image generator in early 2025, its users generated 78 million images *per day* (O'Donnell & Crowhurst, 2025). In comparison, a 5 s video at 16 frames per second (therefore a long way from high definition) uses 700 times the power needed for a still image (O'Donnell & Crowhurst, 2025). Media industries and media users are likely to use increasing amounts of energy as AI becomes integral in all areas of media production and consumption.

From another perspective, we can analyze the power consumption of data centers. These centers are placed among the highest of all consumers of electricity (Crawford, 2021). Data centers that stage AI use more energy than those that do not. The International Energy Agency, working with statistics from 2022, suggests that data centers use about 460 terawatt hours of electricity per year; by 2026 this could increase to between 620 and 1050 TWh, which equates to the same energy use as Sweden or Germany. If the supply of power cannot be increased sufficiently then it is possible that AI could induce energy scarcity and so drive-up the price of energy for everyone. To this direct energy consumption of AI training and operation, we need to add the "embodied" energy use of AI. Embodied energy is the "cumulative energy required to make a device" (Lopez, 2021, p. 154) or product. The power used in mining and transporting the raw materials and manufacturing that comprise the necessary hardware of AI is an example of such embodied energy.

The rapid adoption of AI and its power-hungry operations mean that the shift away from fossil fuels becomes even more imperative than it is already. The growth of AI without the growth of renewable energy must make meeting emission targets much harder. The effects of AI on tech companies emissions targets are already evident. Over the past 5 years, Google's emissions have jumped by a massive 48% due to AI energy demands, and Microsoft is currently exceeding its overall emissions target by roughly 30% (Barnard, 2024); so much for the latter's claim that they would be carbon neutral by 2030 (Crawford, 2021, p. 43). In 2024, Microsoft's president, Matt Smith revealed that the company's plan to be in carbon credit by 2030 had been ended by the AI boom (Gabot, 2024). According to one report, tech companies might also be involved in some "creative accounting" to minimize the appearance of their carbon footprint, for example, in their strategic use of renewable energy certificates (O'Brien, 2024). It seems that much trumpeted environmental commitments are quickly forgotten in the clamor to establish a claim and establish supremacy in the AI gold rush. AI must pose a similar threat to nation states' efforts to meet their environmental targets.

The energy consumption of AI asks important questions about the compatibility of unfettered AI development, the move toward carbon neutrality, and the 2050 targets that many countries have adopted. Taiwan Semiconductor Manufacturing Company, the largest manufacturer of microchips in the world, already consumes 5% of the island's total electricity production and this will only rise in the future. Sam Altman (CEO of OpenAI) has recently conceded that energy systems will be put under serious stress by AI development (Crawford, 2024). In his 2024 speech to the World Economic Forum in Davos, Altman seemed more concerned about the threat of energy shortages on the development of AI and therefore AI profitability, than he did on the effect of AI on the environment. Altman's solution to this energy and profitability challenge was a technocratic one that did not seek greater AI efficiency or impose limits on AI development and use, but rather focused on increasing the availability of cheap power created by two technologies; one that does not yet exist, nuclear fusion, and one that does, solar energy. So, although companies have not been forthcoming about the energy use of their AI systems (O'Donnell & Crowhurst, 2025), their actions to secure sufficient energy supplies speak volumes. They also remind us that our technological infrastructure and the media it has enabled has coevolved with capitalist "ideologies of unlimited growth" (Lopez, 2021, p. 153). Such is tech companies' desire for unlimited growth and the potential for unlimited profits; they have been strenuous in their efforts to secure renewable electricity from wind or solar farms that have not even been built (Meaker, 2024). Meta is paying for solar farms in Denmark; Google is funding wind farms in Norway (Meaker, 2024). Not to be left behind, Microsoft has recently negotiated a $10 billion renewable energy contract, the largest of its kind ever. The deal will secure Microsoft a supply of electricity equal to almost 50% of the entire generating capacity of California's wind and solar farms (Calma, 2024). Such power purchase agreements secure electricity that could otherwise have been used to power homes or other businesses.

Tech companies might argue that such an energy scenario is unnecessarily pessimistic, and they do. They might suggest that the greater efficiencies that will inevitably be achieved as the relevant technologies develop are overlooked or underplayed in such hyperbolic and pessimistic predictions. But while servers will become more energy efficient (Maxwell & Miller, 2012), and the unheralded arrival of DeepSeek in January 2025 promises a vastly reduced energy use when compared with Chatbots like ChatGPT (Enis, 2025), the techno-optimism of the tech companies ignores another possibility. Following the "Jevons paradox" (de Vries, 2023), as efficiencies make AI cheaper, and therefore more profitable, its use will increase, and so efficiencies produce not a reduction in energy consumption but an overall increase. This "efficiency equals increase" pattern has been seen in the development of other technologies. Thinking ecologically, we might also ask how many of these improvements to efficiency will be technologically based, and what might the environmental costs of developing these other more "efficient" technologies be; efficiencies that benefit profitability will not necessarily benefit the environment. With or without such efficiencies, the electricity demands of AI will be massive.

19.3.2 Disruption Two: Raw Materials

The second disruption can be found in terms of raw materials. What is AI made from? What seems like a straightforward question might be difficult to answer when thinking of AI as an assemblage. A rapid increase in the development and use of AI will lead to a spike in demand for its many components. The potential scale of such a disruption is clear when we consider that a microchip might require as many as 300 components. AI is certainly capable of depleting scarce resources in its manufacture, use, and disposal (Brevini & Doctor, 2023); to take just a single example, that of copper. Copper is the third most used mineral and three-quarters of all copper mined goes into electronics. Copper is a key mineral in the manufacture of the semiconductor chips necessary for AI technology, in different components of data centers (like heat exchangers) and in data centers' power systems. The AI revolution is predicted to drive a considerable increase in the global copper deficit, which is already considerable (Desai, 2024). AI will also do the same for other minerals, like tin and gallium, and perhaps for rare earths too. The accelerating demand for resources may divert raw materials/components away from other technologies and manufacturing, inhibiting development in those areas by throttling production and inflating costs. Already there are factories in China whose entire productive capacity is devoted to servers for AI development, some dedicated entirely to one particular company, Nvidia.

In addition to minerals and manufactured components, AI is also a great consumer of water. While the energy consumption of AI is gaining critical attention, AI's water consumption has so far attracted less interest from scholars, policy makers, and the general public. Data centers are as thirsty for water as they are hungry for electricity. Some press reports have projected AI water usage could reach 6.6 billion m^3 by 2027 (Gordon, 2024). Millions of liters of water are needed to train and operate AI. Data centers' cooling systems require up to 9 liters of water for every kwh of energy used. It is also possible to estimate water usage from the perspective of AI users. Lei et al. (2023) suggest that a session with an AI that consists of between 5 and 50 prompts will use 500 ml of water (Lei et al., 2023). This volume of water might not appear excessive at the level of the individual, but the greater impact becomes obvious once we recognize that ChatGPT may have ten million users a day, many who will make multiple prompts (Heikkila, 2023). Moreover, water consumption increases as the technology advances. In 2022, Google's data centers used 25 billion liters of water, an increase of 20% on the previous year. In the same period, Microsoft's total water consumption increased by 34% (Lei et al., 2023).

To the total water used in data centers, we must also add water used in the supply chain before and after actual operations of AI, its "embodied" water consumption (Lei et al., 2023). For example, chip production is a big user of water. The wafers of silicon that are processed into microchips are kept scrupulously clean by millions of liters of water. Taiwan Semiconductor Manufacturing Company's factories used 63 million tons of water in 2019. According to the Georgetown Center for Security and Emerging Technology, the millions of gallons used in a single day's microchip manufacture, in a single factory, is the same volume as that used by a small city, *over a year* (Heilweil, 2023).

As with energy consumption, tech companies are not always forthcoming about AI's water consumption. In some instances, they look close to deceitful. Meta and Microsoft have both been found to have made misleading comments about water consumption. In 2024, when Meta announced the establishment of its south Europe headquarters in Spain, a claim was made by local bureaucrats that it would use virtually no water. Later it was revealed that the center would use up to 665 million liters of water a year. Likewise, a Microsoft data center in Texas that was later found to be using 11 times the water for which it was paying (Gabot, 2024).

Whether it be metals like copper, rare earths or water, the extraction of these materials will only be accelerated by the rush to develop AI. Kate Crawford makes the point, much overlooked, that AI is an "extractive industry": "... demand for rare earth minerals, oil and coal is vast but the true costs of this extraction are never borne by the industry itself" (Crawford, 2021, p. 15).

19.3.3 Disruption Three: E-Waste

A third ecological disruption is found in e-waste. A 2022 report by the World Economic Forum estimated that 53 million tons of e-waste are produced globally each year, with only a meager 20% being recycled responsibly (WEF, 2022). E-waste is the fastest growing waste stream on the planet (Wang et al., 2024), which carries hazardous chemicals like lead, mercury, and cadmium. These substances pose threats to ecological well-being. There are threats to soil and water that endangers both human health and the more-than-human world. Technological development adds to the amount of e-waste generated as "...for every new electrical and electronic equipment ... with better features, aesthetics and quality, a new discarded one has been created" (Munchen et al., 2022, p. 73). One billion devices are discarded over a 4- to 5-year period (Holuzsko et al., 2022). AI is just the latest technology to take us swiftly from innovation to ruin (Gabrys, 2013), and the swifter the innovation the swifter the ruin will be.

There is a strong possibility that AI will increase the volume of e-waste as it is highly likely to accelerate technological obsolescence, reducing the working life of components. AI hardware already gets replaced every 3 years, a pace that is likely to increase. Whether functionally necessary or not, AI is swiftly being integrated into media hardware (smartphones, TVs, gaming consoles) and has become a selling point as companies urge consumers to upgrade their technology; they create the needs their product will satisfy (Marks, 2020). Apple, for example, works to convince users that they need to use Apple Intelligence, perhaps buying a more up-to-date version of the iPhone in the process, to write something as basic as an email. AI-driven obsolescence will also be a feature of production as businesses and industry update hardware used in server farms and data centers—"servers, GPUs, CPUs, memory modules and storage devices" (Wang et al., 2024, p. 818). Consumer and producer e-waste alike contains valuable metals like copper, gold, silver, aluminum, and rare earth elements, as well as "hazardous materials such as lead, mercury, and chromium" (Wang et al., 2024, p. 818). Generative AI produced around 2400 tonnes of e-waste in 2023 (Purtil, 2024), which seems insignificant when taken in the context of the 50 million tonnes of e-waste generated over a year. But "this [AI] e-waste stream will increase, potentially reaching a total accumulation of 1.2–5.0 million tons during 2020–2030, under different future GAI development settings" (Wang et al., 2024, p. 820). Such will be the future "surge" in e-waste, that we need to prepare for it now.

To the embodied energy required for manufacture that I discussed earlier, we must also add the energy used to deal with the resulting e-waste. AI generated e-waste will add to the energy burden of managing this waste stream. As a large majority of e-waste is dispatched to countries in the global south (Gabrys, 2013), the global south will have to deal with the environmental problems created by AI without reaping its fair share of the benefits. The informal e-waste recycling and extraction process that span the global south rely frequently on unsafe practices like acid leaching or burning that release toxic pollutants, and in some cases employ child labor. Tech companies appear free to drive the development of AI without needing to consider e-waste problems, now and in the future. AI is then an environmental justice issue as it entails an unfair distribution of environmental "goods" and "bads" (Brevini, 2021). The global south will bear the brunt of the increases in e-waste but will not feel the full benefits of AI technology. If the treatment of e-waste is combined with considerations of raw material extraction, we can see AI as a "technocolonialist enterprise"; it perpetuates the global south role as the "North's mine and garbage tip" (Brevini, 2023, p. 873).

19.4 Unlimited Computation on a Finite Planet?

In this chapter, I have outlined three ecological disruptions that are already a feature of the.

AI augmented mediascape. Firstly, AI is already affecting both the flows of energy around the world now and plans for the future, making decarbonizing the economy even more complicated and more urgent. Secondly, AI will also disrupt the flows of raw materials, be it copper, rare earths, or water. And thirdly, AI will increase the flows of e-waste as it accelerates the obsolescence of computer hardware. AI will have economic costs and environmental costs; companies might pay the economic cost but side-step the full- and long-term environmental costs.

In recognition perhaps of the environmental impact of AI, under the auspices of UNESCO, over 190 countries have adopted nonbinding recommendations on the ethical use of AI, recommendations that include environmental concerns. In paragraph 17 of the agreement, the signatories acknowledge that "ecosystem flourishing should be recognized, protected and promoted through the life cycle of AI systems" (UNESCO, 2021). This accent on the ethics, environment, and AI is elaborated further:

> all actors involved in the life cycle of AI systems must comply with applicable international law and domestic legislation, standards and practices, such as precaution, designed for environmental and ecosystem protection and restoration, and sustainable development. They should reduce the environmental impact of AI systems, including but not limited to its carbon footprint, to ensure the minimization of climate change and environmental risk factors, and prevent the unsustainable exploitation, use and transformation of natural resources contributing to the deterioration of the environment and the degradation of ecosystems (UNESCO, 2021).

While it is hard to disagree with such statements, it should be remembered that these recommendations are nonbinding on any of the signatories. Such voluntary codes of conduct are generally ineffective. Similarly, at the time of writing, the International Organization for Standardization (IOS) is in the process of developing criteria for what it calls "sustainable AI." Energy, water, resource mining and e-waste, as well as other environmental issues, will all be included in its standards. These standards will allow stakeholders to make informed decisions about AI. Unlike the recommendations of UNESCO, the standards of IOS can be voluntary or mandated via legislation. Standards set by bodies like the IOS are used by the World Trade Organization in trade disputes.

The UNESCO recommendations and the IOS both point to the importance of transparency of AI production and operation. This is especially pertinent when tech companies are often reluctant to be transparent about issues like energy efficiency and water consumption. AI companies hide critical data from the public: it is hard to know what action needs to be taken if the size of the problem faced is not known. Crawford (2021, p. 218) argues that "the opacity of the larger supply chain for computation in general, and AI in particular, is part of a long-established business model of extracting from the commons and avoiding restitution for the lasting damage." Greater transparency would allow government policymakers and the public to make better policy and more informed decisions (Brevini, 2023). As well as greater transparency they are other measures that can be taken to address the ecological impact of AI. According to Kate Crawford (2024), industry has a considerable part to play through the adoption of "sustainable practices" which should be made imperative. Such practices should include, "prioritizing the development of energy-efficient hardware, algorithms, and data centres; and using only renewable energy" (Crawford, 2024). The greater transparency needed could be achieved through external and independent environmental auditing (Crawford, 2024). As part of this auditing, governments could institute "specific environmental disclosure requirements to enhance transparency across the AI supply chain," measures that would foster "... a better understanding of the environmental costs of this emerging technological trend" (de Vries, 2023). Governments could also incentivize the sustainability of AI and punish rule breakers (Crawford, 2024).

19.5 Conclusion

The ecological dimensions of AI that I have outlined in this chapter run contrary to the standard AI evangelism that often dominates discussion about AI in the mediatized public sphere. However, the ecological dimensions of AI are appearing more frequently in public debate about the future of AI and an AI augmented future. The growth and spread of this debate is overdue and a precursor for meaningful change that is necessary if the ecological impact of AI is to be managed for the benefit of all.

References

Barnard, C. (2024). *AI ethics in the news: Summer 2024 roundup*. Institute of Internal Communication. https://www.ioic.org.uk/resource/ai-ethics-in-the-news-summer-2024roundup.html

Brevini, B. (2021). *Is AI good for the planet?* Polity.

Brevini, B. (2023). Myths, techno solutionism and artificial intelligence: Reclaiming AI materiality and its massive environmental costs. In S. Lingren (Ed.), *Handbook of critical studies of artificial intelligence* (pp. 856–867). Edward Elgar.

Brevini, B., & Doctor, D. (2023). Carbon capitalism, artificial intelligence: Placing the climate emergency Centre stage. In A. López, A. Ivakhiv, S. Rust, M. Tola, A. Y. Chang, & K. W. Chu (Eds.), *Routledge handbook of Ecomedia studies* (pp. 171–178). London.

Buell, L. (2005). *The future of environmental criticism: Environmental crisis and literary imagination*. Blackwell.

Calma, J. (2024). Microsoft made the biggest renewable energy agreement ever to fuel its AI ambitions. *The Verge*. https://www.theverge.com/2024/5/2/24147153/microsoft-ai-data-center-record-renewable-energy-purchase

Casemajor, N. (2015). Digital materialisms: Frameworks for digital media studies. *Westminster Papers in Communication and Culture, 10*(1) https://www.westminsterpapers.org/article/id/206/

Citton, Y. (2017). *The ecology of attention*. Polity.

Crawford, K. (2021). *The atlas of AI: Power, politics, and the planetary costs of artificial intelligence*. Yale University Press.

Crawford, K. (2024). Generative AI'S environmental costs are soaring — And mostly secret. *Nature*. https://www.nature.com/articles/d41586-024-00478-x

Dauvergne, P. (2020). *AI in the wild sustainability in the age of artificial intelligence*. MIT Press.

de Vries, A. (2023). The growing energy footprint of artificial intelligence. *Joule, 7*, 2191–2194.

Desai, P. (2024). 'AI could add 1 million tons to copper demand by 2030, says Trafigura', *Reuters* April 9 https://www.reuters.com/markets/commodities/ai-could-add-1-million-tons-copper-demand-by-2030-says-trafigura-2024-04-08/ viewed 11/2/25.

Enis, M. (2025) The environmental cost of AI. Library Journal. http://libraryjournal.com/story/the-environmental-cost-of-ai-climate-crisis

Gabot, M. (2024). *Why we don't know ai's true water footprint*. Tech Policy Press. https://www.techpolicy.press/why-we-dont-know-ais-true-water-footprint/

Gabrys, J. (2013). *Digital rubbish: A natural history of electronic waste*. University of Michigan Press.

Gordon, C. (2024). AI is accelerating the loss of our scarcest natural resource: water. *Forbes*. https://www.forbes.com/sites/cindygordon/2024/02/25/ai-is-accelerating-the-loss-of-our-scarcest-natural-resource-water/

Heikkila, M. (2023). Making an image with generative AI uses as much energy as charging your phone. *MIT Technology Review*. https://www.technologyreview.com/2023/12/01/1084189/making-an-image-with-generative-ai-uses-as-much-energy-as-charging-your-phone/

Heilweil, R. (2023). Want to win a chip war? You're Gonna Need a Lot of Water. *Wired*. https://www.wired.com/story/want-to-win-a-chip-war-youre-gonna-need-a-lot-of-water/

Holuzko, M., Kumar, A, & Espinosa, D. (eds) Electronic Waste; recycling and reprocessing for a sustainable future. Wiley.

Kirschenbaum, K. (2008). *Mechanisms: New media and the forensic imagination*. MIT University Press.

Lei, P., Yang, J., Islam, M, & Ren, S. (2023). *Making ai less "thirsty": uncovering and addressing the secret water footprint of ai models*. https://doi.org/10.48550/arXiv.2304.03271

Lingren, S. (2023). Introducing critical studies of artificial intelligence. In S. Lingren (Ed.), *Handbook of critical studies of artificial intelligence* (pp. 1–19). Edward Elgar.

Lopez, A. (2021). *Ecomedia literacy: Integrating ecology into media education*. Routledge.

Marks, L. U. (2020). Let's deal with the carbon footprint of streaming media. *Afterimage, 47*(2), 46–52.
Maxwell, R., & Miller, T. (2012). *Greening the media*. Oxford University Press.
Meaker, M. (2024). The Big-Tech Clean Energy Crunch is Here. *Wired*. https://www.wired.com/story/big-tech-datacenter-energy-power-grid/
Munchen, D., Dias, P. & Viet, H. (2022). Materials used in electronic equipment and manufacturing perpectivers. In Holuzko, M., Kumar, A, & Espinosa, D. (eds) Electronic waste; recycling and reprocessing for a sustainable future (pp.73-94). Wiley.
Muller, M., & Schurr, C. (2016). Assemblage thinking and actor-network theory: Conjunctions, disjunctions, cross-fertilizations. *Transaction of the Institute of British Geographers, 41*(3), 317–347.
O'Brien, I. (2024). Data center emissions probably 662% higher than big tech claims. Can it keep up the ruse?. *Guardian*. https://www.theguardian.com/technology/2024/sep/15/data-center-gas-emissions-tech
O'Donnell, J., & Crowhurst, C. (2025). We did the math on AI'S energy footprint. Here's the story you haven't heard. *MIT Technology Review*. https://www.technologyreview.com/2025/05/20/1116327/ai-energy-usage-climate-footprint-big-tech/
Purtil, C. (2024). Generative ai will soon generate millions of tonnes of electronic waste, study suggests. *ABC*. https://www.abc.net.au/news/science/2024-10-29/generative-ai-generating-millions-tonnes-electronic-waste-data/104514376
Ross, A. (1990). *The Chicago gangster: Theory of life: Nature's debt of society*. Verso.
Stone Short, C. (2014). The sustainability of our digital environments: The language of the upgrade path and e-waste. *Green Letters: Studies in Ecocriticism, 18*(3), 286–296.
UNESCO. (2021). *Draft recommendation on the ethics of artificial intelligence*. https://www.unesco.org/en/legal-affairs/recommendation-ethics-artificial-intelligence
Vincent, J. (2024). How much electricity does ai consume?. *The Verge*. https://www.theverge.com/24066646/ai-electricity-energy-watts-generative-consumption
Wang, P., Zhang, L.-Y., Tzachor, A., & Chen, W. Q. (2024). E-waste challenges of generative artificial intelligence. *Nature Computational Science, 4*, 818–823.
WEF. (2022). *Top 25 recycling facts and statistics for 2022*. World Economic Forum. https://www.weforum.org/stories/2022/06/recycling-global-statistics-facts-plastic-paper/viewed. 26/6/25
Yigitcanlar, T. (2021). Greening the artificial intelligence for a sustainable planet: An editorial commentary. *Sustainability, 13*(24), 13508.
Yigitcanlar, T., & Cugurullo, F. (2020). The sustainability of artificial intelligence: An urbanistic viewpoint from the lens of smart and sustainable cities. *Sustainability, 12*(20), 8548.
Ziser, M. (2016). Ecomedia. In J. Adamson, W. Gleason, & D. Pellow (Eds.), *Keywords for environmental studies* (pp. 75–76). New York University Press.

Ian Collinson is a lecturer in media at Macquarie University, Sydney. Previously co-director of Macquarie University's environmental humanities research stream, his research focuses on media's many ecological entanglements, including ecocritical approaches to media, media and environmental activism, and explorations of media's ecomateriality.

AI in Media Education and the Training of Media Professionals

20

Anna Jupowicz-Ginalska and Mariola Kinal

Abstract

The rapid development of artificial intelligence (AI) has significantly transformed both the media landscape and the field of education, prompting critical questions about how higher education institutions—particularly those specialising in media and communication—are responding to these shifts. This chapter investigates the intersection between AI, media education, and the professional preparation of future media practitioners. Through a literature review and content analysis, the study explores how AI is being discussed, implemented, and critically assessed within education. Two principal research trajectories are identified: first, the integration of AI into general media education aimed at fostering digital, informational, and critical literacy across various educational stages; and second, the implementation of AI-driven tools and concepts in the training of future media professionals, such as journalists, editors, and media managers. The findings reveal growing attention to the ethical, technical, and pedagogical challenges posed by AI, including issues of data privacy, algorithmic bias, and the credibility of AI-generated content. Moreover, the analysis highlights the need to update existing educational models and syllabi to better reflect the realities of AI-driven media environments. Emphasis is placed on the importance of interdisciplinary collaboration among educators, technologists, policymakers, and industry stakeholders. This chapter concludes that effective media education in the age of AI must go beyond technical training and encompass ethical reasoning, critical thinking, and adaptive skills. By equipping students with both practi-

A. Jupowicz-Ginalska (✉)
Faculty of Journalism, Information and Book Studies, University of Warsaw, Warsaw, Poland
e-mail: a.ginalska@uw.edu.pl

M. Kinal
Institute of Pedagogy, University of Rzeszow, Rzeszow, Poland
e-mail: mkinal@ur.edu.pl

S. Böhm et al. (eds.), *Handbook of AI-based Media Disruption*, Future of Business and Finance, https://doi.org/10.1007/978-3-032-07605-2_20

cal competencies and a critical understanding of AI, higher education can contribute to shaping informed, responsible, and future-ready media professionals.

20.1 Introduction

Technological developments, and in particular the development of artificial intelligence (AI), have brought about a rapid transformation in society's perception of basic services. Immediate access to massive databases and the ubiquity of knowledge, or rather the illusion of knowledge, have caused a change in thinking about education and what tasks educational institutions should perform. Traditional methods, in which the teacher passes knowledge to the passively listening pupils, have been questioned for many years. For example, Freire (2005) criticised this approach, arguing that students who are treated as 'an empty vessel to be filled' (p. 79) inhibit their ability to think critically and perpetuate oppressive structures.

As one of the responses to this problem, AI educational platforms began to be created and developed, promoting individualisation of education and responding more closely to the needs of individuals (Castillo-Martínez et al., 2024). At the same time, the question of what we are educating future generations has arisen (see: Chan & Tsi, 2023). What skills and competences will be necessary? Will some professions— like teachers—disappear and be replaced? How do teachers use technology without demonising it or fostering fear and resistance?

Chan and Tsi (2023) refer to these problems, describing the advantages and disadvantages of interconnections between the education process and AI. In the first group, they observe the reduction of teachers' administrative tasks. This, in turn, allows for time savings and the opportunity to allocate that time to other, more demanding tasks. Researchers also highlight the provision of tools useful in the teaching process, such as supporting language learning, plagiarism detection, automated grading, or monitoring student development (Felix, 2020; Pokrivcakova, 2019; Terzopoulos & Satratzemi, 2019). Among the disadvantages, the following issues are raised: weakening of interpersonal relationships, the lack of emotions in interactions between AI and students, the algorithmisation of social norms and ethics, issues with reliability and credibility, and even social inequalities (Wogu et al., 2018; Schiff, 2021; Felix, 2020).

These concerns refer to all educational stages, from primary school to higher education. However, this chapter focuses on the latter.

As Castillo-Martínez et al. (2024) note, universities face challenges integrating AI into the educational process. Nelson et al. (2024) call its application 'tremendous and fluctuating' and notice that it 'delivers huge difficulties' (p. 14188). Together with Williamson and Eynon (2020) and Bibi et al. (2024), they list problems with 'information protection, moral contemplations, and computerised partition' (p. 14189). On the other hand, they claim that merging AI with the higher educational system enables to 'reconsider education' or even 'customise growth opportunities, upgrade authoritative proficiency, and advance examination capacities'

(Nelson et al., 2024, p. 14194). To achieve this status, 'educators, policymakers, technologists, and specialists' must cooperate (ibid.). Collaboration between different stakeholders is crucial, as in many industries, the ability to work with AI tools and applications is a fundamental factor in a candidate's competitiveness on the job market (World Economic Forum, 2025).

Therefore, knowledge of AI is an essential and valuable part of knowledge of the modern digital world. It is worth remembering that one of its main elements is the media, which accompany humans throughout their lives. Thus, training in media competences and skills, nowadays in AI, is a prerequisite for functioning in a digital society. On the other hand, the media industry itself is a clear example of an AI-driven field. As this book demonstrates, this phenomenon occurs on many levels, ranging from ethical and moral issues (e.g. fake news, deepfakes, authorship of AI-generated content, source credibility) to more operational aspects (such as data processing, datafication, Big Data) and practical tool use (e.g. applications for content creation, analysis and verification, editing, transcription, etc.). It therefore seems legitimate and necessary to educate future media professionals, above all journalists, in using AI. Given the multidimensionality, relevance, and urgency of this topic and the significant interconnections between education, media, and AI, we have drawn two primary directions for this chapter, referring to what issues are brought up in the area of (1) media education and (2) educating media professionals.

As research on implementing artificial intelligence in education is still nascent and growing rapidly, we aim not to analyse it systematically. Instead, we highlight the areas that have already emerged and indicate potential directions for further exploration.

20.2 An Outline of Media Education: From Print to AI

The evolution of media education is inextricably linked to the technological milestones of the development of network society, which reflect the growing recognition of the importance of technology in raising critical awareness and understanding of its role among users about their social and cultural environments.

The first milestone that determined the development of journalism was the advent of printing, which made it possible to reproduce content on a mass scale and create a demand for the work of journalists. The next turning point was the advent of radio and television, which resulted in the rapid growth of the media industry (Bösh, 2021). The next turning point in the 1970s and 1980s was the introduction of the Internet and personal computers. This led to an increased demand for people to create different content and the emergence of new media specialists and professions (Fisher, 2020). As Ptaszek (2019) notes, the Internet was intended to be a space free from the dominance of the mass media industry, which imposed prevailing values, norms, and ways of thinking. Initially, it was thought to be a medium through which individual views could be expressed. On the contrary, Galloway (2004) believes that the basic principle of the Internet was to exercise control over users, not through control of content, but through the technical organisation of the network. Social media's appearance and dynamic development after 2000 created new tools that media professionals could use, causing a diversification of unreliable data sources (Deavours et al., 2022).

Further developments were connected to other modern technologies, like VR and AR. Dodds (2024) analysed how immersive technologies—AR, VR, 360° videos—affect interaction with content audiences. He argued that the new way of journalistic narration allows audiences to become more deeply immersed in the stories being told. A recent turning point in thinking about the phenomenon is artificial intelligence's development and mass availability. In particular, the emergence of ChatGPT in 2022, which understands context and generates natural responses, caused people to think of AI as a creation that can partially replace 'human' journalism (Demmar & Neff, 2023).

Of course, all these breakthroughs required new skills and competencies. Two trends can be observed when analysing the media-related education discourses in the literature (Greenberg, 2007). On the one hand, attention is paid to the practical dimension of education and equipping students with practical skills (i.e. how to use technology, different devices, etc.). On the other hand, the need to improve soft skills such as critical thinking, creativity, collaboration skills, and the ability to perceive and analyse nuances and social, political, and cultural contexts is emphasised.

With the development of digital media, it has become apparent that media education should start as early as possible, as even small children are exposed to their impact without having the tools to evaluate it critically. According to the Erikson Institute Report (2021), early introduction of media education helps teach children to think critically and future-proof their use of new media. As a result, research has emerged looking at the development of media literacy and its shift from focusing on the harmful effects of media to emphasising empowerment and agency. Some studies articulate the need for critical awareness to enable students of all stages to navigate the complexity of media messages. For example, this transition reflects broader sociocultural changes and the growing importance of fostering a community of active media makers who can thoughtfully engage with the media around them (Share et al., 2019). Chan and Tsi (2023) contribute to the discussion by demonstrating practical media literacy applications in high school classrooms, particularly in current events. His study illustrates that media education can improve critical thinking skills, reinforcing that the need for media literacy becomes more important as technology permeates society. Zhang et al.'s (2020) research reinforces the empowerment aspect of media literacy by focusing on racial bias in mass media. Her findings highlight the need to create a curriculum that teaches critical thinking and encourages students to analyse the media they consume. Pro-social attention is consistent with the historical trajectory of media education, which has increasingly recognised the importance of addressing social issues through a critical prism. Riendeau (2019) synthesises historical and theoretical approaches to media literacy, questioning whether current educational practices adequately prepare students for the complexity of contemporary media landscapes. By examining curricular approaches and the role of social media, this review underlines the need to equip students with the skills necessary to assess the bias and credibility of information sources.

Similarly, Polish researchers define the phenomenon of media education. The first attempts of its exploration occurred in the 1990s, when the need to educate society about the media began to be recognised after the political transformation from communism to liberal democracy. At this time, the first educational programmes aimed to develop critical thinking skills in the context of media reception and understanding media impact on society (Bereźnicka, 2023; Waszkiewicz-Raviv, 2015). During this period, media education was often treated as an add-on to traditional school subjects, and its importance was not yet fully appreciated. Another critical moment was Poland's integration into the European Union in 2004, which contributed to an increased interest in media education in the European context. At that time, new standards and curricula began to be introduced, which took into account the development of information technologies and changes in communication (Dereniuk, 2024; Sołtysiak, 2010). The rise of the Internet and social media forced educators to adapt their programmes to the new realities, resulting in numerous initiatives to develop media competence among young people (Pacewicz & Ptaszek, 2019). In recent years, particularly in the COVID-19 pandemic, there has been an explosion in remote education, which has further emphasised the importance of media education. During this time, teachers and students have had to adapt quickly to new forms of learning, highlighting the need for digital literacy skills (Penkowska, 2022). Analyses of the impact of media on young people and the risks associated with their use have also appeared in the literature, prompting reflection on the role of media education in shaping responsible media users (Borawska-Kalbarczyk, 2023; Polcyn, 2018).

With artificial intelligence's dynamic development, media education faces further challenges. It is no longer to provide only formal knowledge, but also to develop and train people for future careers in society, because many will relate to the media. It means that students' knowledge and practical skills must be adapted to the complexity of the digital world. However, to teach efficiently, media educators need to constantly update and develop their skills and knowledge to meet the needs of students (Leja, 2024). No wonder media education is shifting from traditional, offline classrooms orchestrated by old-fashioned pedagogues to digitally skilled teachers who design online learning environments where students are active and independent learners (Schiff, 2021). Technology has become essential for creating such environments, but teachers and students should be prepared to use it effectively.

These considerations go hand in hand with lifelong learning and continuous adaptation to constantly changing situations (Tkach, 2019). Therefore, a readiness to engage with new technologies from the beginning is essential for all stakeholders in media education. At the same time, this foresight in media education raises questions about the need to develop policies as technology is implemented throughout the educational process. They must identify ethical and privacy issues regarding student data, especially when using artificial intelligence technology from third-party companies. Jaskuła (2023) confirms these concerns. She noticed that AI applications in education raise questions about data privacy. This is echoed by Tanaś

(2023), who points to the need to consider the ethical and legal aspects of using AI in pedagogical research.

Another area of development in media education and AI is introducing new tools that could increase learning effectiveness and facilitate the personalisation of the educational process. This, along with instant feedback, may relieve the burden from teachers and allow them to focus on more demanding tasks. Of course, educational adaptive platforms cannot fully replace teachers. Still, they can generate good quality assignments tailored to students' needs and abilities and provide balanced feedback to students on their work. On the other hand, as AI supports adaptive learning platforms, this technology can take over the basic teaching duties and enable quality education for those who do not have access to highly qualified staff (Jing et al., 2023). With the increasingly severe teacher shortage, AI promises universal and quality education.

20.3 An Outline of Educating Media Professionals in Times of AI

AI was identified as the most influential technology expected to impact media-related curricula in the following years (Hossain & Wenger, 2024). As a response, many studies underline the necessity of integrating AI in journalism education programmes, indicating a strong need to adapt education to the changing media landscape and to 'prepare students to report on the coming transformation of AI and equip them to help shape that transformation for society and journalism' (Gordon & Lule, 2019, p. 800). However, to cope with this, the difficulties that stand in the way of implementing AI in higher education media studies programmes need to be identified, explored, and then remedied. Demmar and Neff (2023) point out three major concerns in the discussed area. According to their literature review-based research, there are developing curricula, ethical aspects of AI, and insufficient skills in AI usage by teachers and students.

The central aspect of the problem is integrating AI into curricula. Existing research focuses on twofold development: AI tools and ethics.

Several studies proved that AI can support journalists in various tasks, such as content generation, data analysis, news personalisation, or gatekeeping (Lopezosa et al., 2023; Brigham et al., 2024; Jędrzejewski, 2024). It is also worth noting that AI can support journalists in analysing large data sets and contribute to journalists' efficiency by enabling them to gather information faster and more accurately (Brigham et al., 2024; Dhiman, 2023).

Therefore, teaching students how to work with AI practically would help them carry out future professional duties in editorial offices, the more that it has been confirmed that reaching out for AI tools improves students' 'analytical skills and ability to produce compelling data-driven stories' (Wenger et al., 2024, p. 4). Considering that, current curricula should include data analysis techniques and skills to use AI tools in a journalistic context (Lopezosa et al., 2023; Brigham et al., 2024). In particular, ChatGPT offers new possibilities for content creation, which can be helpful in journalism education (Pavlik & McIntosh, 2023; Tang, 2023; Ifan, 2023). Interestingly, Jaskowska (2023) draws attention to the use of computational models in generating news texts, but she also underlines that these practices may raise legal and ethical concerns.

Considering AI's ambiguities, curricula should teach technical and ethical skills for using these technologies responsibly (Lopezosa et al., 2023; Somorin & Ademola, 2024). Nowicka (2022) adds another layer to ethical considerations by referring to the need for critical thinking in the context of information generated by algorithms in curricula. In general, moral aspects associated with using AI in journalism are an essential thread in the curricula of AI-based development. As mentioned earlier, literature underlines ethical challenges in media professionals' work, such as algorithmic biases, lack of transparency in decision-making processes and accountability for AI-generated content (Borenstein & Howard, 2020; Somorin & Ademola, 2024). In the context of education, it is essential that future journalists are aware of these challenges and can solve them. That means that educational programmes should incorporate modules on AI ethics to prepare students to deal with moral dilemmas that may arise in their work (Borenstein & Howard, 2020; Somorin & Ademola, 2024).

Research on integrating AI in the education of media professionals also focuses on the insufficient skills (or knowledge) of teachers and students. From the staff perspective, studies imply the need to train lecturers. They must be well prepared to teach about AI and its applications in journalism (Chiu et al., 2022; Dinçer, 2024). Higher educational institutions should invest in developing the competencies of their staff so that they can effectively impart knowledge about AI and its impact on journalism, like workshops or constant upgrading of pedagogical skills (Chiu et al., 2022; Dinçer, 2024; Newman, 2023).

Secondly, the hands-on experience in journalism education is also essential. Making lecturers understand the meaning of the practice is crucial. For example, allowing students to work with AI tools in real journalism projects can increase their skills and confidence in using these technologies (Lopezosa et al., 2023; Brigham et al., 2024). As Veenstra et al. (2024) notice, when referring to AI, students 'operate as if they are digital natives as originally understood, but without the actual knowledge and skill assumed by the concept' (preprint). This observation justifies the need to incorporate AI into programmes even at a basic level, by explaining the assumptions behind the phenomenon.

Wenger et al. (2024) share several recommendations for this process. These are 'updating existing courses to AI-related content' and 'a balance between traditional journalism skills and technological advancements', implementing ethics-based courses, and allocating 'resources for long-term professional development to enhance faculty expertise in AI' (p. 13). Dinçer (2024) aligns with these observations; however, he adds that the important element of technical skills is understanding them, and the ability to use AI ethically is connected with personal competencies. He states that 'by learning both, future journalists will be able to use AI tools effectively while still reporting the news honestly and in a way that feels human' (p. 66).

Some researchers have noticed the potential for collaboration with stakeholders (media industry, media educators, technology business, or computer science departments). In this context, cooperation with editors and media organisations can be crucial to provide students with industry-based experience (Lopezosa et al., 2023; Brigham et al., 2024). As Dinçer (2024) concludes, 'by working together, these stakeholders can create an educational environment that prepares students not just to survive but to thrive in the AI era, leveraging technology to enhance reporting while upholding the integrity and social responsibility that are the hallmarks of the profession'. (p. 74).

20.4 Conclusions

Scholars in the fields of media education—both those focused on enhancing media literacy and societal competencies, and those engaged in the academic training of media professionals—increasingly acknowledge the growing impact of artificial intelligence (AI) on the media landscape, including its influence on audiences and content creators alike. There is a clear understanding that AI has become a permanent fixture in everyday human experience, bringing significant advantages and inherent limitations. Given the ubiquity of this technology, researchers emphasise the urgent need to disseminate knowledge about AI, promote its practical and ethical use, and, most importantly, modernise educational curricula across all levels of instruction.

In both domains, scholars advocate for a dual approach to AI education. The first dimension prioritises the development of technical and operational competencies that enable individuals to utilise AI tools effectively. The second dimension underscores the importance of integrating ethical considerations into AI education to ensure its application aligns with fundamental values such as safety, respect for privacy, intellectual authorship, creativity, integrity, and truth. These values are essential for media consumers and professionals, cultivating a democratic and participatory civil society.

Educating individuals in the responsible use of AI is an investment in shaping future generations of media producers and audiences. Additionally, promoting collaborative initiatives among stakeholders opens up pathways for invoking the principle of corporate social responsibility and the role of public institutions in fostering ethical technological engagement.

Current research indicates, however, that integrating AI into university curricula, particularly through courses dedicated exclusively to the application of AI in media, is still in its nascent stages. Salgado (2022), referencing prior studies, identifies several pioneering examples, such as *AI in Media and Society* at the University of Florida, *Algorithms and Automation* at the University of Oregon, *AI and Digital Communication* at Hong Kong Baptist University, *AI & Society* at Carnegie Mellon University School of Design, and *Topics in Journalism & Society: AI, Automation & Journalism* at Northern Illinois University.

It is reasonable to assume that such courses have increased since Salgado's publication. As Babacan et al. (2025) observe, education in this domain continues to face significant challenges. Chief among them is the uneven distribution of AI-focused courses between private and public institutions; the former tend to emphasise industry collaboration, while the latter concentrate on theoretical and research-driven approaches. Geographic disparities also play a role: while institutions in Western countries have begun incorporating 'AI-powered newsroom simulations, computational journalism modules, and hands-on machine learning workshops' (p. n.a.), universities in Latin America often adhere to more traditional, didactic methods of instruction.

Overall, academic programmes offer more courses dealing with ethics and policy than those oriented towards technical subjects such as machine learning or algorithmic content generation.

Given these dynamics, further academic initiatives dedicated to AI in media are anticipated to emerge soon. Babacan et al. (2025) already stress the importance of researching student perceptions and experiences in AI-focused educational programmes. They also advocate for expanding methodological approaches to such studies, including surveys and interviews. Equally critical to advancing AI literacy is empirical research into the perspectives of media educators, ranging from primary and secondary school teachers to university-level instructors. Additionally, understanding the evolving needs of the media industry, particularly about the competencies required of future professionals, is of central importance.

In conclusion, advancing AI education in media remains a complex and ongoing endeavour. It necessitates interdisciplinary collaboration among a diverse array of stakeholders. Only through the alignment of shared goals—practical and ethical—can educational programmes be developed that endow media consumers and producers with meaningful competencies and critical literacies necessary for engaging with AI in a responsible and impactful manner.

References

Babacan, H., Arık, E., Bilisli, Y., Akgun, H., & Ozkara, Y. (2025). Artificial intelligence and journalism education in higher education: digital transformation in undergraduate and graduate curricula in Turkiye. *Journalism and Media, 6*(2), 52. https://doi.org/10.3390/journalmedia6020052

Bereźnicka, M. (2023). Media - szanse, wyzwania i zagrożenia a potrzeba edukacji medialnej. *AUPC Studia Ad Bibliothecarum Scientiam Pertinentia, 20*, 641–660. https://doi.org/10.24917/20811861.20.40

Bibi, A., Yamin, S., Natividad, L. R., Rafique, T., Akhter, N., Fernandez, S. F., & Samad, A. (2024). Navigating the ethical landscape: AI integration in education. *Educational Administration: Theory and Practice, 30*(6), 1579–1585. https://doi.org/10.53555/kuey.v30i6.5546

Borawska-Kalbarczyk, K. (2023). Funkcjonowanie dzieci w przestrzeni informacji cyfrowych—zagrożenia i problemy a edukacyjne strategie rozwoju ich kompetencji informacyjnych. *Edukacja Elementarna w Teorii i Praktyce, 2*(69), 19–30.

Borenstein, J., & Howard, A. (2020). Emerging challenges in AI and the need for AI ethics education. *AI and Ethics, 1*, 1–5. https://doi.org/10.1007/s43681-020-00002-7

Bösh, F. (2021). *Media a przemiany historyczne. Od druku do internetu.* Wydawnictwo Naukowe Scholar.

Brigham, N. G., Gao, C., Kohno, T., Roesner, F., & Mireshghallah, N. (2024). Developing Story: Case Studies of Generative AI's Use in Journalism, <i>arXiv e-prints</i>, Art. no. arXiv:2406.13706, 2024. https://doi.org/10.48550/arXiv.2406.13706

Castillo-Martínez, I. M., Flores-Bueno, D., Gómez-Puente, S. M., & Vite-León, V. O. (2024). AI in higher education: A systematic literature review. *Frontiers in Education, 9*, 1391485. https://doi.org/10.3389/feduc.2024.1391485
Chan, C. K. Y., & Tsi, L. H. Y. (2023). The AI Revolution in Education: Will AI Replace or Assist Teachers in Higher Education? *arXivLabs.* https://doi.org/10.48550/arXiv.2305.01185.
Chiu, C. H., Meng, H., Chai, C.-S., King, I., Wong, S., & Yam, Y. (2022). Creation and evaluation of a pretertiary artificial intelligence (AI) curriculum. *IEEE Transactions on Education, 65*(1), 1–10. https://doi.org/10.1109/te.2021.3085878
Deavours, D., Heath, W., & Broussard, R. (2022). "It's just as whitewashed as ever": Social media sourcing as a diversification tool for journalists. *Journalism Practice, 18*(10), 2647–2666. https://doi.org/10.1080/17512786.2022.2147096
Demmar, K., & Neff, T. (2023). Generative AI in journalism education: Mapping the state of an emerging space of concerns, opportunities and strategies. *Journal of Education, 12*(1), 47–58.
Dereniuk, M. (2024). Development of media education in higher education institutions of Ukraine and the Republic of Poland. *Society and National Interest, 5*(5), 65–73.
Dhiman, B. (2023). Key issues and new challenges in new media technology in 2023: A critical review. *Journal of Media & Management, 5*(1), 1–4.
Dinçer, S. (2024). Hard and soft skills revisited: Journalism education at the dawn of artificial intelligence. *Adnan Menderes Üniversitesi Sosyal Bilimler Enstitüsü Dergisi, 12*(1), 1–15. https://doi.org/10.30803/adusobed.1462061
Dodds, D. (2024). *Immersive journalism: Virtual reality and the future of the news industry.* Routledge.
Erikson Institute. (2021). *A national survey on children's media literacy: Media literacy in early childhood education.* https://www.erikson.edu/wp-content/uploads/2021/06/TEC-MediaLiteracy-Report.pdf
Felix, C. V. (2020). The role of the teacher and AI in education. In E. Sengupta, P. Blessinger, & M. Makhanya (Eds.), *International perspectives on the role of Technology in Humanizing Higher Education* (Vol. 33, pp. 33–48). Emerald Publishing Limited. https://doi.org/10.1108/S2055364120200000033003
Fisher, B. (2020). Otwieranie danych i jego wpływ na rozwój dziennikarstwa danych. *Rocznik Historii Prasy Polskiej, XXIII, 4*(60), 93–109. https://doi.org/10.24425/rhpp.2020.135100
Freire, P. (2005). *Pedagogy of the Oppressed. 30th Anniversary Edition.* New York-London.
Galloway, A. R. (2004). *Protocol: How Control Exists after Decentralisation*, Cambridge–London.
Gordon, C., & Lule, J. (2019). Artificial intelligence and the introductory mass communication class. In P. Guènée, M.-F. Bernier, P. Rodrigues-Rouleau, & S. Puig (Eds.), *Teaching journalism in a disruptive age: Conference proceedings of the 5th world journalism education congress. Paris, July 9–19* (pp. 792–802) http://www.wjec.paris/wp-content/uploads/2020/05/WJEC_proceedings_V2_Final.pdf
Greenberg, S. (2007). Theory and practice in journalism education. *Journal of Media Practice, 8*(3), 289–303. https://doi.org/10.1386/jmpr.8.3.289_1
Hossain, M. S., & Wenger, D. (2024). Has journalism education kept up with digital transformation? *Journalism & Mass Communication Educator, 79*(2), 129–146. https://doi.org/10.1177/10776958231224038
Ifan, M. (2023). Enhancing critical thinking and journalism skills through artificial intelligence literacy: A case study of journalism students in Tajik National University, Tajikistan. *International Journal on Social and Education Sciences, 5*(1), 1–18. https://doi.org/10.46328/ijonse.014
Jaskowska, B. (2023). Książki pisane przez sztuczną inteligencję: Teraźniejszość oraz refleksje i pytania o przyszłość. *Perspektywy Kultury, 42*(3), 39–64. https://doi.org/10.35765/pk.2023.4203.06
Jaskuła, S. (2023). Sztuczna inteligencja w edukacji. *Perspektywy Kultury, 3*(42), 13–26. https://doi.org/10.35765/pk.2023.4203.04
Jędrzejewski, S. (2024). Zdehumanizowany gatekeeping i przyszłość mediów i dziennikarstwa. *Roczniki Kulturoznawcze, 15*(2), 63–85. https://doi.org/10.18290/rkult24152.4

Jing, Y., Zhao, L., Zhu, K., Wang, H., Wang, C., & Xia, Q. (2023). Research landscape of adaptive learning in education: A bibliometric study on research publications from 2000 to 2022. *Sustainability, 15*(4), 3115. https://doi.org/10.3390/su15043115

Leja, B. (2024). Sztuczna inteligencja w mediach—aspekt edukacyjny. *Horyzonty Wychowania, 23, 65*, 43–53. https://doi.org/10.35765/hw.2024.2365.06

Lopezosa, C., Codina, L., Fernández-Planells, A., & Freixa, P. (2023). Journalistic innovation: How new formats of digital journalism are perceived in the academic literature. *Journalism, 24*(4), 821–838.

Nelson, J. C., Orunbon, N. O., Adeleke, A. A., Lee, M. D., al Mamun, M. A., & Natividad, L. R. (2024). The AI revolution in higher education: Navigating opportunities, overcoming challenges, and shaping future directions. *Educational Administration: Theory and Practice, 20*(5), 14187–14195. https://doi.org/10.53555/kuey.v30i5.6422

Newman, N. (2023). *Journalism, media, and technology trends and predictions 2023.* Reuters Institute for the Study of Journalism. Retrieved from https://reutersinstitute.politics.ox.ac.uk/sites/default/files/2023-01/Journalism_media_and_technology_trends_and_predictions_2023.pdf

Nowicka, E. (2022). Edukacja medialna w zmieniającym się społeczeństwie informacyjnym. *Rocznik Lubuski, 48*(2), 185–194. https://doi.org/10.34768/rl.2022.v482.13

Pacewicz, A., & Ptaszek, G. (2019). *Model Edukacji Medialnej.* Centrum Edukacji Obywatelskiej. Retrieved from https://kultura.ceo.org.pl/wp-content/uploads/sites/4/2021/10/memic_publikacja.pdf

Pavlik, J., & McIntosh, S. (2023). *Converging Media: An Introduction to Mass Communication and Digital Innovation.* Oxford.

Penkowska, G. (2022). *Postcovidowa dominacja mediów.* Wydawnictwo Uniwersytetu Gdańskiego.

Pokrivcakova, S. (2019). Preparing teachers for the application of AI-powered technologies in foreign language education. *Journal of Language and Cultural Education, 7*(3), 135–153. https://doi.org/10.2478/jolace-2019-0025

Polcyn, S. (2018). Challenges for media literacy in the context of the destructive phenomenon of patostreamers. *Problemy Opiekuńczo-Wychowawcze, 575*(10), 3–10.

Ptaszek, G. (2019). Od algorytmicznego nadzoru do świadomości algorytmicznej. Edukacja medialna w kontekście nowej ekonomiki mediów i niewidzialnych technologii. In: S. Ratajski (Red.). Edukacja medialna jako wyzwanie. ASP w Warszawie.

Riendeau, R. A. (2019). *Supporting Teacher Collaboration Aimed at Developing High School Students' Digital Media Literacy: A Participatory Action Research Study.* Retrieved from https://scholarcommons.sc.edu/etd/5449

Salgado, L. (2022). From the classroom to the newsroom: A critical route to introduce AI in journalism education. *Facts & Frictions: Emerging Debates, Pedagogies and Practices in Contemporary Journalism, 2*(1), 80–97. https://doi.org/10.22215/ff/v2.i1.04

Schiff, D. (2021). Out of the laboratory and into the classroom: The future of artificial intelligence in education. *AI & SOCIETY, 36*, 331–348. https://doi.org/10.1007/s00146-020-01033-8

Share, J., Mamikonyan, T., & Lopez, E. (2019). *Critical Media Literacy in Teacher Education, Theory, and Practice.* Online publication. https://doi.org/10.1093/acrefore/9780190264093.013.1404

Sołtysiak, W. (2010). Wizja współczesnej edukacji opartej na nowoczesnych technologiach. *Podstawy Edukacji, 3*, 375–394.

Somorin, K., & Ademola, O. (2024). Ethical imperatives in the era of AI journalism: Navigating the intersection of technology and responsibility. *Advances in Multidisciplinary & Scientific Research Journal Publication, 12*(2), 31–36. https://doi.org/10.22624/AIMS/HUMANITIES/V12N2P4

Tanaś, M. (2023). Wspomaganie badań pedagogicznych przez sztuczną inteligencję. *IJONESS, 19, 3*(Special Issue), 25–42. https://doi.org/10.5604/01.3001.0054.4354

Tang, L. (2023). Chinese seafarers' use of the internet and social media to promote labor rights. *Asian and Pacific Migration Journal.* https://doi.org/10.1177/01171968231210327

Terzopoulos, G., & Satratzemi, M. (2019). Voice Assistants and Artificial Intelligence in Education. In *BCI'19: Proceedings of the 9th Balkan Conference on Informatics* (Vol. 34, pp. 1–6). https://doi.org/10.1145/3351556.3351588

Tkach, A. (2019). Lifelong learning as integrational resource of knowledge economy. *Nierówności Społeczne a Wzrost Gospodarczy, 58*(2), 231–239. https://doi.org/10.15584/nsawg.2019.2.18

Veenstra, A. S., Wilder, M., Shimu, F., Schlauder, L., & Dousdebés, F. (2024). Journalism students' use, expectations, and understanding of generative AI tools. *Journalism & Mass Communication Educator, 80*(1), 115–128. https://doi.org/10.1177/10776958241296474

Waszkiewicz-Raviv, A. (2015). Wizualna konsumpcja a komunikacja wizualna. Perswazyjność obrazu w ramach współczesnej komunikacji marketingowej. In W. Patrzałek (Ed.), *Konsumpcja jako forma komunikacji społecznej. Nowe paradygmaty i konteksty badawcze*. Wydawnictwo Uniwersytetu Ekonomicznego we Wrocławiu.

Wenger, D., Hossain, M. S., & Senseman, J. R. (2024). AI and the impact on journalism education. *Journalism & Mass Communication Educator, 80*(1), 97–114. https://doi.org/10.1177/10776958241296497

Williamson, B., & Eynon, R. (2020). Authentic strings, missing connections, and future bearings in artificial intelligence in schooling. *Learning, Media and Innovation, 45*(3), 223–235. https://doi.org/10.1080/17439884.2020.1798995

Wogu, I. A. P., Misra, S., Olu-Owolabi, E. F., Assibong, P. A., & Udoh, O. D. (2018). Artificial intelligence, artificial teachers and the fate of learners in the 21st century education sector: Implications for theory and practice. *International Journal of Pure and Applied Mathematics, 119*(16), 2245–2259.

World Economic Forum. (2025). *Future of Jobs Report 2025.* Retrieved from https://reports.weforum.org/docs/WEF_Future_of_Jobs_Report_2025.pdf

Zhang, L., Zhang, H., & Wang, K. (2020). Media literacy education and curriculum integration: A literature review. *International Journal of Contemporary Education, 3*(1), 55. https://doi.org/10.11114/ijce.v3i1.4769

Anna Jupowicz-Ginalska is an Associate Professor at the University of Warsaw. She specialises in media management, media marketing, and the impact of new technologies on the media and their audiences. She serves as Vice President and is a Board Member of the European Media Management Association. Between 2022 and 2024, she served as Deputy Director of the Doctoral School of Social Sciences at the University of Warsaw. She is the scholarship holder of the 'Poland Fellowships – Schwerpunkt Polen' programme at Johannes Gutenberg University Mainz. She leads an international consortium for the EU project "Beyond Borders" and the Polish team in the EU project "MIA: Media Literacy in Rural Communities." She also manages the UW-financed projects "Social Senior – (Non) Inclusiveness of the Digital World Towards Seniors and Ageing Societies" and "Media Management: An Educational Approach. Mapping and Identifying the Needs of the Academic Community in Poland". She was a member of the research team in the project "Diversity Management as Innovation in Journalism" (POLS, Norway Grants). She also initiated and led the research "FOMO. Poles and the Fear of Missing Out" (2018–2022). Anna was the leader of the global initiatives, The Knowledge-Share Communities (#university & emmahub) and The World Media Economics and Management Conference 2025. Anna is a member of the Editorial Board of the "Journal of Media Business Studies" (Taylor & Francis) and "Humanities and Social Sciences Communications" (Springer Nature), as well as the Reviewers Board of "Future Internet" and "Social Sciences" (MDPI). She serves on the Programme Boards of "Dziennikarstwo i Media" (University of Wroclaw), "Styles of Communication" (University of Bucharest), "Revista Multidisciplinar" (Núcleo Multidisciplinar), and "JOCIS" (MediaXXI/Formalpress).

Mariola Kinal holds a PhD in social sciences and is Assistant Professor at the Institute of Pedagogy of the University of Rzeszów. She specialises in preschool and early school education, with particular emphasis on the use of new media in education, organisational culture and integrated teaching methods. She is a research and educational project manager and author of numerous scientific publications—articles and books—on new technologies in education, communication, organisational culture and pedagogy.

AI and the Hyper-Personalization of News Content

21

Maximilian Eder

Abstract

For decades, editorial decisions and news media organizations' strategic goals have primarily determined the distribution of journalistic content. However, the integration of artificial intelligence (AI) into journalism has significantly altered news content selection in an increasingly digital news media environment. At the same time, there has been a shift toward algorithm-based news recommender systems (NRS) that automate and personalize news content recommendations. While AI presents opportunities to enhance audience engagement and, therefore, higher advertising revenues through hyper-personalized news recommendations, the concept remains underexplored in journalism research. Against this background, this chapter examines the potential of AI-driven hyper-personalization in journalism, analyzing its benefits and challenges. It reviews existing literature on ethical and practical implications of news content personalization and recommendation, while also exploring emerging application areas of AI-powered news recommendations, such as predictive analytics and dynamic paywalls. Additionally, the chapter considers the risks associated with a loss of editorial control and the audience perspective. This chapter contributes to the ongoing debate on AI-driven content personalization and recommendation by providing a comprehensive analysis of AI's role in hyper-personalization, arguing for the need to integrate AI in the news industry responsibly.

M. Eder (✉)
Department of Media and Communication, LMU Munich, Munich, Germany
e-mail: maximilian.eder@ifkw.lmu.de

S. Böhm et al. (eds.), *Handbook of AI-based Media Disruption*, Future of Business and Finance, https://doi.org/10.1007/978-3-032-07605-2_21

21.1 Introduction

Automation and data-driven journalistic processes, partially supported by artificial intelligence (AI), have significantly contributed to a shift in how news is produced and disseminated in a high-choice digital media environment. While the selection and recommendation of news for an (online) audience were mainly determined by the personal taste of a chief editor or a news media organization's strategic goals for decades, algorithm-based news recommender systems (NRS) have enabled the automated dissemination and recommendation of tailor-made news content that accommodates the preferences of individual users, popularity metrics, and/or content-specific features of news items (Bastian et al., 2020; Cools et al., 2021; Feng et al., 2020; Karimi et al., 2018; Mitova et al., 2023). In this context, the term news content refers to "'producer-generated' (journalistic) information, entertainment, their hybrid forms [...], which has to be sourced, aggregated and disseminated in accordance with economic objectives" (Voci et al., 2019, p. 46).

AI and AI-powered technologies hold a specific promise for journalism, particularly in addressing the economic challenges news media organizations face (Diakopoulos, 2019; Kotenidis & Veglis, 2021; Rinehart & Kung, 2022). Against this background, personalized recommendation of news content allows for the distribution of content according to the interests and preferences of the audience to generate traffic and, consequently, higher advertising revenues (Karimi et al., 2018; Thurman & Schifferes, 2012, p. 776). Unsurprisingly, improving (news) content personalization and recommendation with AI is considered one of the most important application areas for the future of journalism (Newman & Cherubini, 2025, p. 31). At the same time, news media organizations struggle to achieve more profound personalization beyond conventional methods such as popularity-based, content-based, or collaborative filtering (Möller et al., 2018), and the application of AI for personalized content recommendation remains largely unexplored (Chen et al., 2024).

Integrating AI into journalism, with the technology's range of possibilities for automated data analysis with machine learning and natural language processing (Deuze & Beckett, 2022, p. 1914), also offers the opportunity to hyper-personalize news content. Borrowing from marketing literature (see Davenport, 2023; Jain et al., 2021; Valdez Mendia & Flores-Cuautle, 2022), such a personalization process describes the use of AI and AI-based technologies regarding (big) data analytics and automation to deliver personalized content and specialized services, intending to provide an enhanced user experience and highly precise services. In journalism, hyper-personalization relates to AI performing extensive data analyses to understand news audience behavior and generate relevant (news) content for users, allowing for dynamic content customization based on real-time user interactions and feedback.[1] Additionally, AI could provide predictive capabilities, enabling proactive

[1] Lim and Zhang (2022) have used the term "AI-powered news," which also relates to personalized news content recommended by digital platforms by using advanced AI and algorithms.

personalization and further applications such as dynamic paywalls (Marín-Sanchiz et al., 2023).

Against this background, this chapter provides an overview of AI's potential for hyper-personalizing news content, associated risks, and responsible usage. First, a review of relevant literature and existing studies on algorithms for content personalization is conducted, beginning with Thurman and Schifferes (2012) and their widely used definition of personalization types on digital platforms such as social media or news websites. Afterward, current developments and debates surrounding the application of AI-based technologies for exponentially improving news content personalization will be summarized and related to hyper-personalization. The chapter concludes with a discussion on the current state of news content personalization, areas for future research, and a conclusion of the AI-induced disruptions in journalism concerning personalized news content recommendations.

By examining these issues, this chapter aims to complement existing research on news recommender systems and AI, offering a comprehensive analysis of how hyper-personalization can be leveraged to enhance user engagement and address the challenges posed by AI-driven disruptions in the digital media environment.

21.2 Literature Review

Since the advent of digital journalism, the production and dissemination of news content have been in constant flux, with recent advancements in AI and algorithm-based NRS offering new opportunities for news media workflows, products, and services. In this context, AI can be described as an umbrella term "for currently dominant computational techniques and technologies that extract statistical correlations (designated as patterns) from large datasets, based on the adjustment of relevant parameters according to either internally or externally generated feedback" (Suchman, 2023). Algorithms primarily refer to "a finite series of precisely described rules or processes to solve a problem. It is a sequence of stages that transform input through specified computational procedures (throughput) into output" (Latzer et al., 2016, p. 397).

21.2.1 Personalization of News Content

Although content personalization has been implemented in digital news aggregation platforms for over a decade, news content personalization remains for many news media organizations "more of an idea than an actual recurrent practice" (Hendrickx et al., 2021, p. 515). However, as digital technologies have advanced, there has been a notable shift in journalism toward news content personalization, influencing how users interact with content and shaping their overall news consumption experience (for an overview, see Mitova et al., 2023).

Thurman and Schifferes (2012) define news personalization as a "form of user-to-system interactivity that uses a set of technological features to adapt the content, delivery, and arrangement of a communication to individual users' explicitly registered and/or implicitly determined preferences" (p. 776). They distinguish between two specific types of personalization used on digital platforms such as social media and news websites: explicit and implicit personalization (Thurman & Schifferes, 2012, pp. 777–778). Explicit personalization refers to content selection, where individuals actively specify their preferences through direct input. This process can involve selecting topics of interest or filtering content based on location and keywords. In contrast, implicit personalization relies on "preferences from data collected [...] via the use of software that monitors activity" (Thurman, 2011, p. 397), inferring user preferences based on browsing history, reading patterns, and engagement metrics.

In the context of implicit personalization, NRS are crucial in structuring and prioritizing news content according to predefined principles (Feng et al., 2020; Karimi et al., 2018; Möller et al., 2018). Two key approaches are content-based filtering (CBF) and collaborative filtering (CF) (Fieiras-Ceide et al., 2023; Möller et al., 2018, pp. 961–962; Møller, 2022, p. 802; Table 21.1).

Through CBF, news content is recommended based on its similarity to "the currently used item or items previously used by the same user on a number of predefined criteria (features)" (Möller et al., 2018, p. 962). In contrast, recommendations based on the news consumption behavior of other users with similar interests are given in CF. This approach relies on aggregated user data to identify patterns in content engagement, thereby requiring a substantial volume of user interactions to produce meaningful recommendations (Raza & Ding, 2022, p. 756).

Although collaborative and content-based filtering are the most widely used approaches by NRS (Schreiner et al., 2020), they are frequently combined to produce more accurate (news) content recommendations (Feng et al., 2020). Moreover, NRS also relate to the business models of news media organizations and their broader organizational goals regarding free, ad-supported, or paid-subscription frameworks, influencing both editorial decisions and technological investments in content recommendations (Joris et al., 2021, p. 592; Möller et al., 2018, p. 962).

Table 21.1 Overview of personalization types

Approach	Type	Description
Content-based filtering	Personalized recommendation	The observed utility of content experienced previously and its attributes for a given user is taken as input to predict the utility of other content to that user
Collaborative filtering	Personalized recommendation	All observed utility for user-content pairs is taken as input to predict utility for unobserved user-content pairs
Editorial filtering	Human selection and ranking	Editors predict the utility of content based on their perception of the audience

Note. Adomavicius et al. (2008), p. 71

21.2.2 AI for Hyper-Personalization of News Content

Personalization has been primarily used to distribute news content according to the interests and preferences of the audience to generate traffic and, therefore, higher advertising revenues (Karimi et al., 2018; Thurman & Schifferes, 2012, p. 776). By leveraging the accelerating capabilities of AI and AI-powered technologies, news media organizations can now provide personalized news content recommendations and optimize their delivery based on incoming streams of user data in ways considered impossible only a few years ago. This new type of personalization goes beyond ranking and recommending news content to fostering individualized engagement by incorporating detailed data analytics of psychographics to understand news audiences and individual users' behavior. Such hyper-personalization aims to dynamically customize, generate, and predictively recommend (news) content based on real-time user interactions and feedback while maintaining the core facts, crafting highly relevant news experiences for individual users.

One of the most important drivers for hyper-personalization is the rapid development of large language models (LLM), enabling NRS to capture sequential, temporal, and contextual information and extract meaningful representations from large-scale data (Chen et al., 2024). The so-called *deep learning-based recommender systems* can simultaneously recommend news content that aligns with individual users' interests and determine the best way to frame it for a specific context. This process can also be applied across different distribution channels, such as newsletters or social media, and in search results on a website. Applying LLM to personalize news content can be beneficial for user engagement. For example, Hagar (2025) shows that when given a choice between human-written and LLM-generated personalized headlines, participants consistently selected the personalized version without knowing it was machine-generated.

Another type of hyper-personalized NRS are *conversational recommender systems*. Through task-oriented user interactions with multi-turn dialogue, these systems collect semi-structured data about users' preferences or process their feedback to recommend and generate personalized (news) content (Gao et al., 2021; Jannach et al., 2022; Pramod & Bafna, 2022). The most prominent examples of such conversational systems are virtual voice assistants (e.g., Amazon Alexa, Apple's Siri, and Microsoft Cortana), which hold the promise of a more engaging user experience. At the same time, they reduce the time and number of real-time interactions required to receive personalized (news) content as they continuously collect data about the individual user.

While hyper-personalization might soon become more relevant to news media organizations due to the release of more advanced AI and AI-powered systems on the commercial market, its current application remains in an exploration phase.

Two current examples of the hyper-personalization of news content can be found within Scandinavian news media organizations. The Norwegian daily newspaper *Aftenposten* has developed an editorially controlled algorithm to optimize digital news distribution. As such, algorithmic personalization has been integrated into their article ranking system and combined with a prediction model that dynamically weighs editorial priorities with individual users' interests. Moreover, the system enhances the discoverability of niche content that users are most likely to be interested in and predicts the likelihood of individual users purchasing a subscription based on editorial metadata and user data, with human oversight maintaining editorial integrity. Results indicate that this personalized news content recommendation has improved subscriber engagement: click-through rates (CTR) increased by approximately 25% over 10 months, and a 40-day test for subscribers with a personalized front page showed an 8% improvement in engagement (Teien, 2024).

The other example is the Swedish media conglomerate *NTM*, whose strategy involves hyper-personalizing the front pages of its owned outlets. For logged-in users, news content is selected and recommended based on their past and predicted behavior and engagement metrics. Additionally, geographical personalization has been integrated into the NRS to ensure that locally relevant news receives prominent placement on the individual front page. Another personalization feature, internally referred to as *best story since last time*, caters to infrequent visitors by highlighting the most relevant articles published since their last visit (Pettersson, 2024).

21.3 Current Developments and Debates of (Hyper-) Personalization

News media organizations have found themselves amid the transformative AI wave, which requires them to navigate several challenges to seize the capabilities of these technologies. The literature discusses several challenges related to current developments and debates surrounding the application of AI and algorithms for improving personalized news content recommendations, particularly regarding when these tools should be used, to what extent users should be informed about them, and broader information obligations (e.g., Diakopoulos & Koliska, 2017).

21.3.1 Attitudes and Awareness

The increasing relevance of AI for (hyper-)personalization concerning NRS raises important questions about audiences' attitudes and awareness of these new technologies. At the same time, studies provided contradictory findings about public attitudes toward personalized news recommendations.

Thurman et al. (2019) provided initial evidence on people's general appreciation of algorithmic news recommendations, while other studies have since hinted at users' limited interest in actively personalizing their news experiences (e.g., Moeller et al., 2023; Ross Arguedas, 2025). Moreover, a cross-country survey by Kozyreva et al. (2021) revealed mixed attitudes toward personalized news content. In Germany and Great Britain, over half of their respondents opposed personalization in both online newspaper front pages (GER: 52%, $N = 1065$; GB: 54%, $N = 1092$) and social media news feeds (GER: 57%; GB: 51%). Conversely, in the United States, a majority of respondents accepted personalized online newspapers (60%, $N = 1059$)

and social media feeds (62%). However, across all three countries, concerns were raised regarding the collection and use of personal data for personalized (news) content recommendations, echoing Ross Arguedas (2025), who has identified a particularly low comfort for using websites or apps with automated news content selection based on previous user preferences in 27 media markets. Moreover, users seem to desire transparency and control of NRS (Mitova et al., 2024).

Several studies have explored the extent to which individuals are aware of personalization algorithms, with mixed results across specific mediated contexts (for an overview, see Mitova et al., 2023). Eslami et al. (2015) examined Facebook users' perceptions of the platform's news feed algorithms. Their findings indicate that the majority of their respondents (62.5%) were completely unaware of the algorithm's presence. Similarly, Gran et al. (2021) reported that almost half of their respondents in Norway (41%, $N = 1624$) had no awareness of algorithms used to present recommendations, advertisements, and other content in social media and online newspapers.

Despite these findings, some studies suggest that users are generally aware of personalized content recommendation practices. In their study on algorithmic curation in Facebook's social media feed, Rader and Gray (2015) found that 73% of their respondents ($N = 505$) recognized that they did not see every post created by their friends on the platform. However, "users vary widely in the degree to which they perceive and understand the behavior of content filtering algorithms in this online social network context" (Rader & Gray, 2015, p. 181). Powers (2017) and Swart (2021) highlighted that younger demographics are generally aware of data collection practices and potential risks associated with content personalization.

Few studies have explicitly investigated audiences' awareness of AI-driven NRS. Kozyreva et al. (2021) found that while respondents across Germany, Great Britain, and the United States were generally aware of AI-related concepts and key entities, significantly fewer individuals recognized the presence of AI-driven news recommenders. Only 34% of German respondents and as few as 12% of British and US respondents reported familiarity with such recommender systems. Moreover, this awareness gap extended to AI being used for social media feed curation (GER: 44%, $N = 1065$; GB: 43%, $N = 1092$; US: 44%, $N = 1059$). Eder and Sjøvaag (2024) explored demographic differences in AI awareness in Germany ($N = 1090$). Their study found that self-reported knowledge of AI-based news selection was highest among older respondents, particularly those aged 55–64 (22.3%), followed by the 45–54 (17.3%) and 35–44 (16.2%) age groups. A statistically significant relationship also emerged between education levels and awareness, with respondents possessing lower educational levels exhibiting greater knowledge gaps concerning algorithmic news recommendations.

21.3.2 Opportunities and Risks

AI offers significant advantages for news media organizations regarding the selection and recommendation of news for online audiences. At the same time, these new opportunities raise critical concerns on different levels, affecting individual users, news media organizations, and society.

Starting with the opportunities of hyper-personalization, first, by leveraging AI for content personalization, news media organizations can maximize revenue by optimizing paywall strategies (e.g., Marín-Sanchiz et al., 2023). Converting online news readers into subscribers has become a common concern in journalism amid a low willingness to pay for online news content (Robertson, 2024) and digital subscribership remaining small (Chyi & Ng, 2020). Dynamic or adaptative paywalls based on (predictive) analytics of user consumption patterns seem to be a viable solution. They allow news media organizations "(1) to individualize access restriction and pricing options based on users' behavior on the website and (2) to identify improved classification schemes with respect to whether specific content should be free or paid content" (Rußell et al., 2020, p. 257). Second, using AI for personalized news content recommendation enables more effective audience segmentation through real-time user clustering with the overarching goal of increasing engagement. For example, the Swiss daily newspaper *Neue Zürcher Zeitung* exemplifies this possibility through its personalized recommender system, which is adapted to accommodate different user segments (anonymous vs. logged-in users) and regional market contexts (Kadar, 2022). Third, AI-driven (hyper-)personalization can be used for product reconfiguration. Not only can front pages be modified, as described earlier, but the writing style, tone, and complexity of content can also be adjusted to suit the interests of different user groups. For example, Pillai et al. (2025) recently tested prompt-driven large language models to rewrite news text on social media in specified language styles.

From an audience perspective, hyper-personalization has the potential to enhance public empowerment by increasing individuals' autonomy in news consumption. Predictively or non-predictively recommended (news) content that cultivates journalistic values such as diversity and transparency can contribute to more diverse news exposure (Heitz et al., 2022; Joris et al., 2024), allowing users to engage with differing perspectives. This, in turn, fosters "self-reflect[ion] on their own viewpoints [...], enhance[s] social and cultural inclusion [...], increases one's familiarity with views oppositional to one's own" (Bodó et al., 2019, p. 208).

At the same time, content recommendation is "a complex problem with the potential to fundamentally shape how news is distributed, received, and how it contributes to political discourse" (Lischka et al., 2024, p. 155). Therefore, risks surrounding news content personalization also need to be addressed.

At the individual level, concerns relate to data privacy, as personalized content recommendations rely on data collection and analysis (Kozyreva et al., 2021; Nielsen, 2016; for an overview, see Friedman et al., 2015). Additional concerns include missing out on diverse perspectives or not being provided with comprehensive information (Joris et al., 2021; Monzer et al., 2020; Sehl & Eder, 2023). Furthermore, there is an ongoing discussion about the influence of content personalization on societal polarization (e.g., Keijzer & Mäs, 2022).

From the perspective of news media organizations, a significant concern is the potential loss of control over their brand identity and editorial content (Thurman,

2011). As third-party platforms have gained influence over how news is curated and delivered, news media organizations may struggle to maintain their editorial independence as gatekeepers of information. Algorithm-driven personalization shifts decision-making power from the newsroom to digital platforms and algorithmic models (Møller, 2022; Schjøtt Hansen & Møller Hartley, 2023). Moreover, discussions within news media organizations about privacy concerns and the lack of auditability have gained prominence in recent years (van Drunen et al., 2019).

At the macro level, concerns about news content personalization extend to broader societal implications, particularly regarding the ideal of inclusive public discourse. However, the rise of algorithm-based NRS challenges this notion by potentially narrowing free access to information and restricting exposure to diverse news sources (Eskens et al., 2017). A key aspect of this debate concerns filter bubbles and echo chambers, both phenomena in which users are primarily exposed to content that aligns with their existing beliefs (Flaxman et al., 2016; Pariser, 2011; Sunstein, 2017). While this concern has been widely discussed, research suggests their impact may be overestimated (Dahlgren, 2021; Zuiderveen Borgesius et al., 2016). Furthermore, their overall effects appear relatively modest, as individuals still encounter diverse perspectives through various media sources and social interactions (Dubois & Blank, 2018; Geiß et al., 2021; Haim et al., 2018).

In AI-powered journalism, the so-called microtargeting of audience members with tailor-made content has also gained importance. This process uses (social media)data to personalize messages for specific segments of a target audience or individual users (Barbu, 2014; Bon et al., 2024). It has particularly been critically examined in the context of targeted political messaging during elections regarding its impact on the democratic public discourse (Bayer, 2020; Gibson et al., 2024; Kozyreva et al., 2021).

21.3.3 Ensuring Responsible Use

It is evident that hyper-personalization will transform the news media ecosystem in one way or another, necessitating a strategic shift in adopting advanced NRS. While news media organizations have historically focused on economic and utility aspects, there is a growing demand to address the ethical challenges posed by content distribution, as "*news recommender systems (NRS)* are a part of the editorial function of news organizations and need to uphold journalistic values" (Bauer et al., 2024, p. 23).

One approach to ensuring the responsible use of hyper-personalization is the development and enforcement of comprehensive policies and guidelines. Despite news media organizations' growing reliance on AI-supported NRS, research on newsroom-specific policies for these technologies remains limited. A comparative analysis of 52 policy guidelines by Becker et al. (2025) highlights the lack of a unified approach among news media organizations regarding human supervision of algorithms. However, the protection of data privacy is frequently emphasized across various policies. Findings by Cools and Diakopoulos (2024), based on interviews with journalists in the Netherlands and Denmark, reveal that guidelines have recently been established for the responsible use of generative AI tools in both countries. Against this background, regulatory frameworks such as the EU Digital Services Act (DSA) represent a "fundamental step by moving beyond empowering users to control their data to enabling them to control the recommendation logic" (Helberger et al., 2021).

Specialized teams of technologists and journalists within news media organizations could also help ensure the responsible use of hyper-personalization by proactively addressing ethical and technical challenges. By conducting regular audits and evaluations, these teams can develop new applications and assess the current use of recommendation algorithms. Public service media in Germany have already taken steps in this direction with the *SWR KI Hub* and the *AI + Automation Lab* at Bayerischer Rundfunk. The *FUNKE Media Group*, one of the largest media companies in Germany, has founded a so-called *AI Task Force*. Cools and Diakopoulos (2024) report that *Berlingske Media* in Denmark and *NRC* and *NOS* in the Netherlands have also established such task forces.

For hyper-personalization to be used responsibly, "designers should understand journalists' professional values and incorporate them into their designs" (Komatsu et al., 2020; see also Bastian et al., 2021). When examining the value-sensitive design of NRS, a broad range of values shaping how these systems operate has been identified (for an overview, see Bauer et al., 2024; Stray et al., 2024). In addition to several *standard values* (i.e., coverage, diversity, novelty, and popularity), there are further values inherent to journalism and news media. These *editorial values* (i.e., authority, credibility, democracy, editorial influence, freedom, journalistic integrity, and objectivity) stem from an organization-centered perspective and align closely with established journalistic and editorial principles. Unlike other recommender systems prioritizing engagement, news personalization must ensure content selection adheres to journalism's public service mission rather than merely optimizing for user preferences or commercial success. Furthermore, Bauer et al. (2024) identified *responsibility values,* including accountability, explainability, fairness, manipulation prevention, privacy, transparency, and trust. These principles highlight the obligations of news providers to their audiences and society at large. For instance, news media organizations are expected to be accountable for the content their algorithms recommend, ensuring that selection mechanisms are explainable and that data privacy is valued. Similarly, manipulation prevention addresses whether recommender systems amplify misinformation or contribute to ideological polarization.

However, the prioritization of journalistic values in the implementation of recommender systems varies across news media organizations and is sometimes not paid attention to at the design level due to epistemological challenges occurring in AI-driven data work (e.g., Møller, 2024; Møller Hartley & Bonde Thylstrup, 2025). Therefore, news media organizations need "to engage internally in an organization-wide process of identifying their core values with regard to ANR [algorithmic news recommender] use, which can subsequently inform their strategies to achieve value-sensitive design" (Bastian et al., 2021, p. 855).

21.4 Discussion

Research on news content personalization and recommendation is a continuously evolving field, primarily in response to increasing levels of digitalization in journalism, accompanied by recent technological developments in AI, which has historically been applied to news content recommendations (Dierickx & Lindén, 2024, p. 143). At the same time, research on hyper-personalization has only recently begun. Despite news media organizations' dedicated resources and significant investments in developing AI, applying such technologies for hyper-personalization remains more of a concept than standard practice. Moreover, responsible AI is still in its infancy due to the lack of systemic frameworks (de-Lima-Santos & Jamil, 2024, p. 337).

Hyper-personalization undeniably offers potential benefits to news media organizations, with AI-based predictive models being used to automatically analyze users' consumption habits to satisfy audience needs and enhance engagement with the news content they create (Beam, 2014). However, studies indicate that there is also a need to ensure the responsible use of hyper-personalization: "From a place of good intention, real-time targeting went from technology that could find groups of target customers for the purpose of marketing efficiency, to hyper-personalisation algorithms that monitor every single thing about you on and offline 24/7" (Nelson-Field, 2020, p. 8).

Despite significant technological advancements, NRS still face several challenges, highlighting the limited application of hyper-personalization today.

From a technical perspective, the so-called *cold-start problem* remains a common issue that hinders the large-scale utility of NRS (for an overview, see Yuan & Hernandez, 2023). For new users with a limited interaction history of a news website or an app, it is difficult to accurately predict their interests and behaviors, leading to inaccurate or even ineffective recommendation results. Additionally, the scalability of real-time news content recommendations and computational efficiency remain relevant concerns. However, natural language processing (e.g., embedding-based and deep learning models) and cloud technology have at least partially mitigated these issues (Raza & Ding, 2022, p. 777).

Another significant challenge in achieving hyper-personalization of news content is predicting users' future preferences due to the dynamic nature of their interests, which shift according to current needs, individual circumstances, and events (Feng et al., 2020; Özgöbek et al., 2014). This variability highlights that news readers often engage with content not solely due to inherent interest but because they perceive it as important or relevant. Moreover, the technical features of the user's device (e.g., mobile phone vs. desktop) must also be considered (Karimi et al., 2018).

Overall, there are differing perspectives on the usefulness of AI-driven hyper-personalization. News media executives consider AI-driven personalization and recommendation an important application area (Newman & Cherubini, 2025, p. 31). Although Sarah McConville, co-president of Harvard Business Publishing, even called it a "game changer" in a 2024 interview with the International New Media Association (INMA) (Verma, 2024), users may disagree. For instance, during the test phase of an AI-based content recommender system at *Corriere della Sera*, Italy's largest daily newspaper, their development team observed that "the recommended feed did not always fit the user's interests, and users wanted to express their preferences and have more control over the news they received" (Cirella & Bernardi, 2023). These findings echo Shin (2020), who states that users indeed want to engage and interact with a recommender system.

21.5 Conclusion

In conclusion, AI has transformed and continues to reshape how news is produced and disseminated. In this context, the hyper-personalization of news content marks a profound transformation in journalism. While editorial decision-making has shaped news dissemination for decades, AI now enables news media organizations to personalize news content more than ever, potentially tailoring it to users' preferences with new levels of precision. This shift presents both opportunities and challenges for the news industry. On one hand, hyper-personalization can enhance user engagement, improve reader retention, and thus generate higher advertising revenues. On the other hand, it raises concerns about data privacy and ethical dilemmas surrounding editorial control and journalistic integrity.

Despite its growing prominence in discussions across the news media industry, AI-powered hyper-personalization of news content is reminiscent of self-driving cars—everybody talks about them, but very few have seen them. Further research is thus required to fully understand the future implications for journalistic practices and news media organizations' strategies, in particular, as AI technologies are "bright, shiny things" (Posetti, 2018), diverting attention and contributing to economic resource overstretch in journalism.

As AI continues to evolve, there is a need to balance economic viability with the public service mission of journalism, ensuring that NRS do not compromise content diversity or journalistic transparency (Bastian et al., 2021; Bauer et al., 2024; Stray et al., 2024). Public service media seem to be particularly sensitive to journalistic values when designing and implementing algorithmic news content personalization, most likely due to their public service mandate (Blassnig et al., 2025; Fieiras-Ceide et al., 2023; van den Bulck & Moe, 2018).

Ultimately, the future of hyper-personalization in journalism will depend on how AI is integrated responsibly, navigating the fine line between the commercial imperatives of news media organizations stemming from declining advertising revenues and shrinking subscription numbers (Tong, 2022), and the fundamental role of journalism in fostering an informed society. As Davenport rightfully remarks: "We don't really yet know the limits of personalization" (Davenport, 2023, p. 35).

References

Adomavicius, G., Huang, Z., & Tuzhilin, A. (2008). Personalization and recommender systems. In Z.-L. Chen, S. Raghavan, P. Gray, & H. J. Greenberg (Eds.), *State-of-the-art decision-making tools in the information-intensive age* (pp. 55–107). Informs.

Barbu, O. (2014). Advertising, microtargeting and social media. *Procedia - Social and Behavioral Sciences, 163*, 44–49. https://doi.org/10.1016/j.sbspro.2014.12.284

Bastian, M., Makhortykh, M., Harambam, J., & van Drunen, M. (2020). Explanations of news personalisation across countries and media types. *Internet Policy Review, 9*(4). https://doi.org/10.14763/2020.4.1504

Bastian, M., Helberger, N., & Makhortykh, M. (2021). Safeguarding the journalistic DNA: Attitudes towards the role of professional values in algorithmic news recommender designs. *Digital Journalism, 9*(6), 835–863. https://doi.org/10.1080/21670811.2021.1912622

Bauer, C., Bagchi, C., Hundogan, O. A., & van Es, K. (2024). Where are the values? A systematic literature review on news recommender systems. *ACM Transactions on Recommender Systems, 2*(3), Article 23. https://doi.org/10.1145/3654805

Bayer, J. (2020). Double harm to voters: Data-driven micro-targeting and democratic public discourse. *Internet Policy Review, 9*(1). https://doi.org/10.14763/2020.1.1460

Beam, M. A. (2014). Automating the news: How personalized news recommender system design choices impact news reception. *Communication Research, 41*(8), 1019–1041. https://doi.org/10.1177/0093650213497979

Becker, K. B., Simon, F. M., & Crum, C. (2025). Policies in parallel? A comparative study of journalistic AI policies in 52 global news organisations. *Digital Journalism, 13*(9), 1578–1598. https://doi.org/10.1080/21670811.2024.2431519

Blassnig, S., Strikovic, E., Mitova, E., Urman, A., Hannák, A., de Vreese, C., & Esser, F. (2025). A balancing act: How media professionals perceive the implementation of news recommender systems. *Digital Journalism, 13*(4), 745–773. https://doi.org/10.1080/21670811.2023.2293933

Bodó, B., Helberger, N., Eskens, S., & Möller, J. (2019). Interested in diversity: The role of user attitudes, algorithmic feedback loops, and policy in news personalization. *Digital Journalism, 7*(2), 206–229. https://doi.org/10.1080/21670811.2018.1521292

Bon, E., Dommett, K., Gibson, R., Kruikemeier, S., & Lecheler, S. (2024). Are certain types of microtargeting more acceptable? Comparing US, German, and Dutch citizens' attitudes. *Media and Communication, 12*, Article 8520. https://doi.org/10.17645/mac.8520

Chen, J., Liu, Z., Huang, X., Wu, C., Liu, Q., Jiang, G., Pu, Y., Lei, Y., Chen, X., Wang, X., Zheng, K., Lian, D., & Chen, E. (2024). When large language models meet personalization: Perspectives of challenges and opportunities. *World Wide Web, 27*(4), Article 42. https://doi.org/10.1007/s11280-024-01276-1

Chyi, H. I., & Ng, Y. M. M. (2020). Still unwilling to pay: An empirical analysis of 50 U.S. newspapers' digital subscription results. *Digital Journalism, 8*(4), 526–547. https://doi.org/10.1080/21670811.2020.1732831

Cirella, C., & Bernardi, G. (2023, June 11). *Corriere della Sera reveals the future of personalised news*. International News Media Association. https://www.inma.org/blogs/ideas/post.cfm/corriere-della-sera-reveals-the-future-of-personalised-news

Cools, H., & Diakopoulos, N. (2024). Uses of generative AI in the newsroom: Mapping journalists' perceptions of perils and possibilities. *Journalism Practice, ahead-of-print*. https://doi.org/10.1080/17512786.2024.2394558

Cools, H., van Gorp, B., & Opgenhaffen, M. (2021). When algorithms recommend what's new(s): New dynamics of decision-making and autonomy in newsgathering. *Media and Communication, 9*(4), 198–207. https://doi.org/10.17645/mac.v9i4.4173

Dahlgren, P. M. (2021). A critical review of filter bubbles and a comparison with selective exposure. *Nordicom Review, 42*(1), 15–33. https://doi.org/10.2478/nor-2021-0002

Davenport, T. H. (2023). Hyper-personalization for customer engagement with artificial intelligence. *Management and Business Review, 3*(1–2), 29–36. https://doi.org/10.1177/2694105820230301006
de-Lima-Santos, M.-F., & Jamil, S. (2024). Bridging the AI divide: Human and responsible AI in news and media industries. *Emerging Media, 2*(3), 335–346. https://doi.org/10.1177/27523543241291229
Deuze, M., & Beckett, C. (2022). Imagination, algorithms and news: Developing AI literacy for journalism. *Digital Journalism, 10*(10), 1913–1918. https://doi.org/10.1080/21670811.2022.2119152
Diakopoulos, N. (2019). *Automating the news: How algorithms are rewriting the media.* Harvard University Press.
Diakopoulos, N., & Koliska, M. (2017). Algorithmic transparency in the news media. *Digital Journalism, 5*(7), 809–828. https://doi.org/10.1080/21670811.2016.1208053
Dierickx, L., & Lindén, C.-G. (2024). From bytes to bylines: A history of AI in journalism practice. In T. Tofalvy & I. Vobič (Eds.), *Histories of digital journalism: The interplay of technology, society and culture* (pp. 136–148). Routledge.
Dubois, E., & Blank, G. (2018). The echo chamber is overstated: The moderating effect of political interest and diverse media. *Information, Communication & Society, 21*(5), 729–745. https://doi.org/10.1080/1369118X.2018.1428656
Eder, M., & Sjøvaag, H. (2024). Artificial intelligence and the dawn of an algorithmic divide. *Frontiers in Communication, 9*. https://doi.org/10.3389/fcomm.2024.1453251
Eskens, S., Helberger, N., & Moeller, J. (2017). Challenged by news personalisation: Five perspectives on the right to receive information. *Journal of Media Law, 9*(2), 259–284. https://doi.org/10.1080/17577632.2017.1387353
Eslami, M., Rickman, A., Vaccaro, K., Aleyasen, A., Vuong, A., Karahalios, K., Hamilton, K., & Sandvig, C. (2015). "I always assumed that I wasn't really that close to [her]": Reasoning about invisible algorithms in news feeds. In *Proceedings of the 33rd annual ACM conference on human factors in computing systems* (pp. 153–162). https://doi.org/10.1145/2702123.2702556
Feng, C., Khan, M., Rahman, A. U., & Ahmad, A. (2020). News recommendation systems: Accomplishments, challenges & future directions. *IEEE Access, 8*, 16702–16725. https://doi.org/10.1109/ACCESS.2020.2967792
Fieiras-Ceide, C., Vaz-Álvarez, M., & Túñez-López, M. (2023). Designing personalisation of European public service media (PSM): Trends on algorithms and artificial intelligence for content distribution. *Profesional de la información, 32*(3), Article e320311. https://doi.org/10.3145/epi.2023.may.11
Flaxman, S., Goel, S., & Rao, J. M. (2016). Filter bubbles, echo chambers, and online news consumption. *Public Opinion Quarterly, 80*(S1), 298–320. https://doi.org/10.1093/poq/nfw006
Friedman, A., Knijnenburg, B. P., Vanhecke, K., Martens, L., & Berkovsky, S. (2015). Privacy aspects of recommender systems. In F. Ricci, L. Rokach, & B. Shapira (Eds.), *Recommender systems handbook* (2nd ed., pp. 649–688). Springer.
Gao, C., Lei, W., He, X., de Rijke, M., & Chua, T.-S. (2021). Advances and challenges in conversational recommender systems: A survey. *AI Open, 2*, 100–126. https://doi.org/10.1016/j.aiopen.2021.06.002
Geiß, S., Magin, M., Jürgens, P., & Stark, B. (2021). Loopholes in the echo chambers: How the echo chamber metaphor oversimplifies the effects of information gateways on opinion expression. *Digital Journalism, 9*(5), 660–686. https://doi.org/10.1080/21670811.2021.1873811
Gibson, R., Bon, E., & Dommett, K. (2024). "I always feel like somebody's watching me": What do the U.S. electorate know about political micro-targeting and how much do they care? *Digital Journal of Quantitative Description: Media, 4*. https://doi.org/10.51685/jqd.2024.001
Gran, A.-B., Booth, P., & Bucher, T. (2021). To be or not to be algorithm aware: A question of a new digital divide? *Information, Communication & Society, 24*(12), 1779–1796. https://doi.org/10.1080/1369118X.2020.1736124

Hagar, N. (2025, January 21). *Personalizing newsletter headlines: Testing LLMs against human editors*. Medium. https://generative-ai-newsroom.com/personalizing-newsletter-headlines-testing-llms-against-human-editors-6f14135089da
Haim, M., Graefe, A., & Brosius, H.-B. (2018). Burst of the filter bubble? Effects of personalization on the diversity of Google news. *Digital Journalism, 6*(3), 330–343. https://doi.org/10.1080/21670811.2017.1338145
Heitz, L., Lischka, J. A., Birrer, A., Paudel, B., Tolmeijer, S., Laugwitz, L., & Bernstein, A. (2022). Benefits of diverse news recommendations for democracy: A user study. *Digital Journalism, 10*(10), 1710–1730. https://doi.org/10.1080/21670811.2021.2021804
Helberger, N., van Drunen, M., Vrijenhoek, S., & Möller, J. (2021, February 26). *Regulation of news recommenders in the Digital Services Act: Empowering David against the very large online Goliath*. Internet Policy Review. https://policyreview.info/articles/news/regulation-news-recommenders-digital-services-act-empowering-david-against-very-large
Hendrickx, J., Smets, A., & Ballon, P. (2021). News recommender systems and news diversity, two of a kind? A case study from a small media market. *Journalism and Media, 2*(3), 515–528. https://doi.org/10.3390/journalmedia2030031
Jain, G., Paul, J., & Shrivastava, A. (2021). Hyper-personalization, co-creation, digital clienteling and transformation. *Journal of Business Research, 124*, 12–23. https://doi.org/10.1016/j.jbusres.2020.11.034
Jannach, D., Manzoor, A., Cai, W., & Chen, L. (2022). A survey on conversational recommender systems. *ACM Computing Surveys, 54*(5), Article 105. https://doi.org/10.1145/3453154
Joris, G., Grove, F. D., van Damme, K., & de Marez, L. (2021). Appreciating news algorithms: Examining audiences' perceptions to different news selection mechanisms. *Digital Journalism, 9*(5), 589–618. https://doi.org/10.1080/21670811.2021.1912626
Joris, G., Vercoutere, S., de Clercq, O., van Damme, K., Mechant, P., & de Marez, L. (2024). Nudging towards exposure diversity: Examining the effects of news recommender design on audiences' news exposure behaviours and perceptions. *Digital Journalism, 12*(8), 1118–1139. https://doi.org/10.1080/21670811.2022.2106445
Kadar, C. (2022, February 22). *Fully redesigned, algorithmic-driven next reads section*. Medium. https://medium.com/nzz-open/fully-redesigned-algorithmic-driven-next-reads-section-on-nzz-ch-4501e5919d66
Karimi, M., Jannach, D., & Jugovac, M. (2018). News recommender systems: Survey and roads ahead. *Information Processing & Management, 54*(6), 1203–1227. https://doi.org/10.1016/j.ipm.2018.04.008
Keijzer, M. A., & Mäs, M. (2022). The complex link between filter bubbles and opinion polarization. *Data Science, 5*(2), 139–166. https://doi.org/10.3233/DS-220054
Komatsu, T., Gutierrez Lopez, M., Makri, S., Porlezza, C., Cooper, G., MacFarlane, A., & Missaoui, S. (2020). AI should embody our values: Investigating journalistic values to inform AI technology design. In *Proceedings of the 11th Nordic conference on human-computer interaction: Shaping experiences, shaping society, Article 11*. https://doi.org/10.1145/3419249.3420105
Kotenidis, E., & Veglis, A. (2021). Algorithmic journalism: Current applications and future perspectives. *Journalism and Media, 2*(2), 244–257. https://doi.org/10.3390/journalmedia2020014
Kozyreva, A., Lorenz-Spreen, P., Hertwig, R., Lewandowsky, S., & Herzog, S. M. (2021). Public attitudes towards algorithmic personalization and use of personal data online: Evidence from Germany, Great Britain, and the United States. *Humanities and Social Sciences Communications, 8*(1), Article 117. https://doi.org/10.1057/s41599-021-00787-w
Latzer, M., Hollnbuchner, K., Just, N., & Saurwein, F. (2016). The economics of algorithmic selection on the internet. In J. M. Bauer & M. Latzer (Eds.), *Handbook on the economics of the internet* (pp. 395–425). Edward Elgar Publishing.
Lim, J. S., & Zhang, J. (2022). Adoption of AI-driven personalization in digital news platforms: An integrative model of technology acceptance and perceived contingency. *Technology in Society, 69*, Article 101965. https://doi.org/10.1016/j.techsoc.2022.101965

Lischka, J. A., Laugwitz, L., & Schaetz, N. (2024). News recommender systems. In S. A. Eldridge II, D. Cheruiyot, S. Banjac, & J. Swart (Eds.), *The Routledge companion to digital journalism studies* (2nd ed., pp. 155–165). Routledge.

Marín-Sanchiz, C.-R., Valero-Pastor, J. M., Carvajal, M., & Arias-Robles, F. (2023). Mapping the use of artificial intelligence for the optimization of paywalls in the news media industry: How firms are taking advantage of machine learning and related technologies to increase reader revenue. In A. Godulla & S. Böhm (Eds.), *Digital disruption and media transformation: How technological innovation shapes the future of communication* (pp. 153–162). Springer.

Mitova, E., Blassnig, S., Strikovic, E., Urman, A., Hannak, A., de Vreese, C. H., & Esser, F. (2023). News recommender systems: A programmatic research review. *Annals of the International Communication Association, 47*(1), 84–113. https://doi.org/10.1080/23808985.2022.2142149

Mitova, E., Blassnig, S., Strikovic, E., Urman, A., de Vreese, C., & Esser, F. (2024). Exploring users' desire for transparency and control in news recommender systems: A five-nation study. *Journalism, 25*(10), 2001–2021. https://doi.org/10.1177/14648849231222099

Moeller, J., Loecherbach, F., Möller, J., & Helberger, N. (2023). Out of control? Using interactive testing to understand user agency in news recommendation systems. In R. G. Lawrence & P. M. Napoli (Eds.), *News quality in the digital age* (pp. 117–133). Routledge.

Møller, L. A. (2022). Recommended for you: How newspapers normalise algorithmic news recommendation to fit their gatekeeping role. *Journalism Studies, 23*(7), 800–817. https://doi.org/10.1080/1461670X.2022.2034522

Møller, L. A. (2024). Designing algorithmic editors: How newspapers embed and encode journalistic values into news recommender systems. *Digital Journalism, 12*(7), 926–944. https://doi.org/10.1080/21670811.2023.2215832

Møller Hartley, J., & Bonde Thylstrup, N. (2025). The algorithmic gut feeling: Articulating journalistic doxa and emerging epistemic frictions in AI-driven data work. *Digital Journalism, 13*(3), 438–456. https://doi.org/10.1080/21670811.2024.2319641

Möller, J., Trilling, D., Helberger, N., & van Es, B. (2018). Do not blame it on the algorithm: An empirical assessment of multiple recommender systems and their impact on content diversity. *Information, Communication & Society, 21*(7), 959–977. https://doi.org/10.1080/1369118X.2018.1444076

Monzer, C., Moeller, J., Helberger, N., & Eskens, S. (2020). User perspectives on the news personalisation process: Agency, trust and utility as building blocks. *Digital Journalism, 8*(9), 1142–1162. https://doi.org/10.1080/21670811.2020.1773291

Nelson-Field, K. (2020). *The attention economy and how media works: Simple truths for marketers*. Palgrave Macmillan.

Newman, N., & Cherubini, F. (2025). *Journalism, media, and technology trends and predictions 2025*. Reuters Institute for the Study of Journalism. https://doi.org/10.60625/RISJ-VTE1-X706

Nielsen, R. K. (2016). People want personalised recommendations (even as they worry about the consequences). In N. Newman, R. Fletcher, D. A. L. Levy, & R. K. Nielsen (Eds.), *Reuters Institute digital news report 2016* (pp. 111–113). Reuters Institute for the Study of Journalism.

Özgöbek, Ö., Gulla, J. A., & Erdur, R. C. (2014). A survey on challenges and methods in news recommendation. In V. Monfort & K.-H. Krempels (Eds.), *Proceedings of the 10th international conference on web information systems and technologies* (Vol. 1, pp. 278–285). SciTePress. https://doi.org/10.5220/0004844202780285

Pariser, E. (2011). *The filter bubble: What the internet is hiding from you*. Viking.

Pettersson, J. (2024, September 16). *NTM'S "fight and unite" project boosts new mobile front page with higher news density*. International News Media Association. https://www.inma.org/blogs/value-content/post.cfm/ntm-s-fight-and-unite-project-boosts-new-mobile-front-page-with-higher-news-density

Pillai, R., Fokkens, A., & van Atteveldt, W. (2025). Engagement-driven persona prompting for rewriting news tweets. In O. Rambow, L. Wanner, M. Apidianaki, H. Al-Khalifa, B. Di Eugenio, & S. Schockaert (Eds.), *Proceedings of the 31st international conference on computational linguistics* (pp. 8612–8622). Association for Computational Linguistics. https://aclanthology.org/2025.coling-main.576.pdf

Posetti, J. (2018). *Time to step away from the "bright, shiny things"? Towards a sustainable model of journalism innovation in an era of perpetual change*. Reuters Institute for the Study of Journalism. https://doi.org/10.60625/risj-kmpg-q993

Powers, E. (2017). My news feed is filtered? Awareness of news personalization among college students. *Digital Journalism, 5*(10), 1315–1335. https://doi.org/10.1080/21670811.2017.1286943

Pramod, D., & Bafna, P. (2022). Conversational recommender systems techniques, tools, acceptance, and adoption: A state of the art review. *Expert Systems with Applications, 203*, Article 117539. https://doi.org/10.1016/j.eswa.2022.117539

Rader, E., & Gray, R. (2015). Understanding user beliefs about algorithmic curation in the Facebook news feed. In *Proceedings of the 33rd annual ACM conference on human factors in computing systems* (pp. 173–182). https://doi.org/10.1145/2702123.2702174

Raza, S., & Ding, C. (2022). News recommender system: A review of recent progress, challenges, and opportunities. *Artificial Intelligence Review, 55*(1), 749–800. https://doi.org/10.1007/s10462-021-10043-x

Rinehart, A., & Kung, E. (2022). *Artificial intelligence in local news: A survey of US newsrooms' AI readiness*. The Associated Press.

Robertson, C. T. (2024). How much do people pay for online news? And what might encourage more people to pay? In N. Newman, R. Fletcher, C. T. Robertson, A. Ross Arguedas, & R. K. Nielsen (Eds.), *Reuters Institute digital news report 2024* (pp. 49–52). Reuters Institute for the Study of Journalism.

Ross Arguedas, A. (2025). How audiences think about news personalization in the AI era. In N. Newman, A. Ross Arguedas, C. T. Robertson, R. K. Nielsen, & R. Fletcher (Eds.), *Reuters Institute digital news report 2025* (pp. 48–52). Reuters Institute for the Study of Journalism.

Rußell, R., Berger, B., Stich, L., Hess, T., & Spann, M. (2020). Monetizing online content: Digital paywall design and configuration. *Business & Information Systems Engineering, 62*(3), 253–260. https://doi.org/10.1007/s12599-020-00632-5

Schjøtt Hansen, A., & Møller Hartley, J. (2023). Designing what's news: An ethnography of a personalization algorithm and the data-driven (re)assembling of the news. *Digital Journalism, 11*(6), 924–942. https://doi.org/10.1080/21670811.2021.1988861

Schreiner, T., Rese, A., & Baier, D. (2020). Success factors for recommender systems from a customers' perspective. *Archives of Data Science, Series A, 6*(2). https://doi.org/10.5445/KSP/1000098012/02

Sehl, A., & Eder, M. (2023). News personalization and public service media: The audience perspective in three European countries. *Journalism and Media, 4*(1), 322–338. https://doi.org/10.3390/journalmedia4010022

Shin, D. (2020). How do users interact with algorithm recommender systems? The interaction of users, algorithms, and performance. *Computers in Human Behavior, 109*, Article 106344. https://doi.org/10.1016/j.chb.2020.106344

Stray, J., Halevy, A., Assar, P., Hadfield-Menell, D., Boutilier, C., Ashar, A., Bakalar, C., Beattie, L., Ekstrand, M., Leibowicz, C., Moon Sehat, C., Johansen, S., Kerlin, L., Vickrey, D., Singh, S., Vrijenhoek, S., Zhang, A., Andrus, M., Helberger, N., & Vasan, N. (2024). Building human values into recommender systems: An interdisciplinary synthesis. *ACM Transactions on Recommender Systems, 2*(3), Article 20. https://doi.org/10.1145/3632297

Suchman, L. (2023). The uncontroversial "thingness" of AI. *Big Data & Society, 10*(2). https://doi.org/10.1177/20539517231206794

Sunstein, C. R. (2017). *#republic: Divided democracy in the age of social media*. Princeton University Press.

Swart, J. (2021). Experiencing algorithms: How young people understand, feel about, and engage with algorithmic news selection on social media. *Social Media + Society, 7*(2). https://doi.org/10.1177/20563051211008828

Teien, K. O. (2024, September 25). *Schibsted blends human insight with algorithms to improve personalisation*. International News Media Association. https://www.inma.org/blogs/ideas/post.cfm/schibsted-blends-human-insight-with-algorithms-to-improve-personalisation

Thurman, N. (2011). Making "the daily me": Technology, economics and habit in the mainstream assimilation of personalized news. *Journalism, 12*(4), 395–415. https://doi.org/10.1177/1464884910388228

Thurman, N., & Schifferes, S. (2012). The future of personalization at news websites: Lessons from a longitudinal study. *Journalism Studies, 13*(5–6), 775–790. https://doi.org/10.1080/1461670X.2012.664341

Thurman, N., Moeller, J., Helberger, N., & Trilling, D. (2019). My friends, editors, algorithms, and I: Examining audience attitudes to news selection. *Digital Journalism, 7*(4), 447–469. https://doi.org/10.1080/21670811.2018.1493936

Tong, J. (2022). *Journalism, economic uncertainty and political irregularity in the digital and data era*. Emerald Publishing.

Valdez Mendia, J. M., & Flores-Cuautle, J. J. A. (2022). Toward customer hyper-personalization experience: A data-driven approach. *Cogent Business & Management, 9*(1), Article 2041384. https://doi.org/10.1080/23311975.2022.2041384

van den Bulck, H., & Moe, H. (2018). Public service media, universality and personalisation through algorithms: Mapping strategies and exploring dilemmas. *Media, Culture & Society, 40*(6), 875–892. https://doi.org/10.1177/0163443717734407

van Drunen, M. Z., Helberger, N., & Bastian, M. (2019). Know your algorithm: What media organizations need to explain to their users about news personalization. *International Data Privacy Law, 9*(4), 220–235. https://doi.org/10.1093/idpl/ipz011

Verma, S. (2024, June 20). *GenAI use cases move news companies towards personalization.* International News Media Association. https://www.inma.org/blogs/Generative-AI-initiative-newsletter/post.cfm/genai-use-cases-move-news-companies-towards-personalisation

Voci, D., Karmasin, M., Nölleke-Przybylski, P., Altmeppen, K.-D., Möller, J., & von Rimscha, M. B. (2019). What is a media company today? Rethinking theoretical and empirical definitions. *Studies in Communication and Media, 8*(1), 29–52. https://doi.org/10.5771/2192-4007-2019-1-29

Yuan, H., & Hernandez, A. A. (2023). User cold start problem in recommendation systems: A systematic review. *IEEE Access, 11*, 136958–136977. https://doi.org/10.1109/ACCESS.2023.3338705

Zuiderveen Borgesius, F. J., Trilling, D., Möller, J., Bodó, B., de Vreese, C. H., & Helberger, N. (2016). Should we worry about filter bubbles? *Internet. Policy Review, 5*(1). https://doi.org/10.14763/2016.1.401

Maximilian Eder is a Research Associate at the Department of Media and Communication, LMU Munich, focusing on artificial intelligence in local journalism. He is also an honorary Research Fellow of the Bundeswehr University Munich. His main research interests include (digital) journalism practice, political journalism, and scandalization dynamics in media.

Toward Transparency of Synthetic Media: EU Regulatory Perspective and Its Implications

22

Mateusz Łabuz

Abstract

The misuse and abuses of synthetic media are one of the social and political challenges accompanying the rapid development of generative artificial intelligence (AI). They have become the subject of interest of regulators around the world. One of the most important regulatory systems dedicated to AI was created by the European Union. The Artificial Intelligence Act (AI Act), adopted in 2024, refers to synthetic media, qualifying them as limited-risk AI systems and introducing safeguards in the form of transparency obligations. It creates a strong regulatory basis rooted in the axiological foundations of democratic legal systems and refers to the concepts of trustworthiness, transparency, and protection of civil rights and freedoms. This system is supplemented, among others, by obligations imposed on digital platforms in the field of mitigating various risks threatening democratic systems. Although the concept of counteracting the harmful use of synthetic media should be assessed positively, the regulations adopted by the EU are not without shortcomings that may in the future affect their effectiveness and the ability to export certain solutions to other jurisdictions. This requires critical analysis and future amendments that can strengthen a comprehensive ecosystem of trust in technology, as well as already adopted countermeasures against media disruptions.

M. Łabuz (✉)
Institute for Peace Research and Security Policy at the University of Hamburg, Hamburg, Germany
e-mail: labuz@ifsh.de

S. Böhm et al. (eds.), *Handbook of AI-based Media Disruption*, Future of Business and Finance, https://doi.org/10.1007/978-3-032-07605-2_22

22.1 Introduction

The rapid development of generative artificial intelligence (AI) has already had a significant impact on the information space, influencing the way information is created and exchanged. The role of machines and automatization has increased significantly over the decades. AI has allowed us to take another step toward replacing humans in the process of creating various types of media, and nowadays their distribution is largely subordinated to the functioning of algorithms that are not always transparent or explainable (Harari, 2024; Hirvonen et al., 2024). The availability and accessibility of AI tools have significantly improved the pace of content production, redefined the concept of journalism, transformed classic content-sharing mechanisms, and thus lowered the entry barriers for new creators (Erman & Furendal, 2024). The emergence of Large Language Models (LLM) and the development of algorithms that enable the almost instant creation of audio and visual content have significantly increased the potential for human–AI collaboration and the volume of content where AI participated in the creation process.

The emergence of such phenomena and the improvement of the quality of available tools have created new legal, political, and social challenges, i.e. the development of new forms of information disorders. AI-generated or AI-manipulated media increasingly challenge our ability to distinguish between synthesized and human-created content, thereby further violating the fundamental paradigm of believing in what we see as well as the epistemic value of the content, which can faithfully imitate reality, but in fact is misleading (Fallis, 2021; Geddes, 2021).

These processes are still gaining momentum, and as technology continues to develop, it is likely that synthetic media will become the dominant form of the content that circulates online (Pereira, 2024). It is difficult to predict the consequences of these changes at the moment. Still, a number of negative phenomena observed in the course of the development of synthetic media have already forced responses at the regulatory level aimed at safeguarding the information space and protecting society's ability to make informed choices. The creators of legal frameworks recognized synthetic media as a risk requiring intervention at the normative level (Romero Moreno, 2024).

One of the first holistic regulatory frameworks for AI was created by the European Union. The Artificial Intelligence Act (AI Act) adopted in 2024 is designed to mitigate risks stemming from AI development while fostering innovation and trust. It also does not remain indifferent to the problem of synthetic media, creating important foundations for a regulatory ecosystem complemented by other EU legislation and based on the overarching democratic values that need to be protected, including transparency, safety, reliability, and trustworthiness of emerging technologies (Łabuz, 2025). These regulations have the potential to influence the regulatory landscape worldwide and will certainly be an important point of reference (Maham & Küspert, 2023). They will also have a significant impact on the media landscape.

Hence, it is necessary to discuss the proposed solutions in detail and take a critical look at their objectives, methods of implementation, internal consistency, or self-correction mechanisms that can help eliminate identified legal loopholes or shortcomings. The main objective of this chapter is to discuss the EU regulatory perspective on synthetic media, taking the provisions of the AI Act as a starting point for analysis. This will allow for including the legal perspective in the multisectoral analysis of AI-based media disruption.

22.2 Key Topics

In this chapter, I focus on analyzing the solutions proposed by the EU to regulate synthetic media, mainly the provisions of the AI Act adopted in 2024. Additionally, I refer to other EU legislation that may complement the AI Act.

First, it is important to distinguish the EU regulatory framework and its significance for introducing different safeguards against and obligations for using synthetic media, especially at particular stages of the AI-powered disinformation supply chain. Therefore, I describe the significance of the AI Act and its potential global impact. I analyze in detail the proposed definitions and descriptions of synthetic media and deepfakes, and the implications of their implementation. I decode the concepts of trustworthiness and transparency, which constitute an important framework for the regulations introduced in the AI Act.

To illustrate the diversity of synthetic media, I point out the importance of regulating deepfakes. The AI Act introduces their first legal definition that might be an important point of reference worldwide, connects deepfakes primarily with their disinformation potential, and separates them from other forms of synthetic media, primarily AI-generated texts. This allows for the creation of separate requirements for both textual and non-textual synthetic content.

I concentrate primarily on Article 50 of the AI Act, which refers to different forms of synthetic media, providing for transparency obligations, and the consequences of its implementation. I point to the need for a two-track approach that includes solutions for synthetic media at large and for deepfakes as a specific subgroup of synthetic media that have great disruptive potential. This distinction is necessary due to the technical specificity of different types of possible synthetic media (text, audio, image, or video) and the lack of universal solutions. I also point to the synergies between various pieces of EU legislation, which complement each other and should be analyzed together as an element of the regulatory ecosystem of trust that the EU pursues to create (Laux et al., 2024).

Then, I focus on the potential consequences of regulating synthetic media in the AI Act and the importance of safeguards based on transparency. Their purpose is to raise the awareness of the recipients, so they can make informed choices. I consider this in the context of the prospects and threats for media that struggle with a crisis of trust severely influenced by the development of new forms of communication and the progressing erosion of the information environment (Newman et al., 2023; van Huijstee et al., 2021). I point to significant problems with marking synthetic content and the need for synergy with actions undertaken by digital platforms.

I criticize the weaknesses of the AI Act, primarily in the semantic layer, and the lack of consistency between selected EU legal acts, which weakens the regulatory ecosystem and negatively affects the assessment of the adopted solutions, or the possibility of their externalization. By pointing out problems with enforcement, I draw attention to future difficulties with the practical implementation of the provisions. I also draw attention to multilevel manipulation with the use of synthetic media, which disrupts the epistemic value of content. This may consequently lead to further erosion of trust in the media and information, and contribute to the weakening of democratic systems.

Overall, I present a critical perspective on the presented solutions, point out shortcomings and necessary future amendments, and underline the necessity of ensuring the internal coherence of EU legislation.

22.3 Literature Review

Due to its importance and potential economic and legal significance, the AI Act has been the subject of numerous analyses. The research considers the impact of the AI Act on the development of AI systems in the EU and its ability to compete in global markets associated with the innovation potential (see: Bradford, 2024; Csernatoni, 2024; Hacker, 2023; Neves, 2023). The legal analyses provide a detailed interpretation of each section, revealing a complex mosaic of interconnections that may be the subject of debate and dispute for many years to come.

Interestingly, regulating synthetic media in the AI Act as a separate, overarching category has not been the subject of research interest so far. The reason for that might be the lack of a clear definition of the term *synthetic media*, which appears in the AI Act only subsidiarily, although it is not devoid of legal significance.

Therefore, the research on the relationship between the AI Act and synthetic media has focused primarily on deepfakes, which have been the subject of numerous analyses since their appearance in the information space in 2017. They have been consistently assessed as a threat to democratic processes (e.g., Pawelec, 2022; Romero Moreno, 2024; van Huijstee et al., 2021) and enhanced negative phenomena such as disinformation by increasing their persuasive potential (Magonara & Malatras, 2022; Vaccari & Chadwick, 2020). Researchers have drawn attention to the process of gradual erosion of the epistemic value of the media, especially in their visual form, which has resulted in predictions of the so-called information or epistemic "apocalypse" (Fallis, 2021; Geddes, 2021; Habgood-Coote, 2023). Many authors focused on specific sectors where deepfakes may have a detrimental impact, which includes analyses made by Delfino (2023) on the judicial system, Weikmann and Lecheler (2023) on journalism, and Rigotti and McGlynn (2022) or Mania (2024) on nonconsensual intimate imagery abuse.

Comprehensive analyses by Łabuz (2023, 2024, 2025) or Romero Moreno (2024) constitute an important summary of the AI Act provisions regarding deepfakes. Shortcomings were also indicated by Toparlak (2022) or Grady (2023) due to the complete omission of the issue of nonconsensual intimate imagery, the ambiguity of the definition, or problems with the enforcement of selected provisions, which was also pointed out by Fernandez (2021) or Veale and Borgesius (2021). The first experimental attempts to measure the impact of disclosure on recipients' behavior were conducted by, among others, Dobber et al. (2023). The transparency regime for AI-generated texts was diligently analyzed by Piasecki et al. (2024). However, this area is understudied and requires additional empirical experiments to verify the effectiveness of transparency obligations.

The literature on regulating synthetic media at large in the AI Act is incomplete and omits an important aspect of the separation between synthetic media (as a superset) and deepfakes (as a subset). Furthermore, the topic of regulating synthetic texts is still understudied, which may result in interpretation difficulties and practical compliance problems in the future. This chapter fills some of the recognized gaps, but it should be emphasized that the problem discussed must be the subject of in-depth academic and legal analyses, which will be one of the challenges for future case law.

22.4 EU AI Act Regulatory Framework and Its Implications

22.4.1 The Artificial Intelligence Act: Its Concept and Significance

The AI Act represents a landmark EU regulatory initiative aimed at harmonizing provisions on AI systems across the EU Member States. It seeks to ensure the safe development and deployment of AI technologies, and at the same time is aimed at fostering innovation (Hacker, 2023; Helberger & Diakopoulos, 2023). Regulations should not hinder European competitiveness and allow for developing business while guaranteeing a high level of protection for the fundamental values of democratic legal systems (Laux et al., 2024; Namysłowska et al., 2023). The AI Act introduces a risk-based approach to the AI systems by categorizing them into four risk levels: unacceptable, high, limited, and minimal (Chamberlain, 2023). Additionally, the regulation refers to the systemic risk category somehow reserved for specific group of general-purpose AI models.

The first draft of the AI Act was presented by the European Commission in 2021, which shows that the EU started work on regulating AI relatively early. In the following years, the document underwent numerous changes and had to be adapted to the dynamically developing technology, especially in the face of the explosion of generative AI (Łabuz, 2024). The AI Act was finally adopted in 2024, and its provisions will enter into force in the following years. The provisions on synthetic media, as a rule, will enter into force 24 months after the adoption of the regulation, i.e., in August 2026 (European Commission, 2024b). During this time, the process of standardization of some solutions will continue, taking into account the best market practices and technological development.

This timeline is important for assessing the effectiveness of the AI Act. At the moment, it is possible to point out shortcomings primarily in the sphere of the wording or general concepts used. A comprehensive assessment of the regulation will only be possible after all provisions have been in force for several months and the interpretation of individual provisions has been consolidated.

The AI Act should be seen as the axis around which the security ecosystem for AI systems is supposed to be built in the EU. Its composition is complemented by other EU legal acts, including the Digital Services Act (DSA), which is key for imposing specific obligations on digital platforms to mitigate systemic risks associated with the amplification of information disorders (Łabuz, 2024; Romero Moreno, 2024).

Proponents of the EU normative soft power indicate that the AI Act can be transposed to other jurisdictions, thus allowing the transfer of values decoded from the EU legal system (Csernatoni, 2024; Siegmann & Anderljung, 2022). The concept of the "Brussels effect" assumes, among other things, building EU soft power based on its global normative influence (Bradford, 2024). In this context, regulating selected AI systems and indicating specific solutions can be a point of reference for other jurisdictions, creating foundations for universal solutions (Manners, 2013). The importance of the AI Act as a comprehensive regulation is all the greater because it also sets certain legislative trends, including by creating catalog of definitions and remedies against inappropriate applications of technology. Even an indirect transfer of these solutions to other jurisdictions may therefore impact the global media ecosystem.

It is too early to assess the validity of these assumptions in the case of the AI Act. The actions taken in other countries are currently characterized by a low degree of harmonization with EU initiatives, although similarities can be seen in the legislation of South American countries and to some extent of South Korea (Gigena & Pisanu, 2024; Shivhare & Park, 2025). Legislation in the USA is developing at its own pace—individual states introduced countermeasures against synthetic media based on various forms of disclosure. However, the lack of harmonization at the federal level leads to fragmentation of solutions, which can make compliance more difficult (Łabuz, 2025).

22.4.2 Definitions of Synthetic Media and Deepfakes

In the introductory remarks, I used the term *synthetic media* to address media that are not created exclusively by humans. However, this term is not self-explanatory and requires deeper analysis, especially since it is not explicitly defined in the AI Act, and the literature does not devote much space to definition, apparently taking the term for granted. The analysis should therefore be guided by the context of use and the common meaning. Cambridge Dictionary (2025) defines "synthetic" as "made artificially" or "made from artificial substances, often copying a natural product," and contrasts it with human-made objects. A very similar concept can be deduced from Recital 133 of the AI Act (European Commission, 2024b), which refers to the notion of *synthetic content*:

> A variety of AI systems can generate large quantities of synthetic content that becomes increasingly hard for humans to distinguish from human-generated and authentic content.

On the one hand, *synthetic content* is identified with what is generated by AI, on the other hand, it is distinguished from *human-generated* and *authentic content*. It can therefore be assumed, *a contrario*, that all content generated with the participation of AI should be classified as synthetic and thus non-authentic. This understanding is shared by Ajder and Glick (2019, p. 9) who see synthetic media as "media that is enabled or modified by artificial intelligence." This also applies to hybrid content, where AI-generated content is mixed with human-generated one.

Although *synthetic media* are not defined in the AI Act, the holistic semantic and substantial analysis of the provisions of the regulation allows one to distinguish four types of synthetic media: texts, audio, image, and video. Such types are listed in Article 50(2). However, there are other possible dividing lines. Millière (2022) distinguishes between *archival* and *synthetic* machine-made media and claims that synthetic media should contain a generative component, which includes modification or independence in generation. Kalpokas (2021) discusses Virtual Reality and Extended Reality in addition to audio and visual forms. Harris (2024) underlines nonbinary distinction between synthetic and non-synthetic, pointing to partly synthetic creations, or automatic additions to pictures made by modern software. Although there are slight differences in these approaches, the generative component seems to be a key and common factor.

Regardless of the definitional weaknesses, the AI Act allows for the clear distinction between the superordinate category of *synthetic content* and the subcategory of *deepfakes*. This distinction is critical for tailoring regulatory responses to address specific risks effectively, which is reflected in the different levels of transparency obligations under Article 50 of the AI Act. Deepfakes are explicitly defined in Article 3(60) of the AI Act as:

> AI-generated or manipulated image, audio or video content that resembles existing persons, objects, places, entities or events and would falsely appear to a person to be authentic or truthful.

This is a broad definition, which might be divided (Łabuz, 2023, 2024) into four aspects relating to: the method of production (AI-generated or AI-manipulated content), the type of the medium used (image, audio, or video), the object/subject of depiction (existing persons, objects, places, entities, or events), and the effect to be achieved (falsely appear to be authentic or truthful). Gils (2024) rightly noted that understanding what *AI-generated* or *AI-manipulated* actually means is problematic. Today, a significant portion of photos taken with our mobile phones are automatically modified to improve quality. It is currently unclear how such modifications will be qualified under the AI Act. This creates an interesting legal issue that requires further clarification.

The typological aspect does not include texts that should be seen as a separate type of synthetic media, and still be subject to transparency obligations. The subject/object aspect has been outlined broadly, as deepfakes, contrary to stereotypical ideas, are not limited to persons only. This classification largely reflects usage trends and takes into account the misleading potential of nonpersons creations (e.g., realistic representations of natural disasters, war damage, desecration of religious symbols) that may have consequences in the real world (Łabuz, 2023).

Deepfakes are a specific type of AI systems regulated in the AI Act. Their separation is justified due to the significant potential for manipulation (which has to do with their ability to faithfully imitate reality) and usage trends, primarily the growing number of deepfakes circulating online. Their regulation is a natural consequence of numerous political and social debates on their potential to amplify disinformation.

22.4.3 Risk Categories in Regulating Synthetic Media

Central to the AI Act's approach to regulating AI systems is the idea of trustworthy AI. The EU is trying to build an ecosystem of trust (Laux et al., 2024), in which the interests of citizens will be taken into account and the development of technology will be subject to supervision. One such element of building an ecosystem of trust is the introduction of transparency obligations, which directly apply to synthetic media, including deepfakes.

On the axiological level (the one referring to certain values), the regulation of synthetic media arises from the need to address the societal risks and ethical concerns associated with AI-generated content (Łabuz, 2025). It also takes into account the fundamental meta-axiology of the democratic systems (Gierycz, 2015), to which the AI Act refers. The need to balance the risks is directly expressed in Recital 133 of the AI Act (European Commission, 2024b), which states:

> A variety of AI systems can generate large quantities of synthetic content that becomes increasingly hard for humans to distinguish from human-generated and authentic content. The wide availability and increasing capabilities of those systems have a significant impact on the integrity and trust in the information ecosystem, raising new risks of misinformation and manipulation at scale, fraud, impersonation and consumer deception.

The AI Act recognizes that synthetic media pose unique challenges for different domains. By establishing clear regulatory frameworks, policymakers aim to mitigate these challenges without hindering the beneficial use of AI technologies. This can be seen as an emanation of the principle of proportionality, in relation to which risk categories are assigned to various AI systems (Mahler, 2022).

In the case of synthetic media, the creators of the AI Act decided on the category of "limited risk," which, however, does not exclude requalification and transfer to, for example, the high risk or systemic risk category. The AI Act itself creates the basis for this, enabling reevaluation in the future. However, the primary qualification is of great importance for regulating synthetic media and creating an appropriate legal regime. At the moment, the basic protection against malicious use of limited-risk AI systems comes down to the disclosure of their synthetic nature. This therefore limits the obligations on the part of providers and deployers, much more restrictive in the case of, for example, high-risk AI systems (Namysłowska et al., 2023).

22.4.4 Transparency Obligations: Disclosure

A key safeguard around which synthetic media provisions in the AI Act are built is the transparent disclosure to explicitly show that AI was used to create specific content (European Commission, 2024b; Łabuz, 2024, 2025). Transparency is a recurring theme in the EU's regulatory framework. The EU emphasizes that transparency obligations reflect a commitment to restore trust in media and technology (European Commission, 2024b), which is particularly important given the epistemic challenges related to the growing volume of synthetic media and their practical indistinguishability from human-made media (Krueger et al., 2023). The strong focus on the transparency of synthetic media also reflects the trends observed by researchers in journalism (Haapanen, 2022), where transparency was one of the key measures to counteract the decline in public trust in the media. It is also a manifestation of building trust in technology as such, which comprises AI systems interacting with humans (Zerilli et al., 2022).

The general principles for transparency obligations are introduced in Chapter IV of the AI Act entitled "Transparency obligations for providers and deployers of certain AI systems." This chapter comprises the single Article 50 that applies, among others, to synthetic media at large and its subordinate categories, different forms of disclosure, and different entities responsible for creating (providers) and deploying (deployers) AI systems.

Therefore, the basic division in the case of disclosure for synthetic media comprises the obligations of providers and deployers. The overarching principle is to inform natural persons that they are interacting with an AI system (intended to interact directly with natural persons), unless this is obvious from the point of view of a natural person who is reasonably well-informed, observant, and circumspect, taking into account the circumstances and the context of use (Article 50(1)). Helberger and Diakopoulos (2023) point out that the use of chatbots, virtual agents, or even news recommenders should be disclosed if they interact with users. This provision might apply to AI systems that can produce content of a different type, although the typological scope is not explicitly outlined in this case.

In the case of AI systems directly capable of generating synthetic media (audio, image, video, or text content), the transparency obligations for providers are clearly described in Article 50(2) which states:

> Providers [...] shall ensure that the outputs of the AI system are marked in a machine-readable format and detectable as artificially generated or manipulated. Providers shall ensure their technical solutions are effective, interoperable, robust and reliable as far as this is technically feasible, taking into account the specificities and limitations of various types of content, the costs of implementation and the generally acknowledged state of the art [...].

This provision is clarified in Recital 133 of the AI Act, which indicates possible solutions and states that providers of those systems shall:

> [...] embed technical solutions that enable marking in a machine readable format and detection that the output has been generated or manipulated by an AI system and not a human.

> Such techniques and methods should be sufficiently reliable, interoperable, effective and robust as far as this is technically feasible, taking into account available techniques or a combination of such techniques, such as watermarks, metadata identifications, cryptographic methods for proving provenance and authenticity of content, logging methods, fingerprints or other techniques, as may be appropriate.

Distinguishing possible forms of disclosure is a significant guidance for providers and will be an important point of reference in the future. It should be emphasized, however, that the final form of disclosure cannot be determined at this moment.

Article 50(2) distinguishes several exceptions from transparency obligations, including AI systems performing an assistive function for standard editing or not substantially altering the input data provided by the deployer or the semantics thereof, as well as selected actions authorized by law to detect, prevent, investigate, or prosecute criminal offences. The consequences of crafting such broad exceptions will be discussed in the following sections.

At the deployers level (Article 50(4)), obligations for labeling deepfakes and AI-generated texts have been separated; however, they are formulated similarly. Importantly, in this case, the AI Act refers to two subcategories: deepfakes and AI-generated texts.

In the case of deepfakes, deployers shall disclose that the content has been artificially generated or manipulated (Article 50(4)). This obligation is further clarified in Recital 134 of the AI Act, as disclosure shall be clear and distinguishable and accomplished by labeling the AI output accordingly and disclosing its artificial origin. The general instructions will be subject to standardization by the EU, so it is not possible to predict at this time what form they will ultimately take. For technical reasons, the marking of audio and visual content will differ (e.g., a message spoken before the broadcast, or a visual notification before the video starts). An important point of reference may be regulations in selected US states, where the form of disclosure is often described in great detail and casuistically (Łabuz, 2024).

An important element of building a regulatory framework that takes into account the axiological foundations of a democratic legal system are guarantees for personal rights and freedoms, including freedom of speech and artistic expression (Łabuz, 2025; Pawelec, 2022; Romero Moreno, 2024). This has significant implications for the media ecosystem and the flow of information. Hence, in the case of deepfakes, broad exceptions from the standard transparency obligations have been outlined, covering selected uses authorized by law, as well as cases where the content forms part of an evidently artistic, creative, satirical, fictional or analogous work, or program. In the latter case, transparency obligations might be limited to disclosure of the existence of such generated or manipulated content in an appropriate manner that does not hamper the display or enjoyment of the work (Article 50(4)). As they currently stand, and without detailed guidance from the EU, the obligations in the case of artistic or satirical creations are not materially different from the basic obligations. However, this approach acknowledges that not all synthetic media are inherently harmful and they should be assessed within their broader contextual and operational environments (Fernandez, 2021; Pawelec, 2022).

In the case of texts, the obligations are outlined very generally, too (disclosure without prejudging the form). They do not apply to all AI-generated texts, and transparency obligations depend on the context of using the output. They cover situations where the text is published "with the purpose of informing the public on matters of public interest" (Article 50(4)). This wording seems unclear without interpretative guidance. Additionally, exceptions apply to selected activities authorized by law, but also to cases where the AI-generated content has undergone a process of human review or editorial control and where a natural or legal person holds editorial responsibility for the publication of the content. The literal wording of the provision indicates that it refers to the established work of journalists and publishers (Piasecki et al., 2024). Furthermore, the provision itself should be understood in the spirit of human oversight, which plays an important role in building a system of trust in AI (Enqvist, 2023).

An important declaration also appears in Recital 135 that states the potential involvement of the Commission in the future, which may:

> [...] encourage and facilitate the drawing up of codes of practice at Union level to facilitate the effective implementation of the obligations regarding the detection and labelling of artificially generated or manipulated content, including to support practical arrangements for making, as appropriate, the detection mechanisms accessible and facilitating cooperation with other actors along the value chain, disseminating content or checking its authenticity and provenance to enable the public to effectively distinguish AI-generated content.

Such an obligation would strengthen transparency based on disclaimers, constituting another layer of protection, which refers to the cooperation with different stakeholders. In the holistic dimension, the AI Act also generally refers to the necessity of raising social awareness and promoting AI literacy (e.g., Article 66 and Recital 56), which can be understood in the context of building societal resilience in the face of information disorders. This is intended to strengthen transparency obligations, which are not sufficient to ensure the integrity of the choices of human audiences if that audiences do not possess at least basic level of technological awareness and media literacy (Helberger & Diakopoulos, 2023). Furthermore, the AI Act outlines penalties for noncompliance that provide legal and financial consequences for violations, which puts financial pressure on entities involved in creating regulated content and is supposed to strengthen the regulatory regime (Chapter XII).

22.4.5 Synergies Between the AI Act and Other EU Legislation

The AI Act should be considered primarily as an element of the EU legal system. This concerns the aforementioned meta-axiology of the democratic systems, as well as the mutual internal connections between individual legal acts. They are not always fully coherent, which may weaken the regulatory framework; however, they allow for regulating various aspects of AI-based media disorders "along the communications pipeline" (Chowdhury, 2024).

The Digital Services Act (DSA) complements the AI Act by imposing obligations on digital platforms to address systemic risks associated with disinformation, including the amplification of synthetic media (Husovec, 2024; Łabuz, 2024; Romero Moreno, 2024). It therefore includes monitoring, moderation, and reporting responsibilities. An indirect consequence of the introduction of these obligations is restrictions imposed by digital platforms on users themselves, including the obligation to label synthetic content (Łabuz, 2024). This can be seen today in social media, where at least some AI-generated or AI-manipulated content has an appropriate note. The DSA also includes a description of deepfakes, which differs slightly from the definition presented in the AI Act by adding the word "appreciably" that precedes the cluster "resembles existing" (European Commission, 2022).

The General Data Protection Regulation (GDPR) intersects with the AI Act and addresses privacy concerns related to the use of personal data in training AI models and generating outputs. GDPR helps to ensure that the use of personal data to generate synthetic media complies with strict privacy standards, helping to prevent misuse and abuses of emerging technologies (Beduschi, 2024).

The advantage of the EU system is its complementarity, although it leads to excessive complexity of the regulations. The above-mentioned "communication pipeline" can be divided into the stages of obtaining training data, including the possible use of data that infringes someone else's image rights, creating AI systems, generating media, distributing media, or interacting with media. This system is supplemented by other legislation that may subsidiarily refer to synthetic media. An example is the *Directive on combating violence against women and domestic violence* adopted by the EU in 2024, in which Member States are obliged to criminalize the creation and sharing of nonconsensual intimate imagery in the form of deepfakes (European Commission, 2024a).

22.5 Discussion

22.5.1 General Assessment of the Proposed Solutions

As indicated, the assessment of the effectiveness of the adopted solutions will be possible *post factum*, i.e., when all the regulations come into force and are implemented. At this moment, the focus should be on the concept itself and its implementation.

The AI Act has come a long way from the conceptual phase to the final version adopted in 2024. The provisions concerning synthetic media have undergone significant changes, as have the definitions used. These changes have usually been for the better and have taken into account the concerns of experts.

The distinction of deepfakes as a special form of synthetic media should be assessed positively. However, the lack of a definition of *synthetic media* or *synthetic content* at large should be assessed negatively. This makes it difficult to systematize and typologize individual forms. The definition of deepfakes in Article 3(60) is comprehensive and covers at least four aspects (Łabuz, 2023). In terms of depicted subjects/objects, the scope is broad enough and reflects the practice of using deepfakes for disinformation purposes that do not necessarily have to focus exclusively on depicting persons. Problems related to the interpretation of what "AI-generated" or "AI-manipulated" means (Gils, 2024; Piasecki et al., 2024), or how to understand cluster ["appreciably"] "resembles existing" will have to be resolved by the EU or jurisprudence (Łabuz, 2025). At the same time, the lack of semantic consistency between the descriptions of deepfakes (within the AI Act itself and between the AI Act and the DSA) is a manifestation of legislative sloppiness (Łabuz, 2024).

In the case of AI-generated or AI-manipulated texts, the provisions of the AI Act are very general and only their practical implementation will be the basis for broader analyses. It is reasonable that the AI Act attaches much importance to labeling AI-generated or AI-manipulated content so that it can be distinguished from human-generated content. However, given the dynamic development of technology and the practice of using LLMs, a valid question arises about the enforceability of these obligations and thresholds for determining what AI's participation in the creation of text actually is. This is, in fact, a broader issue of the admissibility of using synthetic content that the scientific community and education system must face.

The distinction between deepfakes and AI-generated or AI-manipulated texts seems reasonable. It is equally advisable to create a similar, but different in detail, transparency regime. Transparency obligations are supposed to ensure that AI-generated content is properly labeled and thus identifiable, which can help users make informed decisions (European Commission, 2024b), but also mitigate the erosion of trust that has accompanied the rise of synthetic media (Fallis, 2021), which subsequently affects democratic systems and societies.

The focus on transparency obligations is primarily intended to counteract the potential of synthetic media to spread disinformation (Łabuz, 2025). Unfortunately, marking texts generated by LLMs and their subsequent detection seem hardly feasible at the moment, although an increase in the quality of watermarking is also indicated (Dathathri et al., 2024; Fernandez et al., 2024). Attention is also drawn to the large number of errors made by detection software, including false positive indications (Scarfe et al., 2024), or the relative ease of deceiving detection systems (Perkins et al., 2024). Detection of audio and visual synthetic content is more accurate, although technological shortcomings should be noted, too. In an atmosphere of uncertainty and disinformation, these problems may lead to a further decrease in trust in technology, or in the media and information itself. This may even result in a deepening epistemic crisis and lead to questioning the legitimacy of the regulations themselves. This will make the above-mentioned synergies across the entire EU digital ecosystem and strengthening the content moderation regime by digital platforms, e.g., using the DSA, all the more important. The AI Act provides the basis for this by referring directly to its links with the DSA (e.g., Recital 136). These synergies are undoubtedly important for countering information disorders, but will be strongly dependent on the EU's enforcement capabilities, especially when confronted with big-tech companies from the USA.

In that context, an important element of building societal and systemic resilience will be the EU's nonlegal activity. It might be aimed at raising citizens' and stakeholders' awareness, educational and training programs, and increasing trust in technology. It can comprise initiatives on enhancing media literacy and strengthening digital skills to equip citizens with the tools to navigate an increasingly complicated media environment. Programs that build societal resilience also could play a key role, for example, in countering disinformation, which may include fostering critical thinking and addressing important topics in strategic communications. The AI Act enhances support for such activities. They should be seen as part of the ecosystem of diverse safeguards. Moreover, the mere adoption of the AI Act can be seen as a positive signal of readiness to face problems, even if some solutions are not perfect.

22.5.2 Shortcomings

The fundamental concept of regulating synthetic media in the AI Act is linked to countering disinformation, mainly of a political nature (Łabuz, 2025). This in turn means that some detrimental applications of synthetic media, especially the potential of deepfakes to produce nonconsensual intimate imagery, are not addressed (Łabuz, 2023, 2024). The lack of creation of any no-go zones should therefore be assessed negatively. From the perspective of media disruption, this does not play such a significant role, because the AI Act focuses on what audiences perceive, on ensuring their conscious interaction with AI systems and human oversight. However, omitting important negative applications of synthetic media can have social and political consequences.

The mere classification of synthetic media into the category of limited-risk AI systems may raise justified doubts. Romero Moreno (2024) pointed out that such a classification does not guarantee an adequate regime for the protection of fundamental rights. It is therefore considered (Łabuz, 2024; Romero Moreno, 2024), whether in this case, it would not be more advisable to classify at least deepfakes as high-risk or systemic-risk AI systems. In the latter case, this would be in line with the concept used by the DSA that precisely refers to the systemic risks associated with the dissemination of synthetic media and information disorders (Romero Moreno, 2024).

The very phrase "systemic risk" is not understood identically within the EU legal ecosystem. And yet, under the DSA, precisely to mitigate systemic risks, digital platforms are obliged, among others, to ensure that deepfakes are appropriately marked (European Commission, 2022). This discrepancy in qualifications is surprising, especially in view of the numerous risks associated with synthetic media. As a consequence, deepfakes can be considered a systemic risk under the DSA, but only a limited risk under the AI Act (Łabuz, 2024; Romero Moreno, 2024).

There are minor differences in wording that may be significant in interpretative practice. Minor mistakes such as different spellings of "machine-readable" (or "machine readable") are the result of poor legislative technique, but differences in describing deepfakes ("appreciably resembles" from Recital 134 and just "resembles" from Article 3(60)), or disclosure ("sufficiently reliable, interoperable, effective and robust" from Recital 133 and "effective, interoperable, robust and reliable" from Article 50(2)) may cause serious interpretation problems in the future.

This does not speak well of EU legislation, which should provide for reliable legal interpretation. The very definition of deepfakes may be a source of controversy in the future. The use of the term "resembles existing persons" may suggest that in order to create a deepfake presenting a person, it is necessary to use the image of an identifiable person. This calls into question the legal status of completely synthetic creations, without a real-world counterpart (Łabuz, 2024, 2025). The move away from literal interpretation in favor of teleological interpretation, as postulated in the literature, may potentially solve this problem (Łabuz, 2025). The above-mentioned complete lack of definition of *synthetic media* or *synthetic content* does not help either. The problems with what terms *AI-generated* and *AI-manipulated* mean, identified by some authors (e.g., Gils, 2024), will be the subject of discussions and most likely legal tricks in the future to avoid compliance.

The focus on transparency obligations as an almost exclusive technical and legal safeguard against synthetic media is wrong, as it does not take into account forms that should be explicitly prohibited (e.g., nonconsensual synthetic intimate imagery or the production of pedophile content). The key will be the subsequent legislation of the EU Member States, which must adapt to technological developments and create appropriate criminal provisions for cyber-related crimes based on media disruption.

At the level of transparency obligations for providers, there is no distinction made between AI-generated texts and deepfakes. In practice, however, the obligations will vary depending on the type of media, which is primarily justified by the technology used. Broad exceptions to the application of transparency obligations and unclear wording regarding AI-generated or AI-manipulated texts may be more problematic. These will be discussed in the next section.

At this point, it is worth noting the fundamental weakness of transparency obligations, namely, potential noncompliance on the part of disinformation actors and the exclusion of private users from the scope of the definition of deployers under the AI Act. In practice, the enforceability of the regulations will depend on the control mechanisms of the platforms on which the content is made available. It may therefore turn out that the provisions on synthetic media in the AI Act will be strongly dependent on whether the EU can enforce the obligations arising from the DSA. However, this is not a significant internal weakness of the AI Act, but a consequence of how the modern information exchange system is shaped.

22.5.3 Implications for the Media Landscape

The regulation of synthetic media in the AI Act has profound implications for the media landscape and industry, which is already struggling with a crisis of trust (Newman et al., 2023). As the future media landscape may also see shifts in audience expectations and behaviors, regulatory frameworks and media organizations will need to adapt to these changing dynamics, incorporating new solutions to maintain relevance and trust.

It will therefore be extremely important to observe the practical implementation of the transparency obligations arising from the AI Act. The AI Act in Recital 133 presents a non-exhaustive list of solutions that providers could implement to disclose AI synthesis in a machine-readable form. Due to the development of technology, solutions may change and will be subject to standardization and effectiveness evaluation.

Of particular interest will be the outcome of exceptions from the standard transparency obligations. One of them, at the providers level, addresses "standard editing or not substantially altering the input data provided by the deployer or the semantics thereof" (Article 50(2)). This may be a workaround enabling the use of AI for the automatic correction of journalistic texts. Filters used in devices for taking and processing photos, which enable the improvement of quality, or automatic removal of noise from audio recordings, can be assessed similarly. However, in each of the above cases, the boundary between what we consider manipulation and what is "standard editing" will be fluid and discretionary. This may pose interpretational problems, and in some respects negate the idea of transparency.

Piasecki et al. (2024) noted that the wording in Article 50(4) of the AI Act relating to the disclosure of AI-generated texts is vague, too. Namely, terms such as "purpose of informing the public on matters of public interest" or "a process of human review or editorial control" are unclear. Piasecki et al. (2024) also point out that the wording "AI system that generates or manipulates text" may pose problems, and suggest that in each case where AI was involved in writing the text, one can speak of generation or manipulation. Therefore, the priority should be seen in informing the recipient about the content creation process and enabling them to make an informed decision regarding the subsequent interaction with the output (Hacker, 2023; Piasecki et al., 2024).

It is worth noting that the process of human review or editorial control has been somehow equated with transparency and that the very fact that some identifiable third party may be responsible for the dissemination and overseeing of specific content would act as a pre-condition for appropriate verification. And in this case, it can be seen as an attempt to counteract the epistemic crisis, with the leading role of other humans as information signposts. However, given the dynamically changing structure of information exchange, and thus the development of new forms of journalism, practical enforcement of the provision may be difficult or may even be used to circumvent transparency obligations, as some actors could disguise as journalists and pretend to subject the content to appropriate control.

There is also a fundamental question of whether transparency obligations designed in the way the AI Act proposes will work at all and whether, after some time, they will not become "imperceptible" to recipients, or lead to excessive skepticism (Twomey et al., 2023). Empirical research on the effectiveness of various forms of disclosure and their influence on limiting the development of cognitive biases will therefore be key to assessing the appropriateness of the transparency obligations system. At the moment, this topic is still largely understudied.

22.6 Conclusion

The EU's regulatory approach to synthetic media represents a significant step toward addressing the challenges posed by generative AI. By underlining transparency and trust, the AI Act creates the foundation for safer applications of synthetic media. Although the main part concerning safeguards is of a technical and legal nature, the EU also addresses the issue of building societal resilience. However, the complexity of the synthetic media ecosystem requires an adaptive regulatory framework that can address the challenges of a dynamically developing environment.

The AI Act provides a starting point, which now needs to be supplemented by standardization based on strong empirical foundations. At the legal level, it is necessary to develop clear and precise lines of interpretation that will take into account the axiological foundations decoded from the EU legal ecosystem. Future research and policy efforts should focus on refining definitions of synthetic media and its iterations, fostering international and multisectoral cooperation to tackle various challenges, and enhancing the enforceability of transparency obligations. Although we are not yet able to quantify the exact disruptive impact of emerging AI technologies on media, the already observed decline in trust in the media and undermining the epistemic value of content are important warning signals.

Synthetic media are not reduced to any physical borders. The effectiveness of any regulatory framework depends on (international) collaboration. The EU has been proactive in advocating for cross-border regulatory cooperation, and the AI Act can serve as a model for implementing global solutions. The shortcomings identified in this chapter should be subject to further analysis and necessary amendments, which will contribute to improving the quality of legislation and protection regimes at the international level.

International cooperation also extends to research and development. Collaboration between academic institutions, media organizations, and the private sector can drive innovation in watermarking, traceability, or content authentication technologies. These efforts are essential for building a robust infrastructure to support the AI Act's objectives and mitigate the risks associated with synthetic media.

References

Ajder, H., & Glick, J. (2019). *Just joking. Deepfakes, satire and the politics of synthetic media*. WITNESS.

Beduschi, A. (2024). Synthetic data protection: Towards a paradigm change in data regulation? *Big Data & Society, 11*(1), 1–5. https://doi.org/10.1177/20539517241231277

Bradford, A. (2024). The false choice between digital regulation and innovation. *Northwestern University Law Review, 118*(2), 377–454. https://doi.org/10.2139/ssrn.4753107

Cambridge Dictionary. (2025). *Synthetic*. Retrieved January 25, 2025, from https://dictionary.cambridge.org/dictionary/english/synthetic

Chamberlain, J. (2023). The risk-based approach of the European Union's proposed artificial intelligence regulation: Some comments from a tort law perspective. *European Journal of Risk Regulation, 14*, 1–13. https://doi.org/10.1017/err.2022.38

Chowdhury, R. (2024). AI-fuelled election campaigns are here — Where are the rules? *Nature, 628*(237). https://doi.org/10.1038/d41586-024-00995-9

Csernatoni, R. (2024). *Charting the geopolitics and European governance of artificial intelligence*. Carnegie Europe.

Dathathri, S., et al. (2024). Scalable watermarking for identifying large language model outputs. *Nature, 634*, 818–823. https://doi.org/10.1038/s41586-024-08025-4

Delfino, R. (2023). The Deepfake defense—Exploring the limits of the law and ethical norms in protecting legal proceedings from lying lawyers. *Ohio State Law Journal, 84*, 1067–1124. https://doi.org/10.2139/ssrn.4355140

Dobber, T., Kruikemeier, S., Votta, F., Helberger, N., & Goodman, E. P. (2023). The effect of traffic light veracity labels on perceptions of political advertising source and message credibility on social media. *Journal of Information Technology & Politics, 22*(1), 82–97. https://doi.org/10.1080/19331681.2023.2224316

Enqvist, L. (2023). 'Human oversight' in the EU artificial intelligence act: What, when and by whom? *Law, Innovation and Technology, 15*(2), 508–535. https://doi.org/10.1080/17579961.2023.2245683

Erman, E., & Furendal, M. (2024). The democratization of global AI governance and the role of tech companies. *Nature Machine Intelligence, 6*, 246–248. https://doi.org/10.1038/s42256-024-00811-z

European Commission. (2022). *Regulation (EU) 2022/2065 of the European Parliament and of the Council of 19 October 2022 on a Single Market For Digital Services and amending Directive 2000/31/EC (Digital Services Act)*. Retrieved January 25, 2025, from https://eur-lex.europa.eu/legal-content/EN/TXT/PDF/?uri=CELEX:32022R2065

European Commission. (2024a). *Directive (EU) 2024/1385 of the European Parliament and of the Council of 14 May 2024 on combating violence against women and domestic violence*. Retrieved January 25, 2025, from https://eur-lex.europa.eu/legal-content/EN/TXT/PDF/?uri=OJ:L_2024a01385

European Commission. (2024b). *Regulation (EU) 2024/1689 of the European Parliament and of the Council of 13 June 2024 laying down harmonised rules on artificial intelligence*. Retrieved January 25, 2025, from https://eur-lex.europa.eu/legal-content/EN/TXT/PDF/?uri=OJ:L_2024b01689

Fallis, D. (2021). The epistemic threat of deepfakes. *Philosophy & Technology, 34*(4), 623–643. https://doi.org/10.1007/s13347-020-00419-2

Fernandez, A. (2021). "Deep fakes": Disentangling terms in the proposed EU artificial intelligence act. *UFITA, 85*(2), 392–433. https://doi.org/10.5771/2568-9185-2021-2

Fernandez, P., Level, A., & Furon, T. (2024). What Lies Ahead for Generative AI Watermarking. In *2nd Workshop on Generative AI and Law (GenLaw '24)*. Retrieved January 25, 2025, from https://blog.genlaw.org/pdfs/genlaw_icml2024/27.pdf

Geddes, K. G. (2021). Ocularcentrism and Deepfakes: Should seeing be believing? *Fordham Intellectual Property, Media and Entertainment Law Journal, 31*(4), 1042–1083.

Gierycz, M. (2015). The European Union's axiological credo and morality policy tensions. *Studia Philosophiae Christianae, 51*(3), 159–193.

Gigena, F. G., & Pisanu, G. (2024). *Regulatory mapping on artificial intelligence in Latin America*. Access Now.

Gils, T. (2024). A detailed analysis of article 50 of the EU'S artificial intelligence act. In C. N. Pehlivan, N. Forgó, & P. Valcke (Eds.), *The EU artificial intelligence (AI) act: A commentary*. Kluwers Law International.

Grady, P. (2023). *EU Proposals Will Fail to Curb Nonconsensual Deepfake Porn*. Retrieved January 25, 2025, from https://datainnovation.org/2023/01/eu-proposals-will-fail-to-curb-nonconsensual-deepfake-porn

Haapanen, L. (2022). Problematising the restoration of trust through transparency: Focusing on quoting. *Journalism, 23*(4), 875–891. https://doi.org/10.1177/1464884920934236

Habgood-Coote, J. (2023). Deepfakes and the epistemic apocalypse. *Synthese, 201*, 1–23. https://doi.org/10.1007/s11229-023-04097-3

Hacker, P. (2023). *AI regulation in Europe: From the AI Act to future regulatory challenges*. arXiv. https://doi.org/10.48550/arXiv.2310.04072

Harari, Y. N. (2024). *Nexus: A brief history of information networks from the stone age to AI*. London-New York.

Harris, K. R. (2024). Synthetic media detection, the wheel, and the burden of proof. *Philosophy & Technology, 37*(131), 1–20. https://doi.org/10.1007/s13347-024-00821-0

Helberger, N., & Diakopoulos, N. (2023). The European AI act and how it matters for research into AI in media and journalism. *Digital Journalism, 11*(9), 1751–1760. https://doi.org/10.1080/21670811.2022.2082505

Hirvonen, N., Jylhä, V., Lao, Y., & Larsson, S. (2024). Artificial intelligence in the information ecosystem: Affordances for everyday information seeking. *Journal of the Association for Information Science and Technology, 75*(10), 1152–1165. https://doi.org/10.1002/asi.24860

Husovec, M. (2024). The digital services act's red line: What the commission can and cannot do about disinformation. *Journal of Media Law, 16*(1), 47–56. https://doi.org/10.1080/17577632.2024.2362483

Kalpokas, I. (2021). Problematising reality: The promises and perils of synthetic media. *SN Social Sciences, 1*(1), 1–11. https://doi.org/10.1007/s43545-020-00010-8

Krueger, N., Vananmala, M., & Dave, R. (2023). *Recent advancements in the field of deepfake detection*. arXiv. https://doi.org/10.48550/arXiv.2308.05563

Łabuz, M. (2023). Regulating deep fakes in the artificial intelligence act. *Applied Cybersecurity & Internet Governance, 2*(1). https://doi.org/10.60097/ACIG/162856

Łabuz, M. (2024). Deep fakes and the artificial intelligence act—An important signal or a missed opportunity? *Policy & Internet, 16*(24), 783–800. https://doi.org/10.1002/poi3.406

Łabuz, M. (2025). A teleological interpretation of the definition of deep fakes in the EU artificial intelligence act—A purpose-based approach to potential problems with the word "existing". *Policy & Internet*. https://doi.org/10.1002/poi3.435

Laux, J., Wachter, S., & Mittelstadt, B. (2024). Trustworthy artificial intelligence and the European Union AI act: On the conflation of trustworthiness and acceptability of risk. *Regulation & Governance, 18*(1), 3–32. https://doi.org/10.1111/rego.12512

Magonara, E., & Malatras, A. (2022). *Foreign information manipulation and interference (FIMI) and cybersecurity—Threat landscape*. Enisa.

Maham, P., & Küspert, S. (2023). *Governing general purpose AI*. Stiftung Neue Verantwortung.

Mahler, T. (2022). Between risk management and proportionality: The risk-based approach in the EU's Artificial Intelligence Act Proposal. *Nordic Yearbook of Law and Informatics*. Retrieved January 25, 2025, from https://papers.ssrn.com/sol3/papers.cfm?abstract_id=4001444

Mania, K. (2024). Legal protection of revenge and deepfake porn victims in the European Union: Findings from a comparative legal study. *Trauma, Violence, & Abuse, 25*, 117–129. https://doi.org/10.1177/15248380221143772

Manners, I. (2013). Assessing the decennial, reassessing the global: Understanding European Union normative power in global politics. *Cooperation and Conflict, 48*(2), 304–329. https://doi.org/10.1177/0010836713485

Millière, R. (2022). Deep learning and synthetic media. *Synthese, 200*(231), 1–27. https://doi.org/10.1007/s11229-022-03739-2

Namysłowska, M., et al. (2023). On the ethical, legal and social implications of artificial intelligence Systems in the Member States of European Union. Observations against the background of the draft regulation on artificial intelligence. *Przegląd Sejmowy, 6*(179), 61–84. https://doi.org/10.31268/PS.2023.219

Neves, I. (2023). The freedom to conduct a business as a driver for AI governance. *UNIO EU Law Journal, 9*(2), 13–56. https://doi.org/10.21814/unio.9.2.5487

Newman, N., Fletcher, R., Eddy, K., Robertson, C. T., & Nielsen, R. K. (2023). *Reuters institute digital news report 2023*. Reuters Institute for the Study of Journalism.

Pawelec, M. (2022). Deepfakes and democracy (theory): How synthetic audio visual media for disinformation and hate speech threaten core democratic functions. *Digital Society, 19*, 1–37. https://doi.org/10.1007/s44206-022-00010-6

Pereira, D. (2024). *By 2026, Online Content Generated by Non-humans Will Vastly Outnumber Human Generated Content*. Retrieved January 25, 2025, from https://oodaloop.com/analysis/archive/if-90-of-online-content-will-be-ai-generated-by-2026-we-forecast-a-deeply-human-anti-content-movement-in-response

Perkins, M., Roe, J., Vu, B. H., Postma, D., Hickerson, D., McGaughran, J., & Khuat, H. Q. (2024). Simple techniques to bypass GenAI text detectors: Implications for inclusive education. *International Journal of Educational Technology in Higher Education, 21*(53), 1–25. https://doi.org/10.1186/s41239-024-00487-w

Piasecki, S., Morosoli, S., Helberger, N., & Naudts, L. (2024). AI-generated journalism: Do the transparency provisions in the AI act give news readers what they hope for? *Internet Policy Review, 13*(4), 1–28. https://doi.org/10.14763/2024.4.1810

Rigotti, C., & McGlynn, C. (2022). Towards an EU criminal law on violence against women: The ambitions and limitations of the commission's proposal to criminalise image-based sexual abuse. *New Journal of European Criminal Law, 13*(4), 452–477. https://doi.org/10.1177/20322844221140713

Romero Moreno, F. (2024). Generative AI and deepfakes: A human rights approach to tackling harmful content. *International Review of Law, Computers & Technology, 38*(3), 297–326. https://doi.org/10.1080/13600869.2024.2324540

Scarfe, P., Watcham, K., Clarke, A., & Roesch, E. (2024). A real-world test of artificial intelligence infiltration of a university examinations system: A "Turing test" case study. *PLoS One, 19*(6), 1–21. https://doi.org/10.1371/journal.pone.0305354

Shivhare, S., & Park, K. B. (2025). *South Korea's New AI Framework Act: A Balancing Act Between Innovation and Regulation*. Retrieved May 8, 2025, https://fpf.org/blog/south-koreas-new-ai-framework-act-a-balancing-act-between-innovation-and-regulation

Siegmann, C., & Anderljung, M. (2022). *The Brussels effect and artificial intelligence: How EU regulation will impact the global AI market*. Centre for the Governance of AI.

Toparlak, R. T. (2022). Criminalising pornographic deep fakes: A gender-specific inspection of image-based sexual abuse. In *SciencesPo law school the 10th graduate conference*.

Twomey, J., Ching, D., Aylett, M. P., Quayle, M., Linehan, C., & Murphy, G. (2023). Do deepfake videos undermine our epistemic trust? A thematic analysis of tweets that discuss deepfakes in the Russian invasion of Ukraine. *PLoS One, 18*(10), 1–22. https://doi.org/10.1371/journal.pone.0291668

Vaccari, C., & Chadwick, A. (2020). Deepfakes and disinformation: Exploring the impact of synthetic political video on deception, uncertainty, and trust in news. *Social Media + Society, 6*(1), 1–13. https://doi.org/10.1177/2056305120903408

van Huijstee, M., van Boheemen, P., Das, D., Nierling, L., Jahnel, J., Karaboga, M., & Fatun, M. (2021). *Tackling deepfakes in European policy*. European Parliamentary Research Service.

Veale, M., & Borgesius, F. Z. (2021). Demystifying the draft EU artificial intelligence act — Analysing the good, the bad, and the unclear elements of the proposed approach. *Computer Law Review International, 22*(4), 97–112. https://doi.org/10.9785/cri-2021-220402

Weikmann, T., & Lecheler, S. (2023). Cutting through the hype: Understanding the implications of Deepfakes for the fact-checking actor-network. *Digital Journalism, 12*(10), 1505–1522. https://doi.org/10.1080/21670811.2023.2194665

Zerilli, J., Bhatt, U., & Weller, A. (2022). How transparency modulates trust in artificial intelligence. *Patterns, 3*, 1–10. https://doi.org/10.1016/j.patter.2022.100455

Dr. Mateusz Łabuz, PhD is researcher at the Institute for Peace Research and Security Policy at the University of Hamburg (IFSH) and former career diplomat at the Polish Ministry of Foreign Affairs. His PhD thesis defended at the Chemnitz University of Technology was devoted to political uses of deepfakes. He lectures Artificial Intelligence, Cybersecurity, Fact-Checking and Disinformation at the University of the National Education Commission and the Pontifical University of John Paul II in Kraków. His research interests comprise synthetic media, cognitive warfare, and cybersecurity, as well as emerging trends in the disinformation sphere.

MIX
Papier aus verantwortungsvollen Quellen
Paper from responsible sources
FSC® C105338

If you have any concerns about our products,
you can contact us on
ProductSafety@springernature.com

In case Publisher is established outside the EU,
the EU authorized representative is:
Springer Nature Customer Service Center GmbH
Europaplatz 3, 69115 Heidelberg, Germany

Printed by Libri Plureos GmbH
in Hamburg, Germany